T0271215

Impact Evaluation

In recent years, interest in rigorous impact evaluation has grown tremendously in policymaking, economics, public health, social sciences and international relations. Evidence-based policymaking has become a recurring theme in public policy, alongside greater demands for accountability in public policies and public spending, and requests for independent and rigorous impact evaluations for policy evidence. Frölich and Sperlich offer a comprehensive and up-to-date approach to quantitative impact evaluation analysis, also known as causal inference or treatment effect analysis, illustrating the main approaches for identification and estimation: experimental studies, randomisation inference and randomised control trials (RCTs), matching and propensity score matching and weighting, instrumental variable estimation, difference-in-differences, regression discontinuity designs, quantile treatment effects and evaluation of dynamic treatments. The book is designed for economics graduate courses but can also serve as a manual for professionals in research institutes, governments and international organisations evaluating the impact of a wide range of public policies in climate, economic development, education, environment, finance, health, labour and social programmes.

Markus Frölich is Director of the Center for Evaluation and Development (C4ED) in Germany and Switzerland, Professor of Econometrics at Universität Mannheim, Germany and a J-PAL Affiliate. He has twenty years of experience in impact evaluation, including the development of new econometric methods and numerous applied impact evaluations for organisations such as Green Climate Fund, International Fund for Agricultural Development (IFAD), International Labour Organization (ILO), UNDP, UNICEF, World Food Programme (WFP) and the World Bank.

Stefan Sperlich is Full Professor of Statistics and Econometrics at the Université de Genève, has about fifteen years of experience as a consultant, and was co-founder of the 'Poverty, Equity and Growth in Developing Countries' Research Centre, Göttingen. He has published in various top-ranked journals and was awarded the 2000–2002 Tjalling C. Koopmans Econometric Theory Prize.

Impact Evaluation

Treatment Effects and Causal Analysis

MARKUS FRÖLICH

University of Mannheim, Center for Evaluation and Development

STEFAN SPERLICH

University of Geneva

CAMBRIDGE
UNIVERSITY PRESS

University Printing House, Cambridge CB2 8BS, United Kingdom

One Liberty Plaza, 20th Floor, New York, NY 10006, USA

477 Williamstown Road, Port Melbourne, VIC 3207, Australia

314–321, 3rd Floor, Plot 3, Splendor Forum, Jasola District Centre, New Delhi – 110025, India

79 Anson Road, #06–04/06, Singapore 079906

Cambridge University Press is part of the University of Cambridge.

It furthers the University's mission by disseminating knowledge in the pursuit of education, learning, and research at the highest international levels of excellence.

www.cambridge.org
Information on this title: www.cambridge.org/9781107042469
DOI: 10.1017/9781107337008

© Markus Frölich and Stefan Sperlich 2019

First published 2019

A catalogue record for this publication is available from the British Library.

ISBN 978-1-107-04246-9 Hardback
ISBN 978-1-107-61606-6 Paperback

Contents

Acknowledgement

This book is the result of many years of teaching Impact Evaluation at numerous universities and research institutes worldwide. We thank all of our colleagues, PhD and Master students who contributed with discussions, comments, recommendations or simply their encouragement. We would like to mention in particular Michael Lechner and Manuel Arellano.

A special thanks goes to our families for all the support we experienced during the last seven years for finishing this work, Lili, Yvonne, Bianca and Daniel, and to our parents.

Foreword

The treatment effect approach to policy evaluation focuses on evaluating the impact of a yes-or-no policy in place. This approach has inspired a huge amount of empirical work and has become the centerpiece of the econometric toolkit in important branches of applied economics. Markus Frölich and Stefan Sperlich's book is a comprehensive graduate-level treatise on the econometrics of treatment effects. It will appeal to students and researchers who want to have more than a cursory understanding of the whats, whys and hows of treatment effect estimation.

There is much in the book to commend. I like the fact that the authors pay serious attention to both identification *and* estimation problems. In applied work treatment effects are not identified; they are estimated. Reading this book reminds us that it is not always the case that, given identification, an obvious estimation method follows. This is not to the detriment of the book's attention to identification. Formal assumptions involving potential outcomes are discussed alongside Pearl graphical displays of causal models. Causal graphs and the many examples spread over the text help develop intuition in an effective way.

The estimation of treatment effects from non-experimental data – the focus of this book – typically involves conditional arguments, be they conditional exogeneity as in regression and matching approaches, conditional instrumental variable assumptions or conditional difference-in-differences. Conditioning often involves non-trivial choices and trade-offs beyond those associated with identification arrangements. One has to choose the set of variables on which to condition a statistical approach and its implementation. Here the benefits of the in-depth treatment provided by the Frölich–Sperlich partnership are clearly visible. In line with the literature, the authors emphasise non-parametric approaches, providing the reader with an excellent self-contained introduction to local non-parametric methods.

The method of instrumental variables is the central tool for the estimation of endogenous treatments and so it features prominently in this book. Monotonicity of the first-stage equation is required to identify local average treatment effects. Such local effects may or may not be policy-relevant treatment effects. However, the fact that they can all be expressed as weighted averages of marginal treatment effects opens up the possibility of learning from the former about the latter. This is a promising avenue of progress, and the book provides the essential elements to understand the interconnections between local, marginal and other treatment effects. An important lesson from the literature is the major role that the first-stage equation plays in the identification of causal effects. The instrumental-variable method only allows us to identify averages of heterogeneous treatment effects provided that the first-stage equations are not heterogeneous to the same extent. This fact naturally leads to considering structural approaches to modelling treatment choice. This is specially so in the case of non-binary treatments, another situation that is also addressed in the book.

The treatment effect approach has made remarkable progress by boldly focusing on a binary static treatment setting. However, there are economic policies that provide fundamentally dynamic incentives so that their effects cannot be understood in the absence of a dynamic framework of analysis. It is good that Frölich and Sperlich have included a final chapter in which a dynamic potential outcomes model and duration models are discussed.

The authors cover most of the standard tools in the econometrics of treatment effects from a coherent perspective using a common notation. Besides selection of observables and instrumental variables, the book discusses linear and non-linear difference–indifference methods, regression discontinuity designs and quantile models. The econometrics of treatment effects remains an active literature in which new developments abound. High-dimensional regression, Bayesian approaches, bounds and networks are among the many areas of current research in causal inference, so there will soon be material for a second volume.

Frölich and Sperlich's book will be of interest whether you are an applied economist who wants to understand what you are doing or you just want to understand what others do. Estimating the causal effect of a policy from non-experimental data is challenging. This book will help us to better understand and use the existing tools to deal with the challenges. I warmly congratulate Markus and Stefan on their remarkable achievement.

Manuel Arellano
Madrid
April 2018

Manuel Arellano has been a Professor of Economics at CEMFI in Madrid since 1991. Prior to that, he held appointments at the University of Oxford (1985–89) and the London School of Economics (1989–91). He is a graduate of the University of Barcelona and holds a PhD from the London School of Economics. He has served as Editor of the *Review of Economic Studies* (1994–98), Co-Editor of the *Journal of Applied Econometrics* (2006–08) and Co-Chair of the World Congress of the Econometrc Society (2010). He is a Fellow of the Econometric Society and a Foreign Honorary Member of the American Academy of Arts and Sciences. He has been President of the Spanish Economic Association (2003), President of the European Economic Association (2013) and President of the Econometric Society (2014). He has published many research papers on topics in econometrics and labour economics, in particular on the analysis of panel data, being named a Highly Cited Researcher by Thomson ISI (2010). He is the author of *Panel Data Econometrics* (2003). He is a recipient of the Rey Jaime I Prize in Economics (2012).

Introduction

This book on advanced econometrics is intended to familiarise the reader with technical developments in the area of econometrics known as *treatment effect estimation*, or
impact or *policy evaluation*. In this book we try to combine intuitive reasoning in identification and estimation with econometric and statistical rigour. This holds especially for
the complete list of stochastic assumptions and their implications in practice. Moreover,
for both identification and estimation, we focus mostly on non-parametric methods (i.e.
our methods are not based on specific pre-specified models or functional forms) in order
to provide approaches that are quite generally valid. Graphs and a number of examples
of evaluation studies are applied to explain how sources of exogenous variation can be
explored when disentangling causality from correlation.

What makes the analysis of treatment effects different from more conventional econometric analysis methods, such as those covered, for example, in the textbooks of
Cameron and Trivedi (2005), Greene (1997) or Wooldridge (2002)? A first major difference is that the three steps – definition of parameter of interest, identification and
statistical modelling – are clearly separated. This helps first to define the objects one
is interested in, and to clearly articulate the definition and interpretation of counterfactual outcomes. A second major difference is the focus on non-parametric identification
and estimation. Even though parametric models might eventually be used in the empirical analysis, discussing identification without the need to impose – usually arbitrary –
functional forms helps us to understand where the identifying power comes from. This
permits us to link the identification strategy very tightly to the particular policy evaluation problem. A third, and also quite important, difference is the acknowledgement of
possible treatment effect heterogeneity. Even though it would be interesting to model
this heterogeneity of treatment effects, according to the standard literature we take it
as being of unknown form: some individuals may benefit greatly from a certain intervention whereas some may benefit less, while others may even be harmed. Although
treatment effects are most likely heterogeneous, we typically do not know the form of
this heterogeneity. Nonetheless, the practitioner should always be aware of this heterogeneity, whereas (semi-)parametric regression models either do not permit it or do
not articulate it clearly. For example, most of the instrumental variable (IV) literature
simply ignores the problem of heterogeneity, and often people are not aware of the consequences of particular model or IV choices in their data analysis. This can easily render
the presented interpretation invalid.

The book is oriented towards the main strands of recent developments, and it emphasises the reading of original articles by leading scholars. It does not and cannot substitute

for the reading of original articles, but it seeks to summarise most of the central aspects, harmonising notation and (hopefully) providing a coherent road map. Unlike some handbooks on impact evaluation, this book aims to impart a deeper understanding of the underlying ideas, assumptions and methods. This includes such questions as: what are the necessary conditions for the identification and application of the particular methods?; what is the estimator doing to the data?; what are the statistical properties, asymptotically and in finite samples, advantages and pitfalls, etc.? We believe that only a deeper understanding of all these issues (the economic theory that identifies the parameters of interest, the conditions of the chosen estimator or test and the behaviour of the statistical method) can finally lead to a correct inference and interpretation.

Quite comprehensive review articles, summarising a good part of the theoretical work that has been published in the last 15 years in the econometric literature,[1] include, for example, Imbens (2004), Heckman and Vytlacil (2007a), Heckman and Vytlacil (2007b), Abbring and Heckman (2007) and Imbens and Wooldridge (2009). See also Angrist and Pischke (2008). The classical area of application in economics was that of labour market research, where some of the oldest econometric reviews on this topic can be found; see Angrist and Krueger (1999) and Heckman, LaLonde and Smith (1999). Nowadays, the topic of treatment effect estimation and policy evaluation is especially popular in the field of poverty and development economics, as can be seen from the reviews of Duflo, Glennerster and Kremer (2008) and Ravallion (2008). Blundell and Dias (2009) try to reconcile these methods with the structural model approach that is standard in microeconometrics. Certainly, this approach has to be employed with care, as students could easily get the impression that treatment effect estimators are just semi-parametric extensions of the well-known parameter estimation problems in structural models.

Before starting, we should add that this book considers the randomised control trials (RCT) only in the first chapter, and just as a general principle rather than in detail. The book by Guido W. Imbens and Donald B. Rubin, *Causal Inference for Statistics, Social, and Biomedical Sciences: An Introduction*, has appeared quite recently and deals with this topic in considerable detail. (See also the book Glennerster and Takavarasha (2013) on practical aspects of running RCTs). Instead, we have added to the chapters on the standard methods of matching, instrumental variable approach, regression discontinuity design and difference-in-differences more detailed discussions about the use of *propensity scores*, and we introduce in detail *quantile and distributional effects* and give an overview of the analysis of *dynamic treatment effects*, including sequential treatments and duration analysis. Furthermore, unlike the standard econometrics literature, we introduce (for the identification of causality structures) graph theory from the statistics literature, and give a (somewhat condensed) review of non-parametric estimation that is applied later on in the book.

---

[1] There exists an even more abundant statistical literature that we neither cite nor review here simply for the sake of brevity.

1 Basic Definitions, Assumptions and Randomised Experiments

1.1   Treatment Effects: Definitions, Assumptions and Problems

In econometrics, one often wants to learn the *causal effect* of a variable on some other variable, be it a policy question or some mere 'cause and effect' question. Although, at first glance, the problem might look trivial, it can become tricky to talk about causality when the real cause is masked by several other events. In this chapter we will present the basic definitions and assumptions about the casual models; in the coming chapters you will learn the different ways of answering questions about causality. So this chapter is intended to set up the framework for the content of the rest of the book.

We start by assuming we have a variable D which causes variable Y to change. Our principal aim here is not to find the best fitting model for predicting Y or to analyse the covariance of Y; we are interested in the impact of this *treatment* D on the outcome of interest (which is Y). You might be interested in the total effect of D on Y, or in the effect of D on Y in a particular environment where other variables are held fixed (the so-called *ceteris paribus* case). In the latter case, we again have to distinguish carefully between conditional and partial effects. Variable Y could indicate an outcome later in life, e.g. employment status, earnings or wealth, and D could be the amount of education an individual has received, measured as 'years of schooling'. This setup acknowledges the literature on treatment evaluation, where $D \in \{0, 1\}$ is usually binary and indicates whether or not an individual received a particular treatment. Individuals with $D = 1$ will often be called *participants* or *treated*, while individuals with $D = 0$ are referred to as *non-participants* or *controls*. A treatment $D = 1$ could represent, for example, receiving a vaccine or a medical treatment, participating in an adult literacy training programme, participating in a public works scheme, attending private versus public secondary school, attending vocational versus academic secondary schooling, attending a university, etc. A treatment could also be a voucher (or receiving the entitlement to a voucher or even a conditional cash transfer) to attend a private school. Examples of this are the large conditional cash transfer programmes in several countries in Latin America. Certainly, D could also be a non-binary variable, perhaps representing different subjects of university degrees, or even a continuous variable such as subsidy payments, fees or tax policies.

Example 1.1 The Mexican programme PROGRESA, which has been running under the name Oportunidades since 2002, is a government social assistance programme that started in 1997. It was designed to alleviate poverty through the rise of human capital. It has been providing cash payments to families in exchange for regular school attendance, health clinic visits and also nutritional support, to encourage co-responsibility. There was a rigorous (pre-)selection of recipients based on geographical and socioeconomic factors, but at the end of 2006 around one-quarter of Mexico's population had participated in it. One might be interested to know how these cash payments to members, families or households had helped them, or whether there has been any positive impact to change their living conditions. These are quite usual questions that policy makers need to answer on a regular basis. One key feature of PROGRESA is its system of evaluation and statistical controls to ensure its effectiveness. For this reason and given its success, Oportunidades has recently become a role model for programmes instituted in many other countries, especially in Latin America and Africa.

Let us set up the statistical setting that we will use in this book. All variables will be treated as random. This is a notational convenience, but it does not exclude deterministic variables. As measure-theory will not help you much in understanding the econometrics discussed here, we assume that all these random variables are defined in a common probability space. The population of this probability space will often be the set of individuals, firms, households, classrooms, etc. of a certain country, province, district, etc. We are thinking not only of the observed values but of all possible values that the considered variable can take. Similarly, we are not doing finite population theory but thinking rather of a hyper-population; so one may think of a population containing infinitely many individuals from which individuals are sampled randomly (maybe organised in strata or blocks). Furthermore, unlike the situation where we discuss estimation problems, for the purpose of identification one typically starts from the idea of having an infinitely large sample. From here, one can obtain estimators for the joint distribution of all (observed) variables. But as samples are finite in practice, it is important to understand that you can obtain good estimators and reasonable inference only when putting both together: that is, a good identification strategy and good estimation methods. Upper-case letters will represent random variables or random vectors, whereas lower-case letters will represent (realised) numbers or vectors, or simply an unspecified argument over which we integrate.

In most chapters the main interest is first to identify the impact of D on Y from an infinitely large sample of independently sampled observations, and afterwards to estimate it. We will see that, in many situations, once the identification problem is solved, a natural estimator is immediately available (efficiency and further inference issues aside). We will also examine what might be estimated under different identifying assumptions. The empirical researcher has then to decide which set of assumptions is most adequate for the situation. Before we do so, we have to introduce some notation and definitions. This is done in the (statistically probably) 'ideal' situation of having real experimental data, such as in a laboratory.

1.1.1 What Is a Treatment Effect?

There are many ways to introduce the notation of treatment effects. Perhaps the simplest is to imagine two parallel universes, say A and B, containing the same, identical individuals. When in universe A, individual i is now exposed to treatment $D_i = 1$, while in B it is not ($D_i = 0$); then all resulting differences for individual i, say $Y_i^A - Y_i^B$, can be considered as a treatment effect.

Let us formalise this by thinking of data-generating processes. For this, let D and Y be scalar random variables (an extension to vector-valued cases will be discussed later). Also assume in the following setup that Y is observed for every individual, whether it be employment status, earnings of wealth, etc.[1] We want to study the following relationship:

$$Y_i = \varphi(D_i, X_i, U_i), \tag{1.1}$$

where φ is an unknown (measurable) function and (X_i, U_i) are vectors of observed and unobserved characteristics, respectively. The dimension of (X_i, U_i) is not yet restricted. Both might be scalars or of higher dimension; one even might want to drop X_i if only unobserved characteristics matter. If we consider abilities or skills as unobserved characteristics, then U_i can be multidimensional. Nonetheless, inside one equation, all unobserved parts are typically summarised in a one-dimensional variable. When we impose conditions on φ or the distributions of X_i and U_i, this can become relevant. In Equation 1.1 we assume that there exists a common φ for the whole population so that the right-hand variables comprise all heterogeneity when generating outcome Y_i. In this case, U_i plays the same role as the so-called residuals or error terms in regression analysis.

Thinking more generally, not just of one individual i, is important to emphasise that (1.1) does not imply homogeneous (i.e. the same for all individuals) returns to D or X even though we skipped index i from φ. Function φ just describes a structural relationship among the variables, and is assumed to be *not* under the control of the individuals; nor is it chosen or manipulated by them. As an example, it can be a production function. In particular, φ describes the relationship between D and Y not only for the actually observed values, but it should also capture the change in outcome Y if we had changed D externally to some other value.

In fact, our interest is to learn about this function φ or some features of it, so that we can predict what would happen if we changed D exogenously (i.e. without asking i). This idea becomes more clear when we define the concept of potential outcome. Notationally we express the potential outcome as

$$Y_i^d = \varphi(d, X_i, U_i), \tag{1.2}$$

which is the outcome that individual i would experience if (X_i, U_i) were held fixed but D_i were set externally to the value d (the so-called *treatment*). The point here is not to enforce the treatment $D_i = d$, but rather to highlight that we are not interested in a

---

[1] In contrast, a variable like wages would only be observed for those who are actually working. The case is slightly different for those who are not working; clearly it's a latent variable then. This might introduce a (possibly additional) selection problem.

φ that varies with the individual's decision to get treated. The case where changing D_i also has an impact on (X_i, U_i) will be discussed later.

Example 1.2 Let Y_i denote a person's wealth at the age of 50, and let D_i be a dummy indicating whether or not he was randomly selected for a programme promoting his education. Further, let X_i be his observable external (starting) conditions, which were not affected by D_i, and U_i his (remaining) unobserved abilities and facilities. Here, D_i was externally set to d when deciding about the kind of treatment. If we think of a D_i that can only take 0 and 1, then for two values $d = 1$ (he gets the treatment) and $d = 0$ (he doesn't get the treatment), the same individual can have the two different potential outcomes Y_i^1 and Y_i^0 respectively. But of course in reality we observe only one. We denote the realised outcome as Y_i.

This brings us to the notion of a *counterfactual exercise*: this simply means that you observe $Y_i = Y_i^d$ for the realised $d = D_i$ but use your model $\varphi(\cdot)$ to predict $Y_i^{d'}$ for a d' of your choice.

Example 1.3 Let Y_i be as before and let D_i be the dummy indicating whether person i graduated from a university or not. Further, let X_i and U_i be the external conditions as in Example 1.2. In practice, X_i and U_i may impact on D_i for several individuals i such that those who graduate from a different subpopulation from those who do not might hardly be comparable. Note that setting externally D_i to d is a theoretical exercise, it does not necessarily mean that we can effectively enforce a 'treatment' on individual i; rather, it allows us to predict how the individual would perform under treatment (or non-treatment), generating the potential outcomes Y_i^1 and Y_i^0. In reality, we only observe either Y_i^1 or Y_i^0 for each individual, calling it Y_i.

Notice that the relationship (1.2) is assumed on the individual level to be given an unchanged environment: only variation in D for individual i is considered, but not variation in D for other individuals which may impact on Y_i or might generate feedback cycles. We will formalise this assumption in Section 1.1.3. In this sense, the approach is more focused on a microeconometric effect: a policy that changes D for every individual or for a large number of individuals (like a large campaign to increase education or computer literacy) might change the entire equilibrium, and therefore function φ might change then, too. Such kinds of macro effects, displacement effects or general equilibrium effects are not considered here, though they have been receiving more and more attention in the treatment evaluation literature. Certainly, i could be cities, regions, counties or even states.[2] In this sense, the methods introduced here also apply to problems in macroeconomics.

---

[2] Card and Krueger (1994), for example, studied the impact of the increase of the minimum wage in 1992 in New Jersey.

Example 1.4 An example of changing φ could be observed when a large policy is providing employment or wage subsidies for unemployed workers. This may lower the labour market chances for individuals not eligible to such subsidies. This is known as *substitution* or *displacement effects*, and they are expected to change the entire labour market: the cost of labour decreases for the firms, the disutility from unemployment decreases for the workers, which in turn impacts on efficiency wages, search behaviour and the bargaining power of trade unions. In total, we are changing our function φ.

Let us get back to the question of causality in the microcosm and look at the different outcomes for an exogenous change in treatment from d to d'. The difference

$$Y_i^{d'} - Y_i^d$$

is obviously the individual treatment effect. It tells us how the realised outcome for the ith individual would change if we changed the treatment status. This turns out to be almost impossible to estimate or predict. Fortunately, most of the time we are more interested in either the expected treatment effect or an aggregate of treatment effects for many individuals. This brings us to the average treatment effect (ATE).

Example 1.5 As in the last two examples, let $D_i \in \{0, 1\}$ indicate whether or not person i graduated from university, and let Y_i denote their wealth at the age of 50. Then, $Y_i^1 - Y_i^0$ is the effect of university graduation on wealth for person i. It is the wealth obtained if this same individual had attended university minus the wealth this individual would have obtained without attending university. Notice that the 'same individual' is not equivalent to the *ceteris paribus* assumption in regression analysis. We explicitly want to allow for changes in other variables if they were caused by the university graduation. While this is doubtless of intimate interest for this particular person, politicians might be more interested in the gain in wealth on average or for some parts of the population.

Sometimes we want to consider situations explicitly where we are interested in the effects of two (or more) treatment variables. We could then consider D to be vector-valued. Yet, it is useful to use two different symbols for the two treatment variables, say D and X (subsumed in the vector of observable characteristics), for two reasons. The first reason is that we may sometimes have some treatment variables D that are endogenous, i.e. caused by U, whereas the other treatment variables are considered exogenous. Therefore, we distinguish D from the other variables since dealing with the endogeneity of D will require more attention. A second, unrelated reason is that we sometimes like to make it explicit that we are mainly interested in the impacts of *changes* in D by external intervention while keeping X fixed. This is the known *ceteris paribus* analogue, and in the treatment effect literature is typically referred to as a *partial* or *direct effect* of D on Y.

Example 1.6 Let D_i indicate whether individual i attended private or public secondary school, whereas X_i indicates whether the individual afterwards went to university or not. Here, we might be interested in that part of the effect of private versus public school on wealth that is not channelled via university attendance. Clearly, attending private or public school (D) is likely to have an effect on the likelihood to visit a university (X), which in turn is going to affect wealth. But one might instead be interested in a potential direct effect of D on wealth, even if university attendance is externally fixed. From this example we can easily see that it depends heavily on the question of interest, i.e. how the treatment parameter is defined.

To notationally clarify the difference to the above situation, let us define

$$Y_{i,x}^d = \varphi(d, x, U_i) .$$

The function φ is still the same as before, so the only difference is that D and X are both thought of as (separate) arguments that one might want to set externally. Then the *partial* or *direct effect* (i.e. the effect not channelled via university attendance in Example 1.6) of D (public versus private school) is

$$Y_{i,x}^{d''} - Y_{i,x}^{d'} .$$

That is, $Y_{i,0}^1 - Y_{i,0}^0$ in Example 1.6 is the partial effect of private/public when university attendance is set to zero, whereas $Y_{i,1}^1 - Y_{i,1}^0$ is the effect when university attendance is fixed at one (by external intervention). In contrast, the total effect of private versus public secondary school is

$$Y_i^{d''} - Y_i^{d'} .$$

Hence, the reason for using two different symbols for D and X is to emphasise that one is interested in the effects of changes in D while keeping X fixed or not. Sometimes such partial effects can be obtained simply by conditioning X, and sometimes more sophisticated approaches are necessary, as will be seen later.

Example 1.7 Consider the Mincer earnings functions in labour economics, which are often used to estimate the returns to education. To determine them, in many empirical studies log wages are regressed on the job experience, years of schooling and a measure of ability (measured in early childhood, if available). The reasoning is that all these are important determinants of wages. We are not so interested in the effects of ability on wages, and merely include ability in the regression to deal with the selection problem discussed later on. The *ceteris paribus* analysis examines, hypothetically, how wages would change if years of schooling (D) were changed while experience (X) remained fixed. Since on-the-job experience usually accumulates after the completion of education, schooling (D) may have different effects: one plausible possibility is that schooling affects the probability and duration of unemployment or repeated unemployment, which reduces the accumulation of job experience. Schooling outcomes may also affect the time out of the labour force, which also reduces job experience. In some countries it may decrease the time spent in prison. Hence, D affects Y indirectly via X. Another possibility is that years of schooling are likely to have a direct positive effect on wages. Thus, by including X in the regression, we control for the indirect effect and measure only the direct effect of schooling. So, including X in the regression may or may not be a good strategy, depending on what we are trying to identify. Sometimes we want to identify only the total effect, but not the direct effect, and sometimes vice versa.

We are interested in *non-parametric identification* of φ or some features of it. Non-parametric identification basically means that there is no further model than Equation 1.1 without further specification of φ. Thus, the identification will be mainly based on assumptions relating to the causality structure, which in practice have to be based on economic theory. In contrast, most econometric textbooks start by assuming a linear model of the type (keeping our notation of variables)

$$Y_i = \alpha + D_i\beta + X_i\gamma + U_i \tag{1.3}$$

to discuss identification and estimation of β under certain restrictions like

$$E[U_i|D_i, X_i] = 0. \tag{1.4}$$

In other words, they identify the parameters of (1.3), which coincide with the question of interest only if their model is correctly specified. The statistics literature typically discusses the correct interpretation of the parameter whatever the true underlying data-generating process may be, to relate it to the question of interest afterwards. Doubtless, the latter approach is safer, but it might answer the question of interest only unsatisfactorily. However, since the assumption of linearity is almost always an assumption made for convenience but not based on sound economic theory, it is more insightful to discuss what can be identified under which restrictions without imposing a functional form on φ; it might be linear, quadratic or any other form; it need not even be continuous, differentiable or monotonic.

For identification, we will nonetheless have to impose certain restrictions, which are usually much weaker than (1.3), (1.4). Such restrictions often come in the form of differentiability and continuity restrictions on φ (also called smoothness restrictions). There is a large and still growing literature which attempts to find the weakest assumptions under which certain objects can be identified. The function φ is *non-parametrically identified* if we can determine it exactly from an infinitely large sample. Suppose that we have infinitely many observations, so that we effectively know the joint distribution of Y, D and X. The function φ, or some feature of it, is non-parametrically identified if no other function could have generated the same distribution. Or, putting it the other way around, it is not identified if two different functions, say φ and $\tilde{\varphi}$, could generate the same joint distribution of the observed variables. A consequence of the lack of an explicit (parametric) model or function φ is that it is now identified only in some regions but e.g. not outside the support of the observations.

1.1.2   Formal Definitions: ATE, ATET, ATEN

In this section we will formalise different treatment effects 'on average'. We focus on a binary treatment $D \in \{0, 1\}$ case, because it helps a lot to understand the main issues of identification without further complexities; later on we will also discuss some extensions. Recall the university graduation of Example 1.5. There we wanted to estimate the expected wealth effect of attending university for a person randomly drawn from the population, namely

$$E[Y^1 - Y^0].$$

Notice that the expectation operator has the same meaning as averaging over all individuals i of the population of interest. To put things in perspective, let's consider a city in which we send everyone to universities (of course, assuming we have the authority to do so). Somewhat later, we observe their income and take the average for calculating $E[Y^1]$. Now let's imagine we travel back to the past and keep everybody away from university. Again we observe their income and calculate the average to get $E[Y^0]$. Since expectation is linear, this difference is exactly the same as we mentioned before. This is known as an *average treatment effect*, or ATE for short. In reality we cannot send an individual to both states. Some of them will go to university and some won't. So, for the same individual, we cannot observe his outcomes in both states, we observe only one. We can interpret the average causal effect of attending university in two ways: it is the expected effect on an individual randomly drawn from the population and at the same time, and it is the change in the average outcome if D were changed from 0 to 1 for every individual, provided that no general equilibrium effect occurs.

In reality, some of the individuals will go to university and some won't. What we can do is then to take the average of those who attended the university and those who didn't, respectively. To compare the average wealth of those who attended ($D_i = 1$) with those who didn't ($D_i = 0$), we could look at

$$E[Y^1|D = 1] - E[Y^0|D = 0].$$

It is important to see that conceptually this is totally different from an average treatment effect. First of all, we didn't do anything; it was they who decided to go to university or not. This creates the two groups different in many ways. Particularly they might differ in observed and unobserved characteristics. This difference is most apparent when examining the effect only for those who actually did attend universities. This is the so-called *average treatment effect on the treated* (ATET) and it is defined as

$$E[Y^1 - Y^0|D = 1].$$

Again, you do the similar thought experiment as above but not for the whole city; rather, just for those who actually would have attended universities anyhow. This is often of particular interest in a policy evaluation context, where it may be more informative to know how the programme affected those who actually participated in it than how it might have affected others. Here it is even more obvious that simply comparing the observed outcomes of those who did attend university with those who did not will usually not provide a consistent estimate of the ATET. Already intuition tells us that these two groups differ in observed and unobserved characteristics, and might even define different populations while we are now exclusively focusing on the subpopulation for which $D = 1$. Of course, if rolling out the policy to the entire population is intended for the future, then the ATE, or maybe even the *average treatment effect on the non-treated* (ATEN) $E[Y^1 - Y^0|D = 0]$, would be more interesting.

In the university graduation example, the difference between ATET and ATE is often referred to as the *sorting gain*. The decision whether to attend university or not is likely to depend on some kind of individual expectation about their wage gains from attending university. This leads to a sorting of the population. Those who gain most from university are more likely to attend it, whereas those who have little to gain from it will most likely abstain. This could lead to an ATET being much higher than ATE. Hence, the average wage gain for students is higher in the sorted subpopulation than in a world without sorting. This difference between ATET and ATE could be due to differences in observed as well as unobserved characteristics. Hence, the *observed* difference in outcomes among students and non-students can be decomposed as

$$E[Y|D = 1] - E[Y|D = 0] = \underbrace{\text{average return to schooling}}_{ATE} + \underbrace{\text{sorting gain}}_{ATET - ATE}$$

$$+ \underbrace{\text{selection bias}}_{E[Y^0|D=1]-E[Y^0|D=0]} .$$

Example 1.8 Consider an example of formal and informal labour markets. This example will help us to understand that typically $ATET > ATE$ if a larger Y_i means something positive for i. In many parts of the developing and developed world, individuals work in the informal sector (typically consisting of activities at firms without formal registration or without employment contract or without compliance with required social security contributions). Roughly, one can distinguish four different activities: self-employed in the formal sector, i.e. owner of a registered firm; self-employed in the informal sector, i.e. owner of a business without formal registration;[3] worker in the formal sector; and, lastly, worker in the informal sector. Firms in the formal sector pay taxes, have access to courts and other public services but also have to adhere to certain legislation, e.g. adhering to worker protection laws, providing medical and retirement benefits, etc. Informal firms do not have access to public services such as police and courts, and have to purchase private protection or rely on networks. Similarly, employees in the formal sector have a legal work contract and are, at least in principle, covered by worker protection laws and usually benefit from medical benefits like accident insurance, retirement benefits, job dismissal rules, etc.

The early literature on this duality sometimes associated the formal sector with the modern industrialist sector and the informal sector with technologically backward or rural areas. The formal sector was considered to be superior. Those individuals migrating from the rural to the urban areas in search of formal sector jobs who do not find formal employment, accept work in the urban informal sector until they find formal

---

[3] This includes, for example, family firms or various types of street vendors.

employment. Jobs in the formal sector are thus rationed, and employment in the informal sector is a second-best choice.[4] Therefore, a formal and an informal sector coexist, with higher wages and better working conditions in the formal one. Everyone would thus prefer to be working in the latter.

On the contrary, there may be good reasons why some firms and workers voluntarily prefer informality, particularly when taxes and social security contributions are high, licences for registration are expensive or difficult to obtain, public services are of poor quality and returns to firm size (economies of scale) are low. To run a large firm usually means a switch to the formal sector. Similarly, the medical and retirement benefits to formal employees (and worker protection) may be of limited value, and in some countries access to these benefits already exists if a family member is in formal employment. In addition, official labour market restrictions relating to working hours, paid holidays, notice period, severance pay, maternity leave, etc. may not provide the flexibility that firms and workers desire. Under certain conditions, workers and firms could then voluntarily choose informal employment. Firms may also prefer informality, as this may guard them against the development of strong unions or worker representation, e.g. regarding reorganisations, dismissals, social plans for unemployed or precarious workers. Hence, costs (taxes, social security) and state regulations provide incentives for remaining informal.

Now think about individual i who seeks treatment or not, say to employment either in the formal or informal sector, respectively. Let Y_i^1 be his wage if he goes to the formal sector, and Y_i^0 his wage in the informal sector. This outcome may also include non-wage benefits. If individuals self-select their sector they would choose the formal sector when

$$D_i = \mathbb{1}\left\{Y_i^1 > Y_i^0\right\} ,$$

i.e. decide for treatment (or against it), depending on their potential outcomes and ignoring for a moment the uncertainty here. This model is often referred to as the Roy (1951) model.

Under the hypothesis of informality being only an involuntary choice because of the limited size of the formal sector, it should be that $Y_i^1 - Y_i^0 > 0$ for almost everyone. In this case, some individuals would like to join the formal sector but are not successful. But thinking of an efficient allocation, and taking the size of the formal sector as given, we would find that

$$ATET = E\left[Y^1 - Y^0 | D = 1\right] > E\left[Y^1 - Y^0 | D = 0\right] = ATEN , \qquad (1.5)$$

---

[4] Recall also the *efficiency wage theory*: if a worker's effort in the formal sector cannot be monitored perfectly, or only at a considerable cost, to promote workers effort some incentives are required. An implication of efficiency wage theory is that firms pay higher wages to promote effort, which leads to unemployment. The risk of becoming unemployed in the case of shirking provides the incentives for the worker to increase effort. Because most developing countries do not provide generous unemployment insurance schemes, and because the value of money is larger than the utility from leisure, these unemployed enter into low-productivity informal activities where they are either self-employed or where monitoring is less costly.

that is, those who obtained a formal sector job should have a larger gain vis-à-vis non-formal employment than those who did not obtain a formal sector job ($D = 0$).[5] Note that the inequality (1.5) is only a result of economic theory but not a general result from statistics. Further, as

$$ATEN = \{ATE - ATET \cdot P(D = 1)\}/P(D = 0),$$

Equation 1.5 is equivalent to $ATET > ATE$.

1.1.3   Stable-Unit-Treatment-Value Assumption

Recall the concept of potential outcome. When talking about treatment effects, this is perhaps the most important concept. Theoretically, if we could observe the same individual in two different states (with and without treatment) then it would be possible to talk about the effect for the ith individual. But as we mentioned before, in many cases this is not feasible and typically of minor interest for policy and economics. Therefore, we defined the ATE, ATET and ATEN. Let us look at a group of individuals who are treated and another group who are not (our controls). Clearly, in order to think and speak about specific identification problems when measuring impacts, we must have a well-defined control group. We might have a comparison group, but the tricky part is having a well-defined one.

Think about the case where everybody is affected by a policy, then a control subpopulation only exists in theory. Any empirical approach might be in vain in this setting. Moreover, this would clearly change the (partial) equilibrium and therefore change φ anyway (see Example 1.4 and discussion). Even if the entire population does not undergo the treatment directly, and equilibrium is not really affected (φ does not really change), we might face the problem of *spillover effects*. These can destroy the validity of any analysis or its conclusions since it means the individual ith outcome is not only affected by his (non-)treatment but also by the treatment of individual j.

Example 1.9 Typical examples where spillover effects are quite obvious are (medical) treatments to combat contagious diseases. Therefore, studies in which medical treatment is randomised at the individual level potentially underestimate the benefits of treatment. They typically miss externality benefits to the comparison group from reduced disease transmission. Consequently, one fails to estimate the counterfactual situation of no-treatment. Miguel and Kremer (2004) evaluated a Kenyan project in which school-based mass treatment with deworming drugs was randomly phased into schools, rather than to individuals, allowing estimation of overall programme effects. Individuals at the selected school could nonetheless decide not to participate. When accounting for the mentioned spill over effects, they found that the programme reduced school absenteeism in treatment schools by one-quarter. Not surprisingly, deworming substantially improved health and school participation also among the untreated children in both,

---

[5] For a recent application see Arias and Khamis (2008).

treatment schools and even in neighbouring schools. However, they could not find, for example, statistical evidence that the deworming programme had a positive impact on the academic test scores.

A way to express such an assumption of no spillover or no general equilibrium effects on other individuals is known as the *stable-unit-treatment-value assumption* (SUTVA).

The definition of potential outcomes already made implicit use of the assumption of 'no interference between different units' (Cox, 1958, p. 19), which is basically the meaning of SUTVA (Rubin, 1980). It is assumed that the potential outcomes Y_i^0, Y_i^1 of individual i are not affected by the allocation of other individuals to the treatments. Suppose we have a sample of size n. Formally, let $\mathbf{D}$ denote a treatment-allocation vector that indicates for all n individuals the programme in which they participate. Let $\mathbf{Y}$ denote the vector of length n of the observed outcomes of all individuals. Define $\mathbf{Y}(\mathbf{D})$ as the potential outcome vector that would be observed if all individuals were allocated to the policy according to the allocation $\mathbf{D}$. Further let $Y_i(\mathbf{D})$ denote the ith element of this potential outcome vector.

The stable-unit-treatment-value assumption states that, for any two allocations $\mathbf{D}$ and $\mathbf{D}'$,

$$Y_i(\mathbf{D}) = Y_i(\mathbf{D}') \qquad \text{if} \qquad \mathbf{D}_i = \mathbf{D}_i', \qquad (1.6)$$

where $\mathbf{D}_i$ and $\mathbf{D}_i'$ denote the ith element of the vectors $\mathbf{D}$ and $\mathbf{D}'$, respectively. In other words, it is assumed that the observed outcome Y_i depends only on the treatment to which individual i is assigned to, and not on the allocation of other individuals. If we change the allocation of other individuals, keeping the ith allocation fixed, then the outcome of the ith individual shouldn't change.[6]

The SUTVA assumption might be invalidated if individuals interact, either directly or through markets. Let's see some examples.

Example 1.10 Let's assume a firm wants to give training to build a skilled workforce and it needs to evaluate how effective the training is, so that training materials can also be used in future. If the firm wants to see how this training creates an impact on the production or output, it really needs to make sure that lessons from the training do not get to the workers in the control group. It can take two groups from very different parts of the factory, so that they have little or no chance to interact, but then we have different structural setups and it would make little sense to compare them. But if it takes employees from the same part of the production process then there is a possibility that the people who were intentionally not given the training might be interested to know about the contents, ask treated workers and try to implement the ideas. For example, if the training teaches the use of some kind of waste management technique, then some people in the control group might be tempted to use the ideas, too.

---

[6] For an excellent discussion about the history of potential outcomes and SUTVA, please have a look at chapters 1 and 2 of Imbens and Rubin (2015). There they mention two assumptions related to SUTVA: 'No interference', which is same as our no-spillover, and 'No hidden variations of treatments', which means that, for all the observations, the treatment variations should be the same.

Market and general equilibrium effects often depend on the scale of the policy, i.e. on the number of participants in the programmes. In fact, departures from SUTVA are likely to be small if only a few individuals participate in the policy, but with an increasing number of participants we expect larger spillover effects (or other externalities).

Example 1.11 If active labour market programmes change the relative supply of skilled and unskilled labour, all individuals may be affected by the resulting changes in the wage structure. In addition, programmes which affect the labour cost structure, e.g. through wage subsidies, may lead to displacement effects, where unsubsidised workers are laid off and are replaced by subsidised programme participants. Individuals might further be affected by the taxes raised for financing the policy. It is obvious that these interaction or spillover effects can be pretty small if one focuses only on a small economic sector, for example in order to alleviate social hardships when a structural break happens, as was the case for the European coal mining sector or the shipbuilding industry.

A quite different form of interference between individuals can arise due to supply constraints. If the number of programme slots is limited, the availability of the programme for a particular individual depends on how many participants have already been allocated to this programme. Such interaction does not directly affect the potential outcomes and, thus, does not invalidate the microeconometric evaluation approaches discussed subsequently. However, it restricts the set of feasible allocations **D** and could become relevant when trying to change the allocation of participants in order to improve the overall effectiveness of the policy. Supply constraints are often (at least partly) under the control of the programme administration and could be moderated if necessary.

Henceforth, the validity of SUTVA is assumed. Consequently, it is no longer necessary to take account of the full treatment allocation vector **D**, since the outcome of individual i depends only on the treatment received by himself, which is denoted by a scalar variable D_i in the following.

1.1.4 Conditional Independence Assumption and Selection Bias

Unfortunately, SUTVA is necessary but not sufficient for identification. Often a simple estimation of $E[Y^d | D = d]$ will not identify the mean potential outcome due to the obvious problem of selection bias. The reasons for this bias can be various and quite different, such as self-selection or eligibility criteria. In either case, the key problem is the potential differences between the subpopulations of treated and non-treated subjects (or random samples of each). Consequently, neither can be taken as a representative (or sample) of the whole population. Simple estimators will therefore be biased.

However, we will see that if we were to observe all covariates that affect D and the potential outcome, then, conditional on these covariates X, the variables D and Y^d are independent ($\perp\!\!\!\perp$). This at least is the hope that one builds different estimators on. This so-called conditional independence assumption (CIA) can be expressed by

$$Y^d \perp\!\!\!\perp D|X \qquad \forall d \in Supp(D). \tag{1.7}$$

It is also well known as the *selection on observables* assumption.[7]

Let us further discuss here the *selection bias*, as it is basically the key problem of treatment effect estimation. All the methods we introduce in the following chapters simply try to correct for that bias using different sets of assumptions. We start from a most naive estimator of the average treatment effect for the treated (ATET). If you tried to estimate it simply by the difference of sample averages of realised outcomes, you would actually estimate (by the law of large numbers)

$$E[Y|D=1] - E[Y|D=0] = E[Y^1|D=1] - E[Y^0|D=0] \tag{1.8}$$
$$= \underbrace{\left\{ E[Y^1|D=1] - E[Y^0|D=1] \right\}}_{ATET} + \underbrace{\left\{ E[Y^0|D=1] - E[Y^0|D=0] \right\}}_{\text{selection bias}}.$$

For the treatment group the observed outcome equals the potential treatment outcome, and for the control group the observed outcome equals the potential non-treatment outcome. This gives the first equality; adding and subtracting $E[Y^0|D=1]$ gives the second one. This way, we have split up (1.8) into two parts, of which the first term is the ATET, whereas the second term is the selection bias.

Example 1.12 Suppose you want to see whether increased sanitation coverage has any impact on health. In many parts of the developing world, open defecation is still a big problem and the government might be interested in seeing the impact of this policy. Assume we start with a group of households. We seek the households with the worst latrines, or no latrines, and install hygiene latrines there. Then we take the difference of the average of some health measure between those who got the latrines and those who didn't. As we gave treatments to those who were the worst, it might be the case that initially (before treatment) they were already in a worse state for other reasons (people who didn't have the latrines might be poor and their health status is already pretty bad). So even if they hadn't received the treatment, their average health status would be relatively low, i.e. $E[Y^0|D=1]$ might be a lot larger than $E[Y^0|D=0]$. In this case, just taking the difference of simple averages would not reveal the ATE, because *selection bias* would mask the actual treatment effect.

In the example of the impact of university education on earnings or wealth, this selection bias is the difference in the non-graduation wealth between individuals who actually attended university and those who did not. Of central interest is not the association between earnings and schooling, but rather the change in earnings that would result if schooling were changed 'exogenously', i.e. independent of potential earnings to verify the CIA. The fact that university graduates earn, on average, higher wages than non-graduates, could simply reflect differences in ability. Hence, graduates and non-graduates had different observed and unobserved characteristics even before some of

---

[7] This essentially means that there is *no* selection on unobservables that are also affecting the outcome.

them entered university. To identify the individual return to schooling, one would like to compare individuals with the same observed and unobserved characteristics but with different levels of schooling. This argument is actually not that different from the *ceteris paribus* and *exogeneity* discussion in structured regression. The particular interpretation, however, depends essentially on the assumption made about causal chains.

Example 1.13 Consider again the return to schooling on earnings. Even if one identifies the individual return to schooling, the economic interpretation still depends on the causal channels one has in mind. This can easily be seen when contrasting the human capital theory versus the signalling theory of schooling. The human capital theory posits that schooling increases human capital, which increases wages. The signalling theory presumes that attainment of higher education (e.g. a degree) simply signals high unobserved ability to potential employers, even if the content of education was completely useless. In the latter case, from an individual perspective, schooling may well have a high return. On the other hand, if years of schooling were increased for everyone, the overall return would be zero since the ranking between individuals would not change. Then a clear violation of the SUTVA occurs, because now the individual potential outcomes depend on the treatment choices of other individuals. This is also referred to as 'peer effects' or 'externalities'. Individual-level regressions would identify only the private marginal return, not the social return.

Example 1.14 Beegle, Dehejia and Gatti (2006) analyse the effects of transitory income shocks on the extent of child labour, using household panel data in rural western Tanzania collected from 1991 to 1994. Their hypothesis is that transitory income shocks due to crops lost may induce families to use, at least temporarily, more child labour. This effect is expected to be mitigated by family wealth. In other words, the impact will be quite heterogeneous with respect to the wealth of each individual family. If the (relative) size of the transitory income shock depends on this wealth, then we expect $ATET > ATE > ATEN$.

Other examples are the effects of the tax system on labour supply, the public–private sector wage differential or the effects of class size on students' outcomes. Distinguishing the true causal effect from differences in unobservables is the main obstacle to non-parametric identification of the function φ or of features of it such as treatment effects. The challenge will be to work out the assumptions that permit non-parametric identification. While this has always been of concern in econometrics, in recent years much more emphasis has been placed on trying to verify these assumptions and finding weaker assumptions for identification.

1.2   Randomised Controlled Trials

In terms of related literature, experimental economics examines the impact of often hypothetical interventions to study the behaviour of individuals under certain well-defined situations. Typically this proceeds by inviting a number of individuals to play simple games (like public goods, dictator or ultimatum games). Then they are paid actual compensation depending upon how they perform during these games. Most often these experiments take place in a computer laboratory under highly stylised conditions. Although we are not talking about experimental economics here, field experiments are similar to this idea in many ways. A key difference is that we examine the behaviour outside the laboratory (in real-world settings). In these experiments a natural but also essential assumption is that individuals were randomly assigned to one or the other group. So if we have one treatment and one control group then we randomly assign some people to treatment and some to control. Therefore, one speaks of *random* or *randomised experiments* or *trials*.

For several research questions, random or randomised experiments offer the most convincing solution. The obvious reason is that this is not a self-selection procedure in which individuals select their level of treatment. Rather, if we design the experiments we control the assignments. Random(ised) experiments have been extensively studied and are well understood today. Although the vast majority of contributions is linked to biometrics and clinical trials, in economics this idea is also frequently used.

As we will see, in social sciences the problem is less the credibility of results from randomised trials and rather their feasibility. It requires that we are allowed and enabled to randomly assign treatment and can force people to stay in their group. One has to guarantee that people really comply with their assignment, and finally, that there is no (non-random) attrition. So it is obvious that this is a laboratory situation rather than a situation we commonly face in practice.

1.2.1   Definition and Examples for Controlled Trials

To control for differences in observed and unobserved characteristics, controlled experiments can be very helpful. Randomised assignment of D ensures that D is not correlated with observed and unobserved characteristics. Experiments used to be (and still are) rather rare in many OECD countries but have become very popular in developing countries. Examples of deliberate experiments are PROGRESA in Mexico and *Familias en Accion* in Colombia or similar conditional-cash transfer experiments in other Latin American countries. Other examples are the STAR class-size experiment in Tennessee (USA), the Job Training Partnership Act (JTPA) in the USA, a de-worming programme in schools (Miguel and Kremer, 2004) and the random provision of school inputs in Kenya (Glewwe, Kremer, Moulin and Zitzewitz, 2004).

Example 1.15 One of the well-known randomised experiments is the 'Student teacher achievement ratio' or STAR experiment in Tennessee. This experiment took place around the mid-1980s. It was designed to obtain credible evidence on the hotly debated issue of whether smaller classes support student learning and led to better student outcomes. Because reducing class size would imply hiring more teachers and lead to more investment, this experiment was important to observe whether any gains would justify the costs of reducing class sizes. Although there were many observational studies before STAR, the results were highly disputed. Overall non-experimental results suggest that there was very little or no effect of class size on the performance of the students. But class size can be endogenous and there are many observed and unobserved character-istics that can make the students in smaller classes quite different from the students in larger classes. On the one hand, class size may be smaller in richer areas or where parents are very interested in a good education for their children. On the other hand, more disruptive children, and those with learning difficulties, are often placed in smaller classes. Randomised experiments help here to balance the two groups in both observed and unobserved variables. In the STAR experiment, each participating school assigned children to one of three types of classrooms: small classes had a targeted enrolment of 13–17; regular classes had a targeted enrolment of 22–25; and a third class targeted regular enrolment of size 22–25 but adding a full-time teacher's aide in the room.

The design of these experiments ensures that treated and control have the same distribution of observed and unobserved characteristics such that

$$E[Y^1|D = 1] = E[Y^1|D = 0] = E[Y^1].$$

We speak of randomised experiments or controlled trials if a random programme assign-ment is designed such that any differences between the groups are by pure chance and are not systematic. This ensures first that the unobservables are uncorrelated with D, i.e. identically distributed in both groups, which thus eliminates *selection on unobserv-ables*. Therefore, it also guarantees that the distribution of the observed characteristics is almost identical in both groups, and, in particular, that they thus have the same support. This implicates that for any values of concomitant characteristics X that are observed in one group, we could also find individuals with basically the same characteristics in the other group (given an infinitely large number of observations).[8] This implies that $ATE = ATET = ATEN$ and that both treatment effects can be estimated consistently by a naive estimator (like the difference of sample means) because

$$E[Y|D = 1] - E[Y|D = 0].$$

Random experiments, if properly conducted, provide the most convincing identifica-tion strategy, as all the other identification strategies discussed later rest on untestable assumptions that are hardly ever unambiguously accepted. However, notice that all the methods related to randomised experiments are intended to improve ex-ante balance. They are useless if the data have already been collected or if we cannot control the sampling or the treatment assignment.

Example 1.16 Experiments have been conducted in several developing countries for evaluating the impacts of health and education programmes like, for example, PROGRESA in Mexico to increase school participation; see Example 1.1. When the

---

[8] Compare with the *common support condition* discussed in the next chapters.

programme was launched, due to budgetary limits it was introduced only in several pilot regions, which were randomly selected (randomised phasing-in). The unit of randomisation was the community level and data were collected not only for these randomly selected communities but also in several randomly selected non-participating communities. In fact, half of the communities participated in the programme and the other half did not. Participation in the programme was designed as a two-step procedure. In the first step, a number of localities with a high degree of marginality were selected, of which about half were randomised into the programme. In the second step, only poor households living in pilot localities were considered as eligible to the programme, on the basis of a region-specific poverty index at the household level. Data were collected at baseline, i.e. before the introduction of the programme, and in subsequent waves afterwards.

Other than evaluating the impact of different programmes, randomisation can also help us to identify the proper group of beneficiaries. Proper targeting is a common screening problem when implementing different kinds of conditional cash transfer or other welfare programmes. A government needs to separate poor from rich and incorporate them into the programme. But as you might guess, this is not a straightforward problem because rich individuals can always sneak in to get benefits. One of the ways to avoid these problems is to use a self-selection mechanism, which is to incorporate costly requirements for rich, like manual labour requirement, or provide low quality foods so that rich people might not be interested. But this can often produce inefficient outcomes because, just to disincentivise the rich, poor people have to suffer unnecessary costs by painful labour or having bad quality aids. Another way is 'automatic screening', which typically proceeds by some kind of asset test or proxy means test; for example, interviewing the individuals, observing their present status like residence quality, ownership of motorbikes, etc., and then asking other neighbours. But again, this process can also be misleading and lengthy. So the question is whether we can do something better than these suggestions and, if so, what the alternatives might be.

Example 1.17 Alatas, Banerjee, Hanna, Olken, Purnamasari and Wai-poi (2013) used randomised evaluations to see whether it is possible to incorporate some self-targeting mechanism to screen the poor. The idea was to see what happens if the individuals were asked to apply for the test. They used randomisation to select the beneficiaries in Indonesian Conditional Cash Transfer programme PKH and experimentally varied the enrolment process for 400 villages. So they compared those households that were actively applying for the test with those where there was an automatic screening or proxy means test conducted directly by PKH. In the self-targeting villages, the households were asked to go to the registration office first, and only after the asset test was conducted by PKH. In the automatic screening group, PKH conducted the usual proxy means test to see whether they were eligible. They found that villages where the households had to apply for the test had much poorer groups of beneficiaries. The possible explanation is that when households have to apply, then many of them who probably didn't need the aid didn't go for the test.

Like the STAR experiment that we mentioned in Example 1.15, many designs of experiments include the interaction of different treatments. In many cases you may think of one specific treatment, but then you find out that interactions work even better.

Example 1.18 Two major health risks for teenage girls in the sub-Saharan countries are early (adolescent) pregnancy and sexually transmitted infections (STIs) (particularly HIV). In recent reports, WHO reported more than 50 per cent of adolescent births took place in sub-Saharan countries. Both early pregnancy and STIs have negative health effects and social consequences for teenage girls. Often, girls attending primary school have to leave the school, and in many cases adolescent births can lead to further health problems. Duflo, Dupas and Kremer (2015) did an experimental study to see how teenage pregnancy and STI prevalence are affected by two important policy instruments and their interaction: (a) education subsidies and (b) HIV prevention (focused on abstinence until marriage). The experiment was started in 2003 with students of average age from 13.5 to 20.5, enrolled in grade 6 at 328 schools located in the Western part of Kenya. The study followed the project for seven years with 9500 girls and 9800 boys. Schools were randomly assigned to one of four groups: (1) Control (82 schools); (2) Stand-Alone Education Subsidy programme (83 schools); (3) Stand-Alone HIV Education programme (83 schools); and (4) Joint Programme (80 schools). The education subsidy treatment was just like a simple subsidy programme that provided two free school uniforms (it was given to the same students, one at the beginning of 2003 and the other in late 2004) over the last three years of primary school. The HIV education programme was like an education programme about sexually transmitted infections with an emphasis on abstinence until marriage. In every school three teachers were trained by the government to help them deliver Kenya's national HIV/AIDS curriculum. Short, medium and long-term impacts of these two programmes and their interaction were observed on outcome variables like sexual behaviour, fertility and infection with HIV and another STI (Herpes Simplex Virus type 2 [HSV2]). They found only education subsidies reduced adolescent girl dropout, pregnancy and marriage; HIV prevention did not reduce pregnancy or STI. The combined programme reduced STI more, but dropout and pregnancy less, than the education subsidy alone.

1.2.2 Randomisation Methods and Statistical Properties

In principle, the idea of a randomised trial is very simple, though its realisation might not be. Imagine n subjects are supposed to receive either treatment 1 or 0. The sample average treatment effect can be expressed as

$$SATE = \frac{1}{n}\sum_{i=1}^{n}(Y_i^1 - Y_i^0). \tag{1.9}$$

Usually this is of less interest than its population counterpart, namely the ATE, but asymptotically they are same. To maximise the statistical power of a test on ATE = 0, we can distribute half of the individuals in the treatment and the other half in the control group. Therefore we have a sample of $\frac{n}{2}$ subjects who receive treatment 1, whereas $\frac{n}{2}$ subjects receive treatment 0. The estimator would then be

$$\widehat{SATE} = \frac{1}{\frac{1}{2}n}\sum_{D_i=1}Y_i - \frac{1}{\frac{1}{2}n}\sum_{D_i=0}Y_i. \tag{1.10}$$

The hope is to have data such that the $SATE$ can be consistently estimated by $\widehat{SATE}$.

Inference and Error Decomposition

The $\widehat{SATE}$ of (1.10) is a consistent estimator if both the treatment and the control group represent the corresponding sample distribution. It is here where randomisation plays its crucial role. With random assignment we can take this condition to be held. If, in addition, the sample (as a whole) is a good representation of the distribution of the population of interest, then (1.10) is also a consistent estimator for the ATE. A simple t-test applied for the comparison of two means can be used to test whether this difference is significantly different from zero. Note that this is equivalent to an analysis-of-variance with one factor, or a simple linear regression with one dummy (for the treatment).

While this seems to be quite easy, in practice, unfortunately it is not. There are actually a number of issues that are important when sampling and constructing an experimental design. Purely practical issues related to the data collection and reporting will be discussed further on; here we concentrate on issues when planning the sampling and experimental design. To better understand how the latter two differ in their consequence for further inference, let us have a closer look at the difference between the ATE and an estimator as simple as (1.10).

For the sake of simplicity we restrict to $D \in \{0, 1\}$ and φ a separable function such that, depending upon the treatment, the effect from observed and unobserved variables can be separated

$$\varphi(d, X, U) = m_d(X) + \xi_d(U). \tag{1.11}$$

Then we can decompose the difference between ATE and $\widehat{SATE}$ as

$$ATE - \widehat{SATE} = \triangle_{S(X)} + \triangle_{S(U)} + \triangle_{T(X)} + \triangle_{T(U)}, \tag{1.12}$$

where the $\triangle_S$ refers to sample selection and $\triangle_T$ to treatment imbalance differences.[9]

The first term deals with sampling, i.e. how the n subjects were sampled from the population of interest. If individuals were sampled randomly from the population, and each individual could be observed under both states ($d = 0, 1$), then the SATE could be used as an unbiased estimator of the population average treatment effect (ATE $= E[Y^1 - Y^0]$). With random sampling, the empirical distribution function of the observed characteristics X and unobserved characteristics U in the sample is consistent for the distribution function of X and U in the population. Although for any given sample the distribution of X and U may be different from the distribution in the true population, these differences are non-systematic and vanish as sample size increases. Without random sampling, the sample distribution of X and U will typically differ from

---

[9] See also Imai, King and Stuart (2008) and King and Zeng (2006).

the population distribution and the difference would not vanish with increasing smaple size. For example, the individuals who (actively) apply to participate in the experiment are often different from the population we would like to target. This issue is often referred to as *external* versus *internal validity*. The randomised controlled trials have the advantage of high internal validity in the sense that the SATE is consistently estimated, since any difference in observables and unobservables vanishes between treated and controls with increasing sample size. On the other hand, external validity may be low in the sense that SATE is not a consistent indicator for the population ATE when the participants in the experiment (treated and controls) may not be randomly sampled from the population of interest; in other words, the sample may not be a good representative of the population.

Let us formalise the idea. To understand the difference between SATE and ATE better, for now it will be more illuminating to switch to the finite population case (of size N). We can later always conclude for infinite populations by considering $N \to \infty$.[10]

We start by specifying the sampling related differences. Let's make use of the separability in (1.11) to obtain

$$\Delta_{S(X)} = \frac{N-n}{N} \int \{m_1(X) - m_0(X)\} d\{\hat{F}(X|S=0) - \hat{F}(X|S=1)\}, \quad (1.13)$$

$$\Delta_{S(U)} = \frac{N-n}{N} \int \{\xi_1(U) - \xi_0(U)\} d\{\hat{F}(U|S=0) - \hat{F}(U|S=1)\}, \quad (1.14)$$

where $S = 1$ indicates that the individual is in the sample, $S = 0$ otherwise, and $\hat{F}$ refers to the empirical cumulative conditional distribution of either X or U, respectively.

The expressions can be better understood if we focus on each part separately. Let's interpret $\Delta_{S(X)}$. We have two distributions for X, conditional on whether we are looking at the people in the sample or not. If we focus on $\hat{F}(X|S=1)$, this is the empirical cdf of X for the people who are present in the sample, and accordingly, $\int \{m_1(X) - m_0(X)\} d\hat{F}(X|S=1)$ is the ATE related to observed variables that are in the sample. Similarly, it is possible to consider $\hat{F}(X|S=0)$ for the people who are not in the sample. Potential differences are due to the difference in the distribution of X in the two samples. You can think about the term $\frac{N-n}{N}$ as some finite population correction term. For infinite population this vanishes because it goes to 0 as $N \to \infty$. Using the definition of empirical cdf, Equation 1.13 can also be written as

$$\frac{N-n}{N} \left[\frac{1}{N-n} \sum_{i:S_i=0} \{m_1(X_i) - m_0(X_i)\} - \frac{1}{n} \sum_{i:S_i=1} \{m_1(X_i) - m_0(X_i)\} \right].$$

In a similar fashion you can also interpret $\Delta_{S(U)}$. But this portion of the treatment effect is related to the unobserved variables.

---

[10] You may argue that the populations you have in mind are finite, too. This, however, is often not really the case as e.g. the population of a country changes every second, and you want to make a more general statement than one to that resolution. Therefore, it can be quite useful to abstract to an infinite hyperpopulation that might be described by a distribution, and your specific population (of a country, right now) is just a representative sample of it.

Also note that for random(ised) samples, when sample size increases $\hat{F}(X|S = 0)$ should converge to $\hat{F}(X|S = 1)$, and $\hat{F}(U|S = 0)$ to $\hat{F}(U|S = 1)$. So in the limit both $\triangle_{S(X)}$ and $\triangle_{S(U)}$ will approach zero.

Randomisation Method

A second issue refers to the random treatment assignment itself. The simplest strategy, which is often used when treatment decisions have to be made immediately, is to assign each individual with probability 50 per cent either to treatment 1 or 0. Although being a valid randomisation design, this is usually associated with a rather high variance. The intuition is simple, as can be seen from the following example.

Example 1.19 Suppose $n = 100$, of which 50 are men and 50 are women. We randomly assign 50 of these individuals to treatment and 50 to control. By chance it could happen that 40 men and 10 women are assigned to treatment, with the remaining 10 men and 40 women being in the control group. In this case, men are highly overrepresented among the treated, which of course could affect the estimated treatment effect

$$\frac{1}{50}\sum_{D_i=1} Y_i - \frac{1}{50}\sum_{D_i=0} Y_i.$$

Although gender would be balanced in treatment and control group when the sample size goes to infinity, in any given sample it will usually not be. To obtain a quantitative intuition, consider a sample which contains only $0.3n$ women.[11] Half of the sample is randomly allocated to treatment and the other half to the control group. When $n = 50$, in 38 per cent of these experiments the difference in the fraction of women between the treatment and the control group will be larger than 0.1. When $n = 100$, this occurs in only 27 per cent of the experiments. Fortunately, when $n = 400$, such large differences occur only very rarely, namely in 2 per cent of the experiments.

Let us again formalise the balancing issue. Analogously to (1.13) and (1.14), one obtains from the separability (1.11) for our estimation bias (1.12)

$$\triangle_{T(X)} = \int \frac{1}{2}\{m_1(X) + m_0(X)\}d\{\hat{F}(X|D=0, S=1) - \hat{F}(X|D=1, S=1)\}, \quad (1.15)$$

$$\triangle_{T(U)} = \int \frac{1}{2}\{\xi_1(U) + \xi_0(U)\}d\{\hat{F}(U|D=0, S=1) - \hat{F}(U|D=1, S=1)\}. \quad (1.16)$$

Note that we only look at the empirical distributions inside the sample. Looking again at the differences in distributions at the end of each formula, it becomes clear that we have an asymptotic balance in X (and U) between treatment and control group. That is, for increasing samples, $\triangle_{T(X)}$ (and $\triangle_{T(U)}$) disappear.

Taking all together, if we can combine, for example, random sampling with random treatment assignment, we could consistently estimate the ATE simply by appropriate averaging. Otherwise, if random sampling from the population of interest is not possible,

---

[11] The following example is taken from Kernan, Viscoli, Makuch, Brass and Horwitz (1999).

we could attempt to correct for differences in X. For example, if census information on the distribution of X in the population is available, we can correct for these differences by an according weighting.[12] Obviously, to correct for differences in the unobservables U is much harder if not infeasible.

When unbalances happen between the treatment groups like in the gender assignment (Example 1.19), we can correct for them by weighting. The adjustment takes place after the experimental assignment and/or the collection of follow-up data. A smaller variance can be achieved by using blocking or stratification already in the randomisation phase, i.e. before the experiment starts. Here we refer to a blocking and stratification with respect to X when assigning treatment D, not when sampling the observations from the population (i.e. when assigning S).

Blocking and Stratification
Blocking or stratification in the randomisation phase ought to achieve ex-ante balance between the treatment groups. Even if we are provided with reportedly random assignments, it increases the efficiency of estimation and the power of hypothesis tests. As a consequence, it reduces the required sample size for fixed precision or power. Recalling Example 1.19, if we know that 50 women and 50 men participate in the experiment, we can choose to assign randomly exactly 25 women and 25 men to receive treatment 1 and the others to receive treatment 0. This is the concept of *blocking* (or *stratification*): when information on some X is known for the entire subject pool before randomisation starts. Strata with the same values of X are formed, and within each stratum 50 per cent are assigned to treatment 1 versus treatment 0. Evidently, if there are four treatment arms, one would assign 25 per cent to each, within each stratum, etc. This ensures an *exact balance* on these covariates.

When we said 'randomly exactly', which seems to be contradictory or weird, the 'randomly' referred to U but the 'exactly' to X such that we get $\triangle_{T(X)} = 0$ with $\triangle_{T(U)}$ still converging to zero. I.e. the variables X are balanced exactly in the sample and not only in expectation, whereas the U are still balanced in expectation. Such a procedure is sometimes referred to as the *ideal design*: random sample with assignments to treatment which are blocked in X but random in U. Consequently, one has that $\triangle_{T(X)} = 0$ whereas all the other $\triangle$ in (1.12) have expectation zero with an asymptotically vanishing variance. For example, when we do blocking with respect to X, then $\triangle_{T(U)}$ actually becomes

$$\widetilde{\triangle}_{T(U)} = \sum_x w_x \int \frac{1}{2} \{\xi_1(U) + \xi_0(U)\} \{d\hat{F}(U|D = 0, X = x, S = 1)$$
$$- d\hat{F}(U|D = 1, X = x, S = 1)\}$$

hoping that $d\hat{F}(U|D = 0, X = x, S = 1) \approx d\hat{F}(U|D = 1, X = x, S = 1)$ happens thanks to the random assignment in each block. The weight w_x is the probability that value x is observed. The sum is finite because it refers to the observed values of X.

---

[12] Or an according imputation like matching, see the next chapter; also see Exercise 3.

Usually, one would like to stratify on some variables X that are closely related to the outcome variable Y (or one of the several outcome variables of interest) and on variables for which a subgroup analysis is planned (e.g. estimation of treatment effects separately for men and women). Stratification is most helpful when future values of Y can be predicted reasonably well from baseline data. Important predictors are often the lagged values $Y_{t=0}$ of the outcome variable, which should be collected as part of a baseline survey. These variables are most relevant when Y is highly persistent, e.g. when one is interested in school test scores, education, height, wealth, etc. On the other hand, for very volatile outcome variables such as firm profits, lagged values may not predict very well.

The way randomisation was performed has to be taken into account when conducting inference. A large biostatistics literature has examined this issue for clinical trials. Exercises 3 and 4 study how an appropriate weighting modifies the $\widehat{SATE}$ to become a consistent estimator for ATE, and how this weighting changes the variance of the estimator. The latter has to be taken into account when estimating the standard error. For given weights w_x (the proportion x occurs in the population of interest) and independent observations, this is straightforward: the variance expression (1.22) in Exercise 4 can be estimated by $\frac{2}{n} \sum_{x \in \mathcal{X}} w_x \{ \widehat{Var}(Y^1 | X = x) + \widehat{Var}(Y^0 | X = x) \}$, where the conditional variances are estimated separately from the samples of the treated and the untreated, respectively. This can be done parametrically or non-parametrically.[13] Note that we assume we have random samples stratified (or blocked) along X and therefore not being representative for the population. Knowing, however, the population weights w_x allows us to correct for this stratification (or blocking).

In order to be able to afterwards correct the estimator for the bias, one should always choose strata or blocks $\mathcal{X}$ for which the population weights w_x are provided or at least can be obtained.[14] Then, the ATE estimate, standard error and its estimate are as above. In case of using a parametric estimate for the standard error, many authors (compare with Bruhn and McKenzie, 2009) advise correcting the degrees of freedom (d.o.f.) by the number of used strata or blocks. The procedure becomes evident when thinking in a simple linear regression model; compare, for example, with Duflo, Glennerster and Kremer (2008): for J blocks[15] B_j of $\mathcal{X} = \cup_{j=1}^{J} B_j$ with n_j individuals in block j of which half of the subjects (let n_j be even) is treated, consider

$$Y_{ij} = \beta_0 + \beta D_i + \gamma_j + \epsilon_{ij}, \ i = 1, \ldots, n_{ij}, \ j = 1, \ldots, J, \tag{1.17}$$

where γ_j are fixed effects. Let w_j be the population block weights, $w_j = \sum_{x \in B_j} w_x$. If the sample is representative of the population of interest, then the OLS estimate of β is consistent for ATE. Otherwise, one has to use GLS with weights $w_j \cdot n/n_j$. Further

---

[13] While we generally recommend doing this non-parametrically, in practice this will depend on factors like sample size and the nature or dimension of X.

[14] In the above-described procedure, treatment is balanced inside each stratum or block, but we did not say that sampling had to be done along strata, so it might easily be that $w_x = 1$.

[15] You may want to define one block for each potential value x that can be taken by X or to define larger blocks that entail a range of X.

inference should automatically correct the standard error for the degrees of freedom; it is always a remaining question whether to use block-robust standard errors or to assume homoskedasticity.

Obviously, exact stratification is not tractable for continuous variables such as income or wealth. There, only stratification on coarsely defined intervals of those variables is possible (e.g. low, medium and high income). This is defining blocks or strata comprising intervals of the support $\mathcal{X}$. If X is multidimensional, containing some continuous variables, this procedure gets unwieldy. Then an alternative 'randomisation' approach which permits near balance to be achieved on many variables – in contrast to exact balances on very few variables – is more appropriate. A popular approach is the so-called *matched pairs*.

Matched Pairs

If not only gender but also other covariates are known beforehand, one should include these in the randomisation protocol. The more covariates X are observed and included in the blocking, the smaller the variance of the estimated treatment effect will be. One would thus like to block for many covariates and then assign treatment randomly within each stratum or block. When X contains more than one or two covariates, more complex randomisation routines are available. The basic idea of many of these approaches is the use of matched pairs. Suppose the treatment is binary, and a number of pre-treatment covariates X are observed. One proceeds to match pairs of individuals such that the two individuals within each pair have very similar X variables. One individual of each pair is randomly chosen and assigned to treatment. If one has three treatment arms, one would construct triplets instead of pairs.

The more difficult part is the construction of these pairs. Suppose there are $2n$ individuals, and define the distance between individual i and j with respect to their covariates by the Mahalanobis distance[16]

$$\left(X_i - X_j\right)' \Omega^{-1} \left(X_i - X_j\right), \tag{1.18}$$

where Ω is the covariance matrix of X which might be estimated from the sample. One seeks to construct pairs such that the sum of the within-pair distance over all pairs is minimised. This gives the optimal matching of $2n$ subjects into n pairs of two subjects. The problem is that the sequencing in which pairs are matched matters, as examined e.g. in Greevy, Lu, Silver and Rosenbaum (2004). A naive 'greedy' algorithm would first pair the two individuals with the smallest distance, thereafter pairs the two individuals with the second-smallest distance, etc. Such greedy algorithms, however, usually do not produce optimal matches.

---

[16] This is a natural extension of the Euclidean distance, the latter being probably the most intuitive number people can imagine and understand to describe distances in a multidimensional space. In an Euclidean space, however, people subliminally presume orthonormality (90° angles and same scales) for the axes. As this is typically not the case when looking at social economic indicators subsumed in X, the Mahalanobis transformation will first put them in such shape before calculating the Euclidean distance.

Example 1.20 Consider a simple numerical example, with one particular variable X (say 'age') as the only covariate. Suppose we have eight individuals with ages: $\{24, 35, 39, 40, 40, 41, 45, 56\}$. The greedy algorithm would choose $40 : 40$ as the first pair, followed by $39 : 41$, etc. The sum of all within-pair differences is $0+2+10+32 = 44$. In contrast, if we were to match adjacent values, i.e. $24 : 35, 39 : 40, 40 : 41, 45 : 56$, the sum of the differences is $11 + 1 + 1 + 11 = 24$, which is also the optimal pairing. Finding the optimal pairing with multivariate matching is far more complex. Therefore, a distance measure is necessary to project it onto a one-dimensional problem.

The Mahalanobis distance is probably the most common distance metric used, but other distance metrics could be used as well. Instead of applying the Mahalanobis distance to the covariates themselves, one could alternatively apply them to their ranks to limit the impact of a few extreme observations. The Mahalanobis distance has the advantage of requiring only the covariance matrix of X without requiring any knowledge or conjectures as to how these X are related to interesting outcome variables Y. This may be appropriate when multiple and rather diverse outcome variables Y are measured later in the trial. On the other hand, if one is mostly interested in one specific outcome measure, e.g. income or consumption, and has some prior subjective knowledge about the relevance of the X covariates as predictors for Y, one may want to give larger weights in the distance metric to those covariates that are more important.[17]

For inference and hypothesis tests about the estimated treatment effects one should take the method of randomisation into account, i.e. the degrees of freedom. If one does not, the standard errors are underestimated. Again, the simplest solution is to include stratum dummies or pair dummies in the regression model (1.17). Hence, if Mahalanobis matching was used to construct pairs, a dummy for each pair should be included in the linear regression. Clearly, these pair dummies replace the block dummies in (1.17). In other words, for making an inference, one could use what we learnt in the paragraph on *blocking and stratification*.

An alternative approach, which might either be interpreted as blocking or as matching pairs, is the following. In order to avoid introducing more notation, we redefine now the J blocks to be the different matched pairs or blocks with n_{1j} treated and n_{0j} untreated individuals for $j = 1, \ldots, J$, etc. Then, an obvious direct estimator for ATE is

$$\widehat{\alpha}_d = \sum_{j=1}^{J} w_j \left\{ \sum_{i=1}^{n_{1j}} \frac{Y_{ij}^1}{n_{1j}} - \sum_{i=1}^{n_{0j}} \frac{Y_{ij}^0}{n_{0j}} \right\}, \tag{1.19}$$

where we simply compare the differences of outcomes of treated versus outcomes of controls, and adjust for the population weight of each match.

---

[17] If one considers, for example, gender to be a very important variable, then one could require exact matching on gender, by modifying the distance metric such that it takes the value infinity between any two individuals of opposite gender. Similarly, if one wants to ensure that matched individuals differ at most by four years in age, one could simply define the distance to be infinity between individuals who differ in age by more than four years.

There exist several proposals for a variance estimator of $\widehat{\alpha}_d$; a most intuitive and consistent one under weak conditions (see Imai, King and Nall, 2009, for details) is

$$\frac{J}{(J-1)} \sum_{j=1}^{J} \left[w_j \left\{ \sum_{i=1}^{n_{1j}} \frac{Y_{ij}^1}{n_{1j}} - \sum_{i=1}^{n_{0j}} \frac{Y_{ij}^0}{n_{0j}} \right\} - \frac{\widehat{\alpha}_d}{J} \right]^2. \tag{1.20}$$

It is clear that, due to the weighting, we have again that the $\triangle_{S(X)}$ is zero if the weights are exact, and in expectation zero with a variance going to zero if the weights are estimated or simply if we are provided with a random (i.e. representative) sample. The latter is true also for $\triangle_{S(U)}$. The random treatment assignment in the blocks is to obtain $\triangle_{T(X)} = 0$ and $\triangle_{T(U)} = 0$ asymptotically. Then $\widehat{\alpha}_d$ is asymptotically unbiased.

1.2.3 Difficulties and Remedies in Practice

A few recommendations can be drawn from the paragraphs above:

(1) Before the intervention starts, try to achieve ex-ante balance in covariates: this requires us to have access to a few baseline covariates, ideally including lagged values of the most interesting outcome variables. Mahalanobis matched pairs are a useful approach in order to achieve balance on many covariates. Groups or pairs of similar (in X) observations are formed, and within each group or pair, half of them is randomly assigned to treatment. This latter randomisation step can be done repeatedly in order to choose the assignment which produces the best ex-ante balance.[18]

(2) After having achieved balance in X, examine the outcome data Y and calculate average treatment effects. Looking at the outcome data only after having controlled for X has the advantage of minimising the risk of data-mining and pre-testing bias. In other words, this procedure rules out the possibility that the treatment effects themselves can have influenced the model selection and thereby produced biased estimates.

(3) When conducting inference, one should account for the randomisation method used. Correcting for the degrees-of-freedom is the preferred approach due to its simplicity. Randomised inference (see 'further reading') provides exact finite sample inference.

Bruhn and McKenzie (2009) examine recent practices among economists conducting experimental trials and perform a number of simulations with real data sets used for estimating effects on child schooling, child labour, nutrition, micro-enterprise profits, etc. Not surprisingly, they find that stratification and other refinements help for very small sample sizes but lose this advantage for increasing sample sizes. Among the various stratification methods, pair-matching via Mahalanobis distance often performs best in their simulations when X is higher-dimensional. A reason might be that in economic applications it is unlikely that stratification on only one, two or three baseline covariates will explain a large share of the variation in Y. Finally, they also study the trade-off between stratifying or matching on rather few or rather many variables. Based on their

---

[18] Various diagnostics for assessing overall balance are discussed in the section on propensity score matching later in this book.

simulations they suggest that one may want to include rather more than fewer covariates in the stratification/matching, as long as one thinks that they may add additional power in explaining the future outcome. But the theoretical guidance is not unambiguous, because, while adding more covariates is likely to increase the explanatory power in the sample, adding more strata dummies to the regression decreases the d.o.f.

Note that one should not conduct a *test of equality* of X between the two groups, but rather examine the standardised differences in X. The equality-in-means test is a function of the sample size and for a sufficiently low sample size would (almost) always indicate that there are no significant imbalances in X. The concern with pair matching is to reduce relative differences in X and not absolute differences due to the sample size.[19] The following criteria are often suggested instead.[20] Take the propensity score function $\Pr(D = 1|X = x)$ which usually has first to be estimated:

(a) The standardised difference in the mean propensity scores between the two groups should be close to zero.
(b) The ratio of the variance of the propensity score between the two groups should be close to one.
(c) The standardised difference in X should be close to zero.
(d) The ratio of the variance in X between the two groups should be close to one.

Otherwise, in case you use a parametric propensity score (estimate), one repeats this and respecifies the model. Note that at this stage we did not yet look at the outcome data Y. These various diagnostics thus do not depend on the outcome data. Consequently, the pre-specification cannot be influenced by the true treatment effects.

Ideally, all the planned analyses should already be specified before any outcome data is examined in order to avoid the temptation of data mining during the evaluation phase. In practice, however, missing data and partial or non-compliance (e.g. dropout) may nevertheless still require substantial econometric modelling.

Next, organising and conducting an experimental trial can be expensive and may receive a lot of resistance. Heckman and Smith (1995) discuss a variety of resulting problems along the experiment with random assignment to the JTPA training programme in the USA. They also discuss many other sources that may invalidate the experimental evaluation results. If participation in this programme is voluntary, randomisation can only be implemented with respect to the individuals who applied for the programme, which are then randomised in or randomised out. However, these applicants are maybe different from the population of interest. If randomisation covers only parts of the population, the experimental results may not be generalisable to the broader population. In other words, although internal validity is often plausible, external validity may be limited if the selected units are not representative of the population at large. We may speak then of a *sample bias*.

---

[19] Earlier work by Rosenbaum and Rubin had put emphasis on significance testing. Significance testing, however, confuses successful balance with low power. What is relevant for pair matching is the size of the imbalance and not the size of the confidence interval.

[20] See, for example, Lechner (1999), Imai, King and Stuart (2008), Rubin (2001) and Imbens and Rubin (2015).

Even if a policy is mandatory such that all individuals can be randomly assigned to the treatments, full compliance is often difficult to achieve if participants must exercise some effort during the participation and may refuse their cooperation.

One speaks of a *randomisation bias* if the prospect of randomised allocation alters the pool of potential participants because individuals may be reluctant to apply at all or reduce (or increase) any preparatory activities such as complementary training due to the fear of being randomised out (threat of service denial).

A *substitution bias* occurs if members of the control group (the randomised-out non-participants) obtain some treatment or participate in similar programmes, e.g. identical or similar training obtained from private providers. In this case, the experimental evaluation measures only the incremental value of the policy relative to the programmes available otherwise.

A so-called *drop-out bias* occurs if individuals assigned to a particular programme do not or only partly participate. This bias, like the substitution bias, is the results of non-compliance.

As randomised experiments can be expensive and face political obstacles, one often proposes to first perform pilot studies before implementing the actual study. But the pilot-study character of an experiment may change the behaviour of the participants, who may put in additional effort to show that the pilot study works (or does not). This is called the *Hawthorne effect*.

If randomisation proceeds not on the individual but a higher level, *endogenous sample selection* problems may occur. For example, if programme schools receive additional resources, this might attract more parents to send their children to these schools, withdrawing their children from the control schools. Consequently, the resulting allocation is not representative anymore.

Example 1.21 A small number of schools in Kenya received additional inputs such as uniforms and textbooks. This reduced the drop-out rate in the treatment schools. In addition, several students from nearby control schools were transferred to the treatment schools. These two aspects led to a substantial increase in class size in the treatment schools. A large increase in class size leads to downwardly biased treatment effects. The treatment being estimated thus corresponded to a provision of additional school inputs combined with an increase in class size. This had to be taken into account in the cost–benefit calculation, since the increase in class size may be associated, for example, with a cost saving, since teacher salaries usually represent the most expensive input into education.

In such situations, nevertheless, randomisation can still be used to estimate *intention to treat* (ITT) effects. Nonetheless, for programme evaluation a random assignment is generally a good idea, even if people may drop out (or sneak in) later on. For example, there might be randomisation with respect to entitlement or non-entitlement to a particular programme, which can often deliver a credible instrument for an instrumental variables strategy discussed later in this book.

Example 1.22 During the Vietnam war, young American men were drafted to the army on the basis of their month and day of birth, where a certain number of birth dates had been randomly determined to be draft eligible: see Angrist (1998). Hence, the indicator whether being born on a draft-eligible day or not satisfies the above requirements and would deliver the ITT effect. But the main research interest is in the effect of participating in the army on later outcomes. As we will see later, the lottery of birth dates can function as an instrument. The pure participation, however, is no longer random as people could voluntarily enrol or avoid their enrolment in various ways.

Obviously, the potential treatment itself can lead to differential *attrition* or *non-response* in the treatment and/or the comparison group. Take our examples about performance in school: if one obtains outcome data only for those children who are in school on the day a test is administered, the data will be affected by selection bias. One should try to avoid differential non-response or attrition by tracing all students. This may not always be feasible so that non-response (or attrition on collecting longer-term outcomes) may still be high. For such cases, methods to deal with this selection bias[21] are needed.

Often experimental evaluations (randomised controlled trials) are considered as unethical or unfair since some individuals are denied access to the treatment. Yet, if public budgets or administrative capacity are insufficient to cover the entire country at once, it appears fair to choose the participants in the pilot programmes at random. But publicly provided or mandated programmes may partly overcome this problem as follows.

A *randomised phasing-in* will only temporarily deny participation in the programme. In some situations it might even be possible to let all units participate but treat only different subsamples within each unit. Consider, for example, the provision of additional schoolbooks. In some schools, additional books could be provided to the third grade only, and in some other schools to the fifth grade only. Hence, all schools participate to the same degree in the programme (which thus avoids feelings of being deprived of resources relative to others), but the fifth graders from the first half of schools can be used as a control group for the second half of schools and vice versa for the third graders.

Marginal randomisation is sometimes used when the number of available places in a programme or a school is limited, such that those admitted are randomly drawn from the applicants. Consider the application of this method to a particular public school or university, which might (be forced to) choose randomly from the applicants if oversubscribed. In such a situation, those randomised out and randomised in should not differ from each other in their distributions of observable and unobservable characteristics. Otherwise marginal groups may represent only a very tiny fraction of the entire population of interest and the estimated effects may not generalise to the population at large.

---

[21] If one can assume, for example, that it is the weaker students who remain in school when treated but would have dropped out otherwise, the experimental estimates are downward biased.

Hence, randomised assignment can be very helpful for credible evaluation. But not all questions can be answered by experiments (e.g. the effects of constitutions or institutions) and experimental data are often not available. Experimental data alone may also not allow the entire function $\varphi(d, x, u)$ to be determined, for which additional assumptions will be required. Even if a proper experiment is conducted, it might still occur by chance that the treatment and control groups differ substantially in their characteristics, in particular if the sample sizes are small. Although the differences in sample means provide unbiased estimates of average treatment effects, adjusting for the differences in the covariates, as discussed below, can reduce the variance of the estimates; see Rubin (1974).

In practice, randomised experiments hardly ever turn out to be perfect. For example, in the STAR experiment, children who skipped a grade or who repeated a class left the experiment. Also, some pupils entered the school during the trial. Some kind of reassignment happened during the trial, etc. This implies that one needs to know all those details when evaluating the trial, and estimating treatment effects. One should not only know the experimental protocol but also the (smaller and larger) problems that happened during the experimental phase.

Other problems may appear when collecting follow-up data. E.g. an educational intervention may have taken place in kindergarten and we would like to estimate its effects several years later. Attrition and non-response in follow-up surveys may lead to selected samples; e.g. it is be harder to trace and survey individuals who have moved. (In many health interventions, mortality may also be an important reason behind attrition.) Non-experimental methods are needed to deal with this. Nevertheless, it is helpful to keep the ideal setup of a randomised trial in mind when designing or choosing a non-experimental method since some non-experimental designs are in a sense superior than others. As a rule of thumb: collecting pre-treatment data and collecting data from similar but non-treated control observations, e.g. from the same family (twins, siblings), neighbourhood or local labour market is often helpful. In addition, the same survey designs and definitions of the outcome variable should be used for both control and treated, and one should obtain detailed information about the selection process.

1.3 Respecting Heterogeneity: Non-Experimental Data and Distributional Effects

As we have seen in the previous subsection, experiments can be very helpful for credible identification of the average treatment effect. If possible, one should nearly always strive to incorporate some randomised element in an intervention. In many situations, however, we have only access to observational (= non-experimental) data. In addition, even with a perfectly designed experiment, problems such as non-compliance, non-response and attrition often occur in practice, calling for more complex econometric modelling. The source of problems that can arise then for identification and estimation is typically the heterogeneity of individuals, first in their endowments and interests, second in the (resulting) returns. For part of the heterogeneity we can control or at least account for, e.g. via the observed endowments X. We have seen this already when doing blocking or matching. Much more involved is the handling of heterogeneity due to the unobserved part, represented by U in our model. We learnt from the last subsection that randomisation can avoid biased inference. But what happens if we cannot randomly assign treatments? Or, what if heterogeneity is of the first order? Evidently, in the latter case it is much more insightful to study treatment effects conditioned on X or, if it is heterogeneity due to U that dominates, the distributions or quantiles of Y^d.

Consequently, the literature on non-experimental estimators covers a wide array of different parameters (or functions) you might be interested in, and some of these are discussed in the following chapters. Different strategies to estimate them from non-experimental data will be examined there.

1.3.1   Non-Separability and Consequences

As stated, in order to evaluate policy impact, we prefer not to rely too much on pre-specified models. The results would be model-biased, and conclusions prone to the typically strong but often untestable model assumptions. Consequently, we will mainly look for non-parametric identification, and afterwards seek non-parametric estimation and inference. Furthermore, we will mostly consider the non-separable model, maybe with a partial effect:

$$Y = \varphi(D, X, U), \quad Y^d = \varphi(d, X, U) \quad \text{and} \quad Y^d_x = \varphi(d, x, U),$$

where the (hyper)indices d, x indicate that these values are externally fixed. For example, the return to one additional year of schooling for an individual with given characteristics x, u and $d = 8$ is

$$\varphi(9, x, u) - \varphi(8, x, u),$$

which most likely will vary with x and u. If D is continuously distributed, the respective marginal effect is

$$\nabla_d \, \varphi(d, x, u)$$

where ∇_d refers to the partial derivative with respect to the first argument. This model is *non-separable* in the error term, which means that the marginal effect of D on Y can vary among individuals even if all included observables (i.e. x) are equal.

Notice the difference to a model with additively separable errors

$$Y = m(D, X) + U = m_D(X) + U,$$

which implies that the return to one additional year of schooling in this model simplifies to $m(9, X) - m(8, X)$. It does not vary with U.[22] Non-separable models permit heterogeneity in the responses among observably identical persons. The responses to changes in D will therefore have probability distributions. This non-separability will

---

[22] For the sake of notation we have set the error U to be equal to the outcome produced by the unobservables, called $\xi(U)$ before. This does not entail a simplification of the model but just of the notation as $\xi(\cdot)$ is not identified anyway due to the unobservability of its argument.

make these models more realistic and delineate more clearly the nature of the identifying assumptions to be used. On the other hand, it also makes identification more difficult.

Heterogeneity in the responses might itself be of policy interest, and it might therefore often be interesting to try to identify the entire function $\varphi(d, x, u)$. In the familiar linear model $Y = \alpha + D\beta + X\gamma + U$ a common treatment effect β is assumed. It prohibits not only effect heterogeneity conditional on X but also effect heterogeneity in general. This is certainly in line with the practitioners' wish to obtain a parameter that does not depend on U, since U is unobserved and its effect is usually not identified. The average treatment effect is a parameter where the unobserved variables have been averaged out. For the observed X, however, we may want to study the *conditional ATE* or the *conditional ATET* for a given set of observed characteristics x, namely

$$ATE(x) = \int (\varphi(1, x, U) - \varphi(0, x, U)) \, dF_U,$$

$$ATET(x) = \int (\varphi(1, x, U) - \varphi(0, x, U)) \, dF_{U|D=1}.$$

These could also be interpreted as partial treatment effects, and ATE and ATET are just their averages (or integrals).

Sometimes, in the econometric literature, expected potential outcome (for partial and total effects) is also referred to as the *average structural function* (ASF); see Blundell and Powell (2003). More specifically, there we are interested in partial effects where we fixed also some other (treatment) variable X at some value x, namely

$$ASF(d, x) = E[Y_x^d] = \int \varphi(d, x, U) \, dF_U.$$

In contrast, the expected potential outcome conditional on X is

$$E[Y^d | X = x] = \int \varphi(d, X, U) \cdot dF_{U|X=x} = \int \varphi(d, x, U) \, dF_{U|X=x}.$$

If U and X are uncorrelated, which is often assumed, $E[Y_x^d]$ and $E[Y^d | X = x]$ are identical, but otherwise they are not. Both have their justification and interpretation, and one should be careful to not mix them up. Another important point is that these two functions can be much more insightful if the treatment effect varies a lot with X. If the outcome Y depends mainly on X, then this information is politically much more relevant than the average treatment effect over all U and X.

Having defined the ASF, we could imagine various policy scenarios with different distributions of d and x. Consider a policy which assigns d and x according to a weighting function $f^*(d, x)$. To obtain the expected outcome of such a policy, one has to calculate the integral

$$\int \int ASF(d, x) \cdot f^*(d, x) \, dx \, dd.^{23}$$

---

[23] where dd is the differential with respect to continuous d, or else imagine a sum running over the support of D.

1.3.2   Distributional Effects

In addition to the average (conditional) outcome, we might also be interested in the distribution of these hypothetical outcomes. The motivation is obvious: even after having controlled for the heterogeneity in outcomes due to some observables X, heterogeneity can still be of first order (when the outcome $\varphi(D, X, U)$ varies mainly over U). It does not matter whether there is additionally an interaction between U and D, such that the returns to treatment vary over U, or whether this heterogeneity is less complex: if a good part of the heterogeneity is due to unobservables, not the averages but the distributions (or particular quantiles) of Y^d are politically relevant.[24]

Example 1.23 Let us consider the increasing wage inequality. Juhn, Murphy and Pierce (1993) analysed individual wage data from 27 years of the US Population Surveys. Real wages increased by 20 per cent between 1963 and 1989, but with an unequal distribution. Those in the bottom 10 percentile of wages (for the less skilled workers) fell by 5 per cent, whereas those in the 90 percentile increased by 40 per cent. When they repeated these calculations by categories of education and experience, then they observed that wage inequality also increased within categories, especially during the 80s, and that between-group wage differences increased substantially. They interpreted these changes as the result of increased returns to observable and unobservable components of skills (education, experience and ability), e.g. due to the resulting productivity. This, however, was just speculation. It is clear that this increasing wage gap comes from an increase in bargaining power, but this might equally well result from globalisation or weakened trade unions.

The following equations are defined with respect to the two variables D and X (i.e. the included observables), but we could consider X to be the empty set in order to obtain total effects. The *distributional structural function* is the distribution function of $\varphi(\cdot)$ for given x and d:

$$DSF(d, x; a) \equiv \Pr\left[\varphi(d, x, U) \leq a\right] = \int \mathbb{1}\left[\varphi(d, x, u) \leq a\right] d F_U(u).$$

The *quantile structural function* (QSF) is the inverse of the DSF. It is the τth quantile of the outcome for externally set d and x:

$$QSF(d, x; \tau) = Q^\tau[\varphi(d, x, U)] = Q^\tau[Y_x^d], \qquad (1.21)$$

where the quantile refers to the marginal distribution of U.[25] The symbol $Q^\tau(A)$ represents the τth quantile of A, i.e. $Q_A^\tau \equiv Q^\tau(A) \equiv \inf\{q : F_A(q) \geq \tau\}$. While this is the τth quantile of Y if D and X are fixed externally for every individual, in practice it is much easier to estimate from the data the following quantile:

$$Q^\tau[Y|D = d, X = x] = Q^\tau[\varphi(D, X, U)|D = d, X = x]$$

---

[24] In the international organisations it has become customary to speak then of an *integrated approach.*
[25] Quantile and distributional effects will be discussed in detail in Chapter 7.

as it corresponds to the distribution of Y we observe in the data. This is the quantile with respect to the conditional distribution $F_{Y|D,X} = F_{U|D,X}$ instead of the marginal F_U, which is certainly the same if $U \perp\!\!\!\perp (D, X)$. The DSF and the QSF contain the same information, and if the DSF is continuous, $QSF(d, x; \tau) = DSF^{-1}(d, x; \tau)$. Analytically, it is often more convenient to work with the DSF, whereas the QSF is more suited to economic interpretation.

In the treatment effect literature, one is typically interested in something in-between, namely

$$Q^{\tau}[\varphi(d, X, U)|X = x] = Q^{\tau}[Y^d|X = x].$$

But for the following discussion it is easier to work with (1.21) and supposing that U can be condensed to a scalar. It is usually assumed that φ is strictly increasing in this unobserved argument u. This greatly simplifies identification and interpretation.[26] Then we can write

$$Q^{\tau}(\varphi(d, x, U)) = \varphi(d, x, Q_U^{\tau})$$

where Q_U^{τ} represents the quantile in the 'fortune' distribution in the population. Hence, $QSF(d, x; 0.9)$ is the outcome for different values of d and x for an individual at the 90 percentile in the fortune distribution. On the other hand, the observed quantile is

$$Q^{\tau}[Y|D = d, X = x] = \varphi(d, x, Q_{U|D=d,X=x}^{\tau})$$

where $Q_{U|D=d,X=x}^{\tau} = Q^{\tau}[U|D = d, X = x]$ is the quantile in the 'fortune' distribution among those who chose d years of schooling and characteristics x.

Note that since the QSF describes the whole distribution, the ASF can be recovered from the QSF by noticing that

$$ASF(d, x) = E[Y_x^d] = \int_0^1 QSF(d, x; \tau)d\tau.$$

Hence, if the QSF is identified at all quantiles τ, so is the ASF, but not vice versa. As stated, we will more often be interested in

$$E[Y^d|X = x] = \int_0^1 Q^{\tau}[\varphi(d, X, U)|X = x]d\tau.$$

So, when in the following chapters you see a minor x, it simply refers to a realisation of X, i.e. to $\cdot|X = x$, or to an argument you are integrating out. The estimation of distributional effects will be studied in detail in Chapter 7.

So far we have discussed which types of objects we would like to estimate. The next step is to examine under which conditions they can be identified. This means that, suppose we know the distribution function $F_{Y,D,X,Z}$ (e.g. through an infinite amount of data); is this sufficient to identify the above parameters? Without further assumptions, it

---

[26] Note that it is automatically fulfilled when assuming additive separability.

is actually not, since the unobserved variables can generate any statistical association between Y, X and D, even if the true impact of D and/or X on Y is zero. Hence, data alone are not sufficient to identify treatment effects. Conceptual causal models are required, which entail identifying assumptions about the process through which the individuals were assigned to the treatments. The corresponding minimal identifying assumptions cannot be tested formally with observational data, and their plausibility must be assessed through prior knowledge of institutional details, the allocation process and behavioural theory. As we will discuss in the next chapter, the necessary assumptions and their implications are by no means trivial in practice.

1.4   Bibliographic and Computational Notes

1.4.1   Further Reading and Bibliographic Notes

Most of the ideas concerning the appropriate sampling schemes come evidently from sampling theory. As the literature on sampling theory is quite abundant, we only refer to a compendium about model-assisted survey sampling which is maybe the most related to the problem considered here, namely a survey sampling in order to identify and estimate a particular parameter of interest in a given model; see Särndal, Swensson and Wretman (1992). Basically the same can be said about the literature on experimental designs. We therefore just refer to a more recent handbook as being most related to the problems discussed here: Bailey (2008). For economics and social sciences, in Duflo, Glennerster and Kremer (2008) and in Imbens and Rubin (2015) can be found more details on the sampling schemes discussed here, stratification or blocking, randomisation and matching for treatment effect estimation. Bruhn and McKenzie (2009) compare several of these procedures, not on a theoretical level but providing some simulation studies. Estimation methods, asymptotic properties and proposals for variance estimates are presented, discussed and compared, for example, in Imai, King and Stuart (2008), as well as in Imai, King and Nall (2009), and references therein.

A completely deterministic sampling scheme is presented in a working paper by Kasy (2013), who relies on minimising the expected squared error of treatment effect estimators. The author argues that adding noise to an estimation can never decrease risk, and that there must exist a unique optimal non-random treatment assignment if there is at least one continuous covariate. This approach cannot impose balance in terms of potential outcomes, but aims to make the groups at least as similar as possible in terms of the available baseline covariates. The derivation of the balancing approach in Kasy (2013) is based on a Bayesian perspective. He explicitly describes Bayesian and frequentist inference and provides code which implements calculation of risk and discrete optimisation in MATLAB. A somewhat similar idea is presented in a working paper by Barrios (2013). The author shows that, instead of using a distance measure like the Mahalanobis distance for matching, one can calculate the conditional expectation of the outcome given some baseline variables and then use fitted values for one-dimensional pairwise matching. Depending on the first-stage estimation method, such an approach can be semi- or non-parametric, and yields great balance in terms of baseline outcomes.

Barrios (2013) points out that his approach allows for a large number of variables for balancing while maintaining simple inference techniques since only pair-dummies have to be used for proper inference. The author shows that his approach is optimal in the sense that it minimises the variance of the difference in means. Such a randomisation approach might further be very credible, since researchers have to decide before the experiment what they define as their 'outcome of interest'. Barrios (2013) further points out that he only defines optimality with respect to the mean squared error criterion. Further research might focus on alternative criteria like minimising the mean absolute value of the error if one is interested in estimating a conditional quantile function.

The randomisation method is usually not applicable when treatment decisions need to be made immediately every time a new individual enters the trial. Yet, treatment assignment algorithms exist that assign treatments sequentially taking into account the covariate information of the previously assigned individuals, see e.g. Pocock and Simon (1975). Alternative pair-matching algorithms to those being discussed here can be found e.g. in King, Gakidou, Ravishankar, Moore, Lakin, Vargas, Tellez-Rojo and Avila (2007).

After having constructed matched pairs, one can examine the remaining average differences in X between the treated and non-treated group. If these differences appear relatively large, one may start afresh from the beginning with a new randomisation and see whether, after applying the pair-matching process, one would obtain a smaller average imbalance. Of course, such re-randomisation is only possible if treatment has not yet started. If time permits it may be most effective to draw independently a number of randomisation vectors (e.g. 100 times) and choose the assignment vector which gives the smallest imbalance in X. Some re-randomisation methods are also examined in Bruhn and McKenzie (2009). A problem is the correct inference afterwards as our final observations are a result of conditional drawing and therefore follow a conditional distribution. For example, if we re-randomise until we obtain a sample where the Mahalanobis distance of the means of X between the treated subjects and its controls are smaller than a given threshold $\varepsilon > 0$ in each block, then we should be aware that the variance of our ATE estimate is also conditioned on this.

For calculating standard errors in randomised trials we presented regression-based estimators corrected for d.o.f. and potential heteroskedasticity over blocks or strata. An alternative approach to do inference for estimators can be based on randomisation inference. This is mostly based on bootstraps and requires somewhat more complex programming, but has the advantage of providing exact finite sample inference: see Carpenter, Goldstein and Rasbash (2003), Field and Welsh (2007), Have and Rosenbaum (2008), or, for a general introduction, Politis, Romano and Wolf (1999).

More recent is the practice to use hypothesis tests to evaluate balance; see, for example, Lu, Zanuto, Hornik and Rosenbaum (2001), Imai (2005) or Haviland and Nagin (2005). However, Imai, King and Stuart (2008) pointed out the fallacy problem of these methods when matching is mainly based on dropping and doubling observations to reach balance. For further reading on matched sampling we refer to Rubin (2006). A well-known compendium on observational studies in general is Rosenbaum (2002).

A growing literature is now devoted to comparing the performance of experimental versus non-experimental estimators. Whereas earlier studies such as LaLonde (1986) (see also Ham and LaLonde, 1996, for duration models) examined whether and which non-experimental estimators could replicate the results of one particular experimental study, recent research pursued a more comprehensive approach by comparing the results of a large number of non-experimental and experimental estimators; see e.g. Card, Kluve and Weber (2010) or Kluve (2010). An interesting study in this respect is Shadish, Clark and Steiner (2008), who aimed to compare experimental and non-experimental estimation within the same study.

1.4.2   Computational Notes

In **R** the `experiment` package provides various statistical methods for designing and analysing randomised experiments. Many different functions are able to estimate different 'impacts' of the treatment on the variable of interest depending upon the assumptions that the researcher is willing to make about the experimental conditions and the importance of the observed covariates. For example, the `ATEnocov` function estimates the average treatment effect in randomised settings without using pre-treatment covariates, the `ATEbounds` function computes sharp bounds on the average treatment effect when some of the outcome data are missing, and the `ATEcluster` function estimates the average treatment effect in cluster-randomised experiments. The `randomize` function can be used to randomise the treatment assignment for randomised experiments; it also allows for randomised-block and matched-pair designs.

All the previous estimations are appropriate in an experimental environment where the treatment is randomised, but some packages are also available for non-experimental environments. The `nonrandom` package allows data to be analysed if ex-ante stratification and matching by the propensity score is done. A detailed explanation of ex-post matching and propensity score methods will be given in Chapter 3. The `ps.estimate` function can be used to estimate the propensity score-based treatment effects. The default option is to estimate the treatment effects without any additional covariate, but the `ps.estimate` function allows also explanatory variables to be added and to run traditional regressions (`regr`) of the form: *outcome ~ treatment + covariates*. It can further adjust for residual imbalances in strata or in matched data (`adj`).

As will be seen in the next chapters, `Stata` also, like **R**, offers the possibility to compute different estimates in a treatment effect environment. As in this chapter, we just compare simple means; the most interesting ones to mention here are tests to compare two samples (control versus treatment group) for which exist various tests like `ttest`, `oneway`, `ranksum`, `kwallis` (referring to the Kruskal–Wallis test), etc. There is no clear recommendation that can be given, as the choice depends mainly on the data available, and the assumptions you are willing to make. Also interesting for this chapter could be some tests that check the balance between samples; see `tbalance`.

1.5   Exercises

1. Prove the statements (2.1), (2.2) and (2.3).

2. Explain SUTVA and CIA in your own words, and give examples where (a) these assumptions are fulfilled, and (b) where they are violated.

3. Imagine we have data from a random field experiment. We know that the sample is not representative, but balanced along some potential confounders X. (These might be just indicators for confounders, like the historical outcomes of Y.) From some survey data provided by the statistical office we can estimate the population distribution of our observables X. How would you modify the naive estimator (1.10) using this information? What would be a reasonable variance estimator for your estimate?

4. Referring to Exercise 3 for w_x being the weights used to adjust for stratification or blocking (along $x \in \mathcal{X}$), and $D \in \{0, 1\}$, show that the requested estimator has variance

$$\frac{2}{n} \sum_{x \in \mathcal{X}} w_x \{Var(Y^1|X = x) + Var(Y^0|X = x)\}. \tag{1.22}$$

5. Explain the differences between ATE, ATET, ATEN and SATE.

6. Discuss examples where attrition is a problem and those where it is not. Clarify exactly what a sample selection bias means and its consequences for your inference.

7. Explain the difference between blocking and stratification (if there is any). Revise your knowledge on using sampling weights in standard regression problems.

8. Discuss the pros and cons of Randomised Control Trials in social sciences, and in particular in economics.

2   An Introduction to Non-Parametric Identification and Estimation

Data are just either dependent or independent, and such a relation is perfectly symmetric. It is therefore often impossible to draw conclusions on causality out of a purely data explorative analysis. In fact, in order to conclude on a causal effect, one has to have an idea about the causal chain. In other words, you need to have a model. Sometimes it is very helpful to include the time dimension; this leads to the concept of *Granger-causality*. But even this concept is based on a model which assumes that the leading series (the one being ahead in time) is exogenous in the sense of 'no anticipation'. You just have to remind yourself that the croaking of frogs does not cause rain, though it might come first, and is therefore Granger-causal for rain.

In the last chapter, i.e. for randomised experiments, we saw that you actually do not have to specify all details of the model. It was enough to have the *ignorability* of D for (Y^0, Y^1), i.e. $(Y^0, Y^1) \perp\!\!\!\perp D$. This is equivalent to the 'no anticipation' assumption for Granger-causality: whether someone participates or not is not related to the potential outcome. But we did not only introduce basic definitions, assumptions and the direct estimators for randomised experiments; we discussed potential problems of heterogeneity and selection bias, i.e. the violation of the ignorability assumption. And it has been indicated how controlling for characteristics that drive the selection might help. We continue in this line, giving a brief introduction to non-parametric identification via controlling for covariates, mainly the so-called *confounders* (or *confounding variables*). We call those variables X confounders that have an impact on the difference in the potential outcomes Y^d and – often therefore – also on the selection process, i.e. on the decision to participate ($D = 1$). In addition, we discuss some general rules on which variables you want to control for and for which ones you do not. We do this along causal graphs, as they offer quite an illustrative approach to the understanding of non-parametric identification.

The set of control variables used in the classic linear and generalised linear regression analysis often includes variables for mainly two purposes: to control for confounders to eliminate selection bias and/or to control for (filter out) certain covariates in order to obtain the partial effect of D on Y instead of the total effect. In fact, in the classic econometric literature one often does not distinguish between them but includes the consequence of their exclusion in the notation of *omitted variable bias*. We will see, however, that for the identification and estimation of treatment effects, it is typically not appropriate to include all available information (all potential control variables X), even if they exhibit some correlation with Y and/or D. Actually, the inclusion of all those variables does not automatically allow for the identification of partial effects. Unfortunately, in most cases, one can just argue, but not prove, what is the necessary conditioning to obtain total or partial effects, respectively.

The first step is to form a clear idea about the causal chain you are willing to believe, and to think of potential disturbances. This guides us to the econometric model to be analysed. The second step is the estimation. Even though today, in economics and econometrics, most of the effort is put on the identification, i.e. the first step, there is actually no reason why a bad estimate of a neatly identified parameter should contain more (or more helpful) information than a good estimate of an imperfectly (i.e. 'up to a small bias') identified parameter. Even if this 'bad' estimator is consistent, this does not necessarily help much in practice. Recall that in empirical research, good estimators are those that minimise the mean squared error (MSE), i.e. the expected squared distance to the parameter of interest, for the given sample. Unbiasedness is typically emphasised a lot but is actually a poor criterion; even consistency is only an asymptotic property that tells us what happens if $n \approx \infty$. Therefore, as we put a lot of effort into the identification, it would be a pity if it was all in vain because of the use of a bad estimator.

In sum, the first part of this chapter is dedicated to the identification strategies (forming an idea of the causal chain), and the second part to estimation. The former will mainly happen via conditioning strategies on either *confounders* or *instruments*. As this does not, however, tell us much about the functional forms of the resulting models, the second part of the chapter is dedicated to estimation without knowledge of the functional forms of dependencies or distributions. This is commonly known as *non- and semi-parametric estimation*.

2.1   An Illustrative Approach to the Identification of Causality

Assumptions of the *conditional independence* type involving statements about potential outcomes may be somewhat unfamiliar. As similar statements will appear later on with respect to instrumental variables, it is worthwhile gaining a better intuition for this. This is particularly relevant since these 'identifying statements' usually represent the main link between economic theory and empirical analysis, and thus distinguish econometrics from pure statistics.[1] Economic theory often delivers only statements about which variables may or may not affect each other. The other ingredients of empirical analysis, like the choice of the parametric specification of the model, the choice of the estimator, the type of inference, etc., are usually driven by convenience and by the peculiarities of the available data like sample size or the nature of the observed variables.

The conditional independence assumption (CIA), $Y^d \perp\!\!\!\perp D|X$, states that we observe *all* variables X that affected D and the (potential) outcomes. Whether this assumption holds or not in a given application depends largely on the information about the assignment process and the observed data. If the vector X is empty, i.e. no control variables are observed, this condition is almost certainly invalid unless D has been randomly

---

[1] Similar statements apply to biometrics, technometrics, statistics in medicine, etc.

assigned. On the other hand, if the entire information set on which the selection process or assignment mechanism D is based on was observed, then the CIA would hold.

The causal assumptions are to be distinguished from statistical associations. While causal statements can be *asymmetric*, stochastic associations are typically *symmetric*: if D is statistically dependent on X, then X is also statistically dependent on D. Exactly the same can be said about *independence*. This can easily lead to some confusion.

Example 2.1 As an example of such confusion in the literature, take the situation in which some variables X are supposed to be exogenous for potential outcomes, in the sense that D does not cause X. When formalising this, the distribution of X is sometimes assumed to be independent from D given the potential outcomes (Y^0, Y^1), i.e. $F(X|Y^0, Y^1, D) = F(X|Y^0, Y^1)$. However, $X \perp\!\!\!\perp D|(Y^0, Y^1)$ is the same as $D \perp\!\!\!\perp X|(Y^0, Y^1)$, and does not entail any structural assumption on whether X causes D or D causes X. However, the idea in these papers is to use X as a confounder. But then it is quite questionable whether you want to assume that D is (conditionally on Y^0, Y^1) independent from X. What the authors intend to say is that D has no (causal) impact on X if conditioning on the potential outcomes (Y^0, Y^1). But the use of $F(X|Y^0, Y^1, D) = F(X|Y^0, Y^1)$ in subsequent steps or proofs renders the identification strategy of little help when the core idea is the inclusion of X as a confounder.

Some useful rules[2] concerning conditional (in)dependence structures are

$$\{(Y \perp\!\!\!\perp X|Z) \text{ and } (Y \perp\!\!\!\perp Z)\} \iff Y \perp\!\!\!\perp (X, Z) \iff \{(Y \perp\!\!\!\perp Z|X) \text{ and } (Y \perp\!\!\!\perp X)\}. \tag{2.1}$$

For any measurable function $h(\cdot)$ it holds:

$$Y \perp\!\!\!\perp X \implies Y \perp\!\!\!\perp (X, h(X)) \implies Y \perp\!\!\!\perp X|h(X). \tag{2.2}$$

For strictly positive probability distributions we also have

$$\{(Y \perp\!\!\!\perp X|Z) \text{ and } (Y \perp\!\!\!\perp Z|X)\} \iff Y \perp\!\!\!\perp (X, Z). \tag{2.3}$$

For gaining a better intuition about causality and conditional independence assumptions, graphical models encoding the causal assumptions can be very helpful. Following closely the lines of Pearl (2000), we make use of some basic graphical models to develop our intuition for assessing the plausibility of the identifying assumptions. They have the advantage that the causal structure can easily be displayed and that the distinction between causation and correlation becomes much more evident. Essentially, the structural equations, potential outcomes and causal graphs are different approaches to describe and handle the same underlying concept.

2.1.1   Introduction to Causal Graphs and Conditional Independence

Consider the relationship between some variables Y, D and X, and suppose, for convenience, that all variables are *discrete* with a finite number of mass points. Then

---

[2] For further rules see Pearl (2000, p. 11).

the relationship can be described by a probability distribution, say $\Pr(y, d, x)$. To abstract here from any common support problem we assume that $\Pr(y, d, x) > 0$ for all combinations of $y \in Supp(Y)$, $d \in Supp(D)$ and $x \in Supp(X)$. Hence, we suppose that all combinations of y, d and x can be observed with positive probability. Notice that this has quite important implications for causality identification, in particular that the outcome of some variables may have an impact on the probability distribution of other variables but not on their support. In other words, the limitations imposed by this assumption can be severe for some practical situations. Therefore, detailed discussions of the so-called *common support problem* will be given later, in the particular identification and estimation context of the next chapters.

The relationship between the variables can be presented in a graph like Figure 2.1, where V_1, V_2 and U are further (unobserved) variables, which are determined outside the model.

The graph consists of a set of variables (vertices) and a set of (directed or bi-directed) arcs. The set of variables may include observed as well as unobserved variables. The directed arcs represent causal relationships. The *dashed (bi-directed)* arcs represent relationships that might exist even simply due to unobserved common causes. The latter thereby indicate any correlation between the two variables connected. Such correlations may be generated through further unobservables that affect both variables simultaneously. In causal graphs, a priori restrictions can be encoded easily, and simple rules can then be applied to determine whether the effect of one variable on another can be identified. For example, let X be secondary school examination results, D be an indicator of enrolment at university and Y be wealth at age 50. The graph in Figure 2.2 contains the restrictions that Y does not affect D, Y does not affect X, and also D does not affect X. It contains further the restrictions that U, V_1 and V_2 are independent from each

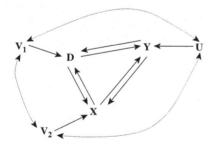

Figure 2.1 Example of a complex causal graph

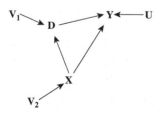

Figure 2.2 Example of a directed acyclic graph

other. Plainly, the missing and the directed arcs encode our a priori assumptions used for identifying the (total) impact of D on Y.

Consequently, a causal structure is richer than the notation of (in)dependence, because X can causally affect Y without X being causally affected by Y. Later on we will be interested in estimating the causal effect of D on Y, i.e. which outcomes would be observed if we were to set D externally. In the non-experimental world, D is also determined by its antecedents in the causal model, here by V_1 and X, and thus indirectly by the exogenous variables V_1 and V_2. When we consider an external intervention that sets D to a specific value d to identify the distribution of Y^d, then this essentially implies that the graph is stripped off all arrows pointing to D.

The graph in Figure 2.2 incorporates only *triangular structure* and *causal chains*. Such a triangular structure is often not sufficient to describe the real world. Like all models it is a simplification. For example, in a market with Q (quantity) and P (price), both variables will have a direct impact on each other, as indicated in the graph of Figure 2.3. This can be solved by simultaneous equations under the (eventual) inclusion of further variables. However, for the ease of presentation we will concentrate in this chapter on graphs that do not entail such feedback or (direct) reverse causality.

A graph where all edges are directed (i.e. a graph without bi-directed dashed arcs) and which contains no cycles is called a *directed acyclic graph* (DAG). Although the requirement of acyclicity rules out many interesting cases, several results for DAG are useful to form our intuition. Note that bi-directed dashed arcs can usually be eliminated by introducing additional unobserved variables in the graph, e.g. in order to obtain a DAG. For example, the left graph in Figure 2.4 can be expressed equivalently by the right graph. In fact, in a DAG you are obliged to specify (or 'model') all relations. This is not always necessary but can make things much easier.[3]

Before coming to the identification of causal relationships, we first discuss explicitly some basic findings on conditional independence to better understand the conditional independence assumption (CIA). We start with some helpful definitions, speaking henceforth of a *path* between two variables when referring to a sequence

Figure 2.3 The mutual effects of quantity and price cannot be presented by triangular structures or causality chains

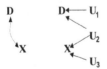

Figure 2.4 Expressing a dashed bi-directed graph as a DAG

---

[3] In other words, identification can only be achieved by being specific.

of consecutive edges of any directionality. First we examine independence between *observed* variables.[4]

DEFINITION 2.1   *Let i, j, m be events described by different random variables. 1. A path is blocked (also called d-separated) by a set of nodes (named $\mathcal{Z}$) iff*

(a) *either the path contains a chain $i \rightarrow m \rightarrow j$ or a fork $i \leftarrow m \rightarrow j$ such that the middle node is in $\mathcal{Z}$*

(b) *or the path contains an inverted fork $i \rightarrow m \leftarrow j$ such that the middle node is* not *in $\mathcal{Z}$, and such that* no *descendant of m is in $\mathcal{Z}$.*

2. A set $\mathcal{Z}$ is said to d-separate X from Y if $\mathcal{Z}$ blocks every path from a node in X to a node in Y.

THEOREM 2.2   *If sets X and Y are d-separated by $\mathcal{Z}$ in a DAG, then X is independent of Y conditional on $\mathcal{Z}$ in every distribution compatible with the graph.*

The intuition behind the first condition of Definition 2.1 is simple: i and j are marginally dependent, but once we compare i and j only when m is observed to take a particular value, i and j will be independent. For example, consider Figure 2.2 without the direct link $D \rightarrow Y$ and choose $X \in \mathcal{Z}$. Then, 1(a) from Definition 2.1 applies, so that Theorem 2.2 gives $D \perp\!\!\!\perp Y|X$ since the only path between D and Y is blocked by X. Further, in Figure 2.4 (right-hand side) one has $X \perp\!\!\!\perp D|U_2$ following 1(b) from Definition 2.1.

The second condition is less obvious at first sight. Here, i and j are marginally independent and become only dependent after conditioning on m. The conditioning *unblocks* the path. For a simple example let us ignore for a moment the common support assumption and consider tossing two coins. Now let the variable m denote whether both coins show the same side. The outcome of each coin-toss is independent of the other, but once we condition on m they will become dependent. Demonstrating this graphically, in Figure 2.4 we have $U_2 \perp\!\!\!\perp U_3$, but following the second condition of Definition 2.1 we have also $U_2 \not\!\perp\!\!\!\perp U_3|X$.

Example 2.2 Let us consider the admission to a certain graduate school which is based on either good grades or high talent in sport. Then we will find a negative correlation between these two characteristics in the school even if these are independent in the entire population. To illustrate this, suppose that both grades and sports were binary variables and independent in the population. There are thus four groups: strong in sports and strong in academic grades, weak in sports and strong in grades, strong in sports and weak in grades, and those being weak in both fields. The first three groups are admitted to the university, which thus implies a negative correlation in the student population. Conditioning on m could also happen inadvertently through the data collection process. In fact, if we obtain our data set from the school register, then we have implicitly

---

[4] For formal details, see definition 1.2.3 and theorem 1.2.4 of Pearl (2000).

conditioned on the event that all observations in the data set have been admitted to the school.

This example helps us to understand the meaning of the conditional independence $Y \perp\!\!\!\perp D|X$. We also see that neither marginal nor conditional independence implies the other, i.e.

$$Y \perp\!\!\!\perp D \qquad \not\Leftrightarrow \qquad Y \perp\!\!\!\perp D|X.$$

Remember that joint independence $(A, B) \perp\!\!\!\perp C$ implies marginal independence $A, B \perp\!\!\!\perp C$ but not vice versa. Our final goal will be the identification of causal links. To this aim we need rather the independence (or conditional independence) of potential outcomes, i.e. $Y^d \perp\!\!\!\perp D|X$. Unfortunately, this is a bit more involved than the independence assumption above.

In the following we will see that one distinguishes between different ways to establish identification. Nonetheless, it is rather the data availability and the complexity of the model (or the data generating processes) that determines which way has to be chosen in a specific practical situation.

2.1.2   Back Door Identification

In this section we study further the meaning of $Y^d \perp\!\!\!\perp D|X$, and why it can help in identifying a causal effect of D on Y when $Y^d \perp\!\!\!\perp D$ does not hold. For a better understanding of the meaning of this conditional independence assumption we have[5]

THEOREM 2.3   *Let $G_{\underline{D}}$ denote the subgraph obtained by deleting all arrows emerging from D, and $G_{\overline{D}}$ the graph obtained by deleting all arrows pointing to D. Then, for a DAG it holds that*

$$\Pr(X^d) = \Pr(X) \quad \text{if } (X \perp\!\!\!\perp D)_{G_{\overline{D}}}, \tag{2.4}$$

$$Y^d \perp\!\!\!\perp D|X^d \quad \text{if } (Y \perp\!\!\!\perp D|X)_{G_{\underline{D}}}, \tag{2.5}$$

$$Y^d \perp\!\!\!\perp D|X \quad \text{if } (Y \perp\!\!\!\perp D|X)_{G_{\underline{D}}} \quad \text{and if } \quad X^d = X. \tag{2.6}$$

In Equation (2.4) we want to make sure that X is not causally influenced by D, which in our context can basically be read as $X^d = X$. Equation (2.5) says that after deleting all arrows emanating from D, the variables Y and D should be independent conditional on X, and Equation 2.6 is a trivial conclusion of the former. Let us once again consider Figure 2.2. There, obviously $X = X^d$ as D has no causal impact on X. Furthermore, as X blocks the left path between Y and D if deleting the arrows emerging from D, we obtain $Y^d \perp\!\!\!\perp D|X$, compare with Definition 2.1 1.(a) and Theorem 2.2.

So, we can express independence relationships regarding potential outcomes by using subgraphs. This should also convince you that, for a specific data generating process, neither of the two statements $Y \perp\!\!\!\perp D|X$ and $Y^d \perp\!\!\!\perp D|X$ strictly implies the other. If the latter is true, the former could be wrong, e.g. because of a non-zero treatment

---

[5] cf. theorem 3.4.1 of Pearl (2000).

effect. If the former is true, the latter is most likely to be true. But in certain situations it could happen that despite Y^d not being independent of D (given X), we still observe $Y \perp\!\!\!\perp D|X$. This would be the (quite unlikely) case when a non-zero treatment effect and non-zero selection bias cancel each other. In sum, generally one has

$$Y \perp\!\!\!\perp D|X \qquad \not\Longleftrightarrow \qquad Y^d \perp\!\!\!\perp D|X.$$

Example 2.3 In his analysis of the effects of voluntary participation in the military on civilian earnings, Angrist (1998) takes advantage of the fact that the military is known to screen applicants to the armed forces on the basis of particular characteristics, say X, primarily on the basis of age, schooling and test scores. Hence, these characteristics are the principal factors guiding the acceptance decision, and he assumes that among applicants with the same observed characteristics, those who finally enter the military and those who do not are not systematically different with respect to some outcome variable Y measured later in life.[6] A similar reasoning applies to the effects of schooling if it is known that applicants to a school are screened on the basis of certain characteristics, but that conditional on these characteristics, selection is on a first come, first served basis.

Theorem 2.3 provides us the tools we need for identifying causal impacts of treatment D on outcome Y. If, for example, due to a conditioning on X or X^d, independence of D from the potential outcomes Y^d is achieved, then the causal impact of D on Y is identifiable. More specifically, one obtains the causal effect of D on Y (i.e. setting D externally from 0 to 1) by

$$E[Y^1 - Y^0] = \int E[Y^1 - Y^0|X]dF_X \qquad (2.7)$$

$$= \int E[Y^1|X, D = 1]dF_X - \int E[Y^0|X, D = 0]dF_X$$

$$= \int E[Y|X, D = 1]dF_X - \int E[Y|X, D = 0]dF_X.$$

That is, one first calculates the expected outcome conditional on $D = d$ and X, to afterwards integrate out X. In practice, the expectations in the last line of (2.7) can be estimated from the sample of the treated ($d = 1$) and the non-treated ($d = 0$), respectively, to afterwards average over these with respect to the distribution of X (but careful: over the entire population and not just to the respective conditional distributions of $X|D = d, d = 0, 1$). This method will be discussed in detail in the next chapter.

Figure 2.2 was a simple though typical situation of identifiability. Let us turn to an example where we cannot identify the effect of D on Y. In Figure 2.5, the original graph and the subgraph needed to apply Theorem 2.3 are given. Not conditioning at all leaves the path $D \dashleftarrow\!\!\!\dashrightarrow X_2 \longrightarrow Y$ unblocked. But conditioning on X_2 unblocks the path $D \dashleftarrow\!\!\!\dashrightarrow X_2 \longleftrightarrow X_1 \longrightarrow Y$. Conditioning on X_1 (or on X_1 and X_2) would block a part of the causal effect of D on Y since X_1 is a descendant of D, i.e. here we do not have $X_1^d = X_1$.

---

[6] Depending on Y, this can be a quite strong assumption.

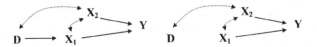

Figure 2.5 Example of non-identifiability of the total impact of D on Y

Figure 2.6 A model where we must not condition on X to identify the impact of D on Y

With this basic intuition developed, we can already imagine which variables need to be included (or not) in order to identify a causal effect of D on Y. The easiest way of thinking about this is to suppose that the true effect is zero, and ascertain whether the impacts of the unobserved variables could generate a dependence between D and Y. Before you continue, try to solve Exercise 3 at the end of this chapter. Then let us conclude this consideration with an example.

Example 2.4 Take a Bernoulli variable D (treatment 'yes' or 'no') with $p = 0.5$. Let the outcome be $Y = D + U$ and further $X = Y + V$. Suppose now that (U, V) are independent and jointly standard normal, and both independent from D, which implies that the support of Y and X is the entire real line. We thus obtain that $E[Y|D = 1] - E[Y|D = 0] = 1$. However, if we condition on $X = 1$ then it can be shown (see Exercise 4) that $E[Y|X = 1, D = 1] - E[Y|X = 1, D = 0] = 0$. This result also holds for other values of X, showing that the estimates for the impact of D on Y (in absolute value) are downward biased when conditioning on X.

In Example 2.4 we have seen that conditioning on third variables is not always appropriate, even if they are highly correlated with D. This becomes also evident in Figure 2.6, where X is neither causally affected by, nor affecting D or Y. Yet, it can still be highly correlated with both variables. The effect of D on Y is well identified if **not** conditioning on X. Conditioning on X would unblock the path via V and U, and thus confound the effect of D.

According to Theorem 2.3 and the proceeding discussion, the effect of D on Y can often be identified by adjusting for a set of variables X, such that X does not contain any descendant of D, and that X blocks every path between D and Y which contains an arrow pointing to D. Pearl (2000) denoted this as the *back-door* adjustment. This set of variables, however, is not necessarily unique. In Figure 2.7, for example, the set $\{X_3, X_4\}$ meets this back-door criterion, as does the set $\{X_4, X_5\}$. The set $\{X_4\}$, however, does not meet the criterion because it unblocks the path from D via X_3, X_1, X_4, X_2, X_5 to Y; neither does $\{X_1, X_2\}$.

Before turning to another identification method, let us recall the structural function notation introduced in equations (1.1) and (1.2). Thinking of classical regression analysis with response Y, regressors (D, X), and the remainder U often called the 'error

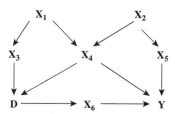

Figure 2.7 Different sets can be used for blocking the paths between D and Y

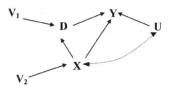

Figure 2.8 Causal graph with unspecified relation between X and U

term', an interesting question to ask would be: what happens if there is also a relation between X and U? Consider Figure 2.8 and note that this graph implies that $U \perp\!\!\!\perp D|X$. It is not hard to see that nonetheless one has

$$E[Y^d] = \int \varphi(d, X, U) dF_{UX} = \int \int \varphi(d, X, U) \, dF_{U|X} \, dF_X$$

$$= \int \int \varphi(d, X, U) \, dF_{U|X, D=d} \cdot dF_X = \int E\left[Y^d | X, D = d\right] dF_X$$

$$= \int E[Y|X, D = d] dF_X = E_X [E[Y|X, D = d]]. \qquad (2.8)$$

Similarly to (2.7), the inner expectation of the last expression can be estimated from the respective subsamples of each treatment group (d) to afterwards average (or integrate) out the X. Thus, the method for identifying the impact of D on Y is the same as in Equation 2.7; it is the so-called *matching* and *propensity score* method discussed in Chapter 3.

2.1.3 Front Door Identification

So far we have mainly considered cases where a direct impact of D on Y was present, sometimes together with an indirect impact. In order to identify correctly the total effect, often a conditioning on some variables in the back door was necessary: so-called *confounders* or *control variables*. Certainly, this is only possible if these are observed. If the variables D and Y are connected by a dashed arc (i.e. an unobservable variable pointing to D and Y), as in the left graph of Figure 2.9, then the effect of D on Y can *not* be identified this way.

We will learn now how a mediating variable, such as Z in the second graph of Figure 2.9, can identify the desired impact. Essentially, one first identifies the effect of D on Z, and subsequently the effect of Z on Y. This also works if there is an effect of some unobserved variables on the mediating one, which can be blocked, e.g. by conditioning on Q as indicated in the right graph. Hence, the usual rule, saying that one should not control for a variable that is on the causal pathway, has some exceptions.

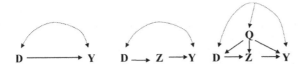

Figure 2.9 Front door identification: left: not identifiable; centre and right: identifiable

One should note, however, that a different formula for identification has to be used then. One example is the so-called *front-door* adjustment.

Example 2.5 Pearl (2000, section 3.3.3) gives an example of front-door identification to estimate the effect of smoking on the occurrence of lung cancer. The advocates of the tobacco industry attributed the observed positive correlation between smoking and lung cancer to some latent genetic differences. According to their theory, some individuals are more likely to enjoy smoking or become addicted to nicotine, and the same individuals are also more susceptible to develop cancer, but not because of smoking. If we were to find a mediating variable Z not caused by these genetic differences, the previously described strategy could be used. The amount of tar deposited in a person's lungs would be such a variable, if we could assume that (1) smoking has no effect on the production of lung cancer except as mediated through tar deposits (i.e. the effect of smoking on cancer is channelled entirely via the mediating variable), (2) that the unobserved genotype has no direct effect on the accumulation of tar, and (3) that there are no other factors that affect the accumulation of tar deposits and (at the same time) have another path to smoking or cancer. This identification approach shows that sometimes it can be appropriate to adjust for a variable that is causally affected by D.[7] Note that our set of assumptions is designed in order to identify the total impact. For just the existence of any effect, you may be able to relax them.

---

[7] Pearl (2000) continues with an insightful and amusing example for the kinds of problems and risks this strategy entails. Suppose for simplicity that all variables are binary with 50% of the population being smokers and the other 50% being non-smokers. Suppose 95% of smokers have accumulated high levels of tar, whereas only 5% of non-smokers have high levels of tar. This implies the population sizes given in the second column of the table below. In the last column the fraction of individuals who have developed lung cancer is given. For example, 10% of non-smokers without tar have lung cancer.

	Population size (%)	Have lung cancer
Non-smokers, No tar	47.5	10 %
Non-smokers, High tar	2.5	5 %
Smokers, No tar	2.5	90 %
Smokers, High tar	47.5	85 %

This table can be interpreted in two ways: overall, smokers seem to have higher lung cancer than non-smokers. One could argue though that this relation is spurious and driven by unobservables. On the other hand, we see that high values of tar seem to have a protective effect. Non-smokers with tar deposits experience less lung cancer than non-smokers without tar. In addition, smokers with tar also have less lung cancer than smokers without tar. Hence, tar is an effective protection against lung cancer such that one should aim to build up tar deposits. At the same time, smoking indeed seems to be a very effective method to develop these protective tar deposits. Following the second interpretation, smoking would even help to reduce lung cancer.

Let us return to the identification of the treatment effect (impact of D on Y) with such a mediating variable in a more general setting. Consider the graph in Figure 2.10. For simplicity we abstract from further covariates X, but as usual, we permit each variable to be further affected by some additional unobservables which are independent of each other. This is made explicit in the left graph. Usually one suppresses these independent unobservables in the graphs, and only shows the simplified graph on the right-hand side.

The graph implies that

$$Z^d \perp\!\!\!\perp U \qquad \text{and} \qquad Z^d \perp\!\!\!\perp D \qquad \text{and} \qquad U \perp\!\!\!\perp Z|D.$$

In terms of cumulative distribution function F, the first statement can also be written as $F_{Z^d,U} = F_{Z^d} F_U$, while the second statement implies that $F_{Z^d} = F_{Z^d|D=d} = F_{Z|D=d}$. We make use of these implications further below when expressing the potential outcomes in terms of observed variables. The potential outcome depends on Z and U in that

$$Y^d = \varphi(Z^d, U),$$

where Z^d is the potential outcome of Z. We have (still suppressing X without loss of generality)

$$E[Y^d] = \int \int \varphi(Z^d, U)\, dF_{Z^d,U} = \int \int \varphi(Z^d, U)\, dF_{Z^d|D=d}\, dF_U$$

$$= \int \left(\int \varphi(Z, U)\, dF_{Z|D=d} \right) dF_U = \int \left(\int \varphi(Z, U)\, dF_U \right) dF_{Z|D=d}.$$

Note that this calculus holds for continuous and discrete variables. It follows that

$$E[Y^d] = \int E\left[E\left[Y|D, Z=z\right]\right] dF_{Z|D=d}, \tag{2.9}$$

where we made use of

$$E\left[E\left[Y|D, Z=z\right]\right] = \int E[Y|D, Z=z]\, dF_D = \int \left(\int \varphi(Z, U)\, dF_{U|D,Z=z} \right) dF_D$$

$$= \int \left(\int \varphi(z, U)\, dF_{U|D,Z=z} \right) dF_D = \int \int \varphi(z, U)\, dF_{U|D}\, dF_D$$

$$= \int \varphi(z, U)\, dF_U \qquad \text{because } U \perp\!\!\!\perp Z|D.$$

The formula (2.9) shows that we can express the expected potential outcome in terms of observable random variables; so it is identifiable. If D and Z are discrete, (2.9) can be written as

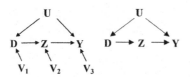

Figure 2.10 Original and simplified graph

$$E[Y^d] = \sum_z \Pr(Z = z|D = d) \left(\sum_{d'} E\left[Y|D = d', Z = z\right] \Pr\left(D = d'\right) \right). \quad (2.10)$$

To obtain an intuition for this, recall that we separately identify the effect of D on Z, and the effect of Z on Y. First, consider the effect of Z on Y, and note that the graph implies $Y^z \perp\!\!\!\perp Z|D$ such that

$$E[Y^z] = \int E[Y|D, Z = z] \, dF_D = E_D[E[Y|D, Z = z]]. \quad (2.11)$$

To obtain the effect of D on Z we note that there is no confounding, i.e. $Z^d \perp\!\!\!\perp D$: in other words, the treatment effect of D on the distribution of Z is directly reflected in the conditional distribution function $F_{Z|D}$. Combining $F_{Z|D}$ with (2.11) gives the formula (2.9). We can summarise this in the following definition:[8]

DEFINITION 2.4   *A set of variables Z is said to satisfy the front-door criterion relative to an ordered pair of variables (D, Y) if:*

(a) *Z intercepts all directed paths from D to Y, and*
(b) *there is no back-door path from D to Z, and*
(c) *all back-door paths from Z to Y are blocked by D.*

Concluding, we can say that again the approach of first regressing Y on D and other observables, here Z, with an appropriate subsequent averaging is a valid identification and estimation strategy. This method is based on it is the so-called *mediation* analysis which today is very popular in statistical methods for psychology, but has largely been ignored in econometrics and applied economics so far. This identification approach via a mediating variable can certainly be combined with the *back door* approach via controlling for confounding variables in order to analyse identification in more complex graphs.

2.1.4   Total versus Partial Effects, Post-Treatment Covariates and Instruments

A main difference between the production-function philosophy and the treatment-effect philosophy in the current econometrics literature is the identification of either the partial or the total effect. The partial effect typically reduces to what we denote in this section also the *direct effect*, whereas the total impact is composed by the direct plus the indirect effects. Even though in both cases people often speak of a *ceteris paribus* interpretation, it has slightly different meanings, depending on the context. The most important difference is that in the production-function philosophy we control for indirect effects due to post-treatment changes in covariates X, whereas in the treatment-effect literature those indirect effects are assigned to the impact of D. Consequently, the production function approach attempts to include all relevant determinants of the output, such that after having included all these factors the term U should be purely random

---

[8] This corresponds to definition 3.3.3 of Pearl (2000).

noise. The treatment-effect philosophy is interested in the effect of only one (or perhaps two) variables D and chooses the other regressors for reasons of identification, according to knowledge about the data-generating process. Then, additional covariates could nonetheless be included or not on the basis of efficiency considerations.

Example 2.6 Often one is interested in the effects of some school inputs, our D (e.g. computer training in school), on 'productivity' Y in adult life (e.g. wages). In the typical Mincer-type equation one regresses wages on a constant, experience (X) and school inputs (D). Here, experience is included to obtain only the direct effect of D on Y, by blocking the indirect effect that D may have on experience (X). This is an example where including an additional variable in the regression may cause problems. Suppose the computer training programme was introduced in some randomly selected pilot schools. Clearly, due to the randomisation the total effect of D on Y is identified. However, introducing experience (X) in the regression is likely to lead to identification problems when being interested in the total effect. Evidently, the amount of labour market experience depends on the time in unemployment or out of the labour force, which is almost certainly correlated with some unobserved productivity characteristics that also affect Y. Hence, introducing X destroys the advantages that could be reaped from the experiment. Most applied labour econometricians are well aware of this problem and use potential experience instead. This, however, does not fully separate the direct from the indirect effect because a mechanistic relationship is imposed, i.e. if education is increased by one year, potential experience decreases automatically by one year.

Whether we are interested in identifying the total or the partial impact is not a question of econometrics but depends on the economic question under study. It is important here to understand the differences when identifying, estimating and interpreting the effect. In practice it can easily happen that we are interested in the total but can identify only the partial effect or vice versa. One might also be in the fortunate situation where we can identify both or in the unfortunate one where we are unable to identify any of them. To illustrate these various cases, let us deviate from the DAGs and examine the more involved analysis in the presence of cycles or feedback.

Consider Figure 2.11 graph (a), where D affects X, and X affects D. This could be due to a direct feedback or simultaneous determination of both variables. It could also be that for some (unknown) subpopulation treatment D affects X, and for the other individuals X affects D. Finally, there is the possibility that the causal influence is in fact

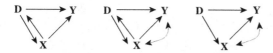

Figure 2.11 Direct and indirect effects, examples (a) to (c) from left to right

unidirectional, but that we simply do not know the correct direction, and therefore do not want to restrict this relationship. Not conditioning on X would lead to confounding. On the other hand, conditioning on X would block the back-door path but would also block the effect of D on Y which mediates through X. By conditioning on X we might be able to estimate the direct effect of D on Y, i.e. the total effect minus the part that is channelled through X. In other words, conditioning on X permits us to estimate partial (here the direct) effect.

Example (b) illustrates once again that conditioning on X does not always guarantee the identification of an (easily) interpretable effect. In this situation, conditioning on X unblocks the path between D and Y via the dashed arc. Hence, even if the true direct effect of D on Y is zero, we still might find a non-zero association between D and Y after conditioning on X. This simple graph demonstrates that attempting to identify direct effects via conditioning can fail.

Graph (c) demonstrates that sometimes, while the direct effect cannot be identified, the total effect might well be. The total effect of D on Y is identified without conditioning. However, the direct effect of D on Y is not because conditioning on X would unblock the path via the dashed arc. Not conditioning would obviously fail, too. A heuristic way to see this is that we could identify the effect of D on X but not that of X on Y; hence we could never know how much of the total effect is channelled by X.

Example 2.7 Consider the example where a birth-control pill is suspected of increasing the risk of thrombosis, but at the same time reduces the rate of pregnancies, which are known to provoke thrombosis. Here you are not interested in the total effect of the pill on thrombosis but rather on its direct impact. Suppose the pill is introduced in a random drug-placebo trial and suppose further that there is an unobserved variable affecting the likelihood of pregnancy as well as of thrombosis. This corresponds to the graph in example (c) in Figure 2.11. The total effect of the pill is immediately identified since it is a random trial. On the other hand, measuring the effect separately among pregnant women and non-pregnant women could lead to spurious associations due to the unobserved confounding factor. Therefore, to measure the direct effect, alternative approaches are required, e.g. to start the randomised trial only after women became pregnant or among women who prevented pregnancy by means other than this drug.

Let us have a another look on the different meanings of a *ceteris paribus* effect, depending on whether we look at the treatment or the production function literature. In the analysis of gender discrimination one frequently observes the claim that women are paid less than men or that women are less likely to be hired. Women and men differ in many respects, yet the central claim is that there is a direct effect of gender on hiring or pay, even if everything else is hold equal. This is exemplified in the graph displayed in Figure 2.12. There, gender may have an effect on education (subject of university degree and type of programme in vocational school), on labour market experience or preferred occupation, and many other factors, in addition to a possible direct effect on

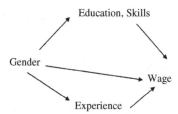

Figure 2.12 Illustrative graph for the impact of gender on wages

wage.[9] In order to attain a real *ceteris paribus* interpretation in the production function thinking, one would like to disentangle the direct effect from the other factors. Even if we abstract from the fact that a large number of unobservables is missing in that graph, it is obvious that gender has also many indirect effects on wages. It has actually turned out to be pretty hard to measure correctly the indirect and therefore the total effect of gender on wages, and many different models have been proposed in the past to solve this problem.[10]

Example 2.8 Rose and Betts (2004) consider the effects of the number and type of maths courses during secondary school on adult earnings. Maths courses are likely to have two effects: First, they could affect the likelihood of continuing with further education. Second, they may have a direct effect on earnings, i.e. given total years of education. Therefore, regressions are examined of the type

wages   on   *maths courses, years of schooling* and *other controls,*

where 'years of schooling' contains the total years of education including tertiary education. The main interest is in the coefficient on *maths courses,* controlling for the *post-treatment variable* total schooling. Rose and Betts (2004) also considered a variant where they control for the two post-treatment variables *college major* (i.e. field of study in university) and *occupation.* In all cases, direct positive effects of maths courses on wages were found. In a similar spirit, they examined the effects of the credits completed during secondary school on wages, controlling for total years of education. The motivation for that analysis was to investigate whether the curriculum during secondary school mattered. Indeed, in classical screening models, education serves only as a screening device such that only the number of years of education (or the degree obtained) should determine wages, while the content of the courses should not matter.

What should become clear from all these examples and discussions is that identifying direct (or partial) effects requires the identification of the distribution of Y_x^d. This can

---

[9] See Moral-Arce, Sperlich, Fernandez-Sainz and Roca (2012), Moral-Arce, Sperlich and Fernandez-Sainz (2013) and references therein for recent non-parametric identification and estimation of the gender wage gap.

[10] A further problem is that we might be able to identify direct and indirect effects of gender on wages, but not all can automatically be referred to as discrimination. For example, if women would voluntarily choose an education that leads to low-paid jobs, one had in a next step to investigate whether the jobs are low-paid just because they are dominated by women; but we could not automatically conclude so.

be different from Y^d where d is set externally and X is observed to be x, as seen in the examples above. An *average direct effect* can be defined as

$$\int E[Y_x^1 - Y_x^0]dF_x$$

which can be different from

$$\int E[Y^1 - Y^0|X = x]dF_x.$$

While the latter can usually be identified from a perfect randomised experiment, identification of the former will require more assumptions. In order to simplify the problem, let us again concentrate on DAGs and establish some rules helping us to identify the distribution of Y_x^d.

Let Y, D, X, V be arbitrary disjoint sets of nodes in a causal DAG, where each of these sets may be empty. Let $Pr(Y^d)$ denote the distribution of Y if D is *externally set* to the value d. Similarly, $\Pr(Y_x^d)$ represents the distribution of Y if D and X are both externally set. In contrast, $\Pr(Y^d|X^d = x)$ is the outcome distribution when D is externally set and x is observed subsequently. In our previous notation, this refers to X^d, i.e. the potential outcome of X when D is fixed externally. Note that as usual $\Pr(Y^d|X^d) = \frac{\Pr(Y^d,X^d)}{\Pr(X^d)}$. As before, let G_D be the subgraph obtained by deleting all arrows emerging from nodes in D. Analogously, $G_{\overline{D}}$ is the graph obtained by deleting all arrows pointing to nodes in D. Then, the rules are summarised in[11]

THEOREM 2.5   *For DAGs, and the notation introduced above one has*

1. Insertion and deletion of observations

$$\Pr(Y^d|X^d, V^d) = \Pr(Y^d|V^d) \qquad if \qquad (Y \perp\!\!\!\perp X|D, V)_{G_{\overline{D}}}$$

2. Action or observation exchange

$$\Pr(Y_x^d|V_x^d) = \Pr(Y^d|X^d, V^d) \qquad if \qquad (Y \perp\!\!\!\perp X|D, V)_{G_{\overline{D}X}}$$

3. Insertion or deletion of actions

$$\Pr(Y_x^d|V_x^d) = \Pr(Y^d|V^d) \qquad if \qquad (Y \perp\!\!\!\perp X|D, V)_{G_{\overline{D,X(V)}}}$$

where $X(V)$ is the set of X-nodes that are not ancestors of any V-node in the subgraph $G_{\overline{D}}$.

We illustrate the use of the rules in Theorem 2.5 by applying them to the graphs in Figure 2.13. In fact, we can show by this theorem that the direct effects are identified. In graph (a) we can apply rule 2 twice: first to obtain

$$\Pr(Y_x^d) = \Pr(Y^d|X^d) \qquad because \qquad (Y \perp\!\!\!\perp X|D)_{G_{\overline{D}X}},$$

and afterwards to show that

$$\Pr(Y^d|X^d) = \Pr(Y|D, X) \qquad as \qquad (Y \perp\!\!\!\perp D|X)_{G_{\underline{D}}}.$$

---

[11] For more details etc. see Pearl (2000), theorem 3.4.1.

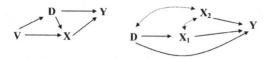

Figure 2.13 How to identify the direct effects in graph (a) [left] and (b) [right]

You can check that both conditions are satisfied in graph (a) such that we finally have $\Pr(Y_x^d) = \Pr(Y|D, X)$. In this situation, conditioning on D and X clearly identifies potential outcomes. Hence, in conventional regression jargon, X can be added as an additional regressor in a regression to identify that part of the effect of D which is not channelled via X. Note however, that the total effect of D on Y cannot be identified.

Also in graph (b), still Figure 2.13, we fail to identify the total effect of D on Y. Instead, with Theorem 2.5, we can identify the distributions of Y_x^d and Y_v^d. For example, by applying rule 2 jointly to D and X we obtain

$$\Pr(Y_x^d|V_x^d) = \Pr(Y|D, X, V) \qquad \text{because} \qquad (Y \perp\!\!\!\perp (D, X)|V)_{G_{(D,X)}}.$$

Furthermore, with $V_x^d = V$ we have $\Pr(Y_x^d|V_x^d) = \Pr(Y_x^d|V) = \Pr(Y|D, X, V)$ (cf. rule 3), and finally

$$E[Y_x^d] = E_V[E[Y|V, D = d, X = x]].$$

It has to be admitted that most of the treatment effect identification and estimation methods we present in the following chapters were introduced as methods for studying the total effect. It is, however, obvious that, if the variation of confounders X is not purely exogenous but has a mutual effect or common driver with D (recall graph (a) of Figure 2.11), then we may want to identify the direct (or partial) effect of D on Y instead.

In later chapters we will also consider the so-called *instrumental variable* estimation, where identification via causal graphs of the kind in Figure 2.14 is applied. A variable Z has a direct impact on D, but is not permitted to have any path to or from Y other than the mediating link via D. So the question is not just to exclude a causal impact of Z on Y; some more assumptions are necessary. The prototypical example for such a situation is the randomised encouragement design. We are, for example, interested in the effect of smoking (D) on health outcomes (Y). One would suspect that the smoking behaviour is not independent of unobservables affecting health outcomes. A randomised trial where D is set randomly is impossible as we cannot force individuals to smoke or not to smoke. In the encouragement design, different doses of encouragement Z 'to stop smoking' are given. For example, individuals could be consulted by their physician about the benefits of stopping smoking or receive a discount from their health insurance provider. These different doses could in principle be randomised. In the simplest design, Z contains only two values: encouragement yes or no. Half of the physicians could be randomly selected to provide stop-smoking encouragement to their patients, while the other half does not. This way, Z would be randomly assigned and thus independent of all unobservables. The resulting graph is given in Figure 2.14. One can immediately obtain the *intention-to-treatment effect* of Z on Y. Identification of the treatment effect of D on

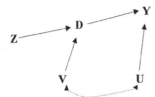

Figure 2.14 How an instrument Z may help to identify the effect of D on Y

Y, however, will require further assumptions, as will be discussed later. One assumption is that Z has no further link with Y, i.e. the stop-smoking campaign should only lead to a reduction in smoking (among those who receive the encouragement) but provide no other health information (e.g. about the harm of obesity) that could also affect Y. In addition, some kind of monotonicity of the effect of Z on D is required, e.g. that the stop-smoking campaign does not induce anyone to start or increase smoking. Clearly, it is only permitted to have an impact (direct or indirect) on those individuals to whom the anti-smoking incentives are offered, but not on anyone else.

2.2   Non- and Semi-Parametric Estimation

Unlike the rest of the book, this section is basically a condensed summary. We introduce here non- and semi-parametric estimation methods that we will frequently apply in the following chapters. The focus is on presenting the main ideas and results (statistical properties), so that you get a feeling for which types of estimators exist and learn their properties. For a deeper understanding of them we recommend that you consult more specific literature on non- and semi-parametric inference, which is now quite abundant.[12] Especially if encountering these methods for the first time, you might find this section a bit too dense and abstract.

In the last section on non-parametric identification we controlled for covariates by means of conditional expectations: recall for example Equation 2.7. Crucial ingredients are conditional mean functions $E[Y|X]$ or $E[Y|X, D]$ and estimates thereof; recall Equation 2.8. Similarly, in the case of a front-door identification with a mediating variable Z, we need to predict conditional expectations in certain subpopulations to apply Equation 2.9. The results for the estimated treatment effects will thus depend on the way we estimate these conditional expectations. Once we have succeeded in identifying treatment effects non-parametrically, i.e. without depending on a particular parametric specification, it would be nice if we could also estimate them without such a restrictive specification. This is the topic of the remaining part of this chapter. The focus is here on the basic ideas. Readers who are already familiar with local polynomial regression can skip the next two sections. To Master-level and PhD students we nonetheless recommend reading Section 2.2.3 where we review exclusively estimators and results of semi-parametric estimation that will be referred to in the subsequent chapters.

---

[12] See for example Härdle, Müller, Sperlich and Werwatz (2004), Henderson and Parmeter (2015), Li and Racine (2007), Yatchew (2003) or Pagan and Ullah (1999).

2.2.1   A Brief Introduction to Non-Parametric Regression

Preliminaries

Non-parametric estimation of a conditional expectation function $E[Y|X]$ differs from parametric regression in that the regression function is not specified parametrically, for example as linear or quadratic, but is permitted to have any arbitrary form. To construct a reasonable estimator it is nonetheless required that some conditions on integrability, continuity and differentiability are fulfilled. There are many different approaches to non-parametric regression, but the approaches closest to the underlying spirit of non-parametric regression are probably the so-called *kernel* and *k-nearest neighbour* (kNN) regression methods which will be introduced and discussed in this section. Both methods are local estimators in the sense that they estimate $m(x) := E[Y|X = x]$ at point x by (weighted) averages of those y_i for which their covariates' vector x_i is close to x. In econometric theory more popular series estimators are often (depending on the series) global estimators and therefore inappropriate for treatment effect estimation, as will be seen and discussed later.

In the following discussion we mostly consider the case where all covariates in vector X are continuously distributed. The handling of discrete covariates will be discussed explicitly somewhat later. The reason is that for discrete covariates the (asymptotic) theory is trivial. This can be seen easily, especially for those with finite support: if the whole vector X were discrete, then the conditional mean $E[Y|X = x]$ could simply be estimated by taking the average of Y over all observations with X being exactly equal to x. As the number of observations with $X = x$ grows proportionally with the sample size, say n, it can be shown that this average is a $\sqrt{n}$ consistent estimator for the conditional mean. In other words, from the perspective of econometric theory the situation is only complex when X is continuously distributed because in that case the number of observations with X being exactly equal to x is zero with probability one. Estimation of $E[Y|X = x]$ then requires the use of observations close to x. One should note, however, that in finite samples some *smoothing* is usually useful even if the X variables are discrete.[13] Although this might introduce some (so-called *smoothing*) bias, it usually reduces the variance a lot and thus the mean squared error (MSE).

The (asymptotic) properties of non-parametric estimators (and of semi-parametric estimators that use non-parametric plug-in estimators) depend on smoothness assumptions on the true regression curve. As usual, the optimal convergence rate of estimators is achieved by balancing bias and variance. Consequently, if we work without assumptions like the knowledge of the functional form (knowledge that may allow for unbiased estimation), the estimator has a bias that disappears at the same rate as the standard deviation goes to zero. Hence, in contrast to parametric regression, we also have to account for this bias when making further inferences. To reach consistency, certain smoothness of $m(x)$ is required.[14] This is often imposed in terms of differentiability (some Hölder or

---

[13] That is, including some observations for which we only have $x_i \approx x$ but not equality.

[14] Typically one adds smoothness conditions for the density of the continuous covariates. This is mainly done for technical convenience but also avoids that the 'left' or 'right' neighbourhood of x is not much more represented in the sample than the other side.

Lipschitz continuity, see below), and sometimes also by boundedness conditions. The idea is pretty simple: if there were a downward jump of $m(\cdot)$ right before x, then a weighted average of the y_i (for x_i being neighbour of x) would systematically overestimate $m(x)$; a 'smoother' is simply not the right approach to estimate functions that are not smooth.[15]

It is useful to present these smoothness concept in real analysis. Let $m : \mathbb{R}^q \to \mathbb{R}$ be a real-valued function. This function m is called *Lipschitz continuous* over a set $\mathcal{X} \subset \mathbb{R}^q$ if there is a non-negative constant c such that for any two values $x_1, x_2 \in \mathcal{X}$

$$|m(x_1) - m(x_2)| \leq c \cdot \|x_1 - x_2\|$$

where $\|\cdot\|$ is the Euclidean norm. Loosely speaking, the smallest value of c for which this condition is satisfied represents the 'steepest slope' of the function in the set $\mathcal{X}$. If there is a c such that the Lipschitz condition is satisfied over its entire domain, one says that the function is *uniformly Lipschitz continuous*.

Example 2.9 Consider $q = 1$, then the function $m(x) = |x|$ is uniformly Lipschitz continuous over the entire real line. On the other hand, it is not differentiable at zero. Note that according to the theorem of Rademacher, a Lipschitz continuous function is differentiable almost everywhere but not necessarily everywhere.[16] As a second example, the function $m(x) = x^2$ is differentiable, but not Lipschitz continuous over $\mathbb{R}$. Hence, neither does differentiability imply Lipschitz continuity nor the other way around. See also Exercise 6.

A generalisation of Lipschitz continuity is the *Hölder continuity* which is satisfied over a set $\mathcal{X}$ if there is a non-negative constant c such that for any two values $x_1, x_2 \in \mathcal{X}$

$$|m(x_1) - m(x_2)| \leq c \cdot \|x_1 - x_2\|^{\alpha}$$

for some $0 < \alpha \leq 1$; see again Exercise 6. This generalisation is useful for several reasons: α allows us to slow down the speed at which $m(x_1)$ approaches $m(x_2)$ when $x_1 \to x_2$. But it also allows us to understand smoothness as an indicator for how well a polynomial approximates locally the true function. This connection is in fact established by the well-known Taylor expansion (cf. Equation 2.12 below).

The class of real-valued functions that are k times differentiable and for which all kth derivatives are Hölder continuous with exponent α is often denoted as $C^{k,\alpha}$.[17] For this class of functions the remainder term of a kth order Taylor series expansion of $m(x + u)$ is of order $\|u\|^{k+\alpha}$. Therefore, one often refers to the 'smoothness' of this class as $k + \alpha$. To be more specific, some more notation is useful. Let $\lambda = (\lambda_1, \ldots, \lambda_q)$ be a q-tuple of non-negative integers, and let $|\lambda| = \lambda_1 + \ldots + \lambda_q$. Define $\lambda! = \lambda_1! \cdots \lambda_q!$, $x^{\lambda} = x_1^{\lambda_1} \cdots x_q^{\lambda_q}$ and the partial derivatives of $m(\cdot)$ by

---

[15] There certainly exist modifications that account for jumps and edges if their location is known.

[16] This means that picking randomly a point from the support, it is for sure that at this point the function is differentiable.

[17] If $\alpha = 1$ one often writes C^k and refers to Lipschitz continuity.

$$\mathcal{D}^\lambda m(x) = \frac{\partial^{|\lambda|}}{\partial x_1^{\lambda_1} \cdots \partial x_q^{\lambda_q}} m(x).$$

Then a Taylor expansion of a function $m(x) \in C^{k,\alpha}$ up to order k is given by

$$m(x+u) = \sum_{0 \leq |\lambda| \leq k} \frac{1}{\lambda!} \cdot \mathcal{D}^\lambda m(x) \cdot u^\lambda + R(x, u) \quad \text{with} \quad |R(x, u)| \leq c \cdot \|u\|^{k+\alpha} \quad (2.12)$$

for some non-negative c. Note that the summation runs over all permutations of the q-tuple λ.

Based on this type of properties it is possible to derive general results on optimal convergence for non-parametric estimators when the only information or restriction on the true function $m(x)$ over some set $\mathcal{X} \subset \mathbb{R}^q$ is that it belongs to the class $C^{k,\alpha}$.[18]

To examine the properties of non-parametric estimators, one also needs to define what *convergence of an estimator $\hat{m}(x)$ to $m(x)$ over some set $\mathcal{X} \subset \mathbb{R}^q$ means*.[19] Different ways to measure the distance between two functions can be used. A popular one[20] is the L_p norm $\|\cdot\|_p$

$$\left\| \hat{m}(x) - m(x) \right\|_p = \left[\int_{\mathcal{X}} |\hat{m}(x) - m(x)|^p \, d\kappa(x) \right]^{\frac{1}{p}} \quad \text{for } 1 \leq p < \infty,$$

where κ is a measure on $\mathcal{X}$; for simplicity imagine the identity or the cumulative distribution function of covariate X. For $p = 2$ you obtain the Euclidean norm. Also quite useful is the *sup-norm* $\|\cdot\|_\infty$ which is defined by

$$\left\| \hat{m}(x) - m(x) \right\|_\infty = \sup_{\mathcal{X}} |\hat{m}(x) - m(x)|.$$

The *Sobolev norm* $\|\cdot\|_{a,p}$ also accounts for distances in the derivatives,

$$\left\| \hat{m}(x) - m(x) \right\|_{a,q} = \left[\sum_{0 \leq |k| \leq a} \int_{\mathcal{X}} \left| D^k \left(\hat{m}(x) - m(x) \right) \right|^q d\kappa(x) \right]^{\frac{1}{q}}.$$

The *sup Sobolev norm* $\|\cdot\|_{a,\infty}$ is defined as

$$\left\| \hat{m}(x) - m(x) \right\|_{a,\infty} = \max_{0 \leq |k| \leq a} \sup_{\mathcal{X}} \left| D^k \left(\hat{m}(x) - m(x) \right) \right|.$$

The Sobolev norms include the L_p and the sup-norm for $a = 0$. These norms express the distance between two functions by a real-valued number so that they can be used for the standard concepts of convergence (*plim, mean square, almost sure*, and *in distribution*).

In the classic regression literature we are used to specify a parametric model and estimate its parameters, say θ. We then speak of an unbiased estimator $\hat{\theta}$ if its expectation

---

[18] See for example Stone (1980, 1982).

[19] We speak of a function, not just of a scalar parameter or finite dimensional vector as it is the case in parametric estimation.

[20] Because it is just the extension of the intuitive Euclidean norm.

equals θ or of asymptotically unbiased if $E[\hat{\theta}] - \theta$ goes to zero for increasing sample size n. This is not a statement about the model, but only about a parameter estimate for a given model. Here now we have no specific model but try to estimate an unknown function (say at point x_0). We know this situation well when we try to estimate a density $f(x_0)$ by the use of histograms. There we have no model but only choose a window or bin-size and cover the range of observations with these bins. Even if x_0 is the centre of the bin, you get that the larger the bins, the larger the bias $E[\hat{f}(x_0)] - f(x_0)$ (the so-called *smoothing bias* due to larger windows), and the smaller the bins, the larger the variance. When we try, instead of using a histogram, to approximate the true density by a flexible parametric model (e.g. a mixture of normal densities), then we would commit a larger bias (so-called *approximation bias*) if the model was too simple but would obtain quite variable estimates (i.e. a large variance) for too flexible models. Certainly, the parameter we estimated in the second approach could again be unbiased for the given model, but the function estimate cannot be unbiased for the true density unless the chosen model corresponds (by chance) exactly to the true density function. Obviously, in regression analysis we face exactly the same problem. The question is therefore not to find an unbiased estimator (which is impossible if the true function is unknown) but to find an estimator that minimises the mean squared error, typically thereby somehow balancing squared bias and variance.

The optimal convergence rate (i.e. the speed at which an estimator converges to the true value) of any non-parametric estimator in L_p norm can already be calculated when the only available information about the true $m(x)$ over some set $\mathcal{X} \subset \mathbb{R}^q$ is its belonging to the class $C^{k,\alpha}$. Specifically, suppose we are interested in estimating the vth order derivative of the function, and all variables are continuous. Then the optimal convergence rate of $\hat{m}(\cdot)$ to $m(\cdot)$ is

$$n^{-\frac{(k+\alpha)-v}{2(k+\alpha)+q}}$$

in L_p norm for any $0 < p < \infty$, and for the sup norm (necessary for getting an idea of the uniform convergence of the function as a whole)

$$\left(\frac{n}{\log n}\right)^{-\frac{(k+\alpha)-v}{2(k+\alpha)+q}} .$$

One can see now that convergence is faster, the smoother the function $m(\cdot)$ is. But we also see that non-parametric estimators can never achieve the convergence rate of $n^{-\frac{1}{2}}$ (which is the typical rate in the parametric world) unless the class of functions is very much restricted. The convergence becomes slower when derivatives are estimated ($v > 0$): in addition, the convergence rate becomes slower for increasing dimension q of X, an effect which is known as the *curse of dimensionality*.

Non-Parametric Smoother

As stated previously, kernel and kNN based methods for non-parametric regression are based on a local estimation approach. The common idea is that only data within a small neighbourhood are used (except for kernels with infinite support). The concept of kernel weighting when estimating the conditional mean $E[Y|X = x_0]$ is to take a (weighted) average of the observed Y in an h-neighbourhood around x_0 with $h > 0$ being called the *bandwidth, smoothing parameter* or *window*. Suppose that X is a scalar ($q = 1$) and that an i.i.d. sample $\{(Y_i, X_i)\}_{i=1}^{n}$ is available. Then, a natural estimate is to take the average of the observed Y in a neighbourhood of range $2h$ giving the estimator

$$\widehat{m}(x_0; h) = \frac{\sum_{i=1}^{n} Y_i \cdot \mathbb{1}\{|X_i - x_0| \leq h\}}{\sum_{i=1}^{n} \mathbb{1}\{|X_i - x_0| \leq h\}}, \qquad (2.13)$$

where the weight is simply a trimming giving a constant weight to the h-neighbourhood of x_0. A weighted average in which different weights are assigned to observations (Y_i, X_i) depending on the distance from X_i to x_0 would look like

$$\widehat{m}(x_0; h) = \frac{\sum_{i=1}^{n} Y_i \cdot K\left(\frac{X_i - x_0}{h}\right)}{\sum_{i=1}^{n} K\left(\frac{X_i - x_0}{h}\right)}, \qquad (2.14)$$

where $K(u)$ is the weighting function called *kernel*. An intuitively appealing kernel would look like for example the Epanechnikov or the Quartic kernel presented in Figure 2.15; they give more weights to the observations being closer to x_0 and no weight to those being far away (except for those with infinite support like the Gaussian). As $K(\cdot)$ almost always appears together with the bandwidth h, often the notation $K_h(u) := K(u/h)/h$ is used.

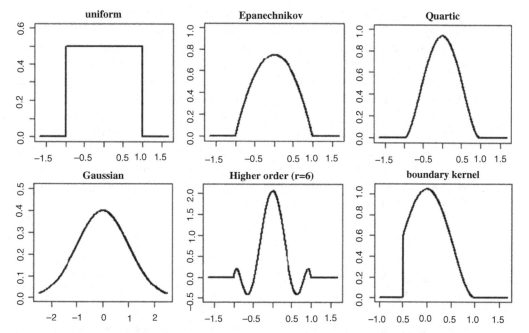

Figure 2.15 Examples of kernel functions: uniform as in (2.13), Epanechnikov, Quartic, Gaussian kernel (all 2nd order), a 6th-order and a boundary (correcting) kernel

Usually, K is positive (but not always, see the 6th-order kernel), has a maximum at 0 and integrates to one. Commonly used kernels are the mentioned Epanechnikov kernel $K(v) = \frac{3}{4}(1 - v^2)\, \mathbb{1}\{-1 < v < 1\}$ or the Gaussian kernel $K(v) = \phi(v)$. While the former is compactly supported, the latter has unbounded support. For the Gaussian kernel the bandwidth h corresponds to the standard deviation of a normal distribution with centre x_0. An also quite popular alternative is the quartic (or biweight) kernel $K(v) = \frac{15}{16}(1 - v^2)^2 \cdot \mathbb{1}\{-1 < v < 1\}$, which is similar to the Epanechniokov but differentiable at the boundaries of its support. In Figure 2.15 we see also the uniform kernel used in Formula 2.13; further, a so-called *higher-order kernel* $K(v) = \frac{35}{256}(15 - 105v^2 + 189v^4 - 99v^6)\,\mathbb{1}\{-1 < v < 1\}$ (discussed later) with some negative weights, and finally a *boundary kernel*. In this example is a truncated quartic kernel which is set to zero outside the support of X (here for all values $\leq x_0 - 0.5h$) but re-normed such that it integrates to one.

It is easy to show that the choice of the kernel is of less importance, whereas the choice of the bandwidth is essential for the properties of the estimator. If h were infinitely large, $\hat{m}(\cdot; h)$ in (2.14) would simply be the sample mean of Y. For h coming close to zero, $\hat{m}$ is the interpolation of the Y_i. As we know, interpolation gives a quite wiggly, rough idea of the functional form of $m(\cdot)$ but is inconsistent as its variance does not go to zero; therefore we need smoothing, i.e. including some neighbours. In fact, for consistent estimation, the number of these neighbours must go to infinity with $n \to \infty$ even when $h \to 0$. Obviously, a necessary condition for identification of $E[Y|X = x_0]$ is that observations at x_0 (if X is discrete) or around it (if continuous) are available. For a continuous density $f(\cdot)$ of X the condition amounts to $f(x_0) > 0$, so that asymptotically we have an infinite number of X_i around x_0. The estimator (2.14) is called the Nadaraya (1965)–Watson (1964) kernel regression estimator. The extension to a multivariate Nadaraya–Watson estimator is immediate; you only have to define multivariate kernel weights $K : \mathbb{R}^q \to \mathbb{R}$ accordingly. The same holds for the next coming estimator (local polynomials), but there you additionally need to use the Taylor expansion (2.12) for $q > 1$ which is notationally (and also computationally) cumbersome. For the sake of presentation we therefore continue for a while with $q = 1$.[21]

Instead of taking a simple weighted average, one could also fit a local model in the neighbourhood around x_0 and take this as a local estimator for $E[Y|X = x_0]$. For example, the *local polynomial estimator* takes advantage of the fact that any continuous function can be approximated arbitrarily well by its Taylor expansion, and applies the idea of weighted least squares by setting

$$\left(\hat{m}(x_0; h), \widehat{m'}(x_0; h), \ldots, \widehat{m^{(p)}}(x_0; h) \right) \tag{2.15}$$

$$:= \underset{m, m', \ldots, m^{(p)}}{\arg\min} \sum_{i=1}^{n} \left(Y_i - m - m' \cdot (X_i - x_0) - \ldots - \frac{m^{(p)}}{p!} \cdot (X_i - x_0)^p \right)^2 K\left(\frac{X_i - x_0}{h} \right)$$

---

[21] Note that this is not a particular pitfall for kernel methods but a difficulty that other non-parametric estimators share in different ways.

for some integer $p > 0$. In the previous expression, m' refers to the first derivative and $m^{(p)}$ refers to the pth derivative. Thus, the local polynomial estimator obtains simultaneously estimates the function $m(\cdot)$ and its derivatives. Fitting a local constant estimator, i.e. setting $p = 0$ gives exactly the Nadaraya–Watson estimator (2.14). According to the polynomial order p, the local polynomial estimator is also called local linear $(p = 1)$, local quadratic $(p = 2)$ or local cubic $(p = 3)$ estimator. Nadaraya–Watson and local linear regression are the most common versions in econometrics. Local polynomial regression of order two or three is more suited when estimating derivatives or strongly oscillating functions in larger samples, but it often is unstable in small samples since more data points in each smoothing interval are required. When the main interest lies in the vth derivative (including $v = 0$, i.e. the function itself), choosing p such that $p - v > 0$ is odd, ensures that the smoothing bias in the boundary region is of the same order as in the interior. If $p - v$ is even, this bias will be of higher order at the boundary and will also depend on the density of X. Finally, it has been shown that the local linear estimator attains full asymptotic efficiency (in a minimax sense) among all linear smoothers, and has high efficiency among all smoothers.[22] By defining $\beta = (\beta_0, \beta_1, \ldots, \beta_p)'$, $\mathbb{X}_i = (1, (X_i - x_0), \ldots, (X_i - x_0)^p)'$, $K_i = K\left(\frac{X_i - x_0}{h}\right)$, $\mathbb{X} = (\mathbb{X}_1, \mathbb{X}_2, \ldots, \mathbb{X}_n)'$, $\mathbb{K} = diag(K_1, K_2, \ldots, K_n)$ and $\mathbb{Y} = (Y_1, \ldots, Y_n)'$, we can write the *local polynomial estimator* as

$$\hat{\beta} = \arg\min_{\beta} (\mathbb{Y} - \mathbb{X}\beta)' \mathbb{K} (\mathbb{Y} - \mathbb{X}\beta) = (\mathbb{X}'\mathbb{K}\mathbb{X})^{-1} \mathbb{X}'\mathbb{K}\mathbb{Y} \qquad (2.16)$$

with $\hat{m}^{(l)}(x_0) := \hat{\beta}_l/(l!)$, $0 \le l \le p$. Note that we are still in the setting where X is one-dimensional and that, for ease of exposition, we have suppressed the dependence on h. We thus obtain

$$\hat{m}(x_0) = e_1' \left(\mathbb{X}'\mathbb{K}\mathbb{X}\right)^{-1} \left(\mathbb{X}'\mathbb{K}\mathbb{Y}\right)$$

where $e_1' = (1, 0, 0, \ldots, 0)$, or equivalently

$$\hat{m}(x_0) = e_1' \begin{pmatrix} Q_0(x_0) & Q_1(x_0) & \cdots & Q_p(x_0) \\ Q_1(x_0) & Q_2(x_0) & \cdots & Q_{p+1}(x_0) \\ \vdots & \vdots & \ddots & \vdots \\ Q_p(x_0) & Q_{p+1}(x_0) & \cdots & Q_{2p}(x_0) \end{pmatrix}^{-1} \begin{pmatrix} T_0(x_0) \\ T_1(x_0) \\ \vdots \\ T_p(x_0) \end{pmatrix}$$

with $Q_l(x_0) = \sum_{i=1}^{n} K\left(\frac{X_i - x_0}{h}\right)(X_i - x_0)^l$ and $T_l(x_0) = \sum_{i=1}^{n} Y_i K\left(\frac{X_i - x_0}{h}\right)(X_i - x_0)^l$. From these derivations we also see that the local polynomial estimator is linear in response $\mathbb{Y}$

$$\hat{m}(x_0) = \frac{1}{n}\sum_{i=1}^{n} w_i Y_i \quad \text{with } w_i = e_1' \cdot \left(\frac{1}{n}\mathbb{X}'\mathbb{K}\mathbb{X}\right)^{-1} \mathbb{X}_i' K_i. \qquad (2.17)$$

[22] For details see for example Fan and Gijbels (1996), Loader (1999a) or Seifert and Gasser (1996, 2000).

The expressions of $\hat{m}(x_0)$ up to polynomial order three are (suppressing the dependence of all T_l and Q_l on x_0 and h)

$$\hat{m}_{p=0}(x_0) = \frac{T_0}{Q_0} = \frac{\sum_{i=1}^{n} Y_i K\left(\frac{X_i - x_0}{h}\right)}{\sum_{i=1}^{n} K\left(\frac{X_i - x_0}{h}\right)} \tag{2.18}$$

$$\hat{m}_{p=1}(x_0) = \frac{Q_2 T_0 - Q_1 T_1}{Q_2 Q_0 - Q_1^2}$$

$$\hat{m}_{p=2}(x_0) = \frac{(Q_2 Q_4 - Q_3^2)T_0 + (Q_2 Q_3 - Q_1 Q_4)T_1 + (Q_1 Q_3 - Q_2^2)T_2}{Q_0 Q_2 Q_4 + 2Q_1 Q_2 Q_3 - Q_2^3 - Q_0 Q_3^2 - Q_1^2 Q_4}$$

$$\hat{m}_{p=3}(x_0) = \frac{A_0 T_0 + A_1 T_1 + A_2 T_2 + A_3 T_3}{A_0 Q_0 + A_1 Q_1 + A_2 Q_2 + A_3 Q_3},$$

where $A_0 = Q_2 Q_4 Q_6 + 2Q_3 Q_4 Q_5 - Q_4^3 - Q_2 Q_5^2 - Q_3^2 Q_6$, $A_1 = Q_3 Q_4^2 + Q_1 Q_5^2 + Q_2 Q_3 Q_6 - Q_1 Q_4 Q_6 - Q_2 Q_4 Q_5 - Q_3^2 Q_5$, $A_2 = Q_1 Q_3 Q_6 + Q_2 Q_4^2 + Q_2 Q_3 Q_5 - Q_3^2 Q_4 - Q_1 Q_4 Q_5 - Q_2^2 Q_6$, $A_3 = Q_3^3 + Q_1 Q_4^2 + Q_2^2 Q_5 - Q_1 Q_3 Q_5 - 2Q_2 Q_3 Q_4$.

Using the above formulae, we can write the *local linear estimator* equivalently as

$$\hat{m}_{p=1}(x_0) = \frac{\sum_{i=1}^{n} K_i^* Y_i}{\sum_{i=1}^{n} K_i^*} \quad \text{where} \quad K_i^* = \{Q_2 - Q_1(X_i - x_0)\} K\left(\frac{X_i - x_0}{h}\right). \tag{2.19}$$

Hence, the local linear estimator is a Nadaraya–Watson kernel estimator with kernel function K_i^*. This kernel K_i^* is negative for some values of X_i and sometimes also called *equivalent kernel*. This may help our intuition to understand what a kernel function with negative values means. Similarly, every local polynomial regression estimator can be written in the form (2.19) with different equivalent kernels K_i^*. They all sometimes take negative values, except for the case $p = 0$, the Nadaraya–Watson estimator.

Ridge Regression

Ridge regression is basically a kernel regression with a penalisation for the roughness of the resulting regression in order to make it more stable (more robust). The name *ridge* originates from the fact that in a simple linear regression context this penalisation term is added to the ridge of the correlation matrix of X when calculating the projection matrix. How this applies to local linear regression is shown below.

In different simulation studies the so-called *ridge regression* has exhibited quite attractive performance qualities such as being less sensible to the bandwidth choice, having a small finite-sample bias, but also numerical robustness against irregular designs (like, for example, data sparseness in some regions of the support of X). A simple presentation and implementation, however, is only known for the one-dimensional case ($q = 1$). To obtain a quick and intuitive idea, one might think of a kind of linear combination of Nadaraya–Watson and local linear regression. More specifically, for $K_h(u) = \frac{1}{h} K\left(\frac{u}{h}\right)$ consider

$$\min_{\beta_0, \beta_1} \sum_{j=1}^{n} \{Y_j - \beta_0 - \beta_1(X_j - \tilde{x}_i)\}^2 K_h\left(X_j - x_i\right) + r\beta_1^2$$

where $\tilde{x}_i = \sum_{j=1}^{n} X_j K_h(X_j - x_i)/\sum_{j=1}^{n} K_h(X_j - x_i)$ and r is the so-called ridge parameter. So $\tilde{x}_i$ is a weighted average of the neighbours of x_i. Define $s_{\alpha(i,j)} = (X_j - \tilde{x}_i)^\alpha K_h(X_j - x_i)$, $\alpha = 0, 1, 2$. Then the ridge regression estimate is

$$\hat{m}(x_i) = \hat{\beta}_0 + \hat{\beta}_1(x_i - \tilde{x}_i) = \sum_{j=1}^{n} w(i, j) Y_j \qquad (2.20)$$

with $w(i, j) = s_0(i, j)/\{\sum_{j=1}^{n} s_0(i, j)\} + s_1(i, j) \cdot (x_i - \tilde{x}_i)/\{r + \sum_{j=1}^{n} s_2(i, j)\}$. Defining $S_\alpha(i) = \sum_{j=1}^{n} s_\alpha(i, j)$, $T_\alpha(i) = \sum_{j=1}^{n} s_\alpha(i, j) Y_j$, and $\bar{r} = S_2(i)/\{r + S_2(i)\}$ we see that

$$\hat{m}(x_i) = (1 - \bar{r})\frac{T_0}{S_0} + \bar{r}\left(\frac{T_0}{S_0} + \frac{(x_i - \tilde{x}_i)T_1}{S_2}\right)$$

being thus a linear combination of the local constant (i.e. Nadaraya–Watson) estimator with weight $(1 - \bar{r})$ and the local linear estimator with weight $\bar{r}$. The mean squared error minimising r is quite complex with many unknown functions and parameters. A simple rule of thumb suggests to set $r = h \cdot |x_i - \tilde{x}_i| \cdot c_r$, $c_r = \max_v\{K(v)\}/\{4\bar{\kappa}_0\}$ which is $c_r = 5/16$ for the Epanechnikov kernel, and $c_r = 0.35$ for the Gaussian one, cf. (2.23).[23]

Statistical Properties of One-Dimensional Kernel Smoothers

An important result is that the exact finite sample bias of local polynomial regression is zero up to order p. To show this, we present some helpful preliminary results. Observe that the weights (2.17) satisfy the orthogonality condition

$$\frac{1}{n}\sum_{i=1}^{n} w_i \mathbb{X}_i = \begin{pmatrix} 1 \\ 0 \\ \vdots \\ 0 \end{pmatrix}, \qquad (2.21)$$

which can immediately be seen by inserting the definition of the weights (2.17); see Exercise 10. The previous expression can be rewritten as

$$\frac{1}{n}\sum_{i=1}^{n}(X_i - x_0)^l \cdot w_i = \begin{cases} 1 & \text{for } l = 0 \\ 0 & \text{for } 1 \le l \le p. \end{cases} \qquad (2.22)$$

These orthogonality conditions imply an exactly zero-finite bias up to order p. This also implies that if the true function $m(x)$ happened indeed to be a polynomial function of order p or less, the local polynomial estimator would be exactly unbiased, i.e. in finite samples for any $h > 0$ and thereby also asymptotically. In this case, one would like to choose the bandwidth $h = \infty$ to minimise the variance. You arrive then in the parametric world with parametric convergence rates etc. because h is no longer supposed to go to zero.

Now we consider the expression as a linear smoother (2.17) and derive the expected value of the estimator. Note that the expected value of the estimator could be undefined if the denominator of the weights is zero. In other words, there could be *local collinearity*

---

[23] For further details we refer to Seifert and Gasser (2000) or Busso, DiNardo and McCrary (2009).

which impedes the calculation of the estimator. Ruppert and Wand (1994) therefore proposed to examine the expected value conditional on the observations $X_1, \ldots, X_n$:

$$E\left[\hat{m}(x_0)|X_1, \ldots, X_n\right] = \frac{1}{n}\sum_{j=1}^{n} E\left[w_j Y_j | X_1, \ldots, X_n\right] = \frac{1}{n}\sum_{j=1}^{n} w_j m(X_j).$$

Using a Taylor series expansion assuming that $m \in C^{p,\alpha}$ you get

$$= \frac{1}{n}\sum_{i=1}^{n} w_i \left(m(x_0) + (X_i - x_0)\frac{\partial m(x_0)}{\partial x} + \ldots + \frac{1}{p!}(X_i - x_0)^p \frac{\partial^P m(x_0)}{\partial x^P} + R(X_i, x_0) \right)$$

$$= m(x_0) + \frac{1}{n}\sum_{i=1}^{n} w_i R(X_i, x_0),$$

where the other terms are zero up to order p because of (2.21). We thus obtain that

$$E\left[\hat{m}(x_0) - m(x_0)|X_1, \ldots, X_n\right] = \frac{1}{n}\sum_{i=1}^{n} w_i R(X_i, x_0),$$

where the remainder term $R(X_i, x_0)$ is of order $(X_i - x_0)^{p+\alpha}$ if $m \in C^{p,\alpha}$, recalling Definition and Equation 2.12. Now inserting (2.17) gives

$$E\left[\hat{m}(x_0) - m(x_0)|X_1, \ldots, X_n\right] = e_1' \left(\frac{1}{n}\mathbb{X}'\mathbb{K}\mathbb{X}\right)^{-1} \frac{1}{n}\sum_{i=1}^{n} \mathbb{X}_i' K_i R(X_i, x_0).$$

As an intuitive argument note that compact kernels are zero outside the interval $[-1, 1]$. Hence, for every i where $|X_i - x_0| > h$, the kernel function K_i will be zero. This implies that the remainder term is at most of order $O_p(h^{p+\alpha})$. We will show later that the expression $\frac{1}{n}\mathbb{X}'\mathbb{K}\mathbb{X}$ is $O_p(1)$. Therefore, the entire expression is $O_p(h^{p+\alpha})$. Since h will always be assumed to converge to zero as $n \to \infty$, the higher the polynomial order p, the lower the order of the finite sample bias (or, say, the faster the bias goes to zero for $h \to 0$).

Before taking a closer look at the asymptotic properties of these estimators, it is useful to work with the following definitions for the one-dimensional kernel function:

$$\kappa_\lambda = \int v^\lambda K(v)\, dv \qquad \text{and} \qquad \bar{\kappa}_\lambda = \int v^\lambda K(v)^2\, dv. \qquad (2.23)$$

One says that a kernel K is of order r if

$$\kappa_0 = 1$$
$$\kappa_\lambda = 0 \quad \text{for} \quad 1 \le \lambda \le \lambda - 1$$
$$\infty > \kappa_\lambda \ne 0 \quad \text{for} \quad \lambda = r.$$

The most common are second-order kernels whereas kernels with $r > 2$ are called higher-order kernels (like the 6th-order kernel in Figure 2.15), and are typically applied where bias reduction is needed. The Epanechnikov, Quartic and Gaussian kernel are of 2nd order. Kernels of higher order require that the 'variance' $\int v^2 K(v)\, dv$ is zero. Hence, these cannot be density functions, and the kernel function $K(v)$ has to be negative for some values of its support. Higher-order kernels are often used in theoretical derivations, particularly for reducing the bias in semi-parametric estimators. They have rarely been used in non-parametric applications, but may be particularly helpful for average treatment effect estimators.

To explicitly calculate bias and variance of non-parametric (kernel) regression estimators we consider first the Nadaraya–Watson estimator for dimension $q = 1$ with a 2nd-order kernel ($r = 2$),

$$\hat{m}(x_0; h) = \frac{\frac{1}{nh} \sum Y_i \cdot K\left(\frac{X_i - x_0}{h}\right)}{\frac{1}{nh} \sum K\left(\frac{X_i - x_0}{h}\right)}.$$

The expected value of the numerator can be rewritten for independent observations (where we also make use of a Taylor expansion) as

$$E\left[\frac{1}{nh} \sum_{i=1}^{n} Y_i \cdot K\left(\frac{X_i - x_0}{h}\right)\right] = \int \frac{1}{h} m(x) \cdot K\left(\frac{x - x_0}{h}\right) f(x)dx$$

$$= \int m(x_0 + uh) f(x_0 + uh) \cdot K(u)\,du$$

$$= m(x_0)f(x_0) \int K(v)\,dv + h \cdot \left(m'(x_0)f(x_0) + m(x_0)f'(x_0)\right) \int u\,K(u)\,du$$

$$+ h^2 \cdot \left(\frac{m''(x_0)}{2} f(x_0) + m(x_0)\frac{f''(x_0)}{2} + m'(x_0)f'(x_0)\right)$$

$$\int u^2 K(u)\,du + O\left(h^3\right) \tag{2.24}$$

$$= m(x_0) f(x_0) + h^2 \cdot \left(\frac{m''(x_0)}{2} f(x_0) + m(x_0)\frac{f''(x_0)}{2} + m'(x_0)f'(x_0)\right)$$

$$\int u^2 K(u)\,du + O\left(h^3\right)$$

for $\kappa_0 = \int K(v)\,dv = 1$ and $\kappa_1 = \int vK(v)\,dv = 0$. Analogously, the expected value of the denominator is[24]

$$E\left[\frac{1}{nh} \sum_{i=1}^{n} K\left(\frac{X_i - x_0}{h}\right)\right] = f(x_0) + h^2 \cdot \frac{f''(x_0)}{2}\kappa_2 + O\left(h^3\right).$$

A weak law of large numbers gives as limit in probability for a fixed h and $n \to \infty$ by showing that the variance converges to zero and applying Chebyshev's inequality. Under some regularity conditions like the smoothness of $m(\cdot)$ or $Var(Y|x) < \infty$, we obtain

[24] The expected value of the denominator may be zero if a kernel with compact support is used. So the expected value of the Nadaraya–Watson estimator may not exist. Therefore the asymptotic analysis is usually done by estimating $m(\cdot)$ at the design points $\{X_i\}_{i=1}^{n}$ as in Ruppert and Wand (1994) or by adding a small number to the denominator that tends to zero as $n \to \infty$; see Fan (1993).

$$plim\left\{\hat{m}(x_0, h) - m(x_0)\right\} = h^2 \frac{\left(\frac{m''(x_0)}{2} f(x_0) + m'(x_0) f'(x_0)\right) \kappa_2 + O\left(h^3\right)}{f(x_0) + h^2 \frac{f''(x_0)}{2} \kappa_2 + O\left(h^3\right)}$$

$$= h^2 \left(\frac{m''(x_0)}{2} + \frac{m'(x_0) f'(x_0)}{f(x_0)}\right) \kappa_2 + O\left(h^3\right).$$

Hence, the bias is proportional to h^2. Exercise 11 asks you to derive the bias resulting from higher-order kernels by revisiting the calculations in (2.24). It is easy to see that in general, the bias term is then of order h^r with r being the order of the kernel.

To obtain an idea of the conditional variance is more tedious but not much more difficult; one basically needs to calculate

$$Var(\hat{m}(x_0, h)) = E\left[\left\{\hat{m}(x_0, h) - E[\hat{m}(x_0, h)]\right\}^2\right]$$

$$= E\left[\left\{\frac{1}{nh} \sum_{i=1}^n \{Y_i - m(X_i)\} K\left(\frac{X_i - x_0}{h}\right)\right\}^2\right]$$

obtaining approximately (i.e. up to higher-order terms) $f(x_0)\frac{Var[Y|x_0]}{nh} \int K^2(v)dv$.

The derivations made implicit use of the *Dominated (Bounded) Convergence Theorem* along Pagan and Ullah (1999, p. 362). It says that for a Borel measurable function $g(x)$ on $\mathbb{R}$ and some function $f(x)$ (not necessarily a density) with $\int |f(x)| dx < \infty$

$$\frac{1}{h^q} \int g\left(\frac{x}{h}\right) f(x_0 - x) dx \longrightarrow f(x_0) \int g(x)dx \text{ as } h \to 0 \qquad (2.25)$$

at every point x_0 of continuity of f if $\int |g(x)| dx < \infty$, $\|x\| \cdot |g(x)| \to 0$ as $\|x\| \to \infty$, and $\sup |g(x)| < \infty$. Furthermore, if f is uniformly continuous, then convergence is uniform. For g being a kernel function, this theorem gives for example that $E\left[\frac{1}{nh} \sum K\left(\frac{X_j - x_0}{h}\right)\right] \longrightarrow f(x_0) \int K(v)dv$. This results extends also to $x \in \mathbb{R}^q$ for $q > 1$.

Let us recall some of the assumptions which have partly been discussed above:

(A1) We consider a model $Y_i = m(X_i) + U_i$ where the unexplained heterogeneity is described by i.i.d. errors U_i with variance function $\sigma^2(X_i)$, the X_i are i.i.d. and independent of U_i, the regression function $m(\cdot)$ and the density $f(\cdot)$ of $X \in \mathbb{R}$ are twice continuously differentiable in a neighbourhood of the point of interest x_0, and the second derivative of the density of X, f_X'', is continuous and bounded in a neighbourhood of x_0.

For the estimation we use

(A2) a kernel K that is of second order ($r = 2$) and integrates to one, and a bandwidth $h \to 0$ with $nh \to \infty$ for $n \to \infty$.

Then we can summarise for the Nadaraya–Watson estimator:

THEOREM 2.6 *Assume that we are provided with a sample $\{X_i, Y_i\}_{i=1}^{n}$ coming from a model fulfilling (A1). Then, for x_0 being an interior point of the support of X, the Nadaraya–Watson estimator $\hat{m}(x_0)$ of $m(x_0)$ with kernel and bandwidth as in (A2) has bias and variance*

$$Bias(\hat{m}(x_0)) = h^2 \frac{\kappa_2}{2f(x_0)} \left(m''(x_0) f(x_0) + 2f'(x_0) m'(x_0) \right) + O\left(\frac{1}{nh}\right) + o(h^2)$$

$$Var(\hat{m}(x_0)) = \frac{\sigma^2(x_0)}{nhf(x_0)} \bar{\kappa}_0 + o\left(\frac{1}{nh}\right), \qquad \bar{\kappa}_0 = \int K^2(v)dv < \infty.$$

Note that for higher-order kernels one generally has $Bias(\hat{m}(x_0)) = O(h^r)$ with $Var(\hat{m}(x_0)) = O(\frac{1}{nh})$ (for $q = 1$), i.e. the kernel order affects directly the first-order bias but not the first-order variance. Recall, however, that larger r requires higher smoothness for the unknown functions. Moreover, we are only talking of an asymptotic effect; higher-order kernels often exhibit bad numerical performance for small and moderate samples. Sometimes you need sample sizes larger than 100,000 before the MSE improves with kernels of order $r > 2$ compared to those with $r = 2$.

For applying Liapunov's central limit theorem to obtain asymptotic normality, and in order to write the convergence of the estimator in a closed form, one needs additional assumptions.

(A3) Kernel K is a real valued function such that $\int |K(v)| \, dv < \infty$, $|v| \, |K(v)| \to 0$ as $v \to \infty$, $\sup |K(v)| < \infty$, and $\bar{\kappa}_0 = \int K^2(v)dv < \infty$.
(A4) $E |U_i|^{2+\delta} < \infty$ and $\int |K(v)|^{2+\delta} \, dv < \infty$ for some $\delta > 0$.

For (A1), (A2), (A3), (A4) given, and

$$\sqrt{nh}h^2 \to c < \infty, \tag{2.26}$$

it has been shown that with the definitions of (2.23)

$$\sqrt{nh} \left\{ \hat{m}(x_0) - m(x_0) \right\} \xrightarrow{D} N\left(c\kappa_2 \left(\frac{m'(x_0) f'(x_0)}{f(x_0)} + \frac{1}{2} m''(x_0) \right), \frac{\sigma^2(x_0)\bar{\kappa}_0}{f(x_0)} \right).$$

For the semi-parametric estimators that we will use later to estimate treatment effects, it is important to know that under these conditions one also obtains uniform convergence.

Let us turn to the more popular local linear estimator. Recall that we motivated it by a local approximation via Taylor expansion. Consequently, we have the chance to (a) estimate simultaneously the function m and its derivatives, and (b) reduce the bias. For example, the local linear estimator does not suffer from a bias in the linear direction; a linear parametric model is therefore perfectly nested in a local linear estimator. In fact, as local polynomial regression of order p provides also estimates of derivatives $m^{(l)}$ up to order p, the bias terms for $\hat{m}$ up to order p are zero. A general result is that the bias at the boundary is of order h^{p+1}. For interior points it is of order h^{p+1} for p being odd, but h^{p+2} for p being even. On the other hand, the extra parameter in the local polynomial do not affect the asymptotic variance, which is always of order $\frac{1}{nh}$, whatever the value of p is.[25]

---

[25] A comprehensive overview is given in Fan and Gijbels (1996).

When we discuss the asymptotic properties of local polynomial regression, we will focus either on the setting $q = 1$ with arbitrary p (higher-order local polynomials for a one-dimensional regression) or examine the setting $p = 1$ for arbitrary q (local linear for several covariates). The main insights of this discussion carry over to the case where $p > 1$ and $q > 1$, i.e. local polynomial estimation for multivariate regressors $(dim(X) = q > 1)$, but the notation becomes much more cumbersome then.

The estimator is defined as in (2.16) by

$$\hat{m}(x_0) = e_1' \left(\mathbb{X}'\mathbb{K}\mathbb{X} \right)^{-1} \mathbb{X}'\mathbb{K}\mathbb{Y}.$$

Let us rewrite the model as

$$Y_i = \mathbb{X}_i' \beta_0 + R_i + U_i,$$

where $\mathbb{X}_i$ is defined as above for (2.16), and β_0 the vector of all coefficients of the Taylor polynomial at x_0. For example, for $q = 1$ one has $\beta_0 = (m(x_0), m'(x_0), \frac{1}{2}m^{(2)}(x_0), \dots, \frac{1}{p!}m^{(p)}(x_0))'$. In other words, $\mathbb{X}_i'\beta_0$ is the Taylor series approximation at the location X_i, and $R_i = m(X_i) - \mathbb{X}_i'\beta_0$ the remainder term of that approximation. One has

$$\hat{\beta}_0 = \beta_0 + \underbrace{\left(\mathbb{X}'\mathbb{K}\mathbb{X} \right)^{-1} \mathbb{X}'\mathbb{K}\mathbb{R}}_{\text{bias term}} + \underbrace{\left(\mathbb{X}'\mathbb{K}\mathbb{X} \right)^{-1} \mathbb{X}'\mathbb{K}\mathbb{U}}_{\text{stochastic term}}. \tag{2.27}$$

The last two terms characterise the bias and the variance of the local polynomial estimator. To go into details let us restrict to the case where $p = 1$ and a kernel function of order 2. Ignore the variance term for a moment and focus on the bias:

$$\left(\frac{1}{nh} \sum_{i=1}^{n} \begin{bmatrix} K_i & (X_i - x_0)K_i \\ (X_i - x_0)K_i & (X_i - x_0)^2 K_i \end{bmatrix} \right)^{-1} \left(\frac{1}{nh} \sum_{i=1}^{n} \begin{bmatrix} K_i \\ (X_i - x_0)K_i \end{bmatrix} \{ m(X_i) - \mathbb{X}_i'\beta_0 \} \right). \tag{2.28}$$

One can show that the first term converges in probability to

$$\left(\begin{bmatrix} f(x_0) & h^2 f'(x_0)\kappa_2 \\ h^2 f'(x_0)\kappa_2 & f(x_0)h^2\kappa_2 \end{bmatrix} \right)^{-1} \quad \text{with } \kappa_l = \int v^l K(v)dv,$$

where $\kappa_1 = 0$ for 2nd-order kernels. The determinant of the matrix $[\cdots]$ is $h^2\kappa_2 f^2(x_0) - o_p(h^2)$. This gives for the first term of (2.28) (only concentrating on the highest-order terms)

$$f(x_0)^{-1} \begin{bmatrix} 1 & -\frac{f'(x_0)}{f(x_0)} \\ -\frac{f'(x_0)}{f(x_0)} & h^{-2}\kappa_2^{-1} \end{bmatrix} \{ 1 + O_p(h) \}.$$

Now consider the second term. By the mean-value theorem one obtains

$$m(X_i) - \mathbb{X}_i'\beta_0 = \frac{m''(x_0) \cdot (X_i - x_0)^2}{2} + \frac{m'''(\bar{x}_i) \cdot (X_i - x_0)^3}{3!},$$

where $\bar{x}_i$ lies between X_i and x_0. So, the second term of (2.28) can be written as

$$\frac{1}{nh} \sum_{i=1}^{n} \begin{bmatrix} K_i \\ (X_i - x_0)K_i \end{bmatrix} \frac{m''(x_0) \cdot (X_i - x_0)^2}{2} \{ 1 + O_p(X_i - x_0) \}.$$

If a second-order kernel function with bounded support is used, the term $(X_i - x_0)^2$ is of order $O_p(h^2)$. If in addition the second derivative is bounded, the bias term as a whole is of order $O_p(h^2)$, and (2.28) becomes

$$= \frac{m''(x_0)}{f(x_0)} \frac{1}{nh} \sum_{j=1}^{n} \left[\frac{1 - \frac{f'(x_0)}{f(x_0)}(X_i - x_0)}{\frac{1}{\kappa_2} \frac{X_i - x_0}{h^2} - \frac{f'(x_0)}{f(x_0)}} \right] K_i \frac{(X_i - x_0)^2}{2} \{1 + O_p(X_i - x_0)\}\{1 + O_p(h)\}$$

$$= \frac{m''(x_0)}{2} h^2 \begin{bmatrix} \kappa_2 \\ \frac{\kappa_3}{h\kappa_2} \end{bmatrix} \{1 + o_p(1)\} \, .$$

Here we can see that the vector-valued estimator converges slower in its second term, i.e. for the derivative by factor h^{-1}, than it does in the first term (the regression function itself).

The last term in (2.27) characterises the conditional variance, which is given by

$$\left(\mathbb{X}'\mathbb{K}\mathbb{X} \right)^{-1} \left\{ \mathbb{X}'\mathbb{K}\Sigma\mathbb{K}\mathbb{X} \right\} \left(\mathbb{X}'\mathbb{K}\mathbb{X} \right)^{-1} . \tag{2.29}$$

Here Σ is an $n \times n$ diagonal matrix with elements $\sigma^2(X_i)$. We already studied the convergence of the outer matrices (when divided by n). Similarly, it can be shown that the middle term in (2.29) converges to

$$\frac{1}{n} \begin{bmatrix} h^{-1}\bar{\kappa}_0 & h\bar{\kappa}_1 \\ h\bar{\kappa}_1 & \bar{\kappa}_2 \end{bmatrix} f(x_0)\sigma^2(x_0) \, , \text{ where } \bar{\kappa}_l = \int v^l K^2(v) dv.$$

Hence, the expressions are such that the bias is at least of order h^{p+1}, while the variance is of order $\frac{1}{nh}$ (similarly to what we saw for higher-order kernels). In sum, we have seen that the analogue to Theorem 2.6, still for $q = 1$, can be written as

THEOREM 2.7 *Assume that we are provided with a sample $\{X_i, Y_i\}_{i=1}^{n}$ coming from a model fulfilling (A1). Then, for x_0 being an interior point of the support of $X \in \mathbb{R}$, the local linear estimator $\hat{m}(x_0)$ of $m(x_0)$ with kernel and bandwidth as in (A2) has bias and variance*

$$Bias(\hat{m}(x_0)) = h^2 \frac{\kappa_2}{2} m''(x_0) + O\left(\frac{1}{nh}\right) + o(h^2),$$

$$Var(\hat{m}(x_0)) = \frac{\sigma^2(x_0)}{nhf(x_0)} \bar{\kappa}_0 + o\left(\frac{1}{nh}\right).$$

Notice that these results hold only for interior points. The following table gives the rates of the bias for interior as well as for boundary points. As already mentioned earlier, for odd-order polynomials the local bias is of the same order in the interior as the boundary, whereas it is of lower order in the interior for even-order polynomials.

Bias and variance in the interior and at boundary points, $dim(X)=1$

	$p = 0$	$p = 1$	$p = 2$	$p = 3$
Bias in interior	$O\left(h^2\right)$	$O\left(h^2\right)$	$O\left(h^4\right)$	$O\left(h^4\right)$
Bias at boundary	$O\left(h^1\right)$	$O\left(h^2\right)$	$O\left(h^3\right)$	$O\left(h^4\right)$

The variance is always of order $(nh)^{-1}$. To achieve the fastest rate of convergence with respect to the mean squared error, the bandwidth h could be chosen to balance squared bias and variance, which leads to the following optimal convergence rates:

Optimal convergence rates in the interior and at boundary points, $dim(X)=1$

Convergence rate	$p=0$	$p=1$	$p=2$	$p=3$
in the interior	$n^{-\frac{2}{5}}$	$n^{-\frac{2}{5}}$	$n^{-\frac{4}{9}}$	$n^{-\frac{4}{9}}$
at the boundary	$n^{-\frac{1}{3}}$	$n^{-\frac{2}{5}}$	$n^{-\frac{3}{7}}$	$n^{-\frac{4}{9}}$

There exist various proposals for how to reduce the bias at the boundary (or say, correct the boundary effects). Especially for density estimation and local constant (Nadaraya–Watson) estimation, the use of boundary kernels (recall Figure 2.15) is quite popular.

For the one-dimensional ridge regression ($q = 1$) asymptotic statements are available for the case where the asymptotically optimal ridge parameter for point x_0 has been used. Though in practice people will rather choose the same (probably a rule-of-thumb) ridge-parameter for all points, this gives us at least an idea of the statistical performance of this method. As it had been proposed as an improvement of the local linear estimator, we give here the variance and mean squared error for $\hat{m}_{ridge}(x_i)$ compared to those of $\hat{m}_{loc.lin.}(x_i)$:

THEOREM 2.8   *Under the same assumptions as for the local linear estimator, see Theorem 2.7, $q = 1$, second order kernel $K(\cdot)$, x_0 being an interior point of X, f the density, and using the asymptotically optimal ridge parameter,*

$$Var[\hat{m}_{ridge}(x_0)] = Var[\hat{m}_{loc.lin}(x_0)] - \frac{2\sigma^4(x_0)\, f'^2(x_0)\, \bar{\kappa}_0^2}{(nh)^2 m'^2(x_0)\, f^4(x_0)\, \kappa_0^4} + o_p\left((nh)^{-2}\right)$$

$$MSE_{ridge}[\hat{m}_{ridge}(x_0)] = MSE_{loc.lin.}[\hat{m}_{loc.lin}(x_0)]$$
$$+ \frac{h\sigma^2(x_0)\, m''(x_0)\, f'(x_0)\, \kappa_2\bar{\kappa}_0}{n\, m'(x_0)\, f^2(x_0)\, \kappa_0^3} + o_p\left(\frac{h}{n}\right).$$

This theorem shows that we indeed improve in the variance by having made the estimator more stable, but we may pay for this in the bias. Whether asymptotic bias and mean squared error are smaller or larger than those of the local linear estimator depends on the derivatives of the underlying regression function $m(\cdot)$ and those of the (true) density f.

Multivariate Kernel Smoothers

Non-parametric regression for a one-dimensional covariate is of limited interest for most econometric applications because usually many covariates are included. There may be situations where the dimension of the covariates can be reduced before non-parametric methods are applied. An example is propensity score matching with a parametric (see Chapter 3) propensity score. Apart from such situations, one usually has to consider non-parametric regression for $\dim(X) = q > 1$ (or a way to efficiently include discrete covariates if X contains some – see further below in this section). The extension of local constant and local linear regression to such multidimensional X is straightforward, especially regarding their implementation. This has already been indicated but so far without being specific. The derivations of its properties are also analogous, although some care in the notation is required.

A multivariate kernel function is needed. Of particular convenience for multivariate regression problems are the so-called *product kernels*, where the multivariate kernel function $K(v) = K(v_1, \ldots, v_q)$ is defined as a product of univariate kernel functions

$$K(v_1, \ldots, v_q) = \prod_{l=1}^{q} K(v_l), \tag{2.30}$$

see Exercise 8, Theorem 2.9 and Subsection 2.2.2. For such product kernels, higher-order kernels are easy to implement.

Further, a $q \times q$ bandwidth matrix H determines the shape of the smoothing window, such that the multivariate analogue of $K_h(v)$ becomes $K_H(v) = \frac{1}{\det(H)} K(H^{-1}v)$. This permits smoothing in different directions and can take into account the correlation structure among covariates. Selecting this $q \times q$ bandwidth matrix by a data-driven bandwidth selector can be inconvenient and time-consuming, especially when q is large. Typically, only diagonal bandwidth matrices H are used. This is not optimal but is done for convenience (computational reasons, interpretation, etc.), such that in practice one bandwidth is chosen for each covariate – or even the same for all. As a practical device, one often just rescales all covariates inside the kernel such that their sample variance is one, but one ignores their potential correlation. After the rescaling simply $H := diag\{h, h \ldots, h\}$ is used; for details see the paragraph on bandwidth choice in Section 2.2.2.

We will see that in such a setting, the bias of the local polynomial estimator at an interior point is still of order h^{p+1} if the order of the polynomial (p) is odd, and of order h^{p+2} if p is even.[26] Hence, these results are the same as in the univariate setting and do not depend on the dimension q. In contrast, the variance is now of order $\frac{1}{nh^q}$, i.e. it decreases for increasing dimension q of X.[27] Recall that it does not depend on p or r. The reason why multivariate non-parametric regression nevertheless becomes difficult is the sparsity of data in higher-dimensional spaces.

Example 2.10 Consider a relatively large sample of size n, and start with a uniformly distributed $X \in [0, 1]$. If we choose a smoothing window of size 0.01 (e.g. a bounded symmetric kernel with $h = \frac{0.01}{2}$), one expects about 1% of the observations to lie in this smoothing window. Then consider the situation where the dimension of X is 2, and X is uniformly distributed on $[0, 1]^2$. With a bandwidth size of $h = 0.005$ you obtain windows of size 0.001 containing in average only 0.1% of all data, etc. If we have $dim(X) = 10$ and want to find a smoothing area that contains 1% of the observations in average, then this requires a 10-dimensional cube with length 0.63. Hence, for each component X_l ($l = 1, \ldots, q$) the smoothing area covers almost two thirds of the support of X_l, whereas it was only 0.01 in the one-dimensional case.

---

[26] Again as before, at a boundary point, the bias is of order h^{p+1}.

[27] What actually matters is the dimension of continuous regressors as we discussed before.

This example illustrates that in higher dimensions we need h (or, in the case of using a non-trivial bandwidth matrix H, all its elements at a time) to go to zero much slower than in the univariate case to control the variance. This in turn implies that the bias will be much larger. Supposing sufficient smoothness of $m(x)$ one could use local polynomials of higher order to reduce the bias. But when $\dim(X) = q$ is large, then a high order of p can become very inconvenient in practice since the number of (interaction) terms proliferates quickly. This could soon give rise to problems of local multicollinearity in small samples. A computationally more convenient alternative is to combine local linear regression with higher-order kernels for bias reduction.

First we need to clarify the properties of kernel functions for $q > 1$. Let λ be a q-tuple of non-negative integers and define $|\lambda| = \lambda_1 + \ldots + \lambda_q$ and $v^\lambda = v_1^{\lambda_1} v_2^{\lambda_2} \cdots v_q^{\lambda_q}$. Define

$$\kappa_\lambda = \int \cdots \int v^\lambda K(v_1, \ldots, v_q) \cdot dv_1 \cdots dv_q \qquad (2.31)$$

$$\text{and} \quad \bar{\kappa}_\lambda = \int \cdots \int v^\lambda K^2(v_1, \ldots, v_q) \cdot dv_1 \cdots dv_q.$$

Again, we say that a kernel K is of order r if $\kappa_0 = 1$, $\kappa_\lambda = 0$ for $1 \leq |\lambda| \leq r - 1$ and $\kappa_\lambda \neq 0$ for $|\lambda| = r$. One again has to normalise the kernel such that it integrates to one, i.e. $\kappa_0 = \int K(v) \, dv = 1$.

Consider the local linear ($p = 1$) estimation of $m(x_0)$. Similarly to before, define the regressor matrices $\mathbb{X}_i = \left(1, (X_i - x_0)'\right)'$, $\mathbb{X} = (\mathbb{X}_1, \mathbb{X}_2, \ldots, \mathbb{X}_n)'$ and $\mathbb{K} = diag(K_1, K_2, \ldots, K_n)$ with $K_i = K_H(X_i - x_0)$. Since $m(x_0)$ is estimated by a weighted least squares regression, we can write the solution as

$$\hat{m}(x_0) = e_1' \left(\mathbb{X}'\mathbb{K}\mathbb{X}\right)^{-1} \sum_{i=1}^n \mathbb{X}_i K_i Y_i = e_1' \left(\mathbb{X}'\mathbb{K}\mathbb{X}\right)^{-1} \sum_{i=1}^n \mathbb{X}_i K_i (Y_i - m(X_i) + m(X_i)),$$

where e_1 is a column vector of zeros with first element being 1. A series expansion gives

$$= e_1' \left(\mathbb{X}'\mathbb{K}\mathbb{X}\right)^{-1} \left\{ \sum_{i=1}^n \mathbb{X}_i K_i (Y_i - m(X_i)) \right.$$

$$+ \left. \sum_{i=1}^n \mathbb{X}_i K_i \left(m(x_0) + (X_i - x_0)' \frac{\partial m(x_0)}{\partial x} + (X_i - x_0)' \frac{1}{2} \frac{\partial^2 m(x_0)}{\partial x \partial x'} (X_i - x_0) + R_i \right) \right\},$$

where $\frac{\partial m(x_0)}{\partial x}$ is the $q \times 1$ vector of first derivatives, $\frac{\partial^2 m(x_0)}{\partial x \partial x'}$ the $q \times q$ matrix of second derivatives, and R_i the remainder term of all third- and higher-order derivatives multiplied with the respective higher-order (interaction) terms of $X_i - x_0$. We can see now what an rth order kernel will do: it will let pass $m(x_0)$ (because the kernel integrates to one) but it turns all further additive terms equal to zero until we reach the rth order terms in the Taylor expansion. Let us assume we used a kernel of the most typical order $r = 2$. Since K_i has bounded support, for x_0 being an interior point the remainder term multiplied with K_i is of order $O(h_{max}^3)$, where h_{max} is the largest diagonal element of bandwidth matrix H. We obtain after some calculations

$$= e_1' \left(\mathbb{X}'\mathbb{K}\mathbb{X}\right)^{-1} \left\{ \sum_{i=1}^{n} \mathbb{X}_i K_i \left(Y_i - m(X_i)\right) + m(x_0) \right. \tag{2.32}$$

$$+ \sum_{i=1}^{n} \mathbb{X}_i K_i \left(\sum_{1 \le |\lambda| \le k} \frac{1}{k!} \mathcal{D}^{\lambda} m(x_0)(X_i - x_0)^{\lambda} + R(x_0, X_i - x_0) \right) \left. \right\}, \tag{2.33}$$

with $|R(x_0, X_i - x_0)| \le O(\|X_i - x_0\|_2^{k+\alpha})$ if $m \in C^{k,\alpha}$ with $r \le k$ for some $0 < \alpha \le 1$. The first term inside the brackets $\{\cdots\}$ gives the variance of the estimator, the second is the wanted quantity, and the two remainder terms give the bias. As for the one-dimensional case, for an rth-order kernel the bias is of order $O(h^r)$ and contains all rth-order partial derivatives but not those of smaller order.

Note that (2.33) divided by n can be approximated by the expectation taken over X_i. Then, by applying the kernel properties, all summands up to $|\lambda| = r$ with $(X_i - x_0)^{\lambda}$ will integrate to zero (do not forget to count also the ones in $\mathbb{X}_n$). Then you obtain for (2.33)

$$\hat{m}(x_0) = e_1' \left(\mathbb{X}'\mathbb{K}\mathbb{X}\right)^{-1} f^{-1}(x_0) \left(\begin{matrix} \frac{\kappa_r}{r!} \sum_{l=1}^{q} h_l^r \frac{\delta^r m(x_0)}{\delta^r x_l} \\ o(H^r \mathbf{1}_q) \end{matrix} \right), \tag{2.34}$$

where $\mathbf{1}_q$ is a q-vector of ones.

To get some intuition about the denominator of the local linear estimator in the multiplicative context with potentially higher-order kernels, let us study $\mathbb{X}'\mathbb{K}\mathbb{X}$ a bit further, but still for $H = diag\{h_1, \ldots, h_q\}$ to simplify notation. Under the assumption that $n \det(H) \to \infty$ and $H \to 0$ element-wise, one can show that for $f(\cdot)$ being the joint density of X, and with $r \ge 2$,

$$\frac{1}{n}\mathbb{X}'\mathbb{K}\mathbb{X} = \frac{1}{n}\sum_{i=1}^{n} \mathbb{X}_i \mathbb{X}_i' K_i$$

$$= \begin{bmatrix} f(x_0) + O_p(h_{max}^r) & h_1^r \frac{\kappa_r}{(r-1)!} \frac{\partial^{r-1} f(x_0)}{\partial x_1^{r-1}} + o_p(h_{max}^r) & \cdots \\ h_1^r \frac{\kappa_r}{(r-1)!} \frac{\partial^{r-1} f(x_0)}{\partial x_1^{r-1}} + o_p(h_{max}^r) & h_1^r \frac{\kappa_r}{(r-2)!} \frac{\partial^{r-2} f(x_0)}{\partial x_1^{r-2}} + o_p(h_{max}^r) & \cdots \\ \vdots & \vdots & \ddots \end{bmatrix}. \tag{2.35}$$

You may imagine the last matrix as a 2×2 block matrix $\begin{pmatrix} a & b \\ b' & c \end{pmatrix}$ with a being mainly the density f at point x_0, b a q-dimensional vector proportional to its $(r-1)$'th partial derivatives times h^r, and c being proportional to the symmetric $q \times q$ matrix of all its (mixed) derivatives of (total) order r. This can be shown element-wise via mean square convergence. Let us illustrate this along the $(2, 2)$ element. The derivations for the other elements work analogously. For $x_0 = (x_{0,1}, x_{0,2}, \ldots, x_{0,q})$ we have

$$\frac{1}{n}\mathbb{X}'\mathbb{K}\mathbb{X} = \frac{1}{n \det(H)} \sum_{i=1}^{n} (X_{i1} - x_{0,1})^2 K\left(H^{-1}\{X_i - x_0\}\right)$$

which has the expected value of

$$E[\frac{1}{n}X'KX] = \frac{1}{\det(H)} \int \cdots \int (z_1 - x_{0,1})^2 K\left(H^{-1}\{z - x_0\}\right) f(z)dz, \quad z = (z_1, \ldots, z_q).$$

With a change in variables $u = H^{-1}(z - x_0) = (u_1, \ldots, u_q)'$, and a Taylor series expansion

$$= \int \cdots \int (h_1 u_1)^2 K(u) f(x_0 + Hu) du$$

$$= \int \cdots \int (h_1 u_1)^2 K(u) \left\{ \frac{h_1^{r-2} u_1^{r-2}}{(r-2)!} \frac{\partial^{r-2} f(x_0)}{\partial u_1^{r-2}} + \frac{h_1^{r-1} u_1^{r-1}}{(r-1)!} \frac{\partial^{r-1} f(x_0)}{\partial u_1^{r-1}} + o_p(h_{max}^r) \right\} du$$

$$= h_1^r \frac{\kappa_r}{(r-2)!} \frac{\partial^{r-2} f(x_0)}{\partial x_1^{r-2}} + o_p(h_{max}^r).$$

To obtain convergence, it has to be shown that the variance converges to zero faster than h_{max}^4. This gives consistent estimators of the first derivatives of $m(\cdot)$ as we are looking at the (2,2) element. We have

$$Var[\frac{1}{n}X'KX] = \frac{1}{(n \det(H))^2} \sum_{i=1}^{n} Var\left[(X_{i1} - x_{0,1})^2 K\left(H^{-1}\{X_i - x_0\}\right)\right]$$

$$= \frac{1}{n \det^2(H)} E\left[(X_{i1} - x_{0,1})^2 K^2\left(H^{-1}\{X_i - x_0\}\right)\right]$$

$$- \frac{1}{n \det^2(H)} E^2\left[(X_{i1} - x_{0,1})^2 K\left(H^{-1}\{X_i - x_0\}\right)\right]$$

$$= \frac{1}{n \det(H)} \int (u_1 h_1)^4 K^2(u) f(x_0 + Hu) du$$

$$- \frac{1}{n} \left\{ \int (h_1 u_1)^2 K(u) f(x_0 + Hu) du \right\}^2$$

$$= O\left(\frac{h_1^4}{n \det(H)}\right) - O\left(\frac{h_{max}^{2r}}{n}\right).$$

As it has been assumed that $n \cdot \det(H) \to \infty$ and $r \geq 2$, the variance converges to zero even faster than h_1^4. In sum, mean square convergence has been shown, which implies convergence in probability by Chebyshev's inequality. Finally, recall that

$$\begin{pmatrix} a & b \\ b' & c \end{pmatrix}^{-1} = \frac{1}{ad - b^2} \begin{pmatrix} c & -b \\ -b' & a \end{pmatrix}.$$

Then it is not hard to see that you get

$$e_1' \left(\frac{1}{n}X'KX\right)^{-1} = \frac{1}{f(x_0)} \begin{pmatrix} 1 + o_p(h_{max}^r) \\ -\left(\frac{\partial^{r-1} f(x_0)}{\partial x_1^{r-1}} \Big/ \frac{\partial^{r-2} f(x_0)}{\partial x_1^{r-2}}\right) \frac{(r-2)!}{(r-1)!} \\ \vdots \\ -\left(\frac{\partial^{r-1} f(x_0)}{\partial x_d^{r-1}} \Big/ \frac{\partial^{r-2} f(x_0)}{\partial x_d^{r-2}}\right) \frac{(r-2)!}{(r-1)!} \end{pmatrix}' + O(h_{max}^r).$$

Putting this together with (2.34) we obtain the bias, and similar calculation would give the variance of the multivariate local linear estimator with higher-order kernels. We summarise:

THEOREM 2.9   *Assume that we are provided with a sample* $\{X_i, Y_i\}_{i=1}^n$ *coming from a model fulfilling (A1) with* $X_i \in \mathbb{R}^q$, $m : \mathbb{R}^q \to \mathbb{R}$. *Then, for* $x_0 \in \mathbb{R}^q$ *being an interior point of the support of X, the local linear estimator* $\hat{m}(x_0)$ *of* $m(x_0)$ *with a multivariate symmetric rth-order kernel* $(r \geq 2)$ *and bandwidth matrix* $H = diag\{h_1, \ldots, h_q\}$ *such that* $h_{max} \to 0$, $n \det(H) \to \infty$ *for* $n \to \infty$ *has*

$$Bias\left(\hat{m}(x_0)\right) = \frac{\kappa_r}{r!} \sum_{l=1}^q h_l^r \frac{\delta^r m(x_0)}{\delta^r x_l} + o(h_{max}^r)$$

$$Var\left(\hat{m}(x_0)\right) = \frac{\sigma^2(x_0)}{n \det(H) f(x_0)} \bar{\kappa}_0 + o\left(\frac{1}{n \det(H)}\right).$$

From the calculations above we obtained an idea of at least three things: how higher dimensions increase the variance in local polynomial kernel regression, its asymptotic performance, and how higher order kernels can reduce the bias for local linear regression. When q is large, local linear estimation with higher-order kernels are easier to implement than higher-order local polynomial regression. The optimal rate of convergence for non-parametric estimation of a k times continuously differentiable regression function $m(x)$, $x \in \mathbb{R}^q$ in L_2-norm is

$$n^{-\frac{k}{2k+q}}$$

and in sup-norm (i.e. uniform convergence)

$$\left(\frac{n}{\log n}\right)^{-\frac{k}{2k+q}}.$$

As stated the rate of convergence is always slower than the parametric $\sqrt{n}$ rate and decreases for increasing $q = dim(X)$ (more precisely the number of continuous variables in X). This is the *curse of dimensionality*, which reflects that non-parametric regression becomes more difficult for higher-dimensional X; recall Example 2.10. One may argue that the optimal rate increases with the number of continuous derivatives of $m(x)$, but this rate can only be reached if one does make use of it, for example by an k-order local polynomial or higher-order kernels. If k is very large we obtain almost the parametric rate $n^{-1/2}$. What does this mean in practice? It simply says that if a k-order Taylor expansion approximates well to the function over the whole support of X, then the bandwidth can be chosen close to infinity, i.e. we can simply take an k-order polynomial and forget about non-parametric estimation. While this is clear in theory, it is little helpful in practice because first, we do not know the right k, and second, it might be that we have to choose such a large k that we run into numerical problems (like local multi-colinearity). For $q > 1$, it is even inconvenient because of all the interactions that have to be included.

2.2.2 Extensions: Bandwidth Choice, Bias Reduction, Discrete Covariates and Estimating Conditional Distribution Functions

Throughout this subsection we keep the definition and notation of kernel moments as introduced in (2.23). Where we have different kernels, say L and K, we specify the moments further by writing e.g. $\kappa_j(K)$ and $\kappa_j(L)$, respectively.

Bandwidth Choice

You can interpret the bandwidth choice as the fine-tuning of model selection: you have avoided choosing a functional form but the question of smoothness is still open. Like in model selection, once you have chosen a bandwidth h (or matrix H), it is taken as given for any further inference. This is standard practice even if it contradicts the philosophy of purely non-parametric analysis. The reason is that an account of any further inference for the randomness of data adaptively estimated bandwidths is often just too complex. It is actually not even clear whether valid inference is possible without the assumption of having the correct bandwidth.[28]

To simplify the presentation let us start with the one-dimensional and local constant regressor case with second-order kernel: $q = 1$, $p = 0$, $r = 2$. Actually, if we just follow the idea of minimising the mean squared error (MSE), then Theorems 2.6 and 2.7 indicate how the bandwidth should be chosen optimally. Suppose we aim to minimise the asymptotic $MSE(\hat{m}(x_0))$. Along with our Theorems, the first-order approximation to the MSE of the Nadaraya–Watson estimator is

$$\left\{ \frac{h^2}{2f(x_0)} \kappa_2 \left(m''(x_0) f(x_0) + 2 f'(x_0) m'(x_0) \right) \right\}^2 + \frac{\sigma^2}{nhf(x_0)} \bar{\kappa}_0.$$

Considering this as a function of h for fixed n, the optimal bandwidth choice is obtained by minimising it with respect to h. The first order condition gives

$$\frac{h^3}{f^2(x_0)} \left(\kappa_2 \left\{ m''(x_0) f(x_0) + 2 f'(x_0) m'(x_0) \right\} \right)^2 - \frac{\sigma^2}{nh^2 f(x_0)} \bar{\kappa}_0 = 0$$

$$\implies h_{opt} = n^{-\frac{1}{5}} \left\{ \frac{\sigma^2 f(x_0) \bar{\kappa}_0}{(\kappa_2 \{ m''(x_0) f(x_0) + 2 f'(x_0) m'(x_0) \})^2} \right\}^{\frac{1}{5}}. \tag{2.36}$$

Hence, the optimal bandwidth for a one-dimensional regression problem under the assumptions of Theorems 2.6 or 2.7 is proportional to $n^{-\frac{1}{5}}$.

Unfortunately, asymptotic properties of non-parametric estimators are often of little guidance for choosing the bandwidth for a particular data set in practice because they contain many unknown terms, and because for your sample size 'higher-order terms' may still be dominant or at least important. A more versatile approach to bandwidth selection is the hitherto very popular *cross-validation* (Stone 1974), based on the principle of maximising the out-of-sample predictive performance. If a quadratic loss function ($= L_2$ error criterion) is used to assess the performance of an estimator of $m(x_0)$ at a particular point x_0, a bandwidth value h should be selected to minimise

---

[28] There is a large literature on model and variable selection already in the parametric world discussing the problems of valid inference after preselection or testing.

$$E\left[\{\hat{m}(x_0; h) - m(x_0)\}^2\right].$$

Moreover, when a single bandwidth value is used to estimate the entire function $m(\cdot)$ at all points, we would like to choose the (global) bandwidth as the minimiser to the mean integrated squared error (MISE), typically weighted by density f:

$$\text{MISE}(h; n) = \int E\left[\{\hat{m}(x; h) - m(x)\}^2\right] f(x)\, dx.$$

In practice, it is more common to look at the minimiser of the integrated squared error

$$\text{ISE}(h; n) = \int \{\hat{m}(x; h) - m(x)\}^2 f(x)\, dx$$

as this gives you the optimal bandwidth for your sample, while minimising the MISE in looking for a bandwidth that minimises the ISE on average (i.e. independent of the sample). Since $m(x)$ is unknown, a computable approximation to minimising the ISE is minimising the average squared error (ASE)

$$\arg\min_h \frac{1}{n}\sum_{i=1}^{n}\{Y_i - \hat{m}(X_i; h)\}^2 \tag{2.37}$$

which converges to $\int\left\{[m(x) - \hat{m}(x)]^2 + \sigma^2(x)\right\} dF(x)$ with $\sigma^2(x)$ not depending on h. However, it is not hard to show theoretically why this criterion must fail. Minimising it leads to the selection of too-small bandwidth values. For example, imagine we had no ties in X (no value is observed more than once). If a kernel with compact support is used and h is very small, the local neighbourhood of X_i would contain only the observation (Y_i, X_i). As the estimate $\hat{m}(X_i)$ is a weighted average of the Y observations in the neighbourhood, the estimate of $m(X_i)$ would be Y_i. Hence, the criterion (2.37) will recommend to set $h = 0$ and interpolate. In order to avoid this, the observation (Y_i, X_i) must be excluded from the sample when estimating $m(X_i)$. The corresponding estimate $\hat{m}_{-i}(X_i)$ is called the *leave-one-out estimate* and represents the out-of-sample prediction with sample $\{(Y_j, X_j)\}_{j\neq i}$. The resulting jackknife cross-validation function is then defined as

$$CV(h; n) = \sum_{i=1}^{n}\left\{Y_i - \hat{m}_{-i}(X_i; h)\right\}^2, \tag{2.38}$$

and h is chosen to minimise (2.38).[29] There exist many different bandwidth selectors; see Köhler, Schindler and Sperlich (2014) for a review. The most promising seem to be some refinements of (2.38), in particular the so-called *Do-validation*.

Instead of out-of-sample-prediction validation, the average squared error criterion (2.37) could be modified to correct the downward bias (the cross validation tends to underestimate $\hat{h}$) by 'penalising' very small bandwidth values. These are similar in spirit to the 'in-sample' model selection criteria in parametric regression, which seek to account for the degrees of freedom by penalising models with a large number of coefficients. A variety of penalised cross-validation criteria have been proposed. Widely

---

[29] For properties of cross-validation bandwidth selection see Härdle and Marron (1987).

used is the so-called *generalised cross-validation*: A linear smoother for the data points $\mathbb{Y} = (Y_1, \ldots, Y_n)'$ can be written as $(\hat{Y}_1, \ldots, \hat{Y}_n)' = \mathbf{A}\mathbb{Y}$ where $\mathbf{A}$ is the $n \times n$ so-called *hat*, *smoothing* or *projection matrix*. Letting a_{ii} denote the (i, i) element of $\mathbf{A}$, the generalised cross-validation criterion is

$$GCV(h) = \frac{1}{n} \frac{\|(I_n - \mathbf{A})\, \mathbb{Y}\|^2}{(tr(I_n - \mathbf{A}))^2} = \frac{1}{n} \frac{\sum_{i=1}^n \left\{ Y_i - \hat{m}(X_i; h) \right\}^2}{\left\{ \sum_{i=1}^n (1 - a_{ii}) \right\}^2}, \quad I_n \text{ identity matrix},$$

(2.39)

which does not require estimating the leave-one-out estimates. However, the approximation that is used here for estimating the degrees of freedom is not generally valid when we turn to more complex estimators.

Usually a single bandwidth h is considered for a given sample to estimate $m(\cdot)$ at different locations x. However, permitting the bandwidth to vary with x (a so-called *local bandwidth* $h(x)$) may yield a more precise estimation if the smoothing window adapts to the density of the available data. One such approach is the kNN regression. In the kNN approach the 'local bandwidth' $h(x)$ is chosen such that exactly k observations fall in the window. I.e. only the k nearest neighbours to x_0 are used for estimating $m(x_0)$.[30]

Generally, when $\dim(X) > 1$, we have to smooth in various dimensions. This would require the choice of a $q \times q$-dimensional bandwidth matrix H (recall our paragraph on multivariate kernel smoothing), which also defines the spatial properties of the kernel, e.g. ellipsoidal support of the kernel. To better understand what a bandwidth matrix plus multivariate kernel is doing, just imagine that for determining nearness a multidimensional distance metric is required. One common choice is the Mahalanobis distance $\sqrt{(X_i - x_0) Var^{-1}[X](X_i - x_0)'}$, which is a quadratic form in $(X_i - x_0)$, weighted by the inverse of the covariance matrix of X. More specifically, it is the Euclidean distance[31] after having passed all variables to a comparable scale (by normalisation). In other words, the simplest solution to deal with this situation is to scale and turn the X_i data beforehand such that each regressor has variance one and covariance zero. This is actually done by the Mahalanobis transformation $\tilde{X} := \hat{V}ar[X]^{-1/2}X$ with $\hat{V}ar[X]$ being any reasonable estimator for the variance–covariance matrix of the covariance vector (typically the sample covariance); recall our discussed of pair matching. Note that then all regressors $\tilde{X}$ are on the same scale (standard deviation $= 1$) and uncorrelated. So you basically use $H := h \cdot \hat{V}ar[X]^{1/2}$. Then, using a single value h for all dimensions combined with a product kernel is convenient.[32]

---

[30] The basic difference between kNN and kernel-based techniques is that the latter estimates $m(x_0)$ by smoothing the data in a window around x_0 of fixed size $2h$, whereas the former smoothes the data in a neighbourhood of stochastic size containing exactly the k nearest neighbours. Furthermore, a kNN assigns the same weight to all neighbours like the uniform kernel does.

[31] Typically the Euclidean distance is understood to be just the square root of the sum of squared distances in each dimension, but supposes linear independence of the dimensions. In our case we have to account for the correlation structure of the regressors spanning a non-right-angled space.

[32] An important exception applies when the optimal bandwidth would be infinity for one of the regressors, which is e.g. the case with Nadaraya–Watson regression when one of the regressors is irrelevant in the conditional mean function. Then separate bandwidths for each regressor would have to be used, such that

One should point out that all known approaches to choose h – see Köhler, Schindler and Sperlich (2014) – are constructed to optimise the estimation of $E[Y|\cdot] = m(\cdot)$ which is not necessarily optimal for the matching or propensity score-based treatment effect estimators. For these, the issue of optimal bandwidth choice is not yet fully resolved, but the results of Frölich (2004) and Frölich (2005) indicate that the bandwidth selectors having been invented for estimating $E[Y|X = x]$ may not perform too badly in this context.

Bias Reduction

Various approaches have been suggested to reduce the asymptotic bias of the non-parametric regression estimator. Unfortunately, most of these approaches have mainly theoretical appeal and seem not really to work well in finite samples. However, as we will see later, for many semi-parametric regression estimators the bias problem is of different nature since variance can be reduced through averaging, whereas bias cannot. Then, the reduction of the bias term can be crucial for obtaining asymptotically better properties.

When introducing local polynomials and higher-order kernels, we could already see their bias reducing properties; their bias was a multiple of h^δ with h being the bandwidth and δ increasing with the order of the polynomial and/or the kernel. Typically, the bandwidth should be chosen to balance variance and squared bias. Nonetheless, if the bandwidth matrix converges to zero such that the squared bias goes faster to zero than the variance, then the former can be neglected in further inference. This reduction of the bias comes at the price of a larger variance and a lower convergence rate, a price we are often willing to pay in the semi-parametric context. This strategy is called *undersmoothing* as we smooth the data less than the smallest MSE would suggest. Note, however, that without further bias reduction (by increasing p or r), this works only for $q \leq 3$ (at most).

An alternative approach to bias reduction is based on the idea of 'jackknifing' (to eliminate the first-order bias term). A jackknife kernel estimator for $q = dim(X) = 1$ is defined by

$$\tilde{m}(x_0) = \frac{\hat{m}(x_0; h) - \frac{1}{c^2}\hat{m}(x_0; c \cdot h)}{1 - \frac{1}{c^2}}$$

where $c > 1$ is a constant,[33] $\hat{m}(x_0; h)$ is the kernel estimator with bandwidth, h and $\hat{m}(x_0; c \cdot h)$ with bandwidth $c \cdot h$. The intuition behind this estimator is as follows: the first-order approximation to the expected value of the kernel estimator is

$$E[\hat{m}(x_0; c \cdot h)] = m(x_0) + \frac{c^2 h^2}{2 f(x_0)}\kappa_2 \left(m''(x_0) f(x_0) + 2 f'(x_0) m'(x_0) \right).$$

Inserting this into the above expression shows that the bias of $\tilde{m}(x_0)$ contains terms only of order h^3 or higher. This is easy to implement for $q = 1$ but else rarely used in practice.

---

automatic bandwidth selectors could smooth out irrelevant variables via choosing infinitely large bandwidths, see e.g. section 2.2.4 of Li and Racine (2007).

[33] For example, $1 < c < 1.1$ is suggested e.g. in Pagan and Ullah (1999).

Combination of Discrete and Continuous Regressors

Many econometric applications contain continuous as well as discrete explanatory variables. While both types of regressors can easily be incorporated in the parametric specification through the choice of an appropriate function, they need also to be accommodated
in the distance metric of the kernel function $K(v)$ defining the local neighbourhood. A
popular method to include discrete regressors, say $x_{q_1+1}, \ldots, x_q$, is to consider a partial
linear model (PLM) of the form $E[Y|X = x] = m(x_1, \ldots, x_{q_1}) + \sum_{j=q_1+1}^{q} \beta_j x_j$ in
which $m(\cdot)$ is still non-parametric but only hosts the continuous regressors.

Building on the work of Aitchison and Aitken (1976), Racine and Li (2004) developed a hybrid product kernel that coalesces continuous and discrete regressors. They
distinguish three types of regressors: continuous, discrete with natural ordering (number of children) and discrete without natural ordering (bus, train, car). Suppose that the
variables in X are arranged such that the first q_1 regressors are continuous, the regressors
$q_1 + 1, \ldots, q_2$ discrete with natural ordering and the remaining $q - q_2$ regressors are
discrete without natural ordering. Then the kernel weights at $(X_i - x)$ are computed as

$$K_{h,\delta,\lambda}(X_i - x) = \prod_{l=1}^{q_1} K\left(\frac{X_{l,i} - x_l}{h}\right) \prod_{l=q_1+1}^{q_2} \delta^{|X_{l,i}-x_l|} \prod_{l=q_2+1}^{q} \lambda^{\mathbb{1}\{X_{l,i} \neq x_l\}}, \qquad (2.40)$$

where $X_{l,i}$ and x_l denote the lth element of X_i and x, respectively, K is a standard (i.e.
as before) kernel with bandwidth h, δ and λ positive smoothing parameters satisfying
$0 \leq \delta, \lambda \leq 1$. This kernel function $K_{h,\delta,\lambda}(X_i - x)$ measures the distance between
X_i and x through three components: the first term is the standard product kernel for
continuous regressors with h defining the size of the local neighbourhood. The second
term measures the distance between the ordered discrete regressors and assigns geometrically declining weights to less narrow observations. The third term measures the
(mis-)match between the unordered discrete regressors. Thus, δ controls the amount of
smoothing for the ordered and λ for the unordered discrete regressors. For example, the
multiplicative weight contribution of the last regressor is 1 if the last element of X_i and
x is identical, and λ if they are different. The larger δ and/or λ are, the more smoothing takes place with respect to the discrete regressors. If δ and λ are both 1, then the
discrete regressors would not affect the kernel weights and the non-parametric estimator would 'smooth globally' over the discrete regressors. On the other hand, if δ and
λ are both zero, then smoothing would proceed only within each of the cells defined
by the discrete regressors but not between them. If in such a situation X contained no
continuous regressors, then this would correspond to the frequency estimator, where Y
is estimated by the average of the observations within each cell. Any value between 0
and 1 for δ and λ thus corresponds to some smoothing over the discrete regressors. By
noting that

$$\prod_{l=1}^{q} \lambda^{\mathbb{1}\{X_{l,i} \neq x_l\}} = \lambda^{\sum_{l=1}^{q} \mathbb{1}\{X_{l,i} \neq x_l\}},$$

it can be seen that the weight contribution of the unordered discrete regressors
depends only on λ and the number of regressors that are distinct between X_i

and x. Racine and Li (2004) analysed Nadaraya–Watson regression based on this hybrid kernel and derived its asymptotic distribution for bandwidths selected by cross-validation.

Principally, instead of using only three bandwidth values h, δ, λ for all regressors, a different bandwidth could be employed for each regressor. But this would increase substantially the computational burden for bandwidth selection and might lead to additional noise due to the estimation of these smoothing parameters. Nevertheless, if the explanatory variables are deemed too distinct, groups of similar regressors could be formed, and each group being then assigned a separate smoothing parameter. Particularly if the ranges assumed by the ordered discrete variables vary considerably, those variables that take on many different values should be separated from those with only few values. In other words, the rule that the different covariates should be brought to the same (or comparable) scale does not only hold for the continuous regressors but also for the discrete ones. This could justify using the same $h, \lambda\delta$ for all regressors.

A different 'solution' is to apply the same kernel function K to both the ordered discrete and the continuous regressors and to rotate them together such that they become orthonormal (by a Mahalanobis transformation as proposed in the paragraph on bandwidth selection). There is no mathematical reason why geometrically declining kernel weights provide a better weighting function. Hence, in practice one can use instead of (2.40) the kernel function

$$
K_{h,\lambda}(X_i - x) = \prod_{l=1}^{q_1} K\left(\frac{X_{l,i} - x_l}{h}\right) \prod_{l=q_1+1}^{q} \lambda^{\mathbb{1}\{X_{l,i} \neq x_l\}}, \tag{2.41}
$$

where the regressors $1, \ldots, q_1$ contain the continuous and the ordered discrete variables. An important aspect in practice is how the information contained in unordered discrete regressors should enter a local model, for example when the same value of λ is used for all.

Example 2.11 Suppose we have two unordered discrete regressors: gender and region, where region takes values in {1=North, 2=South, 3=East, 4=West, 5=North-East, 6=North-West, 7=South-East, 8=South-West} while the dummy variable 'gender' would enter as one regressor in a PLM or in (2.41). The situation with region is more difficult. First, comprising the information on region in one regressor variable in the PLM makes no sense because the values 1 to 8 have no logical meaning. Instead, one would use seven dummy variables for the different regions. However, when the kernel function (2.41) one can use a single regressor variable. If one were to use seven dummy variables instead, then the effective kernel weight used for 'region' would be λ^7 but only λ for gender. The reason is that if two observations j and i live in different regions, they will be different on all seven regional dummies. Hence, the implicit bandwidth would be dramatically smaller for region than it is for gender. This would either require using separate smoothness parameters λ_1, λ_2 for region and gender or a rescaling of them by the number of corresponding dummy variables.

Estimating Conditional Distribution Functions

There are certainly many ways how to introduce non-parametric (kernel) estimators for densities or cumulative distribution functions (cdf). Given what we have learnt so far about nonparametric regression, the easiest way to introduce these estimators at this stage is to derive them as special cases of non-parametric regression.

Recall first that the standard non-parametric estimator for the unconditional cdf is the empirical distribution function

$$\hat{F}(y) = \hat{E}\left[\mathbb{1}\{Y \le y\}\right] = \frac{1}{n}\sum_{i=1}^{n}\mathbb{1}\{Y_i \le y\}. \tag{2.42}$$

As before, conditioning on x could be introduced via kernel weights yielding

$$\hat{F}(y|x) = \hat{E}\left[\mathbb{1}\{Y \le y\}|x\right] = \frac{1}{n}\sum_{i=1}^{n}\mathbb{1}\{Y_i \le y\}\frac{K_h(X_i - x)}{\frac{1}{n}\sum_{j=1}^{n}K_h(X_j - x)}, \tag{2.43}$$

which is simply the Nadaraya–Watson estimator of $E[\mathbb{1}\{Y \le y\}|x]$. Alternatively, one can take any local polynomial estimator of $E[\mathbb{1}\{Y \le y\}|x]$. Following the same lines as above, for the local linear we would get bias $h^2\frac{\kappa_2}{2}F''(y|x)$ and variance $\frac{\bar{\kappa}_0}{nh}\frac{(1-F(y|x))F(y|x)}{f(x)}$ for $dim(x) = 1$ and using a kernel of order $r = 2$. For $dim(x) > 1$ and/or kernels of order $r > 2$ these formulae have to be modified analogously to those in Theorem 2.9.

For conditional densities $f(y|x)$ we may just take the derivative of $\hat{F}(y|x)$ with respect to y. A more direct regression approach, however, would first note that for a kernel L, $E[L_\delta(Y - y)] \xrightarrow{\delta\to 0} f(y)$,[34] and accordingly $E[L(\delta(Y - y))|x] \xrightarrow{\delta\to 0} f(y|x)$. A local linear least squares estimator of $E[L_\delta(Y - y)|x]$ with weights $K_h(X_i - x)$ is then

$$\min_{\beta_0,\beta_1}\frac{1}{n}\sum_{i=1}^{n}\{L_\delta(Y_i - y) - \beta_0 - \beta_1(X_i - x)\}^2 K_h(X_i - x) \tag{2.44}$$

with $\beta_0 = \hat{f}(y|x)$, as long as h and δ tend to zero; with bias

$$\frac{h^2\kappa_2(K)}{2}\frac{\partial^2 f(y|x)}{\partial x^2} + \frac{\delta^2\kappa_2(L)}{2}\frac{\partial^2 f(y|x)}{\partial y^2}$$

and variance (still applying $q = 1$ and second-order kernels L, K)

$$\frac{1}{nh\delta}\bar{\kappa}_0(K)\cdot\bar{\kappa}_0(L)\frac{f(y|x)}{f(x)}.$$

A more direct way is to recall that $f(y|x) = f(y, x)/f(x)$ and to derive standard kernel density estimators for $f(y, x)$, $f(x)$. This actually results in an estimator being equivalent to the local constant estimator of $E[L_\delta(Y - y)|x]$.

---

[34] This is actually much closer to the original idea of 'kernels' than their use as weight functions.

2.2.3   A Brief Introduction to Semi-Parametric Regression

There are many different ways in which semi-parametric models and modelling can be introduced and motivated. Already, from a purely statistical point of view, it is clear that any efficiency gain requires the use of additional information about the model (in particular, the functional form). One could also speak of additional assumptions and restrictions. These, however, should be somehow justified – and this is the point where economic (or econometric) theory comes in. This might concern some separability of impacts, monotonicity or information on the functional form. Moreover, if the response variable is discrete, e.g. binary, it is clear that one would like to work with a particular conditional distribution like a (local) logit or probit for binary, and maybe a Poisson for counting data. Any information about separability or functional form can help to reduce or even overcome the curse of dimensionality. For example, it is well known in non- and semi-parametric statistics that generalised additive models do not suffer from this curse but allow us to estimate each separable component at the optimal one-dimensional rate. We start here with the extension of the local linear estimator to a local parametric regression. Later we will see how both, the use of local logits or probits and the dimension reduction by introducing semi-parametric structure can be used for treatment effect estimators.

Some Typical Semi-Parametric Models

As mentioned above, because of the sparsity of data in higher dimensions, when $\dim(X)$ is large, a larger bandwidth is also required. The reason for the curse of dimensionality is that data are extremely sparse in a high-dimensional regressor space, leading to almost empty neighbourhoods 'almost everywhere'. Even if most of the regressors are discrete, e.g. binary, the number of cells will still proliferate quickly, leading to many empty cells. Estimating $m(x)$ will then require extrapolation from observations that are not as nearby as in the low-dimensional regression context. In finite samples, non-parametric regression is then not that much about averages in small local neighbourhoods but rather about different weighting of the data in large neighbourhoods. Consequently, the choice of the parametric hyperplane being used becomes more important, because regression in finite samples will be based substantially on local extrapolation. (I.e. at location x_0 most of the data points might be relatively far away, so that the local model is used for intra- and extrapolation.)

Example 2.12 The reason why Nadaraya–Watson regression performs poorly is due to its limited use of covariate information, which is incorporated only in the distance metric in the kernel function but not in the extrapolation plane. Consider a simple example where only two binary X characteristics are observed: gender (male/female) and professional qualification (skilled/unskilled) and both coded as 0–1 variables. Expected wages shall be estimated. Suppose that, for instance, the cell skilled males contains no observations. The Nadaraya–Watson estimate with $h > 1$ of the expected wage for skilled male workers would be a weighted average of the observed wages for unskilled male, skilled female and unskilled female workers, and would thus be lower than the expected wage for skilled female workers, which is in contrast to theory and reality. For $h < 1$ the Nadaraya–Watson estimator is not defined for skilled males, as the cell is empty, and $h < 1$ with bounded kernels assigns weight zero to all observations. Now, if the a priori beliefs sustain that skilled workers earn higher wages than unskilled workers and that male workers earn higher wages than female workers, then a monotonic 'additive' extrapolation would be more adequate than simply averaging the observations in the neighbourhood (even if down-weighting more distant observations). Under these circumstances a linear extrapolation e.g. in form of local linear regression would be more appropriate, which would add up the gender wage difference and the wage increment due to the skill level to estimate the expected wage for skilled male workers. Although the linear specification is not true, it is still closer to the true shape than the flat extrapolation plane of Nadaraya–Watson regression. Here, a priori information from economic theory becomes useful for selecting a suited parametric hyperplane that allows the incorporation of covariate information more thoroughly to obtain better extrapolations.

A direct extension of the local linear towards a *local parametric estimator* seems to be a natural answer to our problem. Moreover, if we think of local linear (or, more generally, local parametric) estimators as kernel weighted least squares, one could equally well localise the parametric maximum-likelihood estimator by convoluting it with a kernel function. These will be the first semi-parametric estimators we introduce below. Unfortunately, this does not necessarily mitigate the curse of dimensionality if the imposed parametric structure is not used inside the kernel function. Therefore, other models and methods have been proposed. Among them, the most popular ones are the *partial linear models* (PLM); see Speckman (1988),

$$E[Y|X = x] = x_1'\beta + m(x_2), \ x' = (x_1', x_2') \in I\!\!R^{q_1+q_2}, \ \beta \in I\!\!R^{q_1}, \tag{2.45}$$

where x_1 contains all dummy variables and those covariates whose impact can be restricted to a linear one for whatever reason. Although the method contains non-parametric steps, the β can often[35] be estimated at the parametric convergence rate $\sqrt{n}$. Also quite popular are the *additive partial linear models*; see Hastie and Tibshirani (1990),

$$E[Y|X = x] = x_1'\beta + \sum_{\alpha=q_1+1}^{q} m_\alpha(x_\alpha), \tag{2.46}$$

$$x' = (x_1', x_2, \ldots, x_q) \in I\!\!R^{q_1+q_2}, \ \beta \in I\!\!R^{q_1}, \ x_\alpha \in I\!\!R \ \forall \alpha > q_1.$$

The advantage is that when applying an appropriate estimator, each additive component m_α can be estimated at the optimal one-dimensional non-parametric convergence rate. In other words, this model overcomes the curse of dimensionality. Another class that achieves this is the *single index model*; see Powell, Stock and Stoker (1989) or Härdle, Hall and Ichimura (1993),

$$E[Y|X = x] = G(x'\beta), \ x, \beta \in I\!\!R^q, \ G : I\!\!R \to I\!\!R \text{ unknown}, \tag{2.47}$$

[35] Required are set of assumptions on the smoothness of m, the distribution of X, the dimension of x_2, etc.

which is an extension of the well-known generalised linear models but allowing for an unknown link function G. Under some regularity assumptions, the β can be estimated at the optimal parametric rate, and G at the optimal one-dimensional non-parametric convergence rate. A less popular but rather interesting generalisation of the parametric linear model is the *varying coefficient model*; see Cleveland, Grosse and Shyu (1991):

$$E[Y|X = x] = x_1'\beta(x_2), \quad x' = (x_1', x_2') \in I\!\!R^{q_1+q_2}, \beta(\cdot) : I\!\!R^{q_2} \to I\!\!R^{q_1} \text{ non-parametric},$$

(2.48)

which exist in many forms and modifications. For example, all coefficients of $\beta(\cdot)$ may depend on all covariates of x_2, or each on a certain subset only. Certain covariates can form part of both, x_1 and x_2. Each element of the vector-valued functions β can be estimated at the optimal convergence rate that corresponds to the dimension of its argument.

We do not list here all the combinations of these models or parametric extension like e.g. the inclusion of a parametric transformation of Y or a parametric (i.e. known) link function on the right-hand side of the equation. For those and a list of references, see the section on 'further reading' at the end of this chapter.

We now derive in detail the local parametric estimators, and afterwards introduce the main ideas of partial linear regression, before finally discussing efficiency bounds for semi-parametric estimators. In the next chapters we will see various applications of non-parametric regression, semi-parametric estimation of parameters, and the use of the efficiency bound.

Local Parametric and Local Likelihood Regression

Local parametric estimation proceeds by first specifying a parametric class of functions

$$g(x, \theta_x)$$

(2.49)

where the function g is known, but the coefficients θ_x are unknown, and fitting this local model to the data in a neighbourhood of x. The estimate of the regression function $m(x)$ is then calculated as

$$\hat{m}(x) = g(x, \hat{\theta}_x).$$

The function g should be chosen according to economic theory, taking into account the properties of the outcome variable Y.

Example 2.13 If Y is binary or takes only values between 0 and 1, a local logit specification would be appealing, i.e.

$$g(x, \theta_x) = \frac{1}{1 + e^{\theta_{0,x} + x'\theta_{1,x}}},$$

where $\theta_{0,x}$ refers to the constant and $\theta_{1,x}$ to the other coefficients corresponding to the regressors in x. This local logit specification has the advantage vis-à-vis a local linear one, that all the estimated values $\hat{m}(x)$ are automatically between 0 and 1. Furthermore, it may also help to reduce the high variability of local linear regression in finite samples.

The function g should be chosen to incorporate also other properties that one might expect for the true function m, such as convexity or monotonicity. These properties, however, only apply locally when fitting the function g at location x. It does not imply that $\hat{m}(\cdot)$ is convex or monotonous over the entire support of X. The reason for this is that the coefficients θ_x are re-estimated for every location x: for two different values x_1 and x_2 the function estimates are $g(x_1, \hat{\theta}_{x_1})$ and $g(x_2, \hat{\theta}_{x_2})$, where not only x changes but also $\hat{\theta}_x$.[36]

One should note that the local coefficients θ_x may not be uniquely identified, although $g(x, \hat{\theta}_x)$ may still be. E.g. if some of the regressors are collinear, θ_x is not unique, but all solutions lead to the same value of $g(x, \hat{\theta}_x)$. This was discussed in detail in Gozalo and Linton (2000).

There are several ways to estimate the local model. Local least squares regression estimates the vector of local coefficients θ_x as

$$\hat{\theta}_x = \arg\min_{\theta_x} \sum_{i=1}^{n} \{Y_i - g(X_i, \theta_x)\}^2 \cdot K(X_i - x). \qquad (2.50)$$

It is embedded in the class of local likelihood estimation (see Tibshirani and Hastie 1987, and Staniswalis 1989), which estimates $\hat{\theta}_x$ by

$$\hat{\theta}_x = \arg\max_{\theta_x} \sum_{i=1}^{n} \ln L\left(Y_i, g(X_i, \theta_x)\right) \cdot K(X_i - x), \qquad (2.51)$$

where $L(Y_i, g(X_i, \theta_x))$ is the Likelihood contribution of observation (Y_i, X_i). Evidently, for the log-Likelihood approach one has to specify a likelihood function in addition to the local model, which entails the conjectured properties of the local error term. As in the parametric world, if a normally distributed error is assumed, then the likelihood function in (2.51) is identical to the least squares specification (2.50). If Y is binary, the likelihood for Bernoulli random variables is more appropriate. Although the asymptotic non-parametric results are usually the same for both approaches, the finite sample performance improves when the proposed model is closer to the true data generating process.

The bandwidth h determines the local neighbourhood of the kernel weighting. If h converges to infinity, the local neighbourhood widens and the local estimator converges to the global parametric estimator. In this sense, each parametric model can be nested in a corresponding semi-parametric one. Global parametric regression assumes that the shape of the conditional expectation function is known and correctly specified. Local parametric regression, on the other hand, imposes the $g(\cdot)$ function only locally, i.e. merely as a device for better extrapolations in finite samples.

---

[36] Note that when one is interested in the first derivative, there are two different ways of estimating it: either as $\partial \hat{m}(x)/\partial x$, or from inside the model via $\partial g(x, \hat{\theta}_x)/\partial x$. These are different estimators and may have different properties. E.g. when a local logit model is used, the first derivative $\partial g(x, \hat{\theta}_x)/\partial x$ is always between 0 and 0.25, whereas $\partial \hat{m}(x)/\partial x$ is not restricted but can take any value between $-\infty$ and ∞.

Local least squares (2.50) and local likelihood (2.51) can be estimated by setting the first derivative to zero. Therefore they can also be written as

$$\sum_{i=1}^{n} \Psi\left(Y_i, g(X_i, \theta_x)\right) \cdot K(X_i - x) = 0 \tag{2.52}$$

for some function Ψ that is defined by the first-order condition. They can thus also be embedded in the framework of local estimating equations (Carroll, Ruppert and Welsh 1998), which can be considered as a local GMM estimation but for a more general setup.[37]

Gozalo and Linton (2000) showed uniform consistency of these estimators under quite general assumptions. Simplifying, one could summarise them as follows: to the assumptions used for the local linear regression you have to add assumptions on the behaviour of the criterion function and the existence of (unique) solutions $\hat{\theta}_x$, respectively. Asymptotic normality can be shown when the 'true' vector[38] θ_x^0 is uniquely identified. This again depends on the regularity assumptions applied.

Another interesting result – see Carroll, Ruppert and Welsh (1998) – is that the asymptotic theory becomes quite similar to the results for local polynomial regression when an adequate reparametrisation is conducted. The reparametrisation is necessary as otherwise some (or all) elements of vector θ_x^0 contain (asymptotically) derivatives m^l of different order l, including order 0, i.e. function $m(\cdot)$. A proper reparametrisation separates terms of different convergence rates such that their scores are orthogonal to each other. For example, one wants to achieve that $\theta_{0,x}^0$ contains only $m(x)$, and $\theta_{1,x}^0$ only the gradient of $m(x)$ with scores being orthogonal to the score of $\theta_{0,x}$ giving independent estimates with different convergence rates. This *canonical parametrisation* is setting $\theta_{0,x}^0 = m(x)$ and $\theta_{1,x}^0 = \nabla m(x)$. To get from the original parametrisation of $g(\cdot)$ to a canonical, to be used in (2.52), we look for a $g(X_i, \gamma)$ that solves the system of partial differential equations $g(x, \gamma) = \theta_{0,x}$, $\nabla g(x, \gamma) = \theta_{1,x}$ where γ depends on θ and x. In accordance with the Taylor expansion, the final orthogonal canonical parametrisation then is given by $g(X_i - x, \gamma)$ as will also be seen in the examples below.

Example 2.14 For index models like in Example 2.13 an orthogonal reparametrisation is already given if we use $F\{\theta_{0,x} + \theta_{1,x}'(X_i - x)\}$. But the canonical parametrisation to be used in (2.52) is of the much more complex form

$$F\left\{F^{-1}(\theta_{0,x}) + \theta_{1,x}'(X_i - x)/F'\{F^{-1}(\theta_{0,x})\}\right\}.$$

For such a specifications one obtains for the one-dimensional case with a second-order kernel in (2.50) the bias

---

[37] Local least squares, local likelihood and local estimating equations are essentially equivalent approaches. However, local least squares and local likelihood have the practical advantage over local estimating equations that they can distinguish between multiple optima of the objective function through their objective function value, whereas local estimating equations would treat them all alike.

[38] This refers to the solution for the asymptotic criterion function.

$$E\left[\hat{m}(x) - m(x)\right] = \frac{1}{2}\kappa_2 h^2\left(m''(x) - g''(x, \theta_x^0)\right), \tag{2.53}$$

where θ_x^0 satisfies (2.52) in expectation. The bias is of order h^2 as for the local linear estimator. In addition, the bias is no longer proportional to m'' but rather to $m'' - g''$. When the local model is linear, g'' is zero and the result is the one we obtained for local linear regression. If we use a different local model, the bias will be smaller than for local linear regression if

$$\left|m''(x) - g''(x, \theta_x)\right| < \left|m''(x_0)\right|.$$

Hence, even if we pursue a non-parametric approach, prior knowledge of the shape of the local regression is helpful, especially for bias reduction. If the used prior assumptions are correct, bias will be smaller. If they are wrong, the estimator is still consistent but eventually has a larger bias. Importantly, the first-order term of the variance is $(nh)^{-1}\bar{\kappa}_0\sigma^2(x_0)f^{-1}(x_0)$. So the asymptotic variance of the regression estimator $\hat{m}(x)$ is (in first-order) independent of the parametric model used, and therefore the same as for the local polynomial estimator.

Example 2.15 Recall Example 2.13 with Y being binary, and function $g(\cdot)$ being a logit specification. A quadratic extension would correspond to

$$\frac{1}{1 + e^{\theta_{0,x} + (X_i - x)'\theta_{1,x} + (X_i - x)'\theta_{2,x}(X_i - x)}},$$

where $\theta_{2,x}$ contains also coefficients for mixed terms, i.e. local interactions. This local logit specification with quadratic extensions has the advantage to be bias reducing but requires more assumptions and is more complex to calculate. In fact, with a second-order kernel the bias would be of order h^3 without changing the variance.

Admittedly, the discussion has been a bit vague so far since some further restrictions are required on the local parametric model. If e.g. the local model would be the trivial local constant one, then we should obtain the same results as for Nadaraya–Watson regression, such that (2.53) cannot apply. Roughly speaking, (2.53) applies if the number of coefficients in g is the same as the number of regressors in X plus one (excluding the local constant case). Before we consider the local logit estimator more in detail, we can generally summarise for $\dim(X) = q$ and $\operatorname{order}(K) = r$:

THEOREM 2.10   *Under the assumptions for the local linear regression (and some additional assumptions on the criterion function – see Gozalo and Linton 2000) for all interior points x of the support of X, the local parametric estimator defined as the solution of (2.50) with a kernel of order $r \geq 2$ is uniformly consistent with*

$$\sqrt{nh^q}\{g(x, \hat{\theta}_x) - m(x)\} \to N\left(c_h \frac{1}{r!}\kappa_2(K)\sum_{l=1}^{q}\{m_l^{(r)}(x) - g_l^{(r)}(x, \theta_x^0)\}, \bar{\kappa}_0(K)\frac{\sigma^2(x)}{f(x)}\right),$$

where θ_x^0 as before, $m_l^{(r)}$ and $g_l^{(r)}$ the partial derivatives of order r, $f(\cdot)$ the density of X, $\sigma^2(x)$ the conditional variance of Y, and $c_h = \lim_{n \to \infty} h^r\sqrt{nh^q} < \infty$.

Local Logit Estimation: A Case of Local Likelihood

Because of its particular relevance for the propensity estimation in the context of treatment effect estimation, let us have a closer look at the local logit estimator. For a general introduction to local regression in combination with likelihood based estimation see Loader (1999b). In Examples 2.13 and 2.14, we already discussed the local logit case and a simple orthogonal parametrisation which we will use in the following. We may suppose that the kernel function is a product kernel of order r to facilitate the notation. Define the log likelihood for local logit regression at a location x_0 as

$$
\ln L(x_0, a, b) = \frac{1}{n} \sum_{i=1}^{n} \{ Y_i \ln \Lambda \left(a + b' \left(X_i - x_0 \right) \right)
$$
$$
+ (1 - Y_i) \ln \left(1 - \Lambda \left(a + b' \left(X_i - x_0 \right) \right) \right) \} \cdot K_i
$$

where $\Lambda(x) = \frac{1}{1+e^{-x}}$ and the $K_i = K_h(X_i - x_0)$. We will denote derivatives of $\Lambda(x)$ by $\Lambda'(x)$, $\Lambda''(x)$, $\Lambda^{(3)}(x)$, etc. and note that $\Lambda'(x) = \Lambda(x) \cdot (1 - \Lambda(x))$. Let $\hat{a}$ and $\hat{b}$ be the maximiser of $\ln L(x_0, a, b)$ with a_0, b_0 being the values that maximise the expected value of the likelihood function $E\left[\ln L(x_0, a, b)\right]$. Note that we are interested only in $\hat{a}$, and include $\hat{b}$ only to appeal to the well-known properties that local likelihood or local estimating equations perform better if more than a constant term is included in the local approximation. We estimate $m(x_0)$ by $\hat{m}(x_0) = \Lambda(\hat{a})$. For clarity we may also write $\hat{m}(x_0) = \Lambda(\hat{a}(x_0))$ because the value of $\hat{a}$ varies for different x_0. Similarly, a_0 is a function of x_0, that is $a_0 = a_0(x_0)$. The same applies to $\hat{b}(x_0)$ and $b_0(x_0)$. Most of the time we suppress this dependence to ease notation and focus on the properties at a particular x_0.

In what follows we will also see that $\Lambda(a_0(x_0))$ is identical to $m(x_0)$ up to an $O(h^r)$ term. To derive this, note that since the likelihood function is globally convex, the maximisers are obtained by setting the first-order conditions to zero. The values of $a_0(x_0)$ and $b_0(x_0)$ are thus implicitly defined by the $(1 + \dim(X))$ moment conditions

$$
E \left[\left(Y_i - \Lambda \left(a_0 + b_0' \left(X_i - x_0 \right) \right) \right) \left(\begin{matrix} 1 \\ X_i - x_0 \end{matrix} \right) K_i \right] = 0
$$
$$
\Leftrightarrow E \left[\left(m(X_i) - \Lambda \left(a_0 + b_0' \left(X_i - x_0 \right) \right) \right) \left(\begin{matrix} 1 \\ X_i - x_0 \end{matrix} \right) K_i \right] = 0, \tag{2.54}
$$

written here in vector form.

Let us examine only the first moment condition, as this will give us the estimate for a_0 and thus the regression estimate $\Lambda(\hat{a}_0)$, whereas the others are necessary to identify the gradient or b_0, i.e. the vector of the first-order derivatives of a_0. We obtain

$$
0 = \int \left(m(X_i) - \Lambda \left(a_0 + b_0' \left(X_i - x_0 \right) \right) \right) \cdot K_i \cdot f(X_i) \, dX_i
$$
$$
= \int \left(m(x_0 + uh) - \Lambda \left(a_0 + b_0' uh \right) \right) K(u) \, f(x_0 + uh) du,
$$

where $u = \frac{X_i - x_0}{h}$. Assuming that m is r times differentiable, and noting that the kernel is of order r, we obtain by Taylor expansion that

$$\{m(x_0) - \Lambda(a_0)\} f(x_0) + O(h^r) = 0 \text{ and hence } m(x_0) = \Lambda(a_0) + O(h^r).$$

Combining the previous results we have

$$\hat{m}(x_0) - m(x_0) = \Lambda(\hat{a}(x_0)) - \Lambda(a_0(x_0)) + O_p(h^r),$$

and by Taylor expansion of $\Lambda(\hat{a})$ around $\Lambda(a_0)$ also

$$\hat{m}(x_0) - m(x_0) = \{\hat{a}(x_0) - a_0(x_0)\} \cdot \Lambda'(a_0(x_0)) \cdot \{1 + o_p(1)\} + O_p(h^r). \quad (2.55)$$

Let us now examine $\hat{a}$ in more detail. We denote $(a_0, b_0')'$ by β_0, its estimate by $\hat{\beta} = (\hat{a}, \hat{b}')'$, and set $\mathbb{X}_i = (1, (X_i - x_0)')'$. The first-order condition of the estimator is given by

$$0 = \sum_{i=1}^{n} \left\{ Y_i - \Lambda(\hat{\beta}'\mathbb{X}_i) \right\} K_i \mathbb{X}_i'$$

$$= \sum_{i=1}^{n} \left(Y_i - \Lambda(\beta_0'\mathbb{X}_i) - \Lambda'(\beta_0'\mathbb{X}_i)(\hat{\beta} - \beta_0)'\mathbb{X}_i \right.$$

$$\left. - \Lambda''(\beta_0'\mathbb{X}_i) \cdot (\hat{\beta} - \beta_0)'\mathbb{X}_i\mathbb{X}_i'(\hat{\beta} - \beta_0) - O_p(\|\hat{\beta} - \beta_0\|^3) \right) K_i \mathbb{X}_i'$$

cf. the Taylor expansion. Further we have

$$\hat{\beta} - \beta_0 = \left(\sum_{i=1}^{n} \left\{ \Lambda'(\beta_0'\mathbb{X}_i) + \Lambda''(\beta_0'\mathbb{X}_i)\mathbb{X}_i(\hat{\beta} - \beta_0)' + O_p\left(\|\hat{\beta} - \beta_0\|^2\right) \right\} \mathbb{X}_i\mathbb{X}_i'K_i \right)^{-1}$$

$$\times \sum_{i=1}^{n} \left(Y_i - \Lambda(\beta_0'\mathbb{X}_i) \right) K_i \mathbb{X}_i.$$

As we are only interested in $\hat{a}$ (not in $\hat{b}$), we write

$$\hat{a} - a_0 = e_1' \left(\frac{1}{n} \sum_{i=1}^{n} \left\{ \Lambda'(\beta_0'\mathbb{X}_i) + \Lambda''(\beta_0'\mathbb{X}_i)\mathbb{X}_i(\hat{\beta} - \beta_0)' \right. \right.$$

$$\left. \left. + O_p\left(\|\hat{\beta} - \beta_0\|^2\right) \right\} \mathbb{X}_i\mathbb{X}_i'K_i \right)^{-1} \times \frac{1}{n} \sum_{i=1}^{n} \left(Y_i - \Lambda\{a_0 + b_0'(X_i - x_0)\} \right) K_i \mathbb{X}_i.$$

$$(2.56)$$

For the denominator we start with an approximation to the term

$$\frac{1}{n} \sum_{i=1}^{n} \left\{ \Lambda'(\beta_0'\mathbb{X}_i) + \Lambda''(\beta_0'\mathbb{X}_i)\mathbb{X}_i(\hat{\beta} - \beta_0)' + O_p\left(\|\hat{\beta} - \beta_0\|^2\right) \right\} \mathbb{X}_i\mathbb{X}_i'K_i.$$

Under the assumption that $nh^q \to \infty$ and $h \to 0$, which implies consistency of $\hat{a}$ and $\hat{b}$, one can show that for a kernel of order r this is

$$
= \begin{bmatrix} f(x_0)\Lambda'(a_0) + O_p(h^r) & h^r \frac{\kappa_r}{(r-1)!} \frac{\partial^{r-1}(\Lambda' f(x_0))}{\partial x_1^{r-1}} + o_p(h^r) & \cdots \\ h^r \frac{\kappa_r}{(r-1)!} \frac{\partial^{r-1}(\Lambda' f(x_0))}{\partial x_1^{r-1}} + o_p(h^r) & h^r \frac{\kappa_r}{(r-2)!} \frac{\partial^{r-2}(\Lambda' f(x_0))}{\partial x_1^{r-2}} & \cdots \\ \vdots & \vdots & \ddots \end{bmatrix},
$$

where $\partial^r \left(\Lambda' f(x_0) \right) / \partial x_l^r$ is a shortcut notation for all the cross derivatives of Λ' and $f(x_0)$:

$$
\frac{\partial^r \left(\Lambda' f(x_0) \right)}{\partial x_l^r} \equiv \sum_{l=1}^{r} \Lambda^{(r+1)}(a_0(x_0)) \cdot \frac{\partial^{r-l} f(x_0)}{\partial x_l^{r-l}}. \tag{2.57}
$$

The derivations are similar to those for the local linear estimator and therefore omitted here. An additional complication compared to the derivations for the local linear estimator are the second-order terms, which however are all of lower order when $(\hat{a} - a_0)$ and $(\hat{b} - b_0)$ are $o_p(1)$.

Similarly to the derivations for the local linear estimator one can now derive

$$
e_1' \left(\frac{1}{n} \sum_{i=1}^{n} \left\{ \Lambda'(\beta_0' \mathbb{X}_i) + \Lambda''(\beta_0' \mathbb{X}_i)\mathbb{X}_i (\hat{\beta} - \beta_0)' + O_p \left(||\hat{\beta} - \beta_0||^2 \right) \right\} \mathbb{X}_i \mathbb{X}_i' K_i \right)^{-1}
$$

$$
= \frac{1}{f(x_0)\Lambda'(a_0(x_0))} \left(\begin{array}{c} 1 \\ -h \frac{(r-2)!}{(r-1)!} \left(\frac{\partial^{r-1}(\Lambda' f(x_0))}{\partial x_1^{r-1}} \Big/ \frac{\partial^{r-2}(\Lambda' f(x_0))}{\partial x_1^{r-2}} \right) \\ \vdots \\ -h \frac{(r-2)!}{(r-1)!} \left(\frac{\partial^{r-1}(\Lambda' f(x_0))}{\partial x_d^{r-1}} \Big/ \frac{\partial^{r-2}(\Lambda' f(x_0))}{\partial x_q^{r-2}} \right) \end{array} \right)' \{1 + o_p(1)\}.
$$

$$\tag{2.58}$$

Putting together (2.56) and (2.58) you obtain for (2.55) that

$$
\widehat{m}(x_0) - m(x_0)
$$

$$
= \Lambda'(a_0(x_0)) \cdot e_1' \left(\frac{1}{n} \sum_{i=1}^{n} \left\{ \Lambda'(\beta_0' \mathbb{X}_i) + \Lambda''(\beta_0' \mathbb{X}_i)\mathbb{X}_i (\hat{\beta} - \beta_0)' \right. \right.
$$

$$
\left. \left. + O_p(||\hat{\beta} - \beta_0||^2)\mathbb{X}_i \mathbb{X}_i' \right\} K_i \right)^{-1}
$$

$$
\times \frac{1}{n} \sum_{i=1}^{n} (Y_i - m_i + m_i - \Lambda(a_0 + b_0'(X_i - x_0))) K_i \mathbb{X}_i \cdot (1 + o_p(1)) + O_p(h^r),
$$

$$
= \frac{1}{f(x_0)} \left(\begin{array}{c} 1 \\ -h \frac{(r-2)!}{(r-1)!} \left(\frac{\partial^{r-1}(\Lambda' f(x_0))}{\partial x_1^{r-1}} \Big/ \frac{\partial^{r-2}(\Lambda' f(x_0))}{\partial x_1^{r-2}} \right) \\ \vdots \\ -h \frac{(r-2)!}{(r-1)!} \left(\frac{\partial^{r-1}(\Lambda' f(x_0))}{\partial x_q^{r-1}} \Big/ \frac{\partial^{r-2}(\Lambda' f(x_0))}{\partial x_q^{r-2}} \right) \end{array} \right)'
$$

$$
\times \frac{1}{n} \sum_{i=1}^{n} (Y_i - m_i + m_i - \Lambda \left(a_0 + b_0' (X_j - x_0) \right)) K_i \mathbb{X}_i \cdot (1 + o_p(1)) + O_p(h^r),
$$

where $m_i = m(X_i)$ and $\partial^r \left(\Lambda' f(x_0) \right) / \partial x_1^r$ as defined in (2.57). All in all, we have verified parts of Theorem 2.10 for the local logit case. The calculation of the variance is more tedious, and the normality of the estimator can be derived by the delta method. With similar calculations one could also derive the statistical properties for the derivatives.

The Partial Linear Model and the General Idea of Semi-Parametric Estimation When the Parameter of Interest is Finite

Partially linear models are widely used in the analysis of consumer behaviour, particularly in the analysis of Engel (1857) curves. Let Y be the budget share of a product, X_2 total income and X_1 other household covariates. One often specifies for this a PLM

$$Y = m(X_2) + X_1'\beta + U, \ X_1 \in I\!R^{q_1}, \ X_2 \in I\!R^{q_2},$$

where the relationship between the budget share and income is left completely unspecified. Speckman (1988) introduced several estimators for β which were $\sqrt{n}$ consistent under some smoothness assumptions. The idea is to condition on X_2 and consider

$$Y - E[Y|X_2] = (X_1 - E[X_1|X_2])'\beta + (m(X_2) - E[m(X_2)|X_2]) + (U - E[U|X_2]).$$

Clearly, the second summand and $E[U|X_2]$ equal zero. Hence, one could estimate β by

$$\left(\sum_{i=1}^{n} \left(X_{1,i} - \hat{E}[X_1|X_{2i}] \right) \left(X_{1i} - \hat{E}[X_1|X_{2i}] \right)' \right)^{-1}$$

$$\times \sum_{i=1}^{n} \left(X_{1i} - \hat{E}[X_1|X_{2i}] \right) \left(Y_i - \hat{E}[Y|X_{2i}] \right), \tag{2.59}$$

where the $\hat{E}$ represent non-paramatric estimators. Generally, the statistical properties can be summarised as follows:

THEOREM 2.11   *Under the assumptions of Theorem 2.7 applied to the local linear predictors $\hat{E}[X_1|X_{2i}]$ and $\hat{E}[Y|X_{2i}]$, some additional regularity conditions, and $2r > \dim(X_2)$ for the kernel order, we have for the semi-parametric estimator defined in (2.59) that*

$$\sqrt{n}(\hat{\beta} - \beta) \xrightarrow{d} N\left(0, \sigma^2\varphi^{-1}\right) \tag{2.60}$$

with $\varphi = E\left[(X_1 - E[X_1|X_2])(X_1 - E[X_1|X_2])'\right]$ and $\sigma^2 = E\left[(Y - E[Y|X_2])^2\right]$. Consistent estimates for the variance $\sigma^2\varphi^{-1}$ are given by

$$\hat{\sigma}^2 \left(\frac{1}{n} \sum_{i=1}^{n} \left\{ X_{1i} - \hat{E}[X_1|X_{2i}] \right\} \left\{ X_{1i} - \hat{E}[X_1|X_{2i}] \right\}' \right)^{-1}$$

with $\hat{\sigma}^2 = \frac{1}{n} \sum_{i=1}^{n} \left(\left\{ Y_i - \hat{E}[Y|X_{2i}] \right\} - \left\{ X_{1i} - \hat{E}[X_1|X_{2i}] \right\}'\beta \right)^2.$

Alternative but less efficient estimators are those based on partialling out, i.e.

$$\hat{\beta}_{PO} = \left(\sum_{i=1}^{n} \left\{ X_{1,i} - \hat{E}\left[X_1|X_{2i}\right] \right\} \left\{ X_{1i} - \hat{E}\left[X_1|X_{2i}\right] \right\}' \right)^{-1} \sum_{i=1}^{n} \left\{ X_{1i} - \hat{E}\left[X_1|X_{2i}\right] \right\} Y_i,$$

or on instrumental variable estimation, i.e.

$$\hat{\beta}_{IV} = \left(\sum_{i=1}^{n} \left\{ X_{1,i} - \hat{E}\left[X_1|X_{2i}\right] \right\} X_{1i}' \right)^{-1} \sum_{i=1}^{n} \left\{ X_{1i} - \hat{E}\left[X_1|X_{2i}\right] \right\} Y_i.$$

The condition $2r > \dim(X_2) =: q_2$ is necessary to obtain the parametric $\sqrt{n}$ rate for $\hat{\beta}$ in (2.60). As it is based on non-parametric predictors, one needs to keep their bias small. 'Small' means choosing smoothing parameters for the estimation of the $\hat{E}$ in (2.59) such that their bias is of order $o(n^{-1/2})$. Certainly, as we saw in the section about non-parametric regression, this will slow down the convergence of the variances of the $\hat{E}$. The principle of all semi-parametric estimators is that in the estimator of the parameter of interest, i.e. β in our case, we might be able to average over the n different predictors $\hat{E}\left[X_1|X_{2i}\right]$ and $\hat{E}\left[Y|X_{2i}\right]$, $i = 1, 2, \ldots, n$, respectively. Averaging reduces their impact on the variance by a factor of n, whereas averaging does not help to reduce bias. More specifically, imagine we estimate $\hat{E}\left[Z|X_{2i}\right]$ for $Z = Y$ or $Z = X_1$ with a bias of size $O(h^r)$ (for $r \geq 2$) and a variance of size $O(\frac{1}{nh^{q_2}})$. Then we need to choose h (and r) such that $h^r = o(n^{-1/2})$ and $\frac{1}{nh^{q_2}} = o(1)$. This implicates that we actually need $2r > q_2$, what indicates that for the non-parametric (pre-)estimation of the conditional expectations we must apply bias reducing estimators (higher-order kernels or higher-order local polynomials for example) if the dimension q_2 exceeds 3. Recall that this in turn requires stronger smoothness assumptions, and is computationally more complex. Therefore, the often made statement that the bias reduction methods come for free, is unfortunately wrong.

We now generalise this idea for the case when estimating any finite-dimensional parameter, say β, in the presence of an infinite-dimensional nuisance parameter, say a non-parametric function. Let us denote the data for individual i by the shorthand notation W_i which may contain Y_i, D_i, X_i or any other observed variables of the individuals $i = 1, \ldots, n$. Denote the joint distribution function generating the (observed) data by F. The parameter of interest β could be the average treatment effect or an average outcome for treatment $D = 0$ or $D = 1$. In addition, there is a (possibly non-parametric) function ζ that may depend on β and vice versa. So, when estimating β we call ζ the *infinite nuisance parameter*. This (non-parametric) ζ is also permitted to be a collection of functions, e.g. a regression function $m(x)$ and a density function $f(x)$. Let $\hat{\zeta}$ be any non-parametric estimator, and ζ_0 be the true value.

Consider the score function $M\left(W_i, \beta, \zeta\right)$ or say, the moment condition $E\left[M\left(W, \beta_0, \zeta_0\right)\right] = 0$, where β_0 is the true value. As β_0 and ζ_0 are determined by the data generating process F, for different F we have different β_0 and ζ_0. In other words, the above equation could be written more precisely as

$$E_F\left[M\left(W, \beta_0(F), \zeta_0(F)\right)\right] = 0,$$

where β_0 and ζ_0 are determined by F and the expectation operator is taken with respect to F. A semi-parametric moment estimator $\hat{\beta}$ solves the moment equation

$$\frac{1}{n}\sum_{i=1}^{n} M(W_i, \beta, \hat{\zeta}) = 0. \tag{2.61}$$

If this has a unique solution, under some regularity conditions, the estimator $\hat{\beta}$ converges to β_0 because for $n \to \infty$ also $\hat{\zeta}$ converges to ζ_0, and by the law of large numbers the sample moment converges to the population moment.

For moment estimators it is well established that in the parametric world, i.e. for ζ_0 known, the *influence function* ψ of the moment estimator $\hat{\beta}$, i.e. the one for which $\sqrt{n}\left(\hat{\beta} - \beta_0\right) = \frac{1}{\sqrt{n}}\sum_i \psi(W_i) + O_p(1)$, is given by

$$\psi(W) := -\left(\left.\frac{\partial E[M(W, \beta, \zeta_0)]}{\partial \beta}\right|_{\beta_0}\right)^{-1}\{M(W, \beta_0, \zeta_0)\}, E[\psi(W)] = 0. \tag{2.62}$$

Obviously, the first-order variance of $\hat{\beta}$ is $E[\psi(W)\psi(W)']/n = Var[\psi(W)]/n$.

For β being a non-parametric function, say $\beta(x) = E[Y|x]$, the idea is still the same, except that now $\sqrt{n}\left(\hat{\beta} - \beta_0\right) = \frac{1}{\sqrt{n}}\sum_i \psi(W_i) + b(x) + R(x)$ with $b(x)$ and $R(x)$ being the bias and higher-order terms. For the local linear estimator we have $\psi(Y_i, X_i, x) = \{Y_i - m(X_i)\}K_h(X_i - x)/f(x)$, and it is easy to see that indeed $E[\psi(W)\psi(W)']/n = \frac{1}{n}\sigma^2(x)\kappa_2(K)/f(x)$. For our semi-parametric estimators of a finite dimensional β with infinite dimensional ζ all this looks a bit more complex. Yet, in practice it often has a quite simple meaning as can be seen from the following example.

Example 2.16 For calculating an average treatment effect we often need to predict the expected counterfactual outcome $E[Y^d]$ for a given (externally set) treatment $D = d$.[39] An example of a semi-parametric estimator is the so-called matching estimator, see Chapter 3

$$\widehat{E[Y^d]} = \frac{1}{n}\sum_{i=1}^{n} \hat{m}_d(X_i)$$

with $\hat{m}_d(X_i)$ being non-parametric predictors for the expected outcome Y_i under treatment $D = d$. This can be written as

$$\sum_{i=1}^{n}(\hat{m}_d(X_i) - \beta) = 0$$

resulting from the moment condition

$$E[m_d(X_i) - \beta_0] = 0$$

where $\beta_0 = E[Y^d]$ and $\zeta_0 = m_d$. For more details see the next chapter.

---

[39] Here Y^d denotes the potential outcome Y given D is set externally to d; recall Chapter 1.

In this example the problem of using a non-parametric predictor for the estimation of a finite dimensional parameter is almost eliminated by averaging it to a one-dimensional number. We say almost because we actually need an adjustment term, say $\alpha(\cdot)$, like $b(\cdot) + R(\cdot)$ for the non-parametric regression above. It is called *adjustment term* as it adjusts for the nuisance term (or its estimation). For the semi-parametric estimators we consider, this directly enters the influence function so that we get an estimator of kind (2.61) with variance $E\left[\psi(W)\psi(W)'\right]$ divided by n, where

$$\psi(W) = -\left(\left.\frac{\partial E\left[M\left(W, \beta, \zeta_0\right)\right]}{\partial \beta}\right|_{\hat{\beta}}\right)^{-1} \{M\left(W, \beta_0, \zeta_0\right) + \alpha(W)\} \qquad (2.63)$$

is the influence function, and $\alpha(W)$ the adjustment term for the non-parametric estimation of ζ_0. If ζ_0 contains several components (subsequently or simultaneously), then the adjustment factor is the sum of the adjustment factors relating to each component being previously estimated. This gives the general form of how the asymptotic variance of $\hat{\beta}$ would usually look. One still has to specify precise regularity conditions under which the estimator actually achieves $\sqrt{n}$ consistency (without first-order bias). It also should be mentioned that there may exist situations where $\sqrt{n}$ estimation of the finite-dimensional parameter is not achievable.[40]

How do these adjustment factors look? At least for the case where the nuisance ζ_0 consists of $\partial^\lambda m(x) = \partial^{|\lambda|} m(x)/\partial x_1^{\lambda_1} \cdots \partial x_q^{\lambda_q}$, i.e. partial derivatives of $m(x) = E[\cdot|X = x]$ (including $|\lambda| = 0$, the conditional expectation itself), there exists a general formula.[41] In fact, under some (eventually quite strong) regularity assumptions it holds

$$\alpha(w) = (-1)^{|\lambda|} \cdot \frac{\partial^\lambda \left(\bar{T}(x) \cdot f(x)\right)}{f(x)} \cdot \{y - m(x)\}, \quad f(x) \text{ the density of } X \qquad (2.64)$$

$$\text{where } \bar{T}(x) = E\left[T(W)|X = x\right] \text{ with } T(w) = \left.\frac{\partial M\left(w, \beta_0, \zeta\right)}{\partial \zeta}\right|_{\zeta = \partial^\lambda m(x)}. \qquad (2.65)$$

We will use this frequently, e.g. for the prediction of the expected potential outcome $E[Y^d]$, where d indicates the treatment.

Semi-Parametric Efficiency Bounds

We now have an idea of a way how to get rid of the first order bias and how to determine the variance of the semi-parametric estimators we will need to estimate. But how do we know whether these are 'good' estimators, at least asymptotically? In parametric estimation, the analysis of efficiency is greatly simplified by the Cramér–Rao bounds and the Gauss–Markov theorem. Both these theorems establish, for a large class of models, lower bounds on the variance of any estimator within this class. Hence, no estimator in that class can have a variance lower than this bound, and any estimator that attains this bound is asymptotically efficient.

A similar type of variance bound exists for many semi-parametric problems if $\sqrt{n}$ consistent estimation of the (finite-dimensional) parameter of interest, say β, is possible. Semi-parametric efficiency bounds were introduced by Stein (1956) and further

---

[40] A popular example is the binary fixed effects panel data M-score estimator of Manski.

[41] It also exists if ζ_0 consists of the density $f(x)$ or its derivatives, but we skip it here as we won't use that.

developed by Koshevnik and Levit (1976) and Bickel, Klaassen, Ritov and Wellner (1993). If such a *semi-parametric variance bound* exists, no semi-parametric estimator can have lower variance than this bound, and any estimator that attains this bound is semi-parametrically efficient. Furthermore, a variance bound that is infinitely large tells us that no $\sqrt{n}$ consistent estimator exists.

Not surprisingly, the derivation of such bounds can easily be illustrated for the likelihood context. Consider the log-likelihood

$$\ln L_n (\beta, \zeta) = \frac{1}{n} \sum_{i=1}^{n} \ln L (W_i, \beta, \zeta),$$

that is maximised at the values β_0 and ζ_0 where the derivative has expectation zero. When the nuisance parameter ζ_0 is finite dimensional, then the information matrix provides the Cramér–Rao lower bound β, using partitioned inversion

$$V^* = \left(\mathcal{I}_{\beta\beta} - \mathcal{I}_{\beta\zeta} \mathcal{I}_{\zeta\zeta}^{-1} \mathcal{I}_{\zeta\beta} \right)^{-1} \tag{2.66}$$

where $\mathcal{I}_{\beta\beta}, \mathcal{I}_{\beta\zeta}, \mathcal{I}_{\zeta\zeta}, \mathcal{I}_{\zeta\beta}$ are the respective submatrices of the information matrix for (β, ζ). For maximum likelihood (ML) estimation we obtain

$$\sqrt{n}(\hat{\beta} - \beta) \xrightarrow{d} N(0, V^*).$$

A non-zero $\mathcal{I}_{\beta\zeta}$ indicates that there is an efficiency loss when ζ is unknown.

Now let ζ_0 be non-parametric, i.e. an infinite-dimensional parameter. Then, loosely speaking, the semi-parametric variance bound V^{**} is the largest variance V^* over all possible parametric models that nest $\ln L_n (\beta, \zeta_0)$ for some value of ζ.[42] An estimator that attains the semi-parametric variance bound

$$\sqrt{n}(\hat{\beta} - \beta) \xrightarrow{d} N(0, V^{**}) \tag{2.67}$$

is called *semi-parametrically efficient*. In some situations, the semi-parametric estimator may even obtain the variance V^*, which means that considering ζ as a non-parametric function does not lead to an efficiency loss in the first-order approximation. These are called *adaptive*.

Example 2.17 Take the classical additive linear regression model

$$Y_i = \beta' X_i + \varepsilon_i, \quad \text{where } \varepsilon_i \sim (0, \sigma^2(X_i))$$

with independent observations and unknown function $\sigma^2(\cdot)$. It is known that a generalised least squares estimator with weights being inverse proportional to non-parametric predictors of $\sigma^2(X_i)$ can be optimal.

In some situations, semi-parametric efficiency bounds have been derived but no estimator is known that attains this bound. I.e. although there exist $\sqrt{n}$ consistent estimators, they all have variance larger than V^{**}.

---

[42] This is why in profiled likelihood estimation the estimators of the infinite-dimensional nuisance parameter are often called the *least favourable curve*.

Remains the question how to get V^{**}. Let β denote the object of interest which depends on the true distribution function $F(w)$ of the data W. Let $f(w)$ be the density of the data. Let $\mathcal{F}$ be a general family of distributions and $\{F_\theta : F_\theta \in \mathcal{F}\}$ a one-dimensional subfamily ($\theta \in I\!R$) of $\mathcal{F}$ with $F_{\theta=\theta_0}$ being the true distribution function, and $F_{\theta \neq \theta_0}$ the other distributions from class $\mathcal{F}$. The *pathwise derivative* $\delta(\cdot)$ of $\beta(F)$ is a vector of functions defined by

$$\left.\frac{\partial \beta(F_\theta)}{\partial \theta}\right|_{\theta=\theta_0} = E\left[\delta(W) \cdot S(W)|_{\theta=\theta_0}\right], \qquad (2.68)$$

such that $E[\delta(W)] = 0$ and $E[\|\delta(W)\|^2] < \infty$ with $S(w) = \partial \ln f(w|\theta)/\partial\theta$ the score function. Clearly, the latter has expectation zero for $\theta = \theta_0$ as

$$E_{\theta_0}[S(W)] = \int \left.\frac{\partial \ln f(w|\theta)}{\partial\theta}\right|_{\theta=\theta_0} f(w|\theta_0)dw = \frac{\partial}{\partial\theta}\int f(w|\theta_0)dw = 0,$$

provided conditions for interchanging integration and differentiation. The semi-parametric variance bound V^{**}/n for $\hat{\beta}$ is then given by $Var[\delta(W)]/n$.[43] Not surprisingly, under some regularity conditions, $\delta(\cdot)$ is the influence-function $\psi(\cdot)$ introduced in the preceding paragraph.

Example 2.18 A popular example is the estimation of the finite-dimensional parameter $\beta = E[f(W)]$. This obviously could be estimated by $\frac{1}{n}\sum_{i=1}^{n} \hat{f}(W_i)$ with a non-parametric kernel density estimator $\hat{f}$. Clearly, $\beta = \int f^2(w|\theta_0)dw$ and $\partial\beta(F_{\theta_0})/\partial\theta = \int 2\partial f(w|\theta_0)/\partial\theta \cdot f(w|\theta_0)$. As the score function is simply $\partial f(w|\theta)/\partial\theta \cdot f^{-1}(w|\theta)$, it is easy to verify that function $\delta(w) = 2(f(w|\theta_0) - \beta_0)$ satisfies (2.68) and has also mean zero. Consequently, the semi-parametric variance bound is $Var[\delta(W)] = 4Var[f(W|\theta_0)]$ divided by n.

We will see some more examples in the next chapter. A particularity there is that the binary treatment indicator D acts as a trigger that may change the true joint distribution f of $W_i = (Y_i, X_i)$, where treatment occurs with probability $p(x|\theta) := \Pr(D = 1|x; \theta)$. For finding the $\delta(W)$, it then helps a lot to decompose the score $S(w)$ along the three cases $d = 0$, $d = 1$, and $d - p(x)$. Suppressing the θ inside the functions you use

$$f(Y, X, D) = f(Y|D, X) f(D|X) f(X)$$
$$= \{f_1(Y|X) p(X)\}^D \{f_0(Y|X)(1 - p(X))\}^{1-D} f(x)$$

where $f_d(Y|X) \equiv f(Y|D = d, X)$, $d = 0, 1$. This leads to the score function

$$S(w) = d\frac{\partial \ln f_1(y|x)}{\partial\theta} + (1 - d)\frac{\partial \ln f_0(y|x)}{\partial\theta} + \frac{d - p(x)}{1 - p(x)}\frac{\partial \ln p(x)}{\partial\theta} + \frac{\partial \ln f(x)}{\partial\theta}$$
$$(2.69)$$

giving us the set of zero-mean functions spanning the (proper) tangent space.

---

[43] More specifically, the semi-parametric efficiency bound is equal to the expectation of the squared projection of function $\delta(\cdot)$ on the *tangent space* of the model $\mathcal{F}$ (for more details see Bickel, Klaassen, Ritov and Wellner 1993) which is the space spanned by the partial derivatives of the log-densities with respect to θ.

2.2.4   A Note on Sieves: Series Estimators and Splines

Before concluding this introduction to non- and semi-parametric regression, less localised nonparametric approaches should also be mentioned, in particular sieve estimators such as series regression and splines. For the latter, the localised versions are today the most popular; to some extent they can actually be considered as being equivalent to kernel estimators.[44] In contrast to kernel regression, which is based on smoothing in a local neighbourhood, series estimators are typically global[45] parametric estimators where the number of parameters grows with sample size n. A reasonable sequence of growing parameter subsets will asymptotically span the full parameter space then. This idea is again independent from the estimation approach, whether it be based on a likelihood function, a least squares expression or some generalised moment conditions. Actually, Grenander (1981) suggested performing the optimisation of the objective function (the log-likelihood, sum of least squared errors, etc.) within a subset of the full parameter space, and then allow this subset to 'grow' with the sample size. He called the resulting estimation procedure the *method of sieves*. The advantage of such an approach is that for finite samples the actual specification is a parametric one so that both, the implementation and the mixing of parametric and non-parametric parts seem to be much simpler with lower computational costs. This explains their popularity in practice.[46] Unfortunately, especially in the econometrics literature, there are several papers circulating that also state or insinuate a (statistical) superiority over the smoothing methods. A careful reading of these articles, however, reveals that in their assumptions it is implicitly supposed to have additional information about the (smoothness) class of the non-parametric function. As we learnt in the above sections, such knowledge could also be exploited e.g. by kernel methods, whether by higher-order kernels, higher-order polynomials or appropriate local parametric models. All this leads to bias reduction and/or faster convergence rates, too. Moreover, it is not hard to see that global estimators will always perform worse than smoothers if either the chosen basis or the parameter subspace does not well adapt to the true underlying function, see also Exercise 12.

Global approaches can be convenient to ensure that $\hat{m}$ satisfies certain properties, such as monotonicity or convexity. Other advantages, as mentioned, are the simple implementation and low computational costs. Also, people feel more comfortable with them when they are constructed in such a way that for any finite sample they are simply parametric extensions of well-known parametric models. However, the last point can also be considered as a disadvantage as this can easily induce people to misinterpretations of the empirical results. For smoothing methods, a particular disadvantage of splines is that asymptotic theory turned out to be very hard for the multivariate case, and for many models and procedures, little is known about the asymptotic behaviour of the estimators.

---

[44] For the mathematical details see the work of Schwarz and Krivobokova (2016).

[45] As always, you will certainly find examples that might be considered as exceptions like e.g. wavelet estimators with a Haar basis and high-resolution levels.

[46] This popularity is boosted by the common practice in econometrics (not so in statistics, biometrics, etc.) to resort to the corresponding parametric inference tools, though then it no longer has much to do with non- or semi-parametric analysis.

Throughout this subsection we keep the introduced notation, considering the problem of estimation of the regression function $m(\cdot)$ in a model of the type

$$Y = m(X) + \varepsilon, \qquad E[\varepsilon|X] = E[\varepsilon] = 0, \quad Var[\varepsilon|X] = \sigma^2(X) < \infty \qquad (2.70)$$

and having observed an i.i.d. sample $\{Y_i, X_i\}_{i=1}^n$ with $Y \in \mathbb{R}$ and $X \in \mathbb{R}^q$. Again, function $m(\cdot)$ is assumed to be smooth, and X a vector of continuous variables.

Series Estimators for Regression

Series regression is a global smoothing method like conventional parametric regression but with an increasing number of regressors. Let X be a scalar $(q = 1)$. A series regression based on the (in empirical economics) quite popular *power series* estimates is just a regression on $1, x, x^2, x^3, x^4$, etc. Clearly, for higher dimensions $(q > 1)$ also the interaction terms ought to be included; e.g. for the two-dimensional case

$$1, x_1, x_2, x_1 x_2, x_1^2, x_2^2, x_1^2 x_2, x_1 x_2^2, x_1^3, x_2^3, \ldots$$

The number of regressors included has to grow to infinity with sample size n to make this procedure 'non-parametric'.[47] The number of terms included for a given data set can be obtained by cross-validation. In practice, however, people start with series of already very low order and then use t- or at best F-tests to reduce the series even more. The power series is a particularly bad choice due to several problems, collinearity being one of them. Alternative series are usually more appropriate but less used in econometrics. A large number of more attractive basis functions exists, which one should choose accordingly to the characteristics of $m(x)$. E.g. if $m(x)$ is periodic, then a flexible Fourier series would be adequate. If X has support $[0, 1]$, Chebyshev or Legendre polynomials may be appealing. Clearly, the complexity can be arbitrarily increased up to series that are local smoothers like e.g. wavelets or B-splines.

The motivation for series estimators is given by the result that any square integrable real valued function can be uniquely expressed by a linear combination of linearly independent functions $\{B_j(x)\}_{j=1}^\infty$, s.th.

$$E[Y|x] = m(x) = \sum_{l=1}^\infty b_l \cdot B_l(x).$$

Therefore, a finite series approximation and its estimator is given by

$$m(x) = \sum_{l=1}^L b_l \cdot B_l(x), \qquad \hat{m}(x) = \sum_{l=1}^L \hat{b}_l \cdot B_l(x), \qquad (2.71)$$

for a particular choice of smoothing (or tuning) parameter L. The coefficients b_l can be estimated by ordinary least squares, i.e.

$$\hat{\mathbf{b}} = (\hat{b}_1, \ldots, \hat{b}_L)' = \left(\mathbf{B}^{L'}\mathbf{B}^L\right)^{-1}\left(\mathbf{B}^{L'}\mathbb{Y}\right),$$

---

[47] Actually, there is a general confusion about the notion of what 'non-parametric' means as it actually refers to an infinite-dimensional parameter or, in other words, an infinite number of parameters rather than to 'no parameters'.

where $\mathbb{Y}$ is the vector of all $\{Y_i\}_{i=1}^n$ observations and $\mathbf{B}^L$ is the matrix composed of all $B_1(X_i), \ldots, B_L(X_i)$ for all n observations.

The asymptotic theory for series estimators is different from kernels. For many, no closed-form expressions are derived, or only results on the rates of convergence are available. Certain basis functions that permit a convenient derivation of asymptotic properties may lead to problems of collinearity in estimation. Therefore, they may be used to derive the theoretical properties, but orthogonalised series need to be used in practice, like the *Legendre polynomials*. The trick is that this change in the basis functions does not change the estimators asymptotic properties as long as the two bases span the same space. Most popular series in statistics are the so-called *wavelets* (Daubechies 1992) as they are flexible in the scale and the time domain.

The main disadvantages of global estimators are (1) that they seduce people to extrapolate, (2) people use them like parametric models, and then strongly underestimate confidence intervals, and (3) they often exhibit particularly bad performance for prediction. As we will see in the later chapters, these failures can be especially harmful for our purpose of treatment effect estimation. A different estimation approach with sieves is offered by (penalised) splines; they are local estimators, quite similar to kernels but computationally much more attractive as long as $dim(X) = 1$. As the spline estimators have an analytical parametric representation, the inclusion of dummy variables in the set of covariates is straightforward. In fact, the only reason why we have been giving a preference to kernel smoothing (in the previous and following pages) is that spline estimators are less appealing when two or more continuous covariates are present.

Splines

The term *spline* originates from ship building, where it denoted a flexible strip of wood used to draw smooth curves through a set of points on a section of the ship. There, the spline (curve) passes through all the given points and is therefore referred to as an 'interpolating spline'. In the regression context, interpolation is obviously not the objective; you rather look for a smooth version of such an interpolation. Today, splines have been widely studied in the statistics literature (see Rice 1986, Heckman 1986 or Wahba 1990 for early references) and are extensively used in different domains of applied statistics including biometrics and engineering, but less so in econometrics. Splines are basically piecewise polynomials that are joined at certain *knots* which, in an extreme case, can be all the x_i observations. Therefore, they are also quite popular for non-linear interpolation.

There exist many different versions of spline estimators even when using the same functional basis. Take cubic polynomials, called *cubic splines*. One may differentiate between the three classes: regression splines, smoothing splines and penalised splines (also called P-splines, especially when combined with the B-spline basis – see below). The latter ones are basically compromises between the first two and belong asymptotically to either one or the other class, depending on the rate at which the number of knots increases with the sample size: see Claeskens, Krivobokova and Opsomer (2009).

To simplify notation let us consider the one-dimensional case, setting $q = 1$ with ordered observations $a \leq x_1 < x_2 < \cdots < x_n \leq b$ for some known scalars $a, b \in \mathbb{R}$. Further, we will consider cubic splines for all types of splines we discuss below, i.e. we will always work with piecewise third-order polynomials.

Regression Splines
One starts by defining L values ξ_l, so-called *knots* that separate the interval $[a, b]$ in convenient $L + 1$ non-overlapping intervals, i.e. $a < \xi_1 < \cdots < \xi_L < b$ with $a \leq x_{min}, b \geq x_{max}$. One could introduce the notation $\xi_0 = a$, $\xi_{L+1} = b$. Fitting a cubic polynomial in each interval has at least two obvious drawbacks: one has to estimate $4(L + 1)$ parameters in total, and the function is not continuous as it may exhibit jumps at each knot. Both can be overcome at once by imposing restrictions on the smoothness of the estimate $\hat{m}(x)$ of $E[Y|x]$. Making $\hat{m}$ continuous requires L linear restrictions, and the same holds true for making $\hat{m}$ smooth by imposing linear restrictions that also make the first and second derivative continuous. Then we have only $4(L + 1) - 3L = L + 4$ parameters to be estimated with a piecewise (i.e. in each interval) constant $\hat{m}'''$. One can further reduce the number of parameters to only $L + 2$ by imposing restrictions at the boundaries like making $\hat{m}$ to be a straight line outside $[a, b]$. The result is called a *natural cubic spline*.

Example 2.19 Imagine we choose a single knot $\xi = 0$, so that we consider only two polynomials. Then the conditional expectation of Y given x is represented as

$$m(x) = \begin{cases} m_1(x) & = & \alpha_0 + \alpha_1 x + \alpha_2 x^2 + \alpha_3 x^3 & \text{for} & x \leq 0 \\ m_2(x) & = & \beta_0 + \beta_1 x + \beta_2 x^2 + \beta_3 x^3 & \text{for} & x > 0 \end{cases}.$$

The smoothness restrictions impose: continuity of $\hat{m}(x)$ at $x = 0$ such that $m_1(0) = m_2(0)$ requiring $\beta_0 = \alpha_0$; continuity of $\hat{m}'(x)$ at $x = 0$ such that $m_1'(0) = m_2'(0)$ requiring $\beta_1 = \alpha_1$; and continuity of $\hat{m}''(x)$ at $x = 0$ such that $m_1''(0) = m_2''(0)$ requiring $\beta_2 = \alpha_2$. So we end up with

$$m(x) = \begin{cases} m_1(x) & = & \alpha_0 + \alpha_1 x + \alpha_2 x^2 + \alpha_3 x^3 & \text{for} & x \leq 0 \\ m_2(x) & = & \alpha_0 + \alpha_1 x + \alpha_2 x^2 + \alpha_3 x^3 + \theta_1 x^3 & \text{for} & x > 0 \end{cases}.$$

with $\theta_1 = \beta_3 - \alpha_3$.

The idea of Example 2.19 extends to any number $L > 0$ of knots so that we can generally write a cubic regression spline as

$$m(x) = \alpha_0 + \alpha_1 x + \alpha_2 x^2 + \alpha_3 x^3 + \sum_{l=1}^{L} \theta_l (x - \xi_l)_+^3 \text{ where } z_+ = z\{z > 0\}. \quad (2.72)$$

Although x, x^2 and x^3 are not linearly independent, it is obvious that an orthogonalised version can again be written in terms of (2.71). For equation (2.72) one can estimate all parameters α_k, $k = 0, 1, 2, 3$ and θ_l, $l = 1, \ldots, L$ via a standard OLS procedure. All we have to do in advance is the creation of a design matrix that includes the $1, x, x^2, x^3$

and $(x - \xi_l)^3_+$ terms. However, procedures based on this simple representation are often unstable as for many knots (large L) the projection matrix is often almost singular. In practice one uses so-called B-bases, see below, which lead to the same fit in theory.[48]

As the estimator is a parametric approximation of the true function but without penalising wiggliness or imposing other smoothness than continuity (of the function and some derivatives), the final estimator now has a so-called 'approximation bias' but no 'smoothing bias'. Nonetheless, the number of knots L plays a similar role as the bandwidth h for kernel regression or the number of neighbours in the kNN estimator. For consistency L must converge to infinity but at a slower rate than n does. For L close to n you interpolate (like for $h = 0$), whereas for $L = 0$ you obtain a simple cubic polynomial estimate (like for $h = \infty$ in local cubic regression). One might use generalised cross-validation (2.39) to choose a proper L.

Smoothing Splines

As both the number and location of knots is subject to the individual choice of the empirical researcher, the so-called *smoothing splines* gained rapidly in popularity. They, in the end, are a generalisation of the original interpolation idea based on cubic splines. The motivation for this generalisation is twofold: in model (2.70) one does not want to interpolate the Y with respect to the X but smooth out the errors ε to identify the mean function. This way one also gets rid of the problem that arises when several (but different) responses Y for the same X are observed (so-called *bins*). Pure interpolation is not possible there, and the natural solution would be to predict for those X the average of the corresponding responses. The smoothing now automatically tackles this problem.

Smoothness is related to 'penalisation' if smoothing is a result of keeping the dth derivative $m^{(d)}(\cdot)$ under control. More specifically, one penalises for high oscillations by minimising

$$\frac{1}{n} \sum (y_i - m(x_i))^2 + \lambda \int_a^b \left(m^{(d)}(x)\right)^2 dx, \tag{2.73}$$

with $m(\cdot)$ typically being a polynomial and λ the smoothing parameter corresponding to the bandwidth. It controls the trade-off between optimal fit to the data (first part) and the roughness penalty (second part). Evidently, for $\lambda = 0$ the minimising function would be the interpolation of all data points, and for $\lambda \to \infty$, the function becomes a straight line with $m^{(d)} \equiv 0$ that passes through the data as the least squares fit. As above, it can be chosen e.g. by (generalised) cross-validation.

Reinsch (1967) considered the Sobolev space of C^2 functions with square integrable second derivatives ($d = 2$). Then the solution to (2.73) is a piecewise cubic polynomial whose third derivative jumps at a set of points of measure zero. The knots are the data points $\{x_i\}_{i=1}^n$. Hence, the solution itself, its first and its second derivative are continuous everywhere. The third derivative is continuous almost everywhere and jumps at the knots. The fourth derivative is zero almost everywhere. These conditions provide a finite dimensional set of equations, for which explicit solutions are available. Actually, smoothing splines yield a linear smoother, i.e. the fitted values are linear in $\mathbb{Y}$.

---

[48] See, for example, chapter 2 of Hastie and Tibshirani (1990) for further details.

For a particular case (thin plate splines), see below. Similar to kernel estimators, the method is a penalised (i.e. smoothed) interpolation. Therefore these estimators have only a smoothing (also called shrinkage) but no approximation bias. It disappears with λ going to zero (while $n \to \infty$ as otherwise its variance would go to infinity). Again, cross validation is a popular method for choosing λ.

Penalised Splines
Eilers and Marx (1996) introduced a mixture of smoothing and regression splines. The idea is to use many knots (i.e. large L) such that one does not have to care much about their location and approximation error. For example, for the set of knots one often takes every fifth, tenth or twentieth observation x_i (recall that we assume them to be ordered). As many knots typically lead to a large variance of the coefficients that correspond to the highest order, our θ_l in (2.72), one introduces a penalisation like for the smoothing splines. More specifically, one still considers a regression problem like in (2.72) but restricting the variation of the coefficients θ_l. This can be thought of as a mixed effects model where the α_k, $k = 0, 1, 2, 3$ are fixed effects, and the θ_l, $l = 1, \ldots, L$ are treated like random effects. Then, λ from (2.73) equals the ratio: the variance of θ (σ_θ^2) by the variance of noise ε (σ_ε^2). For a stable implementation one often does not simply use the polynomials from (2.72) but a more complex spline basis; see below for some examples. The final estimator is the minimiser of

$$\sum_{i=1}^{n} \left\{ y_i - \sum_l b_l B_l(x_i) \right\}^2 + \lambda \int_a^b \left\{ \left[\sum_l b_l B_l(x) \right]^{(d)} \right\}^2 dx, \qquad (2.74)$$

where $[\ldots]^{(d)}$ indicates the dth derivative. In Equation 2.74 we have not specified the limits for index l as they depend on the chosen spline basis. How in general a penalised regression spline can be transformed into a mixed effects model in which the penalisation simply converts into an equilibration of σ_θ^2 vs σ_ε^2 is outlined in Curie and Durban (2002) and Wand (2003). Clearly, the bias of this kind of estimator is a combination of approximation and shrinkage bias.

While for the regression splines the main (but in practice often unsolved) question was the choice of number and placing of knots, for smoothing and penalised splines the proper choice of parameter λ is the focus of interest. Today, the main two competing procedures to choose λ (once L is fixed) are generalised cross-validation and the so-called *restricted (or residual, or reduced) maximum likelihood (REML)* which estimates the variances of ε and of the 'random effects' θ simultaneously. Which of these methods performs better depends on the constellation of pre-fixed L and the smoothness of $m(\cdot)$. Not surprisingly, depending on whether L is relatively large or whether λ is relatively small, either the approximation or the shrinkage bias is of smaller order.

Popular Spline Bases and Multivariate Splines
Apart from taking trivial piecewise cubic polynomials, the *thin plate splines* and *B-splines* are probably the most popular ones. The latter is appealing especially for our purpose because it is strictly local. Each basis function is non-zero only over the interval(s) between $p + 2$ adjacent knots, where p is the polynomial order of the basis,

e.g. $p = 3$ for cubic ones. Define knots as before from $a = \xi_0$ to $\xi_{L+1} = b$, and set $\xi_j = \xi_0$ for $j < 0$, $\xi_j = \xi_{L+1}$ for $j > L$ such that the interval over which the spline is to be evaluated lies within $[a, b]$. Recall representation (2.71), but for notational convenience and only for the next formula let us provide the basis functions B_l with a hyperindex indicating the polynomial order, i.e. B_l^p. Then, a B-spline of order p is defined recursively as

$$B_l^p(x) = \frac{x - \xi_l}{\xi_{l+p} - \xi_l} B_l^{p-1}(x) + \frac{\xi_{l+p+1} - x}{\xi_{l+p+1} - \xi_{l+1}} B_{l+1}^{p-1}(x), \quad j = 1, \ldots, k$$

$$\text{with} \quad B_l^0(x) = \mathbb{1}\{\xi_l \le x < \xi_{l+1}\}. \quad (2.75)$$

The use of a B-spline basis within penalised splines led to the expression *P-splines*. They are particularly popular for non-parametric additive models. The often praised simplicity of P-splines gets lost, however, when more complex knot spacing or interactions are required.

Thin plate splines were invented to avoid the allocation of knots, and to facilitate an easy extension of splines to multivariate regression. They are often used for smoothing splines, i.e. to estimate the vector of $E[\mathbb{Y}|x_1, x_2, \ldots, x_n]$ by minimising

$$\|\mathbb{Y} - \mathbf{m}\|^2 + \lambda J_r(m), \quad \mathbf{m} = (m(x_1), m(x_2), \ldots, m(x_n))', \quad x_i \in \mathbb{R}^q, \quad (2.76)$$

where J_r is a penalty for wiggliness $J_r(m) = \int (\partial^r m / \partial u^r)^2 du$ for the univariate case, else

$$J_r(m) = \int \cdots \int \sum_{v_1 + \cdots + v_q = r} \frac{r!}{v_1! \cdots v_q!} \left(\frac{\partial^r m}{\partial u_1^{v_1} \ldots \partial u_q^{v_q}} \right)^2 du_1 d_2 \cdots du_q.$$

For visually smooth results $2r > q + 1$ is required. The calculation of thin plates is computationally costly, so that today only approximations, the so-called *thin plate regression splines* are in use. It can be shown that the solution of them (or their simplification) to estimate $m(\cdot)$ at a given point depends only on the Euclidean distances between the observations x_i, $i = 1, \ldots, n$ and that point. Therefore, for $q > 1$ one also speaks of *isotropic thin plate smoothing*.

An extension of the simple regression cubic splines or B- or P-splines to higher dimensions is much less obvious. The method that's probably most frequently used is applying the so-called *tensor products*. The idea is pretty simple: for each variable X_j, $j = 1, \ldots, q$ calculate the spline basis functions $B_{j,l}(x_{j,i})$, $l = 1, \cdots, L_j$, for all observations $i = 1, \ldots, n$. Then expression (2.71) becomes (for a given point $x_0 \in \mathbb{R}^q$)

$$m(x_0) = \sum_{l_1=1}^{L_1} \cdots \sum_{l_q=1}^{L_q} b_{l_1 \cdots l_q} \prod_{j=1}^{q} B_{j,l_j}(x_{0,j}), \quad b_{l_1 \cdots l_q} \text{ unknown},$$

(here for simplicity without penalisation). This looks quite complex though it is just crossing each basis function from one dimension with all basis functions of all the other dimensions. Already for $q = 3$ this gets a bit cumbersome. Unfortunately, using thin plates or tensor products can lead to quite different figures, depending on the choice of knots and basis functions. These problems lead us to favour kernel based estimation, although splines are attractive alternatives when only one or two continuous covariates are involved or additivity is imposed.

Notes on Asymptotic Properties

A lot of work has been done to study the statistical properties under different conditions. However, without fixing the basis function, knots and design density, typically only convergence rates are obtained. We already noticed that the main difference in their asymptotics is in the bias: regression splines have an approximation bias, smoothing splines a shrinkage bias, and penalised splines a combination of both.

Claeskens, Krivobokova and Opsomer (1998) calculated for $m(\cdot) \in C^{p+1}$ the asymptotics for P-splines, and afterwards related them to regression and smoothing splines, respectively. Generally, the approximation bias of a regression spline estimator is of order $O(L^{-(p+1)})$ for $L = o(n)$ and knots such that $\delta = \max_j (\xi_{j+1} - \xi_j) = o(L^{-1})$, and the variance is of order $O(\frac{L}{n}) + o(\frac{1}{n\delta})$. For smoothing splines with smoothing parameter λ the average mean squared error is of order $O(n^{1/(2d)-1}\lambda^{-1/(2d)}) + O(\frac{\lambda}{n})$ with the first term referring to the squared bias. For P-splines they proved that for $(L + p + 1 - d)(\lambda c/n)^{1/(2d)} < 1$ with c converging to a constant that only depends on d and the design, recall (2.74), the average mean squared error was of order $O(L/n) + O(\{\lambda L^d/n\}^2) + O(1/L^{2(p+1)})$ for $L = o(n)$, but else of order $O(n^{1/(2d)-1}\lambda^{-1/(2d)}) + O(\lambda/n) + O(1/L^{2d})$. This means that for the former case the P-splines behave asymptotically like regression splines (if λ is small enough) but otherwise more like smoothing splines. See Zhou, Shen and Wolfe (1998) for more details on the asymptotics of regression spline estimators, and Utreras (1985) for those of smoothing splines.

2.3   Bibliographic and Computational Notes

2.3.1   Further Reading and Bibliographic Notes

There is a whole bunch of contributions to causality and identification in the statistical literature which we have not mentioned in this chapter: see, for example, Holland (1986). This is especially true for the field of biometrics, though a standard reference is doubtless the seminal paper of Rubin (1974). The discussion is much more diverse and partly controversial in social sciences (see e.g. Moffitt 2004) and economics (see e.g. Meyer 1995). For a critical discussion of the differences between econometric and statistical treatment effect analysis we refer to Heckman (2008) and Heckman (2001). In econometrics, the treatment effect analysis advanced first in labour and development economics, cf. Angrist and Krueger (1999), Duflo (2001) or Duflo, Glennerster and Kremer (2008).

An alternative approach to dealing with post-treatment control variables compared to the one presented in Subsection 2.1.4 has been discussed in Frangakis and Rubin (2002). See also Rosenbaum (1984) for a more traditional statistical approach.

In Section 2.1 we also mentioned the so-called *mediation analysis* for identifying treatment effects. This analysis uses the front-door identification approach introduced in Section 2.1.3 by a reasoning illustrated in the graphs of Figure 2.9 (except the left one, which is a counter-example). To our knowledge this strategy was firstly discussed in detail in Baron and Kenny (1986). In that article they put their main emphasise on the distinction between moderator and mediator variables, respectively, followed by some statistical considerations. More than twenty years later Hayes (2009) revisited this strategy and gave a brief review of the development and potentials. More recent methodological contributions to this approach are, for example, Imai, Keele and Yamamoto (2010) and Albert (2012); consult them also for further references.

Regarding more literature on the identification of treatment effects via the back door, we refer to a paper that tries to link structural regression and treatment effect analysis by discussing how each ATE or ATET estimator relates to a regression estimator in a (generalised) linear model. This was done in Blundell and Dias (2009).

We only gave a quite selective and narrow introduction to non- and semi-parametric regression. The literature is so abundant that we only give some general references and further reading to related literature that could be interesting in the context of treatment effect estimation. For a general introduction to non- and semi-parametric methods for econometricians see, for example, Härdle, Müller, Sperlich and Werwatz (2004), Li and Racine (2007), Henderson and Parmeter (2015), Yatchew (2003) or Pagan and Ullah (1999).

Semi-parametric efficiency bounds were introduced by Stein (1956) and developed by Koshevnik and Levit (1976). Further developments were added by Pfanzagl and Wefelmeyer (1982), Begun, Hall, Huang and Wellner (1983) and Bickel, Klaassen, Ritov and Wellner (1993). You might also consult the survey of Newey (1990), or the same ideas reloaded for the econometrics audience in Newey (1994). Chen, Linton and van Keilegom (2003) extended these results to non-smooth criterion functions, which are helpful e.g. for quantile estimators.

Interesting for estimating the propensity score is also the literature on single index models, see for example Härdle and Stoker (1989) and Powell, Stock and Stoker (1989) for average derivative-based estimators, Klein and Spady (1993) for a semi-parametric maximum-likelihood-based one, and Ichimura (1993) for a semi-parametric least squares approach.

More references to additive and generalised additive (or related) models can be skipped here as they are treated in the mentioned compendia above. Typically not treated there are estimators that guarantee monotonicity restrictions. One approach is to modify the estimator to incorporate the monotonicity restriction in the form of constrained optimisation; see e.g. Mammen (1991), Hall, Wolff and Yao (1999) or Neumeyer (2007), among others. Alternatively, one could rearrange the estimated function; see e.g. Dette, Neumeyer and Pilz (2006), Dette and Pilz (2006) or Chernozhukov, Fernandez-Val and Galichon (2007).

2.3.2   Computational Notes

In **R** there are several packages available for splines (`splines`, `pspline`) and many other packages like `mgcv` or `gam` are mainly spline based. For kernel-based methods, the package np extends the non-parametric methods that were already available in the basic version of **R** (e.g. density) and the somewhat older package KernSmooth. Almost all mentioned packages allow the estimation of various kinds of non- and semi-parametric regression models, univariate and multivariate, and are able to compute data-driven bandwidths. The np package uses the discussed kernel extensions for treating discrete and quantitative variables at once; recall Equation 2.40.

Among the different options present in the np package, there is the possibility to estimate semi-parametric partial linear models with the function npplreg. Also, the package gplm is able to estimate models of the form $E(Y|X_1, X_2) = G\{X_1'\beta + m(X_2)\}$. Both the PLM (2.45) and the generalised PLM with link can be estimated using a Speckman-type estimator or backfitting (setting the kgplm option to speckman or backfit), and partial linear additive models (2.46) can be estimated with gam and mgcv. For single-index models (2.47) and varying coefficient models (2.48), the functions npindex and npscoef are available. Clearly, when using splines or other sieves, these models can also be estimated with the aid of other packages. While the np package uses kernel-based estimators also for semiparametric regression, the SemiPar package uses a (penalised) spline. It has a somewhat larger variety as it includes, for example, mixed effects models via the packages mgcv and lmeSplines, which are both constructed to fit smoothing splines; see also smooth.spline. For more details consult the help files of the respective commands and package descriptions.

Also, Stata offers the possibility to fit several non- and semi-parametric models with different commands. It allows to compute and plot local regression via kernel-weighted local polynomial smoothing (lpoly) but also applies splines (mkspline, bsplines and mvrs), penalised splines (pspline), fractional polynomials (fracploy, mfp) or lowess (the latter two methods were not discussed here). For (generalised or partial linear) additive models you may use gam.

2.4 Exercises

1. Consider the example graphs in Figure 2.16. Which one is a DAG? Can we *d*-separate X and Y by conditioning? For which variables W does $X \perp Y|W$ hold? Justify your answers.

2. Consider in the graphs in Figure 2.17 and decide whether conditioning on X is necessary or not in order to identify the (total and/or direct) causal impact of treatment D on outcome Y. Note that in all these graphs the pointing to Y, D and X are omitted if they come from some unobservables U.

3. Prove the statement made in Example 2.4.

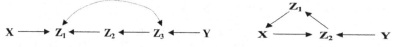

Figure 2.16 Example graphs

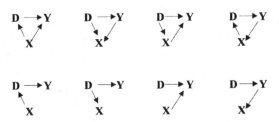

Figure 2.17 Example graphs (a) to (h) from the upper left to the lower right

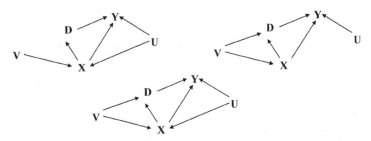

Figure 2.18 Three examples

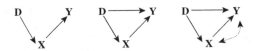

Figure 2.19 Three examples, (a), (b) and (c) from left to right

4. Note that in equation (2.8) the central assumption is $U \perp\!\!\!\perp D|X$. In which of the graphs of Figure 2.18 is this assumption satisfied? Justify your answers.

5. Consider the graph (a) in Figure 2.19. Discuss the identifiability of direct and indirect effects in all three graphs. How could you test $Y \perp\!\!\!\perp D|X$ when comparing (a) with (b), and what are the potential problems when looking at (c)?

6. Note first that a differentiable function is Lipschitz continuous if its first derivative is bounded. Based on this information, discuss to what extent the functions x^2 and $\sqrt{x}$ are Lipschitz continuous. Discuss also if they are Hölder continuous (and on which support).

7. Derive the Nadaraya–Watson estimator from the definition of conditional expectations, using the fact that $\frac{1}{nh} \sum_{i=1}^{n} K\{(x - X_i)/h\}$ and $\frac{1}{nh^2} \sum_{i=1}^{n} K\{(x - X_i)/h, (y - Y_i)/h\}$ are kernel estimators for the densities $f(x)$ and $f(x, y)$, respectively. Here, $K(\cdot, \cdot)$ stands for a bivariate kernel $K : I\!\!R^2 \to I\!\!R$.

8. Recall the definition of multiplicative kernels (2.30). Show that $\prod_{l=1}^{q} K(v_l)$ is an rth-order kernel function if each of the one-dimensional kernels $K(v_l)$ is so.

9. Derive the local quadratic estimator for a two-dimensional regression problem. Give the expressions you obtain for the estimators of the partial first and second derivatives of the regression function. How could this estimator be simplified if we knew that the impact of the two covariates were additively separable?

10. Prove Equation 2.21 by inserting the definition of the weights given in (2.17).

11. Recall the calculations that lead to the result in Equation 2.24. What would have happened if a third-order kernel (instead of a second-order one) had been used? More generally, what bias would result from an rth order kernel (given that nothing else changed)?

12. Imagine you tried to approximate an unknown one-dimensional function by a polynomial of arbitrary degree $p < n$ when the true underlying functional form is a simple log-linear one. Simulate such a regression function $E[Y|X]$ with $X \sim U[0.1, 10]$, $n = 50$ and $Y = \log(X) + e$, where $e \sim N(0, 1)$. Then repeat the exercise with a simple local linear function, alternately setting $h = 0.5$, 1 and 5. The kernel function K might be the Epanechnikov, Quartic or Gaussian kernel. If you take the last one, divide the proposed values for h by 2. For details see Härdle, Müller, Sperlich and Werwatz (2004).

13. Recall the canonical reparametrisation introduced in the context of local parametric estimation. Consider the Cobb–Douglas production function $g(z, \gamma_x) = \gamma_0 \prod_{l=1}^{q} z_l^{\gamma_l}$ and derive its canonical reparametrisation $g(z, \theta_x)$.

14. Let D be binary. Imagine we want to estimate $E[Y^1]$ from the sample $\{(Y_i, X_i, D_i)\}_{i=1}^{n}$ by solving $\frac{1}{n} \sum_{i=1}^{n} Y_i D_i p^{-1}(X_i) - \beta = 0$ with $p(\cdot) := E[D|\cdot]$ the propensity score, such that the solution $\hat{\beta}$ is our estimator.[49] Recall Equation 2.61: show that the influence function (2.63) is equal to

$$\psi(W) = \frac{(Y - m_1(X)) D}{p(X)} + m_1(X) - \beta$$

by finding the correct adjustment factor.

---

[49] Note that here, $p(x)$ is the unknown non-parametric nuisance parameter.

3 Selection on Observables: Matching, Regression and Propensity Score Estimators

In the last chapter we discussed issues concerning non-parametric identification, associated variable (say, confounders) selection and the basics of non- and semi-parametric estimation. In this chapter we put both together to estimate the averages of potential outcomes and treatment effects by adjusting for confounders. We will examine the so-called *matching estimators*, where pairs of treated and non-treated subjects are formed by searching for each treated individual a (most similar) twin in the control group. We will also compare these matching estimators to *(non-parametric) regression* and *(non-parametric) weighting estimators* and will see that these turn out to be rather similar in several respects.

Throughout this chapter we assume the *conditional independence assumption* (CIA), i.e. that all confounding variables are contained in vector $X \in I\!R^q$. In the literature this is often called the *ignorability of D*, and simply means you can ignore D for (Y^0, Y^1) once you have conditioned on X. It is used to derive estimation strategies as well as further tools for inference. Thanks to the ideas outlined in the discussion of causal chains in the last section, we are able to derive the identification of the treatment effects for non-experimental data. A fundamental supposition is, however, that the participation or non-participation is due to a *selection on observables*. We will see that in such a case the proposed identification and estimation procedures could be interpreted as a non-parametric extension of the familiar OLS (ordinary least squares) estimation approaches of marginal impacts.

The necessary assumptions and conditions will be clearly stated; but for their discussion or the verification of their compliance we have to refer to the particular discussions in Chapter 2. It is only in the last section of this chapter that testing strategies are considered. These tests can help to justify, for example, the assumptions of unconfoundedness or the conditional independence. We will see that the latter question will also come up when choosing a model (or just the smoothing parameter) to estimate the *propensity score* $p(x) = \Pr(D = 1|X = x)$, which is the conditional probability of participation of individuals with characteristics x.

3.1 Preliminaries: General Ideas

We start with an introduction to the practical use of the CIA and modified assumptions to identify the average or conditional treatment effect. This is done through the use of feasible regression problems, the matching principle or propensity score weighting. Doing so, we will understand why for the *regression* and *matching estimators* (with or without propensity scores) non-parametric estimators are the most appropriate ones, at least intuitively. Somewhat later we will also learn why semi-parametric methods are quite helpful in practice for *propensity score-based* methods, no matter whether we consider propensity score-based regression, weighting or so-called double robust estimators.

3.1.1 How to Apply the CIA for Identification and Estimation

Recall that, if we were to observe all covariates that affected D and the potential outcome, conditional on these covariates X, the variables D and Y^d are independent ($\perp\!\!\!\perp$). This assumption has been made precise as

$$Y^d \perp\!\!\!\perp D|X \qquad \forall d \in Supp(D) \tag{3.1}$$

and introduced above as the *conditional independence assumption* (CIA). In some literature it is also called the *selection on observables assumption*, which essentially means that there is no further selection on unobservables that is also affecting the outcome Y. This assumption (3.1) implies the *conditional mean independence*

$$E[Y^d|X] = E[Y|X, D = d] , \tag{3.2}$$

which is a much weaker assumption but often sufficient for our purposes. Both assumptions are most easily understood in the treatment evaluation context where the treatment variable D is only binary. Then, by this assumption, we can identify average potential outcomes as

$$E[Y^d] = \int E[Y|X, D = d]\,dF_X .$$

Recalling the calculations (2.7), the ATE is therefore identified by

$$E[Y^1 - Y^0] = \int E[Y|X, D = 1]dF_X - \int E[Y|X, D = 0]dF_X. \tag{3.3}$$

The adjustment for the distribution of covariate-vector X (i.e. integrating with respect to dF_X) is just the application of the law of large numbers applied on $g(X) := E[Y|X, D = d]$. As long as the samples are representative of the population regarding the distribution of X, such an integral can be approximated sufficiently well by the sample average. The remaining statistical task is limited to the prediction of the conditional expectations $E[Y|X, D = d]$ for all combinations of X and D. This approach is also known as the *nonparametric regression method*.

Example 3.1 Let $D \in \{0, 1\}$ indicate whether or not an individual continues to university after secondary school graduation. Suppose that the decision to enrol in a university depends on only two factors: the examination results when finishing secondary school and the weather on that particular day. Without controlling for the secondary school examination results, the conditional independence assumption (3.1) is unlikely to be satisfied: individuals with better grades are more likely to enrol in university and probably also have higher outcomes Y^0 and Y^1. Conditional on the grades, the CIA (3.1) is satisfied if the weather itself has no further[1] effect on wages later in life. Hence, for individuals with the same grades, the decision to enrol no longer systematically depends on factors that are also related to the potential future outcomes. Conditional on grades, there is no selection bias and we can simply compare the outcomes of those deciding to enrol in university with those who do not. Thus, we could compare university graduates and non-graduates with the same values of X and then take the average with respect to X in order to obtain $E[Y^1 - Y^0]$, cf. equation (2.7). Conditioning additionally on the weather of the day of enrolment would not contribute to identification. Rather, it would harm it as it would take out some variation needed for estimation precision. In this simple example, conditioning on weather would actually violate the common support assumption. We will need the so-called common support assumption (see below), which will require that for each value of X we actually observe some individuals enrolling in university and some who do not.

With an analogous derivation as in (2.7), cf. Exercise 1, we can identify the ATET also by

$$E[Y^1 - Y^0|D = 1] = E[Y|D = 1] - \int E[Y|X, D = 0]dF_{X|D=1} \qquad (3.4)$$

where we used $E[Y^1|D = 1] = E[Y|D = 1]$, i.e. that the observed outcome is identical to the potential outcome Y^1 among those actually being treated. We observe a possibly important difference to the identification of the ATE. For the ATET we only need

    (AT1) $\qquad\qquad\qquad\qquad Y^0 \perp\!\!\!\perp D|X$

whereas for identification of ATE we required

    (A1) $\qquad\qquad\qquad Y^0 \perp\!\!\!\perp D|X \qquad$ and $\qquad Y^1 \perp\!\!\!\perp D|X$.

So for identification of ATET we do *not* need that $Y^1 \perp\!\!\!\perp D|X$ and thus also do not need that $(Y^1 - Y^0) \perp\!\!\!\perp D|X$. Hence, we can permit that Y^1 as well as the individual treatment effects may differ between treated and controls, where such differences might be due to unobservables. We could, for example, permit that individuals might have chosen their treatment status D on the basis of their (expected) treatment gains $(Y^1 - Y^0)$ but only if we can rule out that this depends on Y^0 (i.e. that their choice of treatment status was based on Y^0). This is different from identification of the ATE, and this difference could be relevant in applications when we have good predictors for the individual non-treatment outcome Y_i^0, such that by controlling for their X_i we can eliminate selection bias for Y_i^0, even when we know little about the treatment gains $(Y_i^1 - Y_i^0)$ themselves. The latter may largely reflect unobservables that are possibly known to the individuals

---

[1] The whole impact of weather at that day on future earnings is channelled by the enrolment D.

but not to the econometrician. This is not permitted for ATE. In the same way you can argue that for identifying ATEN we only need conditional mean independence of the form $E[Y^1|X, D] = E[Y^1|X]$ whereas we do not need this for Y^0.

This difference can be a relevant relaxation in some applications.[2] The selection-on-observables assumption required for ATE rules out the possibility that individuals can guess their potential outcomes and then choose the treatment with the highest (potential) outcome. In other words, in Chapter 1 we required that the probability of choosing a particular programme must not be affected by the potential outcomes. For CIA now, treatment selection is allowed to depend on anticipated potential outcomes as long as these are anticipated exclusively on the basis of observed characteristics X. But if looking at ATET, we can take advantage of the fact that for the (sub-)population of the treated, their average outcome of Y^1 is the average of their observed outcome Y. Hence, one has only a problem with the prediction of $E[Y^0|D = 1]$. It is just for the non-treatment state Y^0 where one has to control for all relevant factors to estimate its mean. We do not need to predict $E[Y^1|D = 0]$ or $E[(Y^1 - Y^0)|D = 0]$.

To gain some intuition as to what the non-parametric regression treatment effect estimator does, suppose you have a few different values x for X but a reasonably large number of people for each x in all groups. Then we can perform a step-wise averaging: first predict for any observed vector x the conditional expectations $\widehat{E}[Y^d|X = x]$ by $\frac{1}{n_{d,x}} \sum_{i:D_i=d, X_i=x} Y_i$ with $n_{d,x}$ being the number of individuals in group $D = d$ with characteristics $X = x$. Secondly, you set for $n_d = \sum_x n_{d,x}$, $d = 0, 1$

$$\widehat{ATE} = \frac{1}{n} \sum_x (n_{0,x} + n_{1,x})(\widehat{E}[Y^1|X = x] - \widehat{E}[Y^0|X = x]),$$

$$\widehat{ATET} = \frac{1}{n_1} \sum_x n_{1,x}(\widehat{E}[Y^1|X = x] - \widehat{E}[Y^0|X = x]),$$

$$\widehat{ATEN} = \frac{1}{n_0} \sum_x n_{0,x}(\widehat{E}[Y^1|X = x] - \widehat{E}[Y^0|X = x]).$$

In practice you often have too many different x for using such a simple averaging, therefore you include the neighbours. Although this requires more sophisticated non-parametric estimators, the idea stays the same. So we obtain estimates for ATE by first estimating the regression functions $E[Y|X, D]$, then predict the $E[Y|X_i, D = d]$ for all individuals $i = 1, \ldots, n$ for all d, and finally calculate the difference of their sample averages. For the ATET, c.f. (3.4), it is sufficient to do this just for $d = 0$, and to compare it with the average of observed outcomes Y^1. A regression estimator for the ATE is therefore of the form

$$\widehat{ATE} = \frac{1}{n} \sum_{i=1}^n \{\hat{m}_1(X_i) - \hat{m}_0(X_i)\}, \tag{3.5}$$

and analogously for the ATET

---

[2] See, for example, Ham, Li and Reagan (2011).

$$\widehat{ATET} = \frac{1}{n_1} \sum_{i:D_i=1} \{Y_i - \hat{m}_0(X_i)\} \quad \text{with } n_1 = \sum_{i=1}^{n} \mathbb{1}\{D_i = 1\}, \qquad (3.6)$$

where the $\hat{m}_d(x)$ are some regression estimates of $E[Y|X = x, D = d]$.

For the regression or prediction in the first step, traditionally, OLS was the most favoured estimator in such 'selection on observables' situations. In recent years, non- and semi-parametric alternatives have become more popular. This is also because of the parallel development of an estimation strategy called *matching*. The literature actually distinguishes between the non-parametric regression approach and simple matching. We will notice in the following that both are based on the same principles and share common ideas. Differences are less pronounced than they may appear on first sight.

Let us consider for a moment only the estimation of ATET and recall that for its identification it is enough to predict for each participant i ($D_i = 1$) its expected counterfactual outcome Y_i^0. As we assume for the treated and the controls to have observed all confounders X_i, a natural predictor for Y_i^0 would be the outcome of a member j from the control group ($D_j = 0$) with the same characteristics, i.e. take Y_j for predicting Y_i^0 when $X_i = X_j$. As it will be hard to find such a perfect match for each individual, one might take the closest one, where 'closest' has to be specified (X is usually a vector). One could again take the Euclidean or the Mahalanobis distance, see (1.18), recalling our discussion about *matched pairs*. When doing this for each individual i with $D_i = 1$, one would look for such a 'match' in the control group. This is done with or without replacements, where replacements might lead to larger variances, no replacements to larger biases.

But how does this relate to non-parametric regression? In fact, no matter whether one faces the problem of finding either several equally good matches or just many bad matches for i, in both situations one should take the average over their outcomes Y^0 as a predictor for Y_i^0. This is called kNN-matching (referring to k *nearest neighbours*) with fixed k. If we allow k to increase with n, then we have $\hat{Y}_i^0 = \hat{E}[Y^0|X_i]$ being the non-parametric kNN regression estimator introduced in Sections 2.2.1 and 2.2.2.

Alternatively, if one matches participant i ($D_i = 1$) with the average of all members j of the control group having characteristics X_j such that $\|X_i - X_j\| < h$ for a distance measure $\|\cdot\|$ and tolerance threshold $h > 0$, one obtains $\hat{Y}_i^0 = \hat{E}[Y^0|X_i]$ being a kernel regression estimator with bandwidth h and the uniform kernel $K(\|u\|/h) = \frac{1}{2}\|u\| < h\}$ with $dim(u) = dim(X)$. If we apply a $K_h(u)$-weighted average of the outcomes Y^0 for these neighbours, we have the classical kernel regression estimator with kernel K; recall Section 2.2.1.

All this can be repeated equally well to obtain $\hat{m}_1(X_i)$ for equation (3.5), i.e. to predict Y_j^1 for individuals j of the control group using matches (or say, twins) from the treatment group. In other words, our discussion extends to the case of estimating ATE and ATEN.

We conclude that the difference between matching and non-parametric regression is rather of theoretical nature, as for the former we take a fixed number k of neighbours with $k \to \infty$ when sample size n goes to infinity or a fixed distance h, while for the latter we take a fixed distance $k \to \infty$, $h \to 0$ when sample size n goes to infinity. The regression approach has several advantages, though, in permitting more easily bias reduction approaches. The practical difference is that the regression approach is not necessarily non-parametric as we will briefly discuss in the next subsection. Therefore, one advantage often brought forward is that matching estimators (in contrast to regression-based ones) are entirely non-parametric and thus do not rely on functional form assumptions like linearity. This permits in particular a *treatment effect heterogeneity* of any form. This advantage is of special relevance as the distribution of X can – and typically will – be very different inside the treatment and non-treatment group, respectively. In parametric estimation the distribution of X has an essential impact on the parameter estimates (typically ignored in parametric econometrics). Therefore, prediction typically works worse the more the distribution of X differs between treatment and non-treatment group. This, however, is exactly the case in the treatment effect estimation context as only those characteristics X can be confounders that differ (a lot) in distribution between the two groups. In fact, only variables X showing a significant variation between $D = 0$ and $D = 1$ can identify selection.

Note finally that matching will be more efficient the more observations we use for predicting the counterfactual outcome. In other words, matching becomes efficient when it collapses with the non-parametric regression. Therefore we will often use the notation of matching and regression estimation synonymously and only distinguish between them where necessary. Most importantly, whenever we refer to parametric regression, this will be made explicit as this is different from matching and non-parametric regression in several aspects.

3.1.2 Selection Bias and Common Support

A necessary condition in addition to the CIA (which is most evident when thinking of matching) is the so-called *common support condition* (CSC). We can see from (2.7) or (3.3) that for identification reasons it is required that X takes about the same values in both groups, treated and non-treated. This does not refer to the distribution of X which will be importantly different as discussed above (remember that the frequencies will be different simply because X and D are dependent). But, at least theoretically, there should be no value of X that can only be realised in one of the groups, because otherwise we cannot find a counterfacual match – not even in theory! Speaking in terms of Example 3.1, there must exist both university attendees and non-attendees for every value of X. If for some particular values x of X all individuals enrol in university, we obviously cannot compare attendees and non-attendees for those x due to the lack of non-attendees. This is known as the *common support problem* resulting in an additional assumption. Hence, we require two conditions:

Our (**A1**), i.e. that all factors (say confounder X) causing simultaneously D and Y are observed, typically called CIA.

(**A2**) Conditional on X there is still sufficient randomness in the choice of D such that

$$0 < \Pr(D = 1 | X = x) = p(x) < 1 \qquad \forall\, x \in \mathcal{X} \qquad (3.7)$$

where $\mathcal{X}$ was the support of X in the (entire) population, typically called CSC.

The first condition is essentially non-testable. Although it can be tested whether some variables do affect D or Y, it is impossible to ascertain by statistical means whether there is no omitted (unobserved) variable, which consciously or unconsciously affected the process determining the choice of D but has else no impact on Y. In practice, identification by (CIA) is easier to achieve the more bureaucratic, rule-based and deterministic the programme selection process is, provided the common support condition applies.

In contrast, our CSC assumption (A2) can be tested, and if rejected, the object of estimation can be adapted by redefinition of the population of interest such that the CSC holds. How does this work? Let $\mathcal{X}_0$, $\mathcal{X}_1$ be the supports of X within the control and the treatment group respectively, and $\mathcal{X}_{01} = \mathcal{X}_0 \cap \mathcal{X}_1$ (i.e. the intercept) be the common support of the treatment and control group. Note that assumption (A2) is equivalent to

$$\text{(A2) for ATE} : \mathcal{X}_{01} = \mathcal{X}_1 = \mathcal{X}_0. \tag{3.8}$$

Hence, if (A2) fails for your original data, then one can still identify the treatment effects for all people having characteristics from the common support $\mathcal{X}_{01}$. So we can simply declare this subpopulation to be our population of interest. It cannot be answered generally whether this 'solution' always satisfies our curiosity, but at least the subpopulation and its treatment effect are well defined. One therefore speaks of the *common support condition* (CSC) though it is often expressed in terms of the propensity score like in (3.7).

In practice, if the common support condition is violated, the problem is often that the support of X within the treated is just a subset of that within the control group. The reason is that the projects typically target certain subpopulations but on a voluntary basis. It is quite likely that we observe all kind of people among the non-treated whereas among the treated we observe only those who were eligible for the project. The good news is that this reduced common support is all we need to identify the ATET.[3] We define assumption (A2) for ATET as

$$\textbf{(AT2)} \text{ for ATET} : \mathcal{X}_{01} = \mathcal{X}_1 \subseteq \mathcal{X}_0. \tag{3.9}$$

For ATEN you simply exchange the subindices 0, 1.

Example 3.2 If applying for a master programme the university may require a minimum grade (in some examination results). We therefore can find individuals with very low grades in the population not attending university, but we may not find university graduates for particular low values of X. Hence, we will not be able to find a proper comparison group for such levels of X.[4] If we know the rules to enrol in university, we would know exactly which x values cannot be observed in the $D = 1$ population.

---

[3] In addition, recall that for the identification of ATET it was sufficient to have $Y^0 \perp\!\!\!\perp D|X$ instead of requiring the complete CIA. So both necessary conditions are relaxed for identifying ATET compared to ATE.

[4] For example, in active labour market programmes 'being unemployed' is usually a central condition for eligibility. Thus, employed persons cannot be participants as they are not eligible and, hence, no counterfactual outcome is identified for them.

In addition to such formal rules, there are often many other factors unknown to us that make the choice of $D = 1$ or $D = 0$ extremely unlikely. For example, parental income may matter a lot for attending university whereas for very low incomes it might be impossible to attend university. However, we do not know the threshold a priori and would thus not know the common support ex-ante.

Here we have seen another advantage of matching: it highlights the importance of the support condition; although matching does not solve a support problem, it visualises it.

We already gave some intuitive explanations and examples for the selection bias problem we might face in treatment effect estimation. Let us briefly revisit this problem more formally. We are interested in estimating average potential or differences in outcomes, i.e.

$$E[Y^d], \qquad E[Y^{d_2} - Y^{d_1}],$$

where the outcome could be for example wages or wealth after the treatments d_1 and d_2. The endogeneity of D due to (self-) selection implies that

$$E[Y^d | D = d] \neq E[Y^d]$$

so that a simple estimation of $E[Y^d | D = d]$ will not identify the mean potential outcome. The literature on matching estimators largely evolved around the identification and estimation of treatment effects with a binary variable D. Following this discussion we consider the problem of estimating the ATET, i.e. $E[Y^1 - Y^0 | D = 1]$. Recall that a naive estimator would build upon

$$E[Y | D = 1] - E[Y | D = 0]$$

by simply comparing the observed outcomes among the treated and the non-treated. With non-experimental data (where D is not randomly distributed), this estimator is usually biased due to differences in observables and unobservables among those who chose $D = 1$ and those who chose $D = 0$. This bias is

$$E[Y^0 | D = 1] - E[Y^0 | D = 0],$$

which can also be written and decomposed as

$$= \int_{\mathcal{X}_1} E[Y^0 | X = x, D = 1] dF_{X|D=1}(x) - \int_{\mathcal{X}_0} E[Y^0 | X = x, D = 0] dF_{X|D=0}(x)$$

$$= \int_{\mathcal{X}_1 \setminus \mathcal{X}_{01}} E\left[Y^0 | X = x, D = 1\right] dF_{X|D=1}(x) - \int_{\mathcal{X}_0 \setminus \mathcal{X}_{01}} E\left[Y^0 | X = x, D = 0\right] dF_{X|D=0}(x) \tag{3.10}$$

$$+ \int_{\mathcal{X}_{01}} E\left[Y^0 | X = x, D = 0\right] \cdot (dF_{X|D=1}(x) - dF_{X|D=0}(x)) \, dx \tag{3.11}$$

$$+ \int_{\mathcal{X}_{01}} \left(E[Y^0 | X = x, D = 1] - E[Y^0 | X = x, D = 0]\right) \cdot dF_{X|D=1}(x). \tag{3.12}$$

The third part (3.12) is the bias due to differences in the expected outcomes between the participants $(D = 1)$ and the non-participants $(D = 0)$ conditional on X inside the population of the participants.[5] This component is zero if there are no systematic unobserved differences after controlling for X, because in case that X includes all confounding variables we have

$$E[Y^0|X, D = 0] \equiv E[Y^0|X, D = 1] \qquad \text{i.e. CIA holds.} \qquad (3.13)$$

This third part is what is traditionally understood by *selection bias*. Nevertheless the first and the second part form also part of the bias showing that there are still some other issues, namely differences in the conditional distributions of observed covariates as well as different supports of these covariates.

The first component (3.10) is due to differences in the support of X in the participant and non-participant subpopulation. When using the simple estimator $E[Y|D = 1] - E[Y|D = 0]$ we partly compare individuals to each other for whom no counterfactual could ever be identified simply because $\mathcal{X}_1 \setminus \mathcal{X}_{01}$ is non-zero. There are participants with characteristics x for whom no counterpart in the non-participant $(D = 0)$ subpopulation could ever be observed. Analogously, if $\mathcal{X}_0 \setminus \mathcal{X}_{01}$ is non-zero, there will be non-participants with characteristics for whom no participant with identical characteristics could be found. In other words, part (3.10) is zero if the CSC for ATE (A2) holds, but only the first term of (3.10) is zero if CSC holds just for (AT2). The second term in (3.10) disappears by not using individuals from $\mathcal{X}_1 \setminus \mathcal{X}_{01}$.

Example 3.3 If it happened that individuals with characteristics $\mathcal{X}_1 \setminus \mathcal{X}_{01}$ have on average large outcomes Y^0, and those with characteristics $\mathcal{X}_0 \setminus \mathcal{X}_{01}$ have on average small outcomes Y^0, then the first bias component of the experimental estimator would be positive. The reason is that the term $E[Y|D = 1]$ contains these high-outcome individuals (i.e. $\mathcal{X}_1 \setminus \mathcal{X}_{01}$), which are missing in the $D = 0$ population. Analogously, $E[Y|D = 0]$ contains individuals with low outcome (i.e. $\mathcal{X}_0 \setminus \mathcal{X}_{01}$) whose characteristics have zero density in the $D = 1$ population. Therefore the term $E[Y|D = 1]$ would be too large as it contains the individuals with high outcome, and the term $E[Y|D = 0]$ would be too small as it contains those low-outcome individuals. In the case of randomised experiments the supports are identical, $\mathcal{X}_0 = \mathcal{X}_1$, and common support is guaranteed. With observational studies this is typically not the case.

The second part of the bias (3.11) is due to differences in the distributions of the X characteristics among participants and non-participants (on the common support). An adequate estimator will have to adjust for this difference. For example, to deal with the

---

[5] We switch here from the notion of 'treatment group' to 'participants' by intention though, admittedly, it is often used synonymously. This is to emphasise here a frequent reason for selection biases in practice: people might be assigned to a treatment (or the control) group but decide (voluntarily or not) afterwards to change the group. For the estimation, however, the treatment (i.e. participation) itself is crucial, not the assignment. The ATE for D = 'assignment' instead of D = 'actual participation' is called *intention-to-treat effect*.

second component one has to weight the non-parametric estimates of $E\left[Y^0|X, D = 0\right]$ with the appropriate distribution of $X|D = d$.

Note that all this discussion could be repeated now for

$$E[Y^1|D = 1] - E[Y^1|D = 0]$$

which adds to the bias above if the objective was to estimate the ATE. It has a similar decomposition as that of (3.10) to (3.12). You can try as an exercise, and you will note that these terms do not cancel those of (3.10) to (3.12) when calculating the bias of ATE.

3.1.3   Using Linear Regression Models?

One might think that, given Formula 3.5, the ATE (and similarly the ATET) can equally well be estimated based on linear regression. If linear and log-linear models are well accepted in the classical econometric literature for structural models, why not stick to them? Moreover, we only need them to average over the resulting predictors. This brings us to the question how our above-elaborated identification strategy relates to the classical, though maybe old-fashioned, way of estimating an impact by simply including a dummy for 'treatment' to a conventional econometric regression equation. In formal terms this is

$$Y_i = \alpha + \beta D_i + \gamma' X_i + U_i. \tag{3.14}$$

Note that the CIA corresponds to assuming

$$U \perp\!\!\!\perp D|X , \tag{3.15}$$

which we might call *conditional exogeneity*. For estimating average treatment effects it would be sufficient to ask for conditional linear independence or conditional zero-correlation. Condition (3.15) implies

$$E[U_i|D_i, X_i] = E[U_i|X_i].$$

The assumption typically invoked for OLS in (3.14) is actually stronger, namely

$$E[U_i|D_i, X_i] = 0.$$

Indeed, for estimating the linear model we ask that U is mean-independent from D and X, or at least from those elements of X which are correlated with D. For the non-parametric identification as well as for the treatment effect estimators, we have seen that this assumption is not needed. So the news is that U is allowed to be correlated with X. More generally, in the matching approach for treatment effect estimation, the confounders X are permitted to be endogenous in (3.14).

How is the above-introduced matching approach related to ordinary least squares (OLS) regression of (3.14)? This is easier to see when starting with parametric matching, also based on simple linear models for m_0 and m_1 having

$$\hat{m}_d(x) = \hat{a}_d + x'\hat{b}_d,$$

where $\hat{a}_d, \hat{b}_d$ are the coefficients estimated from group $\{i \ : \ D_i = d\}$. The average potential outcome is then

$$\widehat{E}\left[Y^d\right] = \hat{a}_d + \bar{X}'\hat{b}_d,$$

where $\bar{X}$ are the average characteristics in the entire sample. The ATE estimate is then

$$\widehat{E}\left[Y^1 - Y^0\right] = \hat{a}_1 - \hat{a}_0 + \bar{X}'(\hat{b}_1 - \hat{b}_0). \tag{3.16}$$

Instead, an OLS estimation of (3.14) would deliver $\hat{\alpha} + d\hat{\beta} + \bar{x}'\hat{\gamma}$ where $\hat{\alpha}, \hat{\beta}, \hat{\gamma}$ were obtained from the entire sample. The corresponding direct estimate of ATE is then $\hat{\beta}$. The first thing that has to be recalled is that, in both cases, one must only use covariates X that are confounders. Second, in (3.16) used assumption (3.15) whereas a stronger assumption is needed for OLS. Third, the matching approach accounts automatically for possible interaction of D and X on $(Y^0 - Y^1)$ whereas in (3.14) one would have to model this explicitly. It is clear that this is also true for any other functional modification or extension; try e.g. with any polynomial extension of (3.14). An immediate conclusion is that while for the partial, marginal *ceteris paribus* effect of D one might still argue that an OLS estimate $\hat{\beta}$ from (3.14) is a consistent estimate for the linear part of this effect. There is not such a clear interpretation available when the parameter of interest was the ATE. However, when introducing double robust estimators, then we will see that the negligence of having different distributions of X in the two groups harms less in (3.16) than it does in (3.14) while it causes no problems when using local estimators. This partly explains the importance of non-parametric estimates for the treatment effect estimation: the parametric simplification complicates the correct interpretation instead of simplifying it.

3.2   ATE and ATET Estimation Based on CIA

We have seen what kind of biases can emerge from a direct mean comparison. They reflect an identification problem due to (auto-)selection of the different treatment groups. We saw how CIA and CSC help to identify ATE and ATET if all important confounders were observed and $\mathcal{X}_{01}$ is the population of interest. A simple comparison of classical structural equation analysis and the matching based approach has further illustrated why the misspecification of the functional form has maybe even more severe consequences for the correct interpretation than it typically has in the classical regression context.

The CIA is basically used in two different ways to estimate treatment effects: either for a direct matching of individuals being treated with those not being treated, or via their propensity (expressed in probability) to be treated or not. The second approach opens different ways of how to continue: using the propensity either for matching or for readjusting the distributions of subjects in the two subpopulations (treated vs non-treated) to make them comparable. We will see that matching and propensity score weighting can even be combined to increase the robustness of the treatment effect estimator.

3.2.1   Definition of Matching and Regression Estimators

So why does the CIA and CSC based matching (or regression) solve our bias problem? Consider again ATET and bias (3.10)–(3.12). We saw that CIA eliminates (3.12). Next, the average potential outcome among the treated is

$$E\left[Y^0|D=1\right] = \int E[Y|X, D=0]dF_{X|D=1} = \int m_0(x)f_{X|D=1}(x)dx.$$

If we succeed to estimate the conditional expectation $m_0(x) = E[Y|X = x, D = 0]$ among the non-participants and integrate it over the distribution of X among the participants, then (3.11) is eliminated. Suppose that $\mathcal{X}_1 \subseteq \mathcal{X}_0$ giving the CSC for ATET. An intuitive and adequate estimator for $E\left[Y^0|D=1\right]$ is obtained by replacing $F_{X|D=1}$ by the empirical distribution function $\hat{F}_{X|D=1}$ and m_0 by a (non-parametric) estimator, i.e.

$$\hat{E}\left[Y^0|D=1\right] = \frac{1}{n_1} \sum_{i:D_i=1} \hat{m}_0(X_i),$$

which gives our proposal (3.6) $\hat{E}\left[Y^1 - Y^0|D=1\right] = \frac{1}{n_1}\sum_{i:D_i=1}\left\{Y_i^1 - \hat{m}_0(X_i)\right\}$. As this matching estimator automatically 'integrates empirically' over $F_{X|D=1}$ (i.e. *averages*) we have to replace in (3.10) and (3.11) $F_{X|D=0}$ by $F_{X|D=1}$. This eliminates (3.11).

Concerning the second component of (3.10), recall that we redefine the ATET by restricting it to the region $\mathcal{X}_{01}$.[6] As $F_{X|D=1}(x) = 0$ for $x \in \mathcal{X}_0 \backslash \mathcal{X}_{01}$ the second component in (3.10) is also zero. Thus, restricting to the common support region, our ATET estimate is actually

$$\hat{E}\left[Y^1 - Y^0|D=1\right] = \frac{1}{n_{01}} \sum_{\mathcal{X}_{01}}\left\{Y_i^1 - \hat{m}_0(X_i)\right\}, \quad n_{01} = \sum_{i}^{n} \mathbb{1}\{X_i \in \mathcal{X}_{01}\}, \quad (3.17)$$

and accordingly the ATE

$$\hat{E}\left[Y^1 - Y^0\right] = \frac{1}{n_{01}} \sum_{\mathcal{X}_{01}}\left\{\hat{m}_1(X_i) - \hat{m}_0(X_i)\right\} \quad (3.18)$$

with $\hat{m}_1$ being an estimate of the expected outcome Y under treatment. The next step is to find an appropriate predictor $\hat{m}_0$ (and $\hat{m}_1$ in case we want to estimate ATE); afterwards one can study the statistical properties of the final estimators.

Popular non-parametric methods in this context are the kernel regression estimator, local polynomial regression, and kNN estimators. A very popular version of the latter is the simple first-nearest-neighbour regression: for predicting $m_0(X_i)$ for an individual i taken from the treated, the individual from the control group with characteristics X_j being the closest to the characteristics X_i is selected and its value Y_j is taken as predictor: $\hat{m}_0(X_i) := Y_j$. The use of the nearest-neighbour regression estimators provides actually the origin of the name *matching*: 'pairs' or 'matches' of similar participants and non-participants are formed, and the average of their outcome difference is taken to

---

[6] Recall also that a non-parametric estimate of $m_0(x)$ is only defined where $f_{X|D=0}(x) > 0$.

estimate the treatment effect. There existed the discussion on whether controls can be matched (i.e. used) repeatedly or only once. In case of ATET estimation, for example, the latter requires $n_0 \geq n_1$ and leads to a larger bias but reduces the variance. One may be wondering why the simple one-to-one matching estimators have been so popular. One reason is that it can help to reduce the cost of data collection if matching is used ex-ante.

Example 3.4 Suppose we have a data set from medical records on 50 individuals who were exposed to a certain drug treatment and 5000 individuals who were not exposed. For the 5000 controls some basic X variables are available but not the Y variable of interest. We would thus have to still collect data on Y. Collecting these Y data is often costly, and may e.g. require a blood test with prior consent of the physician and the individual. Thus, instead of following-up all 5000 individuals, it makes sense to use the available X data to choose a smaller number of control observations, e.g. 50, who are most similar to the 50 treated individuals (in terms of X) and to collect additional data (namely their Y) only on these individuals.

Example 3.4 gives a reason for why the one-to-one matching is helpful before data collection is done. Nevertheless, after data collection has been completed it does not preclude the use of estimators that use a larger smoothing area. Obviously, using a single-nearest neighbour for predicting $m_0(x)$ leads (asymptotically) to the lowest bias but rather high variance. Therefore a wider window (larger $k = $ 'number of neighbours' for kNN or larger bandwidth for kernel and local polynomial smoothers) might be appropriate. Having said this, it is clear that in such cases several individuals will be used repeatedly for matches. Matching with kNN methods or kernel regression with bandwidth h are likely to perform very similarly if k and h are chosen optimally. Some people argue that in practice, k nearest neighbour matching may perform somewhat better since the smoothing region automatically adapts to the density and thus ensures that never less than k observations are in the smoothing region. Recall that this corresponds to local bandwidths in kernel regression. However, 'matching' based on local polynomial regression or with higher-order kernels can reduce the bias of the matching estimator, which is not possible with kNN regression.

Let us come back to the CSC in theory and practice. In theory, m_0 is simply not well defined outside $\mathcal{X}_0$. So if there exist x in $\mathcal{X}_1 \backslash \mathcal{X}_{01}$, then their potential outcome Y^0 is not defined (or say 'identified') and consequently not their treatment effect. Then, neither ATE nor ATET are defined for a population that includes individuals with those characteristics. The same story could be told exchanging subindices 0, 1 and we conclude that neither ATE nor ATEN were defined. This is the theoretical part. In practice, we simply cannot (or should not try to) extrapolate non-parametrically too far. For example, if there is no individual j in the control group exhibiting an x_j close to x_i for some i from the treatment group, then there is no match. With kernels it is similar; if there is no match for x in the h-neighbourhood (h being the bandwidth), the prediction of $m_0(x)$ is not possible. Here we see the practical meaning of the CSC for non-parametric matching and regression estimators.

3.2.2 Statistical Properties of Matching

We summarise the main findings. For details of the quite technical proofs one should consult the original papers which we cite where possible. Let us start by specifying kNN matching when the number of neighbours k is fixed to K (but not growing with sample size). This includes the standard pair-matching estimator ($K = 1$). So let us consider the traditional matching estimator where a counterfactual match to (Y_i, X_i) is constructed by the average of the K responses Y_j of those subjects (from the counterfactual group) whose characteristics X_j are closest to X_i. To be exact about the statistical properties we need first to be exact in defining the estimator.[7] Let $J(i)$ be the set of indices $(j_1(i), \ldots, j_K(i))$ pointing to these closest neighbours. Then the matches can be formalised for $d \in \{0, 1\}$ by

$$\hat{Y}_i(d) = \begin{cases} Y_i & , \quad if \quad D_i = d \\ \frac{1}{K} \sum_{j \in J(i)} Y_j & , \quad if \quad D_i = 1 - d \end{cases} \tag{3.19}$$

for which we implicitly assume $n_1 \geq K \leq n_0$.

Typically one allows for repetitions defining $R(j) = \sum_{i=1}^{n} \mathbb{1}\{j \in J(i)\}$ as the number of times that subject j is used for a match. Then the matching estimators are

$$\widehat{ATE} = \frac{1}{n} \sum_{i=1}^{n} \hat{Y}_i(1) - \hat{Y}_i(0) = \frac{1}{n} \sum_{i=1}^{n} (2D_i - 1) \left(1 + \frac{R(i)}{K}\right) Y_i, \tag{3.20}$$

$$\widehat{ATET} = \frac{1}{n_1} \sum_{i:D_i=1} Y_i(1) - \hat{Y}_i(0) = \frac{1}{n_1} \sum_{i=1}^{n} \left(D_i - (1 - D_i)\frac{R(i)}{K}\right) Y_i. \tag{3.21}$$

For studying their asymptotic properties it is helpful to consider the decompositions

$$\widehat{ATE} - ATE = \overline{ATE(X)} - ATE + B_K + S_K, \text{ with}$$

average conditional treatment effect $\quad \overline{ATE(X)} = \frac{1}{n} \sum_{i=1}^{n} m_1(X_i) - m_0(X_i),$

conditional bias $\quad B_K = \frac{1}{n} \sum_{i=1}^{n} (2D_i - 1) \left[\frac{1}{K} \sum_{k=1}^{K} m_{1-D_i}(X_i) - m_{1-D_i}(X_{j_k(i)})\right],$

and stochastic term $\quad S_K = \frac{1}{n} \sum_{i=1}^{n} (2D_i - 1) \left(1 + \frac{R(i)}{K}\right) \varepsilon_i,$

where $\varepsilon_i = Y_i - m_{D_i}(X_i)$, and analogously

$$\widehat{ATET} - ATET = \overline{ATET(X)} - ATET + BT_K + ST_K, \text{ with}$$

conditional ATET $\quad \overline{ATET(X)} = \frac{1}{n_1} \sum_{i:D_i=1} E[Y|X_i, D_i = 1] - m_0(X_i),$

---

[7] We follow here mainly the work of Abadie and Imbens (2006).

$$\text{conditional bias} \quad BT_K = \frac{1}{n_1} \sum_{i:D_i=1} \frac{1}{K} \sum_{k=1}^{K} m_0(X_i) - m_0(X_{j_k(i)}),$$

$$\text{and stochastic term} \quad ST_K = \frac{1}{n} \sum_{i=1}^{n} (2D_i - 1) \left(1 + \frac{R(i)}{K}\right) \varepsilon_i.$$

These decompositions show nicely what drives potential biases and variance of the treatment effect estimates. Obviously, the main difficulty in calculating the bias and variance for these estimators is the handling of the stochastic matching discrepancies $X_i - X_{j_k(i)}$. Recalling the common support assumption, it is clear that for discrete variables, fixed K but $n \to \infty$, these discrepancies will become zero, and so will be B_K and BT_K. For continuous variables in X, Abadie and Imbens (2006) gave their explicit distribution (densities and the first two moments). These enabled them to derive the asymptotics for (3.20) and (3.21) as given below. As the continuous confounders will dominate the asymptotic behaviour, let us assume without loss of generality that X is a vector of q continuous variables. The adding of discrete ones is asymptotically for free. Let us first summarise the assumptions to be made:

(A1) and **(A2)**   We use the CIA and the common support, i.e. there exist an $\epsilon > 0$ such that $\epsilon < P(D = 1|X = x) < 1 - \epsilon$ for all x.

(A3)   We are provided with a random sample $\{(Y_i, X_i, D_i)\}_{i=1}^{n}$.

Recall that if the common support condition is not fulfilled, or if we cannot find reasonable matches for some of the observed x, then the population of interest has to be redefined restricting the analysis on a set, say $\mathcal{X}$, where this condition holds. As already discussed, for estimating the ATET we need to assume a little bit less, specifically

(AT1) and **(AT2)** $Y^0 \perp D|X$ and $P(D = 1|X = x) < 1 - \epsilon$ for all x.

(AT3)   Conditional on $D = d$ the sample consists of independent draws from $(Y, X)|D = d$ for $d = 0, 1$, and for some $r \geq 1$, $n_1^r/n_0 \to \rho$ with $0 < \rho < \infty$.

With these we can state

THEOREM 3.1   *Under assumptions (A1) to (A3) and with $m_1(\cdot)$, $m_0(\cdot)$ Lipschitz, then $B_K = O_p(n^{-1/q})$, and the order of the bias term $E[B_K]$ is not in general lower than $n^{-2/q}$. Furthermore, $Var[\widehat{ATE}|\mathbf{X}, \mathbf{D}] = \frac{1}{n^2} \sum_{i=1}^{n} \left(1 + \frac{R(i)}{K}\right)^2 Var[Y|X_i, D_i]$.*

Set $f_d := f_{X|D=d}$. Under assumptions (AT1) to (AT3) and with $m_0(\cdot)$ Lipschitz, one has $BT_K = O_p(n_1^{-r/q})$, and for $\mathcal{X}_{01}$ being a compact subset of the interior of $\mathcal{X}_0$ with $m_0(\cdot)$ having bounded third derivatives, and $f_0(x)$ having first bounded derivatives, one has

$$E[BT_K] = n^{-2r/q} \left(\frac{-1}{K} \sum_{k=1}^{K} \Gamma\left(\frac{kq+2}{q}\right) \frac{1}{(k-1)!q}\right) \rho^{2/q}$$

$$\times \int \left(f_0(x) \frac{\pi^{q/2}}{\Gamma(1+q/2)}\right)^{-2/q} \left\{f_0^{-1}(x) \frac{\partial f_0}{\partial x'}(x) \frac{\partial m_0}{\partial x'}(x) + \frac{1}{2} tr\left(\frac{\partial^2 f_0}{\partial x' \partial x}(x)\right)\right\}$$

$$f_1(x) \, dx + o(n_1^{2r/q}).$$

Furthermore, $Var[\widehat{ATET}|\mathbf{X}, \mathbf{D}] = \frac{1}{n_1^2} \sum_{i=1}^{n} \left(D_i - (1 - D_i)\frac{R(i)}{K}\right)^2 Var[Y|X_i, D_i]$.

If additionally $Var[Y|X, D]$ is Lipschitz and bounded away from zero, and the fourth moments of the conditional distribution of $Y|(x, d)$ exist and are uniformly bounded in x, then

$$\sqrt{n} \frac{\left(\widehat{ATE} - ATE - B_K\right)}{\left\{E[(ATE(X) - ATE)^2] + nVar[\widehat{ATE}|X, D]\right\}^{1/2}} \xrightarrow{d} N(0, 1),$$

$$\sqrt{n_1} \frac{\left(\widehat{ATET} - ATET - BT_K\right)}{\left\{E[(ATET(X) - ATET)^2] + n_1 Var[\widehat{ATET}|X, D]\right\}^{1/2}} \xrightarrow{d} N(0, 1).$$

In the bias expressions we see what we called the *curse of dimensionality* in non-parametric estimation: the larger the number q of continuous conditioning variables x, the larger the bias, and the slower the convergence rate. What is somehow harder to see is the impact of the number of neighbours K, and therefore also that of replicates $R(i)$. However, if we let K increase with n, then we are in the (non-parametric) regression context which we will study later.[8]

One might argue that Theorem 3.1 indicates that the fewer (continuous) conditioning variables we include, the better the performance of the estimator. However, the correct statement is that 'the fewer (continuous) conditioning variables are necessary, the easier the estimation'. Actually, without an excellent estimator for the bias (that one would have to use for bias reduction by subtracting it from the treatment effect estimate) we only get the parametric $\sqrt{n}$ convergence rate for $q \leq 2$ when estimating ATE. To ignore the bias we even need $q = 1$. Not surprisingly, for the ATET, the convergence rate depends on n_1 and on the ratio n_1/n_0, recall assumption (AT3). Consequently, even with more than one conditioning variable (i.e. $q > 1$) one might reach a $\sqrt{n_1}$ convergence rate if n_0 increased accordingly faster ($n_1/n_0 \to 0$). The good news is that in both cases, the inclusion of covariates that are discrete with finite support has asymptotically no impact on the bias. It should be said, however, that in finite samples the inclusion of many discrete variables, and in particular of those with 'large support' (relative to sample size), does have an impact. Unfortunately, little is known about the 'how much'.

It is important to keep in mind that the Theorem holds only under the assumptions (A1) to (A3) or (AT1) to (AT3), respectively. If the CIA fails because we did not include enough conditioning variables, then an additional bias term adds to B_K (or BT_K when estimating ATET). That does not asymptotically disappear and gives therefore an inconsistent estimator. But as in practice we are only provided with finite samples, also B_K (BT_K) is indeed always present, so that we have at least two trade-offs to handle:

---

[8] The appearance of the other expressions like the number π or the Gamma-function Γ come directly from the density and moments of the used matching discrepancy $X_i - X_{j_k(i)}$ in $\mathbb{R}^q$. When looking for the closest neighbours in the Euclidean sense, then the volume of the unit q sphere is of particular interest which is in fact $2\pi^{q/2}/\Gamma(q/2)$. This explains the appearance of these terms in the bias.

the bias–bias trade-off when choosing the number of conditioning variables[9], and a bias–variance trade-off, especially when choosing K and therewith $R(i)$.[10]

We should add at this point a comment regarding these trade-offs. For about two decades the identification aspect has been dominating a large part of the economics and econometrics literature. It basically puts most of the emphasise on identifying exactly the parameter of interest. For theory and academic papers this might be fair enough. For empirical research it can be misleading because there, people face finite samples and have to estimate the parameter with the data and information at hand. The unbiasedness can only be attained thanks to untestable (and mostly disputable) assumptions. The potential bias effect when these are violated is little studied. Furthermore, the unbiasedness is often just an asymptotic phenomenon while in practice the finite sample bias and variance (i.e. the finite sample mean squared error) are quantities that matter and should worry us as well. An empirical researcher should always look for a compromise between all potential biases and variances of the estimators and data at hand. His objective must be to minimise the finite sample mean squared error.

In practice the correction for bias is often much harder than the estimation of the variance. One tries therefore to use bias-reducing methods, and in particular undersmoothing, such that the squared bias becomes negligible compared to the variance. But what about the variance? Theorem 3.1 gives explicit formulae for the $Var[\widehat{ATE}|\mathbf{X}, \mathbf{D}]$, $Var[\widehat{ATET}|\mathbf{X}, \mathbf{D}]$ which can be used directly when replacing $Var[Y|\mathbf{X}, \mathbf{D}]$ by nonparametric estimates. For doing inference on our treatment effect estimates we need

$$Var[\widehat{ATE}] = n^{-1} \left\{ E\left[nV(\widehat{ATE}|\mathbf{X}, \mathbf{D}) + (ATE(X) - ATE)^2 \right] \right\}$$

and

$$Var[\widehat{ATET}] = n_1^{-1} \left\{ E\left[n_1 V(\widehat{ATET}|\mathbf{X}, \mathbf{D}) + (ATET(X) - ATET)^2 \right] \right\}$$

respectively. Recalling the formulae for

$$Var[\widehat{ATE}|\mathbf{X}, \mathbf{D}], \ Var[\widehat{ATET}|\mathbf{X}, \mathbf{D}],$$

definition (3.19) of

$$\hat{Y}_i(d), \ d = 0, 1,$$

and

$$E\left[(\hat{Y}_i(1) - \hat{Y}_i(0) - ATE)^2 \right] \simeq E[(ATE(X) - ATE)^2] + E\left[\varepsilon_i^2 + \frac{1}{K^2} \sum_{k=1}^{K} \varepsilon_{j_k(i)}^2 \right],$$

$$\frac{1}{n} \sum_{i=1}^{n} E\left[\varepsilon_i^2 + \frac{1}{K^2} \sum_{k=1}^{K} \varepsilon_{j_k(i)}^2 | \mathbf{X}, \mathbf{D} \right] = \frac{1}{n} \sum_{i=1}^{n} \left(1 + \frac{R(i)}{K^2} \right) Var[Y|X_i, D_i],$$

---

[9] Choosing too many confounders increases B_K or BT_K unnecessarily, but choosing too few counfounders leads to the violation of CIA leading to an additional (the *selection*) bias.

[10] The number of confounders has an impact on both, the total bias (B_K or BT_K plus selection bias) and the variance, but their choice is mostly driven by the first mentioned concern. The 'smoothing' bias B_K (BT_K) is increasing with K, while a small K increases the variance.

we get the following immediate and intuitive estimators[11]

$$\hat{V}ar[\widehat{ATE}]$$

$$= \frac{1}{n^2} \sum_{i=1} \left(Y_i - \hat{Y}_i(0) - \widehat{ATET} \right)^2 + \left[\left(\frac{R(i)}{K} \right)^2 + \frac{(2K-1)R(i)}{K^2} \right] \hat{V}ar[Y|X_i, D_i],$$

$$\hat{V}ar[\widehat{ATET}]$$

$$= \frac{1}{n_1^2} \sum_{i:D_i=1} \left(\hat{Y}_i(1) - \hat{Y}_i(0) - \widehat{ATET} \right)^2 + \frac{1}{n_1^2} \sum_{i:D_i=0} \left(\frac{R(i)\{R(i)-1\}}{K^2} \right) \hat{V}ar[Y|X_i, D_i].$$

3.2.3 Statistical Properties of Regression Estimators

The discussion about convergence rates and biases has brought us to reflections about the very much related *regression methods*. How close they are to matching becomes evident when recognising that the above-discussed matching estimator is a kNN regression estimator if $K \xrightarrow[n\to\infty]{} \infty$. We realise that we could not achieve $\sqrt{n}$ consistency when considering kNN regression unless X contained only one (continuous[12]) variable. To achieve $\sqrt{n}$ convergence, the bias has to be kept sufficiently small. For $q > 1$ this requires bias reduction methods like higher order local polynomials or higher-order kernels.[13] Both approaches can be shown to be first-order equivalent to a weighted kernel regression estimator with a particular weighting function. This weighting function is such that some of the weights are actually negative, a construction that does not exist so easily for kNN.

There are different articles studying some of the asymptotic properties for regression-based estimators. The differences concern not only the pre-estimation of the $m_d(\cdot)$ but also the use of the propensity score $p(x) = P(D = 1|X = x)$. Each article works with different assumptions, but they have in common that they show under certain conditions $\sqrt{n}$-consistency for the estimators. Without saying so explicitly, they also show implicitly that for each additional (continuous) covariate X more bias reduction has to be conducted. Consequently, the regularity conditions on the functions m_0, m_1 and densities f_0, f_1 are getting stronger for larger dim(X). If only ATET is of interest (or ATEN), then we usually only need such conditions for m_0, f_0 (or m_1, f_1, respectively).

---

[11] Abadie and Imbens (2006) show the consistency of these estimators for reasonable estimators $\hat{V}ar[Y|X_i, D_i]$.

[12] Again as a reminder: discrete covariates with finite support do not affect the asymptotic properties; depending on their number and support size. However, they can essentially affect the finite sample performance and thus are important in practice. This is why we set 'continuous' in parentheses.

[13] Readers who are more familiar with non- and semi-parametric regression might be somewhat confused, as for semi-parametric estimators the so-called curse of dimensionally starts at dimension $q > 3$ and not for $q > 1$. This is true for all generally used methods like kernels, kNN, splines or any other sieves estimator – but here the K is fixed. A further difference to estimation problems which are subject to the less restrictive rule ($q < 4$) is that in our case – take, for the example, the ATE estimation problem – we consider the average of differences of predictors from two non-parametrically estimated functions, m_0 and m_1, estimated from two different independent samples with probably different densities. This is a somewhat more complex problem than the classical semi-parametric estimation problems.

We are not going to examine the different regularity conditions in detail here. They are hard or impossible to check anyway, and therefore simply tell us what we have to believe. In some approaches, the regularity conditions may look very strong.[14] In brief, either higher-order local polynomial regression or higher-order kernels are required if we want to make the bias negligible in order to get $\sqrt{n}$-convergence. It is often stated that this can also be achieved – or even done better – by sieves. Unfortunately, this is not true, especially not for the 'global' ones, recall our discussions in Section 2.2. There, people just work with much stronger assumptions on the $m_d(\cdot)$.

For the non-parametric treatment effect estimators exist asymptotic variance bounds, always assuming sufficient smoothness for all unkonwn functions.[15] We will later see that there exist several estimators that indeed meet these bounds and can therefore be called 'efficient'.

THEOREM 3.2   *Under the CIA and CSC, i.e. assumptions (A1) and (A2), for a binary treatment D the asymptotic variance bound for ATE is generally*

$$E\left[\left(E\left[Y^1 - Y^0|X\right] - ATE\right)^2 + \frac{Var[Y^1|X]}{\Pr(D=1|X)} + \frac{Var[Y^0|X]}{1 - \Pr(D=1|X)}\right].$$

Analogously, under the modified CIA and CSC (AT1) and (AT2), for a binary treatment D the asymptotic variance bound for ATET is generally

$$\Pr{}^{-2}(D=1) \cdot E\left[\Pr(D=1|X)\left\{E[Y^1 - Y^0|X] - ATET\right\}^2\right.$$
$$\left. + \Pr(D=1|X)Var[Y^1|X] + \frac{\Pr{}^2(D=1|X)Var[Y^0|X]}{1 - \Pr(D=1|X)}\right].$$

In the special case when the propensity score is known, the efficiency bound for ATE stays the same whereas for the ATET estimation it changes to

$$\Pr{}^{-2}(D=1) \cdot E\left[\Pr{}^2(D=1|X)\left\{E[Y^1 - Y^0|X] - ATET\right\}^2\right.$$
$$\left. + \Pr(D=1|X)Var[Y^1|X] + \frac{\Pr{}^2(D=1|X)Var[Y^0|X]}{1 - \Pr(D=1|X)}\right].$$

In order to prove these statements one can resort to the ideas of pathwise derivatives in Section 2.2.3, recall Equation 2.68. There we already calculated the score function $S(Y, D, X)$, Equation 2.69, which gives the *tangent space* of our model as a set of functions that are mean zero and exhibit the additive structure of the score

$$\Im = \left\{d \cdot s_1(y|x) + (1-d) \cdot s_0(y|x) + (d - p(x)) \cdot s_p(x) + s_x(x)\right\} \qquad (3.22)$$

---

[14] Hirano, Imbens and Ridder (2003) assume that the propensity score is at least $7q$ times continuously differentiable. Others work with infinitely many continuous derivatives for the m_d, f_d, p functions. This is still less restrictive than directly working with a purely parametric approach with a fixed functional specification.

[15] Here we follow mainly Hahn (1998).

for any functions s_1, s_0, s_p, s_x satisfying:

$$\int s_d (y|x) f_d (y|x) dy = 0 \quad \forall x , \qquad \int s_x (x) f (x) dx = 0 \tag{3.23}$$

and $s_p(x)$ being a square-integrable measurable function of x.

Let us briefly sketch the calculations of the variance bound for the estimation of ATE. For a *regular parametric submodel*[16] F_θ (with θ_0 being the true parameter) we can write

$$ATE(F_\theta) = \int \{E_\theta [Y|x, D = 1] - E_\theta [Y|x, D = 0]\} dF_\theta(x)$$

$$= \int \left(\int y f_1 (y|x, \theta) dy - \int y f_0 (y|x, \theta) dy \right) dF_\theta(x).$$

Computing the pathwise derivative along θ and evaluating it at θ_0 gives

$$\frac{\partial ATE(F_\theta)}{\partial \theta}|_{\theta=\theta_0} = \cdots = \int \int y \{f_1' - f_0'\} f(x) dy dx + \int (m_1(x) - m_0(x)) f'(x) dx,$$

where the f_d' are the derivatives of the respective density of X in group $D = d$ with respect to θ. If you find a function $\delta(y, d, x)$ such that

$$\frac{\partial ATE(F_\theta)}{\partial \theta}\bigg|_{\theta=\theta_0} = E [\delta(Y, D, X) \cdot S(Y, D, X)]|_{\theta=\theta_0} , \tag{3.24}$$

then we know that for its projection on the tangent space $\mathfrak{I}$ its variance $E[\delta^2(Y, D, X)] = Var[\delta(Y, D, X)]$ is the variance bound for the ATE estimators. Consider now

$$\delta(y, d, x) = \{m_1(x) - m_0(x) - ATE\} + d\frac{y - m_1(x)}{p(x)} + (1 - d)\frac{m_0(x) - y}{1 - p(x)}$$

and verify (3.24), and that it lies in space $\mathfrak{I}$, i.e. is identical to its projection on $\mathfrak{I}$. To calculate $E[\delta^2(Y, D, X)]$ is straightforward then.

What can we see from the obtained results? On a first glimpse the importance of the propensity score in these bounds might be surprising. But it is not when you realise that we speak of binary treatments and thus $E[D|X] = \Pr(D = 1|X)$. Furthermore, the treatment effect estimation problem conditioned on X is affected by 'selection on X', and therefore must depend on $\Pr(D = 1|X)$. A corollary is that for constant propensity scores, $\Pr(D = 1|X) = E[\Pr(D = 1|X)] = P$, i.e. when we are back in the situation of random treatment assignment with $ATE = ATET$, we have the variance bound

$$E \left[\left(E\left[Y^1 - Y^0|X\right] - ATE \right)^2 + \frac{Var[Y^1|X]}{P} + \frac{Var[Y^0|X]}{1 - P} \right] . \tag{3.25}$$

This would not change if we knew P, and therefore knew also that we are in the case of random assignment. It tells us that for estimating ATE one does not asymptotically gain in efficiency by knowing that random assignment has taken place.

Why does knowledge of the propensity score (like, for example, in a controlled experiment) not change the variance bound for the ATE but reduces that of ATET? The main

---

[16] I.e. a model with the parameters belonging to an open set, non-singular Fisher information and some more regularity conditions.

reason for this is that knowledge of the propensity score helps to improve the estimation of $f_1 := f_{X|D=1}$ which is needed for the ATET but not for the ATE. The propensity score provides information about the ratio of the density in the control and the treated population and thus allows control observations to identify the density of X in the treated population and vice versa. The estimation of $E[Y^0|D = 1]$ can therefore be improved. The (Y, X) observations of both treatment groups identify the conditional expectation. This conditional expectation is weighted by the distribution of X among the treated, say f_1, which can be estimated from the treated group. Usually, the non-participant observations are not informative for estimating that distribution. If, however, the relationship between the distribution of X among the treated and the one among the controls was known, then the X observations of the controls would be useful for estimating f_1. The propensity score ratio provides exactly this information as it equals the density ratio times the size ratio of the subpopulations: $\frac{p(X)}{1-p(X)} = \frac{f_1(X)}{f_0(X)} \frac{\Pr(D=1)}{\Pr(D=0)}$ with $f_0 := f_{X|D=0}$. Since the relative size of the treated subpopulation $\Pr(D = 1) = 1 - \Pr(D = 0)$ can be estimated precisely, for known $p(x)$ the observations of both, the treated and the controls can be used to estimate f_1.

Example 3.5 In the case of random assignment with $p(x) = \frac{1}{2}$ for all x, the distribution of X is the same among the treated and the non-participants, and using only the treated observations to estimate f_1 would neglect half of the informative observations. But as we know that $f_1 = f_0$ you can use all observations. In fact, with knowledge of the propensity score the counterfactual outcome for the treated $E[Y^0|D = 1]$ could be predicted even without observing the treated.

This example demonstrates heuristically that for estimating the ATET we expect an improvement when knowing the propensity score. For estimating ATE, this knowledge is not helpful: the (Y, X) observations of the treated sample are informative for estimating $E[Y^1|X]$, whereas the (Y, X) observations of the controls are informative for estimating $E[Y^0|X]$. Since the joint distribution of Y^1, Y^0 is not identified, the observations of the treated sample cannot assist in estimating $E[Y^0|X]$ and vice versa. Knowledge of the propensity score is of no use here. Theorem 3.2 has some practical use. Sometimes we know an estimation procedure coming from a different context but which may be applied to our problem. We would like to check, then, if this leads to an efficient estimator in our setting or not.

Example 3.6 Imagine we have experimental data and can separate the treatment impact from the confounders impact in an additive way: $E[Y|X = x, D = d] = d'\alpha + m(x)$. Obviously, we then face a partial linear model as discussed in the section on non- and semi-parametric estimation. Recall now the estimator (2.59) of Speckman (1988) to get α, i.e.

$$\hat{\alpha} = \sum_{i=1}^{n} \left(y_i - \hat{E}\,[Y|x_i] \right) \left(d_i - \hat{E}\,[D|x_i] \right) / \sum_{i=1}^{n} \left(d_i - \hat{E}\,[D|x_i] \right)^2 ,$$

which corresponds to the treatment effect. As we have experimental data, $\Pr(D = 1|X) = P$ is constant, and it can be shown that its asymptotic variance is

$$E\left[Var[Y^1|X]/P + Var[Y^0|X]/(1-P)\right] + \left\{\frac{1}{P(1-P)} - 3\right\} Var[ATE(X)].$$

(3.26)

It is easy to verify that this estimator only reaches the asymptotic efficiency bound if we have a propensity score of $P = 1 - P = 0.5$.

The next direct corollary from Theorem 3.2 is that for estimators of the sample analogues, i.e. estimators of the SATE (sample ATE) and the SATET, we obtain the same lower bounds for the variances minus the respective first term. Take for example the ATE: the first term is $Var\left[Y^1 - Y^0 - ATE|X\right]$ which only describes the contribution of the sampling variance, and therefore $Var\left[Y^1 - Y^0 - SATE|X\right] = 0$.

As already discussed, sometimes we are interested in a weighted treatment effect

$$\frac{E\left[\omega(X) \cdot E[Y^1 - Y^0|X]\right]}{E\left[\omega(X)\right]},$$

where the weighting function $\omega(X)$ may take values in $[0, \infty)$ but is mostly used for trimming (defining particular strata or blocks). The semi-parametric efficiency bound for such a weighted treatment effect is, along the lines of Theorem 3.2,

$$\frac{E\left[\omega(X)^2\left\{\frac{Var[Y^1|X]}{p(X)} + \frac{Var[Y^0|X]}{1-p(X)} + \left(E\left[Y^1 - Y^0|X\right] - ATE\right)^2\right\}\right]}{E\left[\omega(X)^2\right]}.$$

(3.27)

The 'problem' is now to construct treatment effect estimators that reach this lower bound. In any case we have to admit that this 'optimality' is asymptotic; it can only be attained conditionally on assumptions that allow for a bias reduction when necessary, and it does not tell us much about optimality when our sample is of moderate size.

For kernel smoothing based estimators it is not that hard to derive a consistency proof for $\widehat{ATET}$ estimators.[17] In order to achieve $\sqrt{n}$-consistency one needs a set of conditions:

(B1) Both, the density of X, $f(x)$, and the function $m_0(x)$ have Hölder continuous derivatives up to the order $p > q$.

(B2) Let $K(\cdot)$ be a Lipschitz continuous kernel function of order p with a compact support with Hölder continuous derivatives of order 1 at least.

It should be evident to readers of Section 2.2 that this condition is needed as a bias reduction tool. This can also be seen from the next condition which can only hold if $2p > q$, which is automatically fulfilled by condition $p > q$ in (B1). As discussed in the section about non-parametric kernel regression, there is always the possibility of using higher-order local polynomials instead of higher-order kernels (or even a mix of both).

---

[17] Here we follow the lines of Heckman, Ichimura and Todd (1998). In their article, however, they mix estimators with and without a prior estimation of the unknown propensity score, what led Hahn and Ridder (2013) to the conjecture that their derivation was wrong. Note that our result refers to a special case which is not affected by this criticism.

(B3) Bandwidth h satisfies $nh^q / log(n) \to \infty$ but $nh^{2p} \to c < \infty, c \geq 0$.

What we try to get by (B2) is a bias of order h^p which by (B3) is then of order $\sqrt{n}$.

(B4) Function $m_0(\cdot)$ is only predicted for interior points of $\mathcal{X}_0.$[18]

There exist many versions of regression estimators for ATET; a most intuitive one is

$$\widehat{ATET} = \frac{1}{n_1} \sum_{i:D_i=1} Y_i - \hat{m}_0(X_i) , \qquad \hat{m}_0(x) = \frac{\sum_{j:D_j=0} Y_j K_h(X_j - x)}{\sum_{j:D_j=0} K_h(X_j - x)}. \qquad (3.28)$$

You may equally well replace $\hat{m}_0(\cdot)$ by a local polynomial estimator. This allows you to accordingly relax assumption (B2). Let us consider only continuous confounders for the reasons we discussed. Then one can state

THEOREM 3.3   *Given a random sample $\{Y_i, X_i\}_{i=1}^n$ with $X_i \in \mathbb{R}^q$ and $Y_i \in \mathbb{R}$ with finite variance. Under assumptions (B1) to (B4), (AT1) to (AT3) with $r = 1$, for (3.28) it holds*

$$\sqrt{n_1} \left\{ \widehat{ATET} - \frac{1}{n_1} \sum_{i:D_i=1} B(X_i) - ATET \right\} \xrightarrow[n_1 \to \infty]{} N(0, Var)$$

where the variance is

$$Var = V_X \left[E[Y^1 - Y^0|X, D = 1]|D = 1 \right] + E_X \left[Var[Y^1|X, D = 1]|D = 1 \right]$$
$$+ \rho E_X \left[\frac{Var[Y^0|X, D = 0] f^2(X|D = 1)}{f^2(X|D = 0)} |D = 0 \right]$$

with $\rho = \lim(n_1/n_0)$, cf. (AT3), and $B(x)$ is the bias of $\hat{m}_0(x)$. For a product kernel (2.30) we can write

$$B(x) = h^p f^{-1}(x) \sum_{l=1}^p \frac{1}{l!(p-l)!} \sum_{j=1}^q \int u_j^p K(u) du \cdot \frac{\partial^l m_0(x)}{\partial x_j^l} \frac{\partial^{p-l} f(x)}{\partial x_j^{p-l}} .$$

The bias term can be reduced by the use of higher-order polynomials: the general rule is that the higher the order of the local polynomial, the later starts the first sum $\sum_{l=1}^p$; e.g. when using local linear estimation we obtain $B(x)$ as above but with $\sum_{l=2}^p$. Moreover, we can choose p large enough to extend (B3) such that $nh^{2p} \to 0$ leading to an asymptotically negligible bias.

---

[18] This says that $\mathcal{X}_1$ is not only a subspace of $\mathcal{X}_0$ (which is the ATET analogue of the CSC), it demands the sometimes not realistic assumption that the h-neighbourhood of all points of $\mathcal{X}_1$ are in $\mathcal{X}_0$. In the articles this assumption sometimes is weakened by introducing a trimming function to get rid of boundary effects of the non-parametric estimator. Although for microdata sets where h (and therefore the boundary) is relatively tiny such that the boundary effects become negligible, this is necessary for exact asymptotic theory. The trimming also allows you to directly define a subpopulation S for which one wants to estimate the treatment effect. In practice people do this automatically and thereby actually redefine the population under consideration. We therefore have decided to present the version without trimming to simplify notation and formulae, but we apply (B4) for mathematical correctness.

Both terms, Var and $B(x)$ can straightforwardly be derived from standard results known in non-parametric regression; see our Section 2.2 and Exercise 8. The difference between estimator (3.28) and the true $ATET$ can be rewritten as

$$\frac{1}{n_1} \sum_{i:D_i=1} \{Y_i - m_1(X_i)\} + \{m_1(X_i) - m_0(X_i) - ATET\} + \{m_0(X_i) - \hat{m}_0(X_i)\}.$$

It is clear that the expectation of the first two terms is zero while from the last term we get the smoothing bias as given in Theorem 3.3; compare also with Section 2.2.

To obtain now the variance, note that under our assumptions the first two terms converge to the first two terms of Var. For the last term it is sufficient to consider the random part of $\hat{m}_0(\cdot)$. From Section 2.2 we know that it is asymptotically equivalent[19] to

$$\varepsilon_i \frac{1}{n_0} K_h(X_i - X) f_x^{-1}(X|D=0), \quad \text{with } \varepsilon_i = Y_i - m_0(X_i),$$

where all (Y_i, X_i) are taken from the control group $\{i : D_i = 0\}$. Their average over all $X = X_i$ with $D_i = 1$ converges to the conditional expectation

$$E\left[\varepsilon_i \frac{1}{n_1} K_h(X_i - X) f_x^{-1}(X)|D=1, (Y_i, X_i, D_i = 0)\right]$$
$$= \int \varepsilon_i K_h(X_i - w) f_x^{-1}(w|D=0) f_x(w|D=1) \, dw$$

which for $h \to 0$ converges to the zero-mean variable $\varepsilon_i f_x^{-1}(X_i|D=0) f_x(X_i|D=1)$ with the (ε_i, X_i) restricted to $D_i = 0$. From this expression one can easily calculate the variance. As $Var[U] = E[U^2] - E^2[U]$ one only needs to calculate $E[\varepsilon_i^2 f_x^{-2}(X_i|D=0) f_x^2(X_i|D=1)|D_i = 0]$ giving the last term of Var. Evidently, the same way one can derive kernel-based estimators and their asymptotic properties for ATE or $ATEN$.

It remains the question to what extent such a kernel estimator is efficient. Looking at Theorem 3.2 one realises that Var indeed corresponds to the efficiency bound as $\rho = \Pr(D=1)/\Pr(D=0)$.[20] To achieve (full) asymptotic efficiency, all we need is a sufficient bias reduction.

As an alternative there exist different suggestions based on series estimators for $m_0(\cdot)$, $m_1(\cdot)$ which again consider both, estimation of $ATET$ and ATE by

$$\frac{1}{n_1} \sum_{i:D_i=1} Y_i - \hat{m}_0(X_i), \quad \text{and} \quad \frac{1}{n} \sum_{i=1}^{n} \hat{m}_1(X_i) - \hat{m}_0(X_i), \tag{3.29}$$

---

[19] We say 'asymptotically equivalent' because – without loss of generality – we substituted the true density f_x for its estimate in the denominator.

[20] Check term by term and note that the second term of Var in Theorem 3.3 is

$$E[Var(Y^1|X, D=1)|D=1] = \int Var[Y^1|x, D=1] \, f_x(x|D=1) \, dx$$
$$= \int Var[Y^1|x, D=1] \, \Pr(D=1|X)\Pr^{-1}(D=1) f_x(x) \, dx$$
$$= E\left[\int (Y^1 - m_1(X))^2 f(y^1|X)\Pr^{-1}(D=1) \, dy^1 \, \Pr(D=1|X)\Pr^{-1}(D=1)\right]$$

respectively, with $m_1(\cdot)$, $m_0(\cdot)$ being estimated from the subsets of treated, respectively non-treated. Again, where authors state a presumable superiority of those series estimators one will note that it is always at the cost of stronger assumptions which, heuristically stated, shall guarantee that the chosen series approximates sufficiently well the functions $m_0(\cdot)$, $m_1(\cdot)$. Then the bias reduction is automatically given.[21] As discussed at the end of Chapter 2, a general handicap of too-simple sieves like the popular power series is that they are so-called 'global' estimators. They do not adapt locally and depend strongly on the density of X in the estimation sample. This makes them particularly inadequate for extrapolation (prediction), especially when extrapolating to a (sub-)population with a density of X that is different from the one used for estimation. Remember that this is exactly what we expect to be the case for the confounders X (our situation).

3.3   Propensity Score-Based Estimator

3.3.1   Propensity Score Matching

We have already seen in Section 1.2.2 how propensity scores can be used to check the validity of the randomised experiment assumption and to readjust the design accordingly. As we are in the situation where we have different distributions of X (i.e. different populations) in the different treatment groups, the propensity scores could be used to adjust retroactively for this difference. Before we come to the explicit propensity score weighting, consider a quite popular alternative. Let us rethink whether for a comparison of potential outcomes it is really necessary that two individuals are similar to each other in all confounders. Is it not enough to compare individuals who just have the same chance to be under treatment, respectively not to be treated? In fact, instead of using a matching estimator with respect to the covariates X, one could match individuals with respect to their propensity score. More formally, this *propensity score matching* is motivated on the observation that CIA, the conditional independence assumption (3.1), also implies that for propensity score $p(x) := \Pr(D = 1|X = x)$

$$Y^d \perp\!\!\!\perp D|P. \tag{3.30}$$

where $P = p(X)$. The proof is very simple: to show that (3.30) holds, i.e. that the distribution of D does not depend on Y^d given $p(X)$, it needs to be shown that $\Pr(D = 1|Y^d, p(X)) = \Pr(D = 1|p(X))$, and analogously for $D = 0$. Because $\Pr(D = 1|\cdot)$ and $\Pr(D = 0|\cdot)$ have to add to one for binary D, it suffices to show this relationship for one of them. Now, $\Pr(D = 1|Y^d, p(X)) = E[D|Y^d, p(X)] = E[E[D|X, Y^d, p(X)]|Y^d, p(X)]$ by iterated expectation. As $p(X)$ is deterministic given X, by the CIA this equals

$$E[E[D|X, Y^d]|Y^d, p(X)] = E[E[D|X]|Y^d, p(X)] = E[p(X)|Y^d, p(X)] = p(X).$$

---

[21] Hahn (1998) does this for a sequences of polynomials which in practice are hardly available, whereas Imbens, Newey and Ridder (2005) propose the use of power series which in practice should not be used; recall our earlier discussions.

Analogously, for the right-hand side you have

$$\Pr(D = 1|p(X)) = E[D|p(X)] = E[E[D|X, p(X)]|p(X)] = p(X).$$

So we see that the justification of propensity score matching does not depend on any property of the potential outcomes. Note, however, that (3.30) does not imply CIA.

Propensity score matching and matching on covariates X will always converge to the same limit since it is a mechanical property of iterated integration.[22] Hence, in order to eliminate selection bias due to observables x, it is indeed not necessary to compare individuals that are identical in all x; it suffices that they are identical in the propensity score. This suggests to match on the one-dimensional propensity score $p(x)$, because

$$E\left[Y^0|D = 1\right] = E_X\left[E[Y^0|p(X), D = 1]|D = 1\right]$$
$$= E_X\left[E[Y^0|p(X), D = 0]|D = 1\right] = E_X\left[E[Y|p(X), D = 0]|D = 1\right],$$

where the subindex X emphasises that the outer expectation is integrating over X. Finally, it is not hard to see from (3.30) that you also can obtain

$$Y^d \perp\!\!\!\perp D|\delta(P) \tag{3.31}$$

for any function $\delta(\cdot)$ that is bijective on the interval $(0, 1)$. While this knowledge is useless for propensity score weighting, it can directly be used for propensity score matching noticing that then

$$E\left[Y^0|D = 1\right] = E_X\left[E[Y^0|\delta\{p(X)\}, D = 1]|D = 1\right]$$
$$= E_X\left[E[Y|\delta\{p(X)\}, D = 0]|D = 1\right].$$

In practice the propensity score is almost always unknown and has to be estimated first.[23] Estimating the propensity score non-parametrically is usually as difficult as estimating the conditional expectation function $m_0(x)$ since they have the same dimensionality.[24] Whether matching on x or on $\hat{p}(x)$ yields better estimates depends on the particular problem and data; for example on whether it is easier to model and estimate $p(x)$ or the $m_d(x)$.

So what are the advantages of doing propensity matching? Isn't it just one more estimation step but else giving the same results? There are actually some potential advantages of propensity score matching: First, as indicated, it might be that the modelling and estimation of the multivariate propensity score regression is easier than it is

---

[22] For further details see Frölich (2007b).

[23] In fact, instead of the propensity score one can also use any balancing score $b(x_i)$ with the property that in expectation it is proportional to the propensity score.

[24] It is general practice in applied econometrics to estimate the propensity score by a probit or logit model. Such a parametric estimator would turn the matching estimator essentially into a much simpler semi-parametric estimator due to the parametrisation of the propensity score. It is often believed that a logit estimate of the propensity score works well and does not lead to important difference compared to the use of a non-parametric propensity score. This is unfortunately not correct as misspecifications of $p(x)$ can easily have a leverage effect inside the matching so that even small mistakes here lead to large ones in the final treatment effect estimate.

for the $m_d(x)$. Second, it relaxes the common support restriction in practice: we only need to find matches for people's propensity (what is much easier than finding a match regarding a high dimensional vector of characteristics). Moreover, if we can estimate the propensity score semi-parametrically, then this two-step procedure does indeed lead to a dimensionality reduction. If, however, also the propensity score has to be estimated non-parametrically, then the dimensionality problem has just been shifted from the matching to the propensity score estimation – and concerning the theoretical convergence rate nothing is gained.

The most important advantage of propensity score based estimation is that it avoids model selection based on the outcome variable: one can specify the model of the selection process without involving the outcome variable Y. Hence, one can respecify a probit model several times e.g. via omitted-variables tests, balancing tests or the inclusion of several interaction terms until a good fit is obtained, *without* this procedure being driven by Y or the treatment effects themselves. This is in contrast to the conventional regression approach: if one were to estimate a regression of Y on D and X, all diagnostics would be influenced by Y or treatment effect such that a re-specification of the model would already depend on Y and thus on the treatment effect, and therefore be endogenous by construction. In an ideal analysis, one would specify and analyse the propensity score without ever looking at the Y data. This can already be used for designing an observational study, where one could try to balance groups such that they have the same support or (even better) distribution of the propensity score. Also in the estimation of the propensity score diagnostic analysis for assessing the balance of covariate distributions is crucial and should be done without looking at the outcome data Y. If the outcome is not used at all, the true treatment effects cannot influence the modelling process for balancing covariates. The key advantage of propensity score analysis is that one conducts the design, analysis and balancing of the covariates before ever seeing the outcome data.

Another point one should mention is that once a good fit of the propensity score has been obtained, it can be used to estimate the treatment effect on several different outcome variables Y, e.g. employment states at different times in the future, various measures of earnings, health indicators etc., i.e. as the final outcome is not involved in finding $\hat{p}(x)$, the latter can be used for the analysis of any outcome Y for which $Y^d \perp\!\!\!\perp D|P$ can be supposed.

We still permit heterogeneity in treatment effects of arbitrary form: if we are interested in the ATET and not the ATE, we only need that $Y^0 \perp\!\!\!\perp D|P$ but do not require $Y^1 \perp\!\!\!\perp D|P$ or $\{Y^1 - Y^0\} \perp\!\!\!\perp D|P$. In other words, we can permit that individuals endogeneously select into treatment. The analogue holds for identifying ATEN. Like before in the simple matching or regression context, endogenous control variables X are permitted, i.e. correlation between X and U is allowed to be non-zero.

We turn now to the actual implementation of the estimator. To guarantee that we calculate a treatment effect only for population $\mathcal{X}_{01}$, the propensity score estimate $\hat{p}$ will be used for both matching and trimming: for

$$\mu_d(p) := E[Y^d|P = p]$$

(analogously to the definition of m_d with arguments X) and all for population $\mathcal{X}_{01}$

$$\widehat{ATET} = \widehat{E}\left[Y^1|D=1\right] - \widehat{E}\left[Y^0|D=1\right]$$

$$= \frac{\sum\limits_{i:D_i=1} \left\{Y_i - \hat{\mu}_0(\hat{p}_i)\right\} \mathbb{1}\{\hat{p}_i < 1\}}{\sum\limits_{i:D_i=1} \mathbb{1}\{\hat{p}_i < 1\}}$$

$$\widehat{ATE} = \widehat{E}\left[Y^1\right] - \widehat{E}\left[Y^0\right]$$

$$= \frac{\sum\limits_{i=1}^{n} \left\{\hat{\mu}_1(\hat{p}_i) - \hat{\mu}_0(\hat{p}_i)\right\} \mathbb{1}\{1 > \hat{p}_i > 0\}}{\sum\limits_{i=1}^{n} \mathbb{1}\{1 > \hat{p}_i > 0\}}.$$

Although we give no explicit theorem, it is known that if the propensity score $\Pr(D = d|X = x)$ can be estimated at the same convergence rate as the conditional expectation $E[Y|X = x, D = d]$, then propensity score matching estimators with predicted propensity have the same distribution limits as we found them for the direct matching (or regression) estimators;[25] see also Section 3.5.1. If you can improve in rate due to some prior knowledge which, for example, enables you to use a dimension-reducing semi-parametric model for $\Pr(D = d|X = x)$, then this improvement allows you to relax the smoothness conditions otherwise necessary to avoid the curse of dimensionality. An extreme case of this strategy is when people do parametric propensity score estimation and use this for kNN matching. From Theorem 3.1 we know that we can only allow for a one-dimensional matching variable if we want the squared bias to converge faster than the variance. It is obvious that this also works if the confounder is parametrically generated (i.e. predicted). However, one should still account for this prediction when calculating the variance and standard errors. For details on this particular case of kNN matching with a fixed number of neighbours and the true propensity score being of type $F(x'\theta)$ for known F with finite dimensional unknown parameter θ, see Abadie and Imbens (2016).

Another possibility of dimension reduction comes from structural modelling.[26] A first step is to realise that the CIA (3.1) implies not only independence conditional on the propensity score $p(x)$ but may also be thought of as

$$Y^d \perp\!\!\!\perp D|(p(X_1), X_2), \qquad \text{where } X = (X_1, X_2) \text{ and } X_2 \text{ is assumed to not}$$

$$\text{affect the propensity score, i.e.,} \qquad (3.32)$$

This originates from the idea of simultaneous equations like

$$Y^d = m_d(X_2) + U^d, \qquad \Pr(D = d|X) = \Pr(D = d|X_1)$$

with $\{Y^d - m_d(X_2)\} \perp\!\!\!\perp D|p(X_1)$. Note that (3.32) is automatically implied by $Y^d \perp\!\!\!\perp D|p(X)$; it does in fact not introduce a new assumption but a maybe more meaningful modelling option.

---

[25] For more details see Frölich (2007b). See Sperlich (2009) and Hahn and Ridder (2013) for general results on non- and semi-parametric regression with generated regressors.

[26] These approaches are especially pronounced in different oeuvres of Heckman. Here we refer to ideas of Heckman, Ichimura and Todd (1998).

Example 3.7 Let X_2 comprise only (a few) components like gender and age. Hence, if we were interested in estimating the average potential outcome separately for men and women at different age categories, we could use (assuming full common support)

$$E\left[Y^0 | D = 1, gender, age\right]$$
$$= E\left[E[Y^0 | p(X_1), D = 1, gender, age] | D = 1, gender, age\right]$$
$$= E\left[E[Y^0 | p(X_1), D = 0, gender, age] | D = 1, gender, age\right]$$
$$= E\left[E[Y | p(X_1), D = 0, gender, age] | D = 1, gender, age\right],$$

where the outer expectation integrates over $p(X_1)$. Interestingly, we can use the same propensity score to estimate the potential outcome for both genders and all ages. Thus, we can use the same estimated propensity score for estimating the average potential outcome in the entire population; predicting the propensity scores only once will suffice. Obviously, the analysis of common support has to be done separately for each subpopulation.

We see an additional advantage of this structural approach here: as one would typically expect both X_1 and X_2 to be of smaller dimension than X, for both, $p(\cdot)$ and the $m_d(\cdot)$ fewer smoothness conditions (and fewer bias reducing methods) are necessary than were needed before. That is, the structural modelling entails dimension reduction by construction.

The propensity score has mainly an ex-post balancing function whereas the regression has the matching approach interpretation. So it could be that from a regression point of view we were (by chance) to match only on noise, then the $m_d(\cdot)$ are almost constant functions for each. However, an unbalanced sampling will still show a variation of $p(\cdot)$ in X. It is often helpful to make use of (3.32) and to match not only on the propensity score but also on those characteristics that we deem to be particularly important (or interesting) with respect to the outcome variable. Including some covariates in addition to the propensity score in the matching estimator can improve, apart from the advantage of interpretability, also the finite sample performance since a better balancing of these covariates is obtained. Further advantages of combining regression and propensity weighting will be discussed in Subsection 3.3.3.

Example 3.8 If we are interested in effects on wages or earnings, we might want to include *gender* as an additional matching variable in addition to the propensity score in order to study also the treatment effect by gender. Note that gender might nonetheless also be included in the estimation of the propensity score. This guarantees a good balance of gender, even if the effect of gender in the propensity score is zero or close to it. In this example one can simply impose exact matching on gender in the matching estimator, combined with propensity score weighting as proposed in the next subsection.

We conclude the subsection with a remark that might be obvious for some readers but less so for others. Propensity score matching can also be used for estimating *counterfactual distribution functions*. Furthermore, its applicability is not confined to treatment evaluation. It can be used more generally to adjust for differences in the distribution of covariates between the populations we compare. For this, certainly, propensity score *weighting*, discussed next, can be used as well.

Example 3.9 Frölich (2007b) studied the gender wage gap in the labour market with the use of propensity score matching. The fact that women are paid substantially lower wages than men may be the result of wage discrimination in the labour market. On the other hand, part of this wage gap may be due to differences in education, experience and other skills, whose distribution differs between men and women. Most of the literature on discrimination has attempted to estimate how much of the gender wage gap would remain if men and women had the same distributions of observable characteristics.[27] Not unexpectedly, the conclusion drawn from his study depends on which and how many characteristics are observed. For individuals with tertiary education (university, college, polytechnic) the choice of subject (or college major) may be an important characteristic of subsequent wages. A wide array of specialisations is available, ranging from mathematics, engineering, economics to philosophy, etc. One observes that men and women choose rather different subjects, with mathematical and technical subjects more often chosen by men. At the same time 'subject of degree' (= field of major) is not available in most data sets. In Frölich (2007b) this additional explanatory power of 'subject of degree' on the gender wage was examined. Propensity score matching was applied to analyse the gender wage gap of college graduates in the UK to see to which extent this gap could be explained by observed characteristics. He also simulated the entire wage distributions to examine the gender wage gap at different quantiles. It turned out that subject of degree contributed substantially to reducing the unexplained wage gap, particularly in the upper tail of the wage distribution. The huge wage differential between high-earning men and high-earning women was thus to a large extent the result of men and women choosing different subjects in university.

3.3.2   Propensity Score Weighting

An alternative but obvious estimation strategy to adjust for the differences in the covariate composition among treated and control population relies on weighting the observed outcomes by the inverse of the propensity score. Since, for example, values of x for which $p(x)$ is large may be relatively over-represented among the treated and values of x with small $p(x)$ over-represented among the non-treated, we could rectify this by

---

[27] If one attempts to phrase this in the treatment evaluation jargon, one would like to measure the direct effect of gender on wage when holding skills and experience fixed.

weighting along the propensity score. This idea is exactly what one traditionally does in (regression) estimation with missing values or with sample weights when working with strata.[28] Therefore, there exists already a huge literature on this topic but we limit our considerations to what is specific to the treatment effect estimation.

For the sake of presentation we again focus first on the ATET estimation and even start with the simpler case of known propensity scores and common support. Certainly, all calculations are based on the CIA in the sense of $Y^d \perp\!\!\!\perp D|p(X)$. The main challenge is to predict the average potential outcome Y^0 for the participants. As by Bayes' law we have, again with notation $f_d := f_{X|D=d}$

$$p(x) = \frac{f_1(x)\Pr(D=1)}{f_X(x)} \Rightarrow \frac{p(x)}{1-p(x)} = \frac{f_1(x)\Pr(D=1)}{f_0(x)\Pr(D=0)}, \text{ it follows}$$

$$E\left[Y^0|D=1\right] = \int m_0(x)f_1(x)dx = \int m_0(x)\frac{p(x)}{1-p(x)}\frac{\Pr(D=0)}{\Pr(D=1)}f_0(x)dx$$

$$= \frac{\Pr(D=0)}{\Pr(D=1)}E\left[m_0(X)\frac{p(X)}{1-p(X)}|D=0\right] = \frac{\Pr(D=0)}{\Pr(D=1)}E\left[Y\cdot\frac{p(X)}{1-p(X)}|D=0\right].$$

A natural estimator would therefore be

$$\widehat{E}\left[Y^0|D=1\right] = \frac{\Pr(D=0)}{\Pr(D=1)}\frac{1}{n_0}\sum_{i:D_i=0}Y_i\cdot\frac{p(x_i)}{1-p(x_i)}$$

$$\approx \widehat{E}\left[Y^0|D=1\right] = \frac{1}{n_1}\sum_{i:D_i=0}Y_i\cdot\frac{p(x_i)}{1-p(x_i)}$$

with $\frac{\Pr(D=0)}{\Pr(D=1)} \approx \frac{n_0}{n_1}$. Note that this estimator uses only the observations Y_i from the controls, cf. Example 3.5. All you need is a ('good') estimator for the propensity score. Comparing the average outcome of the treated with this predictor gives a consistent ATET estimator.

It is obvious that along similar steps we can obtain predictions of the potential treatment outcomes Y^1 for the non-participants for an ATEN estimator. Putting both together can be used to get an ATE estimator. Specifically, with a consistent predictor $\hat{p}$ we estimate the ATET by .

$$\frac{1}{n_1}\sum_{i=1}^{n}Y_iD_i - Y_i(1-D_i)\frac{\hat{p}(X_i)}{1-\hat{p}(X_i)}. \tag{3.33}$$

Analogously, the ATE is identified as

$$E\left[Y^1 - Y^0\right] = E\left[\frac{YD}{p(X)} - \frac{Y(1-D)}{1-p(X)}\right]$$

---

[28] How is this problem related to ours? Directly, because you can simply think of participants being the missings when estimating $m_0(\cdot)$ and the controls being the missings when estimating $m_1(\cdot)$.

and can be estimated by

$$\frac{1}{n} \sum_{i=1}^{n} \frac{Y_i D_i}{\hat{p}(X_i)} - \frac{Y_i (1 - D_i)}{1 - \hat{p}(X_i)}. \tag{3.34}$$

What are the advantages or disadvantages of this estimator compared to the matching? It has the advantage that it only requires a first step estimation of $p(x)$ and does not require $m_0(x)$ or $m_1(x)$. Hence, we would avoid their explicit non-parametric estimation. In small samples, however, the estimates can have a rather high variance if some propensity scores p_i are close to zero or one. In the latter case, term $\frac{p_i}{1-p_i}$ can get arbitrarily large and lead to variable estimates. In practice, it is then recommended to impose a cap on $\frac{p_i}{1-p_i}$. One could either trim (i.e. delete) those observations or censor them by replacing $\frac{p_i}{1-p_i}$ with $min(\frac{p_i}{1-p_i}$, prefixed upper bound). The typical solution to the problem is to remove (or rescale) observations with very large weights and check the sensitivity of the final results with respect to the trimming rules applied. We will discuss the general problem of trimming or capping somewhat later in this chapter.

The reason for the high variance when p_i is close to one is of course related to the common support problem. The remedies and consequences are somewhat different from that in the matching estimator, though. In the matching setup discussed before, if we are interested in the ATET we would delete the $D = 1$ observations with high propensity scores. Then we could compare the descriptive statistics of the deleted $D = 1$ observations with the remaining observations to understand the implications of this deletion and to assess external validity of our findings. If e.g. the deleted observations are low-income individuals compared to the remaining $D = 1$ observations, we know that our results do mainly hold for high-income individuals.

Applying some kind of trimming or capping with the weighting estimator also changes the population for which the effect is estimated. But depending on the implementation of this capping, the implications might be less obvious. To simplify, consider only the ATET comparing the average of observed Y^1 with the above proposed predictor for $E[Y^0|D = 1]$. Trimming would only happen in the latter term, but there are used only observations from the control group. Now, if any of the $D = 0$ observations with large values of $\frac{p}{1-p}$ are trimmed or censored, we do not see how this changes the treatment group (for which the ATET is calculated). A simple solution could be to trim (i.e. delete) the $D = 0$ observations with large values of $\frac{p}{1-p}$ in the calculation of $\hat{E}[Y^0|D = 1]$ and to use the same trimming rule for the treated when averaging over the Y_i^1. You may then compare those $D = 1$ observations that have been deleted with those $D = 1$ observations that have not been deleted to obtain an understanding of the implications of this trimming.

Concerning the asymptotic properties of estimators (3.33) and (3.34), there exist several results in the literature deriving them for different estimators of the propensity scores, see for example Hirano, Imbens and Ridder (2003), Huber, Lechner and Wunsch (2013) and references therein. The non-parametric versions are typically calculating the asymptotics for series estimators, namely power series. Applying slightly different (non-testable) conditions they all show asymptotic efficiency, i.e. that the estimators reach the variance bounds presented in Theorem 3.2 with asymptotically ignorable (smoothing or approximation) bias. Although the asymptotics are admittedly important, they alone give hardly recommendations for practical estimation and inference. A main problem is that practitioners underestimate the lever effect of an estimation error in the propensity score for the final treatment effect estimate: a small estimation error for $p(\cdot)$ may have a large impact on the treatment effect estimate. As $p(\cdot)$ is usually a smooth monotone function, the errors are virtually small. This is also a reason, though not a good one, why propensity score based methods are so enticing. Above all, do not forget that we already have seen in preceding discussions that in a semi-parametric estimation procedure you need to keep the non-parametric bias small, i.e. you have to undersmooth. When suffering from the curse of dimensionality you even have to use bias-reducing methods.

How should one proceed if the true propensity score $p(x\cdot)$ is known, as it is for example in an experiment where the treatment assignment is under control? From Theorem 3.2 we see that the answer is different for ATE and ATET because the asymptotics change only for ATET when $p(\cdot)$ was known. Nonetheless it might be surprising that for ATE it is asymptotically more efficient to weight by the estimated than by the true propensity score if the used propensity estimators are consistent and fulfil certain efficiency conditions.[29] Recalling the discussion that followed Theorem 3.2 we must realise that the knowledge of the propensity score only provides important information for the ATET, because there we need the conditional distribution $F(X|D = 1)$, and $p(\cdot)$ provides information about $F(X|D = 1)$. Theorem 3.2 reveals that the knowledge of $p(\cdot)$ reduces the variance part that comes from the sampling; it does not reduce the variance parts coming from the prediction of $m_0(x_i)$ or $m_1(x_i)$. So the variance part coming from sampling (referring to the difference between the sample distribution and the population distribution) can be reduced for the ATET estimates. The possibly surprising thing is that replacing $\hat{p}$ by p in the ATE estimator does lead to a larger variance. The reason is quite simple: the weighting with $\hat{p}(X_i)$ (the sample propensity score) is used to ex-post (re-)balance the participants in your sample. Using $p(X_i)$ does this asymptotically (i.e. for the population) but not so for your sample.[30]

Both aspects, that the knowledge of p does only help for reducing the sampling variance correcting for the conditioning in $F(X|D = 1)$ but not regarding the balancing, becomes obvious when looking at the following three ATET estimators using p, $\hat{p}$ or both:

$$\frac{1}{n_1} \sum_{i=1}^{n} \hat{p}(X_i) \left(\frac{Y_i D_i}{\hat{p}(X_i)} - \frac{Y_i (1 - D_i)}{1 - \hat{p}(X_i)} \right)$$

$$\frac{1}{n_1} \sum_{i=1}^{n} p(X_i) \left(\frac{Y_i D_i}{p(X_i)} - \frac{Y_i (1 - D_i)}{1 - p(X_i)} \right)$$

[29] See Robins and Rotnitzky (1995) for the case where the propensity score is estimated parametrically, and Hirano, Imbens and Ridder (2003) where it is estimated non-parametrically.

[30] See also Hirano, Imbens and Ridder (2003) who show that including the knowledge of $p(\cdot)$ as an additional moment condition leads to exactly the same estimator for ATE as if one uses a direct ATE estimator with estimated $p(\cdot)$.

$$\frac{1}{n_1} \sum_{i=1}^{n} p(X_i) \left(\frac{Y_i D_i}{\hat{p}(X_i)} - \frac{Y_i (1 - D_i)}{1 - \hat{p}(X_i)} \right). \tag{3.35}$$

In the first one we do the balancing well but do not appreciate the information contained in p to improve the estimation of the integral $\int dF(X|D = 1)$; in the second we do this but worsen the balancing; in the last one we use p for estimating $\int dF(X|D = 1)$ but keep $\hat{p}$ for the right sample balancing. Consequently, the last one is an efficient estimator of ATET whereas the others are not. Still, in practice one should be careful when estimating $p(\cdot)$ and keep the bias small. You get rewarded by asymptotically reaching the efficiency bound.

We conclude with a practical note. It might happen that the weights $\frac{\hat{p}(x_i)}{1-\hat{p}(x_i)}$ do not sum up to one in the respective (sub-)sample. It is therefore recommended to normalise by the sum of the weights, i.e. to actually use

$$\text{for the ATET} \quad \frac{\sum_{i=1}^{n} Y_i D_i}{\sum_{i=1}^{n} D_i} - \frac{\sum_{i=1}^{n} Y_i (1 - D_i) \frac{\hat{p}(X_i)}{1-\hat{p}(X_i)}}{\sum_{i=1}^{n} (1 - D_i) \frac{\hat{p}(X_i)}{1-\hat{p}(X_i)}} \tag{3.36}$$

$$\text{and for the ATE} \quad \frac{\sum_{i=1}^{n} \frac{Y_i D_i}{\hat{p}(X_i)}}{\sum_{i=1}^{n} \frac{D_i}{\hat{p}(X_i)}} - \frac{\sum_{i=1}^{n} \frac{Y_i(1-D_i)}{1-\hat{p}(X_i)}}{\sum_{i=1}^{n} \frac{1-D_i}{1-\hat{p}(X_i)}}. \tag{3.37}$$

3.3.3 Combination of Weighting and Regression: Double Robust Estimators

We already saw a combination of matching and propensity score weighting in the context of structural modelling. Another, obvious combination of non-parametric regression and propensity score weighting is the following.[31] One can construct

$$\widehat{ATE} = \frac{1}{n} \sum_{i=1}^{n} \hat{m}_1(X_i) - \hat{m}_0(X_i), \text{ and}$$

$$\widehat{ATET} = \frac{1}{n_1} \sum_{i:D_i=1} \hat{m}_1(X_i) - \hat{m}_0(X_i) \text{ with}$$

$$\hat{m}_0(x) = \hat{E}[Y(1-D)|X = x]\{1-\hat{p}(x)\}^{-1},$$
$$\hat{m}_1(x) = \hat{E}[YD|X = x]\hat{p}^{-1}(x),$$

which can be estimated non-parametrically from the sample. Both treatment effect estimators are efficient under sufficient regularity conditions (mainly to keep the biases small for $\hat{p}$, $\hat{m}_0$ and $\hat{m}_1$). When using non-parametric estimators for the conditional expectations, then we do not gain in efficiency when weighting (afterward) with $\hat{p}$, but even need more assumptions and nonparametric estimators than before. Therefore this estimator only becomes interesting when you do not want to use non-parametric estimators for the conditional expectation or $p(\cdot)$, and therefore risk to run into misspecification problems. So we try to find a way of combining propensity score weighting

---

[31] For more details see Hahn (1998).

and regression in a way that we can model $m_d(\cdot)$ and/or $p(\cdot)$ parametrically or semi-parametrically, and get consistency if either the $m_d(\cdot)$ or $p(\cdot)$ are correctly specified. This would really be a helpful tool in practice as it simplifies interpretation and estimation in the prior step.

In order to do this, let us rewrite the propensity score weighting ATET estimator:

$$E\left[Y^1 - Y^0|D = 1\right] = \frac{1}{\Pr(D = 1)} E\left[Y_i \cdot \left\{D_i - \frac{1 - D_i}{1 - p(X_i)} p(X_i)\right\}\right]$$

$$= \frac{1}{\Pr(D = 1)} E\left[p(X) \cdot E[Y^1 - Y^0|X]\right].$$

Note that the weights are negative for the $D = 0$ observations. In addition, the weights have mean zero: $E\left[D_i - \frac{1 - D_i}{1 - p(X_i)} p(X_i)\right] = 0$.

Alternatively, one can show that the weighting estimator can be written as a linear regression:

$$\text{regress} \quad Y_i \quad \text{on} \quad constant, D_i$$

using weighted least squares (WLS) with weights

$$\omega_i = D_i + (1 - D_i) \frac{p(X_i)}{1 - p(X_i)} \tag{3.38}$$

to obtain an ATET estimate. The ATE estimation works similar but with weights[32]

$$\omega_i = \frac{D_i}{p(X_i)} + \frac{1 - D_i}{1 - p(X_i)}. \tag{3.39}$$

One can extend this idea to include further covariates at least in a linear way in this regression. For estimating ATE we

$$\text{regress} \quad Y \quad \text{on} \quad constant, D, X - \bar{X} \text{ and } (X - \bar{X})D \tag{3.40}$$

using weighted least squares (WLS) with the weights ω_i (3.39) ($\bar{X}$ denoting the sample mean of X). Basically, this is a combination of weighting and regression. An interesting property of these estimators is the so-called 'double robustness property', which implies that the estimator is consistent if either the parametric (i.e. linear) specification (3.40) or the specification of $p(\cdot)$ in the weights ω_i is correct, i.e. that the propensity score is consistently estimated. The notion of being robust refers only to model misspecification, not to robustness against outliers.

Before we discuss this double robustness property for a more general case, let us consider (3.40). Suppose we can estimate the weights (3.39) consistently (either parametrically or non-parametrically). To see that the estimated coefficient of D estimates the ATE consistently even if the linear model (3.40) is misspecified, note that the *plim* of the coefficient of D, using weights (3.39) and setting $\tilde{X} := X - \bar{X}$ is indeed

---

[32] See Exercise 12.

$$e_2' \begin{bmatrix} E[\omega] & E[\omega D] & E\left[\omega \tilde{X}\right] & E\left[\omega \tilde{X} D\right] \\ E[\omega D] & E\left[\omega D^2\right] & E\left[\omega \tilde{X} D\right] & E\left[\omega \tilde{X} D^2\right] \\ E\left[\omega \tilde{X}\right] & E\left[\omega \tilde{X} D\right] & E\left[\omega \tilde{X}^2\right] & E\left[\omega \tilde{X}^2 D\right] \\ E\left[\omega \tilde{X} D\right] & E\left[\omega \tilde{X} D^2\right] & E\left[\omega \tilde{X}^2 D\right] & E\left[\omega \tilde{X}^2 D^2\right] \end{bmatrix}^{-1} \begin{bmatrix} E[\omega Y] \\ E[\omega DY] \\ E\left[\omega \tilde{X} Y\right] \\ E\left[\omega \tilde{X} DY\right] \end{bmatrix}$$

$$= e_2' \begin{bmatrix} 2 & 1 & 0 & 0 \\ 1 & 1 & 0 & 0 \\ 0 & 0 & 2Var(X) & Var(X) \\ 0 & 0 & Var(X) & Var(X) \end{bmatrix}^{-1} \begin{bmatrix} E[\omega Y] \\ E[\omega DY] \\ E\left[\omega \tilde{X} Y\right] \\ E\left[\omega \tilde{X} DY\right] \end{bmatrix}$$

$$= -E[\omega Y] + 2E[\omega DY] = E\left[\frac{D}{p(X)}Y - \frac{1-D}{1-p(X)}Y\right] = E\left[Y^1 - Y^0\right] = ATE.$$

To estimate the ATET we need to use the weights (3.38) and run the regression

$$\text{regress by WLS} \quad Y \quad \text{on} \quad constant, D, X - \bar{X}_1 \text{ and } (X - \bar{X}_1)D,$$

where $\bar{X}_1$ indicates now the average of X among the $D = 1$ observations. With this scaling of the regressors one can show analogously (in Exercise 11) that the ATET is consistently estimated even if the linear regression specification was wrong. This double robustness holds also when permitting non-linear specifications. Set $m_d(x) = E[Y|D = d, X = x]$ but $\hat{m}_i^d := m_d(x_i; \hat{\beta}_d)$ being parametric estimators with finite dimensional coefficient vectors $\hat{\beta}_1$ and $\hat{\beta}_0$. These parametric models can be linear or non-linear. In addition, let $\hat{p}_i := p(x_i; \hat{\beta}_p)$ be a parametric estimator of the propensity score. An efficient estimator of $E[Y^1]$ is then obtained by

$$\frac{1}{n} \sum_{i=1}^{n} \left(\frac{D_i Y_i}{\hat{p}_i} - \frac{(D_i - \hat{p}_i)\hat{m}_i^1}{\hat{p}_i} \right). \tag{3.41}$$

Analogously, one can estimate $E[Y^0]$ by

$$\frac{1}{n} \sum_{i=1}^{n} \left(\frac{(1 - D_i) Y_i}{1 - \hat{p}_i} - \frac{\{(1 - D_i) - (1 - \hat{p}_i)\}\hat{m}_i^0}{1 - \hat{p}_i} \right)$$

such that the ATE estimate is finally

$$\frac{1}{n} \sum_{i=1}^{n} \left(\frac{D_i Y_i}{\hat{p}_i} - \frac{(D_i - \hat{p}_i)\hat{m}_i^1}{\hat{p}_i} \right) - \frac{1}{n} \sum_{i=1}^{n} \left(\frac{(1 - D_i) Y_i}{1 - \hat{p}_i} + \frac{(D_i - \hat{p}_i)\hat{m}_i^0}{1 - \hat{p}_i} \right).$$

We can easily show that it is consistent if either the parametric specification of the propensity score or that of the outcome equation is correct. In other words, one of the parametric models may be misspecified, but we still attain consistency. We show this only for the estimator of $E[Y^1]$ because the derivations for $E[Y^0]$ are analogous. Let β_1^* and β_p^* be the probability limits of the coefficient estimates in the outcome and the propensity score model. Then the estimator of $E[Y^1]$ in (3.41) converges to

$$E\left[\frac{DY}{p(X;\beta_p^*)} - \frac{\left\{D - p(X;\beta_p^*)\right\}m_1(X;\beta_1^*)}{p(X;\beta_p^*)}\right].$$ (3.42)

Note that we can write

$$\frac{DY}{p(X;\beta_p^*)} = \frac{DY^1}{p(X;\beta_p^*)} = Y^1 + \frac{\left\{D - p(X;\beta_p^*)\right\}Y^1}{p(X;\beta_p^*)}.$$

Inserting this in the previous expression we obtain that (3.42) equals

$$E[Y^1] + E\left[\frac{\left\{D - p(X;\beta_p^*)\right\}\left\{Y^1 - m_1(X;\beta_1^*)\right\}}{p(X;\beta_p^*)}\right].$$ (3.43)

We have only to show that the last expression is zero if either the outcome model or the propensity score is correctly specified.

Consider first the case where the outcome model is correct, i.e. $m_1(X;\beta_1^*) = E[Y|X, D = 1]$ a.s. (but $p(x, \beta_p^*)$ may not). The second term in (3.43) can be written, after using iterated expectations with respect to D and X, as

$$E\left[\frac{\left\{D - p(X;\beta_p^*)\right\}\left\{Y^1 - m_1(X;\beta_1^*)\right\}}{p(X;\beta_p^*)}\right]$$

$$= E\left[E\left[\frac{\left\{D - p(X;\beta_p^*)\right\}\left\{Y^1 - m_1(X;\beta_1^*)\right\}}{p(X;\beta_p^*)}\Bigg|D, X\right]\right]$$

$$= E\left[\frac{D - p(X;\beta_p^*)}{p(X;\beta_p^*)}\underbrace{\left\{E\left[Y^1|D, X\right] - m_1(X;\beta_1^*)\right\}}_{=0}\right],$$

where the inner term is zero because of the conditional independence assumption, i.e. $E[Y^1|D, X] = E[Y^1|D = 1, X] = E[Y|D = 1, X] = m_1(X;\beta_1^*)$, and because the function $m_1(\cdot)$ has been assumed to be correctly specified.

Now consider the case where the propensity score model is correct, $p(X;\beta_p^*) = \Pr(D = 1|X)$ a.s. The second term in (3.43) becomes, after using iterated expectations,

$$E\left[\frac{\left\{D - p(X;\beta_p^*)\right\}\left\{Y^1 - m_1(X;\beta_1^*)\right\}}{p(X;\beta_p^*)}\right]$$

$$= E\left[E\left[\frac{\left\{D - p(X;\beta_p^*)\right\}\left\{Y^1 - m_1(X;\beta_1^*)\right\}}{p(X;\beta_p^*)}\Bigg|Y^1, X\right]\right]$$

$$= E\left[\underbrace{\left\{E\left[D|Y^1, X\right] - p(X;\beta_p^*)\right\}}_{=0}\frac{Y^1 - m_1(X;\beta_1^*)}{p(X;\beta_p^*)}\right],$$

where the first term is zero because $E\left[D|Y^1, X\right] = E\left[D|X\right] = \Pr(D = 1|X)$ by the conditional independence assumption, and because the propensity score model is correctly specified.

It should be mentioned once again that in addition to the double robustness, these estimators attain also the efficiency bound. Hence, if one intends to use parametric models to estimate treatment effects, the combination of weighting and regression is very appealing due to efficiency and robustness considerations. When using fully non-parametric approaches, then both methods, weighting and matching, can achieve efficiency on their own; the combination cannot improve this, yet Firpo and Rothe still show advantages with respect to regularity conditions.

3.4 Practical Issues on Matching and Propensity Score Estimation

3.4.1 Summary of Estimators, Finite Sample Performance and Inference

We first briefly summarise the considered estimators, including also some of the modified versions that have been developed to improve their performance. Here, 'performance' does not refer to asymptotic properties but to bias, standard error, mean squared error and robustness in finite samples. While asymptotic theory is helpful to analyse the general properties of estimators, it is not always helpful to guide the empirical researcher how to choose an estimator in practice. In fact, it might happen that estimators being asymptotically efficient have worse finite sample properties than some simpler estimators. A recent summary is given in Frölich, Huber and Wiesenfarth.

We start with a summary of matching estimators. To simplify notation we do this for estimating the ATET.[33] They can basically be summarised as

$$\widehat{ATET} = \frac{1}{n_1} \sum_{i:D_i=1} \left\{ Y_i - \sum_{j:D_j=0} w(i, j) Y_j \right\}, \tag{3.44}$$

where the weights $w(i, j)$ are determined by the applied method like for example kNN, Nadaraya–Watson and local linear regression (which we discussed in Section 2.2.1 and above). Alternatively used (or recommended) methods are blocking (as an extension of kNN), ridge regression or radius matching (as a special case of kernel regression).[34] A particularity of the radius matching is that the worst match, i.e. the largest distance from a participant to a control, determines the bandwidth size. The weights $w(i, j)$ may refer to the distance of either the vectors of confounders, or of the propensity scores $p(X_i) - p(X_j)$, or even a mixture of both. As discussed, sometimes it is also proposed to include variables that have strong predictive power for outcome Y but are not really confounders i.e., having no impact on the propensity to participate.

---

[33] Remember that you can analogously estimate ATEN by simply replacing D_i by $(1 - D_i)$, i.e. declaring the treatment group to be the controls and vice versa.
[34] See Lechner, Miquel and Wunsch (2011).

For the (re-)weighting estimators, there are quite a few proposals. Consider

$$\widehat{ATET} = \frac{1}{n_1} \sum_{i:D_i=1} Y_i - \frac{1}{n_0} \sum_{j:D_j=0} w(j)Y_j, \tag{3.45}$$

where for $w(j)$ you can use

$$\frac{n_0}{n_1} \frac{\hat{p}(X_j)}{1 - \hat{p}(X_j)} \quad \text{or} \quad \frac{\hat{p}(X_j)}{1 - \hat{p}(X_j)} \frac{n_0}{\sum_{i:D_i=0} \frac{\hat{p}(X_i)}{1-\hat{p}(X_i)}}$$

$$\text{or} \quad \frac{(1-c_j)\hat{p}(X_j)}{1 - \hat{p}(X_j)} \frac{n_0}{\sum_{i:D_i=0}(1-c_i)\frac{\hat{p}(X_i)}{1-\hat{p}(X_i)}}$$

$$\text{with } c_i = \frac{\left(1 - \frac{n\hat{p}(X_i)}{n_1}A_i\right)\frac{1}{n}\sum_{j=1}^{n}\left(1 - \frac{n\hat{p}(X_j)}{n_1}A_j\right)}{\frac{1}{n}\sum_{j=1}^{n}\left(1 - \frac{n\hat{p}(X_j)}{n_1}A_j\right)^2}$$

$$\text{in which } A_j = \frac{1 - D_j}{1 - \hat{p}(X_j)}.$$

The latter results from a variance minimising linear combination of the former weights.[35]

Another alternative is the *inverse probability tilting* which criticises that the propensity score estimate $\hat{p}$ used in the (re-)weighting estimators may maximise the likelihood for estimating the propensity but is not optimal for estimating treatment effects. A method tailored towards the treatment effect estimation is to re-estimate (after having calculated $\hat{p}$) the two propensity function(s) (say, $(\tilde{p}_0, \tilde{p}_1)$) by solving the moment conditions[36]

$$1 = \frac{1}{n} \sum_{i=1}^{n} \frac{1 - D_i}{\frac{1}{n}\sum_{j=1}^{n}\hat{p}(X_j)} \frac{\hat{p}(X_i)}{1 - \tilde{p}_0(X_i)} \quad \text{and}$$

$$\frac{1}{n} \sum_{i=1}^{n} \frac{\hat{p}(X_i)}{\frac{1}{n}\sum_{j=1}^{n}\hat{p}(X_j)} X_i = \frac{1}{n} \sum_{i=1}^{n} \frac{1 - D_i}{\frac{1}{n}\sum_{j=1}^{n}\hat{p}(X_j)} \frac{\hat{p}(X_i)}{1 - \tilde{p}_0(X_i)} X_i,$$

and the same way $\tilde{p}_1$ by substituting D_i for $1 - D_i$ and $1 - \tilde{p}_0(X_i)$ by $\tilde{p}_1(X_i)$.[37] Then, as an ATET estimator is suggested

$$\widehat{ATET} = \sum_{i:D_i=1} \frac{\hat{p}(X_i)}{\tilde{p}_1(X_i)\sum_{j=1}^{n}\hat{p}(X_j)} Y_i - \sum_{j:D_j=0} \frac{\hat{p}(X_j)}{\{1 - \tilde{p}_0(X_j)\}\sum_{i=1}^{n}\hat{p}(X_i)} Y_j. \tag{3.46}$$

---

[35] See Lunceford and Davidian (2004) for the ATE case.
[36] See Graham, Pinto and Egel (2011) and Graham, Pinto and Egel (2012) for details and further discussion.
[37] Both, $\tilde{p}_0$ and $\tilde{p}_1$ are estimates for the propensity score, but obtained from the two different groups.

There exist some proposals for correcting these kind of estimators for their finite sample bias.[38] This bias correction may be attractive if a simple but reasonable estimate of the bias is available. It is not hard to see that for $w(j)$ as in (3.45) or setting $w(j) = \frac{n_0}{n_1} \sum_{i:D_i=1} w(i,j)$ with $w(i,j)$ as in (3.44), the bias of the above estimator of $E[Y^0|D=1]$ can be approximated by

$$\frac{1}{n_0} \sum_{j:D_j=0} w(j)\hat{Y}_j^0 - \frac{1}{n_1} \sum_{i:D_i=1} w(i)\hat{Y}_i^0 , \qquad (3.47)$$

where $\hat{Y}_i^0$ are the predictors for the non-treatment outcome in (3.45) or (3.44), respectively.

In order to do further inference, even more important than estimating the bias is the problem of estimating the standard error of the estimators. There exist few explicit variance estimators in the literature but many different proposals how to proceed in practice. A popular but coarse approach is to take an asymptotically efficient estimator for the wanted treatment effect, and to (non-parametrically) estimate the efficiency bounds given in Theorem 3.2. These bounds, however, can be far from the true finite sample variances. Therefore it is common practice to approximate variances via *simple*[39] bootstrapping due to convenience and seemingly improved small sample results.[40] Potential alternative resampling methods are *wild bootstrap*[41] and *subsampling*,[42] but this is still an open field for further research.

There exists, however, a generally accepted method for estimating the variance of linear estimators, i.e. those that can be written in terms of $\sum_{i=1}^n w(i)Y_i$ when the observations are independent. Let us consider the ATET estimator

$$\widehat{ATET} = \frac{1}{n_1} \sum_{i:D_i=1} \left\{ Y_i^1 - \hat{m}_0(X_i) \right\} , \text{ with } Y^d = m_d(X_i) + U_i^d .$$

For all kind of estimators we have considered so far, we have (for some weights, say $w(j,i)$)

$$\hat{m}_0(X_i) = \sum_{j:D_j=0} w(j,i)Y_j^0 = \sum_{j:D_j=0} w(j,i)\{m_0(X_j) + U_j^0\}$$

$$= \sum_{j:D_j=0} w(j,i)m_0(X_j) + \sum_{j:D_j=0} w(j,i)U_j^0 ,$$

---

[38] See for example Abadie and Imbens (2011) or Huber, Lechner and Steinmayr (2013).

[39] We call *simple bootstrap* the resampling procedure where random samples $\{(Y_i, X_i, D_i)^*\}_{i=1}^n$ are drawn with replacement directly from the original sample, maybe stratified along treatment.

[40] Moreover, Abadie and Imbens (2008) showed that bootstrapping is inconsistent for the kNN matching estimator.

[41] See Mammen (1992). In *wild bootstrap* one relies on the original design $\{(X_i, D_i)\}_{i=1}^n$ but generates $\{Y_i^*\}_{i=1}^n$ from estimates $\hat{m}_d$ and some random errors. Note that generally, naive bootstrap is estimating the variance of the conditional treatment effects, say $ATE(x)$, inconsistently.

[42] See Politis, Romano and Wolf (1999).

which equals $m_0(X_i)$ plus a smoothing bias $b(X_i)$ and the random term $\sum_{j:D_j=0} w(j,i)U_j^0$. Therefore we can write

$$\widehat{ATET} = \sum_{i:D_i=1} \frac{1}{n_1}Y_i^1 + \sum_{j:D_j=0}\sum_{i:D_i=1} \frac{-w(j,i)}{n_1}Y_j^0$$

$$= \sum_{i:D_i=1} \frac{1}{n_1}\{m_1(X_i)+U_i^1\} + \sum_{j:D_j=0}\sum_{i:D_i=1} \frac{-w(j,i)}{n_1}\{m_0(X_j)+U_j^0\}$$

$$= \frac{1}{n_1}\sum_{i:D_i=1}\{ATE(X_i)+b(X_i)\} + \sum_{i:D_i=1}w(i)U_i^1 + \sum_{j:D_j=0}w(j)U_j^0$$

with $w(i) := \frac{1}{n_1}$ for $D_i = 1$ and $w(j) = \sum_{i:D_i=1}\frac{-w(j,i)}{n_1}$ for $D_j = 0$. Note that each weight is composed out of all X_i from the treated, and X_j from the control group. Consequently, these weights are neither independent from each other nor from Y_i. They are, however, conditionally independent, i.e. when knowing or fixing the X and D. So we can continue calculating

$$Var[\widehat{ATET}|x_1,\ldots,x_n,d_1,\ldots,d_n] = \sum_{i=1}^{n} w(i)^2 Var[U^D|X=x_i, D=d_i]. \quad (3.48)$$

Generally, it is not hard to show that conditional on the covariates, i.e. on confounders X and treatment D, Formula 3.48 applies to basically all the here presented estimators.

Nonetheless, there are two points to be discussed. The first is that we still need to estimate the $Var[U^D|X = x_i, D = d_i]$; the second is that we have conditioned on the sample design. This implicates that we neglect variation caused by potential differences between the sample distribution of X, D compared to the population distribution. Whether this makes a big difference or not depends on several factors like whether we used global or local smoothers (the impact is worse for the former ones) and also on the variance of $ATET(X)$. Some resampling methods are supposed to offer a remedy here.

Coming back to (3.48) and knowing the $w(i)$, for the prediction of $Var[U^D|X = x_i, D = d_i]$ different methods have been proposed in the past.[43] It might be helpful to realise first that in order to get a consistent estimator in (3.48), we only need asymptotically unbiased predictors. This is similar to what we discussed in Section 2.2.3 in the context of root-n-consistent semi-parametric estimators: the (though weighted) averaging over i provides the variance with a rate of $1/n$ such that only the bias has to be shrunken to $O(n^{-1/2})$ for obtaining root-n convergence. Consequently, you may in (3.48) simply replace $Var[U^D|X = x_i, D = d_i]$ by $(Y - \hat{m}_{d_i}(X_i))^2$. A quite attractive and intuitive procedure is to go ahead with exactly the same smoother $\hat{m}_d$ used for obtaining the treatment effect estimate. Certainly, as for ATET you only needed $\hat{m}_0$ (or for ATEN only $\hat{m}_1$), the lacking regression m_{1-d} has also to be estimated for ATE. But it is still the same procedure.

Simulation-based comparison studies have mainly looked at the finite sample performance of the treatment effect estimates, not on estimators of the variance or bias. These

---

[43] See Dette, Munk and Wagner (1998) for a review of non-parametric proposals.

revealed, among others, the following findings: bias correction with (3.47) can generally be recommend but increases variance. For the (re-)weighting estimators trimming can be important to obtain reliable estimates of treatment effects, but the discussion about the question of an adequate trimming is still controversial; we will discuss trimming in the context of practical issues when using the propensity score. Moreover, there is an interplay between trimming and bandwidth choice partly due to the so-called boundary problems in non-parametric regression. Generally, cross validation (CV) that evaluates the prediction power of $m_0(\cdot)$ seems to be reasonable bandwidth selection criteria for our purpose. While it is true that CV aims to minimise the mean squared error of the non-parametric predictors but not for ATE or ATET estimation, its tendency to undersmooth in the non-parametric part is exactly what we need for our semi-parametric estimation problem. As already mentioned, the ridge regression based estimates are less sensible to bandwidth choice, and so are bias corrected versions as these try to correct for the smoothing bias. For the rest, the main findings are that – depending on the underlying data generating process, the (mis-)specification of the propensity score function, or the compliance of the common support condition – most of the introduced estimators have their advantages but also their pitfalls, so that further general recommendation can hardly be given. Maybe surprisingly, even for a given data generating process, the ranking of estimators can vary with the sample size. The main conclusion is therefore that it is good to have different estimators, use several of them and try to understand the differences in estimation results by the above highlighted differences in construction and applied assumptions.[44] For further results see Frölich, Huber and Wiesenfarth (2017).

3.4.2 When Using Propensity Scores

The propensity score plays two central roles. First, it is a very helpful tool to highlight and handle the common support condition (CSC). Second, it can additionally be used to simplify the estimation process via propensity score matching or weighting (or both). Even if one does not pursue this second aspect and uses matching on X or parametric regression, the propensity score nevertheless remains very helpful to visualise common support issues, for example by plotting the histograms or kernel densities for the distributions of the predicted propensity scores separately for the $D = 0$ and the $D = 1$ population. This is often emphasised to be the essential advantage of using propensity score matching or weighting: the visualisation of the CSC issue. As it is a one-dimensional variable ranging from zero to one, you can plot its density for any set of potential confounders and look at its distribution. You even see the proportion of the sample for which you may have problems with the CSC and propensity score weighting. An example is given in Figure 3.1 which shows how the distributions of the propensity scores could look like. This graph helps us to visualise the differences in observed characteristics between the treated and controls in a simple way. First, we see roughly how much the distributions differ. If D had been randomly allocated with probability 0.5, the distributions should be very similar and all density mass about 0.5. If the D are

---

[44] See also the section on further reading.

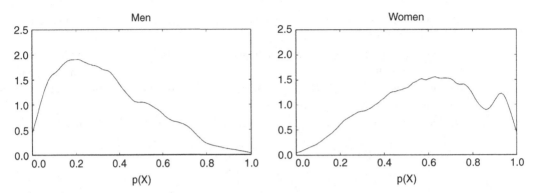

Figure 3.1 Density $f_{P|D=0}$ for men (left), and density $f_{P|D=1}$ for women (right)

not randomly allocated over the entire population, the distributions for the different D would be more dissimilar, for example with most of the mass to the left for the controls and most of the mass to the right for the treated.

Propensity Scores for Trimming

We often find that there is little density mass above 0.7 or 0.8 in the $D = 0$ population, whereas naturally much of the density mass lies above 0.7 in the $D = 1$ population. If we are interested in the ATET, we would then drop all treated observations above the largest value of $P := p(X)$ in the control sample. Hence, if the largest value of P among the controls is 0.7, all treated above this threshold are deleted since we could not find matches (i.e. individuals with similar treatment propensity) in the control group. Usually, we would often be stricter in the implementation of the common support in that we drop all treated above, say, the tenth-largest value of P in the control population. If we are interested in the ATE, we would implement common supports on both sides in that we delete treated with very high values of P, and controls with very low values of P. Defining the trimming and thus consequently $\mathcal{X}_{01}$ only on the basis of the propensity score avoids that the treatment effects themselves can influence the selection of this set.

Obviously, the deletion of these observations changes the population for which we estimate an effect, and we therefore should always compare the descriptive statistics of the observations deleted with those remaining. If we lose only about 2 to 5 per cent of the observations due to imposition of common support and if the sample means are similar among those deleted and those remaining, we would be relatively confident that the estimates obtained can be interpreted more broadly. However, we should be aware that an exact interpretation of our estimates only refers to the remaining subpopulation and acknowledge that external validity is limited.

One might generally consider only subsets of the common support regions. E.g. using only the subset $0.1 < P < 0.9$ is a frequent choice to obtain more precise estimates.[45] A first motivation is that one would expect more precise estimates for this region where

---

[45] Similarly, Black and Smith (2004) define the 'thick support' region as $0.33 < P < 0.67$ and examine an additional analysis for this region and give arguments for this choice.

most of the data are. Additional reasons are for example that a very high value of P_i for individual i with recorded $D_i = 0$ could be an indication of measurement error in D_i or X_i. There may be less reason for suspecting measurement errors when P_i takes intermediate values. Another reason is that, under certain assumptions, the bias due to any remaining selection-on-unobservables is largest in the tails of the distribution of P.[46] Finally, trimming at the boundaries typically improves the performance of the non-parametric estimator. There is certainly always a bias-variance trade-off; the trick is that, as the bias is the expected distance to *the parameter of interest*, a simple redefinition of this *parameter of interest* can make the bias disappear. Specifically, we declare the parameter of interest to be the ATE or ATET for the finally chosen set $\mathcal{X}_{01}$. Trimming changes this set towards a set on which the non-parametric estimator works pretty well (has small variance) while the theoretical bias increases due to the suppression of certain observations. This is eliminated by our (re-)definition of the parameter of interest. Consequently, trimming can achieve a (seemingly free-lunch) variance reduction. However, as trimming is only used to improve the finite sample variance, we should be aware of the fact that for increasing sample size the estimation improves even where the propensity score is extremely low or high. For this reason, alternative trimming procedures were proposed in the literature; see Section 3.5.1.

Estimation of the Propensity Score in Practice

In principle, we could estimate the propensity score non-parametrically. Many researchers, though, prefer at least a semi-parametric probit or logit model, i.e. keeping a parametric log-likelihood approach but allowing the argument (index) to be non-parametric. As we learnt in Section 2.2.3, there exist either the possibility to look at smoothed log-likelihoods or at standard log-likelihoods with spline functions in the index. In practice, people often take simple power series instead, despite their bad local fitting properties. In either case, there is a smoothing parameter to be chosen. Additionally, one has to decide about the set of confounders X that should be included. Ideally, economic theory helps to answer the latter question. In practice one would prefer not to have too many variables in X but eliminate the insignificant ones. Including variables that are not significant predictors of D might not hurt in principle but could unnecessarily add some noise to the propensity score prediction, in particular due to their contribution to the curse of dimensionality.

Example 3.10 If in the true model there is only one strong predictor of D, estimating the propensity score with only this variable would ensure that we compare only observations with the same characteristic. If, on the other hand, we include many additional insignificant variables in X, the estimated propensity scores would then contain a lot of noise and it would be more or less random which control individual is matched to a given treated individual.

---

[46] See Black and Smith (2004, pp. 111–113) for an illustrative example of such a situation.

On the other hand, if they are good predictors for Y, then they can equally well reduce the variance of treatment effect estimates. If pre-programme outcome data $Y_{t=0}$ or even $Y_{t=-1}$, $Y_{t=-2}$, etc. are available, it is also helpful to examine a regression of $Y_{t=0}$ on various X variables. If we expect Y to be rather persistent over time, this provides us with guidance on likely important predictors of the outcome variable, which should be included in X even if they affect D only little. The reason for this, though, is a different one. It actually refers exactly to the problem which we discussed in the context of randomised experiments: it is about variance reduction (while the inclusion of real confounders is about bias reduction, or say 'identification').

Example 3.11 When analyzing effects of some treatment on incomes, gender might be a good predictor of income. Even when gender is balanced between treatment and control (e.g. RCT), i.e., it is not a confounder, controlling for gender reduces variance, as we estimate treatment effects by gender with subsequent averaging across gender by their proportions.

This example shows nicely the pros and cons of including 'additional' (in the sense of not being confounders in its strict definition) covariates. Obviously, it is not always easy to decide which of those variables one should include or not. This can only be found out by analysing the impact of X on Y and D. The proper set of confounders does not change when switching from matching to propensity score matching or weighting.[47] Similarly, also the choice of smoothing parameter (like the number of knots for splines or the order of the polynomial for power series) is not trivial. In order to decide this it is helpful to remember that in the context of experimental designs we used the propensity function to assess balance in covariates. What we want to reach in the context of matching and regression is a conditional balance: we require

$$X \perp\!\!\!\perp D | p(X).^{48} \tag{3.49}$$

What does this mean in practice and how can we make use of it? Imagine all confounders were discrete. Then it simply says that for all $x \in \mathcal{X}_{01}$ you should get

$$n_x^1 / p(x) \approx n_x^0 / (1 - p(x)), \tag{3.50}$$

where n_x^d is the number of individuals i with $(D_i = d, X_i = x)$. If we have also continuous confounders one has to build accordingly strata and blocks to perform a similar analysis. Similarly to what has been said in the context of randomised experiments, a testing of conditional balance is not recommended particularly if sample size varied after trimming. Especially attractive for continuous confounders, one could proceed along $p(X)$ instead of checking along X: for any value of $p(X)$ or a subset of values, the variables X should be balanced between the $D = 1$ and the $D = 0$ group in the sense

---

[47] However, as we have seen, from a structural modelling point of view one could ask which confounders should be used for modelling the selection, and which (only) for the regression part.

[48] Although $Y^d \perp\!\!\!\perp D | p(X)$ is the real goal. But this is not testable.

that the number of observations are very similar when inversely weighted by $p(X)$ and $(1 - p(X))$, cf. Equation 3.50. If this is not the case, the propensity score model is likely to be misspecified and has to be respecified until balance is achieved.[49] One way to proceed is to sort the estimated propensity scores and group them into five or ten strata i.e. using quintiles or deciles. By the balancing property of the propensity score we have

$$E\left[\frac{X \cdot D}{p(X)}\,\middle|\,a \le p(X) \le b\right] = E\left[\frac{X \cdot (1 - D)}{1 - p(X)}\,\middle|\,a \le p(X) \le b\right]$$

Then in each block the absolute difference of the weighted (by $p(X)$) average of X in the $D = 1$ and the $D = 0$ group is examined, standardised by the standard deviation of X. If the absolute difference is large, the propensity score model is respecified by making it more flexible (less smooth by decreasing the bandwidth, increasing the knots or the order of the polynomial, etc.). In any case we are looking for a weighted (by the inverse of $\Pr(D = d|X = x)$) balance in X between the different treatment groups. A test tells us only if we were able to statistically prove (weighted) imbalances. Already a generous number of confounders can reduce the power of any such a test to an extent that it hardly ever finds significant imbalances and may therefore lead to wrong conclusions.

Propensity Score Matching with Choice-Based Samples
You might want to perform propensity score matching with non-random sampling. In other words, the available data may often not be representative for the true population proportions, with certain groups (such as treatment participants, foreigners, low-income individuals or residents of particular regions) being oversampled. This may also occur when the treated and controls stem from separate surveys or data sources. In those cases, the sampling distribution $F_{Y,X,D}$ is different from the population distribution. In the context of treatment evaluation, it is helpful to distinguish between non-random sampling with respect to D (or the propensity) from those with respect to $F_{Y,X|D}$. Non-random sampling with respect to D is particularly frequent in the treatment evaluation context, where treatment participants are often oversampled. This is referred to as *choice-based sampling*. It is evident that choice-based sampling leads to inconsistent estimates, say $\tilde{p} := \delta(p)$ with bijective δ, of the true propensity score. If participants are over-represented, the propensity score gets over estimated ($E[\tilde{p}_i] > p_i$) throughout; if participants are under-sampled, then it gets under estimated throughout. Nevertheless, the estimation of the ATET using these inconsistent predictors $\tilde{p}_i$ is often still consistent because of (3.31). This is evident as there is no selection bias regarding (Y, X); both groups represent well their population (the population of participants and the one of controls, respectively). So any averaging inside each group will give a consistent estimator of the wanted mean. We can predict consistently $E[Y^0|\tilde{p}_i]$ from the control group, and estimate the ATET by $\frac{1}{n_1}\sum_{i:D_i=1} Y_i - \hat{E}[Y^0|\tilde{p}_i]$. The same holds true for the ATEN. For estimating the ATE, however, we need to know the sampling weights.

---

[49] We say here 'likely' because it can well be that very different X values predict the same or similar treatment propensity allowing for those imbalances.

In contrast, non-random sampling with respect to $F_{Y,X|D}$ requires a modification of the matching estimator. Non-random sampling with respect to X or Y given D can occur e.g. due to oversampling of foreigners or low-income individuals in a given treatment group (for binary D: either treated or controls). Non-random sampling could be present only in one of the groups, for example, if different sampling designs were used. A survey might over-sample pregnant women or women with small children among those who take a new medical drug ($D = 1$), while using random sampling for the control group. In this case, at least one modification of the propensity score matching estimator is required. More specifically, when taking the average of $\widehat{E}[Y^0|\tilde{p}_i]$ over the treated observations, sampling weights have to be included. In the estimation of $E[Y^0|\tilde{p}_i]$ from the controls, sampling weights have to be included only if the sampling was done along the pairs (Y, X) (e.g. strata along combinations of X and Y). But these are not necessary if the sampling was either random or only done along X, and local smoothers were used.[50] In the case that the sampling scheme was the same in both subpopulations (treatment groups), weighting can be ignored completely.[51] In any case, the most secure procedure is to use in each step the sampling weights that correspond to the (sub-)population you are referring to.

3.4.3   Testing the Validity of the Conditional Independence Assumption

In the economic theory literature can be found a controversy about the plausibility of the conditional independence assumption in social and economic settings. Some are opposed to accept this as a viable strategy arguing that agent's optimising behaviour intrinsically precludes their participation being independent of the potential outcomes, whether or not conditional on covariates. A quite obvious counterargument is that any quantitative evaluation involves pooling and thus comparisons of subjects that made choices based on their expectations. We only have to be cautious about the question which subjects can be compared to each other and the correct interpretation. The hope is that economic theory tells us along which covariates such a comparison is reasonable, or for which variables one has to control for. The question whether all these can be observed is an empirical one. It does by no means invalidate the principle of CIA. Moreover, the argument of the critics is a pretty weak one if the output of interest Y is not the direct target of the agent's utility optimisation. It even becomes invalid if the agents are provided with about the same amount of information as the empirical researcher. Finally, researchers from behavioural economics would generally doubt the agent's rationality and effective optimising behaviour, may it be due to the lack of information or capacity, non-rational actions, switching targets, etc. And indeed, as we have seen, variables being essential for the selection process can even be omitted if they have no impact on the potential outcome of interest other than the impact channelled by the selection ($D = d$).

---

[50] We do not refer to local smoothing parameters but to local smoothers. Global smoothers will also be seriously affected by sampling along X whereas local smoothers like kNN, kernels or splines will not.

[51] In the example mentioned above, the relevant condition is Pr (individual is in sample$|X, D = 1$) $\propto$ Pr (individual is in sample$|X, D = 0$). Notice that this proportionality condition refers to the marginal sampling probability with respect to X only.

Example 3.12 Imbens (2004) considers an example where production is a stochastic variable of technological innovation measured as a binary decision of implementing it or not: $Y_i = \varphi(D_i, e_i)$. Here, e_i are random factors not being under the firm's control. Profits are measured by output minus costs: $\pi_i = Y_i - c_i \cdot D_i$, where c_i are the costs for firm i if implementing the new technology. The agent's optimising behaviour would predict

$$D_i = \underset{d \in \{0,1\}}{argmax} \; E[\pi(d)|c_i] \, .$$

As $E[\pi(d)|c_i] = E[\varphi(d, e_i) - c_i d|c_i]$, where the expectation runs only over e_i, the rest is given, one has $D_i = \mathbb{1}\{E[\varphi(1, e_i) - \varphi(0, e_i) \geq c_i|c_i]\}$ which is just a deterministic (though unknown) function of c_i. If c_i is independent of the e_i, then you get $(\varphi(1, e_i), \varphi(0, e_i)) \perp\!\!\!\perp c_i$. In this case we have even unconfoundedness without conditioning. So one could identify the treatment effect on production without observing the c_i although the firms knew their c_i and use it for the selection decision. But we could not identify the treatment effect on profits without observing all c_i. If X comprises all information about c_i, it is sufficient to condition on X. See also Exercise 9.

In any case, the conditional mean independence assumption might be the minimal identifying assumption and cannot be validated from the data. Its assertion must be based on economic theory, institutional knowledge and beliefs. It could only be rigorously tested if one were willing to impose additional assumptions. With such over-identifying assumptions it can be tested whether given a certain set of assumptions, the remaining assumptions are valid. If under these conditions the latter assumptions were not rejected, the identification strategy would be considered as being credible.

Nonetheless, simply claiming that one believes in the independence assumption might be unsatisfactory. In order to get some more insight, it is common to conduct *falsification tests*, also called *pseudo-treatment tests*. For example, an indirect test of the CIA is to examine whether we would obtain a zero treatment effect when comparing sub-populations for which we knew that they were either both treated or both untreated. In these test situations we know that the estimated effects should be zero if the CIA were true. Hence, if nonetheless the estimated treatment effect is significantly different from zero, one concludes that the CIA fails. Examples are: split the controls into two groups, and see whether you find $ATE \neq 0$ comparing them; another example is given below. If such a falsification test fails, one would be doubtful about the CIA. If one is able to conduct different falsification tests and hardly any of them fails, one would be more inclined to believe the CIA.[52] Let us consider another example.

Example 3.13 Access to social programmes often depends on certain eligibility criteria. This leads to three groups: ineligibles, eligible non-participants and (eligible) participants. We are only interested in the ATET as the ineligibles will never be treated.

---

[52] For a good example of how falsification analysis helps to increase the credibility of the findings see Bhatt and Koedel (2010).

Therefore it is sufficient to check $Y^0 \perp\!\!\!\perp D|X$. The first two groups are non-participants and their Y^0 outcome is thus observed. Usually both groups have different distributions of X characteristics. If one strengthens the conditional independence assumption to

$$Y^0 \perp\!\!\!\perp \tilde{D}|X \text{ , where } \tilde{D} \in \{\text{ineligibles, eligible non-participants, participants}\},$$

then a testable implication is that

$$Y \perp\!\!\!\perp \tilde{D}|X \text{ , with } \tilde{D} \in \{\text{ineligibles, eligible non-participants}\}.$$

The (average) outcome of Y among the ineligibles and among the eligible non-participants should be about identical when adjusting for differences in the distribution of X. This is testable and might indicate whether $Y^0 \perp\!\!\!\perp D|X$ holds.

So we see that you may simply split the control group into two ($T \in \{0, 1\}$, e.g. eligibles vs. non-eligibles) for testing $Y^0 \perp\!\!\!\perp T|X$ or the treatment group for testing $Y^1 \perp\!\!\!\perp T|X$. These test are interpreted then as indicators for the validity of $Y^0 \perp\!\!\!\perp D|X$ and $Y^1 \perp\!\!\!\perp D|X$, respectively.

An especially interesting situation for this pseudo-treatment approach is the case where information on the outcome variable before the treatment happened is available, e.g. in the form of panel data. One can then examine differences between participants and non-participants before the treatment actually happened (and hopefully before the participants knew about their participation status as this might have generated anticipation effects). Since the treatment has not yet happened, there should be no (statistically significant) difference in the outcomes between the subpopulation that is later taking treatment, and the subpopulation that is later not taking treatment (at least after controlling for confounders X). This is known as the *pre-programme* test or *pseudo-treatment* test.

Let us discuss such a situation more in detail. Suppose that longitudinal data on participants and non-participants are available for up to $k + 1$ periods before treatment started (at $t = 0$). As an example think of an adult literacy programme that starts at time $t = 0$ and where we measure the outcome at time 1. Let us consider the CIA condition for ATET. Before time 0, all individuals are in the non-treatment state. We assume that there are no *anticipation effects*, such that $Y^0_{t=0} = Y_{t=0}$ is fulfilled. Assume that conditional independence holds at time $t = 1$:

$$Y^0_{t=1} \perp\!\!\!\perp D_{t=0}|X, Y^0_{t=0}, Y^0_{t=-1}, Y^0_{t=-2}, \ldots, Y^0_{t=-k} , \qquad (3.51)$$

where X contains time invariant characteristics. We also condition on lagged outcome values as these are often important determinants of the programme participation decision. It is reasonable to assume that the potential outcomes are correlated over time such that any unobserved differences might be captured by the control variables in earlier time periods. We could therefore assume conditional independence to hold also in previous periods, i.e.[53]

---

[53] Imbens (2004) refers to this as assuming stationary and exchangeability.

$$Y^0_{t=l} \perp\!\!\!\perp D_{t=0} | X, Y^0_{t=l-1}, Y^0_{t=l-2}, Y^0_{t=l-3}, \dots, Y^0_{t=-(k+1)}, \qquad l = 0, -1, -2, \dots \tag{3.52}$$

This assumption is testable, because at time $t = 0$ we observe the non-treatment outcome Y^0 as well for those with $D_{t=0} = 0$ as for those with $D_{t=0} = 1$, i.e. those who will later participate in treatment. Assumption 3.51 is untestable because at time 1 the outcome $Y^0_{t=1}$ for those with $D_{t=0} = 1$ is counterfactual (could never be observed because these individuals received treatment); in other words, only $Y^1_{t=1}$ can be observed. Hence, if we are willing to accept equivalence of (3.51) and (3.52), we could estimate the treatment effects in those previous periods and test whether they were zero. If they are statistically different from zero, participants and non-participants were already different in their unobserved confounders before the treatment started, even conditional on X. To be able to use this test, we needed to have additional lags of $Y^0_{t=-l}, l > k$, that were not included as control variables in (3.51). To implement this test it is useful to think of it as if some *pseudo-treatment* had happened at time zero or earlier. Hence, we retain the observed indicator $D_{t=0}$ as defining the participants and non-participants and pretend that the treatment had started already at time -1. Since we know that actually no treatment had happened, we expect treatment effect to be zero. Statistically significant non-zero estimates would be an indication for CIA violation. A simple and obvious case is that where you check $Y^0_{t=1} \perp\!\!\!\perp D_{t=0} | X$ by testing $Y^0_{t=0} \perp\!\!\!\perp D_{t=0} | X$. Here $k = 0$ is such that the lagged outcome is not included in the original conditioning but only used for the pre- or pseudo-treatment test.

So far we tried to check the CIA for ATET but can we extend this idea in order to check also

$$Y^1_{t=1} \perp\!\!\!\perp D_{t=0} | X, Y^0_{t=0}, Y^0_{t=-1}, Y^0_{t=-2}, \dots, Y^0_{t=-k},$$

i.e. the assumption we need for ATE and ATEN? In fact, it cannot, since pre-treatment periods only provide information about Y^0 but not Y^1.

What if we find significant pseudo-treatment effects? We might consider them as an estimate of the bias due to unobserved confounders and be willing to assume that this bias is constant over time. Then we could first proceed as if CIA held to afterwards correct the resulting estimate by substracting the bias estimate. This is the basic idea of difference-in-difference (DiD) estimators and DiD-Matching to be discussed in a later chapter of this book, and it is also essentially the intuition behind fixed effects estimators for panel data models.

3.4.4 Multiple Treatment Evaluation

In principle, we could extend all ideas of this chapter to the situation where D is non-binary. Consider the case of multiple (and thus discrete) treatments, where D can take values in $\{0, 1, \dots, M\}$.[54] These $M + 1$ different treatments are typically to be defined as mutually exclusive, i.e. each individual will receive exactly one of these treatments.

---

[54] See for example Lechner (2001) or Imbens (2000).

These do not have to be ordered.[55] The average treatment effect for two different treatments m and l would thus be

$$ATE(m, l) := E[Y^m - Y^l], \qquad m \neq l \in \{0, 1, \ldots, M\} \qquad (3.53)$$

and the ATET correspondingly

$$ATET(m, l) := E[Y^m - Y^l | D = m]. \qquad (3.54)$$

The corresponding conditional independence assumption is

$$Y^d \perp\!\!\!\perp D | X \qquad \forall d \in \{0, 1, \ldots, M\},$$

and a common support assumption looks like

$$\Pr(D = d | X) > 0 \qquad a.s. \qquad \forall d \in \{0, 1, \ldots, M\}.$$

With these assumptions we can identify and estimate all ATE or ATET for any combination $m \neq l$ of programmes.

More specifically: if D is discrete with only a few mass points M, $M << n$, we could estimate $m_d(x)$ separately in each sub-population, i.e. for each value of d in $Supp(D)$. But if D takes on many different values, e.g. M large or D being continuous (or multivariate) and thus ordered, then the estimator of $m_d(x)$ also has to smooth over D. Hence, we could still use

$$\widehat{E\left[Y^0\right]} = \frac{1}{n} \sum_{i=1}^{n} \hat{m}_0(X_i),$$

where $\hat{m}_d(x)$ is a non-parametric regression estimator of $E[Y | X = x, D = d]$ which smoothes over X **and** D. In other words, when D was binary, we estimated $m_0(x)$ by using only the non-participant ($D = 0$) observations. But when D is continuously distributed, the probability that any observation with $D = d$ is observed is zero, and we have to rely also on observations with $D \neq d$ to estimate $m_d(x)$. Therefore, we might use all observations but assign a larger weight to those observations j for which D_j is close to d. A propensity score matching approach would be more difficult to implement (since $P(D = d | X = x) = 0$), and we usually had to rely on higher-dimensional non-parametric regression.

Yet, you can extend the approach of propensity score matching to the case with $M << n$. A quite useful result is that a dimension reducing balancing property is available also for that case. Define the probabilities

$$p^l(x) \equiv \Pr(D = l | X = x) \text{ and}$$

$$p^{l|ml}(x) \equiv \Pr(D = l | X = x, D \in \{m, l\}) = \frac{p^l(x)}{p^l(x) + p^m(x)}.$$

---

[55] I.e. treatments 0, 1 and 2 can be different training programmes with arbitrary ordering. If, however, they represented different dosages or intensities of the same treatment, then one would like to invoke additional assumptions such as monotonicity, which would help to identify and improve the precision of the estimates.

It is easy to show that

$$E\left[Y^m\right] = \int E\left[Y|D = m, p^m\right] dF(p^m),$$

$$E\left[Y^m|D = l\right] = \int E\left[Y|D = m, p^{m|ml}\right] dF(p^{m|ml}|D = l). \qquad (3.55)$$

The latter result is obtained by showing that the conditional independence also implies

$$Y^d \perp\!\!\!\perp D|p^{m|ml}, \qquad D \in \{m, l\}.$$

Instead of conditioning on $p^{m|ml}$ it is also possible to jointly condition on p^m and p^l, because $p^{m|ml}$ is a function of them. Hence, we also could consider

$$Y^d \perp\!\!\!\perp D|(p^m, p^l), \qquad D \in \{m, l\}.$$

These results suggest different estimation strategies via propensity score matching. If one is interested in all pairwise treatment effects, one could estimate a discrete choice model such as multinomial probit (MNP) (or a multinomial logit (MNL) if the different treatment categories are very distinct),[56] which delivers consistent estimates of the marginal probabilities $p^l(x)$ for all treatment categories.

If computation time for the MNP is too demanding, an alternative is to estimate all the $M(M - 1)/2$ propensity scores $p^{m|ml}$ by using binary probits for all pairwise comparisons separately. From a modelling perspective, the MNP model might be preferred because if the model is correct, all marginal and conditional probabilities would be consistently estimated. The estimation of pairwise probits, on the other hand, does not seem to be consistent with any well-known discrete choice model.[57] On the other hand, specification tests and verification of balancing are often easier to perform with respect to binary probits to obtain a well-fitting specification. Using separate binary probits has also the advantage that misspecification of one of the binary probit models does not imply that all propensity scores are misspecified (as would be the case with an MNP model). So far, comparison studies of these various methods have found little difference in their relative performance.[58] Overall, estimating separate binary probit models seems to be a flexible and convenient approach.

Whichever way one chooses to estimate the propensity scores, one should define the common support with respect to all the propensity scores. Although it would suffice for the estimation of $E[Y^m - Y^l|D = m]$ to examine only $p^{m|ml}$ for the support region, the interpretation of various effects such as $E[Y^m - Y^l|D = m]$ and $E[Y^m - Y^k|D = m]$

---

[56] The MNL is based on stronger assumptions than the MNP. A well-known implication is the Independence of Irrelevant Alternatives (IIA), which is often not plausible if some of the choice options are more similar than others. A nested logit approach might be an alternative, e.g. if the first decision is whether to attend training or not, and the exact type of training is determined only as a second decision. This, however, requires a previous grouping of the categories. For semi-parametric MNL see Langrock, Heidenreich and Sperlich (2014). MNP is therefore a more flexible approach if computational power permits its use.

[57] I.e. the usual discrete choice model would assume that all choices made and the corresponding characteristics X have to be taken into account for estimation. A pairwise probit of m versus l, and one for l versus k, etc. would not be consistent with this model.

[58] Compare for example the studies and applications in Gerfin and Lechner (2002), Lechner (2002a) or Gerfin, Lechner and Steiger (2005).

would be more difficult if they were defined for different subpopulations due to the common support restriction. A comparison of the estimates could not disentangle differences coming from different supports compared to differences coming from different effects.

One (relatively strict) way to implement a joint common support is to delete all observations with at least one of their estimated probabilities larger than the smallest maximum and smaller than the largest minimum of all subsamples defined by D. For an individual who satisfies this restriction we can thus be sure that we find at least one comparison observation (a match) in each subgroup defined by D. Instead of matching, a propensity score weighting approach is also possible. In fact, it is straightforward to show that, recall (3.55),

$$E[Y^m | D = l] = \int E\left[Y^m | X = x, D = m\right] dF(x|l)$$

$$= E\left[Y^m \cdot \frac{1 - p^{m|ml}(X)}{p^{m|ml}(X)} \frac{\Pr(D = m)}{\Pr(D = l)} \Big| D = m\right].$$

The latter can be estimated by

$$\frac{1}{n_m} \sum_{i:D_i = m} Y_i \frac{1 - \hat{p}^{m|ml}(X_i)}{\hat{p}^{m|ml}(X_i)} \frac{n_m}{n_l} \quad \text{with } n_k = \sum_{i=1}^{n} \mathbb{1}\{D_i = k\}.$$

A difference between the evaluation of a single programme and that of multiple programmes is that some identification strategies that we will learn for the evaluation of a single programme are less useful for the evaluation of multiple treatments.

3.5   Bibliographic and Computational Notes

3.5.1   Further Reading and Bibliographic Notes

Again, compare the literature in biometrics and statistics like e.g. Robins, Rotnitzky and Zhao (1994), Rotnitzky and Robins (1995), Rotnitzky and Robins (1997), Rotnitzky, Robins and Scharfstein (1998) which introduced different kinds of matching, propensity matching and weighting estimators, the so-called augmented *inverse propensity weighted* (AIPW) estimator being one of the most popular ones. Actually, in Robins and Rotnitzky (1995) and Robins, Rotnitzky and Zhao (1995) you see that the AIPW is the same as what in econometrics we call the *double robust estimator* combining regression and weighting, but with most parts of the model being fully parametric. For a nice summary and computational issues see Glynn and Quinn (2010). In the case where the propensity score is estimated parametrically, the analytical variance of the propensity weighting estimators can be obtained straightforwardly from the theory of sequential GMM estimators. This makes the weighting estimator attractive particularly in more complex settings; see Hernan, Brumback and Robins (2001), Hirano, Imbens and Ridder (2003), Lechner (2009), Robins and Rotnitzky (1995) or Robins, Rotnitzky and Zhao (1995).

As stated different authors have made a major effort to compare all kind of proposed matching, regression, (re-)weighting and double robust estimators: see, for example, Lunceford and Davidian (2004), Frölich (2004), Zhao (2004) for early studies, Busso, DiNardo and McCrary (2009), Huber, Lechner and Wunsch (2013) or Busso, DiNardo and McCrary (2014), Frölich, Huber and Wiesenfarth (2017), Frölich and Huber (2017, J RSS B) for more recent ones. Frölich (2005) contributed a study on the bandwidth choice. A number of recipes for one-to-one propensity score matching have been suggested, e.g. in Lechner (1999), Brookhart, Schneeweiss, Rothman, Glynn, Avorn and Stürmer (2006) and Imbens and Rubin (2015) among many others. Some other estimators proposed in the literature use the propensity score just to get estimates for the functions m_0, m_1. For example you may take

$$\hat{m}_1(X_i) := \widehat{E}[D_i Y_i | X_i] / \hat{p}(X_i), \qquad \hat{m}_0(X_i) := \widehat{E}[(1 - D_i) Y_i | X_i] / \{1 - \hat{p}(X_i)\} \tag{3.56}$$

with $\hat{p}(X_i) := \widehat{E}[D_i | X_i]$. When using in (3.56) proper non-parametric estimators of the conditional expectation, then it can be shown that for those

$$\widehat{ATE} = \frac{1}{n} \sum_{i=1}^{n} \hat{m}_1(x_i) - \hat{m}_0(x_i)$$

is asymptotically linear in the sense of the ATE estimator defined by

$$\sqrt{n}(\widehat{ATE} - ATE) = \frac{1}{\sqrt{n}} \sum_{i=1}^{n} \psi(y_i, x_i, d_i) + O_p(1) \tag{3.57}$$

with $E[\psi(Y, X, D)] = 0$, $\quad Var[\psi(Y, X, D)] < \infty$.

One again obtains the so-called *influence function*

$$\psi(y_i, x_i, d_i) = E[Y | x_i, d_i = 1] - E[Y | x_i, d_i = 0] - ATE + \frac{d_i}{p(x_i)} (y_i - E[y | x_i, d_i = 1]) - \frac{1 - d_i}{1 - p(x_i)} (y_i - E[y | x_i, d_i = 0]). \tag{3.58}$$

As $Var[\widehat{ATE}] = Var[\psi(Y, X, D)]/n$, it is easy to see that these estimators reach the lower bound of variance. It is evident then how this procedure can be extended to ATET or ATEN.

These again have typically been proposed using power series estimators. Therefore, let us briefly comment on a common misunderstanding. Recall that reducing the bias is reducing this approximation error; 'undersmoothing' is thus equivalent to including that many basis functions that the variance (the difference between sample and population coefficients) clearly dominates the squared approximation error. Note that this cannot be checked by simple t or F tests – and not only because of the well-known pre-testing problem that invalidates further inference. For example, for propensity score based estimation with (power) series it is stated that efficiency could be reached when the number L of basis functions is in the interval $(n^{2(\delta/q-2)}, n^{1/9})$ with $\delta/q \geq 7$, and δ being the number of times the propensity score is continuously differentiable.[59] This would mean that even for $n = 10,000$ people would take only two basis functions; for $n = 60,000$ just three, etc. For power series is proposed the basis $1, x_1, x_2, \ldots, x_q, x_1^2, x_2^2, \ldots, x_q^2, x_1 x_2, \ldots$ etc.[60] Along this reasoning you might conclude that using a linear model with $L = q + 1$ you strongly undersmooth (actually, more than admitted), which obviously does not make much sense. Even if you interpreted the series in the sense that $L - 1$ should be the order of the used polynomial, then for $n = 10,000$ you would still work with a linear model, or for $n = 60,000$ with a quadratic one. However, these will typically have very poor fitting properties. A more appropriate way to understand the rate related statement is to imagine that one needs $L = n^v \cdot C$ where v is just about the rate but C is fixed and depends on the adaptiveness of the used series, the true density and the true function, and should be much larger than 1. But this does still not solve the problem of poor extrapolation (or prediction) to other populations and thus the inappropriateness for the estimation of counterfactual outcomes.

Concerning further discussion on trimming, especially that based on the propensity score, Crump, Hotz, Imbens and Mitnik (2009) propose choosing the subset of the support of X that minimises the variance of the estimated treatment effect. Since the exact variances of the estimators are unknown, their approach is based on the efficiency bound, i.e. the asymptotic variance of an efficient non-parametric estimator. This solution only depends on the propensity score and conditional variances of Y. Under homoskedasticity, a simpler formula is obtained which depends only on the marginal distribution of the propensity score. Trimming all observations with $p_i \leq 0.1$ or $p_i \geq 0.9$ works as a useful rule of thumb.

Huber, Lechner and Wunsch (2013) criticise the various trimming proposals since they all ignore the asymptotic nature. Unless the propensity score is in fact 0 or 1 for some values, the need for trimming vanishes when the sample size increases. Trimming is only used as a small-sample tool to make the estimator less variable when n is small. Therefore, the proportion of observations being trimmed should go to zero when n increases. They suggest a trimming scheme based on the sum of weights each observation receives in the implicit weighting of the matching estimator. Observations with very large weights are discarded. Since each weight is obtained by dividing by the sample size, the weights automatically decrease with sample size and thus the proportion of trimmed observations decreases to zero unless the treatment probability is really 0 or 1 for that x. If the latter were true, we could suspect this from knowledge of the institutional details and exclude those x values before estimating the propensity score.

Much more recent is literature on treatment effect estimation with high-dimensional data. Given the increasing size of data sets on the one hand, and the fear that one might not have included enough confounders to reach CIA validity on the other, it would be

---

[59] Hirano, Imbens and Ridder (2003) give slightly different bounds in their theorem but the ones given here coincide with those in their proof and some other, unpublished work of theirs.

[60] Sometimes the notation is careless if not wrong when constructing these series such that they are of little use for the practitioner. Most of them additionally require rectangle supports of X, i.e. that the support of X is the Cartesian product of the q intervals $[min(X_j), max(X_j)]$. This basically excludes confounders with important correlation like for example 'age' and 'tenure' or 'experience'.

interesting to know how to do inference on the ATE estimate after having performed an extensive selection of potential confounders. This problem is studied in Belloni, Chernozhukov and Hansen (2014) who allow for a number of potential confounders being larger than the sample size. Certainly, you need that the correct number q is much smaller than n, and that potentially committed selection errors are (first-order) orthogonal to the main estimation problem (i.e. the estimation of the ATE). So far, this has been shown to work at least for some (generalised) partial linear models.

What has been discussed less is the identification and estimation of multivalued treatment (which will be considered in later chapters), i.e. when we have various treatments but each individual can participate at most in one. As was indicated, idea and procedure are the same as for binary D; see e.g. Cattaneo (2010), who introduced a double robust estimator for multivariate treatment effects.

3.5.2   Computational Notes

There exists a variety of packages for matching and propensity score based methods in **R**, Stata, SAS, Matlab, Gauss, etc. Again we concentrate here on **R** and Stata. Many of them, however, are either based on parametric estimation or kNN matching.

Matching is an **R** package which provides functions for multivariate and propensity score matching and for finding optimal covariate balance based on a genetic search algorithm. It uses automated procedures to select matches based on univariate and multivariate balance diagnostics. The package provides a set of functions to do the matching (Match) and to evaluate how good covariate balance is before and after matching (MatchBalance). Match is the fastest multivariate and propensity score matching function so far. Maximum speed is achieved when one uses the replace=FALSE and/or ties=FALSE options.

The GenMatch function finds optimal balance using multivariate matching where a search algorithm determines the weight each covariate is given. Balance is determined by examining cumulative probability distribution functions of a variety of standardised statistics. These statistics include paired t-tests, univariate and multivariate Kolmogorov–Smirnov (KS) tests, etc. A variety of descriptive statistics based on empirical-QQ plots are also offered. GenMatch supports the use of multiple computers, CPUs or cores to perform parallel computations.

The R package TMLE (published in 2014 for targeted maximum likelihood estimation) is a quite comprehensive collection of parametric and semi-parametric procedures to estimate effects of binary treatment. Coming from biometrics it also allows for the handling of missings and longitudinal data, see Gruber and van der Laan (2012) for details.

Another recent (published in 2013) R package for (semi-)parametric causal inference is iWeigReg. It offers methods based on inverse propensity score weighting and potential outcome regression (for both, causal inference and missing data problems) based on double robust likelihood estimation along Tan (2006), Tan (2010) and Tan (2013).

The **R** package CausalGAM works with non-parametric generalised additive models (GAM). It implements various estimators for ATE, namely an inverse propensity score weighting, an augmented inverse probability weighting, and a standard regression estimator that makes use of GAM for both, the treatment assignment and/or the outcome model.

Finally, `ATE` is a very recent **R** package to estimate the ATE or the ATET based on a quite recent estimation idea; see Chan, Yam and Zhang (2016). This function uses a covariate balancing method which creates weights for each subject without the need to specify a propensity score or an outcome regression model.

Until recently `Stata` didn't have many explicit built-in commands for propensity score based methods or other non-experimental methods that produced control groups with distributions of confounders similar to that of the treated group. However, there are several user-written modules, of which the maybe most popular ones were: `psmatch2` and `pscore`, and more recently `nnmatch`. All three modules support pair-matching as well as subclassification. In addition, `ivqte` also permits estimation of distributional effects and quantile treatment effects.

The command `psmatch2` – see Leuven and Sianesi (2014) – has been the preferred tool to perform propensity score matching. It performs full Mahalanobis and propensity score matching, common support graphing (`psgraph`) and covariate imbalance testing (`pstest`). It allows kNN matching, kernel weighting, Mahalanobis matching and includes built-in diagnostics. It further includes procedures for estimating ATET or ATE. The default matching method is single nearest-neighbour (without caliper). However, standard errors are calculated by naive bootstrapping which is known to be inconsistent in this context. The `common` option imposes a common support by dropping treatment observations based on their propensity score; see the help file for details.

The command `pscore` estimates treatment effects by the use of propensity score matching techniques. Additionally, the program offers balancing tests based on stratification. The commands to estimate the average treatment effect on the treated group using kNN matching are `attnd` and `attnw`. For radius matching, the average treatment effect on the treated is calculated with the module `attr`. In the programs `attnd`, `attnw`, and `attr`, standard errors are estimated analytically or approximated by bootstrapping using the `bootstrap` option. Kernel matching is implemented in `attk`. Users can choose the default Gaussian or the Epanechnikov kernel. Stratification can be used in `atts`. By construction, in each block defined by this procedure, the covariates are balanced and the assignment to treatment can be considered as random. No weights are allowed.

If you want to directly apply nearest-neighbour matching instead of estimating the propensity score equation first, you may use `nnmatch`. This command does kNN matching with the option of choosing between several different distance metrics. It allows for exact matching (or as close as possible) on a subset of variables, bias correction of the treatment effect and estimation of either the sample or population variance with or without assuming a constant treatment effect.

However, as we have seen, the two main problems in practice are the choice of the proper method for the present data set, and an appropriate estimator for the standard error. So it is recommendable to always try not just different methods but also different implementations. For instance, if `pscore` and `nnmatch` give similar results, then the findings are assumed to be quite reliable; if not, then you have a problem. For a review see Becker and Ichino (2002) and Nichols (2007). Related implementations of the reweighting propensity score estimator are for example the `stata` routine `treatrew` (Cerulli, 2012).

With STATA 13 the command `teffects` was introduced. This command takes into account that the propensity score used for matching was estimated in a first stage. Adjusted standard errors are implemented in the command `teffects psmatch`. This command also provides regression adjustment (`teffects ra`), inverse probability weighting (`teffects ipw`), augmented inverse probability weighting (`teffects aipw`), inverse probability weighted regression adjustment (`teffects ipwra`), and nearest neighbour matching (`teffects nnmatch`). There is also a rich menu of post-estimation inference tools. However, many (if not most) methods are purely parametric, typically based on linear regression techniques. For more details visit the manual and related help files. For extensions to multivalued treatment effects see Cattaneo, Drucker and Holland (2013), who discuss in detail the related `poparms` command. The command `ivqte` permits estimation of quantile treatment effects and distributional effects.

3.6 Exercises

1. Derive the analogue to (2.7) for the identification of $ATET = E[Y^1 - Y^0 | D = 1]$.

2. List and explain different advantages of matching and non-parametric regression compared to the OLS-regression-based approach when estimating ATE and ATET with CIA.

3. Repeat the discussion from Subsection 3.1.3 when using parametric quadratic and cubic models, including interaction terms. Try now to interpret an ATE estimate based on a linear model if these (quadratic and cubic) were the correct functional forms.

4. Recall Subsection 3.1.2, and in particular the decomposition of the bias, Equations 3.10 to 3.12. How would this look like for the ATE estimation? Discuss, basically by repeating our arguments, how the ATE matching or regression-based estimator eliminates the different bias terms you face in the ATE estimation problem.

5. Consider the variance and bias terms of the matching-based estimator given in Theorem 3.1. What is the impact of K (number of neighbours)? How does it affect the variance and bias if we increase K along n?

6. Consider now the semi-parametric efficiency bounds for the variances when estimating ATE or ATET, Theorem 3.2.

7. Recall Example 3.6. Derive the variance expression given in (3.26) and show that it reaches the efficiency bound for $P = 0.5$.

8. Calculate the bias in Theorem 3.3 for the case $p = 2, q = 1$. How would it change when using a local linear estimator for $m_0(\cdot)$?

9. Prove the statement from Section 3.3.1, where it was said that taking (3.58) with $E[Y|x_i, d_i = d]$ replaced by $\mu_d(p(x_i))$ plus the term

$$\{p(x_i) - d_i\} \left\{ \frac{E[Y|x_i, d_i = 1] - \mu_1(p(x_i))}{p(x_i)} + \frac{E[Y|x_i, d_i = 0] - \mu_0(p(x_i))}{1 - p(x_i)} \right\} \tag{3.59}$$

would again give the original influence function (3.58).

10. Let us extend Example 3.12 taken from Imbens (2004). Imagine we were provided with a vector of firm characteristics x_i that affected production and costs, and consequently also potential profits. Then the production is still a stochastic function $Y_i = \varphi(D_i, x_i, e_i)$, influenced by technological innovation D_i, random factors not being under the firms control e_i, and some observable(s) x_i. Profits are again measured by output minus costs: $\pi_i = Y_i - c(x_i, v_i) \cdot D_i$, where c is the cost function depending also on x_i and unknown random factors v_i. Discuss the (in-)validity of the CIA along the same lines as we discussed the unconfoundedness in Example 3.12.

11. Recall the double robustness of the ATE estimator presented in Subsection 3.3.3. Show that running a WLS regression with weights (3.38)

$$\text{regress} \quad Y \quad \text{on} \quad constant, D, X - \bar{X}_1 \text{ and } (X - \bar{X}_1)D,$$

where $\bar{X}_1$ is the average of X among the $D = 1$ observations, gives a propensity score weighting ATET estimator.

12. For the double robust estimator recall the weights for ATE in (3.39). Show then that

$$e_2' \begin{bmatrix} \sum \omega_i & \sum \omega_i D_i \\ \sum \omega_i D_i & \sum \omega_i D_i^2 \end{bmatrix}^{-1} \begin{bmatrix} \sum \omega_i Y_i \\ \sum \omega_i D_i Y_i \end{bmatrix} = \frac{\sum_{i=1}^n \frac{Y_i D_i}{\hat{p}(X_i)}}{\sum_{i=1}^n \frac{D_i}{\hat{p}(X_i)}} - \frac{\sum_{i=1}^n \frac{Y_i(1-D_i)}{1-\hat{p}(X_i)}}{\sum_{i=1}^n \frac{1-D_i}{1-\hat{p}(X_i)}}.$$

4 Selection on Unobservables: Non-Parametric IV and Structural Equation Approaches

In many situations we may not be able to observe all confounding variables, perhaps because data collection has been too expensive or simply because some variables are hard or impossible to measure. This may be less of a concern with detailed administrative data, but more often when only a limited set of covariates is available, these may perhaps even have been measured with substantial error if obtained by e.g. telephone surveys. Often data of some obviously important confounders have not been collected because the responsible agency did not consider this information relevant for the project. In these kinds of situations the endogeneity of D can no longer be controlled for by conditioning on the set of observed covariates X. In the classic econometric literature the so-called *instrumental variable* (IV) estimation is the most frequently used technique to deal with this problem. An *instrument*, say Z, is a variable that affects the endogenous variable D but is unrelated to the potential outcome Y^d. In fact, in the selection-on-observables approach considered in the previous chapter we also required the existence of instrumental variables, but without the need to observe them explicitly. In fact, in order to fulfil the common support condition (CSC) you need some variation in $D|X$ (i.e. variation in D that cannot be explained by X) that is independent of Y^d.

4.1 Preliminaries: General Ideas and LATE

We first stress the point that instruments Z are supposed to affect the observed outcome Y only indirectly through the treatment D. Hence, any observed impact of Z on Y must have been mediated via D. Then a variation in Z permits to observe changes in D without any change in the unobservables, allowing us to identify and estimate the effect of D on Y.

Example 4.1 A firm can choose between adopting a new production technology ($D = 1$) or not ($D = 0$). Our interest is in the effect of technology on production output Y. The firm, on the other hand, chooses D in order to maximise profits, i.e.

$$D_i = \arg\max_{d \in \{0,1\}} pY_i^d - c_i(d),$$

where p is the price of a unit of output. This is common to all firms and not influenced by the firm's decision. Here the firm is a price-taker without market power. As before, $c_i(d)$ is the cost of adopting the new technology. A valid instrument Z could be a subsidy or a regulatory feature of the environment the firm operates in. It typically will change the costs and thus the profits without affecting the production output directly. Suppose that the cost function of adopting the new technology is the same for every firm, i.e. $c_i(\cdot) = c(\cdot)$ and that it only depends on d and the value of the subsidy z or regulation. Hence, the cost function is $c(d, z)$ and the firm's decision problem becomes

$$D_i = \arg\max_{d \in \{0,1\}} p Y_i^d - c(d, z).$$

Notice that the cost enters in the choice problem of the firm but the potential outputs Y^d $(d = 0, 1)$ is not affected by them. This is important for identification. We may be able to use the subsidy as an instrument to identify the effect of technology on output. However, we cannot use it to identify the effect of technology on profits or stock prices, since the subsidy itself changes the profits.

Unfortunately, while many users of IVs emphasise the exogeneity of their instrument regarding the economic process, they ignore the fact that they actually need to assume its stochastic independence from the potential outcomes, which is often hard to justify. This idea is pretty much the same as what is known and used in classical econometric regression analysis. There are mainly two differences we should have in mind: first, we are still interested in the total impact of D on Y, not in a marginal one. Second, we consider non-parametric identification and estimation. Thus, we will allow for heterogeneous returns to treatment D. This reveals another fundamental problem one has with the IV approach. In the treatment effect literature the latter is reflected in the notion of *local average treatment effects* (LATE), which will be explained in this chapter. To get around that, one needs to either make more assumptions or resort to structural modelling.

To better highlight these issues we again start with Y, D and Z being scalar variables, with the latter two being just binary. Somewhat later we will reintroduce confounders X and discuss extensions to discrete and continuous instruments. We begin with preliminary considerations for illustration before formalising the identification and estimation procedure.

4.1.1   General Ideas

Recall the classical instrumental variables strategy. As we just look at one binary regressor D, one might start by considering the simple linear model

$$Y = \alpha_0 + D\alpha_1 + U \tag{4.1}$$

where $cov(D, U) \neq 0$ is the endogeneity problem to be dealt with. It is assumed then that an instrument Z is provided, such that

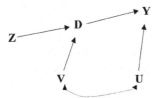

Figure 4.1 Treatment effect identification via an instrument Z

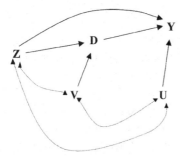

Figure 4.2 When treatment effect identification via instrument Z fails

$$cov(U, Z) = 0, \qquad cov(D, Z) \neq 0,$$

i.e. Z is not correlated with the unobservables but is correlated with D. This leads to some versions of parametric (standard) IV estimators, which will be discussed in the next sections. This procedure does not change if D is, for example, continuous. Then, however, the linearity in model (4.1) is chosen for convenience, but does not necessarily emanate from economic theory.

It is most helpful to better understand the merits and limits of instrumental variables by analysing non-parametric identification. A simple illustration of the situation without control variables in which the effect of Z on Y is channelled by D is given in Figure 4.1. We are going to see why we often need three assumptions: first, that the instrument Z has no direct effect on Y and, second, that the instrument itself is not confounded. The meaning of these assumptions can be seen by comparing Figure 4.2 with 4.1. The assumption that Z has no direct effect on Y requires that the direct arc from Z to Y should not exist nor an inverse analogue. Furthermore, the assumption of no confounding requires that there are no dashed arcs between Z and V, and no ones between Z and U, or more generally. In sum, there must be no further (dashed or solid) arcs between Z and Y. In practice you find mainly arguments that tell you why there is no direct impact $Z \rightarrow Y$ but ignore the dashed arcs. The third assumption is that Z has predictive power for D. (Fourth, we will need some monotonicity assumption.)

Example 4.2 The determinants of civil wars are an important research topic. A number of contributions have stressed that civil wars, particularly in Africa, are more often driven by business opportunities than by political grievances. The costs of recruiting fighters may therefore be an important factor for triggering civil wars. In this respect, poor young men are more willing to be recruited as fighters when their income opportunities in agriculture or in the formal labour market are worse. Therefore, it would be interesting to estimate the impact of economic growth or GDP per capita on the likelihood of civil war in Africa. It is quite obvious that at the same time civil wars heavily effect GDP p.c. and economic growth. A popular causal chain assumption[1] is that, in countries with a large agricultural sector (which is mainly rain fed), negative weather shocks reduce GDP, which, as a proxy for the economic situation, increases the risk of civil war. The price for recruiting fighters may be one of the channels. But another could be the reduced state military strength or road coverage. Whereas weather shocks are arguably exogenously driven, the absence of any other stochastic dependence between weather and civil war incidence is a quite arguable assumption.

In the next section we will begin with the simplest situation where D and Z are both binary and no other covariates are included. Later we will relax these assumptions by permitting conditioning on additional covariates X, hoping that this conditioning makes the necessary assumptions hold. Hence, observed X will then allow us to 'block' any further arc between Z and Y.

Example 4.3 Edin, Fredriksson and Aslund (2003) studied the effect of living in highly concentrated ethnic area $(D = 1)$ on labour success Y in Sweden. Traditionally, the expected outcome was ambiguous: on the one hand the residential segregation should lower the acquisition rate of local skills preventing access to good jobs. But on the other hand, these ethnic enclaves also act as an opportunity to increasing networks by disseminating information to immigrants. The raw data say that immigrants in ethnic enclaves have 5% lower earnings, even after controlling for age, education, gender, family background, country of origin and year of immigration. However, the resulting negative association may not be causal if the decision to live in such an enclave depended on one's expected opportunities related to unobserved abilities.

From 1985 to 1991 the Swedish government assigned initial areas of residence to all refugees, motivated by the belief that dispersing immigrants would promote integration. Let now Z indicate the initial assignment eight years before measuring D, with $Z = 1$ meaning that one was – though randomly – assigned (close) to an ethnic enclave. It seems to be plausible to assume that Z was independent of potential earnings Y^0, Y^1 but affected D (eight years later). Then all impact from Z on Y is coming through D. One might, however, want to control for some of the labour market conditions X of the region people were originally assigned to. Formally stated, X should contain all relevant information about the government's assignment policy that could confound our analysis. This way one could ensure that there was no further relation between Z and Y.

---

[1] See, for example, Miguel, Satyanath and Sergenti (2004) or Collier and Höffler (2002).

Example 4.4 An individual may choose to attend college or not, and the outcome Y is earnings or wealth later in the life cycle. The individual's decision depends on the expected payoff, i.e. better employment chances or higher wages, and also on the costs of attending college, which includes travel costs, tuition, commuting time but also fore-gone earnings. Only some of them are covered by confounders X. A popular though problematic instrument Z is, for example, the distance to college. Suppose the individual chooses college if Y_i^1 is larger than Y_i^0. Albeit knowing X, he may not be able to forecast the potential outcomes perfectly as he has only a noisy signal of ability, reflected in U. The same problem has the empirical researcher who observes X and Z but not the proneness to school (reflected in V) which influences the cost function. The participation decision is (most likely)

$$D_i = \mathbb{1} \left\{ E\left[Y_i^1 | U_i, X_i, Z_i\right] - c(1, X_i, V_i, Z_i) > E\left[Y_i^0 | U_i, X_i, Z_i\right] \right. $$
$$\left. -c(0, X_i, V_i, Z_i)\right\}.$$

Here is a difference between the objective function of the individual (outcomes minus costs) and the production function that the econometrician is interested in (namely $Y_i^1 - Y_i^0$). The tricky point is that the instruments should shift the objective function of the individual without shifting the production function.

But what do we actually estimate by IV methods? Generally, a correct and informative interpretation of the treatment effect identified by IVs is obtained by explicitly modelling the decision to participate (or selection into a treatment group). In order to do so we add a second equation to the outcome equation

$$D_i = \zeta(Z_i, X_i, V_i), \quad Y_i = \varphi(D_i, X_i, U_i), \tag{4.2}$$

where the endogeneity of D arises from statistical dependence between U and V, where U and V are vectors of unobserved variables, suppressing potential model misspecification. In this triangular system U could be unobserved cognitive and non-cognitive skills, talents, ability, etc., while V could be dedication to academic study or any other factor affecting the costs of schooling. That is, one might think of U as fortune in the labour market and V as ability in schooling. Most of the time we will consider only cases where we are interested in identifying the second equation.

We know from the classical literature on triangular or simultaneous equation systems that given (4.2) with unobserved U, V we identify and estimate the impact of those D on $Y|X$ that are predicted by (Z, X); or say, the impact of that variation in D (on variation in $Y|X$) which is driven by the variation of (Z, X).

In the introduction to this chapter we have already used the notion of LATE but without explaining it further. The question is where this *local* stands for. Remember that we distinguished between the general ATE and the ATET or ATEN referring to the ATE for different (sub-)populations. This distinction made sense always when we allowed for heterogeneous returns to treatment as otherwise they would all be equal. Calling it *local* makes explicit that the identified treatment effect refers (again) only to a certain subpopulation. One could actually also say that ATET and ATEN are *local*. The notion LATE is typically used when this subpopulation is defined by another variable, here instrument Z or (Z, X). The interpretability or say the usefulness of LATE depends thus on the extent to which the particular subpopulation is a reasonable target to look at. In the statistics literature, LATE is usually referred to as Complier Average Causal Effect (CACE), which makes it very explicit that we are referring to the average effect for the subpopulation defined as Compliers.

4.1.2   Local Average Treatment Effect: LATE

There are many other ways how to introduce the instrumental variable approach for treatment effect estimation. Also, the assumptions used seem to differ a bit. However, as long as they lead to equivalent estimators – which is mostly the case – they are certainly equivalent. What we present here is the classical way how to introduce the LATE idea in econometrics.[2] Consider a triangular model with potentially non-separable errors, where Y and D are scalar, Z and D binary, and ignoring confounders X for notational convenience

$$Y_i = \varphi(D_i, Z_i, U_i) \quad \text{with} \quad Y_{i,z}^d = \varphi(d, z, U_i) \quad \text{and} \quad Y_{i,Z_i}^{D_i} = Y_i$$
$$D_i = \zeta(Z_i, V_i) \quad \text{with} \quad D_{i,z} = \zeta(z, V_i) \quad \text{and} \quad D_{i,Z_i} = D_i.$$

You can think of Example 4.4 where D indicates 'attending' college and Z being an indicator of living close to or far from a college. The latter was commonly considered to be a valid instrument as living close to a college during childhood may induce some children to go to college but is unlikely to directly affect the wages earned in their adulthood. So one argues with Figure 2.14 and ignores potential problems coming from the dashed lines in Figure 4.2.

According to the reaction of D on an external intervention on Z (family moves further away or closer to a college but because of reasons not related with the college),[3] the units i can be distinguished into different types: For some units, D would remain unchanged if Z were changed from 0 to 1, whereas for others D would change. With D and Z binary, four different latent types $T \in \{n, c, d, a\}$ are possible:

$T_i = a$	if $D_{i,0} = 1$ and $D_{i,1} = 1$	Always-taker
$T_i = n$	if $D_{i,0} = 0$ and $D_{i,1} = 0$	Never-taker
$T_i = c$	if $D_{i,0} = 0$ and $D_{i,1} = 1$	Complier/compliant
$T_i = d$	if $D_{i,0} = 1$ and $D_{i,1} = 0$	Defier

---

[2] This is based on the ideas outlined in Angrist, Imbens and Rubin (1996), Imbens (2001) and Frölich (2007a).

[3] This excludes the cases where people move closer to a college because the children are supposed to attend it.

Example 4.5 In this situation it is quite easy to imagine the two first groups: people who definitely will go to the college, no matter how far they live from one. The second group is the exact counterpart, giving us the subpopulation of people who will not go to the college independently of the distance. The third group consists exactly of those who go to the college because it is close but would not have done so if it were far away. The last group is composed of people who go to college because it is far from home but might not have done so if it were close by or vice versa. But who are these people and why should that group exist at all? First, one has to see that they have one thing in common with the former group, the so-called *compliers*: both groups together present people who are basically indifferent to attending a college but are finally driven by the instrument 'distance'. The last group just differs in the sense that their decision seems counter-intuitive to what we expect. But if you imagine someone living far away, who had to stay home when deciding for an apprenticeship but could leave and move to a new place when choosing 'college', then we can well imagine that this latter group exists and is even not negligibly small compared to the group size of compliers.

We might say that compliers and defiers are generally indifferent to D (get treated or not) but their final decision is induced by instrument Z. Note that we have the same problem as we discussed at the beginning for Y^d: we observe each individual's D_z only under either $z = 0$ or $z = 1$. Consequently we cannot assign the individuals uniquely to one of the four types. For example, individual i with $D_{i,0} = 1$ might be an always-taker or a defier, and $D_{i,1} = 1$ might be either an always-taker or a complier. Furthermore, since the units of type always-taker and of type never-taker cannot be induced to change D through a variation in the instrumental variable; the impact of D on Y can at most be ascertained for the subpopulations of compliers and defiers. Unfortunately, since changes in the instrument Z would trigger changes in D for the compliers as well as for the defiers, but with the opposite sign, any causal effect on the compliers could be offset by opposite flows of defiers. The most obvious strategy is to rule out the existence of subpopulations that are affected by the instrument in an opposite direction (i.e. assume 'no defiers' are observed). It is also clear – and will be seen in further discussion below – that we need compliers for identification. In sum, we assume:

Assumption (A1), *Monotonicity*: The subpopulation of defiers has probability measure zero:

$$\Pr\left(D_{i,0} > D_{i,1}\right) = 0.$$

Assumption (A2), *Existence of compliers*: The subpopulation of compliers has positive probability:

$$\Pr\left(D_{i,0} < D_{i,1}\right) > 0.$$

Monotonicity ensures that the effect of Z on D has the same direction for all units. The monotonicity and the existence assumption together ensure that $D_{i,1} \geq D_{i,0}$ for all

i and that the instrument has an effect on D, such that $D_{i,1} > D_{i,0}$ for at least some units (with positive measure). These assumptions are not testable but are essential.

Example 4.6 Thinking of Example 4.4, where college proximity was used as an instrument to identify the returns to attending college, monotonicity requires that any child which would not have attended college if living close to a college, would also not have done so if living far from a college. Analogously, any person attending college living far away would also have attended if living close to one. The existence assumption requires that the college attendance decision depends at least for some children on the proximity to the nearest college (in both directions).

Actually, Assumption (A2) corresponds to the classical assumption that Z is relevant for the endogenous regressor D. The next assumptions we make on instrument Z sound more familiar to us as they correspond to the 'exogeneity' condition imposed on instruments in standard regression analysis. However, Assumption (A3) actually has no direct analog in the classic IV-regression. It is used to fix the latent types – something not necessary in classic IV-regression as there the returns are often supposed to be constant. It requires that the fraction of always-takers, never-takers and compliers is independent of the instrument.

Assumption (A3), *Unconfounded instrument*: The relative size of the subpopulations always-takers, never-takers and compliers is independent of the instrument:

$$\Pr(T_i = t|Z_i = 0) = \Pr(T_i = t|Z_i = 1) \qquad \text{for } t \in \{a, n, c\}.$$

Example 4.7 Recall Example 4.1 on adopting (or not) a new production technology with Z being subsidies for doing so. For identification we need a variation in the level of Z. The unconfoundedness assumption requires that the mechanism that generated this variation in Z should not be related to the production function of the firms nor to their decision rule. A violation of these assumptions could arise, e.g. if particular firms are granted a more generous subsidy after lobbying for favourable environments. If firms that are more likely to adopt the new technology only if subsidised are able to lobby for a higher subsidy, then the fraction of compliers would be higher among firms that obtained a higher subsidy than among those that did not, violating Assumption (A3). The monotonicity assumption is satisfied if the cost function $c(d, z)$ is not increasing in z. The LATE is the effect of technology on those firms which only adopt the new technology because of the subsidy. It could be plausible that the effect for the always-takers is larger than LATE, and that the effect on never-takers would be smaller. While for engineers who want to know the total technology impact, this LATE is uninteresting, for policymakers it is probably the parameter of interest.

Assumption (A4), *Mean exclusion restriction*: The potential outcomes are mean independent of the instrumental variable Z in each subpopulation:

$$E\left[Y_{i,Z_i}^0 | Z_i = 0, T_i = t\right] = E\left[Y_{i,Z_i}^0 | Z_i = 1, T_i = t\right] \qquad \text{for } t \in \{n, c\}$$

$$E\left[Y_{i,Z_i}^1 | Z_i = 0, T_i = t\right] = E\left[Y_{i,Z_i}^1 | Z_i = 1, T_i = t\right] \qquad \text{for } t \in \{a, c\}.$$

In order to keep things easy we restricted ourselves here to the equality of conditional means instead of invoking stochastic independence. Exclusion restrictions are also imposed in classical IV regression estimation, even though that is not always clearly stated. Here it is slightly different in the sense that it includes the conditioning on type T. It rules out a different path from Z to Y than the one passing D. This is necessary as in treatment effect estimation we are interested in identifying and estimating the total effect of D. Any effect of Z must therefore be channelled through D such that the potential outcomes (given D) are not correlated with the instrument.

To gain a better intuition, one could think of Assumption (A4) as actually containing two assumptions: an unconfounded instrument and an exclusion restriction. Take the first condition

$$E\left[Y_{i,0}^0 | Z_i = 0, T_i = t\right] = E\left[Y_{i,1}^0 | Z_i = 1, T_i = t\right] \qquad \text{for } t \in \{n, c\}$$

and consider splitting it up into two parts, say Assumptions (A4a) and (A4b):[4]

$$E\left[Y_{i,0}^0 | Z_i = 0, T_i = t\right] = E\left[Y_{i,1}^0 | Z_i = 0, T_i = t\right]$$

$$= E\left[Y_{i,1}^0 | Z_i = 1, T_i = t\right] \qquad \text{for } t \in \{n, c\}.$$

The first part is like an exclusion restriction on the **individual** level and would be satisfied e.g. if $Y_{i,0}^0 = Y_{i,1}^0$. It is assumed that the potential outcome for unit i is unaffected by an exogenous change in Z_i. The second part represents an unconfoundedness assumption on the population level. It assumes that the potential outcome $Y_{i,1}^0$ is identically distributed in the subpopulation of units for whom the instrument Z_i is observed to have the value zero, and in the subpopulation of units where Z_i is observed to be one. This assumption rules out selection effects that are related to the potential outcomes.

Example 4.8 Continuing our Examples 4.4 to 4.6, where D is college attendance and Y the earnings or wealth later in the life cycle, if we have for potential outcomes $Y_{i,0}^1 = Y_{i,1}^1$, then college proximity Z itself has no direct effect on the child's wages in its later career. So it rules out any relation of Z with the potential outcomes on a unit level, cf. Assumption (A4a).[5] Assumption (A4b) now requires that those families who decided to reside close to a college should be identical in all characteristics (that affect their children's subsequent wages) to the families who decided to live far from a college. Thus, whereas the second part refers to the composition of units for whom $Z = 1$ or

---

[4] Obviously, the following assumption is stronger than the previous and not strictly necessary. It helps, though, to gain intuition into what these assumptions mean and how they can be justified in applications.

[5] This implies the assumption that living in an area with higher educational level has no impact on later earnings except via your choice to attend or not a college.

$Z = 0$ is observed, the first part of the assumption refers to how the instrument affects the outcome Y of a particular unit.

___

Note that the second part of the assumption is trivially satisfied if the instrument Z is randomly assigned. Nevertheless randomisation of Z does not guarantee that the exclusion assumption holds on the unit level (Exercises 1 and 2). On the other hand, it is rather obvious that if Z is chosen by the unit itself, selection effects may often invalidate Assumption (A4b). In our college example this assumption is invalid if families who decide to reside nearer to or farther from a college are different. This might be the case due to the job opportunities in districts with colleges (especially for academics) or because of the opportunity for the children to visit a college. In this case it is necessary to also condition on the confounders X, i.e. all variables that affect the choice of residence Z as well as the potential outcomes Y^0_{i,Z_i} and Y^1_{i,Z_i}. How to include them is the topic of the next section. As typically Z is assumed to fulfil $Z \perp\!\!\!\perp Y^z | X$, we could calculate the ATE_Z, clearly related to the *intention to treat effect* (ITT), the total effect of Z on Y. More interestingly, note that one implication of the mean exclusion restriction is that it implies unconfoundedness of D in the complier subpopulation. As $D_i = Z_i$ for a complier you have

$$E\left[Y^0_{i,Z_i}|D_i = 0, T_i = c\right] = E\left[Y^0_{i,Z_i}|D_i = 1, T_i = c\right]$$
$$E\left[Y^1_{i,Z_i}|D_i = 0, T_i = c\right] = E\left[Y^1_{i,Z_i}|D_i = 1, T_i = c\right].$$

Hence, conditioning on the complier subpopulation, D is not confounded with the potential outcomes. If one were able to observe the type T, one could retain only the complier subpopulation and use a simple means comparison (as with experimental data discussed in Chapter 1) to estimate the treatment effect. The IV Z simply picks a subpopulation for which we have a randomised experiment with $Y^d \perp\!\!\!\perp D$ (or conditioned on X). In other words, Z picks the compliers; for them the CIA holds and we can calculate their ATE. This is the $LATE_Z$ inside the population. However, we do not observe the type. The ATE on the compliers is obtained by noting that both the ITT as well as the size of the complier subpopulation can be estimated.

How now to get the ITT? First note that

$$E[Y_i|Z_i = z]$$
$$= E\left[Y^{D_i}_{i,Z_i}|Z_i = z, T_i = n\right] \cdot \Pr(T_i = n|Z_i = z)$$
$$+ E\left[Y^{D_i}_{i,Z_i}|Z_i = z, T_i = c\right] \cdot \Pr(T_i = c|Z_i = z)$$
$$+ E\left[Y^{D_i}_{i,Z_i}|Z_i = z, T_i = d\right] \cdot \Pr(T_i = d|Z_i = z)$$
$$+ E\left[Y^{D_i}_{i,Z_i}|Z_i = z, T_i = a\right] \cdot \Pr(T_i = a|Z_i = z)$$
$$= E\left[Y^0_{i,Z_i}|Z_i = z, T_i = n\right] \cdot \Pr(T_i = n) + E\left[Y^{D_i}_{i,Z_i}|Z_i = z, T_i = c\right] \cdot \Pr(T_i = c)$$
$$+ E\left[Y^{D_i}_{i,Z_i}|Z_i = z, T_i = d\right] \cdot \Pr(T_i = d) + E\left[Y^1_{i,Z_i}|Z_i = z, T_i = a\right] \cdot \Pr(T_i = a)$$

by Assumption (A3) and the definition of the types $\mathcal{T}$. By the mean exclusion restriction (A4) the potential outcomes are independent of Z in the always- and in the never-taker subpopulation. Hence, when taking the difference $E[Y|Z = 1] - E[Y|Z = 0]$ the respective terms for the always- and for the never-takers cancel, such that

$$E[Y_i|Z_i = 1] - E[Y_i|Z_i = 0]$$
$$= \left(E\left[Y_{i,Z_i}^{D_i}|Z_i = 1, \mathcal{T}_i = c\right] - E\left[Y_{i,Z_i}^{D_i}|Z_i = 0, \mathcal{T}_i = c\right] \right) \cdot \Pr(\mathcal{T}_i = c)$$
$$+ \left(E\left[Y_{i,Z_i}^{D_i}|Z_i = 1, \mathcal{T}_i = d\right] - E\left[Y_{i,Z_i}^{D_i}|Z_i = 0, \mathcal{T}_i = d\right] \right) \cdot \Pr(\mathcal{T}_i = d)$$
$$= \left(E\left[Y_{i,Z_i}^1|Z_i = 1, \mathcal{T}_i = c\right] - E\left[Y_{i,Z_i}^0|Z_i = 0, \mathcal{T}_i = c\right] \right) \cdot \Pr(\mathcal{T}_i = c)$$
$$+ \left(E\left[Y_{i,Z_i}^0|Z_i = 1, \mathcal{T}_i = d\right] - E\left[Y_{i,Z_i}^1|Z_i = 0, \mathcal{T}_i = d\right] \right) \cdot \Pr(\mathcal{T}_i = d).$$

Exploiting the mean exclusion restriction for the compliers (and defiers) gives

$$= E\left[Y_{i,Z_i}^1 - Y_{i,Z_i}^0|\mathcal{T}_i = c\right] \cdot \Pr(\mathcal{T}_i = c) - E\left[Y_{i,Z_i}^1 - Y_{i,Z_i}^0|\mathcal{T}_i = d\right] \cdot \Pr(\mathcal{T}_i = d). \quad (4.3)$$

The difference $E[Y|Z = 1] - E[Y|Z = 0]$ thus represents the difference between the ATE of the compliers (who switch into treatment as a reaction on a change in the instrument from 0 to 1) and the ATE of the defiers. Often, an estimate of (4.3) is not very informative since, for example, an estimate of zero could be the result of a treatment without any effect, or of offsetting flows of compliers and defiers. Hence, the exclusion restriction is not sufficient to isolate a meaningful treatment effect of D on Y unless $\Pr(\mathcal{T}_i = d) = 0$ but $\Pr(\mathcal{T}_i = c) \neq 0$. So if an instrument is found that induces all individuals in the same direction, e.g. that either induces individuals to switch into participation or leaves their participation status unchanged but does not induce any individual to switch out of treatment, the ATE on the responsive subpopulation (i.e. the compliers) is identified. Under the monotonicity (Assumption 1) we get that the LATE is the ITT by size, i.e.

$$LATE := E\left[Y^1 - Y^0|T = c\right] = \frac{E[Y|Z = 1] - E[Y|Z = 0]}{\Pr(T = c)},$$

so that it just remains to find $\Pr(T = c)$. Noticing that

$$E[D|Z = 0] = \Pr(D = 1|Z = 0) = \Pr(T = a) + \Pr(T = d),$$
$$E[D|Z = 1] = \Pr(D = 1|Z = 1) = \Pr(T = a) + \Pr(T = c),$$

and using that $\Pr(T = d) = 0$ by Assumption 1, the relative size of the subpopulation of compliers is identified as

$$\Pr(T = c) = E[D|Z = 1] - E[D|Z = 0].$$

It follows that the (local) ATE in the subpopulation of compliers is

$$LATE = E\left[Y^1 - Y^0|T = c\right] = \frac{E[Y|Z = 1] - E[Y|Z = 0]}{E[D|Z = 1] - E[D|Z = 0]}. \quad (4.4)$$

which can be estimated by

$$\widehat{LATE} = \frac{\widehat{E}[Y|Z=1] - \widehat{E}[Y|Z=0]}{\widehat{E}[D|Z=1] - \widehat{E}[D|Z=0]}. \tag{4.5}$$

This is also called the *Wald estimator* since Wald (1940) suggested this particular estimator. Obviously, for binary Z and D the estimator is simply given by

$$\frac{\frac{\sum Y_i Z_i}{\sum Z_i} - \frac{\sum Y_i(1-Z_i)}{\sum (1-Z_i)}}{\frac{\sum D_i Z_i}{\sum Z_i} - \frac{\sum D_i(1-Z_i)}{\sum (1-Z_i)}} = \frac{\sum(1-Z_i)\sum Y_i Z_i - \sum Z_i(\sum Y_i - \sum Y_i Z_i)}{\sum(1-Z_i)\sum D_i Z_i - \sum Z_i(\sum D_i - \sum D_i Z_i)}$$

$$= \frac{n\sum Y_i Z_i - \sum Y_i \sum Z_i}{n\sum D_i Z_i - \sum D_i \sum Z_i},$$

which is actually an estimator for $Cov(Y, Z)/Cov(D, Z)$. This in turn leads us to the conjecture that we could equally well have used a standard instrumental variable regression approach to estimate the $LATE$. We conclude:

THEOREM 4.1   *The LATE estimator given in (4.5) is identical to the (two-step least-squares) instrumental variable estimator.[6] Under Assumptions (A1) to (A4) this estimator is consistent and*

$$\sqrt{n}(\widehat{LATE} - LATE) \rightarrow N(0, V)$$

such that the variance of the estimator can be approximated by

$$Var(\widehat{LATE}) \approx \frac{1}{n}V = \frac{E^2[\{Y - E[Y] - LATE \cdot (D - E[D])\}^2\{Z - E[Z]\}^2]}{n \cdot Cov^2(D, Z)}. \tag{4.6}$$

The variance can easily be estimated by replacing the unknown moments by sample estimates. The problem of weak instruments is visible in the formula of the Wald estimator and its variance; we are dividing the intention to treat effect $E[Y|Z=1] - E[Y|Z=0]$ by $E[D|Z=1] - E[D|Z=0]$. If the instrument has only a weak correlation with D, then the denominator is close to zero, leading to very imprecise estimates with a huge variance.

Clearly, if the treatment effect is homogeneous over the different types $\mathcal{T}$, then LATE, ATE, ATET and ATEN are all the same. Then we do not even need Assumption (A1), i.e. the non-existence of defiers, as we get then

$$\frac{E[Y|Z=1] - E[Y|Z=0]}{E[D|Z=1] - E[D|Z=0]}$$

$$= \frac{E[Y^1 - Y^0|\mathcal{T}=c] \cdot \Pr(\mathcal{T}=c) - E[Y^1 - Y^0|\mathcal{T}=d] \cdot \Pr(\mathcal{T}=d)}{\Pr(\mathcal{T}=c) + \Pr(\mathcal{T}=a) - \Pr(\mathcal{T}=d) - \Pr(\mathcal{T}=a)}.$$

In fact, we only need that the complier- and defier-treatment effects are identical, and both subpopulations not of equal size, then the Wald estimator is consistent. Note that

---

[6] See Exercise 3.

all the statements made in this paragraph become invalid or have to be modified if conditioning on some additional confounders X is necessary.

We are thus identifying a parameter of an abstract subpopulation. Moreover, this subpopulation is defined by the choice of instruments, because the compliers are those who react positively to this specific set. That is, different IVs lead to different parameters even under instrument validity. Note that we are not just speaking of numerical differences in the estimates; different instruments identify and estimate different parameters. So the question is to what extent the parameter identified by a particular instrument is of political or economic relevance. This could have partly been answered already by introducing the whole IV story in a different way, namely via using again the propensity score. This becomes clear in the later sections of this chapter. In any case, most relevant LATEs are those based on political instruments like subsidies, imposition of regulations, college fees, or eligibility rules for being treated. The latter can even be of such kind that only those people can participate in treatment that were randomly assigned (without enforcement but random assignment as a eligibility criterion).

4.1.3   Special Cases and First Extensions

Let us first discuss this easy-to-interpret instrument: the eligibility criteria, i.e. an indicator variable Z_i telling us whether individual i is allowed to participate or not. Taking eligibility rules as instrument will automatically lead to the so-called *one-sided non-compliance* design (i.e. individuals assigned to the control group cannot gain access to the treatment). This situation has attracted particular attention not just because it is a quite common one – for clinical trials but also for many other programmes, especially social programmes to which only assigned underprivileged people have access – but also because it is much easier to understand for whom we have identified the treatment effect. In other words, it is pretty easy to understand who this subpopulation of compliers is.

Example 4.9 Individuals in a clinical trial are randomly assigned to a new treatment against cancer or to a control treatment. Individuals assigned to the treatment group may refuse the new treatment. But individuals assigned to the control group cannot receive the new treatment. Hence, individuals in the treatment group may or may not comply, but individuals in the control group cannot get access to the treatment. This is called *one-sided non-compliance*. The decision of individuals to decline the new treatment may be related to their health status at that time. Individuals in particularly bad health at the time when being administered the new drug may refuse to take it. As the decision to take the drug may be related with health status at that time (which is likely to be related to the health status later) D is endogenous. Nevertheless, the random assignment could be used as an instrumental variable Z. The unconfoundedness of this instrument is guaranteed by formal randomisation. Defiers are people being assigned but refuse the treatment. But as they cannot do vice versa, they technically become never-takers. If all individuals would comply with their assignment, the treatment effect could be estimated by simple means comparisons. With non-compliance, still the Intention to Treat effect of Z on Y can be estimated, but this does not correspond to any treatment effect of D on Y. The exclusion restriction requires that the assignment status itself has no direct effect on health, which could well arise e.g. through psychological effects on the side of the patient or the physician because of the awareness of assignment status. This is actually the reason for double-blind placebo trials in medicine.

Formally, with one-sided non-compliance ($D_{i,0} = 0$ for all individuals), monotonicity is automatically satisfied as all potential defiers become nevertakers since $D_{i,0} = 1$ can never happen. So it is often said that if $Z_i = 0$ rules out obtaining the treatment, then the groups of defiers and always-takers do not exist. Consequently, $\Pr(D = 1|Z = 0) = E[D|Z = 0] = 0$ and $\Pr(Z = 1|D = 1) = 1$ and one has

$$E(Y|Z = 1) = E(Y_0) + E[(Y_1 - Y_0)D|Z = 1]$$

$$= E(Y_0) + E(Y_1 - Y_0|D = 1, Z = 1) \cdot E(D|Z = 1)$$

$$E(Y|Z = 0) = E(Y_0) + E(Y_1 - Y_0|D = 1, Z = 0)E(D|Z = 0) = E(Y_0).$$

As by eligibility rule $E[Y_1 - Y_0|D = 1, Z = 1] = E[Y_1 - Y_0|D = 1]$ we can summarise

$$LATE = \frac{E[Y|Z = 1] - E[Y|Z = 0]}{E[D|Z = 1] - 0} = E[Y_1 - Y_0|D = 1, Z = 1] = ATET$$

without the need of thinking about defiers. In sum, one-sided non-compliance makes Assumption (A1) unnecessary. Unfortunately, this equivalence no longer holds when we additionally include confounders X. Adequate modifications are the topic of the next sections.

What if the treatment is discrete or continuous? When we still have Z binary[7] but D discrete $\in \{0, 1, 2, 3, \ldots\}$ we need to extend the non-existence of defiers to all treatment levels; that is, for setting instrument Z from 0 to 1, all individuals D move in the same direction or stay unchanged, i.e. $D_i^1 - D_i^0 \geq 0$ for all i (or alternatively $D_i^1 - D_i^0 \leq 0$ for all individuals i). Then the expression

$$\frac{E(Y|Z = 1) - E(Y|Z = 0)}{E(D|Z = 1) - E(D|Z = 0)} \text{ gives}$$

$$\sum_{j=1} w_j \cdot E[Y^j - Y^{j-1}|D^1 \geq j > D^0], \quad w_j = \frac{\Pr(D^1 \geq j > D^0)}{\sum_{k=1} \Pr(D^1 \geq k > D^0)}, \quad (4.7)$$

which implies $\sum_{j=1} w_j = 1$, and delivers us a weighted average per-treatment-unit effect. So, while the estimator and inference do not change compared to above, the interpretation does, cf. also the literature on partial identification. A more precise discussion is given in section 4.4.

---

[7] More complex situations are discussed during, and in particular at the end of, this chapter.

What if, for binary treatment, our instrument is discrete or even continuous? Then look at the identification strategy we used for the Wald estimator $Cov(Y, Z)/Cov(D, Z)$. This could be interpreted as the weighted average over all LATEs for marginal changes in the instrument Z (e.g. the incentive for D). Let us imagine Z to be discrete with finite support $\{z_1, \ldots, z_K\}$ of K values with $z_k \leq z_{k+1}$. Then we need to assume that there are no defiers at any increase (or decrease if Z and D are negatively correlated) of Z. In such a case we could explicitly set

$$LATE = \sum_{k=2}^{K} w_k \alpha_{k-1 \to k} \tag{4.8}$$

where $\alpha_{k-1 \to k}$ is the LATE for the subpopulation of compliers that decide to switch from $D = 0$ to $D = 1$ if their Z is set from z_{k-1} to z_k. The weights w_k are constructed from the percentage of compliers and the conditional expectation of Z:

$$w_k = \frac{\{\Pr(D = 1|z_k) - \Pr(D = 1|z_{k-1})\} \sum_{l=k}^{K} \Pr(Z = z_l)(z_l - E[Z])}{\sum_{j=2}^{K} \{\Pr(D = 1|z_j) - \Pr(D = 1|z_{j-1})\} \sum_{l=j}^{K} \Pr(Z = z_l)(z_l - E[Z])}$$

It is not hard to see that the variance is the analogue to the one of the Wald estimator given in (4.6), Theorem 4.1, and can therefore be estimated the same way. The extension to continuous instruments Z is now obtained by substituting integrals for the sums, and densities for the probabilities of Z. For details on LATE identification and estimation with continuous Z see Section 4.2.4.

Another question is how to make use of a set of instruments, say $Z \in \mathbb{R}^\delta$; $\delta > 1$. This is particularly interesting when a single instrument is too weak or does not provide a sensible interpretation of the corresponding LATE. Again, the extension is pretty straight; you may take the propensity score $\Pr(D = 1|Z)$ instead of Z. It is, however, sufficient to take any function $g : Z \to \mathbb{R}$ such that $\Pr(D = 1|Z = z) \leq \Pr(D = 1|Z = \tilde{z})$ implies $g(z) \leq g(\tilde{z})$ for all $z, \tilde{z}$ from the $Supp(Z)$.[8] Then we can work with

$$LATE = \sum_{k=2}^{K} w_k' \alpha_{k-1 \to k} \tag{4.9}$$

with the (slightly) modified weights

$$w_k' = \frac{\{\Pr(D = 1|z_k) - \Pr(D = 1|z_{k-1})\} \sum_{l=k}^{K} \Pr(Z = z_l)\{g(z_l) - E[g(Z)]\}}{\sum_{j=2}^{K} \{\Pr(D = 1|z_j) - \Pr(D = 1|z_{j-1})\} \sum_{l=j}^{K} \Pr(Z = z_l)\{g(z_l) - E[g(Z)]\}}.$$

In cases where the propensity score (or g) has to be estimated, the variance will change.[9]

For combinations of these different extensions, potentially combined with (additional) confounders, see the sections at the end of this chapter. Note finally that this instrumental

---

[8] Alternatively, $\Pr(D = 1|Z = z) \leq \Pr(D = 1|Z = \tilde{z})$ implies $g(z) \geq g(\tilde{z})$ for all $z, \tilde{z}$ from the $Supp(Z)$.
[9] To our knowledge, no explicit literature exists on the variance and its estimation, but an appropriate wild bootstrap procedure should work here.

variable setup permits us not only to estimate the ATE for the compliers but also the distributions of the potential outcomes for the compliers, namely

$$F_{Y^1|T=c} \quad \text{and} \quad F_{Y^0|T=c} \tag{4.10}$$

if we extend the assumptions from mean-independence to general (conditional) independence. This will be studied in detail in Chapter 7.

4.2   LATE with Covariates

As alluded to several times above, often the IV assumptions are not valid in general but may become so only after conditioning on certain confounders X. In fact, it is very much the same problem as the one we considered when switching from the randomized trials with $Y^d \perp\!\!\!\perp D$ to the CIA $Y^d \perp\!\!\!\perp D|X$. Now we switch from $Y^d \perp\!\!\!\perp Z$ in the last section to $Y^d \perp\!\!\!\perp Z|X$. Certainly, the other assumptions will have to be modified accordingly such that for example D still exhibits variation with respect to instrument Z even when conditioned on confounders X. You may equally well say that Z is still relevant for D even when knowing X.

Example 4.10 In the distance-to-college example, it appears unreasonable that those living close to a college and those living at a distance from a college are identical in terms of their characteristics. Deliberate residential choice by their parents is likely to lead to confounding between Z and other characteristics of the individuals. Their choice is quite likely related to characteristics that affect their children's subsequent wages directly. In addition, cities with a college may also have other facilities that can improve their earnings capacity (city size might matter). However, if we are able to condition on relevant parental characteristics and other covariates we might be able to intercept (or 'block') all confounding paths between Z and further heterogeneity U and/or V, and might also be able to intercept all directed paths of Z to Y.

Parental education is another example of an instrumental variable that is often used to identify the returns to schooling. It may appear reasonable to assume that parental schooling itself has no direct impact on their children's wages. Nevertheless, it is likely to be correlated with parents' profession, family income and wealth, which may directly affect the wage prospects of their offspring even if excluding the upper-class people who manage to place their children in well-paid positions anyhow. It could be discussed whether this information should be included as confounder.

4.2.1   Identification of the LATE by Conditioning

By speaking of blocking we applied our graph theory introduced in Chapter 2. To be a bit more specific, let us look at Figure 4.3. The graphs shall help to illustrate the crucial conditions needed for IV identification and relate them to our discussion on

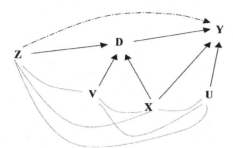

Figure 4.3 A case where neither matching nor IV will help to identify the impact of D on Y; for ease of illustration we suppressed here the arrowheads of the dashed-dotted lines

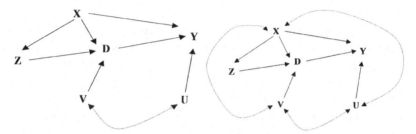

Figure 4.4 Left: (a) example of exogenous X; Right: (b) confounder X might be endogenous

selection on observables. A more thorough discussion follows later. This graph shows the situation where neither matching estimation nor IV identification is possible. IV identification (without blocking) is not possible since Z has a direct impact highlighted by the dashed-dotted line on Y, but also because Z has other paths to Y. (e.g. correlated with U).

A crucial assumption for identification will be our new CIA analogue:

$$\textbf{(CIA-IV)} \qquad (Y^d, \mathcal{T}) \perp\!\!\!\perp Z | X \qquad a.s. \qquad \text{for } d = 0, 1, \qquad (4.11)$$

although some kind of mean independence would suffice. This is the *conditional independence assumption for instruments* (CIA-IV). Consider first a situation where Z has no direct impact on Y, i.e. skipping the dashed-dotted line. Then there are still paths left that could cause problems. Some of them can be blocked by X, but let us go step by step. Note that for the sake of simplicity we neglect the independence condition w.r.t. $\mathcal{T}$ for now.

In Figure 4.4 both graphs (a) and (b) satisfy the independence assumption (4.11) conditional on X. The difference between these two graphs is that in (a) X is exogenous whereas in (b) X is correlated with V and U. We will see that non-parametric identification can be obtained in both situations. Note that in classical two-step least-squares (2SLS), situations like (b) with endogenous X are not permitted.[10]

In Figure 4.5 we have added the possibility that Z might have another effect on Y via the variables X_2. In the left graph (a) we can achieve (CIA-IV) if we condition on

---

[10] Think of the situation where φ and ζ of Equation 4.2 are parametric with additive errors U, V where you first estimate ζ to then estimate φ using $\hat{\zeta}$ instead of D.

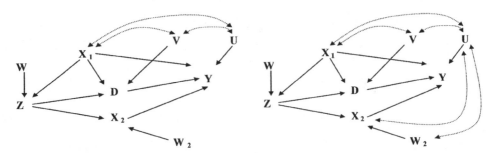

Figure 4.5 Left: (a) exogenous X_2 with endogenous X_1; Right: (b) X_1 and X_2 are both endogenous

X_1 and X_2. Hence, we can control for variables that confound the instrument and also for those which lie on a mediating causal path other than via D. There is one further distinction between X_1 and X_2, though. Whereas X_1 is permitted to be endogenous, X_2 is **not** permitted to be so. This can be seen well in graph (b). If we there condition on X_2, we unblock the path $Z \rightarrow X_2 \leftarrow U$ and also the path $Z \rightarrow X_2 \leftarrow W_2$. Hereby we introduce another confounding link between Z and the outcome variable Y. On the other hand, if we do not condition on X_2, the instrument Z has an effect on Y via X_2 and would thus not satisfy (4.11). Hence, while the X_1 are permitted to be endogenous, the X_2 (those being affected by Z) must be exogenous.

Example 4.11 In order to discuss an example let us simplify Figure 4.5 to

$$Z \rightarrow D \rightarrow Y$$

$$X$$

Hong and Nekipelov (2012) consider an empirical auction model in which they are interested in the effect of early bidding (D) in an internet auction on eBay on the variance of the bids (Y). Their concern is that the two variables D and Y may be correlated due to the visibility of the auctioned object. To overcome this endogeneity problem, the authors artificially increase the supply of the auctioned object by themselves auctioning additional objects on eBay. $Z = 0$ refers to the period with normal supply before, whereas $Z = 1$ refers to the period with enlarged supply. The authors argue that the larger supply should have an effect on D but no direct effect on Y. Since the authors themselves create the larger supply ($Z = 1$), they also changed the average characteristics X of the auctioned objects. Relevant characteristics X in eBay auctions are the seller's reliability (as perceived by previous buyers), and the geographical location of the seller (which affects shipping costs). These variables have been affected by the authors' supply inflation in the market, in particular the geographic location of the auctioned objects. These X variables have thus been caused by the instrument Z, and should be controlled for.

In sum we have seen that introducing covariates, say confounders X, may serve four different purposes here:

1. To control for potential confounders of the instrument Z.
2. To intercept or block all mediating causal paths between Z and Y, i.e. all paths other than those via D.
3. To separate total effects from partial effects (as discussed in earlier chapters).
4. To increase efficiency, as will be discussed later.

Controlling for such X, however, may not always be a valid approach. Let us consider the setup where the unobservable U affects Y but also X, and perhaps (but not necessarily) D. More specifically, you may think of our Example 4.11 but being enlarged by unobserved U:

$$
\begin{array}{c}
Z \rightarrow D \rightarrow Y \\
\searrow \quad \nearrow \quad \nwarrow \\
X \quad \leftarrow \quad U
\end{array}
$$

Conditioning on X opens the path $Z \rightarrow X \leftarrow U \rightarrow Y$ such that the instrumental variable approach is inconsistent. In Example 4.11 such an X variable is the 'number of bidders' in an auction. The active intervention Z by the researchers increased substantially the supply of the objects. Since the demand side is unchanged, it is likely (and in fact even visible) that the number of bidders per auction decreases unless each buyer bids for all auctioned objects. With the number of bidders per auction decreasing, also the variance of the bids Y decreases. There are actually many auctions with zero or only one bidder, implying a variance of zero. Hence, X has a direct effect on Y. At the same time, however, it is likely that the unobserved visibility U – which was the authors main motivation for using an IV approach – has also a direct effect on the number of bidders per auction. Hence, neither the IV approach with nor without conditioning on the number of bidders is therefore consistent in that example.

Before we continue let us revise and summarise the notation to describe the relation between variables more formally. To keep things simple we may think first of the case where both, the endogenous regressor D and the instrument Z are binary. Extensions to non-binary D and Z are discussed later. We incorporate a vector of covariates X:

$$
\begin{aligned}
Y_i &= \varphi(D_i, Z_i, X_i, U_i) \quad &\text{with} \quad && Y_{i,z}^d &= \varphi(d, z, X_i, U_i) \quad &\text{and} \quad && Y_{i,Z_i}^{D_i} &= Y_i \\
D_i &= \zeta(Z_i, X_i, V_i) \quad &\text{with} \quad && D_{i,z} &= \zeta(z, X_i, V_i) \quad &\text{and} \quad && D_{i,Z_i} &= D_i.
\end{aligned}
$$

Recall that if D has also an effect on X in the sense that changing D would imply a change in X, only the direct effect of D on Y would be recovered with our identification strategy, but not the total effect, as discussed in Chapter 2.

The previous instrumental variable conditions are assumed to hold conditional on X. Note that this also requires that conditioning on X does not introduce any dependencies and new confounding paths. The extension to incorporate covariates is assumed not to affect the decision of the compliance types $\mathcal{T}$, which is as before. More specifically, we modify all assumptions but keep the same numbering.

Assumption (A1C), *Monotonicity*: The subpopulation of defiers has probability measure zero:

$$\Pr\left(D_{i,0} > D_{i,1}|X_i = x\right) = 0 \qquad \forall x \in \mathcal{X}.$$

Assumption (A2C), *Existence of compliers*: The subpopulation of compliers has positive probability: for any x for which we want to estimate a treatment effect we have

$$\Pr\left(D_{i,0} < D_{i,1}|X_i = x\right) > 0.$$

As before, these assumptions rule out the existence of subpopulations that are affected by the instrument in an opposite direction, and guarantees that Z is relevant for $D|X$. This has not changed compared to the case when we ignored covariates X. Monotonicity just ensures that the effect of Z on D has the same direction for all individuals with the same X. Later we will see that the assumption can be weakened by dropping the conditioning on X.

Assumption (A3C), *Unconfounded instrument*: The relative size of the subpopulations always-takers, never-takers and compliers is independent of the instrument: for all $x \in$ *Supp* (X)

$$\Pr\left(\mathcal{T}_i = t|X_i = x, Z_i = 0\right) = \Pr\left(\mathcal{T}_i = t|X_i = x, Z_i = 1\right) \qquad \text{for } t \in \{a, n, c\}.$$

Validity of Assumption (A3C) requires that the vector X contains all variables that affect (simultaneously) the choice of Z and $\mathcal{T}$. Without conditioning on covariates X this assumption may often be invalid because of selection effects.

Example 4.12 Recalling the college attendance example we already discussed the problem that it is quite likely that parents who want their children to visit later on a college tend to live closer to one than those who care less. This would imply that there live more compliers close than far away which would violate our former, i.e. unconditional Assumption (A3) where no X were included. In this case, the subpopulation living close to a college would contain a higher fraction of compliers than those living far away. If this effect is captured by variables X (i.e. that control for these kind of parents) we would satisfy the new version of Assumption (A3), namely our (A3C).

We further need to rule out a relation of Z with $Y|X$ not channelled by D. This time, however, it suffices to do this conditional on X. In other words, conditional on X any effect of Z should be channelled through D such that the potential outcomes are not related with the instrument.

Assumption (A4C), *Mean exclusion restriction*: Conditional on X the potential outcomes are mean independent of the instrumental variable Z in each subpopulation: for all $x \in$ *Supp* (X)

$$E\left[Y^0_{i,Z_i}|X_i = x, Z_i = 0, T_i = t\right] = E\left[Y^0_{i,Z_i}|X_i = x, Z_i = 1, T_i = t\right] \quad \text{for } t \in \{n, c\}$$

$$E\left[Y^1_{i,Z_i}|X_i = x, Z_i = 0, T_i = t\right] = E\left[Y^1_{i,Z_i}|X_i = x, Z_i = 1, T_i = t\right] \quad \text{for } t \in \{a, c\}.$$

Again, without conditioning on X, this assumption may often be invalid. However, recall from Chapter 2 that conditioning can also create dependency for variables that without this conditioning had been independent.

Often you see in the literature the Assumptions (A2C) and (A4C) replaced by modifications of the CIA, namely asking for $Z \not\!\perp\!\!\!\perp D|X$ and $Y^d \perp\!\!\!\perp Z|X$, where the latter obviously corresponds to (A4C), and the former to (A2C) which is also called the *relevance condition*. Assumption (A3C) is often ignored.

Finally, since we are going to be interested in estimating some kind of average complier effect (LATE) we will impose an additional assumption:

Assumption (A5C), *Common support*: The support of X is identical in both subpopulations:

$$Supp\,(X|Z = 1) = Supp\,(X|Z = 0).$$

Assumption (A5C) requires that for any value of X (in its support) both values of the instrument can be observed. Clearly, an equivalent representation of the common support condition is that $0 < \Pr(Z = 1|X = x) < 1 \,\forall x$ with $f_X(x) > 0$. As for the CSC we are certainly free to (re-)define our population of interest such that χ fulfils Assumptions (A1C) to (A5C).

With these assumptions, the LATE is identified for all x with $\Pr\,(T = c|X = x) > 0$ by

$$LATE(x) = E[Y^1 - Y^0|X = x, T = c] = \frac{E\,[Y|X = x, Z = 1] - E\,[Y|X = x, Z = 0]}{E\,[D|X = x, Z = 1] - E\,[D|X = x, Z = 0]}.$$

If we could restrict to the subpopulation of compliers, this IV method is simply the matching method. This is by no means surprising: as in the case with binary Z, one could think of compliers being exactly those for whom always $D = Z$. The proof is analogous to the case without covariates X. So for our crucial assumption for identification

$$Y^d \perp\!\!\!\perp Z|X, T = c$$

we may equally well write

$$Y^d \perp\!\!\!\perp D|X \text{ restricted to subpopulation } T = c \tag{4.12}$$

being exactly the selection on observables assumption (CIA) but restricted to compliers, saying that conditional on X, the compliers were randomly selected into $D = 0$ or $D = 1$. Again, as the CIA does not hold for the entire population, the IV picks from the population a subpopulation for which it does hold.

4.2.2 A Feasible LATE Estimator with Confounders: The unconditional LATE

Although one has identified LATE for every value of X, in policy applications one is typically interested in obtaining an average effect for the whole population or at least certain parts of it. Particularly if X contains many variables, there would be many different LATE(x) to be interpreted. Moreover, if X contains continuous variables, the estimates might be rather imprecise and we would also not be able to attain $\sqrt{n}$ convergence for our LATE(x) estimators. In these cases we are interested in some kind of average effects.

One possibility would be to weight LATE(x) by the population distribution of x, which would give us an average treatment effect of the form

$$\int LATE(x) \, dF_X = \int \frac{E[Y|X=x, Z=1] - E[Y|X=x, Z=0]}{E[D|X=x, Z=1] - E[D|X=x, Z=0]} dF_X. \quad (4.13)$$

However, this approach may be problematic in two respects. First, the estimates of

$$\frac{E[Y|X, Z=1] - E[Y|X, Z=0]}{E[D|X, Z=1] - E[D|X, Z=0]}$$

will sometimes be quite imprecise, especially if X contains continuous variables. The non-parametrically estimated denominator $\hat{E}[D|X, Z=1] - \hat{E}[D|X, Z=0]$ might often be close to zero, thus leading to very large estimates of $LATE(x)$. In addition, the above weighting scheme represents a mixture between the effects on compliers and always-/never-takers that might be hard to interpret: $LATE(x)$ refers only to the effect for compliers exhibiting x, whereas dF_X refers to the distribution of x in the entire population (consisting of compliers, always- and never-takers – defiers do not exist by assumption). That is, (4.13) mixes different things.

An alternative is to examine the effect in the subpopulation of all compliers, which is in fact the largest subpopulation for which a treatment effect is identified without further assumptions. This treatment effect over all compliers is

$$E\left[Y^1 - Y^0|T = c\right] = \int E[Y^1 - Y^0|X = x, T = c] dF_{X|T=c}$$

$$= \int LATE(x) \, dF_{X|T=c}, \quad (4.14)$$

where $F_{X|T=c}$ denotes the distribution function of X in the subpopulation of all compliers. This distribution is not directly identified, since the subpopulation of compliers is not. However, by Bayes' theorem $dF_{X|T=c} = \frac{\Pr(T=c|X)}{\Pr(T=c)} dF_X$ we have

$$E\left[Y^1 - Y^0|T = c\right] = \int LATE(x) \frac{\Pr(T=c|X=x)}{\Pr(T=c)} dF_X.$$

Furthermore, the size of the complier-subpopulation with characteristics x is identified as

$$\Pr(T = c|X = x) = E[D|X = x, Z = 1] - E[D|X = x, Z = 0]. \quad (4.15)$$

Now inserting the formula for $LATE(x)$ defined in (4.14) gives

$$E\left[Y^1 - Y^0|T = c\right] = \frac{1}{\Pr(T=c)} \int \{E[Y|X = x, Z = 1] - E[Y|X = x, Z=0]\} \, dF_X,$$

and using that $\Pr(T = c) = \int \Pr(T = c|X = x) \, dF_X$ together with (4.15) gives

$$E\left[Y^1 - Y^0|T = c\right] = \frac{\int E[Y|X = x, Z = 1] - E[Y|X = x, Z = 0] \, dF_X}{\int E[D|X = x, Z = 1] - E[D|X = x, Z = 0] \, dF_X}. \quad (4.16)$$

By (A5C) the conditional expectations are identified in the $Z = 1$ and $Z = 0$ subpopulations. That is, we can identify and estimate the LATE, i.e. the average treatment effect for all compliers (with respect to instrument Z) by taking the expectations of numerator and denominator separately over the entire population. Obviously, as long as the compliers represent a well understood and interesting group (due to a proper choice of Z), this is a quite useful parameter. We discussed already the eligibility criterion but should add examples for Z such as tax incentives, subsidies, grants, lowering (or raising) fees for which the compliers might be our target group. In addition to being a well defined treatment effect, the formula (4.16) has two nice properties. First, instead of being an integral of a ratio, it is a ratio of two integrals, which thus reduces the risk of very small denominators. Second, the expression (4.16) corresponds to a ratio of two matching estimators, which have been examined in detail in Chapter 3.

Defining the conditional mean functions $m_z(x) = E[Y|X = x, Z = z]$ and $p_z(x) = E[D|X = x, Z = z]$, a non-parametric estimator of $E\left[Y^1 - Y^0|T = c\right]$ is given by

$$\frac{\sum_i \left(\hat{m}_1(X_i) - \hat{m}_0(X_i) \right)}{\sum_i \left(\hat{p}_1(X_i) - \hat{p}_0(X_i) \right)},$$

where $\hat{m}_z(x)$ and $\hat{p}_z(x)$ are corresponding non-parametric regression estimators. Alternatively, we could use the observed values Y_i and D_i as predictors of $E[Y_i|X_i, Z = z]$ and $E[D_i|X_i, Z = z]$, whenever $Z_i = z$. This gives the estimator:

$$\widehat{LATE} = \frac{\sum\limits_{i:Z_i=1} \left(Y_i - \hat{m}_0(X_i) \right) - \sum\limits_{i:Z_i=0} \left(Y_i - \hat{m}_1(X_i) \right)}{\sum\limits_{i:Z_i=1} \left(D_i - \hat{p}_0(X_i) \right) - \sum\limits_{i:Z_i=0} \left(D_i - \hat{p}_1(X_i) \right)}. \tag{4.17}$$

As this is a combination of matching estimators, its asymptotic properties can be derived similarly – with adopted assumptions – as it has been done for the matching and/or regression estimators in Chapter 3. Keep in mind that we only consider here binary instruments Z. The following theorem provides both, the efficiency bound for semiparametric LATE estimators and a feasible (kernel) estimator.

THEOREM 4.2   *Under Assumptions (A1C) to (A5C), provided with a random sample, and the following regularity conditions*

(i) *$f_{X|Z=1}$, $m_z(\cdot)$ and $p_z(\cdot)$, $z = 0, 1$ are s-times continuously differentiable with the s-th derivative being Hölder continuous with $s > q = dim(X)$*
(ii) *$K(\cdot)$ is a compact and Lipschitz continuous $(s + 1)$-order kernel*
(iii) *The bandwidth h satisfies $n_0 h^q / \ln(n_0) \to \infty$ and $n_0 h^{2s} \to 0$ for $n_0 \to \infty$ where n_0 is the smallest subsample size out of the following four: $\sum_{i=1}^n \mathbb{1}\{z_i = 0\}$, $\sum_{i=1}^n \mathbb{1}\{z_i = 1\}$, $\sum_{i=1}^n \mathbb{1}\{d_i = 0\}$, $\sum_{i=1}^n \mathbb{1}\{d_i = 1\}$.*

Then, if the $m_d(x)$ and $p_d(x)$ are obtained by local polynomial regression of order $< s$, one obtains for the estimator given in (4.17)

$$\sqrt{n}(\widehat{LATE} - LATE) \longrightarrow N(0, V)$$

with variance V reaching the efficiency bound for semi-parametric LATE estimators which is given by

$$\gamma^{-2} E \left[\{m_1(X) - m_0(X) - \alpha p_1(X) + \alpha p_0(X)\}^2 \right.$$

$$\left. + \sum_{z=0}^{1} \frac{\sigma_Y^2(X,z) - 2\alpha \sigma_{Y,D}(X,z) + \alpha^2 \sigma_D^2(X,z)}{\Pr(Z = z|X)} \right]$$

where $\alpha = LATE$, $\gamma = \int \{p_1(x) - p_0(x)\} dF_X$, $\sigma_{Y,D}(X,z) = Cov(Y,D|X, Z = z)$, $\sigma_Y^2(X,z) = Var[Y|X, Z = z]$, and $\sigma_D^2(X,z)$ analogously.

4.2.3   LATE Estimation with Propensity Scores

Having seen that the treatment effect can be estimated by a ratio of two matching estimators, you will suspect that some kind of propensity score matching approach or propensity score weighting should also be available. Defining the analogue of the propensity score for the binary instrument Z by

$$\pi(x) = \Pr(Z = 1|X = x)$$

and noting that

$$E\left[\frac{YZ}{\pi(X)}\right] = \int \frac{1}{\pi(x)} E[YZ|x] dF_X = \int m_1(x)\, dF_X$$

it is not hard to see that the LATE can also be expressed as

$$E\left[Y^1 - Y^0|T = c\right] = E\left[\frac{YZ}{\pi(X)} - \frac{Y(1-Z)}{1-\pi(X)}\right] / E\left[\frac{DZ}{\pi(X)} - \frac{D(1-Z)}{1-\pi(X)}\right] \quad (4.18)$$

which in turn can obviously be estimated by the so-called *propensity score weighting estimator*

$$\widehat{LATE} = \sum_{i=1}^{n}\left(\frac{Y_iZ_i}{\pi(X_i)} - \frac{Y_i(1-Z_i)}{1-\pi(X_i)}\right) / \sum_{i=1}^{n}\left(\frac{D_iZ_i}{\pi(X_i)} - \frac{D_i(1-Z_i)}{1-\pi(X_i)}\right). \quad (4.19)$$

It has been shown that the efficiency bound is reached as given in Theorem 4.2. In many applications, the propensity score $\pi(x)$ is unknown and needs to be estimated. But due to the efficiency results for the propensity score-based estimators in Chapter 3 it is expected that even if it was known, using an estimated propensity score would be preferable.

As in Chapter 3 one might use the propensity score – here the one for Z given X – not for weighting but as a substitute for the regressor X. Due to this analogy one speaks again of propensity score matching though it refers to the propensity score for the binary instrument. Let us first derive the identification of the LATE via $\mu_z(p) := E[Y|\pi(X) = p, Z = z]$ and $\nu_z(p) := E[D|\pi(X) = p, Z = z]$ for $z = 0, 1$. Obviously, for a given (or predicted) π these four functions can be estimated non-parametrically, e.g. by kernel regression. Now reconsider equation (4.18) noting that

$$E\left[\frac{YZ}{\pi(X)}\right] = E_\rho\left\{E\left[\frac{YZ}{\pi(X)}|\pi(X) = \rho\right]\right\}$$

$$= E_\rho\left\{\frac{1}{\rho}E[Y|\pi(X) = \rho, Z = 1]\Pr(Z = 1|\pi(X) = \rho)\right\}$$

$$= E_\rho\{E[Y|\pi(X) = \rho, Z = 1]\} = \int \mu_1(\rho)\,dF_\pi$$

where F_π is the c.d.f. of $\rho = \pi(x)$ in the population. Similarly we obtain $E\left[\frac{Y(1-Z)}{1-\pi(X)}\right] = \int \mu_0(\rho)\,dF_\pi$, $E\left[\frac{DZ}{\pi(X)}\right] = \int v_1(\rho)\,dF_\pi$, and $E\left[\frac{D(1-Z)}{1-\pi(X)}\right] = \int v_0(\rho)\,dF_\pi$. Replacing the expectation by sample averages and the μ_z, v_z by non-parametric estimates, we can estimate (4.18) by

$$\left[\sum_{i=1}^n \hat{\mu}_1\{\pi(X_i)\} - \hat{\mu}_0\{\pi(X_i)\}\right] / \left[\sum_{i=1}^n \hat{v}_1\{\pi(X_i)\} - \hat{v}_0\{\pi(X_i)\}\right]. \tag{4.20}$$

Asymptotically, however, this estimator is inefficient as its variance does not meet the efficiency bound of Theorem 4.2 unless some very particular conditions are met.[11] In fact, its variance is

$$\gamma^{-2}E\left[\{\mu_1(\pi) - \mu_0(\pi) - \alpha v_1(\pi) + \alpha v_0(\pi)\}^2\right.$$

$$\left. + \sum_{z=0}^1 \frac{\sigma_Y^2(\pi, z) - 2\alpha\sigma_{Y,D}(\pi, z) + \alpha^2\sigma_D^2(\pi, z)}{z + (-1)^z\pi}\right]$$

where again $\alpha = LATE$, $\sigma_{Y,D}(\pi, z) = Cov(Y, D|\pi, Z = z)$, $\sigma_Y^2(\pi, z) = Var(Y|\pi, Z = z)$, and $\sigma_D^2(\pi, z)$ analogously.

Often the propensity score $\Pr(Z = 1|X)$ is not known, counterexamples are situations where Z is the assignment to treatment along (eligibility) criteria contained in X. For the other cases it will have to be estimated. Again it depends on the particular application whether this estimation is simple; for example, could be done parametrically or as complex as the non-parametric estimation of $\mu_z(X)$ and $v_z(X)$. In the latter case the above-proposed propensity weighting or propensity matching estimators are not really attractive. There is, however, still a reason to estimate this propensity score: it allows us to identify the *ATE for treated compliers* (LATET), i.e. $E[Y^1 - Y^0|D = 1, T = c]$. To see this you first write it as

$$\int E[Y^1 - Y^0|X = x, Z = 1, T = c]\,dF_{X|Z=1,T=c}(x)$$

$$= \int E[Y^1 - Y^0|X = x, T = c]\,dF_{X|Z=1,T=c}(x)$$

---

[11] See Frölich (2007a) for details.

which follows from the exclusion restriction, Assumption 4. Then, following Bayes' rule we have

$$dF_{X|Z=1,T=c}(x) = \frac{\Pr(Z=1, T=c|x)\, dF_X(x)}{\Pr(Z=1, T=c)}$$

$$= \frac{\Pr(T=c|x, Z=1)\pi(x)\, dF_X(x)}{\int \Pr(Z=1, T=c|x)\, dF_X(x)} = \frac{\Pr(T=c|x)\pi(x)\, dF_X(x)}{\int \Pr(T=c|x)\pi(x)\, dF_X(x)}$$

by the unconfoundedness condition, Assumption 3. Consequently the effect is now identified as

$$E\left[Y^1 - Y^0 | D=1, T=c\right]$$
$$= \frac{\int (E[Y|X=x, Z=1] - E[Y|X=x, Z=0])\,\pi(X)\, dF_X}{\int (E[D|X=x, Z=1] - E[D|X=x, Z=0])\,\pi(X)\, dF_X}, \quad (4.21)$$

and in terms of propensity scores as

$$E\left[Y^1 - Y^0 | D=1, T=c\right] = \frac{\int (\mu_1(\rho) - \mu_0(\rho))\,\rho\, dF_\pi}{\int (\nu_1(\rho) - \nu_0(\rho))\,\rho\, dF_\pi}. \quad (4.22)$$

As usual, you replace the unknown functions μ_z, ν_z, π (and thus ρ) by (non-)parametric predictions and the integrals by sample averages. A weighting type estimator could be derived from these formulae as well, see Exercise 4.

Why is this interesting? In the situation of one-sided non-compliance, i.e. where you may say that the subpopulations of always-takers and defiers do not exist, the treated compliers are the only individuals that are treated.[12] The ATET is then identified as

$$E\left[Y^1 - Y^0 | D=1\right] = E\left[Y^1 - Y^0 | D=1, T=c\right].$$

Note that formula (4.21) is different from (4.16). Hence, with one-sided non-compliance the ATET is the LATET (4.21) but **not** the LATE. This is different from the situation without confounders X. Simply check by setting X constant; then the formulae (4.21) and (4.16) are identical in the one-sided non-compliance design such that ATET = LATE.

What can be said about the (local) treatment effect for the always- and the never-takers? With similar arguments as above we can identify $E[Y^1|T=a]$ and $E[Y^0|T=n]$. More specifically, from (4.3) combined with (A4C) we get that

$$E\left[Y^1|T=a\right]\Pr(T=a) = \int E[YD|X, Z=0]\, dF_X$$

$$\text{with } \Pr(T=a) = \int E[D|X, Z=0]\, dF_X$$

$$E\left[Y^0|T=n\right]\Pr(T=n) = \int E[Y(1-D)|X, Z=1]\, dF_X$$

$$\text{with } \Pr(T=n) = \int E[1-D|X, Z=1]\, dF_X.$$

[12] As discussed earlier, in various experimental situations, only one-sided non-compliance is possible: Individuals assigned to treatment $Z=1$ may decide to refuse or drop out ($D=0$), whereas individuals assigned to control cannot gain access to treatment, such that the event $Z_i=0 \wedge D_i=1$ cannot be observed.

Following the same strategy, can we also identify $E[Y^0|T = a]$ and $E[Y^1|T = n]$? For this we would need to suppose that the selection on observables holds not only for the compliers but also for the always- and never-takers. But in such a case we had CIA for the entire population, and used the IV only for splitting the population along their types T without any need.[13] In other words, in such a case the IV Z was of interest on its own (eligibility, subsidies, incentives, ...) but was not needed for ATE or ATET identification. On the other hand, in some situations such a strategy could be helpful in some other respects: first, we obtained the average treatment effects $Y^1 - Y^0$ separately for the compliers, the always-participants and the never-participants. This gives some indication about treatment effect heterogeneity. Second, the comparison between $E\left[Y^0|T = c\right]$ and $E\left[Y^0|T = a\right]$, and $E\left[Y^0|T = n\right]$ may be helpful to obtain some understanding what kind of people these groups actually represent. Note that this still requires (A1C) to (A5C) to hold.

Example 4.13 Imagine Y is employment status and we find that $E\left[Y^0|T = a\right] < E\left[Y^0|T = c\right] < E\left[Y^0|T = n\right]$. This could be interpreted in that the never-takers have the best labour market chances (even without treatment) and that the always-takers have worse labour market chances than the compliers. This would help us to understand which kind of people belong to a, c and n for a given incentive Z. In addition to this, we can also identify the distributions of X among the always-, and the never-takers and the compliers, which provides us with additional insights into the labour market.

Chapter 7 will discuss how the same identification strategy can help us to recover the entire hypothetical distributions of Y^0, Y^1, and therefore also the quantiles.

4.2.4   IV with Non-Binary Instruments

Most of our discussion so far assumed that the instrument Z is binary. We can extend this to a non-binary instrument or to having several instruments, i.e. Z being a vector. The latter we already discussed briefly at the end of Section 4.1.2 with binary D. Permitting the instrument Z to be non-binary, we can derive a formula similar to (4.16) which compares only observations (Y_i, X_i, D_i, Z_i) with values of Z_i lying at the end-points of the support of the instrument. Suppose we have a single non-binary instrument Z, which has bounded support $Supp(Z) = [z_{min}, z_{max}]$. Obviously, a local average treatment effect could be defined with respect to any two distinct values of Z. However, this would

[13] For completeness let us mention here that then,

$$E[Y^0|T = a] = \frac{E[Y^0] - E[Y^0|T = c]P(T = c) - E[Y^0|T = n]P(T = n)}{P(T = a)}$$

$$E[Y^1|T = n] = \frac{E[Y^1] - E[Y^1|T = c]P(T = c) - E[Y^1|T = a]P(T = a)}{P(T = n)}.$$

yield a multitude of pairwise treatment effects, each of them referring to a different (sub-)population. Instead of estimating many pairwise effects, one might prefer to estimate the average treatment effect in the largest (sub-)population for which an effect can be identified, which is the population of individuals who react to the instrument, see next subsection. Under certain assumptions one can also show that a weighted average of all pairwise LATE (weighted by the respective number of compliers) is identical to the LATE using only $z_{\min}$ and $z_{\max}$.

Define the subpopulation of compliers as that of all individuals i with $D_{i,z_{\min}} = 0$ and $D_{i,z_{\max}} = 1$. The compliers comprise all individuals who switch from $D = 0$ to $D = 1$ at some point when the instrument Z increased from $z_{\min}$ to $z_{\max}$. The value of z which triggers the switch can be different for different individuals. If monotonicity holds with respect to any two values z and z', each individual switches D at most once. The following assumptions are extensions of Assumptions (A1C) to (A5C) to a still one-dimensional but non-binary instrument.

Assumption (A1C'), *Monotonicity*: The effect of Z on D is monotonous

$$\Pr\left(D_z > D_{z'}\right) = 0 \text{ for any values } z, z' \text{ with } z_{\min} \leq z < z' \leq z_{\max}.$$

You could replace this by only looking at (z_{min}, z_{max}).

Assumption (A2C'), *Existence of compliers*: The subpopulation of compliers has positive probability

$$\Pr\left(T = c\right) > 0 \text{ where for all } i \quad T_i = c \text{ if } D_{i,z_{\min}} < D_{i,z_{\max}}.$$

Assumption (A3C'), *Unconfounded instrument*: For any value $z \in Supp\,(Z)$, any $(d, d') \in \{0, 1\}^2$ and for all $x \in Supp\,(X)$

$$\Pr\left(D_z = d, D_{z'} = d' \,|X = x, Z = z\right) = \Pr\left(D_z = d, D_{z'} = d' \,|X = x\right).$$

Assumption (A4C'), *Mean exclusion restriction*: For any value $z \in Supp\,(Z)$, any $d, d' \in \{0, 1\}$ and for all $x \in Supp\,(X)$

$$E\left[Y_Z^d|X = x, D_z = d, D_{z'} = d', Z = z\right] = E\left[Y_Z^d|X = x, D_z = d, D_{z'} = d'\right].$$

Assumption (A5C'), *Common support*: The support of X is identical for $z_{\min}$ and $z_{\max}$

$$Supp\,(X|Z = z_{\min}) = Supp\,(X|Z = z_{\max}).$$

Given these assumptions it can be shown that the LATE for the subpopulation of compliers is non-parametrically identified as

$$E[Y^1 - Y^0|T = c] = \frac{\int (E\,[Y|X = x, Z = z_{\max}] - E\,[Y|X = x, Z = z_{\min}])\,dF_X}{\int (E\,[D|X = x, Z = z_{\max}] - E\,[D|X = x, Z = z_{\min}])\,dF_X}.$$

(4.23)

This formula is analogous to (4.16) with $Z = 0$ and $Z = 1$ replaced with the endpoints of the support of Z. If Z is discrete with finite support, previous results would apply and $\sqrt{n}$ consistency could be attained. This is certainly just a statement about the asymptotic behaviour; it actually throws away all information in-between $z_{\min}$ and $z_{\max}$. In practice you might therefore prefer to estimate the LATE for each increase in Z and then average over them. This is actually the idea of the next section. For a continuous instrument, $\sqrt{n}$-consistency can no longer be achieved, unless it is mixed continuous-discrete with mass points at z_{min} and z_{max}. The intuitive reason for this is that with continuous Z the probability of observing individuals with $Z_i = z_{max}$ or z_{min} is zero. Therefore we also have to use observations with Z_i a little bit smaller than z_{max}, and for non-parametric regression to be consistent we will need the bandwidth to converge to zero. (A similar situation will appear in the following situation on regression discontinuity design.)[14]

Now consider the situation with multiple instrumental variables, i.e. Z being vector valued. There is a way to extend the above assumptions and derivations accordingly. Set the sign of all IVs such that they are all positively correlated with D and ask the selection function ζ to be convex and proceed as before. Another, simpler way is to recall the idea of propensity score matching. The different instrumental variables act through their effect on D, so the different components of Z can be summarised conveniently by using $p(z, x) = \Pr(D = 1|X = x, Z = z)$ as instrument. If D follows an index structure in the sense that D_i depends on Z_i only via $p(Z_i, X_i)$,[15] and Assumptions (A1C') to (A5C') are satisfied with respect to $p(z, x)$, then the LATE is identified as

$$E[Y^1 - Y^0|T = c]$$
$$= \frac{\int \left(E[Y|X = x, p(Z, X) = \bar{p}_x] - E[Y|X = x, p(Z, X) = \underline{p}_x] \right) dF_X}{\int \left(E[D|X = x, p(Z, X) = \bar{p}_x] - E[D|X = x, p(Z, X) = \underline{p}_x] \right) dF_X}, \quad (4.24)$$

where $\bar{p}_x = \max_z p(z, x)$ and $\underline{p}_x = \min_z p(z, x)$. This is equivalent to

$$E[Y^1 - Y^0|T = c]$$
$$= \frac{\int \left(E[Y|X = x, p(Z, X) = \bar{p}_x] - E[Y|X = x, p(Z, X) = \underline{p}_x] \right) dF_X}{\int \left(\bar{p}_x - \underline{p}_x \right) dF_X}. \quad (4.25)$$

Again, this formula is analogous to (4.16). The two groups of observations on which estimation is based are those with $p(z, x) = \bar{p}_x$ and those with $p(z, x) = \underline{p}_x$. In the first representation (4.24), exact knowledge of $p(z, x)$ is in fact not needed; it is sufficient to identify the set of observations for which $p(Z, X)$ is highest and lowest, respectively, and compare their values of Y and D. Only the ranking with respect to $p(z, x)$ matters, but not the values of $p(z, x)$ themselves.[16] For example, if Z contains two binary variables (Z_1, Z_2) which for any value of X are known to have a positive effect on D,

---

[14] From (4.23) a bias-variance trade-off in the estimation of the LATE with non-binary Z becomes visible. Although (4.23) incorporates the proper weighting of the different complier subgroups and leads to an unbiased estimator, only observations with Z_i equal (or close) to z_{min} or z_{max} are used for estimation. Observations with Z_i between the endpoints z_{min} and z_{max} are neglected, which might lead to a large variance. Variance could be reduced, at the expense of a larger bias, by weighting the subgroups of compliers differently or by choosing larger bandwidth values.

[15] So $D_{i,z} = D_{i,z'}$ if $p(z, X_i) = p(z', X_i)$. In other words, D_i does not change if Z_i is varied within a set where $p(\cdot, X_i)$ remains constant, see also next section.

[16] In Equation 4.25 the consistent estimation of $p(z, x)$ matters, though.

then the observations with $Z_1 = Z_2 = 0$ and those with $Z_1 = Z_2 = 1$ represent the endpoints of the support of $p(Z, X)$ given X, and are used for estimation.

4.3   Marginal Treatment Effects

An often-expressed criticism is that the LATE identifies a parameter that is not of inter-est. Since it is the effect on the complier subpopulation and this subpopulation is then induced by the instrument, any LATE is directly tied to its instrument and cannot be interpreted on its own. For example, if Z represents the size of a programme (the num-ber of available slots), the LATE would represent the impact of the programme if it were extended from size z to size z' on the subpopulation which would participate only in the enlarged programme. So is it interesting for decision-makers? As we discussed in the previous sections, this depends on the context, and in particular on the applied instrument Z. Especially if Z represents a political instrument (fees, taxes, eligibility rules, subventions, etc.) LATE might actually even be more interesting than ATE or ATET themselves, as it tells us the average effect for those who reacted on these policy intervention.

This interpretation becomes more complex if we face non-binary treatments or instru-ments. On the other hand, if we directly think of continuous instruments, which in practice should often be the case, interpretation becomes simpler as this will allow us to study the *marginal treatment effect* (MTE). Contrary to what we are used from the com-mon notion when speaking of marginal effects, the MTE refers to the treatment effect for a marginal change in the propensity to participate and therefore a marginal change in the instrument.Most interestingly, we will see that this will enable us to redefine the ATE, ATET, ATEN and LATE as a function of MTE and link it (more generally) to what sometimes is called *policy related treatment effects* (PRTE). As stated, in order to do so it is necessary from now on to have a continuous instrument (or a vector of instruments with at least one continuous element).

4.3.1   The Concept of Marginal Treatment Effects

So far we have mainly discussed changes of Z from z_{min} to z_{max} which can be a huge step, and at the same time considerably reduce the useable sample. Instead of examining the effects of very large changes in Z, we could also be interested in what would happen if we changed Z only a little bit. Moreover, for a continuous Z one could think of infinitesimal small changes in Z to define a treatment effect for the individuals just at the margin to change D. Thinking it this way one might say that the MTE is basically the limit version of LATE.

We remain in the setup with a single binary endogenous regressor $D \in \{0, 1\}$ as then the MTE can easily be understood as the treatment effect of a marginal propensity change being equivalent to the marginal change of the participating population. The model is

$$Y_i^1 = \varphi_1(X_i, U_i^1) \qquad Y_i^0 = \varphi_0(X_i, U_i^0), \qquad D_i = \mathbb{1}\{\zeta(Z_i, X_i) - V_i \geq 0\}$$

with unknown functions φ_d, ζ and the assumptions:[17]

Assumption MTE.1 *relevance*: $\zeta(Z, X)$ is a non-degenerate random variable conditional on X

Assumption MTE.2 *unconfoundedness*: $(U^1, V) \perp\!\!\!\perp Z|X$ and $(U^0, V) \perp\!\!\!\perp Z|X$.

Assumption MTE.3 *(technical)*: The distribution of V is absolutely continuous (with respect to Lebesgue measure).

Assumption MTE.4 *common support*: $0 < \Pr(D = 1|X) < 1$ *almost sure.*

It is obvious that this latent index threshold-crossing model together with its assumptions is similar to the one we used when introducing the LATE (conditional on X). The main difference is that now, for modelling D we work with a latent model for the selection process that has an additive stochastic (unobserved) term V, and the assumptions have to be adjusted accordingly. This presentation puts in evidence how the instruments help to overcome the endogeneity problem: they are used for modelling the selection of D that takes place and in this way identify the treatment effect for those that got selected along the mechanism (4.26). This is useful for sharpening one's intuition about the economic (or policy) implications: $(\zeta(Z_i, X_i) - V_i)$ is determining the choice of D and could be considered as a latent index representing the net gain or utility from choosing $D = 1$. If this net utility is larger than zero, $D = 1$ is chosen, otherwise $D = 0$.

You may ask where the monotonicity is gone to, i.e. the assumption of absence of defiers. It is implicitly given by the selection rule (4.26) with additive heterogeneity V being conditionally independent from Z (Assumption MTE.2). This guarantees that for all people given $X = x$ and $Z = z$ the effect of a change in the instrument to z' has the same direction regarding their propensity to participate. Always-takers could be characterised as those individuals i with $V_i \leq \min_{x,z} \zeta(z, x)$ and never-takers as those with $V_i > \max_{x,z} \zeta(z, x)$. Moreover, assuming V as being continuous allows us to ease the interpretation by normalising the distribution of V (conditional on X): As its distribution function $F_{V|X}(\cdot)$ is strictly increasing, the following equivalences hold

$$\zeta(Z_i, X_i) \geq V_i \iff F_{V|X=X_i}(\zeta(Z_i, X_i)) \geq F_{V|X=X_i}(V_i) \iff p(X_i, Z_i) \geq F_{V|X=X_i}(V_i),$$

where $p(x, z) = \Pr(D = 1|X = x, Z = z)$ denotes the participation propensity. The last equivalence holds because

$$p(z, x) = \Pr(D = 1|Z = z, X = x) = \Pr(\zeta(Z, X) - V \geq 0|Z = z, X = x)$$
$$= \Pr(V \leq \zeta(z, x)|Z = z, X = x) = F_{V|Z=z,X=x}(\zeta(z, x)) = F_{V|X=x}(\zeta(z, x)),$$

as $V \perp\!\!\!\perp Z|X$. $F_{V|X}(V)$ is uniformly $[0, 1]$ distributed.[18] Therefore the model can actually be written as

---

[17] In the literature is often added the technical, non-restrictive (i.e. in practice typically given) assumption that Y^0 and Y^1 have finite first moments.

[18] To see this consider (for a strictly increasing distribution function) $\Pr(F_V(V) \leq c) = \Pr\left(V \leq F_V^{-1}(c)\right)$
$= F_V\left(F_V^{-1}(c)\right) = c$. Hence, the distribution is uniform. The same applies conditional on X, i.e.
$\Pr\left(F_{V|X}(V) \leq c|X\right) = \Pr(V \leq F_{V|X}^{-1}(c)|X) = F_{V|X}(F_{V|X}^{-1}(c)) = c.$

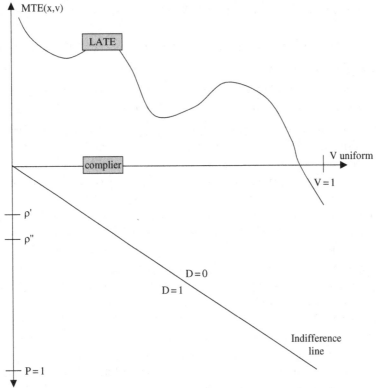

Everything conditional on $X = x$

$$Y^1 = \varphi_1(X, U^1), \qquad Y^0 = \varphi_0(X, U^0) \qquad (4.26)$$
$$D = \mathbb{1}\left\{p(Z, X) - \bar{V} \geq 0\right\} \quad \text{with} \quad \bar{V}|Z, X \sim \bar{V}|X \sim U(0, 1) \qquad (4.27)$$

where $\bar{V} \equiv F_{V|X}(V)$, which is (mean) independent of Z given X by construction. Hence, the distribution of the error term can be normalised to be uniform, conditional on X and Z. So we write for notational convenience V but refer to $\bar{V}$ throughout. Intuitively, individuals can be thought of as being ordered on the real line from 0 to 1 in terms of their inclination to participate. Individuals with a low value of V are very likely to participate, while those with a high value are unlikely to participate. By varying $p(Z, X)$ through variation in Z, each individual can be made more or less inclined to participate. Therefore, in the following $P_i = p(X_i, Z_i)$ is considered as being our instrument. Recall how multiple instruments can be handled: they all enter in the one-dimensional participation probability. In practice, $p(z, x)$ needs to be estimated, which makes the incorporation of multiple instruments not that trivial.

Examine everything in the following conditional on X i.e., conditioning on X is implicit. If Z were to take only two different values (keeping X fix), i.e. $Z \in \{z', z''\}$, also P would take only two different values, i.e. $P \in \{\rho', \rho''\}$ and suppose that $\rho' < \rho''$. Individuals with $V_i < \rho'$ would participate irrespective of the value of P, whereas individuals with $V_i > \rho''$ would never participate. Those with $\rho' \leq V_i \leq \rho''$ are individuals who would be induced to switch if the instrument were changed from z' to z''. For these compliers we have

$$LATE(x, \rho', \rho'') = E[Y^1 - Y^0|X = x, \rho' \le P \le \rho''] = \frac{E[Y|x, \rho''] - E[Y|x, \rho']}{\rho'' - \rho'} \tag{4.28}$$

for $\rho' < \rho''$. We used that $E[D|X = x, P = \rho''] = E[E[D|X, Z, P(Z, X) = \rho'']$ $|X = x, P = \rho'']$ is equal to $E[E[D|X, Z]|X = x, P = \rho''] = \rho''$. To see this, notice that

$$E[Y|X = x, P = \rho] = E[Y|X = x, P = \rho, D = 1]\Pr(D = 1|X = x, P = \rho)$$
$$+ E[Y|X = x, P = \rho, D = 0]\Pr(D = 0|X = x, P = \rho)$$
$$= \rho \cdot \int_0^\rho E[Y^1|X = x, P = v]\frac{dv}{\rho} + (1 - \rho) \cdot \int_\rho^1 E[Y^0|X = x, P = v]\frac{dv}{1 - \rho}. \tag{4.29}$$

This gives the *surplus* for setting Z from z' to z'':

$$E[Y|X = x, P = \rho''] - E[Y|X = x, P = \rho']$$
$$= \int_{\rho'}^{\rho''} E[Y^1|X = x, V = v]dv - \int_{\rho'}^{\rho''} E[Y^0|X = x, V = v]dv$$
$$= \int_{\rho'}^{\rho''} E[Y^1 - Y^0|X = x, V = v]dv = (\rho'' - \rho') \cdot E[Y^1 - Y^0|X = x, \rho' \le V \le \rho''].$$

So the surplus refers to the expected return to the treatment for the (sub)population with $X = x$. In case you are interested in the LATE return for the participants induced by this change in Z you will have to divide this expression by $(\rho'' - \rho')$.

Once again we notice that if Z takes on many different values, different LATE could be defined for any two values of Z, recall (4.8). If Z is continuous, we can take the derivative of (4.29)

$$\frac{\partial E[Y|X = x, P = \rho]}{\partial \rho} = \frac{\partial}{\partial \rho}\int_0^\rho E[Y^1|X = x, P = v]dv$$

$$+ \frac{\partial}{\partial \rho}\int_\rho^1 E[Y^0|X = x, P = v]dv$$

$$= E[Y^1|X = x, V = \rho] - E[Y^0|X = x, V = \rho]$$
$$= E[Y^1 - Y^0|X = x, V = \rho].$$

The *marginal treatment effect* (MTE) is now defined as

$$MTE(x, p) = E[Y^1 - Y^0|X = x, V = p] = \frac{\partial E[Y|X = x, P = v]}{\partial v}\bigg|_{v=p},$$

provided $E\left[Y|X=x, P=p\right]$ is differentiable in the second argument at the location p. This is the average treatment effect among those with characteristics $X = x$ and unobserved characteristic V such that $V = p$. For this reason the MTE is often expressed by $MTE(x, v)$ where v refers to the unobserved characteristics in the selection equation. So we talk about the individuals being indifferent between participating and non-participating if $P = p$.

It can be obtained by estimating the derivative of $E[Y|X, P]$ with respect to P which is therefore often called *local instrumental variable estimator* (LIVE). An evident non-parametric estimator is the local linear regression estimator with respect to $(X_i - x)$ and $(P_i - p)$ where the coefficient of $(P_i - p)$ gives the estimate of the partial derivative at point p for $X = x$. This will certainly be a non-parametric function in p **and** x. Only when either having a parametric specification, or if integrating (afterwards) over x **and** p will provide us with a $\sqrt{n}$-rate (consistent) estimator. This will be briefly discussed later.

4.3.2   Relating Other Treatment Effects to MTEs

As the marginal treatment effect is a function of both, the confounders X which were expected to match people being similar in observables, and the unobserved heterogeneity v it controls for the treatment effect heterogeneity. Let us fix the X to x. Depending over which support of P or V we integrate the MTE, it reveals the ATE, ATET, ATEN or LATE. In fact it can be shown that

$$ATE(x) = E[Y^1 - Y^0|X = x] = \int_0^1 MTE(x, v)\, dv$$

$$ATET(x) = E[Y^1 - Y^0|X = x, D = 1]$$

$$= \int_0^1 E[Y^1 - Y^0|X = x, P, D = 1]\, dF_{P|X=x, D=1}$$

$$= \int_0^1 E[Y^1 - Y^0|X = x, P = \rho, D = 1]$$

$$= \int_0^\rho MTE(x, v)\frac{dv}{\rho}dF_{P|X=x, D=1}$$

$$= \int_0^1 MTE(x, v)\frac{1 - F_{P|X=x}(v)}{\Pr(D = 1|X = x)}\, dv$$

$$ATEN(x) = \int_0^1 MTE(x, v)\frac{F_{P|X=x}(v)}{1 - \Pr(D = 1|X = x)}\, dv$$

$$LATE(x, \rho', \rho'') = E[Y^1 - Y^0|X = x, \rho' \le P \le \rho''] = \int_{\rho'}^{\rho''} MTE(x, v)\frac{dv}{\rho'' - \rho'}.$$

Hence, all these treatment effects can be written as a weighted average of the MTE. The support of $p(Z, X)$ determines which effects we can identify. If Z is continuous and has a substantial impact on D, the support of $p(Z, X)$ given X will be large and many different effects can be identified. On the other hand, if Z induces only few individuals to change treatment status, then only little is identified. This shows also that a strong impact of Z on D is important. Recall that extrapolation has to be done with care – if at all – and is only possible in parametric models. So the question is whether you get for any given x estimates of $MTE(x, p)$ over the whole range of p from 0 to 1, and the same can certainly be questioned for $F_{P|X=x}$.

So you may say that we should at least attempt to estimate the treatment effect for the largest subpopulation for which it is identified. Let $S_{\rho|x} = Supp(p(Z, X)|X = x)$ be the support of ρ given X, and let $\underline{p}_x$ and $\bar{p}_x$ be the inf and sup of $S_{\rho|x}$. Then the treatment effect on the largest subpopulation with $X = x$ is $LATE(x, \underline{p}_x, \bar{p}_x)$. Certainly, if $\underline{p}_x = 0$ and $\bar{p}_x = 1$, the ATE conditional on X could be obtained. So we are again in the typical dilemma of IV estimation: on the one hand we would like to have a strong instrument Z such that $p(Z, X)$, conditional on X, has a large support. On the other hand, the stronger the instrument the less credible are the necessary assumptions to hold. Moreover, if we would like to average the obtained treatment effects over various values of x, only the effect for the $\sup_x \underline{p}_x$ and $\inf_x \bar{p}_x$ over this set of values x is identified, which reduces the identification set even further. However, if X is exogenous, i.e. independent of U^1 and U^0, and our interest is the average effect over all values of x, then we can increase our identification region, see below.

An interesting question is when LATE(x) (as a function of x) equals ATE boils down to the question of where (for a given IV) $MTE(x, p)$ is constant in p. Many ways can be found to give answers to this. What you basically need is that for a given IV and x, the gain or return to participation $(Y^1 - Y^0) = \{\varphi_1(x, U^1) - \varphi_0(x, U^0)\}$; recall (4.27) does not vary with the unobserved heterogeneity V in the participation decision. How can this be formalised? First let us assume additive separability of the unobserved part in the outcome equation redefining $\varphi_d(x) = E[Y^d|X = x]$ and $U^d := Y^d - E[Y^d|X = x]$ for $d = 0, 1$. Then you would ask for $(U^1 - U^0) \perp\!\!\!\perp V|_{X=x}$. Recalling that $Y = DY^1 + (1 - D)Y^0 = Y^0 + D(Y - Y^1 - Y^0)$ we have

$$E[Y|P = p, X = x] = E[Y^0|P = p, X = x]$$
$$+ E\left[\{\varphi_1(x) - \varphi_0(x) + U^1 - U^0\}\mathbb{1}\{p > V\}\right]$$
$$= E[Y^0|P = p, X = x]$$
$$+ p \cdot ATE(x) + \int_0^P E[U^1 - U^0|V = v]\, dv,$$

keeping in mind that $V \sim U[0, 1]$. The MTE is the derivative with respect to p, therefore

$$MTE(x, p) = \frac{\partial E[Y|P = p, X = x]}{\partial p} = ATE(x) + E[U^1 - U^0|V = p].$$

If $(U^1 - U^0) \perp\!\!\!\perp V|_{X=x}$, then $E[U^1 - U^0|V = p]$ cannot be a function of p because of this (conditional) independence. Therefore, if $E[Y|P = p, X = x]$ is a linear function of p, then one concludes that $MTE(x, p) = ATE(x)$. Then it also holds $MTE(x) = ATE(x) = LATE(x)$. In other words, the heterogeneity of treatment effect can be explained sufficiently well by x. There exist a large set of non-parametric specification tests to check for linearity, see Gonzalez-Manteiga and Crujeiras (2013) for a review on non-parametric testing. Which of these tests is the most appropriate for which situation depends on the smoothing method you plan to use for the estimation.[19] As we recommended a local linear or local quadratic estimator for $E[Y|P = p, X = x]$ to get directly an estimate for $MTE(x, p)$, a straightforward strategy would be to check whether $MTE(x, p)$ is constant in p or not. The obvious problem is that one would have to check this for any x ending up in a complex multiple testing problem. A simple solution can only be given for models with a parametric impact of x and p.

As the MTE defines the gain in Y for a marginal change in 'participation' induced by an instrument Z, it would be interesting to see how the general formula for a social welfare gain caused by a policy change looks like.

Example 4.14 A policy could increase the incentives for taking up or extending schooling through financial support (without directly affecting the remuneration of education in the labour market 20 years later). If the policy only operates through changing Z without affecting any of the structural relationships, the impact of the policy can be identified by averaging over the MTE appropriately. As usual, a problem occurs if Z is also correlated with a variable that has a relation with the potential remuneration, except if you can observe all those and condition on them.

Consider two potential policies denoted as a and b, which differ in that they affect the participation inclination, but where the model remains valid under both policies, in particular the independence of the instrument. Denote by P_a and P_b the participation probabilities under the respective policy a and b. If the distributions of the potential outcomes and of V (conditional on X) are the same under policy a and b, the MTE remains the same under both policies and is thus invariant to it. Any utilitarian welfare function (also called a Benthamite welfare function) sums the utility of each individual in order to obtain society's overall welfare. All people are treated the same, regardless of their initial level of utility. For such a social welfare function of Y, say $\mathcal{U}$, the MTE is

$$MTE_{\mathcal{U}}(x, v) = E[\mathcal{U}(Y^1) - \mathcal{U}(Y^0)|X = x, V = v]$$

and the policy impact for individuals with a given level of X is

$$E[\mathcal{U}(Y_a)|X = x] - E[\mathcal{U}(Y_b)|X = x] = \int_0^1 MTE_{\mathcal{U}}(x, v) \left\{ F_{P_b|X}(v|x) - F_{P_a|X}(v|x) \right\} dv,$$

where $F_{P_b|X}$ and $F_{P_a|X}$ are the respective distributions of the participation probability. In the literature one often speaks of *policy relevant treatment parameters*. If the distribution of P can be forecasted for the different policies, it gives us the appropriate weighting of the MTE for calculating the impact of the policy.

---

[19] See Sperlich (2014) for details of bandwidth choice in testing problems.

4.3.3 Extensions: Identification of Distributions of Potential Outcomes and Increasing the Identification Region

A number of extensions of the basic marginal-treatment-effect concept have been developed. Consider first the identification of the entire potential outcome distributions. Note that

$$E[YD|X, P = \rho] = E[Y^1|X, P=\rho, D=1] \cdot \rho = E[\varphi_1(X, U^1)|X, P=\rho, V \leq \rho] \cdot \rho$$
$$= \rho \int_0^\rho E[\varphi_1(X, U^1)|X, P = \rho, V = v] \cdot f_{V|X,P=\rho,V\leq\rho}(v) \, dv \,.$$

(4.30)

Using that P is a deterministic function of X and Z, $(U^1, V) \perp\!\!\!\perp Z|X$ and $V \sim U[0, 1]$ (also independent of X given Z), we obtain for (4.30)

$$= \int_0^\rho E[Y^1|X, V = v] dv.$$

Differentiating this expression with respect to ρ gives therefore

$$\frac{\partial E[YD|X, P = \rho]}{\partial \rho} = E[Y^1|X, V = \rho].$$

(4.31)

Similar calculations for Y^0 deliver

$$\frac{\partial E[Y(D-1)|X, P = \rho]}{\partial \rho} = E[Y^0|X, V = \rho].$$

Hence, the mean potential outcomes Y^0 and Y^1 are identified separately. Therefore, we can analogously identify the potential outcome distributions by substituting $\mathbb{1}\{Y \leq c\}$ (for any $c \in (0, 1)$) for Y to obtain $F_{Y^1|X,V=\rho}$ and $F_{Y^0|X,V=\rho}$.

We can estimate (4.31) by non-parametric regression of YD on X and P. In order to avoid a sample with many zeros when regressing the product of Y and D on the regressors you may rewrite this as

$$E[Y^1|X, V = \rho] = \frac{\partial E[YD|X, P = \rho]}{\partial \rho} = \frac{\partial}{\partial \rho} (E[Y|X, P = \rho, D = 1] \cdot \rho)$$
$$= \rho \frac{\partial E[Y|X, P = \rho, D = 1]}{\partial \rho} + E[Y|X, P = \rho, D = 1]. \quad (4.32)$$

Hence, one can estimate the potential outcome from the conditional mean of Y and its derivative in the $D = 1$ population.

The distribution functions $F_{Y^1|X,V}$ and $F_{Y^0|X,V}$ can be estimated in two ways. One approach is substituting $\mathbb{1}\{Y \leq c\}$ for Y as mentioned above. Alternatively one can use the structure of the additively separable model with

$$Y_i^1 = \varphi_1(X_i) + U_i^1 \quad \text{and} \quad Y_i^0 = \varphi_0(X_i) + U_i^0. \quad (4.33)$$

which implies for the conditional densities

$$f_{Y^d|X,V}(c|x, v) = f_{U^d|X,V}(c - \varphi_d(x)|x, v) = f_{U^d|V}(c - \varphi_d(x)|v).$$

The latter can be obtained as a density estimate after having estimated $\varphi_d(x)$.

Almost as a by-product, the above calculations reveal how an increase of the identification region could work. Above we briefly discussed the problem of treatment effect identification when instrument Z does not cause much variation in the propensity score once X has been fixed. In fact, $E[Y^1|X, V = \rho]$ and $F_{Y^1|X,V=\rho}$ are only identified for those values of ρ which are in the support of the conditional distribution of P, i.e. $P|(X, D = 1)$, whereas $E[Y^0|X, V = \rho]$ and $F_{Y^0|X,V=\rho}$ are only identified for those values of ρ which are in the support of $P|(X, D = 0)$. Since P is a deterministic function of X and Z only, any variation in $P|X$ can only be due to variation in Z. Unless the instruments Z have strong predictive power such that for each value of X they generate substantial variation in $P|X$, the set of values of (X, V) where $F_{Y^1|X,V}$ and $F_{Y^0|X,V}$ are identified may be small for given x. A remedy would be if we could integrate over X, enlarging the identification region substantially.

Though extensions to non-separable cases might be thinkable, we continue with the more restrictive model (4.33). Much more restrictive and hard to relax is the next assumption, namely that the errors U^d, V are jointly independent from Z and X, i.e. $(U^0, V) \perp\!\!\!\perp (Z, X)$ and $(U^1, V) \perp\!\!\!\perp (Z, X)$. Repeating then the calculations from above we get

$$E[Y|X, P = \rho, D = 1] = \int_0^\rho E[Y^1|X, V = v]\frac{dv}{\rho} = \varphi_1(X) + \int_{-\infty}^\rho E[U^1|V = v]\frac{dv}{\rho}$$

$$= \varphi_1(X) + \lambda_1(\rho), \text{ with } \lambda_1(\rho) := \int_0^\rho E[U^1|V = v]\frac{dv}{\rho}.$$

(4.34)

Note that we can identify the function $\varphi_1(X)$ by examining $E[Y|X, P = \rho, D = 1]$ for different values of X but keeping ρ constant. Analogously we can proceed for φ_0. These results are helpful but do not yet provide us with the marginal treatment outcomes

$$E[Y^d|X, V = \rho] = \varphi_d(X) + E[U^d|X, V = \rho] = \varphi_d(X) + E[U^d|V = \rho], \quad d = 0, 1,$$

since the rightmost terms are missing. But with a few calculations we obtain

$$E[U^d|V = \rho] = \rho\frac{\partial E[Y - \varphi_d(X)|P = \rho, D = d]}{\partial \rho} + E[Y - \varphi_d(X)|P = \rho, D = d], \quad d = 0, 1$$

because P is a deterministic function of X and Z, and $U^d \perp\!\!\!\perp (Z, X)|V$.

What makes this expression different from (4.32)? The main difference is that this is identified for all values of ρ which are in the support of $P|D = 1$, so without conditioning on X. In (4.32) we had identification only in the support of $P|(X, D = 1)$. The support region $P|D = 1$ can be much larger because variation in P can now also be generated by X. In contrast, when we looked at the support of $P|(X, D = 1)$ only variation in Z could move P. Hence, we no longer require that strong instruments to obtain a large identification region because sufficiently many covariates X can move P from very small to very large values. The disadvantage of this approach are the assumptions of additive separability of U^d and the above-mentioned independence assumptions requiring also exogeneity of X.

Before turning to the non-binary models, it is worth emphasising that identification of MTE hinges crucially on the additive separability in the choice equation index: $D_{i,z} = \mathbb{1}\{p(z, X_i) - V_i \geq 0\}$. This representation entails monotonicity from two different perspectives. First, a change in z shifts the participation index in the same direction for every individual conditional on X. So if an increase in z makes individual i more inclined to participate, then it also makes individual j more inclined to participate if they both have the same x. This is part of the monotonicity discussed in the LATE framework which rules out defiers, i.e. it rules out the possibility that shifting the instrument shifts treatment inclination in different directions for different people even when controlling for x. The second perspective, again conditional on X, is like a rank invariance assumption between individuals: If V_i is smaller than V_j, individual i will always be more inclined to participate than individual j whatever the value of the instrument is. In other words, the individuals can be ordered according to their inclination to participate: Individuals with small V are always more inclined to participate than individuals with large V. In the binary models both definitions of monotonicity are essentially equivalent and one can use the formulation which is more intuitive or easier to verify by economic reasoning. Whereas monotonicity with respect to the impact of the instrument has been discussed frequently in the binary world, the monotonicity assumption in terms of ranking (or ordering individuals by their participation inclination) is important when estimating treatment effects on outcome quantiles or distributions, and it becomes dominant on the following subsections in non-binary models.

4.4 Non-Binary Models with Monotonicity in Choice Equation

The previous sections examined identification for a scalar binary endogenous regressor D. This is a simple situation, though sufficient in many situations. In the case with D discrete, the methods introduced above can often be extended. If now the treatment D is continuous and confounders X are included, non-parametric identification becomes more complex. To keep things relatively easy, the models examined here are based on restrictions in the (selectivity or) choice equation. Specifically, we still work with *triangularity*

$$Y = \varphi(D, X, U) \qquad \text{with} \qquad D = \zeta(Z, X, V), \qquad (4.35)$$

where it is assumed that Y does not affect D. In other words, we still impose a causal chain in that D may affect Y but not vice versa. Such a model may be appropriate because of temporal ordering, e.g. if D represents schooling and Y represents some outcome 20 years later. In other situation like that of a market equilibrium where Y represents supply and D demand, such a triangular model is no longer appropriate.

4.4.1 Continuous Treatment with Triangularity

We start with the triangular type and continuous D, but impose no particular restriction on the support of Y. We examine mainly identification issues. Non-parametric estimation with endogenous, continuous D can actually be quite difficult. A popular way to do so is the so-called generalised *control variable* approach.[20] The basic idea is to control for potential endogeneity of D by conditioning on the predicted V when estimating $\varphi(\cdot)$. As throughout this chapter the basic intuition for identification is that function ζ is assumed to be strictly monotonous in its third argument, it can be inverted with respect to V. Since the inverse function depends only on observed variables (D, Z, X), it is identified. Assuming that there is no measurement error and no endogeneity due to functional misspecification (as we are in the non-parametric context), conditioning Y on this inverse function should control for the remaining (potential) sources of endogeneity of D in the first equation. Note that U can be of any dimension and we might even think of U^D as in the previous (sub)sections – but not so V.

To be more specific, let us formalise the necessary assumptions and see what can be identified by applying them. Note that they are very similar to what we have seen above.

Assumption IN.1: $(U, V) \perp\!\!\!\perp (X, Z)$

This assumption can be decomposed into $(U, V) \perp\!\!\!\perp Z|X$ and $(U, V) \perp\!\!\!\perp X$. The first part is similar to the assumptions in the previous sections. The second part requires that the variables X are exogenous too, i.e. unrelated to U and V.

Assumption IN.2: V is a scalar and ζ is strictly monotone in its third argument, with probability 1.

Let us imagine ζ to be normalised in the sense that it is always increasing in v. As before, we could also normalise V to be a uniform random variable. The assumption that ζ is (weakly) monotonous corresponds to a *rank invariance assumption* in the endogenous regressor D.

Example 4.15 Let D be the years of schooling. An individual i with value v_i larger than v_j for an individual j (with identical characteristics X and getting assigned the same z) will always receive at least as much schooling as individual j regardless of the value of the instrument Z. This assumption may often appear more plausible when we include many variables in X as all heterogeneity these can capture is no longer contained in V.

The assumption of strict monotonicity essentially requires D to be continuous. The assumption also implies that we do not permit for a general reverse causality without imposing further structure. Suppose the true model was such that

$$Y = \varphi(D, X, U), \qquad D = \zeta(Z, X, V, Y),$$

i.e. where D is also a function of Y. We could insert the first equation into the second to obtain

$$Y = \varphi(D, X, U), \qquad D = \zeta(Z, X, V, \varphi(D, X, U))$$

---

[20] More often you may find the notion of *control function*; this typically refers to the special case where the effect of V appears as a separate function in the model.

which implies that D depends on two unobservables. Now we see that the unobservables affecting D are two-dimensional such that we cannot write the model in terms of an invertible function of a one-dimensional unobservable. Consequently, the problem can only be solved simultaneously and imposing more structure.

Turning back to the triangular model. As stated, there exists as a simple and straightforward way the so-called *control function* approach. The idea is to condition on V when studying the impact of D on Y as V should capture all endogeneity inherited by D. Let us go step by step. Assumption IN.2 implies that the inverse function of ζ with respect to its third argument exists: $v = \zeta^{-1}(z, x, d)$, such that $\zeta(z, x, \zeta^{-1}(z, x, d)) = d$. Hence, if ζ was known, the unobserved V would be identified by z, x, d. For ζ unknown, with Assumption IN.1 you still have

$$F_{D|ZX}(d|z, x) = \Pr(D \le d|X = x, Z = z) = \Pr(\zeta(z, x, V) \le d|X = x, Z = z)$$
$$= \Pr(V \le \zeta^{-1}(z, x, d)) = F_V(\zeta^{-1}(z, x, d)) = F_V(v).$$

If V is continuously distributed, $F_V(v)$ is a one-to-one function of v. Thus, controlling for $F_V(v)$ is identical to controlling for V.[21] Hence, two individuals with the same value of $F_{D|ZX}(D_i|Z_i, X_i)$ have the same V. Since $F_{D|ZX}(d|z, x)$ depends only on observed covariates, it is identified. We know from Chapter 2 that this can be estimated by nonparametric regression noting that $F_{D|ZX}(d|z, x) = E[\mathbb{1}(D \le d)|Z = z, X = x]$.

After conditioning on V, observed variation in D is stochastically independent of variation in U such that the effect of D on the outcome variable can be separated from the effect of U. But it is required that there is variation in D after conditioning on V and X, which is thus generated by the instrumental variable(s) Z. The endogeneity of D is therefore controlled for in a similar way as in the selection on observables approach, i.e. the matching approach.

To simplify notation, define the random variable

$$\bar{V} \equiv F_V(V) = F_{D|ZX}(D|Z, X)$$

and let $\bar{v}$ be a realisation of it. $\bar{V}$ can be thought of as a rank-preserving transformation of V to the unit interval. For example, if V were uniformly $[0, 1]$ distributed, then $\bar{V} = V$ (this is basically equivalent to what we did in Section 4.3.1). In the context of treatment effect estimation one often finds the notation of the *average structural function* (ASF) which is the average outcome Y for given x and treatment d. To identify the ASF, notice that conditional on $\bar{V}$, the endogeneity is controlled by

$$f_{U|D,X,\bar{V}} = f_{U|X,\bar{V}} = f_{U|\bar{V}}.$$

As we have

$$E[Y|D = d, X = x, \bar{V} = \bar{v}] = \int \varphi(d, x, u) \cdot f_{U|DX\bar{V}}(u|d, x, \bar{v})du$$
$$= \int \varphi(d, x, u) f_{U|\bar{V}}(u|\bar{v})du$$

---

[21] If V is not continuously distributed, $F_V(v)$ contains steps, and the set $\{v : F_V(v) = a\}$ of values v with the same $F_V(v)$ is not a singleton. Nevertheless, only one element of this set, the smallest, has a positive probability, and therefore conditioning on $F_V(v)$ is equivalent to conditioning on this element with positive probability.

you get as the ASF for $(D, X) = (d, x)$

$$ASF(d, x) := \int E[Y|D = d, X = x, \bar{V} = \bar{v}] \cdot f_{\bar{V}}(\bar{v})d\bar{v}$$

$$= \int \int \varphi(d, x, u) \cdot f_{U|\bar{V}}(u|\bar{v})du \cdot f_{\bar{V}}(\bar{v})d\bar{v}$$

$$= \int \varphi(d, x, u) \left(\int f_{U,\bar{V}}(u, \bar{v})d\bar{v} \right) du = \int \varphi(d, x, u) f_U(u)du \quad (4.36)$$

assuming that all the conditional moments in the expressions are finite, and provided the term $E[Y|D = d, X = x, \bar{V} = \bar{v}]$ is identified for all $\bar{v}$ where $f_{\bar{V}}(\bar{v})$ is non-zero. The latter requires that the support of $\bar{V}|(D, X)$ is the same as the support of $\bar{V}$, which in practice can be pretty restrictive. This certainly depends on the context.

Example 4.16 Take once again our schooling example. If we want to identify the ASF for $d = 5$ years of schooling and suppose the distribution of 'ability in schooling' $\bar{V}$ ranges from 0 to 1, it would be necessary to observe individuals of all ability levels with $d = 5$ years of schooling. If, for example, the upper part of the ability distribution would always choose to have more than five years of schooling, the $E[Y|D = 5, X, \bar{V}]$ would not be identified for all large ability values $\bar{V}$. In other words, in the sub-population observed with five years of schooling, the high-ability individuals would be missing. If this were the case, then we could never infer from data what these high-ability individuals would have earned if they had received only five years of schooling.

From this example it becomes obvious that we need such an assumption, formally

Assumption IN.3 *(Full range condition)*: For all (d, x) where the ASF shall be identified,

$$Supp(\bar{V}|X = x, D = d) = Supp(\bar{V}).$$

So, as in the sections before, since the support of $\bar{V}$ given d and x depends only on the instrument Z, this requires a large amount of variation in the instrument. Regarding Example 4.16, this requires that the instrument is sufficiently powerful to move any individual to 5 years of schooling. By varying Z, the individuals with the highest ability for schooling and the lowest ability have to be induced to choose 5 years of schooling.

An analogous derivation shows the identification of the *distribution structural function* (DSF) and thus the *quantile structural function* (QSF):

$$\int E[\mathbb{1}\{Y \le a\}|D = d, X = x, \bar{V} = \bar{v}] \cdot f_{\bar{V}}(\bar{v})d\bar{v}$$

$$= \int \int \mathbb{1}\{\varphi(d, x, u) \le a\} \cdot f_{U|\bar{V}}(u|\bar{v})du \cdot f_{\bar{V}}(\bar{v})d\bar{v}$$

$$= \int \mathbb{1}\{\varphi(d, x, u) \le a\} f_U(u)du,$$

which is identified as

$$DSF(d, x; a) = \int F_{Y|DX\bar{V}}[a|D = d, X = x, \bar{V} = \bar{v}] \cdot f_{\bar{V}}(\bar{v})d\bar{v}. \qquad (4.37)$$

If we are only interested in the expected potential outcomes $E[Y^d]$, i.e. the ASF as a function of d only and not of x, we could relax the previous assumptions somewhat. Notice that the expected potential outcome is identified by

$$E[Y^d] = \int \int E[Y|D = d, X = x, \bar{V} = \bar{v}] \cdot f_{X\bar{V}}(x, \bar{v})dxd\bar{v}, \qquad (4.38)$$

see Exercise 9. For this result we could even relax Assumption IN.1 to $(U, V) \perp\!\!\!\perp Z|X$ and would no longer require $(U, V) \perp\!\!\!\perp X$. We would have to change notation somewhat in that we should permit the distribution function F_V to depend on X. Furthermore, the common support Assumption IN.3 changes to: for all d where $E\left[Y^d\right]$ shall be identified we need

$$Supp(\bar{V}, X|D = d) = Supp(\bar{V}, X).$$

To compare this assumption to the original one, you may rewrite it as

$$Supp\left(\bar{V}|X, D = d\right) = Supp(\bar{V}|X) \quad \text{and} \quad Supp\left(X|D = d\right) = Supp(X).$$

The first part is in some sense weaker than Assumption IN.3 in that $Supp(\bar{V}|X = x, D = d)$ needs to contain only those 'ability' values $\bar{V}$ that are also observed in the $X = x$ population instead of all values observed in the population at large. Hence, a less powerful instrument could be admitted. However, this assumption is not necessarily strictly weaker than Assumption IN.3 since this assumption is required to hold for all values of X. The second part of the above assumption is new and was not needed before.

Example 4.17 Think of X as family income. Ability $\bar{V}$ is likely to be positively correlated with family income. Consider $X = $ low income families. The previous Assumption IN.3 would require that all ability values of the entire population would also be observed in the low income population with $D = d$. The first part of the above assumption requires only that all ability values observed in low-income families are also observed in the $D = d$ subpopulation.

Nonetheless, Assumption IN.3 is quite strong and may not be satisfied. It is not needed, however, for identifying *Average Derivatives*. Suppose φ is continuously differentiable in the first element with probability one. Recall again the equality

$$E[Y|D = d, X = x, \bar{V} = \bar{v}] = \int \varphi(d, x, u) \cdot f_{U|\bar{V}}(u|\bar{v})du,$$

and what we can estimate:

$$E\left[\frac{\partial E[Y|D, X, \bar{V}]}{\partial d}\right] = E\left[\frac{\partial \int \varphi(D, X, u) \cdot f_{U|\bar{V}}(u|\bar{V})du}{\partial d}\right].$$

However, we were looking for

$$
ADer = E\left[\frac{\partial\varphi(D, X, U)}{\partial d}\right] = E\left[E\left[\frac{\partial\varphi(D, X, U)}{\partial d} | D, X, \bar{V}\right]\right]
$$
$$
= E\left[\int \frac{\partial\varphi(D, X, u)}{\partial d} \cdot f_{U|D,X,\bar{V}}(u|D, X, \bar{V})du\right]
$$
$$
= E\left[\int \frac{\partial\varphi(D, X, u)}{\partial d} \cdot f_{U|\bar{V}}(u|\bar{V})du\right].
$$

If differentiation and integration are interchangeable, the expressions are identical such that

$$
ADer = E\left[\frac{\partial E[Y|D, X, \bar{V}]}{\partial d}\right].
$$

No large support condition is needed since the derivative of $E[Y|D, X, \bar{V}]$ is evaluated only where it is observed.

4.4.2   Ordered Discrete Treatment with Triangularity

Consider the situation where the endogenous regressor D is discrete but not necessarily binary, say $D \in \{0, .., K\}$. To simplify the presentation let us assume to have a binary instrument Z. With D taking many different values, the so-called *compliance intensity* can differ among individuals. Some might be induced to change from $D_i = d$ to $D_i = d + 1$ as a reaction on changing Z_i from 0 to 1. Other might change, for example, from $D_i = d'$ to $D_i = d' + 2$. Hence, a change in Z induces a variety of different reactions in D which cannot be disentangled. Since D is not continuous, the previously discussed approach cannot be used to identify the value of V. If many different instruments are available, they might help to disentangle the effects of different changes in treatment status.

Example 4.18 Suppose D is years of schooling and Z an instrument that influences the schooling decision. If Z was changed exogenously, some individuals might respond by increasing school attendance by an additional year. Other individuals might increase school attendance by two or three years. But have in mind that even if Z was set to zero for all individuals, they would 'choose' different numbers of years of schooling.

Here we consider the situation when only a single binary instrument is available like for example a random assignment to drug versus placebo. Only a weighted average of the effects can then be identified. According to their reaction on a change in Z from 0 to 1, the population can be partitioned into the types $c_{0,0}, c_{0,1}, \ldots, c_{K,K}$, where the treatment choice made by individual i is denoted by

$$
\tau_i = c_{k,l} \qquad \text{if } D_{i,0} = k \text{ and } D_{i,1} = l. \tag{4.39}
$$

Assuming monotonicity, the defier-types $c_{k,l}$ for $k > l$ do not exist. The types $c_{k,k}$ represent those units that do not react on a change in Z. In the setup where D is binary these are the always-takers and the never-takers. The types $c_{k,l}$ for $k < l$ are the compliers, which comply by increasing D_i from k to l. These compliers comply at different base levels k and with different intensities $l - k$. In order to simplify identification you might want restrict your study on the average returns accounting for intensities $(l - k)$.

Example 4.19 In our returns to schooling example, $E[Y^{k+1} - Y^k | X, \tau = c_{k,k+1}]$ measures the return to one additional year of schooling for the $c_{k,k+1}$ subpopulations. $E[Y^{k+2} - Y^k | X, \tau = c_{k,k+2}]$ measures the return to two additional years of schooling, which can be interpreted as twice the average return of one additional year. Similarly, $E[Y^{k+3} - Y^k | X, \tau = c_{k,k+3}]$ is three times the average return to one additional year. Hence, the effective weight contribution of the $c_{k,l}$ subpopulation to the measurement of the return to one additional year of schooling is $(l - k) \cdot \Pr(\tau = c_{k,l})$. Then a weighted $LATE(x)$, say $\gamma_w(x)$, for all compliers with characteristics x could be defined as

$$
\gamma_w(x) = \frac{\sum_k^K \sum_{l>k}^K E\left[Y^l - Y^k | x, \tau = c_{k,l}\right] \cdot \Pr\left(\tau = c_{k,l} | x\right)}{\sum_k^K \sum_{l>k}^K (l - k) \cdot \Pr\left(\tau = c_{k,l} | x\right)}.
\tag{4.40}
$$

The problem is now triple: to estimate $E\left[Y^l - Y^k | X, \tau = c_{k,l}\right]$ and $\Pr\left(\tau = c_{k,l} | X\right)$ for unobserved τ (you again have only treated and controls, you do not know to which partition $c_{k,l}$ the individuals belong to, nor their proportions), and the integration of $\gamma_w(x)$. This function is the effect of the induced treatment change for given x, averaged over the different complier groups and normalised by the intensity of compliance. To obtain the weighted average effect for the subpopulation of all compliers (i.e. all subpopulations $c_{k,l}$ with $k < l$), one would need to weight $\gamma_w(x)$ by the distribution of X in the complier subpopulation:

$$
\int \gamma_w(x) \, dF_{x|complier}(x),
\tag{4.41}
$$

where $F_{x|complier}$ is the distribution of X in the all-compliers subpopulation. Unfortunately, the distribution of X in the all-compliers subpopulation is not identified if D takes more than two different values. In particular, the size of the all-compliers subpopulation is no longer identified by the distribution of D and Z.

Example 4.20 Imagine, for D taking values in $\{0, 1, 2\}$, the population can be partitioned in the subpopulations: $\{c_{0,0}, c_{0,1}, c_{0,2}, c_{1,1}, c_{1,2}, c_{2,2}\}$ with the all-compliers subpopulation consisting of $\{c_{0,1}, c_{0,2}, c_{1,2}\}$. The two partitions with proportions $\{0.1, 0.1, 0.3, 0.3, 0.1, 0.1\}$ and $\{0.1, 0.2, 0.2, 0.2, 0.2, 0.1\}$, respectively, generate the same distribution of D given Z; namely $\Pr(D = 0|Z = 0) = 0.5$, $\Pr(D = 1|Z = 0) = 0.4$, $\Pr(D = 2|Z = 0) = 0.1$, $\Pr(D = 0|Z = 1) = 0.1$, $\Pr(D = 1|Z = 1) = 0.4$, $\Pr(D = 2|Z = 1) = 0.5$. But already the size of the all-compliers subpopulation is different for the two partitions (0.5 and 0.6, respectively). Hence the size of the all-compliers subpopulation is not identified from the observable variables.

Now, if one defines the all-compliers subpopulation together with *compliance inten-sities* $(l - k)$, the distribution of X becomes identifiable. Each complier is weighted by its compliance intensity. In the case of Example 4.20 where $D \in \{0, 1, 2\}$, the sub-population $c_{0,2}$ receives twice the weight of the subpopulation $c_{0,1}$. In the general case one has

$$f^w_{x|complier}(x) = \frac{\sum_k^K \sum_{l>k}^K (l-k) \cdot f_{x|\tau=c_{k,l}}(x) \Pr(\tau = c_{k,l})}{\sum_k^K \sum_{l>k}^K (l-k) \cdot \Pr(\tau = c_{k,l})}. \tag{4.42}$$

With respect to this weighted distribution function, a weighted LATE is identified.

Example 4.21 Considering the years-of-schooling example, the subpopulation $c_{0,2}$ complies with intensity $= 2$ additional years of schooling. If the returns to a year of schooling are the same for each year of schooling, an individual who complies with two additional years can be thought of as an observation that measures twice the effect of one additional year of schooling or as two (correlated) measurements of the return to a year of schooling. Unless these two measurements are perfectly cor-related, the individual who complies with two additional years contributes more to the estimation of the return to schooling than an individual who complies with only one additional year. Consequently, the individuals who comply with more than one year should receive a higher weight when averaging the return to schooling over the distribution of X. If each individual is weighted by its number of additional years, the weighted distribution function of X in the all-compliers subpopulation, where $D \in \{0, 1, 2\}$, is

$$f^w_{x|complier} = \frac{f_{x|\tau=c_{0,1}} \Pr(\tau = c_{0,1}) + f_{x|\tau=c_{1,2}} \Pr(\tau=c_{1,2}) + 2 f_{x|\tau=c_{0,2}} \Pr(\tau = c_{0,2})}{\Pr(\tau = c_{0,1}) + \Pr(\tau = c_{1,2}) + 2 \Pr(\tau = c_{0,2})}.$$

Suppose that D is discrete with finite support, the instrument Z is binary and Assump-tions (A1C), (A2C) and (A5C) are satisfied as well as (A3C), (A4C) with respect to all types $t \in \{c_{k,l} : k \leq l\}$, defined in (4.39). It can be shown (Exercise 10) that the weighted LATE for the subpopulation of compliers is non-parametrically identified as

$$\int \gamma_w(x) \cdot f^w_{x|complier}(x)dx = \frac{\int (E[Y|X=x, Z=1] - E[Y|X=x, Z=0]) \, dF_X}{\int (E[D|X=x, Z=1] - E[D|X=x, Z=0]) \, dF_X}. \tag{4.43}$$

This is actually not hard to estimate (even non-parametrically). All we have to do is to replace the conditional expectations by non-parametric predictors – which is not very difficult given that these involve only observables; and the integrals with $d F_X$ can be replaced by sample averages.

4.5   Bibliographic and Computational Notes

4.5.1   Further Reading and Bibliographic Notes

In this chapter, we could not hope to cover all the findings of the last years concerning causal inference under endogeneity. Estimation with instruments (though using different notation) and simultaneous equations is rather old in statistics. The classic approach of using control functions, to our knowledge, was introduced by Telser (1964). Non-parametric causal inference through instrumental variables was introduced to the econometric literature, among others, by Imbens and Angrist (1994), Angrist, Imbens and Rubin (1996), Heckman and Vytlacil (1999) and Imbens (2001). In this context, the identification and estimation of the causal impact of an endogenous regressor via the solution of integral equations, so-called *ill posed inverse problems*, has become quite topical; see, for example, Florens (2003), Darolles, Fan, Florens and Renault (2011) or Newey and Powell (2003) for the econometric approach. A recent contribution to the control function approach is, for example, Florens, Heckman, Meghir and Vytlacil (2008).

As discussed several times, the propensity scores either of the binary instrument or of the participation can be used for dimension reduction and – as we saw especially in the context of MTE identification and estimation – has a clear interpretation. However, in order to reach this we either need to know or to estimate the propensity score $\pi(X)$. For some applications of this method, see e.g. Frölich and Lechner (2010), Henderson, Millimet, Parmeter and Wang (2008) or Arpino and Aassve (2013).

It is interesting to point out the relationship of LATE or MTE to the over-identification tests in IV regression. Suppose we have two (binary) instruments, Z_1 and Z_2. In IV regression, if we have more instruments than endogenous variables, we can use an over-identification test. We would use the two moment conditions implied by Z_1, Z_2 and compare a 2SLS estimate obtained from Z_1 with the one obtained from Z_2. If they are very different, one rejects the assumption of both moment conditions being valid. In our non-parametric setting, we can estimate one LATE referring to the binary Z_1 and another one referring to the binary instrument Z_2. These two estimated LATE, however, refer to different subpopulations, since the compliers with Z_1 will usually be different from the compliers with Z_2. Hence, if treatment effects are permitted to be heterogeneous, we estimate two effects for two different populations and there is no reason to expect these two parameters to be similar. Based on this insight, we can see the over-identification test of 2SLS in a different light. If the test fails, this might simply mean that the treatment effect is different for different subpopulations. In other words, an alternative interpretation of rejections in over-identification tests is that the effects of interest vary over individuals, rather than that some of the instruments are invalid. Without assuming homogenous effects there exist no such tests for checking the validity of instruments.

Presently, the literature is mainly developing further methods for models with non-separable errors and consequently focuses on quantile regression or random effects models. We will study the former in more detail in Chapter 7. Furthermore, as already mentioned in the context of matching, there exists some quite recent research on post-confounder-selection inference. In particular, Belloni, Chernozhukov, Fernández-Val and Hansen (2017) consider the case with binary treatment and a binary instrument Z but a huge vector of potential counfounders. The number of confounders on which you indeed have to condition on in order to make the IV assumptions hold has to be sparse (q is much smaller than n), and potential selection errors have to be ignorable (first-order orthogonal). Then you can reach valid post-selection inference on treatment effects with a binary IV in high-dimensional data.

In the spirit of the control function approach, Imbens and Newey (2009) consider extensions of the ASF approach that allow for the simulation of an alternative treatment regime where the variable D is replaced by some known function $l(D, X)$ of D and/or X. The potential outcome of this policy is $\varphi(l(D, X), X, U)$ and the average treatment effect compared to the status quo is

$$E\left[\varphi(l(D, X), X, U)\right] - E[Y]. \tag{4.44}$$

As an example, they consider a policy which imposes an upper limit on the choice variable D. Hence, $l(D, X) = \min\{D, \bar{d}\}$, where $\bar{d}$ is the limit.

Identification in simultaneous equations with monotonicity in both equations, namely the outcome and the selection equation, say

$$Y = \varphi(D, X, U, V), \qquad D = \zeta(Y, X, Z, U, V),$$

is discussed in various articles by Chesher (Chesher 2005, Chesher 2007, Chesher 2010). For non-separable models see Chesher (2003) and Hoderlein and Mammen (2007). Why is monotonicity in both equations of interest? Because then we can write by differential calculus (using the chain rule):

$$\frac{\partial y}{\partial z} = \frac{\partial\varphi(d, x, u, v)}{\partial d}\frac{\partial d}{\partial z} + \underbrace{\frac{\partial\varphi(d, x, u, v)}{\partial z}}_{=0}, \text{ and}$$

$$\frac{\partial d}{\partial z} = \frac{\partial\zeta(y, x, z, u, v)}{\partial y}\frac{\partial y}{\partial z} + \frac{\partial\zeta(y, x, z, u, v)}{\partial z}.$$

And with the exclusion restriction, you obtain

$$\frac{\partial\varphi(d, x, u, v)}{\partial d} = \left.\frac{\partial y/\partial z}{\partial d/\partial z}\right|_{d, x, z, u, v},$$

where the right-hand side depends only on the variables d, x, z, u, v but no longer on the unknown function. But as u, v are unobserved, you need monotonicity. The implicit rank invariance was relaxed to rank similarity by Chernozhukov and Hansen (2005).

Back to some modelling for easier identification and estimation. A quite useful compromise between parametric and non-parametric modelling is the varying coefficient models

$$E[Y|X = x_i] = x_i'\beta_i, \quad x_i' \in I\!\!R^q, \beta_i \in I\!\!R^q \text{ non- or semi-parametric,}$$

which we briefly introduced in Section 2.2.3. There, recall (2.48), we modelled β_i as a vector of functions of observables. An alternative would be to consider them as random coefficients; see Hoderlein and Mammen (2010) for the non-parametric case. The latter has been used for modelling the selection model when treatment D is binary – see Gautier and Hoderlein (2014) – or for the main equation with potentially continuous treatment, see Hoderlein and Sasaki (2014). While the idea of estimating directly the distribution of return is quite attractive, a main problem is the necessary assumption regarding the independence of β_i from other parts of the data generating process, and in practice also the difficulty of interpretation. These problems are relaxed in the first mentioned alternative of modelling β_i as a function of observables or of a sum of such a deterministic function plus a random term (similar to mixed effect models). Moreover, as they allow for directly modelling the heterogeneity of returns they can essentially reduce the variation over LATE that refer to different instruments, and even make the IV assumptions more credible. This has been studied for example in Moffitt (2008); see also Sperlich and Theler (2015), Benini, Sperlich and Theler (2016) and Benini and Sperlich (2017).

There is, however, still room to develop feasible, numerically robust estimators for intuitive and straightforwardly interpretable models which nonetheless achieve the necessary functional flexibility. The latter is essential as any systematic deviation can easily bias the final result even more seriously than omitted confounders or reversed causality would do when applying matching without IVs.

4.5.2   Computational Notes

While there exist different commands in **R** and `stata` for IV estimation, most of them are written for the classic IV regression analysis, and even this only for linear models, i.e. for $\varphi(\cdot)$ and $\zeta(\cdot)$ being linear with additive errors.

As discussed, when a binary variable Z is a valid instrument for D without conditioning on further covariates, then the LATE can be estimated by a standard IV estimator being equivalent to the Wald estimator. In **R**, the command `ivreg(Y ~ D | Z)` of the package `AER` produces such a Wald estimate. In `stata` the respective command is `ivregress 2sls Y (D=Z)` which applies a linear 2SLS estimator (consult the remark at the end of this subsection).

When the inclusion of some confounders X is required for the validity of Z, things can complicate or not, depending on how you want to condition on X. For instance, in case you assume that a linear inclusion of X is sufficient, i.e. you assume that they enter the outcome as well as the treatment (selection) equation linearly, then you can just use `ivreg(Y ~ D+X | Z+X)` in **R**, and `ivregress 2sls Y X (D=Z)` in `stata`. An alternative is `etregress Y X, treat (D=Z X)` (estimation by full maximum likelihood, a two-step consistent estimator or a control-function estimator) which is based on the assumption of joint normality for (U, V). The latter is especially interesting if the treatment is not continuous but binary (as it is used to be in most of our considerations in this book). As we have seen, for estimating ζ a more sophisticated regression is more appropriate than logit or probit. The stata command eteffects and its extensions offer further alternatives. These can also be used in order to apply for example a probit in the first stage, and a simple linear one in the second step. If we assume that the treatment effect is different for the treated and non-treated individuals (grouped heterogeneity), ivtreatreg is another alternative; see Cerulli (2014). It is unfortunately not always very clear what the particular differences between these commands are and which one should be used.

For estimating the different LATE or MTE non-parametrically, it is recommended to switch to **R**. In Exercises 6, 7 and 8 you are asked to implement general estimators out of kernel and/or spline smoothers. When mainly the MTE is of interest, then the estimated $\frac{\delta E(Y_i|P_i,X_i)}{\delta P_i}$ can be obtained from local polynomial regression. For example, you obtain it using the command reg$grad[,1] consecutive to h=npregbw(Y ~ P + X, gradient = TRUE) and reg = npreg(h), where P is the vector of propensity scores. In this case, the local polynomial kernel estimator of at least order 2 is a privileged method because it provides the estimated gradient required to infer the MTE.

Only very broadly discussed was the control function approach; recall Section 4.4.1. Now, in additive models one can always include a control function, i.e. a non-parametric function of the residual of the selection model, in order to switch from a standard matching or propensity score weighting model to an IV model. There are no specific packages of commands available for this approach. However, a simple implementation for binary D is provided if in the second stage you assume to have an additively separable model (also for the control function), i.e. you regress (using e.g. a command from the gam or np package from **R**)

$$E[Y|D, X, \hat{V}] = \alpha D + m_{inter}(DX) + m_X(X) + m_v(\hat{V})$$

with $m_{inter}(\cdot)$, $m_X(\cdot)$ and $m_V(\cdot)$ being non-parametric functions. When allowing for individual heterogeneity of the treatment effect as well as complex interactions between covariates and treatment, a conditional LATE on grouped observations of the values taken by the confounders X is more appropriate.

Finally a general remark: many commands were constructed for linear additive models. You certainly know that you can always define polynomials and interactions in a straightforward way. Similarly you can extend this to non-parametric additive models semi-parametric varying coefficient models using splines. Especially R allows you almost always to build out of a variable a spline basis such that you get a non-parametric additive model simply by substituting this spline basis for the original covariate. See also npLate and Frölich and Melly.

4.6   Exercises

1. Recall Assumptions (A3), (A4) of the LATE estimator in Section 4.1.2. Show that the second part of Assumption (A4), which we also called Assumption (A4b), is trivially satisfied if the instrument Z is randomly assigned.

2. Again recall Assumptions (A3), (A4) of the LATE estimator in Section 4.1.2. Show that randomisation of Z does not guarantee that the exclusion assumption holds on the unit level, i.e. Assumption (A4a).

3. Recall the Wald estimator for LATE (4.5) in Section 4.1.2. Show that this estimator is identical to the 2SLS estimator with D and Z being binary variables.

4. Analogously to Chapter 3, derive for (4.21) and (4.22) propensity weighting estimators of the LATE.

5. Discuss the validity of the necessary assumptions for the following example: The yearly quarter of birth for estimating returns to schooling, as e.g. in Angrist and Krueger (1991). They estimated the returns to schooling using the quarter of birth as an instrumental variable for educational attainment. According to US compulsory school attendance laws, compulsory education ends when the pupil reaches a certain age, and thus, the month in which termination of the compulsory education is reached depends on the birth date. Since the school year starts for all pupils in summer/autumn, the minimum education varies with the birth date, which can be exploited to estimate the impact of an additional year of schooling on earnings. The authors show that the instrument birth quarter Z has indeed an effect on the years of education D. On the other hand, the quarter of birth will in most countries also have an effect on *age at school entry* and *relative age in primary school*. In most countries, children who are born, for example, before 1st September enter school at age six, whereas children born after this date enter school in the following year. Although there are usually deviations from this regulation, there are still many children who comply with it. Now compare two children, one born in August and one born in September of the same year. Although the first child is only a few weeks older, it will tend to enter school about one year earlier than the second one. The first child therefore starts schooling at a younger age and in addition will tend to be younger relative to his classmates during elementary (and usually also secondary) school. Discuss now the validity of the exclusion restriction.

6. Write R code for calculating a $LATE$ estimator by averaging over non-parametrically predicted $LATE(X_i)$. Use local linear kernel regression for the $E[Y|Z = z, X_i]$ and either Nadaraya–Watson estimators or local logit estimation for $E[D|Z = z, X_i]$. Start with the case where X is a continuous one-dimensional variable; then consider two continuous confounders, and then a general partial linear model for $E[Y|Z = z, X_i]$, and a generalised partial linear model with logit link for $E[D|Z = z, X_i]$.

7. As Exercise 6 but now use for $E[Y|Z = z, X_i]$ some additive (P-) splines and for $E[D|Z = z, X_i]$ a logit estimator with additive (P-) splines in the index. i.e. for the latent model.

8. Repeat Exercises 6 for estimating the MTE. As you need the first derivatives, you should again use either local linear or local quadratic estimators.

9. Prove Equation 4.38 using the assumptions of Section 4.4.1.

10. Prove Equation 4.43 using Equations 4.40, 4.41 and 4.42, and recalling the definition of expectations for discrete variables. Proceed by first separating $f(x)$ from the joint and conditional distributions, using that for X, a continuous, and D, a discrete variable, the joint distribution is $f(x, d) = f(x|d)\Pr(D = d)$. You may first want to prove that

$$\sum_{k}^{K}\sum_{l>k}^{K}(l - k) \cdot \Pr\left(\tau = c_{k,l}\right) = E\left[D|X = x, Z = 1\right] - E\left[D|X = x, Z = 0\right].$$

5 Difference-in-Differences Estimation: Selection on Observables and Unobservables

The methods discussed in previous sections could be applied with data observed for a treated and a control group at a single point in time. In this section we discuss methods that can be used if data are observed at several points in time and/or if several control groups are available. We discuss first the case where data are observed at two points in time for the control group and for the treated group. This could for example be panel data, i.e. where the same individuals or households are observed repeatedly. But it could also be independent cross-section observations from the same populations at different points in time. Longitudinal data on the same observations is thus not always needed for these methods to be applied fruitfully, which is particularly relevant in settings where attrition in data collection could be high.

Data on cohorts (or even panels) from before and after a treatment has taken place are often available as in many projects data collections took place at several points in time. The obvious reason is that before a project is implemented, one already knows if at some point in time an evaluation will be required or not. The most natural idea is then to either try to implement a randomised design (Chapter 1) or at least to collect information on Y (and potentially also on X) before the project starts. Therefore, as before, we have $\{Y_i\}_{i=1}^n$ for a treatment and a control group, but additional to the information on final outcomes you have the same information also for the time before treatment.

Example 5.1 Card and Krueger (1994) are interested in the employment effects of a change in the legal minimum wage in one state, and take a neighbouring state, where no change in the minimum wage occurred, as a comparison state. The effects of the minimum wage change are examined over time, and the variation in employment over time in the comparison state is used to identify the time trend that presumably would have occurred in the absence of the raise in the minimum wage.

In this chapter we will see how this information over time can be exploited to relax the assumptions necessary for identification of the treatment effect. In the setting with two groups observed at two points in time, there are different ways how to look at the *difference-in-differences* (DiD henceforth) idea introduced here. The crucial insight is that for the control group we observe the non-treatment outcome Y^0 before and after the intervention, because the control group is not affected by the intervention. On the other hand, for the treatment group we observe the potential outcome Y^1 *after* the intervention, but before the intervention we observe the non-treatment outcome Y^0 also for the treatment group, because the intervention had not yet started.

Thinking of the regression or matching approach one might think of the situation where at time t the additionally available information on which we plan to condition are the individuals past outcomes $Y_{i,t-1}$, i.e. before treatment started. Let D be the indicator for affiliation of the individual to either the treatment ($D_i = 1$) or control group ($D_i = 0$). Being provided with this information, a simple way to predict the average Y_t^0 for the treated individuals is

$$\widehat{E}[Y_t^0|D = 1] := \frac{1}{n_1} \sum_{i:D_i=1} Y_{i,t-1} + \frac{1}{n_0} \sum_{i:D_i=0} (Y_{i,t} - Y_{i,t-1}) \qquad (5.1)$$

with $n_1 = \sum_i D_i = n - n_0$. An alternative way to look at it is to imagine that we are interested in the average return increase due to treatment, i.e. $E[Y_t^1 - Y_{t-1}^0] - E[Y_t^0 - Y_{t-1}^0]$, rather than the difference between treated and non-treated. This is actually the same, because $E[Y_t^1 - Y_{t-1}^0] - E[Y_t^0 - Y_{t-1}^0] = E[Y_t^1 - Y_t^0]$, and this shows also where the name *difference-in-differences* comes from. Obviously you need only to assume ($Y_t^d - Y_{t-1}^0$) $\perp\!\!\!\perp D$ for applying a most simple estimator like in randomised experiments.

Recall that treatment effect estimation is a prediction problem. Having observed outcomes from the time before treatment started will help us to predict the potential non-treatment outcome, in particular $E[Y^0|D = 1]$. But this does not necessarily provide additional information for predicting the treatment outcome for the control group. Therefore we focus throughout on identification of the ATET $E[Y_t^1 - Y_t^0|D = 1]$. The treatment outcome $E[Y_t^1|D = 1]$ can be directly estimated from the observed outcomes, the focus will be on finding assumptions under which $E[Y_t^0|D = 1]$ is identified.

We will first discuss non-parametric identification of $E[Y^0|D = 1]$ but also examine linear models and the inherent assumptions imposed on $E[Y^0|D = 1]$. While linear models impose stronger assumptions on the functional form, they provide the useful link to well known results and estimators in panel data analysis. After the different possibilities to combine the DiD idea with RDD or matching we have to think about the possibility that the development of Y had already been different for the treatment group before treatment took place. Related to this problem is that the DiD is scale-dependent: if the trend of Y^0 is the same for both treatment groups, this is no longer true for the log of Y^0. A remedy to this problem is to look at the entire distribution of Y^0 (and Y^1) resulting in the so-called *changes-in-changes* approach we introduce later on.

5.1   The Difference-in-Differences Estimator with Two Time Periods

As indicated above, DiD identification can be applied in situations where we observe both a treatment and a control group already earlier in an untreated state. A typical example may be a (policy) change at a time t which affects only a part of the population, e.g. only some specific geographical area of a country. We could examine differences in the outcomes between the affected and unaffected parts of the population after this (policy) change, but we might be worried that these differences in outcomes might, at least partly, also reflect other, say unobserved, differences between these regions. This may generate a spurious correlation between treatment status and outcomes. If we have outcome data for the period before or until t, i.e. when the population was not yet affected by the policy change, we could examine whether differences between these regions already existed before. If these differences are time-invariant, we could subtract them from the differences observed after t. This is nothing other than taking differences in differences.

5.1.1   Diff-in-Diff, the Simple Case

Consider the arrival of a large number of refugees in one city at a particular time. One would like to estimate the impacts of this increase in refugees on local markets, employment, crime or diseases. Take the Rwandan genocide, which led to a massive increase in refugee populations and internally displaced people in neighbouring regions. Consider a city A and suppose we have data on an outcome variable Y, say number of crimes per month, for a time period t after the influx of refugees and for a time period $t - 1$ before. I.e. the immigrants arrived at some time between $t - 1$ and t. The before–after difference is $Y_t - Y_{t-1}$. If the time periods are sufficiently far apart, we would be concerned that other changes might also have happened during this time. Therefore we would like to subtract the time trend that would have happened if no influx of refugees had occurred. If there are neighbouring unaffected regions, these could help us to identify this counterfactual trend.

If we also have data for a city B where no refugees (or at least not more than what we would consider as the usual immigration flow) have arrived, then one could correct for this by comparing the differences, i.e.

$$\Delta Y_{t,A} - \Delta Y_{t,B} = \underbrace{(Y_{t,A} - Y_{t-1,A})}_{\text{diff over time}} - \underbrace{(Y_{t,B} - Y_{t-1,B})}_{\text{diff over time}}$$

$$= \underbrace{(Y_{t,A} - Y_{t,B})}_{\text{diff between cities}} - \underbrace{(Y_{t-1,A} - Y_{t-1,B})}_{\text{diff between cities}}.$$

Clearly, taking the difference in the differences over time gives the same answer as taking the difference in the differences between cities. It should also be clear that we have estimated by this only the treatment effect for the treated (ATET). That is, we use the changes of the outcomes in the control group to construct the counterfactual outcome for the treated.

The assumption we implicitly made in the examples above was that the time trend was the same in the control group, which is usually referred to as the common trend assumption. In the following we denote these two time periods by $t = 1$ for the post-intervention period and by $t = 0$ for the pre-intervention period. In addition to SUTVA we assume for identification.

Assumption 1 *common trend (CT)* or *bias stability (BS)*: During the period $[t-1,t]$ (or t_0 to t_1) the potential non-treatment outcomes Y^0 followed the same linear trend in the treatment group as in the control group. Formally,

$$Common\,Trend \quad E[Y_{t=1}^0 - Y_{t=0}^0 | D = 1] = E[Y_{t=1}^0 - Y_{t=0}^0 | D = 0] \quad \text{or}$$

$$Bias\,Stability \quad E[Y_{t=0}^0 | D = 1] - E[Y_{t=0}^0 | D = 0] = E[Y_{t=1}^0 | D = 1] - E[Y_{t=1}^0 | D = 0]$$

Often the *common trend* is synonymously called the *parallel path*. The main difference is that *parallel path* always refers to the development of Y whereas the notation of *common trend* is sometimes maintained when people actually refer to *parallel growth*, i.e. a common trend of the growth (or first difference) of Y.

With the CT or BS assumption we can identify the counterfactual non-treatment outcome as

$$E[Y_{t=1}^0 | D = 1] = E[Y_{t=0}^0 | D = 1] + E[Y_{t=1}^0 - Y_{t=0}^0 | D = 0]$$

and since the potential outcome Y^0 corresponds to the observed outcome Y if being in non-treatment state we obtain

$$E[Y_{t=1}^0 | D = 1] = E[Y_{t=0} | D = 1] + E[Y_{t=1} - Y_{t=0} | D = 0].$$

We can now estimate the counterfactual outcome by replacing expected values with sample averages

$$\hat{E}[Y_{t=1}^0 | D = 1] = \hat{E}[Y | D = 1, T = 0] + \hat{E}[Y | D = 0, T = 1] - \hat{E}[Y | D = 0, T = 0].$$

and

$$\hat{E}[Y_{t=1}^1 | D = 1] = \hat{E}[Y | D = 1, T = 1].$$

Putting all pieces together we obtain an estimate of the ATET as

$$\hat{E}[Y_{t=1}^1 - Y_{t=1}^0 | D = 1] = \hat{E}[Y | D = 1, T = 1] - \hat{E}[Y | D = 1, T = 0]$$
$$- \hat{E}[Y | D = 0, T = 1] - \hat{E}[Y | D = 0, T = 0].$$

The CT, BS or parallel path assumption can easily be visualised, especially if we are provided with data that contain observations from several time points before and after treatment. This is illustrated in two examples in Figure 5.1. In both panels we have three time points ($t = -2, -1, 0$) before, and three after ($t = 1, 2, 3$) treatment. The thin black line represents the unaffected development of the control group, the thick black line the one of the treatment group. In both panels they run in parallel and hence fulfil the CT assumption. The right panel simply illustrates that the trend does neither has to be linear or monotone e.g. a seasonal pattern such as unemployment rate. After treatment many developments are thinkable for the treatment group: a different, e.g. steeper, trend (dashed), a parallel trend but on a different level than before treatment (dotted), or unaffected (semi-dashed). We do not observe or know the exact development between $t = 0$ to $t = 1$; in the left panel we may speculate about it due to the linearity, but preferred to suppress it in the right panel.

An alternative, but numerically identical, estimator of ATET can be obtained via a linear regression model. Such representation can be helpful to illustrate the link to linear

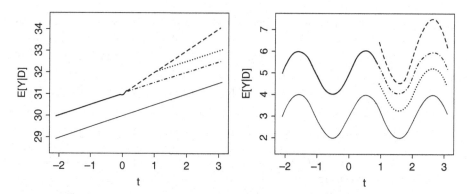

Figure 5.1 The CT, BS or parallel path assumption. Until $t = 0$, before treatment takes place, $E[Y|D] = E[Y^0|D]$ (solid lines) is developing in parallel in both D groups with thin line for the control group $E[Y|D = 0]$, and the thick lines indicating different scenarios for the treatment group as after treatment has taken place, $E[Y|D = 1]$ may develop in different ways

panel models and also exemplifies how diff-in-diff estimation can be expressed in linear models. More precisely, we can write the DiD estimator in the regression representation, by including the interaction term:

$$Y = \alpha + \beta \cdot \mathbb{1}\{time = t\} + \underbrace{\gamma \cdot \mathbb{1}\{city = A\}}_{\text{time constant}} + \delta \cdot \mathbb{1}\{time = t\} \cdot \mathbb{1}\{city = A\} + U.$$

One can easily show that the coefficient δ on the interaction term is identical to the DiD estimator given before. Here, γ is a time constant city effect and β is a city-invariant time effect. Writing the regression model in first differences

$$\Delta Y = \beta \cdot \Delta time + \delta \cdot \Delta \mathbb{1}\{time = t\} \cdot \mathbb{1}\{city = A\} + \Delta U,$$

we observe the relationship to linear panel data models. However, we actually do not need individual level nor panel data, but only city averages of Y taken from cohorts. This is a quite important advantage, since panel data is often plagued by attrition, panel mortality, etc.

Example 5.2 Duflo (2001) took advantage of a rapid school expansion programme that occurred in Indonesia in the 1970s to estimate the impact of building schools on schooling and subsequent wages. Identification is made possible by the fact that the allocation rule for the school is known – more schools were built in places with low initial enrolment rates – and by the fact that the cohorts participating in the programme are easily identified. Children of 12 years or older when the programme started did not participate in the programme. The increased growth of education across cohorts in regions that received more schools suggests that access to schools contributed to increased education. The trends were quite parallel before the programme and shifted clearly for the first cohort that was exposed to the programme, thus reinforcing confidence in the identification assumption.

Certainly, in practice regression models on the individual level are more frequently used. Suppose a policy change at $t = 1$ in the unemployment insurance law. Affected individuals become unemployed only if they are older than 50 at the time of unemployment registration. Let Y be some outcome measure, e.g. employment status after one year, whereas time period $t = 0$ refers to a period before the change. We could run the regression

$$Y_t = \beta_0 + \beta_1 \cdot \mathbb{1}_{time=1} + \beta_2 \cdot \mathbb{1}_{age>50} + \gamma \cdot \mathbb{1}_{age>50} \cdot \mathbb{1}_{time=1} + U_t, \qquad (5.2)$$

where the selection $age > 50$ refers to $t = 0$ so that it does not have a time index. Here, γ measures the treatment effect of the policy change, β_1 captures (time constant) differences between the two age groups, and β_2 captures time trends (in the absence of the policy change) that are assumed to be identical for both age groups.

It is easy to see that the OLS estimate of γ in (5.2) can be written as

$$\hat{\gamma} = \left(\bar{y}_{50+,t=1} - \bar{y}_{50+,t=0}\right) - \left(\bar{y}_{50-,t=1} - \bar{y}_{50-,t=0}\right) \qquad (5.3)$$

or equivalently as

$$\hat{\gamma} = \left(\bar{y}_{50+,t=1} - \bar{y}_{50-,t=1}\right) - \left(\bar{y}_{50+,t=0} - \bar{y}_{50-,t=0}\right), \qquad (5.4)$$

where $\bar{y}$ is the group average outcome, 50+ refers to the group older than 50 years, and 50− are those below or equal to 50 years.

What is then the difference of these presentations? Only the way of thinking: in representation (5.4) the DiD estimate compares the outcomes in time period 1 and subtracts the bias from permanent (time constant) differences between the two groups. In representation (5.3) the average outcome gain for age group 50+ is estimated and a possible bias from a general trend is removed. This works only under the assumption that the trend was the same in the 50− group. But both give the same.

Note again that for (5.2) cohorts are all what you need for estimation. In fact, not even individual data is needed since only group averages are required, as is seen from (5.3) and (5.4). For estimation, the four averages $\bar{y}_{50+,t=1}$, $\bar{y}_{50-,t=1}$, $\bar{y}_{50+,t=0}$ and $\bar{y}_{50-,t=0}$ would be sufficient.

An alternative way of writing (5.2) is to represent the potential non-treatment outcome Y^0 as

$$Y_i^0 = \beta_0 + \beta_1 T_i + \beta_2 G_i + U_i \qquad \text{with} \qquad U_i \perp\!\!\!\perp (G_i, T_i),$$

where $G_i \in \{50-, 50+\}$ is the group indicator and $T_i \in \{0, 1\}$ the time indicator. G_i takes the value one for the older group, and the value zero for the younger group. Treatment status is defined as $D = G \cdot T$. That is, only the older group is treated and only in the later time period. In the earlier time period this group is untreated.

Instead of having a group fixed effect $\beta_2 G_i$ we could consider a model with an individual time-invariant fixed effect C_i.

$$Y_i^0 = \beta_0 + \beta_1 T_i + C_i + U_i \qquad \text{with} \qquad U_i \perp\!\!\!\perp (C_i, T_i),$$

where the C_i could be correlated with G_i. If we are interested in the ATET then we do not need a model for Y^1, because without any assumptions $E[Y^1 - Y^0|D = 1] =$

$E[Y|D = 1] - E[Y^0|D = 1]$. Since $E[Y|D = 1]$ is directly identified we do not need any assumptions on Y^1. We only need a model for Y^0. This discussion also implies that we do not restrict the treatment effects $Y_i^1 - Y_i^0$ themselves, since we impose structure only on Y_i^0.

We always obtain the same estimator for ATET, identified as

$$E\left[Y^1 - Y^0|D = 1\right] = E\left[Y|G = 1, T = 1\right] - E\left[Y|G = 1, T = 0\right]$$
$$- \{E\left[Y|G = 0, T = 1\right] - E\left[Y|G = 0, T = 0\right]\}.$$

This is directly estimated from either differences of independent means or a parameter estimator of a simple linear panel regression.

However, although DiD is a very useful approach, one should not take identification for granted. The assumption of parallel trends across groups may easily be violated.

Example 5.3 Chay, McEwan and Urquiola (2005) consider a policy in Chile where poorly performing schools were given additional financial resources. The DiD estimator compares average school outcomes between treated and control schools before and after the intervention. The school outcomes are measured in the same grade before and after the intervention (i.e. these are therefore different pupils). The treated schools are selected according to the average performance of their pupils on an achievement test. All schools with such a test-based ranking that is below a certain threshold receive a subsidy. Test scores, however, are noisy measures of the true performance; also because different pupils are tested before and after the intervention. Imagine two schools with identical true average performance, which is close to the threshold. Suppose testing takes place in grade 3. One of the schools happens to have a bad test-based ranking in this year (e.g. due to a cohort of unusually weak students, bad weather, disruptions during the test etc.). This school thus falls below the threshold and receives the subsidy. The other school's test-based ranking is above the threshold and no subsidy is awarded. Suppose the true effect of the subsidy is zero. In the next year, another cohort enters grade 3 and is tested. We would expect both schools to have the same test-based ranking (apart from random variations). The DiD estimate, however, would give us a positive treatment effect estimate because the school with the bad shock in the previous year is in the treated group. This result is also often referred to as 'regression to the mean'. The spurious DiD estimate is due to the random noise or measurement error of the test-based ranking. If this is just within the usual variation or test outcomes, then a correctly estimated standard error of our ATET estimate should warn us that this effect is not significant. But if this trend is stronger, then it is hard to see from the data whether it was just a random variation, and the common trend assumption is no longer valid. Since this ranking is based on the average performance of all pupils in grade 3, we expect the variance of this error to be larger in small classes.

In this example, the common-trend assumption might be violated. Also in many other applications, we are at least doubtful about the plausibility of identical trends.

Sometimes we may have several pre-treatment waves of data for treated and control group, which would permit us to examine the trends for both groups before the intervention. We discuss this further below.

5.1.2   Diff-in-Diff, Conditional on Confounders

In the previous subsection we discussed the simple difference-in-differences estimator without further covariates. The required common-trend assumption may often not be satisfied directly. It might, however, be more credible conditional on some covariates: Therefore we now examine a DiD estimator for situations in which the CS or BS assumption is assumed to hold (only) conditional on some observable confounders X. As in Chapter 3 for matching and propensity score weighting, the X covariates are permitted to enter in a non-parametric way. It is common then to speak of *matching-DiD* (MDiD) or *conditional DiD* (CDiD). Conditional on X, the analysis is similar to the above. Recall first that for estimating ATET, matching estimators relied on the selection-on-observables assumption (or CIA)

$$Y_t^0 \perp\!\!\!\perp D|X_t, \tag{5.5}$$

where D denotes treatment group and X represents characteristics that are not affected by treatment. Often one does therefore only consider predetermined X or those that do (or did) not change from $t = 0$ to $t = 1$ such that their time index can be skipped. This corresponds to assuming that, conditional on X_t, the distribution of Y_t^0 does not differ between treated and controls. The MDiD approach now essentially replaces this assumption by

$$\left(Y_1^0 - Y_0^0\right) \perp\!\!\!\perp D|X \tag{5.6}$$

or in its weaker mean independence version:

Assumption 1x For confounders not affected by treatment, i.e. $X^0 = X^d = X$ we have

$$E\left[Y_1^0 - Y_0^0|X, D = 1\right] = E\left[Y_1^0 - Y_0^0|X, D = 0\right], \tag{5.7}$$

where X may comprise information about both time points t. Moreover, we need the common support condition (CSC) in the sense that[1]

$$\Pr(TD = 1|X = x, (T, D) \in \{(t, d), (1, 1)\}) > 0 \quad \forall x \in \mathcal{X}, \forall (t, d) \in \{(0, 0), (1, 0), (0, 1)\}. \tag{5.8}$$

Hence again, we permit differences in levels but assume that the trends (i.e. the change over time) are the same among treated and controls, or simply assumption CT or BS conditional on X. Note that for a visual check we are now asking and looking for a parallel path of the $E[Y^0|X]$ instead of just Y^0 in the control and treatment

---

[1] Note that we can identify with DiD at most the ATET anyway, so that we do not need the symmetric assumptions for Y^1, and just a strictly positive propensity score.

group. This implies that the conditional ATET, say $\alpha(X) = E\left[Y_1^1 - Y_1^0 | X, D = 1\right]$ is identified as

$$\alpha(X) = E\left[Y_1 | X, D = 1\right] - E\left[Y_1 | X, D = 0\right] - \{E\left[Y_0 | X, D = 1\right] - E\left[Y_0 | X, D = 0\right]\}.$$
(5.9)

Integrating X out with respect to the distribution of $X|D = 1$, i.e. among the treated, will provide the

$$ATET = E\left[\alpha(X) | D = 1\right].$$
(5.10)

This approach is based on a similar motivation as the pre-programme test: if the assumption (5.5) is not valid, we would expect also systematic differences in the pre-programme outcomes between treated and controls (unless we have conditioned for X). By having pre-programme outcomes, we could in a sense, test whether the outcomes Y_i^0 are on average identical between treated and controls. If we detect differences, these differences may be useful to predict the magnitude of selection bias in the post-programme outcomes. Estimating this bias and subtracting it leads to the DiD estimator.

If X does not contain all confounding variables, i.e. Assumption (5.5) was not valid, adjusting for X via matching will not yield a consistent estimate of the ATET because

$$E\left[Y_t^1 | D = 1\right] - \int E\left[Y_t^0 | X_t, D = 0\right] dF_{X_t | D = 1}$$

$$\neq E\left[Y_t^1 | D = 1\right] - \int E\left[Y_t^0 | X_t, D = 1\right] \cdot dF_{X_t | D = 1} = E\left[Y_t^1 - Y_t^0 | D = 1\right]$$

since $E[Y_t^0 | X_t, D = 1] \neq E[Y_t^0 | X_t, D = 0]$. The difference

$$\int \left(E[Y_t^0 | X_t, D = 1] - E[Y_t^0 | X_t, D = 0]\right) dF_{X_t | D = 1} =: B_{t,t}$$

is the systematic bias in the potential outcome Y_t^0 in period t that still remains even after adjusting for the different distributions of X. The conditional BS assumption says that pre-programme outcomes permit to estimate this systematic bias, as for a period τ before treatment

$$B_{\tau,t} = \int \left(E[Y_\tau^0 | X_\tau, D = 1] - E[Y_\tau^0 | X_\tau, D = 0]\right) dF_{X_t | D = 1}$$
(5.11)

is equal to $B_{t,t}$.

Example 5.4 Consider the evaluation of training programmes. If the individuals who decided to participate have on average more abilities to increase Y, it is likely that their labour market outcomes would also have been better even without participation in the programme. In this case, the average selection bias $B_{\tau,t}$ would be positive. If the potential outcome in the case of non-participation Y_t^0 is related over time, it is likely that these differences between the treatment groups would also persist in other time periods including periods before the start of the programme. In other words, the more able persons would also had enjoyed better labour market outcomes in periods previous to treatment.

If the pre-programme outcome in period τ (before treatment) is not affected by the programme, i.e. no effects due to anticipation, the 'non-participation' outcomes $Y_\tau^0 = Y_\tau$ are observed for the different treatment groups and the corresponding average selection bias in period τ equals $B_{\tau,t}$ which in turn is identified from the observed pre-programme data. Thus, the ATET is identified as

$$E\left[Y_t^1 - Y_t^0 | D = 1\right] = E\left[Y_t^1 | D = 1\right] - \left(\int E\left[Y_t^0 | X_t, D = 0\right] dF_{X_t | D=1} dx + B_{t,t}\right)$$

$$= E\left[Y_t | D = 1\right] - \left(\int E\left[Y_t | X_t, D = 0\right] dF_{X_t | D=1} dx + B_{\tau,t}\right).$$

It now becomes clear that even the BS assumption is not strictly necessary. It suffices that $B_{t,t}$ can be estimated consistently from the average selection biases in pre-programme periods, called also *predictable-bias assumption*. If several periods with pre-programme outcomes are observed, the average selection bias can be estimated in each period $\hat{B}_{\tau,t}$, $\hat{B}_{\tau-1,t}$, $\hat{B}_{\tau-2,t}$. Any patterns in the estimates $\hat{B}_{\tau,t}$, $\hat{B}_{\tau-1,t}$, $\hat{B}_{\tau-2,t}$ may lead to improved predictions of $B_{t,t}$. A nice example is that their average is expected to mitigate potential biases due to the regression to the mean problem mentioned in Example 5.3.

It is also clear now that the classic CIA requires $B_{t,t} = 0$ whereas for the MDiD we require that $B_{t,t}$ is estimable from pre-programme periods. Note that these assumptions are not nested. For example, when imposing CIA we often include pre-programme outcomes Y_τ as potential confounders in X. However, when using the DiD approach we cannot include the lags of the outcome variable Y since we have to be able to calculate $B_{\tau,t}$, cf. also Section 5.1.3.

The non-parametric estimation of (5.9) and (5.10) is not really a challenge, unless X is of dimension larger than 3 and therefore affected by the curse of dimensionality. We simply replace all conditional expectations in (5.9) by local polynomial estimators for all X_i for which $D_i = 1$, and then average over them to obtain an estimator for the ATET; see (5.10). As discussed in Chapter 3, one could alternatively pre-estimate the propensity scores P_i for all X_i, and condition the expectations in (5.9) on them instead of conditioning on the vector X; see *propensity score matching*. The justification is exactly the same as in Chapter 3. Note that, as we can separate the four conditional expectations and estimate each independently from the other, we again do not need panel data; repeated cross sections, i.e. cohort data would do equally well.

Recall Assumption 1x and define $\psi_1 = \{D - \Pr(D = 1|X)\}\{\Pr(D = 1|X)\Pr(D = 0|X)\}^{-1}$ for $\Pr(D = 1|X) > 0$ (you may set $\psi_1 = 1$ else). Then

$$E\left[\psi_1(Y_1 - Y_0)|X\right] = E\left[\psi_1(Y_1 - Y_0)|X, D = 1\right] \cdot \Pr(D = 1|X) \qquad (5.12)$$

$$+ E\left[\psi_1(Y_1 - Y_0)|X, D = 0\right] \cdot \Pr(D = 0|X)$$

$$= E\left[Y_1 - Y_0|X, D = 1\right] - E\left[Y_1 - Y_0|X, D = 0\right],$$

which is the conditional ATET(X), see (5.9). Moreover,

$$E\left[Y_1^1 - Y_1^0 | D = 1\right] = \int E\left[\psi_1(Y_1 - Y_0)|x\right] f(x|D = 1)dx$$

$$= E\left[\psi_1(Y_1 - Y_0)\frac{\Pr(D = 1|X)}{\Pr(D = 1)}\right]$$

$$= E\left[\frac{Y_1 - Y_0}{\Pr(D = 1)}\frac{D - \Pr(D = 1|X)}{\Pr(D = 0|X)}\right],$$

cf. Exercise 6. Once we have predictors for the propensity score, the ATET can be obtained by weighted averages of outcomes Y before and after treatment. When using cohorts instead of panels, then we need to modify the formulae as follows: Define $\psi_2 = \psi_1 \cdot \{T - \lambda\}\{\lambda(1 - \lambda)\}^{-1}$ with λ being the proportion of observations sampled in the post-treatment period. We then get the conditional ATET $\alpha(X) = E[\psi_2 \cdot Y|X]$, where the expectation is taken over the distribution of the entire sample. Finally, and analogously to above you get the unconditional ATET by $\alpha = E\left[\psi_2 \cdot Y \cdot \Pr(D = 1|X)\Pr^{-1}(D = 1)|D = 1\right].$

5.1.3 Relationship to Linear Panel Models

We extend our discussion regarding the relationship to linear panel data models but now introducing observed confounders X. These may include time-varying as well as time-constant variables. We still consider the case with only two time periods, $t \in \{0, 1\}$. Let

$$Y_{it} = \alpha_t + \beta D_{it} + \gamma_t X_{it} + C_i + U_{it} \tag{5.13}$$

where α_t are time effects and D_{it} is the indicator for treatment which is only for the treatment group and only in time period $t = 1,$[2] C_i is a time constant individual effect and U_{it} some error term.[3] In standard panel data analysis one assumes U_{it} to be uncorrelated not just with D_{it} but also with X_{it}. Recall that the variables X_{it} must not be affected by treatment. By taking first differences we eliminate C_i and obtain

$$\Delta Y_i = \bar{\alpha} + \beta \Delta D_i + \bar{\gamma} X_{i,t=1} + \gamma_0 \Delta X_i + \Delta U_i,$$

where $\bar{\gamma} = \gamma_1 - \gamma_0$ and $\bar{\alpha} = \alpha_1 - \alpha_0$. Since we are only interested in β, by rearranging we can write this as

$$\Delta Y_i = \bar{\alpha} + \beta \Delta D_i + \gamma_1 X_{i,t=1} + \gamma_2 X_{i,t=0} + \Delta U_i.$$

This approach requires that we observe also the covariates X at two time points. In many policy evaluation applications, X_{it} is only observed in a baseline study or constant over time (like e.g. gender) as practitioners worry about potential impacts of treatment on X. In this situation we have no time-varying confounders such that we can write

$$Y_{it} = \alpha_t + \beta D_{it} + \gamma_t X_i + C_i + U_{it},$$

[2] In other words, it corresponds to the interaction term TD of our initial simple panel model.
[3] When working with cohorts you must skip C_i but can still include time-invariant confounders.

where taking first differences gives

$$\Delta Y_i = \bar{\alpha} + \beta \Delta D_{it} + \bar{\gamma} X_i + \Delta U_{it}.$$

Here we control for characteristics that are considered to be related to the dynamics of the outcome variable and D. Hence, although we do not observe the changes in X_i, we admit that the coefficients γ_t may change over time. If the variables X_i are unbalanced between treatment and control group but not included in the model, they may generate differences in ΔY_{it} between treatment and control even if the true treatment effect β is zero, unless one controls for these variables. In other words, we control for differences between treated and control that are due to dynamics in the coefficients.

As a special case of the above discussion consider the situation where we include in X_{it} the lagged outcome $Y_{i,t-1}$, and where we assume that the timing is such that $Y_{i,t=0}$ is included in the X variable. The reason for including $Y_{i,t-1}$ is that it may be an important determinant of D_{it}. For simplicity, assume that there are no other variables in X such that (5.13) becomes

$$Y_{it} = \alpha_t + \beta D_{it} + \gamma_t Y_{i,t-1} + C_i + U_{it}, \tag{5.14}$$

and where $D_{it} = \xi(Y_{i,t-1}, C_i, V_{it})$ is some function of $Y_{i,t-1}$, C_i, and some unobserved heterogeneity V_{it}, see Figure 5.2. Here we have two confounding variables: $Y_{i,t-1}$ and C_i. If we had only one of these variables, we could either use simple DiD or matching. If $Y_{i,t-1}$ did not enter in the above equation, we could use simple DiD. If C_i did not enter in the above equation, we could use a matching estimator. However, with both confounders we can use neither technique. This is illustrated in the following in order to show that matching and unconditional DiD rest on fundamentally different assumptions.

Taking first differences eliminates the C_i

$$Y_{i,1} - Y_{i,0} = \Delta Y_{i,t=1} = \bar{\alpha} + \beta \Delta D_{i,t=1} + \bar{\gamma} Y_{i,t=0} + \gamma_0 \Delta Y_{i,t=0} + \Delta U_{i,t=1}, \tag{5.15}$$

where $\bar{\gamma} = \gamma_1 - \gamma_0$. We could estimate this expression by regressing $\Delta Y_{i,t=1}$ on $D_{i,t=1}$, $Y_{i,t=0}$ and $Y_{i,t=-1}$. The usual concern is that $Y_{i,t=0}$ is correlated with $\Delta U_{i,t=1}$. On first sight one might think that we would not be concerned about this correlation as we are only interested in the coefficient β and do not care about the other coefficients. One might think that if we were to control non-parametrically for $Y_{i,t=0}$ and $Y_{i,t=1}$ we would be able to ignore this endogeneity in the control variables. This requires that

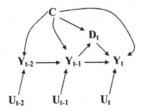

Figure 5.2 Dynamic causality graph for understanding DiD

$$\Delta U_{i,t=1} \perp\!\!\!\perp \Delta D_{i,t=1} | Y_{i,t=0}, Y_{i,t=-1}.$$

But this is in general not true because we do not have

$$U_{i,t=0} \perp\!\!\!\perp D_{i,t=1} | Y_{i,t=0}, Y_{i,t=-1}.$$

As $Y_{i,t=0}$ is a function of C_i and $U_{i,t=0}$ (inverted fork, see Figure 5.2), conditioning on $Y_{i,t=0}$ introduces a dependence.

Hence, in a situation where $Y_{i,t-1}$ and C_i are both confounders, neither unconditional DiD nor matching can be applied. Therefore, one turns to some kind of Arellano–Bond dynamic panel data approach, using $Y_{i,t=-2}$ as excluded instrument. This is certainly only valid if $U_{t-2} \perp\!\!\!\perp U_{t-1}$ (no persistent shocks, no auto-correlation).

Certainly, if we can eliminate $\gamma_t Y_{i,t-1}$ in (5.14), i.e. assuming that all relevant unobserved heterogeneity is time constant, then we obtain

$$\Delta Y_{i,t=1} = \bar{\alpha} + \beta \Delta D_{i,t=1} + \Delta U_{i,t=1},$$

which gives the DiD estimator (at least, if we have two time periods). Extending the previous discussion to incorporate (additional) exogenous X is straightforward. Alternatively, if we can assume $Y_t^d \perp\!\!\!\perp D_t | Y_{t-1}$, then matching or propensity weighting will work.

5.2 Multiple Groups and Multiple Time Periods

In several applications we may have several groups and/or several time periods. Suppose different states of a country are affected by a policy change at different time periods. We may have panel data on these states for several years. The policy change occurs at the state level, yet for reasons of estimation precision we may sometimes also want to add individual characteristics to the regression. We need to acknowledge that entire groups of individuals are affected simultaneously by the policy change: for example all individuals aged 50 years or older in a certain state. Hence, the treatment indicator does not vary at the individual but rather at the group level. In the following, let g index different groups (e.g. 50+, 50− in regions A and B). The model for the mean outcome $\bar{Y}_{gt}$ can be written as

$$\bar{Y}_{gt} = \delta_{gt} + D_{gt}\beta + V_{gt}$$

where δ_{gt} is a set of group by time period constants and D_{gt} is one if (already) treated, and zero otherwise. As we just consider group averages, the model is completely general so far. Without further restrictions it is not identified, though.

Possible identifying restrictions in this case are to assume

$$\bar{Y}_{gt} = \alpha_g + \lambda_t + D_{gt}\beta + V_{gt}$$

together with uncorrelatedness of D_{gt} and V_{gt}. With this restriction, the model is identified as long as we have more than four observations and at least two time periods and two groups. One can use panel data analysis with the appropriate asymptotic inference depending on whether groups or time go to infinity.

While the previous discussion only requires observation of the group level averages $\bar{Y}_{gt}$, this changes when including covariates – no matter whether this is done for efficiency reasons or for making the Common Trend assumption more plausible. Clearly, if the observed characteristics X changed over time, this assumption is less plausible. We would thus like to take changes in X into account and assume only that the differences due to unobservables are constant over time. In a linear model one could simply include the group by time averages $\bar{X}_{gt}$ in the model

$$\bar{Y}_{gt} = \alpha_g + \lambda_t + D_{gt}\beta + \bar{X}'_{gt}\gamma + V_{gt}.$$

To gain efficiency one could additionally include individual characteristics Z_i:

$$Y_{igt} = \left\{ \alpha_g + \lambda_t + D_{gt}\beta + \bar{X}'_{gt}\gamma + V_{gt} \right\} + Z'_{igt}\delta_{gt} + U_{igt}. \tag{5.16}$$

This is an example of a multilevel model, where the regressors and error terms are measured at different aggregation levels. Simply calculating standard errors by the conventional formula for i.i.d. errors and thereby ignoring the group structure in the error term $V_{gt} + U_{igt}$ usually leads to bad standard error estimates and wrong t-values. Therefore one might want to combine treatment effect estimation with methods from *small area statistics*. For calculating the standards errors one would like to permit serial correlation and within-group correlation, while assuming that the errors are independent across groups or modelling the dependency.

How to do inference now? Consider Equation 5.16 and ignore any covariates X and Z. The error term has the structure $V_{gt} + U_{igt}$. Suppose that U_{igt} and V_{gt} are both mean-zero i.i.d. and neither correlated between groups nor over time. Consider the case with two groups and two time periods. The DiD estimator of β is then

$$\hat{\beta} = \left(\bar{Y}_{11} - \bar{Y}_{10}\right) - \left(\bar{Y}_{01} - \bar{Y}_{00}\right).$$

With a large number of individuals in each group, the group-time averages $\bar{Y}_{gt}$ will converge to $\alpha_g + \lambda_t + D_{gt}\beta + V_{gt}$ by the law of large numbers. The DiD estimator will thus asymptotically have mean

$$E[\hat{\beta}] = \beta + V_{11} - V_{10} - V_{01} + V_{00},$$

and is therefore inconsistent. Unbiasedness would require $V_{11} - V_{10} - V_{01} + V_{00} = 0$, which is assumed by the simple DiD estimator. But we cannot conduct inference since we cannot estimate σ_v^2 which in turn is not going to zero. If we assumed that there were only individual errors U_{igt} and no group errors V_{gt} (or, in other words, that the group error V_{gt} is simply the average of the individual errors) then the estimates would usually be consistent. If we further assume that U_{igt} is neither correlated over time nor between individuals, we obtain that

$$\sqrt{n}(\hat{\beta} - \beta) \xrightarrow{d} N(0, Var),$$

$$Var = \frac{\sigma_{U_{11}}^2}{\Pr(G=1,T=1)} + \frac{\sigma_{U_{10}}^2}{\Pr(G=1,T=0)} + \frac{\sigma_{U_{01}}^2}{\Pr(G=0,T=1)} + \frac{\sigma_{U_{00}}^2}{\Pr(G=0,T=0)},$$

where the variances $\sigma_{U_{gt}}^2 = Var(U_{igt})$ are estimable from the data.

With multiple groups and time periods we can consider other approaches, e.g. considering the number of groups G and time periods T to go to infinity, when the sample size increases (Hansen 2007a and Hansen 2007b). The analysis is then akin to conventional linear panel data analysis with grouped and individual errors and one could also permit a richer serial correlation structure. The relevance of this is for example documented in the Monte Carlo study of Bertrand, Duflo and Mullainathan (2004), who found that simple DiD estimation inference can exhibit severely bias standard errors, for example when regions are affected by time persistent shocks, (i.e. auto-correlated errors) that may look like programme effects. This is also discussed in the next sections.

So unless we do not impose some more assumptions and restrictions, it seems that the inclusion of several time periods is a bane rather than a boon; that including several time periods before and after the treatment may be problematic (without further assumptions) becomes already clear when only reconsidering the idiosyncratic shocks U_{igt} – although we could equally well find similar arguments when looking at the group shocks V_{gt}. For $d = g \in \{0, 1\}$ and neglecting potential confounders X (or Z) one has that

$$E[\hat{\alpha}_{DiD}] = \alpha_{ATET} + E[U_{ig1} - U_{ig0}|g = 1] - E[U_{ig1} - U_{ig0}|g = 0].$$

A low U among the treated in the past period may often be the cause which triggered a policy change. I.e. bad shocks may have prompted the policy change. Unless these bad shocks are extremely persistent, the DiD estimator would overestimate the ATET because we expect $E[U_{ig1} - U_{ig0}|g = 1] > E[U_{ig1} - U_{ig0}|g = 0]$. This is the so-called *Ashenfelter's dip* yielding a positive bias for the DiD estimators for ATET:

Example 5.5 Suppose a training programme is being evaluated. An enrolment to this programme is much more likely for individuals that experienced a temporary dip in earnings just before the programme takes place. The same is true for individuals who experienced a fairly long stagnancy in their salaries. These are exactly the people with quite negative U_{ig0} but more likely to participate.

The idea is that among the treated those individuals are over-represented that have $U_{ig0} < 0$ and analogously individuals with $U_{ig0} > 0$ are over-represented in the control group. This is not a problem if this is also true for U_{ig1} (i.e. if shocks are persistent). However, the *regression-to-the-mean* effect says that generally all have the tendency to converge to the (regression) mean so that for individuals with negative residuals we expect a different trend than for individuals with positive residuals. In other words, the idea of a *regression-to-the-mean* effect combined with the Ashenfelter dip contradicts the Common Trend assumption.[4] Having said this, two obvious solutions are thinkable. Either we include and average over several periods before and after the treatment so that this 'dip' is smoothed out, or we have to correct for different trends in the control compared to the treatment group. The former, simpler solution, can be

---

[4] It is important that only this combination causes a problem: neither the Ashenfelter dip nor the regression to the mean principle alone can cause a problem.

carried out by considering longer panels, the latter can be handled by the so-called *difference-in-differences-in-differences* estimator which we consider next.

5.2.1　Triple Differences and Higher Differences

As mentioned, the CT assumption which basically means that the trends are parallel, is questionable in many situations. There are several approaches to relax this assumption. One is to include (time-varying) covariates, another one is to include several time periods, both discussed in the sections above. Alternatively – or in addition – we may include several control groups. In this direction goes the *difference-in-differences-in-differences* (DiDiD) approach estimator. Take our age-group example from above right at the beginning of Section 5.2; you might be concerned that the assumption of a common time trend (our parallel trends in the absence of treatment) between the 50+ and the 50− group could be too strong. Particularly, if the periods $t = 0$ and $t = 1$ are in fact some time apart (e.g. 10 years), different trends could have affected these groups. In other words, the composition of the unobserved characteristics could have changed over time. This may be due to changes in their characteristics or due to changes in the effects of these characteristics on Y. We might then be able to remove the bias due to such non-identical trends if we had another control group that was not affected by the policy change.

Imagine that only the 50+ group living in certain regions, called A, were affected by the policy, whereas individuals in neighbouring regions, called B, were not affected.[5] If provided with those data, for people living in region B one could calculate

$$\left(\bar{y}_{B,50+,t=1} - \bar{y}_{B,50-,t=1}\right) - \left(\bar{y}_{B,50+,t=0} - \bar{y}_{B,50-,t=0}\right).$$

Because no policy change happened in region B, this expression should be zero if time trends were identical, i.e. if the unobserved differences between 50+ and 50− remained identical over time. If not, we could take this as an estimate of the bias due changing time trends. This recommends an ATET estimate of the form

$$\left(\bar{y}_{A,50+,t=1} - \bar{y}_{A,50-,t=1}\right) - \left(\bar{y}_{A,50+,t=0} - \bar{y}_{A,50-,t=0}\right)$$
$$- \left\{\left(\bar{y}_{B,50+,t=1} - \bar{y}_{B,50-,t=1}\right) - \left(\bar{y}_{B,50+,t=0} - \bar{y}_{B,50-,t=0}\right)\right\}$$

called DiDiD, or equivalently

$$\Delta\bar{y}_{A,50+} - \Delta\bar{y}_{A,50-} - \Delta\bar{y}_{B,50+} + \Delta\bar{y}_{B,50-}, \tag{5.17}$$

where Δ refers to the difference over time.

Note that this DiDiD is numerically equivalent to the coefficient γ on the triple interaction term $\mathbb{1}_{age\ 50+} \cdot \mathbb{1}_{time=1} \cdot \mathbb{1}_A$ in model

$$Y = \beta_0 + \beta_1 \cdot \mathbb{1}_{age\ 50+} + \beta_2 \cdot \mathbb{1}_{time=1} + \beta_3 \cdot \mathbb{1}_A$$
$$+ \beta_4 \cdot \mathbb{1}_{age\ 50+} \cdot \mathbb{1}_{time=1} + \beta_5 \cdot \mathbb{1}_{age\ 50+} \cdot \mathbb{1}_A$$
$$+ \beta_6 \cdot \mathbb{1}_{time=1} \cdot \mathbb{1}_A + \gamma \cdot \mathbb{1}_{age\ 50+} \cdot \mathbb{1}_{time=1} \cdot \mathbb{1}_A + U.$$

---

[5] See Lalive (2008) for details from which is taken this example.

In order to prove that the population equivalent, i.e. the expected value of (5.17), is identical to γ, rewrite the above regression equation in order to express the expected value of $\bar{y}_{A,50+,t=1}$ as $\beta_0 + \beta_1 + \beta_2 + \beta_3 + \beta_4 + \beta_5 + \beta_6 + \gamma$. With analogous calculations for the other groups, and plugging these expressions into (5.17), one obtains that the expected value corresponds indeed to γ.

A similar idea can be used when three time periods, say $t = -1, 0, 1$ are available of which two are measured before the policy change. If the assumption of identical time trends for both groups were valid, the following expression should have mean zero:

$$\left(\bar{y}_{50+,t=0} - \bar{y}_{50-,t=0} \right) - \left(\bar{y}_{50+,t=-1} - \bar{y}_{50-,t=-1} \right).$$

If not, we could use this expression to measure the difference in the time trend before the treatment. Hence, the slope of the time trend is permitted to differ between the 50+ and the 50− group (as before treatment). If we assume that the change of the slope, i.e. the second difference or acceleration, is the same in both groups, then we could predict the counterfactual average outcome for $\bar{y}_{50+,t=1}$ in the absence of a policy change. The DiDiD estimate is

$$
\begin{aligned}
&\left(\bar{y}_{50+,t=1} - \bar{y}_{50-,t=1} \right) - \left(\bar{y}_{50+,t=0} - \bar{y}_{50-,t=0} \right) \\
&\quad - \left\{ \left(\bar{y}_{50+,t=0} - \bar{y}_{50-,t=0} \right) - \left(\bar{y}_{50+,t=-1} - \bar{y}_{50-,t=-1} \right) \right\} \\
&= \left(\bar{y}_{50+,t=1} - \bar{y}_{50+,t=0} \right) - \left(\bar{y}_{50+,t=0} - \bar{y}_{50+,t=-1} \right) \\
&\quad - \left\{ \left(\bar{y}_{50-,t=1} - \bar{y}_{50-,t=0} \right) - \left(\bar{y}_{50-,t=0} - \bar{y}_{50-,t=-1} \right) \right\} \\
&= \Delta\Delta \bar{y}_{50+,t=1} - \Delta\Delta \bar{y}_{50-,t=1}.
\end{aligned}
$$

Generally, with more than two time periods, we can use second differences to eliminate not only 'individual fixed effects' but also 'individual time trends'. This concept can certainly be extended to higher order differences; see Mora and Reggio (2012).

The basic idea in all these situations is that we have only one treated group in one time period, and several[6] non-treated groups in earlier time periods. We thus use all the non-treated observations to predict the counterfactual outcome for that time period in which the treated group was affected by the policy change. For predicting the counterfactual outcome we could also use more elaborate modelling approaches.

The DiDiD goes one step further than (5.7) by permitting differences in levels and trends, but requires that the acceleration (second difference) is the same for treated and controls. Sometimes one speaks also of *parallel path* instead of *common trend* (CT), and of *parallel growth* instead of *common acceleration*. More specifically, let $\Delta Y_t^0 = Y_t^0 - Y_\tau^0$ be the first difference and $\Delta\Delta Y_t^0 = \Delta Y_t^0 - \Delta Y_\tau^0$ be the second difference. Both DiDiD extensions can be further developed to the case where we additionally condition on potential confounders X to make the underlying assumptions more credible. Then the CIA for the DiD approach requires that

$$\Delta Y_t^0 \perp\!\!\!\perp D | X \tag{5.18}$$

---

[6] This makes it different from the matching approach of Chapter 3.

while DiDiD requires that

$$\Delta\Delta Y_t^0 \perp\!\!\!\perp D|X. \qquad (5.19)$$

The so-called *pre-programme* tests in the DiD approach test whether there are differences in levels between treated and controls. The pre-programme test in the DiDiD approach tests whether there are differences in trends between treated and controls. If one has several periods after treatment, one could test for parallel paths or parallel growth after the treatment. However, without having comparable information about the periods before treatment, the correct interpretation remains unclear. Recall finally that, as long as we only work with averages or conditional averages, we do not need to be provided with panel data; cohorts would do as well.

5.3   The Changes-in-Changes Concept

In the previous sections we introduced the DiD idea and studied different scenarios of alternative assumptions and resulting modifications of our ATET estimator. However, we have not studied so far the problem that the Assumptions (5.18) and (5.19) are not scale-invariant. In fact, the parallel path or growth assumptions are by nature intrinsically related to the scale of Y; if, for example, the Y^0 in group $D = 1$ follow a parallel path to Y^0 in group $D = 0$, than for the $log Y^0$ this can no longer be the case, and vice versa. While this is often presented as a major disadvantage, as a scale-invariant assumption can hardly be justified only based on economic theory. On the other hand, it could also be considered as an advantage if you have observations from at least two periods before treatment started. Because in this case you just have to find the scale on which the necessary assumptions apply. After such a prior study that finds the transformation of Y for which either the assumptions required for DiD or those required for DiDiD hold, you can apply the respective method. All what you need are data of several pre-treatment periods.

A quite different approach would be to get rid of the scale by no longer focusing directly on the mean but the cumulative distribution function of Y. The simple reason is that this is scale invariant. It has also the advantage that we can reveal the impact of D on the entire distribution of Y. This is certainly much more informative than just looking at the mean; it actually can still be useful when the treatment effect is quite heterogeneous. For that reason we also dedicate an entire chapter (Chapter 8) on quantile treatment effect estimation.

This particular extension of the DiD approach is known as *changes-in-changes* (CiC). As stated, it does not just allow for treatment effect heterogeneity but even explores it by looking at the identification and estimation of distributional effects. The effects of time and of treatment are permitted to differ systematically across individuals. In order to simplify we still discuss only the situation with two groups $g \in \{0, 1\}$ and two time periods $t \in \{0, 1\}$. The group 1 is subject to the policy change in the second time period. For this, the outcome $Y_{G=1,T=1}^1$ is observed, but the counterfactual outcome $Y_{G=1,T=1}^0$ is not. The focus is on estimation of (a kind of) ATET. As in DiD, to estimate the counterfactual outcome Y^0 in case of non-treatment we can use the information from the other three group-by-time combinations. We use the fact that Y^0 is observed for the groups $(G = 1, T = 0)$, $(G = 0, T = 0)$ and $(G = 0, T = 1)$. As we look at the entire distributions of Y^0 and Y^1, we need to express their quantiles or their c.d.f. in terms of observed outcomes. We can estimate quantiles and c.d.f. for Y^0 for the groups $(G = 1, T = 0)$, $(G = 0, T = 0)$, $(G = 0, T = 1)$, and the ones of Y^1 for group $(G = 1, T = 1)$ directly from the observations inside each group. What we cannot estimate directly are the counterfactual distributions $F_{Y^0|11}$ to be compared with $F_{Y^1|11}$ when interested in the treatment effect for the treated, or the counterfactual c.d.f. $F_{Y^1|01}$ of $F_{Y^0|01}$ for the non-treated. In the following we concentrate on the identification and estimation of $F_{Y^0|11}$; the one for $F_{Y^1|01}$ works analogously. In other words, for CiC we cannot only derive identification and estimation of ATET but also of ATENT and ATE.

We consider first the case without covariates. It will not be hard to see, however, that one can incorporate covariates X simply by conditioning on them in all of the following derivations. Unconditional treatment effects for the treated can then be obtained by integrating out the X. Note that like before in the DiD case, we do not require individual panel data, repeated cross-sections in the treatment and the control group are sufficient.

5.3.1   Changes-in-Changes with Continuous Outcome Y

Each individual i is characterised by the variables U_i and G_i, where U_i is some unobserved characteristic and G_i is the group that individual i belongs to (i.e. treatment or control groups). Both $(U$ and $G)$ are considered as random variables that are permitted to be dependent, i.e. the policy change could have happened in regions where U was particularly low or high. It will thus also be permitted that the treatment group adopted the policy because they expected greater benefits than for the control group. We start with some basic assumptions.

Assumption CiC 1 $Y_i^0 = \varphi(U_i, T_i)$ and φ is strictly increasing in its first argument.

This assumption requires that the non-treatment outcome Y_i^0 is only a function of U and time but not of the group G. Hence, while G and U are permitted to be correlated, G does not affect Y_i^0. This assumption requires the function φ to not depend on G. Strict monotonicity in U permits us to invert the function φ to map from the observed outcomes Y_i^0 to the unobserved U_i. Since U is usually continuously distributed, also the outcomes Y must be so. For Y discrete, only set identification is obtained – or stronger assumptions are needed.

Assumption CiC 2 $U \perp\!\!\!\perp T | G$

This assumption requires that, within each group, the distribution of U is the same over time. Hence, while specific individuals are permitted to have different values of U in time period 0 and 1, the distribution of U in the entire group remains unchanged.

These first two assumptions together imply that all differences in Y^0 between group 1 and group 0 in the same time period are only due to differences in U. Any differences over time are only because the function $\varphi(u, t)$ changes with t, and not due to changes in the distribution of U.

Assumption CiC 3 $Supp(U|G = 1) \subseteq Supp(U|G = 0)$

This is a common support assumption on U. For every value of U in the $G = 1$ population, we need to infer the counterfactual outcome in the $t = 1$ period, which can only be achieved from the $G = 0$ population.

Groups and time periods are treated asymmetrically. The important assumptions are thus: First, within each time period, the production function (for the non-treatment outcome) $\varphi(U, t)$ is the same in both groups. Second, the defining feature of a group is that the distribution of U does not change over time (although for each individual it is permitted to change). Note, however, that we can reverse the roles of G and T, which leads to a different model with different assumptions and different estimates. More specifically, in the *reversed CiC* model, the assumption is that the production function φ does not change over time, but is permitted to be different between groups. In contrast, the distribution of U has to be the same in both groups, but is permitted to change over time.

Example 5.6 Consider as groups G the cohort of 60-year-old males and females. We may be willing to assume that the distribution of U is the same for males and females. But even when conditioning on all kind of observables, we may still want to allow the outcome φ_G to be different for different gender. As age is fixed to 60, we have different cohorts over time, and thus the distribution of U should be allowed to change over time, whereas the φ_G functions should not. One may think here of a medical intervention; the health production function(s) φ_G for Y^0 (i.e. without treatment) may depend on U and also on group membership (i.e. gender), but it does not change over time.

Hence, the model applies when either T or G does not enter in the production function $\varphi(U, T, G)$ and the distribution of U (i.e. the quantiles) remains the same in the other dimension (i.e. in the one which enters in φ). Whichever of these two potential model assumptions is more appropriate depends on the particular empirical application. The estimates can be different. However, since the model does not contain any overidentifying restrictions, neither of these two models can be tested for validity. Note that we have placed no restrictions on Y_i^1. This implies that we permit arbitrary treatment effect heterogeneity $Y_i^1 - Y_i^0$, thereby also permitting (as indicated above) that individuals were partly selected into treatment on the basis of their individual gain.

We first sketch an intuitive outline of the identification for the counterfactual distribution. As stated, the basic idea is that in time period $T = 0$, the production function φ is the same in both groups G. Different outcome distributions of Y in the $G = 0$ and $G = 1$ groups can be attributed to different distributions of U in the two groups. Therefore, while, from time period 0 to 1 the production function changes, the distribution of U remains the same. This means that someone at quantile q of U will remain at quantile q in time period 1. The inverse distribution function (i.e. quantile function) will frequently be used and is defined for a random variable Y as

$$F_Y^{-1}(q) = \inf\{y : F_Y(y) \geq q, \quad y \in Supp(Y)\}.$$

This implies that $F_Y(F_Y^{-1}(q)) \geq q$. This relation holds with equality if Y is continuous or, when Y is discrete, at discontinuity points of $F_Y^{-1}(q)$. Similarly, $F_Y^{-1}(F_Y(y)) \leq y$. This relation holds with equality at all $y \in Supp(Y)$ for continuous or discrete Y but not necessarily if Y is mixed.

Consider an individual i in the $G = 1$ group, and suppose we knew the value of U_i. We use the notation of 'individual' only for convenience. In fact, only the quantile in the U distribution is important. So whenever it is referred to an individual, we actually refer to any individual at a particular quantile of U. One would like to know $\varphi(U_i, 1)$ for which only the group $G = 0$ and $T = 1$ is informative, because the $G = 1, T = 1$ group is observed only in the treatment state, and because the $G = 0, T = 0$ or $G = 1, T = 0$ group is only informative for $\varphi(U_i, 0)$. We do not observe U_i in the $G = 0$ group, but by assuming monotonicity we can relate quantiles of Y to quantiles of U.

We start from an individual of the $(G = 1, T = 0)$ group with a particular value U_i. We map this individual first into the $G = 0, T = 0$ group and relate it then to the $G = 0, T = 1$ group. Define $F_{U|gt} = F_{U|G=g,T=t}$ and note that $F_{U|gt} = F_{U|g}$ by Assumption CiC.2. Suppose the value U_i corresponds to the quantile q in the $(G = 1, T = 0)$ group

$$F_{U|10}(U_i) = q.$$

We observe the outcomes Y^0 in the non-treatment state for both groups in the 0 period. In the $G = 0, T = 0$ group, the value of U_i is associated with a different quantile q', i.e.

$$F_{U|00}(U_i) = q'$$

or in other words, the individual with U_i is at rank q' in the $G = 0, T = 0$ group such that

$$q' = F_{U|00}(F_{U|10}^{-1}(q)). \tag{5.20}$$

More precisely, the observation at rank q in the $G = 1, T = 0$ group has the same value of U as the observation at rank q' in the $G = 0, T = 0$ group.

Because the function $\varphi(U_i, t)$ is strictly increasing in its first element (Assumption CiC 1), the rank transformation is the same with respect to U or with respect to Y, and from (5.20) follows

$$q' = F_{Y|00}(F_{Y|10}^{-1}(q)). \tag{5.21}$$

Now use Assumption CiC 2 which implies that the quantile q' in the $G = 0$ group is the same in $T = 0$ as in $T = 1$. Then the outcome for rank q' in the U distribution in $T = 1$ is

$$F_{Y|01}^{-1}(q').$$

Because the function φ depends only on U and T but not on G (Assumption CiC 1) this implies that this is the counterfactual outcome for an individual with U_i of group 1 in time period $T = 1$. In addition, by Assumption CiC 2 this individual would also be at rank q in time period 1. More formally, the counterfactual outcome $F_{Y^0|11}^{-1}(q)$ for an individual with U_i that corresponds to rank q in the $G = 1$ and $T = 0$ population is

$$F_{Y^0|11}^{-1}(q) = F_{Y|01}^{-1}(q') = F_{Y|01}^{-1}(F_{Y|00}(F_{Y|10}^{-1}(q))). \tag{5.22}$$

The following graph illustrates the logic of this derivation:

$$
\begin{array}{cc}
(G = 1, T = 1) & (G = 0, T = 1) \\
\uparrow & \uparrow \\
(G = 1, T = 0) \quad\longrightarrow\quad & (G = 0, T = 0) \\
rank\ q & rank\ q'
\end{array}
$$

We consider an individual in the $G = 1, T = 0$ group at rank q. The qth quantile of Y^1 in the $G = 1, T = 1$ population is the observed outcome after treatment. The counterfactual outcome Y^0 is obtained by first mapping the rank q into the rank q' in the $G = 0, T = 0$ population, and then taking the q' quantile of Y in the $G = 0, T = 1$ population.

Hence, using (5.22), the quantile-TE on the treated for quantile q is

$$
QTET_q = \alpha_q^{CiC} := F_{Y|11}^{-1}(q) - F_{Y|01}^{-1}(F_{Y|00}(F_{Y|10}^{-1}(q))). \tag{5.23}
$$

Inverting the quantile function (5.22) we obtain the counterfactual distribution function

$$
F_{Y^0|11}(y) = F_{Y|10}\left\{ F_{Y|00}^{-1}\left(F_{Y|01}(y) \right) \right\}. \tag{5.24}
$$

From the above derivations it is obvious that for every value of $U \in Supp(U|G = 1)$ we need to have also observations with U in the $G = 0$ group, which is made precise in Assumption CiC 3.

A formal derivation can be obtained as follows. One first shows that

$$
F_{Y^0|gt}(y) = \Pr\left(\varphi(U, t) \le y | G = g, T = t \right) = \Pr\left(U \le \varphi^{-1}(y, t) | G = g, T = t \right)
$$

$$
= \Pr\left(U \le \varphi^{-1}(y, t) | G = g \right) = F_{U|g}\left(\varphi^{-1}(y, t) \right).
$$

This implies $F_{Y|00}(y) = F_{U|0}\left(\varphi^{-1}(y, 0) \right)$, and replacing y by $\varphi(u, 0)$ we obtain $F_{Y|00}\left(\varphi(u, 0) \right) = F_{U|0}(u)$ from which follows, provided $u \in Supp(U|G = 0)$,

$$
\varphi(u, 0) = F_{Y|00}^{-1}\left(F_{U|0}(u) \right). \tag{5.25}
$$

With similar derivations for $G = 0$ and $T = 1$ one obtains

$$
F_{Y|01}(y) = F_{U|0}\left(\varphi^{-1}(y, 1) \right) \implies F_{U|0}^{-1}\left(F_{Y|01}(y) \right) = \varphi^{-1}(y, 1). \tag{5.26}
$$

Now starting from (5.25), substituting $u = \varphi^{-1}(y, 1)$ and entering (5.26) gives

$$
\varphi\left(\varphi^{-1}(y, 1), 0 \right) = F_{Y|00}^{-1}\left(F_{Y|01}(y) \right). \tag{5.27}
$$

Further,

$$
F_{Y|10}(y) = F_{U|1}\left(\varphi^{-1}(y, 0) \right) \implies F_{Y|10}(\varphi\left(\varphi^{-1}(y, 1), 0 \right)) = F_{U|1}\left(\varphi^{-1}(y, 1) \right), \tag{5.28}
$$

where we substituted y with $\varphi\left(\varphi^{-1}(y, 1), 0 \right)$. By entering (5.28) and plugging in (5.27) gives

$$
F_{Y^0|11}(y) = F_{U|1}\left(\varphi^{-1}(y, 1) \right) = F_{Y|10}\left\{ \varphi\left(\varphi^{-1}(y, 1), 0 \right) \right\} = F_{Y|10}(F_{Y|00}^{-1}(F_{Y|01}(y))),
$$

which is identical to (5.24).

This can be used to identify the ATET. Consider an individual i from the $G = 1$ population with outcome $Y_{i,t=0}$ in the first period and $Y_{i,t=1}$ after the treatment. As derived in (5.21) the rank of this individual in the $G = 0$ population is

$$q' = F_{Y|00}(Y_{t=0})$$

and the corresponding Y^0 outcome in the period $T = 1$ is thus

$$F_{Y|01}^{-1}(F_{Y|00}(Y_{t=0})),$$

which is thus the counterfactual outcome for this individual. By conditioning only on population $G = 1$ we obtain the ATET (making again use of Assumption CiC 2)

$$ATET = E\,[Y|G = 1, T = 1] - E\left[F_{Y|01}^{-1}(F_{Y|00}(Y))\,|G = 1, T = 0\right].$$

In order to estimate $ATET$ let us assume that

(i) Conditional on $T_i = t$ and $G_i = g$, Y_i is a random draw from the subpopulation with $G_i = g$ in period t with $i = 1, \ldots, n$.
(ii) For all $t, g \in \{0, 1\}$, $p_{gt} = \Pr(T_i = t, G_i = g) > 0$.
(iii) The random variables Y_{gt} are continuous with densities $f_{Y|gt}$ that are continuously differentiable, bounded from above by $\bar{f}_{gt}$, and from below by $\underline{f}_{gt} > 0$ with support $\mathcal{Y}_{gt} = [\underline{y}_{gt}, \bar{y}_{gt}]$.
(iv) We have $[\underline{y}_{10}, \bar{y}_{10}] \subseteq [\underline{y}_{00}, \bar{y}_{00}]$.

We use now the shortcut notation $ATET = E[Y_{11}^1] - E[Y_{11}^0]$ and $\alpha^{CiC} = E[Y_{11}] - E[F_{Y|01}^{-1}(F_{Y|00}(Y_{10}))]$, which are identical if the identification assumptions hold. One may estimate the distribution functions F and their inverse simply by the use of the empirical counterparts

$$\hat{F}_{Y|gt}(y) = \frac{1}{n_{gt}} \sum_{i=1}^{n_{gt}} \mathbb{1}\{Y_{gt,i} \leq y\} \qquad (5.29)$$

$$\hat{F}_{Y|gt}^{-1}(q) = \inf\{y \in \mathcal{Y}_{gt} : \hat{F}_{Y|gt}(y) \geq q\} \qquad (5.30)$$

so that $\hat{F}_{Y|gt}^{-1}(0) = \underline{y}_{gt}$. With these one can obtain

$$\alpha^{CiC} = \frac{1}{n_{11}} \sum_{i=1}^{n_{11}} Y_{11,i} - \frac{1}{n_{10}} \sum_{i=1}^{n_{10}} \hat{F}_{Y|01}^{-1}\left(\hat{F}_{Y|00}(Y_{10,i})\right). \qquad (5.31)$$

In order to derive the statistical (asymptotic) behaviour it is useful to define

$$P(y, z) = \left[f_{Y|01}(F_{Y|01}^{-1}(F_{Y|00}(z)))\right]^{-1} \left(\mathbb{1}\{y \leq z\} - F_{Y|00}(z)\right), \quad p(y) = E\left[P(y, Y_{10})\right]$$

$$Q(y, z) = -\left[f_{Y|01}\{F_{Y|01}^{-1}(F_{Y|00}(z))\}\right]^{-1} \left(\mathbb{1}\{F_{Y|01}(y) \leq F_{Y|00}(z)\} - F_{Y|00}(z)\right)$$

$$r(y) = F_{Y|01}^{-1}\left(F_{Y|00}(y)\right) - E\left[F_{Y|01}^{-1}\{F_{Y|00}(Y_{10})\}\right], \quad q(y) = E[Q(y, Y_{10})],$$

$$s(y) = y - E[Y_{11}]$$

with variances $V_p = E[p(Y_{00})^2]$, $V_q = E[q(Y_{01})^2]$, $V_s = E[s(Y_{11})^2]$ and $V_r = E[r(Y_{10})^2]$.

THEOREM 5.1 *Under the above assumptions one has*

$$\hat{\alpha}^{CiC} - \alpha^{CiC} = O_p(n^{1/2})$$
$$\sqrt{n}(\hat{\alpha}^{CiC} - \alpha^{CiC}) \to N(0, V_p/p_{00} + V_q/p_{01} + V_r/p_{10} + V_s/p_{11}).$$

The idea is to linearise the estimator and decompose it into α^{CiC} and some mean-zero terms

$$\frac{1}{n_{00}}\sum_{i=n}^{n_{00}} p(Y_{00,i}) + \frac{1}{n_{01}}\sum_{i=n}^{n_{01}} q(Y_{01,i}) + \frac{1}{n_{10}}\sum_{i=n}^{n_{10}} r(Y_{10,i}) + \frac{1}{n_{11}}\sum_{i=n}^{n_{11}} s(Y_{11,i}) + o_p(n^{-1/2}).$$

Note that the variance of the CiC estimator either neither generally larger than the variance of the standard DiD estimator, nor it is generally smaller, it might even be equal. To estimate the asymptotic variance of $\hat{\alpha}^{CiC}$ one has to replace expectations with sample averages, using empirical distribution functions and their inverses, and using any uniformly consistent non-parametric estimator for the density functions to obtain estimates of $P(y,z)$, $Q(y,z)$, $r(y)$, $s(y)$, $p(y)$ and $q(y)$. Finally, one has to calculate

$$\hat{V}_p = \frac{1}{n_{00}}\sum_{i=1}^{n_{00}} \hat{p}(Y_{00,i})^2, \quad \hat{V}_q = \frac{1}{n_{01}}\sum_{i=1}^{n_{01}} \hat{q}(Y_{01,i})^2,$$

$$\hat{V}_r = \frac{1}{n_{10}}\sum_{i=1}^{n_{10}} \hat{r}(Y_{10,i})^2, \quad \hat{V}_s = \frac{1}{n_{11}}\sum_{i=1}^{n_{11}} \hat{s}(Y_{11,i})^2, \tag{5.32}$$

and estimate the p_{gt} by $\sum_{i=1} \mathbb{1}\{G_i = g, T_i = t\}/n$. It can be shown that combining these estimators gives a consistent one for the variance of $\hat{\alpha}^{CiC}$.

Fortunately, in order to estimate the treatment effect α_q^{CiC} for a given quantile q of the distribution of Y, see (5.23), we can use almost the same notation and method: replace in (5.23) all distribution functions by its empirical counterpart and define

$$p_q(y) = P(y, F_{Y|10}^{-1}(q)), \quad q_q(y) = Q(y, F_{Y|10}^{-1}(q))$$

$$r_q(y) = -\frac{f_{Y|00(F_{Y|10}^{-1}(q))}}{f_{Y|01}(F_{Y|01}^{-1}(F_{Y|00}(F_{10}^{-1}(q)))) f_{Y|10}(F_{Y|10}^{-1}(q))} \left(\mathbb{1}\left\{F_{Y|10}(y) \le q\right\} - q\right)$$

$$s_q(y) = -\left[f_{Y|11}(F_{Y|11}^{-1}(q))\right]^{-1}\left(\mathbb{1}\left\{y \le F_{Y|11}^{-1}(q)\right\} - q\right)$$

with corresponding variances $V_p^q = E[p_q(Y_{00})^2]$, $V_q^q = E[q_q(Y_{01})^2]$, $V_r^q = E[r_q(Y_{10})^2]$ and $V_s^q = E[s_q(Y_{11})^2]$. Then one can state:

THEOREM 5.2 *Under the above assumptions one has*

$$\hat{\alpha}_q^{CiC} - \alpha_q^{CiC} = O_p(n^{1/2})$$

$$\sqrt{n}(\hat{\alpha}^{CiC} - \alpha^{CiC}) \to N(0, V_p^q/p_{00} + V_q^q/p_{01} + V_r^q/p_{10} + V_s^q/p_{11})$$

for $\min_{y \in \mathcal{Y}_{00}} F_{Y|10}(y) < q < \bar{q} = \max_{y \in \mathcal{Y}_{00}} F_{Y|10}(y)$.

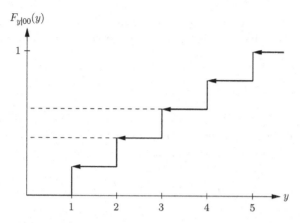

$F_{y|00}(y)$

Figure 5.3 Non-invertible cdf

5.3.2 Changes-in-Changes with Discrete Outcome Y and Interval Identification

Consider now the situation when the outcome variable Y is discrete with a finite number of support points $Supp(Y) = \{\lambda_0, \ldots, \lambda_L\}$ where $\lambda_l < \lambda_{l+1}$. The previous model needs to be modified to be a realistic model of the observed data. Since the assumption of discrete U is not very attractive, we maintain the assumption that U is continuously distributed in the $G = 0$ and $G = 1$ population, but permit the function φ to be just weakly monotonously increasing in U. Without loss of generality let us assume that $U|G = 0, T = 0$ is uniformly distributed on $[0, 1]$.

Without further assumptions, the counterfactual distribution is not point identified anymore. We first discuss the general case, and show later how to restore point identification under additional assumptions. The reason why point identification is lost is that we cannot invert $F_{Y|00}$ any longer to obtain the value of U. Consider Figure 5.3 and remember that we normalised $U|G = 0$ to be uniformly distributed. When we observe $Y = 3$, we only know that U lies in the half-open interval $(F_{Y|00}(2), F_{Y|00}(3)]$, i.e. U lies between the two dashed lines in the figure.

If Y was continuously distributed, the value of U would be exactly identified. With discrete Y we only know that for a non-decreasing function φ one has

$$u = \Pr(U \leq u|G = 0) = \Pr(U \leq u|G = 0, T = 0)$$
$$\leq \Pr(\varphi(U, 0) \leq \varphi(u, 0)|G = 0, T = 0). \tag{5.33}$$

The inequality follows because $U \leq u$ implies $\varphi(U, 0) \leq \varphi(u, 0)$ but not vice versa. Let $\mathbb{Q}$ denote the set of all values of $q \in [0, 1]$ such that $\exists y \in \mathcal{Y}_{00}$ with $F_{Y|00}(y) = q$. If $u \in \mathbb{Q}$, then the statements $U \leq u$ and $\varphi(U, 0) \leq \varphi(u, 0)$ imply each other. We thus obtain for $u \in \mathbb{Q}$

$$u = \Pr(U \leq u|G = 0) = \Pr(U \leq u|G = 0, T = 0)$$
$$= \Pr(\varphi(U, 0) \leq \varphi(u, 0)|G = 0, T = 0)$$
$$= \Pr(Y \leq \varphi(u, 0)|G = 0, T = 0) = F_{Y|00}(\varphi(u, 0)). \tag{5.34}$$

Hence, for $u \in Q$ we have $\varphi(u, 0) = F_{Y|00}^{-1}(u)$. However, all values of U in $(F_{Y|00}(\lambda_{l-1}), F_{Y|00}(\lambda_l)]$ will be mapped onto $Y = y$. Define a second inverse function

$$F_{Y|00}^{-1}(q) = \inf \{y : F_{Y|00}(y) \geq q \quad , \quad y \in \mathcal{Y}_{00}\}, \text{ and}$$

$$F_{Y|00}^{(-1)}(q) = \sup \{y : F_{Y|00}(y) \leq q \quad , \quad y \in \mathcal{Y}_{00} \cup \{-\infty\} \}$$

where $\mathcal{Y}_{00} = Supp(Y|G = 0, t = 0)$. These two inverse functions also permit to describe the interval of values of U that are mapped onto the same value of Y. Consider a value q such that $F_{Y|00}^{-1}(q) = y$. Then all values of $U_i = u$ with

$$F_{Y|00}(F_{Y|00}^{(-1)}(q)) < u \leq F_{Y|00}(F_{Y|00}^{-1}(q))$$

will be mapped on $Y_i = y$.

Regarding the two inverse functions, we note that for values of q such that $\exists y \in \mathcal{Y}_{00}$ with $F_{Y|00}(y) = q$ it follows that $F_{Y|00}^{(-1)}(q) = F_{Y|00}^{-1}(q)$. Let Q denote the set of all values of $q \in [0, 1]$ that satisfy this relationship. These are the jump points in Figure 5.3. For all other values of $q \notin Q$ we have that $F_{Y|00}^{(-1)}(q) < F_{Y|00}^{-1}(q)$. For all values of q it therefore follows that

$$F_{Y|00}(F_{Y|00}^{(-1)}(q)) \leq q \leq F_{Y|00}(F_{Y|00}^{-1}(q)), \tag{5.35}$$

and for $q \in Q$ even $F_{Y|00}(F_{Y|00}^{(-1)}(q)) = q = F_{Y|00}(F_{Y|00}^{-1}(q))$. Likewise, we can show that $F_{U|G=1}(u)$ is identified only for $u \in Q$. We derived in (5.34) above that for those, $F_{Y|00}(\varphi(u, 0)) = u$ and $\varphi(u, 0) = F_{Y|00}^{-1}(u)$. Now consider $F_{U|G=1}(u)$ for a given value of $u \in Q$:

$$F_{U|G=1}(u) = \Pr(U \leq u|G = 1) = \Pr(U \leq u|G = 1, T = 0)$$
$$= \Pr(\varphi(U, 0) \leq \varphi(u, 0)|G = 1, T = 0) = \Pr(Y \leq \varphi(u, 0)|G = 1, T = 0)$$
$$= F_{Y|10}(\varphi(u, 0)) = F_{Y|10}(F_{Y|00}^{-1}(u)).$$

Consequently, $F_{U|G=1}(u)$ is point identified only for $u \in Q$. For all other values, $F_{U|G=1}(u)$ can only be bounded, similarly to (5.33), as is shown further below.

To illustrate the identification area of $F_{U|G=1}(u)$, let us consider an example where $Y \in \{1, 2, 3, 4\}$, and imagine we had observed the frequencies

	$F_{Y|00}$	$F_{Y|10}$	$F_{Y|01}$	
$y = 1$	0.1	0.3	0.2	
$y = 2$	0.4	0.5	0.6	(5.36)
$y = 3$	0.7	0.9	0.8	
$y = 4$	1	1	1.	

Figure 5.4 shows the distribution function $F_{U|G=1}(u)$ as a function of u. Note also that $F_{U|G=0}(u) = u$ because u has been normalised to be uniform in the $G = 0$ group. The graph on the left indicates the values of $F_{U|G=1}(u)$ where it is identified from $F_{Y|00}$ and $F_{Y|10}$. Since distribution functions are right-continuous and non-decreasing, the shaded areas in the graph on the right show the lower and upper bounds for $F_{U|G=1}(u)$, i.e. function $F_{U|G=1}$ must lie in the shaded areas.

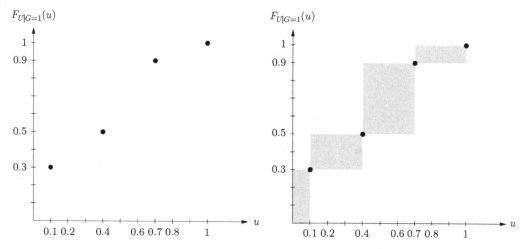

Figure 5.4 The cumulative distribution function $F_{U|G=1}(u)$

Having (partly) identified the function $F_{U|G=1}$, we can proceed with identifying the distribution of the counterfactual outcome $F_{Y^0|11}$. Note first that

$$F_{Y|0t}(y) = \Pr(\varphi(U, t) \leq y | G = 0)$$
$$= \Pr(U \leq \sup\{u : \varphi(u, t) = y\} | G = 0) = \sup\{u : \varphi(u, t) = y\}$$

because U is uniformly distributed in the $G = 0$ population. Note further that

$$F_{Y^0|1t}(y) = \Pr(\varphi(U, t) \leq y | G = 1) = \Pr(U \leq \sup\{u : \varphi(u, t) = y\} | G = 1)$$
$$= \Pr\left(U \leq F_{Y|0t}(y) | G = 1\right) = F_{U|G=1}(F_{Y|0t}(y)). \quad (5.37)$$

This implies

$$F_{Y^0|11}(y) = F_{U|G=1}(F_{Y|01}(y)). \quad (5.38)$$

Hence, we can derive $F_{Y^0|11}(y)$ from the distribution of $F_{U|G=1}$. For the numerical example (5.36) given above we obtain

$$F_{Y^0|11}(1) = F_{U|G=1}(F_{Y|01}(1)) = F_{U|G=1}(0.2) \in [0.3; 0.5]$$
$$F_{Y^0|11}(2) = F_{U|G=1}(F_{Y|01}(2)) = F_{U|G=1}(0.6) \in [0.5; 0.9]$$
$$F_{Y^0|11}(3) = F_{U|G=1}(F_{Y|01}(3)) = F_{U|G=1}(0.8) \in [0.9; 1]$$
$$F_{Y^0|11}(4) = F_{U|G=1}(F_{Y|01}(4)) = F_{U|G=1}(1) = 1.$$

This is also illustrated in Figure 5.5.

The formal derivation of these bounds is as follows. Start from (5.37) with $T = 0$ and set y to $F_{Y|00}^{(-1)}(F_{Y|01}(y))$. We obtain

$$F_{Y|10}(F_{Y|00}^{(-1)}(F_{Y|01}(y))) = \Pr\left(U \leq F_{Y|00}(F_{Y|00}^{(-1)}(F_{Y|01}(y))) | G = 1\right)$$
$$\leq \Pr\left(U \leq F_{Y|01}(y) | G = 1\right) = F_{Y^0|11}(y)$$

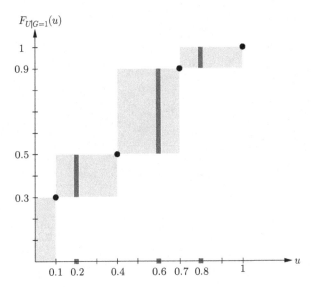

Figure 5.5 $F_{Y^0|11}$ for the numerical example (5.36)

because of (5.35) and (5.38). Similarly,

$$F_{Y|10}(F_{Y|00}^{-1}(F_{Y|01}(y))) = \Pr\left(U \leq F_{Y|00}(F_{Y|00}^{-1}(F_{Y|01}(y)))|G=1\right)$$
$$\geq \Pr\left(U \leq F_{Y|01}(y)|G=1\right) = F_{Y^0|11}(y).$$

We thus obtain the lower and upper bound (Lb and Ub) distributions[7] for $y \in \mathcal{Y}_{01}$

$$F_{Y^0|11}^{Lb}(y) := F_{Y|10}(F_{Y|00}^{-1}(F_{Y|01}(y))) \leq F_{Y^0|11}(y) \leq F_{Y|10}(F_{Y|00}^{-1}(F_{Y|01}(y))) =: F_{Y^0|11}^{Ub}(y) \tag{5.39}$$

which bound the distribution of the counterfactual outcome of interest $F_{Y^0|11}(y)$.

Both, the upper and the lower bound c.d.f. can be estimated by replacing in Equation 5.39 the different distribution functions by its empirical counterparts, and applying numerical inversion. The upper and lower bound of the ATET can be estimated by

$$\hat{\alpha}_{Ub} = \frac{1}{n_{11}} \sum_{i=1}^{n_{11}} Y_{11,i} - \frac{1}{n_{10}} \sum_{i=1}^{n_{10}} F_{Y|01}^{-1}\left(\underline{\widehat{F}}_{Y|00}(Y_{10,i})\right) \tag{5.40}$$

$$\hat{\alpha}_{Lb} = \frac{1}{n_{11}} \sum_{i=1}^{n_{11}} Y_{11,i} - \frac{1}{n_{10}} \sum_{i=1}^{n_{10}} F_{Y|01}^{-1}\left(\widehat{F}_{Y|00}(Y_{10,i})\right), \tag{5.41}$$

where $\underline{F}_{Y|00}(y) = \Pr(Y_{00} < y)$ which can be estimated by $\frac{1}{n_{00}} \sum_{i=1}^{n_{00}} \mathbb{1}\{Y_{00,i} < y\}$, whereas $\widehat{F}_{Y|00}(y)$ is estimated like always, i.e. by $\widehat{\Pr}(Y_{00} < y) = \frac{1}{n_{00}} \sum_{i=1}^{n_{00}} \mathbb{1}\{Y_{00,i} \leq y\}$.

---

[7] C.f. Theorem 4.1 of Athey and Imbens (2006). They show also that these bounds are tight, i.e. that no narrower bounds can exist.

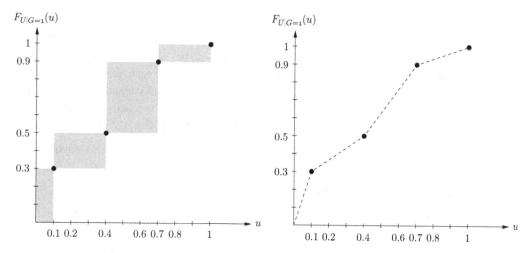

Figure 5.6 How we reach point identification: an illustration

THEOREM 5.3   *With the same assumptions and p_{gt}, V_s as for the continuous case (Theorem 5.1) we obtain for the estimators defined in (5.40) and (5.41) that*

$$\sqrt{n}\left(\hat{\alpha}_{Ub} - \alpha_{Ub}\right) \rightarrow N\left(0, V_s/p_{11} + \underline{V}/p_{10}\right)$$
$$\sqrt{n}\left(\hat{\alpha}_{Lb} - \alpha_{Lb}\right) \rightarrow N\left(0, V_s/p_{11} + \overline{V}/p_{10}\right)$$

with $\underline{V} = Var\left(F_{Y|01}^{-1}(\underline{F}_{Y|00}(Y_{10}))\right)$, *and* $\overline{V} = Var\left(F_{Y|01}^{-1}(\overline{F}_{Y|00}(Y_{10}))\right)$.

5.3.3   Changes-in-Changes with Discrete Outcome Y but Point Identification

As just shown, for discrete Y with weak assumptions we obtain only interval identification. There are different ways to restore point identification: using an additional independence assumption or by imposing some exclusion restrictions. We consider here only the first approach. In addition to the previous assumptions for the discrete Y case, and the normalisation of U to be uniform in the $G = 0, T = 0$ population, we now further impose

Assumption CiC 4.1 $U \perp\!\!\!\perp G|T, Y$.

Hence, the distribution of U may still differ between the $G = 1$ and the $G = 0$ population. For those observations with the same value of Y but for whom we know only the interval in which U lies, it is assumed that they are distributed the same way in the $G = 1$ as in the $G = 0$ population. Assumption CiC 4.1 is automatically satisfied when Y is continuous with φ strictly increasing. In that case we have $U = \varphi^{-1}(Y, T)$ such that U is degenerate conditional on Y and T, and therefore trivially independent of G.

The intuition why we obtain point identification can be obtained from Figure 5.6. Recall that U is uniformly distributed in the $G = 0, T = 0$ population, so it is also uniformly distributed in the $G = 0, T = 0, Y = y$ population. In our simple numerical example we have seen that $F_{U|G=1}(u)$ was point-identified only for some values of u.

But with Assumption CiC 4.1 we can reach point identification for $F_{U|G=1}(u)$ for all values of u as U is then also uniformly distributed in the $G = 1, T = 0, Y = y$ population. Hence, the distribution function $F_{U|G=1}(u)$ has to be a diagonal between the bounds on $F_{U|G=1}(u)$ derived above. These bounds are replicated in the left graph below, while the graph on the right shows $F_{U|G=1}(u)$ with Assumption CiC 4.1. For a formal proof you need some more assumptions. Let us discuss here only the proof for binary Y.[8] The assumptions for this binary Y case are, in addition to $U \perp\!\!\!\perp T|G$,

Assumption CiC 4.2   The random variable $Y_{G=0,T=0}$ is discrete with possible outcomes $\mathcal{Y}_{00} = \{0, 1\}$.

Assumption CiC 4.3   The function $\varphi(u, t)$ is non-decreasing in u.

Assumption CiC 4.4   The variables $U|G = 1$ and $U|G = 0$ are continuously distributed.

Still assume that $U|G = 0$ is normalised to be uniform. Define $\tilde{u}(t) = \sup(u \in [0, 1] : \varphi(u, t) = 0)$ as the largest value of u such that $\varphi(u, t)$ is still zero. This implies that $E\left[Y^0|G = g, T = t\right] = \Pr(U > \tilde{u}(t)|G = g, T = t)$. Now consider

$$\Pr(U \leq u|U \leq \tilde{u}(t), G = 1) = \Pr(U \leq u|U \leq \tilde{u}(t), G = 1, T = t)$$

because of $U \perp\!\!\!\perp T|G$. By the definition of $\tilde{u}(t)$, conditioning on $U \leq \tilde{u}$ implies $Y = 0$, such that

$$= \Pr(U \leq u|U \leq \tilde{u}(t), G = 1, T = t, Y = 0)$$
$$= \Pr(U \leq u|U \leq \tilde{u}(t), G = 0, T = t, Y = 0)$$

because of Assumption (A4.4). Now again using the definition of $\tilde{u}(t)$ we obtain

$$= \Pr(U \leq u|U \leq \tilde{u}(t), G = 0, T = t) = \Pr(U \leq u|U \leq \tilde{u}(t), G = 0)$$
$$= \min\left(\frac{u}{\tilde{u}(t)}, 1\right) \tag{5.42}$$

because of $U \perp\!\!\!\perp T|G$; the last equality follows because $U|G = 0$ is uniform. Analogously one can show that

$$\Pr(U > u|U > \tilde{u}(t), G = 1) = \min\left(\frac{1 - u}{1 - \tilde{u}(t)}, 1\right).$$

Recall the following equalities:

$$E[Y|G = 1, T = 0] = \Pr(U > \tilde{u}(0)|G = 1)$$
$$E[Y|G = 0, T = t] = \Pr(U > \tilde{u}(t)|G = 0, T = t) = \Pr(U > \tilde{u}(t)|G = 0) = 1 - \tilde{u}(t).$$

With them we get

$$E\left[Y^0|G = 1, T = 1\right] = \Pr(U > \tilde{u}(1)|G = 1, T = 1) = \Pr(U > \tilde{u}(1)|G = 1)$$
$$= \Pr(U > \tilde{u}(1)|U > \tilde{u}(0), G = 1)\Pr(U > \tilde{u}(0)|G = 1)$$
$$+ \Pr(U > \tilde{u}(1)|U \leq \tilde{u}(0), G = 1)\Pr(U \leq \tilde{u}(0)|G = 1). \tag{5.43}$$

---

[8] The general case can be found for example in Athey and Imbens (2006).

Now consider the situation where

$$E[Y|G = 0, T = 1] > E[Y|G = 0, T = 0]$$
$$\Leftrightarrow 1 - \tilde{u}(1) > 1 - \tilde{u}(0) \Leftrightarrow \tilde{u}(1) < \tilde{u}(0).$$

Inserting this result in (5.43) gives

$$E\left[Y^0|G = 1, T = 1\right]$$
$$= \Pr(U > \tilde{u}(0)|G = 1) + \Pr(U > \tilde{u}(1)|U \le \tilde{u}(0), G = 1)\Pr(U \le \tilde{u}(0)|G = 1)$$
$$= \Pr(U > \tilde{u}(0)|G = 1) + (1 - \Pr(U \le \tilde{u}(1)|U \le \tilde{u}(0), G = 1))\Pr(U \le \tilde{u}(0)|G = 1).$$

And inserting (5.42) gives

$$= \Pr(U > \tilde{u}(0)|G = 1) + \left(1 - \frac{\tilde{u}(1)}{\tilde{u}(0)}\right)\Pr(U \le \tilde{u}(0)|G = 1).$$

Making use of the other previous derivations gives

$$= 1 - \frac{1 - E[Y|G = 0, T = 1]}{1 - E[Y|G = 0, T = 0]}(1 - E[Y|G = 1, T = 0])$$
$$= E[Y|G = 0, T = 1] + \frac{1 - E[Y|G = 0, T = 1]}{1 - E[Y|G = 0, T = 0]}$$
$$\times (E[Y|G = 1, T = 0] - E[Y|G = 0, T = 0]).$$

In the situation where $E[Y|G = 0, T = 1] < E[Y|G = 0, T = 0]$, which implies $\tilde{u}(1) > \tilde{u}(0)$, we obtain with similar calculations $E\left[Y^0|G = 1, T = 1\right] =$

$$E[Y|G=0, T = 1] + \frac{E[Y|G = 0, T = 1]}{E[Y|G = 0, T = 0]}(E[Y|G=1, T = 0] - E[Y|G = 0, T = 0]).$$

Finally, consider the situation where $E[Y|G = 0, T = 1] = E[Y|G = 0, T = 0]$. This implies $\tilde{u}(1) = \tilde{u}(0)$ and gives (after analogous calculations)

$$E\left[Y^0|G = 1, T = 1\right] = E[Y|G = 1, T = 0].$$

5.3.4   Relationship to Panel Data Analysis and Selection on Observables

The CiC methods discussed so far were applicable to cohort data and therefore also to panel data. With panel data we index the data by i and t and have

$$Y_{it}^0 = \varphi(U_{it}, t) \tag{5.44}$$

where we permit that $U_{i0} \ne U_{i1}$, i.e. the unobserved variable may vary over time for the same individual. For example, $U_{it} = v_i + \varepsilon_{it}$ would be permitted. Let us compare the CiC approach to a selection-on-observables approach in this setting with two time periods. With two time periods we could use the $Y_{t=0}$ outcome as a control variable in a matching estimator, perhaps together with additional X. The basic assumption of unconfoundedness is that there is no selection bias left when conditioning on these control variables (here, conditioning on $Y_{t=0}$). Define the treatment indicator $D_i = G_i T_i$ such that only the $G_i = 1$ group is treated and only in the period $t = 1$.

Consider first the matching approach. If $Y_{t=0}$ is the only confounding variable, then by applying the logic of selection-on-observables identification we can write $F_{Y^0_{t=1}|G=1}(y)$

$$= \Pr\left(Y^0_{t=1} \le y | D = 1\right) = E\left[\mathbb{1}\left(Y^0_{t=1} \le y\right) | G = 1\right]$$

$$= E\left[E\left[\mathbb{1}\left(Y^0_{t=1} \le y\right) | Y_{t=0}, G = 1\right] | G = 1\right]$$

$$= E\left[E\left[\mathbb{1}\left(Y^0_{t=1} \le y\right) | Y_{t=0}, G = 0\right] | G = 1\right]$$

$$= E\left[F_{Y_{t=1}|Y_{t=0},G=0}(y|Y_{t=0}) | G = 1\right]. \tag{5.45}$$

This result is different from the above CiC method. With the selection on observables approach it is assumed that conditional on $Y_{t=0}$ the unobservables are *identically distributed in both groups* (in the second period). The above introduced CiC method did not assume that the unobservables are identically distributed between groups (conditional on $Y_{t=0}$), but rather required that the unobservables were identically distributed over time, cf. with (5.44). Hence, as we already showed for the DiD model, the CiC method is not nested with the selection-on-observables approach.

However, selection on observables and CiC are identical when $U_{i0} = U_{i1}$. To see this, note first that the conditional distribution

$$F_{Y_{t=1}|Y_{t=0},G=0}(y|v)$$

is degenerate if $U_{i0} = U_{i1}$. Assuming this implies perfect rank correlation: for i with U_{i0} such that $Y_{i,t=0} = v$ we have $Y^0_{i,t=1} = F^{-1}_{Y|01}(F_{Y|00}(v))$ which is the mapping of ranks. This implies

$$F_{Y_{t=1}|Y_{t=0},G=0}(y|v) = 0 \quad \text{if} \quad y < F^{-1}_{Y|01}(F_{Y|00}(v)) \tag{5.46}$$

$$F_{Y_{t=1}|Y_{t=0},G=0}(y|v) = 1 \quad \text{if} \quad y \ge F^{-1}_{Y|01}(F_{Y|00}(v)) .$$

Starting from (5.45) we have

$$F_{Y^0_{t=1}|G=1}(y) = E\left[F_{Y_{t=1}|Y_{t=0},G=0}(y|Y_{t=0}) | G = 1\right]$$

$$= \int F_{Y_{t=1}|Y_{t=0},G=0}(y, v) \cdot f_{Y_{t=0}|G=1}(v)dv.$$

Making use of (5.46) we obtain

$$= \int \mathbb{1}\left\{y \ge F^{-1}_{Y|01}(F_{Y|00}(v))\right\} \cdot f_{Y_{t=0}|G=1}(v)dv = \Pr\left(y \ge F^{-1}_{Y|01}(F_{Y|00}(Y_{t=0})) | G = 1\right)$$

$$= \Pr\left(F^{-1}_{Y|00}(F_{Y|01}(y)) \ge Y_{t=0} | G = 1\right) = \Pr\left(Y_{t=0} \le F^{-1}_{Y|00}(F_{Y|01}(y)) | G = 1\right)$$

$$= F_{Y|10}\left(F^{-1}_{Y|00}(F_{Y|01}(y))\right)$$

which is identical to (5.24). Hence, Assumptions CiC 1 to CiC 3 are valid and also $U_{i,t=1} = U_{i,t=0}$. Therefore CiC and matching (selection-on-observables) deliver the same results.

To enhance our understanding of the relationship between the CiC and the selection-on-observables approach, note that the latter only requires

$$Y^0_{t=1} \perp\!\!\!\perp D | Y_{t=0},$$

(or at least mean independence if interest is in average effects). If $Y_{it}^0 = \varphi(U_{it}, t)$ and φ is strictly monotonous in the first element, this is identical to

$$U_{i,t=1} \perp\!\!\!\perp G_i | U_{i,t=0}. \tag{5.47}$$

The selection-on-observables approach thus requires that all information that affects $U_{t=1}$ and the treatment decision is incorporated in $U_{t=0}$. This assumption (5.47) is, for example, not satisfied in a fixed-effect specification $U_{it} = v_i + \varepsilon_{it}$ where v_i is related with the treatment decision and ε_{it} some independent noise. For (5.47) to be satisfied would require that $U_{i,t=0}$ contains all information about v_i because it is the confounding element. However, in the fixed-effect model our $U_{i,t=0}$ reveals v_i only partly since the noise $\varepsilon_{i,t=0}$ is also contained.

Example 5.7 Consider the simple example where $G_i = \mathbb{1}\,(v_i - \eta_i > 0)$ and η_i some noise. For the (5.47) we need for identification $E\left[U_{i,t=1}|G_i = 1, U_{i,t=0}\right] - E\left[U_{i,t=1}|G_i = 0, U_{i,t=0}\right] = 0$, which is not true here since $E\left[U_{i,t=1}|G_i = 1, U_{i,t=0} = a\right] = E\left[v_i + \varepsilon_{i,t=1}|v_i > \eta_i, v_i + \varepsilon_{i,t=0} = a\right] = E\left[v_i|v_i > \eta_i, \varepsilon_{i,t=0} = a - v_i\right]$ which is larger than $E\left[v_i|v_i \le \eta_i, \varepsilon_{i,t=0} = a - v_i\right]$. This is similar to situations with measurement errors in the confounder or the treatment variable.

The CiC model requires, in addition to the monotonicity and the support assumption, that

$$U \perp\!\!\!\perp T | G.$$

This does not permit that the distribution of U changes over time. It does not permit e.g. an increase in the variance of U, which would not be a concern in the selection-on-observables approach. In the CiC method, an increase in the variance of U or any other change in the distribution of U, is not permitted because we attribute any change in the observed outcomes Y (over time) to a change in the function from $\varphi(u, 0)$ to $\varphi(u, 1)$. If the distribution of U changed between the time periods, we could not disentangle how much of the changes in Y is due to changes in U and how much due to changes in the function φ.

Another difference between the selection-on-observables approach and the CiC method is the assumption that $\varphi(u, t)$ is monotonous in u, an assumption which is not required for matching. Hence, the CiC approach requires that the unobservables in the outcome equation are one-dimensional, i.e. all individuals can be ranked on a one-dimensional scale with respect to their outcomes, irrespective of the value of the treatment. In the selection-on-observables approach, on the other hand, unobservables are permitted to be multi-dimensional. This emphasises once again that both approaches rest on different assumptions which cannot be nested. Only in the case where the joint distribution of $U_{i,t=1}$ and $U_{i,t=0}$ is degenerate, which trivially implies (5.47), the selection-on-observables approach rests on weaker assumptions. One example is $U_{i,t=0} = U_{i,t=1}$.

Finally, note that the CiC method can also be used to analyse the effects of changes in the distribution of U over time if these occur only in one of the two groups. This can be applied e.g. to the analysis of wage discrimination.

Example 5.8 Suppose we are interested in the wage differential between Black and White, after having purged the effects due to differences in some pre-specified observables X. Let U be an unobserved skill and $\varphi(U, T)$ the equilibrium wage function, which may change over time, but is assumed to be identical for the two groups $G = 1 = blacks$ and $G = 0 = whites$. Suppose that the distribution of U did not change over time for white workers but that it did change for black workers. The treatment effect of interest here is not the effect of a particular intervention, but rather the impact on the wage distribution due to the change in the unobservables for the black. We observe the wage distribution for the black after the change in the distribution of U had taken place. The counterfactual is the wage distribution that would have been observed if the distribution of U had remained constant over time for the black. Under the maintained assumption that the distribution of U for the white was constant over time this situation fits exactly the CiC model assumptions for Y^0 with $U \perp\!\!\!\perp T | G$. The difference between the observed wage distribution for black and their counterfactual is thus attributed to the change in the distribution of U over time for the blacks (under the maintained assumption that the distribution of U did not change for white workers).

It is not hard to imagine that there are many situations in which the assumptions necessary for the CiC method are to some extent credible. As always, we never know whether all model assumptions hold perfectly true. In fact, as models are always a simplification, often this may not be 100% true; what we hope for is that the artificial simplification is not too strong, i.e. that potential deviations from the made assumptions are not too strong and to a good part accounted for by the (estimated) standard errors.

5.4   Bibliographic and Computational Notes

5.4.1   Further Reading and Bibliographic Notes

We have seen that the DiD and the appropriateness of the particular technique again depends crucially on the validity of several assumptions we discussed in the previous sections. Typically, empirical researchers focus on parametric models, in particular the linear regression approach. Lechner (2011) provides a brief overview of the literature on the DiD estimation. His survey gives a somewhat different view on DiD than the standard literature discussion of the DiD model but also contains a couple of extensions like suggestions for non-linear DiD as well as DiD based on propensity-score type matching. Abadie (2005) discusses semi-parametric adjustments for potential endogeneity e.g by using propensity score methods. From this article you also learn how to correct for confounders by propensity score weighting instead of using (direct) matching.

    Some are worried about the accuracy of the existing inference methods and try to develop alternatives or improvements, see Donald and Lang (2007) or Bertrand, Duflo and Mullainathan (2004). It has to be admitted, however, that for non-linear and semi-parametric methods the development of correct estimation of standard errors (or p-values for tests) is still an open research field.

The extension of the basic DiD idea to more situations, different assumption sets or data is often quite straight (even if then the consistency proofs etc may be more tedious) such that the literature in this domain is abundant, and we therefore can only give a very limited review. We else refer to Lechner (2011).

As already mentioned, Mora and Reggio (2012) study the parallel paths assumption and extend it to a much more general set of assumptions. More precisely, we have seen that whether the interaction of time and group identifies the treatment effect of interest will depend on the trend modelling strategy and the definition of the trend variable. For example, with group-specific invariant linear trends, this interaction does not identify the treatment effect under the parallel paths assumption used in this chapter, but it does identify the treatment effect for output first differences (rather than for output levels); recall the DiDiD. They generalise this idea by proposing a family of alternative parallel assumptions which widen the set of alternative estimators under fully flexible dynamics.

Other articles generalise the DiD in order to identify the entire counterfactual distribution of potential outcomes – as we outlined it in the context of the CiC approach; see also Bonhomme and Sauder (2011). Alternative ways to study the distribution instead of the mean are the quantile regression approaches that we will discuss in a later chapter.

Inference in the multiple period or multiple group case has been considered, among many others, by Donald and Lang (2007), Hansen (2007a) and Hansen (2007b). But again, unless you use just linear parametric panel models, this is still an open field.

5.4.2 Computational Notes

Generally, as the DiD approach coincides to some extent with the fixed effects panel estimation, the corresponding ATET estimates and standard errors can be obtained from the standard commands in Stata and R used for panel regression if you are provided with panel data. Even when substituting the parallel growth for the parallel path assumption, you can use this methods simply by including the corresponding interaction terms, see Mora and Reggio (2012).

For Stata, linear fixed effect estimation can be done by the xtreg command (for non-linear extensions, see xtlogit, xtpoisson, xtnbreg and xtgee). For linear dynamic panels fixed effects estimators there exist xtabond, known as the Arellano–Bond or dynamic GMM estimator, and the less recommendable (see Roodman 2009a, Roodman 2009b) counterpart xtdpdsys for the so-called dynamic GMM or Blundell–Bond estimator. In R almost all of these procedures – at least those you need for the methods introduced here and their straightforward extensions – are provided in the package plm (panel linear models); see Croissant and Millo (2008) for details.

Now, the difference-in-differences estimators introduced here are usually calculated including two dummy variables, one for being in the treated group (*treatment*), and one for being in the post-treatment sample (*post*). Formally, gen $post = 1$ if the observation is in the post period, zero otherwise, and gen $treatment = 1$ if the observation is in the treatment group and zero otherwise. Then generate the post-period treatment dummy gen $pt = post * treatment$ and run the regression of interest with the three dummies (two dummies for the groups plus the interaction). The coefficient on pt then represent the ATET estimator. To test the difference in the two groups, use the t-statistic on that coefficient. A popular correction for potential heteroscedasticity is to cluster standard errors at the group level adding the `cl("group var")` option in the regression command.

For combining fixed effects model estimation with weighting in R, see Imai and Kim (2015). They show how weighted linear fixed effects estimators can be used to estimate the average treatment effects (for treated) using different identification strategies. These strategies include stratified randomised experiments, matching and stratification for observational studies, difference-in-differences, and a method they call *first differencing*. Their R package `wfe` provides a computationally efficient way of fitting weighted linear fixed effects estimators for causal inference with various weighting schemes. The package also provides various robust standard errors and a specification test for standard linear fixed effects estimators.

You further will find in `Stata` the user-written ado commands `diff`, `diffbs`, presently available at `econpapers.repec.org/software/bocbocode/s45 7083.htm`. Along the description of its release in 2015 it performs several diff-in-diff estimations of the treatment effect of a given outcome variable from a pooled base line and follow up dataset(s): Single Diff-in-Diff, Diff-in-Diff controlling for covariates, Kernel-based Propensity Score Matching diff-in-diff, and Quantile Diff-in-Diff; see Chapter 7. It is also suitable for estimating repeated cross section Diff-in-Diff, except for the kernel option. Note that this command ignores the grouping variable and does not take the pairing of the observations into account, as is usual when you `xtset` your data before using `xtreg`.

5.5   Exercises

1. In a simple DiD without confounders, how can you test the validity of the made assumptions before and after treatment when provided with additional panel waves or cohorts? How can you *make these assumptions hold*?

2. Now think of conditional DiD with confounders and the accordingly modified parallel path assumption. Again imagine you are provided with data from at least two waves before and after the treatment has taken place. How can you (a) test these assumptions, (b) select an appropriate set of confounders, and (c) if necessary, find the right scale for Y?

3. Think about the difference between DiD with panels vs with cohorts. What is the advantage of having panels compared to cohorts?

4. No matter whether you do DiD with panels or with cohorts, when including covariates (e.g. necessary when they are confounders) – why now it is no longer sufficient to have the cohort or panel aggregates for each group?

5. Show that parallel path fails in the log-linear model (looking at $log(Y)$) when it holds for the linear model. Discuss, how to choose the scale if you do not have data from several time points before treatment was implemented.

6. Recall DiD-matching/propensity weighting: prove the steps of (5.13) using Bayes' rule.

7. Have you thought about DiD with instruments (IVs)? Recall that it is very hard to find IVs that indeed fulfil the necessary conditions and at the same time improve in the finite sample mean squared error of your treatment effect estimate (compared to matching or propensity score weighting). Furthermore, as you only identify the LATE, only a reasonable structural model provides a useful estimate. Having the time dimension in the DiD already, you may work with lagged variables as IV. What are you identifying and estimating then? Which estimators do you know already from panel data analytics – even if maybe just in the linear model context?

8. Above we have discussed how to check the parallel path assumption and how to adapt if it is not fulfilled (change scale, condition on an appropriate set of covariates, etc.). You may, however, end up with a data transformation or set of confounders that are hard to justify with economic theory or that even contradict it. An alternative is to change to the parallel growth model. Write down the new model and answer for it Exercises 5.1 to 5.5.

9. You may end up with the question as to whether you should use parallel path, parallel growth, CiC, etc. Discuss the various possibilities of checking or testing which assumptions are most likely to hold.

6   Regression Discontinuity Design

Sometimes treatments or interventions happen around a certain 'threshold', which can be the size of a firm, age of an applicant, score in an admission test etc. This threshold is usually defined along with some eligibility criteria. Think about a minimum score to obtain a grant or to get access into some programmes, like a poverty-score for a means-tested government assistance programme or a credit scoring for loan eligibility. For many interventions, assignment rules are based on a cut-off or threshold that determines the allocation of resources. It can be some explicit number, such as poverty score or family income, or it can be a set of rules for giving treatments. And of course it may also reflect some budget rules, for example if the budget permits only 200 schools in disadvantaged areas to be supported, so the worst 200 schools are selected. However, one important thing to note is that these cut-offs often arise from some political or social goals or reasons. The relevant question that we have to answer is whether we can use this threshold to identify the treatment effect. The answers is yes, at least if certain conditions hold. These designs around a certain threshold are known as Regression Discontinuity Designs (RDD) and will be explored in this chapter.

Recall Chapter 4: we discussed examples where eligibility criteria could not only be valid instruments but even provide a LATE that referred to an easy to understand subpopulation (compliers) and thereby provided a useful interpretation. Here now, 'eligibility' has to be understood in a broader way. For example, Hahn, Todd and van der Klaauw (1999) analysed the effect of anti-discrimination laws on the employment of minority workers by exploiting the fact that only firms with more than 15 employees were subject to these laws. An important thing to note is that often these eligibility criteria turn out not to be valid instrumental variables as they might violate the exclusion restriction.

Example 6.1 Consider a summer school remediation programme for poorly performing school children. Participation in this mandatory remediation programme is based on a grade in Mathematics. Students with low scores on the math test are obliged to attend the summer school programme during the holidays. On the other hand, students with high scores are not eligible for the programme. We want to learn whether these remedial education programme during the summer break actually helped the children, e.g. in performing better in school in the following years. Treatment D is defined as participation in the programme. All students with math test score Z below the threshold z_0 are assigned to treatment, whereas those with Z above the threshold z_0 are not.

Clearly, Z cannot be a valid instrumental variable since the test score Z is most likely related to (unobserved) ability and skills, which will also affect school performance in the future. Yet, perhaps we can use it if we restricted ourselves only to students in the neighbourhood of z_0.

We will see that such rules sometimes generate a *local* instrumental variable, i.e. an instrumental variable that is valid only at a particular threshold (not for the entire population). We will exploit this local behaviour at the margin of z_0. But one should always keep in mind that the identification is obtained only for the individuals at (or close to) threshold value z_0, which often may not be the primary population of interest. Sometimes it may be, e.g. when the policy of interest is a marginal change of the threshold z_0. In sum, the identification around this threshold may provide internal validity, but not external.

Example 6.2 Leuven, Lindahl, Oosterbeek and Webbink (2007) examined a programme in the Netherlands, where schools with at least 70% disadvantaged minority pupils received extra funding. Schools slightly above this threshold would qualify for extra funding whereas schools slightly below the threshold would not be eligible. While comparing schools with 0% disadvantaged pupils to schools with 100% disadvantaged pupils is unlikely to deliver the true treatment effect since these schools are likely to also differ in many other unobserved characteristics, comparing only schools slightly below 70% to those slightly above 70% could be a valid approach since both groups of schools are very similar in their student composition even though only one group qualifies for the extra funding.

Note, that one could say that the expectation of D, i.e. the probability of getting treated depends in a discontinuous way on the test score Z, while there is no reason to assume that the conditional expectations $E[Y^d|Z = z], d = 0, 1$ should be discontinuous at z_0.

Example 6.3 Lalive (2008) studied the effects of maximum duration of unemployment benefits in Austria. In clearly defined regions of Austria the maximum duration of receiving unemployment benefits was substantially extended for job seekers aged 50 or older at entry into unemployment. Basically, two control group comparisons can be examined: those slightly younger than 50 to those being 50 and slightly above, and those living in the treatment region but close to a border to a non-treatment region to those on the other side of the border.

The age-based strategy would compare the 50-year-old to 49-year-old individuals. This way we would compare groups of workers who are very similar in age (and in other characteristics like health and working experience), but where only one group gets the benefit of extension. To increase sample size, in practice we would compare job seekers e.g. in the age bracket 45 to 49 to those of age 50 to 54. Similar arguments apply top the strategy based on comparing people from different administrative regions but living very close to each other and therefore sharing the same labour market.

Whether these strategies indeed deliver a consistent estimate of the treatment effect depends on further conditions that are discussed below.

As seen in the last example, such a threshold could also be given by a geographical or administrative border; so whether you get treatment or not depends on which side of the border you reside. Then these geographical borders can also lead to regression discontinuity. For example, two villages can be very close to an administrative border but located on different sides of the border. If commuting times are short between these two villages, they might share many common features. But administrative regulations can differ a lot between these villages due to their belonging to different provinces. Such kinds of geographic or administrative borders provide opportunities for evaluation of interventions. We can think about individuals living close but on different sides of an administrative border, they may be living in the same labour market, but in case of becoming unemployed they have to attend different employment offices with potentially rather different types of support or training programmes.

Example 6.4 Frölich and Lechner (2010) analyse the impact of participation in an active labour market training programme on subsequent employment chances. They use the so-called 'minimum quota' as an instrument for being assigned to a labour market programme. When active labour market programmes were introduced on a large scale in Switzerland, the central government wanted to ensure that all regions (so-called 'cantons') would get introduced to these new programmes at the same time. The fear was that otherwise (at least some of) the cantons might have been reluctant to introduce these new programmes and prefer a wait-and-see strategy (as they enjoyed a very high degree of autonomy in the implementation of the policy). To avoid such behaviour, the central government demanded that each canton had to provide a minimum number of programme places (minimum quota). Since the calculation of these quota was partly based on population share and partly on unemployment share, it introduced a differential in the likelihood of being assigned to treatment between neighbouring cantons. This means that people living close to a cantonal border but on different sides of it, faced essentially the same labour market environment, but their chances of being assigned to treatment in case of becoming unemployed depended on their side of the border.

Thinking about Example 6.4 you will probably agree that there is no particular reason why the potential employment chances should be discontinuous at the frontier of a canton, but the chance to be involved in an active labour market training programme might be discontinuous, and this happens because of different quota. In evaluating impacts of policies, today it has become a frequently used tool to identify interventions where certain rules, especially bureaucratic ones (less often natural[1]), increase the likelihood of D to change discontinuously from 0 to 1.

---

[1] 'Natural' like mountain chains or language borders may cause a discontinuity in $E[Y^d|Z]$ at $Z = z_0$ for at least one d, and might therefore not be helpful.

Example 6.5 Black (1999) used this idea to study the impact of school quality on the prices of houses. In many countries, admission to primary school is usually based on the residency principle. Someone living in a particular school district is automatically assigned to a particular school. If the quality of school varies from school to school, parents have to relocate to the school district where they want their child to attend the school. Houses in areas with better schools would thus have a higher demand and thus be more expensive. If the school district border runs, for example, through the middle of a street, houses on the left-hand side of the street might be more expensive than those on the right-hand side of the street because of its belonging to a different school district.

The original idea was that around such threshold you observe something like a random experiment. Some units, firms or individuals happen to lie on the side of the threshold at which a treatment is administered, whereas others lie on the other side of the threshold. Units close to the threshold but on different sides can be compared to estimate the average treatment effect. Often the units to the left of the threshold differ in their observed characteristics from those to the right of the threshold. Then, as in the CIA case, accounting for these observed differences can be important to identify the treatment effect.

So we have two ways to relate RDD to preceding chapters and methods: either one argues that the threshold acts like a random assignment mechanism, i.e. you are 'by chance' right above or right below z_0; or we can argue that such rules generate a *local instrumental variable*, i.e. an instrument that is valid only at or around a particular threshold z_0. In the former case we consider the observations around z_0 like data obtained from a randomised experiment but in both cases it is obvious that our argument looses its validity as we move away from z_0: In Example 6.1 pure hazard is not placing a student far above or far below the threshold as we can always argue ability has played an important role. Similarly, in Example 6.4 people living away from the frontier inside one or the other province most likely face different labour markets.[2]

6.1 Regression Discontinuity Design without Covariates

For the ease of presentation we first consider the case without further covariates. How can we employ RDD to identify and estimate treatment effects?

6.1.1 Identification in the Regression Discontinuity Designs

Imagine a new education programme is designed to give extra funding to schools with larger shares of immigrants. The fraction of immigrant students, say Z, is measured per school on a particular day. Let us say we have our threshold at z_0 (e.g. $= 25\%$). The

---

[2] Although it is not a necessary condition, we only use methods that assume knowledge of the location of the discontinuity, that is, that know the threshold value z_0. One could extend the methods to allow for estimated break points z_0, but most of the credibility of the design gets lost, then.

assignment rule is that schools with $Z \geq z_0$ receive some additional funding but schools with $Z < z_0$ receive nothing. We are interested in the effect of this extra funding D on some student outcomes Y. As stated, the basic idea of RDD is to compare the outcomes of schools with Z just below z_0 to those with Z just above z_0. Note that we cannot use Z as an instrumental variable as we suspect that Z has a direct impact on school average outcomes Y (the fraction of immigrant children Z is expected to have a down side effect on Y). But when we compare only schools very close to this threshold, this direct effect of Z should not really matter.

Generally, RDD can be used when a continuous variable[3] Z, which we will call *assignment score*, influences an outcome variable Y and also the treatment indicator D, which itself affects the outcome variable Y. Hence, Z has a direct impact on Y as well as an indirect impact on Y via D. This latter impact, however, represents the causal effect of D on Y. This can only be identified if the direct and the indirect (via D) impact of Z on Y can be told apart. Think about the cases where the direct impact of Z on Y is known to be smooth but the relationship between Z and D is discontinuous. Then any discontinuity (i.e. a jump) in the observed relationship between Z and Y at locations where the relation of Z to D is discontinuous, can be attributed to the indirect impact of D.

The graphs in Figures 6.1 and 6.2 give an illustration of this idea. While the two functions $E[Y^0|Z]$ and $E[Y^1|Z]$ are continuous in Z, the function $E[D|Z]$ jumps at a particular value. For values of Z smaller than z_0 the $E[D|Z=z]$ is very small, for

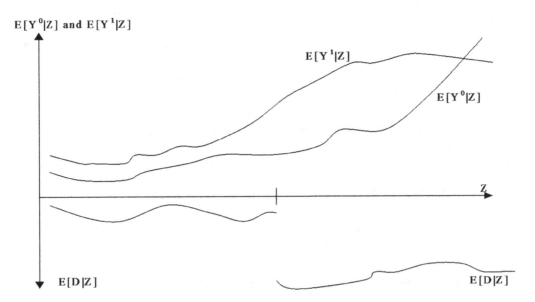

Figure 6.1 Expectations of the potential outcomes Y^0, Y^1 and D for given Z

---

[3] Mathematically it has to be continuous around z_0 in a strict sense. In practice it is sufficient that the distance to z_0 is measured on a reasonable scale such that the here presented ideas and arguments still apply, and the later on presented assumptions make at least intuitively some sense. As an exercise you might discuss why 'years of age' for adults often might work whereas 'number of children' with $z_0 \leq 2$ often would not.

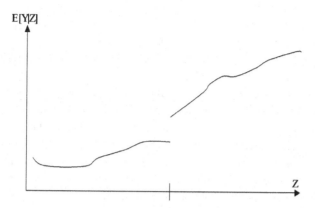

Figure 6.2 The observed outcomes and the treatment effect at the threshold

values of Z larger than z_0 the $E[D|Z = z]$ is large. This discontinuity will generate a jump in $E[Y|Z]$. A special case is the 'sharp design' where $E[D|Z]$ jumps from 0 to 1 as in the examples discussed earlier. Hence, although Z is not 'globally' a valid instrumental variable since it has a direct impact at Y^0 and Y^1, visible in the graphs, it can 'locally' be a valid instrument if we compare only those observations slightly below (control group) with those slightly above z_0 (treatment group).

For the moment we distinguish two different situations (or designs): the *sharp design* where D_i changes for all i (i.e. everyone) at the threshold, and the *fuzzy design*, where D_i changes only for some individual i. In the former, the participation status is determined by

$$D_i = \mathbb{1}\{Z_i \geq z_0\}, \tag{6.1}$$

which is a deterministic function of Z_i: all individuals change their programme participation status exactly at z_0. This requires a strictly rule-based programme selection process such as age limits or other strictly respected eligibility criteria. In Example 6.3 we clearly focus on two sharp designs (age and region) as the criteria define tight, impermeable borders. Any flexibility in the application of these criteria or a certain margin of appreciation (whether to admit an individual or not) will violate (6.1) and cause a fuzzy design.

For sharp designs it is obvious that in a small neighbourhood around the discontinuity at z_0, the direct impact of Z on the potential outcomes Y^d hardly varies with Z. So if the randomised experiment and the instrumental variable assumptions are satisfied locally, we can identify the causal effect at or around z_0, namely $E[Y^1 - Y^0|Z = z_0]$. This is in fact the treatment effect for the subpopulation with Z equal to z_0, but it may not generalise to the population at large. The conceptual framework is such that we imagine we could take an individual and hypothetically change D from zero to one, e.g. by either moving Z or by shifting the threshold z_0 by external intervention.

Let us turn to fuzzy designs. The general idea is the same but with slight modifications. In many applications the participation decision is not completely determined by Z, even in a rule-based selection process. For example, the assignment to active labour market programmes is guided by factors such as previous work history, occupation, educational attainment and mobility etc. Often the case workers have some power of discretion about whom they offer a programme, so they may base their decision on criteria that are unobserved to the econometrician. They might consider the motivation of the unemployed for participating in such programmes or include wishes of unemployed in their decisions. Additionally, individuals may be allowed to decline participation. So in brief, not all individuals would change programme participation status from $D = 0$ to $D = 1$ if Z were increased from $z_0 - \varepsilon$ to $z_0 + \varepsilon$ (for $\varepsilon > 0$). Rather, the relation between Z and D may be discontinuous at z_0 only on average. So, in the fuzzy design the expected value of D given Z (which is the probability of treatment receipt) is still supposed to be discontinuous at z_0 but not jumps from 0 to 1.

Example 6.6 Van der Klaauw (2002) analyses the effect of financial aid offered to college applicants on their probability of subsequent enrolment. College applicants are ranked according to their test score achievements into a small number of categories. The amount of financial aid offered depends largely on this classification. Yet, he finds that the financial aid officer also took other characteristics into account, which are not observed by the econometrician. Hence the treatment assignment is not a deterministic function of the test score Z, but the conditional expectation function $E[D|Z]$ nonetheless displays clear jumps because of the test-score rule.

We can state our first assumption formally by

Assumption RDD-1: $\lim_{\varepsilon \to 0} E[D|Z = z_0 + \varepsilon] - \lim_{\varepsilon \to 0} E[D|Z = z_0 - \varepsilon] \neq 0$ (6.2)

Obviously, for sharp designs the difference is exactly equal to 1. As therefore the fuzzy design includes the sharp design as a special case, much of the following discussion focuses on the more general fuzzy design but implicitly includes the sharp designs (as a trivial case).

A third case you may observe from time to time, is a *mixed design*, which is a mixture of sharp and fuzzy design or, more specifically a design with only one-sided non-compliance. This occurs if the threshold is strictly applied only on one side. A frequent case arises when *eligibility* depends strictly on observed characteristics but participation in treatment is voluntary. Obvious examples are all projects where eligibility to certain treatments are means like food stamp programmes, with a strict eligibility threshold z_0, but take-up of the treatment is typically less than 100 percent (people who got the stamps might not go for the treatment). Consequently we expect

$$\lim_{\varepsilon \to 0} E[D|Z = z_0 - \varepsilon] = 0 \quad \text{but} \quad \lim_{\varepsilon \to 0} E[D|Z = z_0 + \varepsilon] \in (0, 1]. \quad (6.3)$$

Example 6.7 Think about an eligibility to a certain labour market programme. It may depend on the duration of unemployment or on the age of individuals. The 'New Deal for Young People' in the UK offers job-search assistance (and other programmes) to all individuals aged between eighteen and twenty-four who have been claiming unemployment insurance for six months. Accordingly, the population consists of three subgroups (near the threshold): ineligibles, eligible non-participants and participants. Often data on all three groups is available.

You can also find mixed designs where theoretically everyone is allowed to get treated but some people below (or above) threshold z_0 have the permission to resign. Then you would get

$$\lim_{\varepsilon \to 0} E\left[D|Z = z_0 - \varepsilon\right] \in [0, 1) \qquad \text{but} \qquad \lim_{\varepsilon \to 0} E\left[D|Z = z_0 + \varepsilon\right] = 1, \qquad (6.4)$$

(depending on the sign of Z). Note, however, that (6.3) and (6.4) are equivalent; you simply have to redefine the treatment indicator as $1 - D$. To simplify the discussion we can therefore always refer to (6.3) without loss of generality.

Like in the sharp design, the setup in mixed designs rules out the existence of (local) *defiers*[4] close to z_0, i.e. that an individual i enters treatment for $Z_i < z_0$ but sorts out else. In the sharp design they are not allowed to chose, and in the mixed design, by definition (6.3) potential defiers are either not allowed to participate or they equal never-takers (recall the one-sided compliance case). For the rest one could say that all discussion on fuzzy designs also applies to mixed designs though with somewhat simpler formulae and fewer assumptions. For example in (6.3) also the group of (local) always-takers is redundant as they either are not eligible or become *local compliers*.[5] The adjective *local* refers now to the fact that we are only looking at the location around z_0.[6]

We will always use the Assumption RDD-1 (6.2), which is therefore supposed to be fulfilled for this entire chapter. Later on we will also discuss that we need the non-existence of defiers. Further, in many of our examples we have seen that Z may also be linked to the potential outcomes Y^d directly, so that the treatment effect cannot be identified without further assumptions. Supposing that the direct influence of Z on the potential outcomes is continuous, the potential outcomes hardly changes with Z within a small neighbourhood, e.g. around z_0. So, identification essentially relies on analysing the outcomes of those individuals being located around the threshold and that the conditional mean function is continuous at the threshold:

Assumption RDD-2: $\qquad E[Y^d|Z = z]$ is continuous in z at z_0 for $d \in \{0, 1\}$ $\qquad (6.5)$

because if there were a jump in Y^0 or Y^1 at z_0 anyway, then the underlying idea of the RDD identification and estimation would no longer apply. This again is assumed to be fulfilled for the entire chapter. The previous assumptions are sufficient for identifying average treatment effects, but if we are interested in distributional or quantile treatment effects (Chapter 7), one often finds the stronger condition in terms of conditional independence, namely

---

[4] The meaning and notation corresponds exactly to that of Chapter 4.
[5] Again, the meaning of *compliers* corresponds exactly to that of Chapter 4.
[6] In LATE, the 'local' refers to 'only compliers'.

$$Y_i^d \perp\!\!\!\perp Z_i \qquad \text{near } z_0. \tag{6.6}$$

This clearly implies the previous condition (6.5).

The continuity assumption requires that the *potential outcomes* are essentially the same on both sides of the threshold. This assumption can be violated if other things happen at threshold z_0. In the study of anti-discrimination law effects, only firms with more than 15 employees were affected. But there might also be other (public) programmes or regulations which set in at a firm size of 15. In that case, the RDD analysis would measure the effect of these different programmes together. So if we define the potential outcomes as those outcomes referring to the presence or absence of the anti-discrimination law, Assumption RDD-2 is clearly violated because outcome Y^0 (the potential outcome in the absence of the anti-discrimination law) jumps at z_0 for various reasons. This is also a concern if other programmes and regulations set in at some values close to z_0, except if our sample only contains observations directly at the cut-off.

In a sharp design, Assumption RDD-2 is sufficient for the identification of ATE=ATET=ATEN at (or near) point z_0. It is can be defined as

$$ATE(z_0) = E\left[Y^1 - Y^0 | Z = z_0\right] = \lim_{\varepsilon \to 0} E\left[Y|Z = z_0 + \varepsilon\right] - \lim_{\varepsilon \to 0} E\left[Y|Z = z_0 - \varepsilon\right], \tag{6.7}$$

where we have to estimate the terms on the right-hand side. You might ask why near z_0 ATE=ATET=ATEN; the intuitive answer follows directly from the above-mentioned motivation. The RDD with sharp design equals a randomised experiment (conditional on being close to $Z = z_0$) for which we know that ATE=ATET=ATEN; both subpopulations, treated and control, are supposed to be identical respective to the means of Y^d, $d = 0, 1$, because in a sharp design everybody is a complier by default.

An important consideration in every RDD is a potential manipulation of Z (which we study in more detail in Section 6.3.1). This is a serious concern because it can easily violate the assumptions needed for identification. Let's first explain what is meant when people speak of *perfect manipulation*. Roughly, perfect manipulation is achieved when three things hold: first, agents need to have perfect control of their value of Z; second, they have reasons to manipulate; and third, they need to know the threshold z_0. Especially if treatment effects are quite heterogeneous, there are good reasons for the agents to act against our Assumption RDD-2 (6.5). In those situations, we expect a discontinuity of the distribution of Z at the threshold, and also of other characteristics. On the other hand, a continuous density f_Z is neither a sufficient nor a necessary condition for RDD. To put things in perspective, imagine the situation when teachers want to reduce the number of students in the revision courses. They may marginally upgrade some randomly chosen students, being otherwise right below the threshold z_0. In such cases, f_Z should be discontinuous at z_0, but the assumptions of the RDD are still satisfied. But if the teachers do not select them randomly, either because they want to exclude some trouble-makers or pupils who have the abilities and knowledge but were just too lazy (or unfortunate) this year, then we can no longer apply the argument of randomised experiments. Especially if manipulation is monotonic, i.e. excluding from the programme the smartest pupils by raising their scores to z_0, then f_Z has a discontinuity, and (6.5) is violated. If it is not monotonic but goes in both directions in the sense that we upgrade the smartest for which the score was below z_0 but lowering the score for some bad pupils who had a score right above z_0, then despite the fact the density f_Z may be continuous at z_0, assumption (6.5) is also violated.

Now, instead of manipulating scores, in practice it is more likely that one simply relaxes the selection rules in the sense that people around z_0 were allowed or animated to switch into or out of treatment. Then we should be in the above introduced *fuzzy design*. But then Assumption RDD-2 is no longer sufficient. In fact, we need additionally to assume

Assumption RDD-3: $\qquad (Y_i^1 - Y_i^0) \perp\!\!\!\perp D_i | Z_i \qquad$ for Z_i near z_0 $\qquad\qquad$ (6.8)

or just the mean-analogue if not interested in the entire distribution[7]

$$E[(Y_i^1 - Y_i^0)D_i | Z_i \approx z_0] = E[(Y_i^1 - Y_i^0) | Z_i \approx z_0] \cdot E[D_i | Z_i \approx z_0].$$

It is some kind of a 'selection on observables' assumption to identify $E[Y^1 - Y^0 | Z = z_0]$ once we condition on $Z = z_0$.[8] However, this assumption has been criticised as being too restrictive and thus not credible in many applications.

An alternative approach refers to a type of *local compliers* concept. Let $D_i(z)$ be the treatment status of individual i if Z was exogenously set to z. If we were to move z a little bit around the threshold z_0, then we could have four types of people: the local always-takers would be those for whom $D_i(z_0 - \varepsilon) = 1$ and $D_i(z_0 + \varepsilon) = 1$, the local never-takers for whom $D_i(z_0 - \varepsilon) = 0$ and $D_i(z_0 + \varepsilon) = 0$, the local compliers with $D_i(z_0 - \varepsilon) = 0$ and $D_i(z_0 - \varepsilon) = 1$, and finally the local defiers for whom $D_i(z_0 - \varepsilon) = 1$ and $D_i(z_0 + \varepsilon) = 0$. As usual, the latter are assumed not to exist. Then you may replace RDD-3 by

Assumption RDD-3*: $\qquad \left\{ Y_i^1 - Y_i^0, D_i(z) \right\} \perp\!\!\!\perp Z_i$ near z_0 $\qquad\qquad$ (6.9)

$$\text{and there exists } e > 0 \text{ such that for all } \quad 0 < \varepsilon < e$$

$$D_i(z_0 + \varepsilon) \geq D_i(z_0 - \varepsilon)$$

which provides the identification of a LATE for the local compliers. The first line is very similar to the instrument exclusion restriction of Chapter 4, whereas the second line represents a type of local monotonicity restriction, requiring the absence of defiers in a neighbourhood of z_0.

It has been argued that in many applications this assumption would be easier to justify (but is not testable anyway). Its handicap is that it is some kind of instrumental variable approach and therefore only identifies the treatment effect for a group of local compliers induced by the chosen instrument and threshold, i.e.

$$LATE(z_0) = \lim_{\varepsilon \to 0} E\left[Y^1 - Y^0 | D(z_0 + \varepsilon) > D(z_0 - \varepsilon), Z = z_0 \right].$$

---

[7] We slowly switch now from the mean-independence notation to the distributional one because in the future, see especially Chapter 7, we study not just mean but distributional effects.

[8] This is often still supposed to be equal to ATET and ATEN at z_0 because this assumption says that conditioning on Z near z_0 gives a randomised trial.

Like in Chapter 4 it can be shown (Exercise 2) that the ATE on the *local compliers* is identified as

$$LATE(z_0) = \frac{\lim_{\varepsilon \to 0} E\,[Y|Z = z_0 + \varepsilon] - \lim_{\varepsilon \to 0} E\,[Y|Z = z_0 - \varepsilon]}{\lim_{\varepsilon \to 0} E\,[D|Z = z_0 + \varepsilon] - \lim_{\varepsilon \to 0} E\,[D|Z = z_0 - \varepsilon]}. \tag{6.10}$$

It has the property of being 'local' twice: first for $Z = z_0$ and second for compliers, i.e. the group of individuals whose Z value lies in a small neighbourhood of z_0 and whose treatment status D would change from 0 to 1 if Z were changed exogenously from $z_0 - \varepsilon$ to $z_0 + \varepsilon$. Now you see why we called this a handicap: depending on the context, this subpopulation and parameter might be helpful and easy to interpret or it might not. The good news is, whichever of the two alternative assumptions, i.e. RDD-3 or RDD-3*, is invoked, the existing estimators are actually the same under both identification strategies. So there is no doubt for us what we have to do regarding the data analysis; we might only hesitate when it comes to interpretation. Moreover, as in Chapter 4, the fact that we can only estimate the treatment effect for the compliers needs not necessarily be a disadvantage: sometimes this may just be the parameter one is interested in:

Example 6.8 Anderson, Dobkin and Gross (2012) examined the effect of health insurance coverage on the use of medical services. They exploited a sharp drop in insurance coverage rates at age 19, i.e. when children 'age out' of their parents' insurance plans. Many private health insurers in the USA cover dependent children up to age 18. When these children turn 19, many drop out of their parents' insurance cover. In fact, about five to eight percent of teenagers become uninsured shortly after the nineteenth birthday. The authors exploited this age discontinuity to estimate the effect of insurance coverage on the utilisation of medical services and find a huge drop in emergency department visits and inpatient hospital admissions. The estimated treatment effects represent the response of 'compliers', i.e. individuals who become uninsured when turning 19. The parameter of interest for policy purposes would be the average effect of insurance coverage for these uninsured since most current policies focus on expanding rather than reducing health insurance coverage. The 'compliers' represent a substantial fraction of uninsured young adults. Providing insurance coverage to this population would have a significant policy relevance, particularly since this group represents a large share of the uninsured population in the US. In addition, there are also local never-takers, yet the authors argue that their treatment effects should be similar to those of the compliers since the pre-19 insurance coverage is mostly an artifact of their parents' insurance plans rather than a deliberate choice based on unobserved health status. Therefore the typical adverse selection process is unlikely to apply in their context. Indeed they did not find evidence that never-takers were significantly less healthy or consumed less health care services than uninsured 'compliers'.

Let us turn to the discussion of subpopulations in mixed designs. It should be emphasised that in the fuzzy design the non-existence of defiers (forth- and back-switching of D for increasing Z) is effectively an assumption while for the other designs they are not an issue by construction. Notice that the RDD assumption implies the existence of compliers as else there was no discontinuity. Fuzzy designs allow for never- and/or always-takers, though this 'never' and 'always' refers to 'nearby z_0'. In the *mixed design* Assumptions RDD-1 and RDD-2 are sufficient if you aim to estimate the ATET (if it is sharp with respect to treatment admission but fuzzy in the sense that you may refuse the treatment, cf. equation (6.3)).[9] Then ATET and LATE are even the same at the threshold. To obtain this, recall

$$ATET(z_0) = E[Y^1 - Y^0 | D = 1, Z = z_0],$$

where we need to identify the counterfactual outcome $E[Y^0 | D = 1, Z = z_0]$. The only assumption needed is that the mean of Y^0 is continuous at z_0. Then $\lim E\left[Y^0 | Z = z_0 + \varepsilon\right] = \lim E\left[Y^0 | Z = z_0 - \varepsilon\right]$. In fact, we do not need Assumption RDD-3 or RDD-3*. Still considering (6.3), note that due to $Y = D(Y^1 - Y^0) + Y^0$ we obtain

$$\lim_{\varepsilon \to 0} E\left[Y | Z = z_0 + \varepsilon\right] - \lim_{\varepsilon \to 0} E\left[Y | Z = z_0 - \varepsilon\right]$$

$$= \lim_{\varepsilon \to 0} E\left[D(Y^1 - Y^0) + Y^0 | Z = z_0 + \varepsilon\right] - \lim_{\varepsilon \to 0} E\left[D(Y^1 - Y^0) + Y^0 | Z = z_0 - \varepsilon\right]$$

$$= \lim_{\varepsilon \to 0} E\left[D(Y^1 - Y^0) | Z = z_0 + \varepsilon\right] - \lim_{\varepsilon \to 0} E\left[D(Y^1 - Y^0) | Z = z_0 - \varepsilon\right]$$

$$= \lim_{\varepsilon \to 0} E\left[D(Y^1 - Y^0) | Z = z_0 + \varepsilon\right]$$

$$= \lim_{\varepsilon \to 0} E\left[Y^1 - Y^0 | D = 1, Z = z_0 + \varepsilon\right] \lim_{\varepsilon \to 0} E\left[D | Z = z_0 + \varepsilon\right]. \tag{6.11}$$

The second equality follows because the left and right limits for Y^0 are identical by Assumption RDD-2, the third equality follows because $D = 0$ on the left of the threshold, and the last equality follows by RDD-1 and because D is binary. We thus obtain

$$\frac{\lim_{\varepsilon \to 0} E\left[Y | Z = z_0 + \varepsilon\right] - \lim_{\varepsilon \to 0} E\left[Y | Z = z_0 - \varepsilon\right]}{\lim_{\varepsilon \to 0} E\left[D | Z = z_0 + \varepsilon\right] - \lim_{\varepsilon \to 0} E\left[D | Z = z_0 - \varepsilon\right]}$$

$$= \lim_{\varepsilon \to 0} E\left[Y^1 - Y^0 | D = 1, Z = z_0 + \varepsilon\right], \tag{6.12}$$

which is the average treatment effect on the treated for those near the threshold, i.e. ATET(z_0).

Note finally that if pre-treatment data on Y is available, we can also consider a *DiD-RDD* approach, which we discuss further below.

---

[9] Analogously, if rules are inverted such that you can switch from control to treatment but not vice versa, then these assumptions are sufficient for estimating ATENT.

6.1.2   Estimation of RDD-Based Treatment Effects

In the last section, Equations 6.7, 6.10 and 6.12 provided the identification of treatment effects under sharp, fuzzy and mixed design. These parameters are composed by limits of conditional expectations. It is not hard to see that these limit expressions, namely of $E[Y|Z = z_0 \pm \varepsilon]$ and $E[D|Z = z_0 \pm \varepsilon]$, can be estimated, for example, by local linear regression. The only challenge in their estimation is the fact that these limits define boundary points of else continuous (and smooth) functions. Consequently – see Chapter 2 – local linear estimators are more convenient as they are expected to have better boundary properties than many other estimators. In practice one could apply for each of these conditional expectations a standard local linear estimator where one uses only the data points either to the left or only those to the right of z_0. There exist also special boundary correction kernels that could be used, especially when applying the local constant (Nadaraya–Watson) kernel estimator. As discussed for propensity score estimation, there also exist alternative semi-parametric methods which are more appropriate when the response variable is binary, as it is for our D. In all these cases the optimal bandwidth selection is a crucial problem. Under conventional smoothness assumptions the (generalised) cross-validation method remains a feasible though not optimal choice. Certainly, one should use only the data points within some (not too narrow) neighbourhood of z_0 to calculate the criterion, as otherwise the observations very distant from z_0 would affect the bandwidth value too much.

One immediately notices the similarity of (6.10) to the Wald estimator for binary treatment with binary instruments. Recall that the Wald estimator is equivalent to a two-step least-squares instrumental variable regression of Y on a constant and D using Z as an instrument, cf. Exercise 3 and Theorem 4.1 of Chapter 4. The same would apply here although only in the limit case, i.e. when using exclusively observations infinitesimally close to z_0. Many applied papers use for convenience separated linear regressions (two for the sharp and four for the fuzzy design, respectively) in a neighbourhood around z_0, what corresponds to a local linear estimator with uniform kernel and huge bandwidths.

To see how this works, let us first consider the sharp design. There, everyone is a complier at z_0. We can estimate $m_+ := \lim_{\varepsilon \to 0} E[Y|Z = z_0 + \varepsilon]$ by one-sided local linear kernel regression via

$$(\hat{m}_+, \hat{\beta}_+) = \underset{m,\beta}{\arg\min} \sum_{i=1}^{n} \{Y_i - m - \beta (Z_i - z_0)\}^2 K\left(\frac{Z_i - z_0}{h_+}\right) \cdot \mathbb{1}\{Z_i \geq z_0\}$$

$$(6.13)$$

with a bandwidth h_+, and analogously $m_- := \lim_{\varepsilon \to 0} E[Y|Z = z_0 - \varepsilon]$ by

$$(\hat{m}_-, \hat{\beta}_-) = \underset{m,\beta}{\arg\min} \sum_{i=1}^{n} \{Y_i - m - \beta (Z_i - z_0)\}^2 K\left(\frac{Z_i - z_0}{h_-}\right) \cdot \mathbb{1}\{Z_i < z_0\},$$

$$(6.14)$$

with bandwidth h_- to finally obtain an estimator for $E[Y^1 - Y^0|Z = z_0]$, namely

$$\widehat{ATE}(z_0) = \hat{m}_+ - \hat{m}_-.$$

$$(6.15)$$

The exact list of necessary assumptions and the asymptotic behaviour of this estimator is given below, together with those for the estimator when facing a fuzzy design. (Recall that the sharp design can be considered as a special – and actually the simplest – case of fuzzy designs.) But before we come to an ATE estimator for the fuzzy design, let us briefly discuss some modifications of (6.14) and (6.15), still in the sharp design context.

We can rewrite the above expressions to estimate $\widehat{ATE}(z_0)$ in a single estimation step. Suppose that we use the same bandwidth left and right of z_0, i.e. $h_- = h_+ = h$. Define further $1_i^+ = \mathbb{1}\{Z_i \geq z_0\}$, $1_i^- = \mathbb{1}\{Z_i < z_0\}$, noticing that $1_i^+ + 1_i^- = 1$. The previous two local linear expressions can also be expressed as minimisers of quadratic objective functions. Since $\hat{m}_+$ and $\hat{m}_-$ are estimated from separate subsamples, these solutions are numerically identical to the minimisers of the *sum* of the two objective functions. To obtain the following formula, we just add the objective functions of the previous two local linear regressions. We obtain a joint objective function, which is minimised at $(\hat{m}_+, \hat{\beta}_+)$ and $(\hat{m}_-, \hat{\beta}_-)$:

$$\sum_{i=1}^{n} (Y_i - m_+ - \beta_+ (Z_i - z_0))^2 \, K\left(\frac{Z_i - z_0}{h}\right) \cdot 1_i^+$$

$$+ \sum_{i=1}^{n} (Y_i - m_- - \beta_- (Z_i - z_0))^2 \, K\left(\frac{Z_i - z_0}{h}\right) \cdot 1_i^-$$

$$= \sum_{i=1}^{n} \left(Y_i 1_i^+ - m_+ 1_i^+ - \beta_+ (Z_i - z_0) \, 1_i^+ \right.$$

$$\left. + Y_i 1_i^- - m_- 1_i^- - \beta_- (Z_i - z_0) \, 1_i^- \right)^2 \cdot K\left(\frac{Z_i - z_0}{h}\right).$$

Noting that in the sharp design 1_i^+ implies $D_i = 1$ and 1_i^- implies $D_i = 0$, such that we obtain

$$= \sum \left\{ Y_i - m_+ 1_i^+ - m_-(1 - 1_i^+) - \beta_+ (Z_i - z_0) \, D_i \right.$$

$$\left. - \beta_- (Z_i - z_0) \, (1 - D_i) \right\}^2 K\left(\frac{Z_i - z_0}{h}\right)$$

$$= \sum \left\{ Y_i - m_- - (m_+ - m_-) \, D_i - \beta_+ (Z_i - z_0) \, D_i \right.$$

$$\left. - \beta_- (Z_i - z_0) \, (1 - D_i) \right\}^2 K\left(\frac{Z_i - z_0}{h}\right)$$

$$= \sum \left\{ Y_i - m_- - (m_+ - m_-) \, D_i - \beta_-(Z_i - z_0) \right.$$

$$\left. - (\beta_+ - \beta_-)(Z_i - z_0) D_i \right\}^2 K\left(\frac{Z_i - z_0}{h}\right). \tag{6.16}$$

Since this function is minimised at $(\hat{m}_+, \hat{\beta}_+)$ and $(\hat{m}_-, \hat{\beta}_-)$, the coefficient on D would be estimated by $(\hat{m}_+ - \hat{m}_-)$. It gives a local linear estimator for $ATE(z_0)$ that is equivalent to the one above if $h = h_+ = h_-$. We can thus obtain the treatment effect directly by a local linear regression of Y_i on a constant, D_i, $(Z_i - z_0)$ and $(Z_i - z_0) D_i$, which is identical to the separate regressions given above.

If we want to permit different bandwidths, we have to replace the simple kernel function in (6.16) with

$$K\left(\frac{Z_i - z_0}{h_+}\right)^{1_i^+} K\left(\frac{Z_i - z_0}{h_-}\right)^{1_i^-}. \tag{6.17}$$

This implies that the bandwidth h_+ is used for smoothing on the right of z_0, and h_- is used for smoothing on the left of z_0. Kernel function (6.17) will also be applicable for the derivations for the fuzzy design.

We can estimate (6.16) as a regression of

$$Y_i \qquad \text{on} \qquad \text{a constant, } D_i, (Z_i - z_0) \quad \text{and} \quad (Z_i - z_0) D_i \tag{6.18}$$

using weighted least squares with weights (6.17). The coefficient of D_i corresponds to the estimator (6.15). If for convenience one used a uniform kernel with equal bandwidths, then the estimator would correspond to a simple (unweighted) OLS regression where all observations further apart from z_0 than h are deleted.

In some applications, the restriction is imposed that the derivative of $E[Y|Z]$ is identical on the two sides of the threshold, i.e. that

$$\lim_{\varepsilon \to 0} \frac{\partial E[Y|Z = z_0 + \varepsilon]}{\partial z} = \lim_{\varepsilon \to 0} \frac{\partial E[Y|Z = z_0 - \varepsilon]}{\partial z}.$$

This assumption appears particularly natural if one aims to test the hypothesis of a zero treatment effect, i.e. the null hypothesis that $E[Y^1 - Y^0|Z = z_0] = 0$. In other words, if the treatment has no effect on the level, it appears plausible that it also has no effect on the slope. This can easily be implemented in (6.16) by imposing that $\beta_- = \beta_+$. In the implementation we would then estimate the treatment effect by a local linear regression on a constant, D_i and $(Z_i - z_0)$ without interacting the last term with D_i. If one is not testing for a null effect, this restriction is less appealing because a non-zero treatment effect may not only lead to a jump in the mean outcome but possibly also in its slope. Note moreover that if we do not impose the restriction $\beta_- = \beta_+$ and estimate expression (6.16) including the interaction term $(Z_i - z_0)D_i$, we ensure that only data points to the left of z_0 are used for estimating the potential outcome $E[Y^0|Z = z_0]$ while only points to the right of z_0 are used for estimating the potential outcome $E[Y^1|Z = z_0]$. In contrast, when we impose the restriction $\beta_- = \beta_+$, then data points from both sides of z_0 are always used for estimating the average potential outcomes. Consequently, some Y^0 outcomes are used to estimate $E[Y^1|Z = z_0]$, and analogously, some Y^1 outcomes are used to estimate $E[Y^0|Z = z_0]$, which is counter-intuitive unless treatment effect is zero everywhere.

In the fuzzy design we implement the Wald type estimator along identification strategy (6.10) by estimating (6.13) and (6.14), once with respect to the outcome Y, and once with respect to D. For notational convenience set $m(z) = E[Y|Z = z]$, $p(z) = E[D|Z = z]$ with m_+, m_-, p_+, p_- being the limits from above and below, respectively, when $z \to z_0$. Imagine now that all these are estimated by local linear regression. The same way we define for its first and second derivatives m'_+, m'_-, p'_+, p'_- and $m''_+, m''_-, p''_+, p''_-$. Let us further define

$$\sigma_+^2 = \lim_{\varepsilon \to 0} Var(Y|Z = z_0 + \varepsilon), \qquad \rho_+ = \lim_{\varepsilon \to 0} Cov(Y, D|Z = z_0 + \varepsilon),$$

and σ_-^2, ρ_- analogously, being the limits from below. Then we can state the asymptotic behaviour of the Wald type RDD-(L)ATE estimator[10]

THEOREM 6.1 *Suppose that Assumptions RDD-1, RDD-2 and RDD-3 or RDD-3* are fulfilled. Furthermore, assume that m and p are twice continuously differentiable for $z > z_0$. For consistent estimation we need the following regularity assumptions:*

(i) *There exists some $\varepsilon > 0$ such that $|m_+|$, $|m'_+|$, $|m''_+|$, and $|p_+|$, $|p'_+|$, $|p''_+|$ are uniformly bounded on $(z_0, z_0 + \varepsilon]$, and $|m_-|$, $|m'_-|$, $|m''_-|$, and $|p_-|$, $|p'_-|$, $|p''_-|$ are uniformly bounded on $[z_0 - \varepsilon, z_0)$.*

(ii) *The limits off m_+, m_-, p_+, p_- in z_0 exist and are finite. The same holds for its first and second derivatives.*

(iii) *The conditional variance $\sigma^2(z_i) = Var(Y_i|z_i)$ and covariance $\rho(z_i) = Cov(Y_i, D_i|z_i)$ are uniformly bounded near z_0. Their limits σ_+^2, σ_-^2, ρ_+, ρ_- exist and are finite.*

(iv) *The limits of $E\left[|Y_i - m(Z_i)|^3|z_i = z\right]$ exist and are finite for z approaching z_0 from above or below.*

(v) *The density f_z of z is continuous, bounded, and bounded away from zero near z_0.*

(vi) *The kernel function $K(\cdot)$ is continuous, of 2nd order, and > 0 with compact support. For the bandwidth we have $h = \varrho n^{-1/5}$.*

Then, with $\hat{m}_+$, $\hat{m}_-$, $\hat{p}_+$ and $\hat{p}_-$ being local linear estimators of m_+, m_-, p_+ and p_- respectively, we have for the RDD-LATE estimator

$$n^{2/5}\left(\frac{\hat{m}_+ - \hat{m}_-}{\hat{p}_+ - \hat{p}_-} - \frac{m_+ - m_-}{p_+ - p_-}\right) \longrightarrow N(B, V)$$

where bias and variance are given by

$$B = \frac{v_+ m''_+ - v_- m''_-}{p_+ - p_-} - \frac{(m_+ - m_-)(v_+ p''_+ - v_- p''_-)}{(p_+ - p_-)^2}$$

with
$$v_+ = \frac{\varrho^2}{2} \frac{\left(\int_0^\infty u^2 K(u)\, du\right)^2 - \left(\int_0^\infty u K(u)\, du\right)\left(\int_0^\infty u^3 K(u)\, du\right)}{\left(\int_0^\infty K(u)\, du\right)\left(\int_0^\infty u^2 K(u)\, du\right) - \left(\int_0^\infty u K(u)\, du\right)^2},$$

$$V = \frac{w_+ \sigma_+^2 + w_- \sigma_-^2}{(p_+ - p_-)^2} - 2\frac{m_+ - m_-}{(p_+ - p_-)^3}\left(w_+ \rho_+^2 + w_- \rho_-^2\right)$$
$$+ \frac{(m_+ - m_-)^2}{(p_+ - p_-)^4}\left(w_+ p_+\{1 - p_+\} + w_- p_-\{1 - p_-\}\right)$$

with
$$w_+ = \frac{\int_0^\infty \left\{\int_0^\infty s^2 K(s)\, ds - u \int_0^\infty s K(s)\, ds\right\}^2 K^2(u)\, du}{\varrho f_z(z_0)\left\{\int_0^\infty u^2 K(u)\, du \cdot \int_0^\infty K(u)\, du - \left(\int_0^\infty u K(u)\, du\right)^2\right\}^2}$$

and v_-, w_- being defined as v_+, w_+ but for integral limits $(-\infty, 0)$.

---

[10] See Hahn, Todd and van der Klaauw (1999) for further details and proof.

To conclude so far: The regression-discontinuity approach permits the estimation of a treatment effect under weak conditions. In particular, a type of instrumental variable assumption needs to hold only locally. On the other hand, the ATE is identified only for the local compliers, i.e. for compliers around z_0. Due to its double local nature, no $\sqrt{n}$-consistent estimator can exist for estimating it, because we require a continuous variable Z for this approach and have to rely on smoothing around z_0 with bandwidth converging to zero for consistency.

In practice, since $E[D|Z = z]$ is typically expected to be smoother (as a function of z) than $E[Y|Z = z]$, one would tend to choose a larger bandwidth for estimating the terms appearing in the denominator of (6.10) than for those terms appearing in the numerator. In case we have a sharp design, the denominator is no longer necessary, and therefore all terms related to the estimation of p_+, p_- will disappear.

When thinking of the RDD as an instrumental variable approach, one might ask whether our Wald-type RDD estimator could also be written as a two step least squares (2SLS) estimator. This is indeed the case if we use the same bandwidth values in all expressions of (6.10). If we used different bandwidths in the numerator and denominator of (6.10), then the following representation as a 2SLS estimator would not be correct. For simplicity we use a uniform kernel in the following. The uniform kernel implies that all observations with $|Z_i - z_0| \leq h$ receive a weight of one and all other observations receive a weight zero. Consider the 2SLS regression using only observations with $|Z_i - z_0| \leq h$: regress

$$Y_i \quad \text{on} \quad \text{a constant, } D_i, \ (Z_i - z_0)\,1_i^+ \quad \text{and} \quad (Z_i - z_0)\,1_i^- \qquad (6.19)$$

with the following instruments: a constant, 1_i^+, $(Z_i - z_0)\,1_i^+$ and $(Z_i - z_0)\,1_i^-$. So 1_i^+ is the excluded instrument for the endogenous regressor D_i. The coefficient on D_i is numerically identical to the Wald estimator (6.10) based on (6.13) and (6.14) and the corresponding expressions for D. As mentioned, the previous result is also obtained when using a kernel function (6.17), as long as the same bandwidth is used throughout.

The 2SLS regression equation (6.19) can be extended by adding further polynomial terms e.g. $(Z_i - z_0)^2\,1_i^+$ and $(Z_i - z_0)^2\,1_i^-$, which would then correspond to estimating the terms in (6.10) by local quadratic regression. Similarly, higher-order polynomials can be included, which is done in some applied articles. Analogously, one could also include squares and polynomials in $(Z_i - z_0)$ in (6.18) for the sharp design. Including polynomials in $(Z_i - z_0)$ would become relevant if one is using a large bandwidth value such that also observations rather distant from z_0 enter in the regression model, particularly if one uses a uniform kernel where close and distant observations get the same weight. Since Z is likely to be related to the outcomes, controlling for the influences of Z in possibly non-linear ways becomes important. In contrast, with a small bandwidth value h the linear terms are sufficient. (This situation is akin to the discussion of local polynomial non-parametric regression with the practical trade-off of a small bandwidth versus a more complex local model.) The fact that the expression (6.10) can also be estimated via (6.19) appears to be only of theoretical value, but it shows again the link between the RDD and a local IV identification. The 2SLS approach in (6.19) will be particularly helpful, though, when we examine multiple thresholds. Another convenient advantage of (6.19) is that it easily permits the inclusion of additional covariates X or some fixed effects in a linear way. In addition, expression (6.19) can be convenient to obtain standard errors, where one should use robust 2SLS standard errors. All this is conditioned on using only observations i with $|Z_i - z_0| \leq h$.

6.1.3 RDD with Multiple Thresholds

The RDD method has been designed to use a discontinuity at one unique point z_0 in order to identify and afterwards estimate the treatment effect at or around z_0. In practice you may easily face a situation where you actually have several discontinuity points, say z_{01}, z_{02}, z_{03}, etc. For example, when Lalive, Wüllrich and Zweimüller (2008) considered a policy in Austria where firms were obliged to hire one severely disabled worker per 25 non-disabled workers, or to pay a fee instead, this rule obviously implied a threshold at $z_{01} = 25$, $z_{02} = 50$, $z_{03} = 75$ etc. Another example (Van der Klaauw 2002) for a mixed design is (increasing) financial aid as a function of an ability test score: the test score is more or less continuous, but for administrative purposes it is grouped into four categories, $Z < z_{01}$, $z_{01} < Z < z_{02}$, $z_{02} < Z < z_{03}$ and $Z > z_{03}$. At each of these thresholds the probability of treatment rises discontinuously and may or may not remain constant between these thresholds. In these two examples we are not really facing the same problem: while in the first example the treatment is the same at each threshold (one disabled worker per 25 non-disabled), in the second example the financial aid is steadily increasing for the same person depending on his test score. Consequently, to expect about the same treatment effect at each threshold is more plausible in the first than in the second example. When dealing a multiple threshold case, we first need to clarify whether each threshold is actually combined with the same kind of treatment. If not, for each treatment we might want to identify and estimate its own treatment effect. In those cases we would apply the method(s) we have learnt above to each z_{0j}, $j = 1, 2, 3$. But more interesting is the case where we have the same treatment and/or assume the same average treatment effect at each threshold. We certainly could still use the above methods to estimate the treatment effect separately at each threshold, and then take a (weighted) average of all these estimates. An alternative approach may be helpful for two reasons: first, if the (average) treatment effect is indeed the same, we would expect to obtain more precise inference. Second, it helps us to link the methods derived above to more conventional parametric modelling, which may be helpful if we would like to incorporate further specific features in a particular application. Let us consider an example that revisits several of the problems discussed so far:

Example 6.9 Angrist and Lavy (1999) used that in Israel 'class size' is usually determined by a rule that splits classes when class size would be larger than 40. This policy generates discontinuities in class size when the enrolment in a grade grows from 40 to 41 – as class size changes from one class of 40 to one class of size 20 and 21. The same applies then to 80–81, etc. Enrolment (Z) has thus a discontinuous effect on class size (D) at these different cut-off points. Since Z may directly influence student achievement (e.g. via the size or popularity of the school), it is not a valid instrumental variable as it clearly violates the exclusion restriction. But it produces thresholds at 41, 81, 121, etc. such that, if we compared only classes with enrolment of size 40 to those with 41, those of size 80 to those with 81, etc. we could apply the RDD idea. Furthermore, it is plausible to assume to have the same average treatment effect at each threshold. The authors imposed more structure in form of a linear model to estimate the impact of class size on student achievement. Nevertheless, the justification for their approach essentially relied on the considerations above.

We discuss the case of multiple thresholds for the sharp design first. For further simplification, imagine that around z_0 we can work with a more or less constant treatment effect β. If we had just one threshold z_0:

$$Y_i = \beta_0 + \beta D_i + U_i, \tag{6.20}$$

where endogeneity arises because of dependency between D_i and U_i. In the sharp design one has $D_i = \mathbb{1}\{Z_i \geq z_0\}$ such that we obtain

$$E[Y_i|Z_i, D_i] = \beta_0 + \beta D_i + E[U_i|Z_i, D_i], \tag{6.21}$$

where $E[U_i|Z_i, D_i] = E[U_i|Z_i]$ because D_i is a deterministic function of Z_i. We can rewrite the previous equation by adding Y_i on both sides, i.e.

$$Y_i = \beta_0 + \beta D_i + E[U_i|Z_i] + \underbrace{W_i}_{Y_i - E[Y|Z_i, D_i]} .$$

The 'error' term W_i has the nice properties $E[W_i] = 0$ for all i, $cov(W_i, D_i) = 0$ and $cov(W_i, E[U_i|Z_i]) = 0$. This can be shown by straightforward calculations using iterated expectations. Suppose further that $E[U_i|Z_i]$ belongs to a parametric family of functions, e.g. polynomial functions, which we denote by $\Upsilon(z, \delta)$ (with δ a vector of unknown parameters; infinite number if Υ is non-parametric) and is continuous in z at z_0. You must suppress the intercept in the specification of $\Upsilon(\cdot)$ because we already have β_0 in the above equation as a constant. Hence, we cannot identify another intercept (what is not a problem as we are only interested in β). We assume that there is a true vector δ such that $E[U_i|Z_i] = \Upsilon(Z_i, \delta)$ *almost surely*.[11] If $E[U_i|Z_i]$ is sufficiently smooth, it can always be approximated to arbitrary precision by a polynomial of sufficiently large order. The important point is to have the number of terms in $\Upsilon(z, \delta)$ sufficiently large.[12] By using $E[U_i|Z_i] = \Upsilon(Z_i, \delta)$ we can rewrite the previous expression as

$$Y_i = \beta_0 + \beta D_i + \Upsilon(Z_i, \delta) + \underbrace{W_i}_{Y_i - E[Y|Z_i, D_i]} , \tag{6.22}$$

---

[11] There is a vector δ such that for all values $z \in \mathbb{R}\backslash A$, where $\Pr(Z \in A) = 0$, it holds
$E[U|Z = z] = \Upsilon(z, \delta)$.

[12] You may take a second-order polynomial $\delta_1 z + \delta_2 z^2$ but with a high risk of misspecification. Alternatively, you may take a series and, theoretically, include a number of basis functions that increases with sample size. This would result in a non-parametric sieve estimator for $E[U|Z]$.

where we now consider the terms in $\Upsilon(Z_i, \delta)$ as additional regressors, which are all uncorrelated with W_i. Hence, $\Upsilon(Z_i, \delta)$ is supposed to control for any impact on Y_i that is correlated with Z_i (and this way with D_i without being caused by D_i). Then the treatment effect β could be consistently estimated.

Interestingly, the regression in (6.22) does not make any use of z_0 itself. The identification nevertheless comes from the discontinuity at z_0 together with the smoothness assumption on $E[U|Z]$. To see this, consider what would happen if we used only data to the left (respectively, right) side of z_0. In this case, D_i would be the same for all data points such that β could not be identified. Actually, in (6.22) the variable Z_i has two functions: its discontinuity in D at z_0 to identify β, and then its inclusion via $\Upsilon(\cdot)$ to avoid an omitted variable bias. Moreover, endogeneity of D in (6.20) with the treatment effect being constant around z_0 is only caused by the omission of Z. In sum, from the derivations leading to (6.22) it is not hard to see that the regression (6.22) would be the same if there were multiple thresholds z_{0j}, $j = 1, 2, \ldots$ But we have to redefine D_i accordingly; see below and Exercise 4.

Example 6.10 Recall Example 6.9 of splitting school classes in Israel if class size exceeds 41 pupils having thus thresholds at 41, 81, 121, etc. We could either just ask whether they have been split, or divide the set of all positive integers in non-overlapping sets on which D_i is either equal to one (school is considered as being treated) or zero. This shows our 'dilemma': a school with 60 enrolments, is it considered as treated (since $60 > 40$) or not (since $60 < 81$)?

A remedy to this and the above-mentioned problems is to use only observations that are close to a threshold z_{0j}, $j = 1, 2, \ldots$ This also makes the necessary assumptions more credible. Firstly, for sharp designs, near the thresholds it is clear whether D_i takes the value zero or one. Secondly, to approximate $E[U_i|Z_i]$ by (different) local parametric functions in (each) threshold neighbourhood should be a valid simplification. Recall also that we are interested in the average of all treatment effects, i.e. the average over all individuals over all thresholds. If β is constant, $E[U_i|Z_i]$ should be almost constant around a given $Z_i = z$ as otherwise the assumptions we made on U_i above might become implausible.[13] If you want to allow for different treatment effects at different thresholds, then you would estimate them separately. In sum, obtaining $\hat{\beta}$ by estimating (6.22) with a partial linear model (recall Chapter 2) only using data around the thresholds is a valid strategy.

The case of multiple thresholds becomes more complex when facing a fuzzy design. We still work with a constant treatment effect as above. Recall Assumption RDD-3: Generally, we do not permit that individuals may select into treatment according to their gain $(Y_i^1 - Y_i^0)$ from it. Note that the assumption of a constant treatment effect automatically implies that this is satisfied, because then $(Y_i^1 - Y_i^0)$ is the same for everyone. As

---

[13] Note that U represents all deviations from the mean model, including those that are caused by potential heterogeneous returns to treatment.

stated, an alternative is to work with Asumption RDD-3*, resulting in the same estimator but with a more complex interpretation. We start again from Equation 6.20 with only one threshold z_0 and aim to rewrite it such that we could estimate it by OLS. Because D_i is no longer a deterministic function of Z_i, we consider only expected values conditional on Z_i, i.e. we do not condition on Z_i and D_i jointly:

$$Y_i = \beta_0 + \beta D_i + U_i \Rightarrow E[Y_i|Z_i] = \beta_0 + \beta E[D_i|Z_i] + E[U_i|Z_i],$$
$$Y_i = \beta_0 + \beta \cdot E[D_i|Z_i] + E[U_i|Z_i] + \underbrace{W_i}_{Y_i - E[Y_i|Z_i]},$$

where W_i is not correlated with any of the other terms on the right-hand side of the equation. As before we suppose that $E[U_i|Z_i] = \Upsilon(Z_i, \delta)$ belongs to a parametric family of functions that are continuous at z_0, and write

$$Y_i = \beta_0 + \beta \cdot E[D_i|Z_i] + \Upsilon(Z_i, \delta) + \underbrace{W_i}_{Y_i - E[Y|Z_i]}. \tag{6.23}$$

If we knew the function $E[D_i|Z_i] = \Pr(D_i = 1|Z_i)$, we could estimate the previous equation by (weighted) OLS to obtain β. Since we do not know $E[D_i|Z_i]$ we could pursue a two-step approach in that we first estimate it and plug the predicted $E[D_i|Z_i]$ in (6.23). What is new here is that for an efficient estimation of $E[D_i|Z_i]$ one could and should use the priori knowledge of a discontinuity at z_0. In practice, people just use linear probability models with an indicator function $\mathbb{1}\{Z_i > z_0\}$, see also Exercise 3. In such cases one could invoke the following specification

$$E[D_i|Z_i] = \gamma + \bar{\Upsilon}(Z_i, \bar{\delta}) + \lambda \cdot \mathbb{1}\{Z_i \geq z_0\}, \tag{6.24}$$

where $\bar{\Upsilon}(\cdot, \bar{\delta})$ is a parametric family of functions indexed by $\bar{\delta}$, e.g. a polynomial. In (6.24) one uses the knowledge of having a discontinuity at z_0. (It is, however, well known that linear probability models are inappropriate; see also our discussion in Chapter 3.)

What would happen if we chose the same polynomial order for Υ and $\bar{\Upsilon}$, e.g. a third-order polynomial? With exact identification, IV and 2SLS were identical because the solution to (6.23) is identical to IV regression of Y_i on a constant, D_i, Z_i, Z_i^2, Z_i^3 with instruments: a constant, Z_i, Z_i^2, Z_i^3 and $\mathbb{1}\{Z_i \geq z_0\}$, where the latter is the excluded instrument.

If we have multiple thresholds e.g. z_0, z_1, z_2 we replace (6.24) by

$$E[D_i|Z_i] = \gamma + \bar{\Upsilon}(Z_i, \bar{\delta}) + \lambda_0 \cdot \mathbb{1}\{Z_i \geq z_0\} + \lambda_1 \cdot \mathbb{1}\{Z_i \geq z_1\} + \lambda_2 \cdot \mathbb{1}\{Z_i \geq z_2\}. \tag{6.25}$$

In this case we have three excluded instruments: $\mathbb{1}\{Z_i \geq z_0\}$, $\mathbb{1}\{Z_i \geq z_1\}$, $\mathbb{1}\{Z_i \geq z_2\}$ giving over-identification.

These approaches would also apply if D_i was a non-binary treatment variable as long as the wanted effect is just a constant β (and therefore a linear structure $\beta \cdot D_i$ sufficient). For example, van der Klaauw (2002) considered the amount of financial aid offered (continuous). Of course, in this case and with constant returns to treatment the assumption (6.20) becomes more restrictive because of the linearity in D_i. An example in which (6.25) is estimated and its predicted values are plugged into (6.23) is the class size rule in Angrist and Lavy (1999).

Matsudaira (2008) considered a mandatory summer school programme for pupils with poor performance on school. Pupils with low scores on maths and readings tests were obliged to attend a summer school programme during the holidays. Students who scored below a certain threshold on either of these tests had to attend the programme, i.e.

$$Z = \mathbb{1}\{Z_{math} < z_{0,math} \text{ or } Z_{reading} < z_{0,reading}\}. \tag{6.26}$$

The structure with these two test scores thus permits to control for maths ability while using the RDD with respect to the reading score and vice versa.

6.2 Regression Discontinuity Design with Covariates

6.2.1 Motivations for Including Covariates

In the RDD setup, if we have data beyond what is exactly required for RDD, i.e. other than Y, D and Z, they can sometimes be helpful. This additional data could be in the form of pre-treatment outcomes $Y_{i,t-1}$ or Y_{t-2}, as will be examined in the subsection on DiD-RDD, or it can be included as covariates, denoted by X. These covariates may be known to be unaffected by treatment, often labelled as pre-treatment covariates, or they may have been affected by D or Z. This section is based on Frölich and Huber (2018).

First we discuss the case when X are covariates that are not affected by treatment. In that case we generally expect that the conditional distribution of such covariates $F(X|Z)$ should be continuous at z_0. For example, we would expect that $\lim_{\varepsilon \to 0} E[X|Z = z_0 - \varepsilon] = \lim_{\varepsilon \to 0} E[X|Z = z_0 + \varepsilon]$. If, on the other hand, the mean function $E[X|Z]$ is discontinuous at z_0, this may be an indication that the variable Z may have been manipulated, which would often raise suspicions regarding the validity of the RDD design. Therefore, one often tests for discontinuities in $E[X|Z]$ or $F(X|Z)$ either by a formal statistical test or by visual exploration. As an alternative, one often sees regression discontinuity estimates with and without covariates. If all covariates are indeed continuous at the threshold z_0, the estimates with and without covariates should be similar as they converge to the same limit. Hence, by comparing both estimates, which should be similar, one can also judge the credibility of the RDD assumptions.

Below we will examine a non-parametric approach when including those X. But before going into details of identification and estimation of treatment effects based on RDD with covariates, we should answer to the question why and when someone should include covariates additional to Z. A first simple reason could be that one is interested in ATE(x) rather than the overall average. The inclusion of covariates is mostly motivated on the grounds that they may help to reduce small sample imbalances. Another obvious reason is that if these covariates are good predictors of the outcome, then they can reduce the variance of the treatment effect estimate quite importantly. Therefore, even with excellent experimental data for which no selection bias is suspected, researchers include covariates that are good predictors of the outcome variable Y. For the RDD case, a typical example is when educational support programme is offered to children from poor families. Children can participate in this programme if their parents' income Z falls below a certain threshold z_0. The outcome of interest Y is the maths test one year later. Good predictors of the maths test outcome Y are usually the maths tests in the previous years. These could be added as additional control variables X to obtain more precise estimates. So already in this example there are at least two reasons to include X; first, for a better control of heterogeneous returns to treatment and thus making the RDD assumptions more likely to hold; and second, the reduction of the standard errors. The first point is less important if all covariates are perfectly balanced between treated and non-treated in the sample used for estimation. Certainly, one might argue that this should be the case anyway if all subjects are very close or equal to z_0. Note that all mentioned arguments are also valid if we first include X for the regression, but later on integrate them out to obtain an unconditional treatment effect.

Maybe more frequently, covariates X are added for a robustness when moving away from z_0. In many applications we might have only few observations close to the threshold at our disposal. In practice we might thus be forced to also include observations with values of Z not that close to z_0 (in other words, choose a rather large bandwidth). While it appears plausible that locally pre-treatment covariates should be randomly distributed about z_0 (such that each value of X is equally likely observed on the left and on the right of z_0), further away from z_0 there is no reason why the distributions of X should be balanced. Consequently, the omission of X could lead to sample biases akin to omitted variables. Although this problem would vanish asymptotically (when data become abundant close to z_0) the small sample imbalances in X can be serious in practice. In sum, we see why including covariates X can help then to reduce the risk of a bias when using observations (far) away from z_0.

Example 6.11 Black, Galdo and Smith (2005) evaluate the finite sample performance of the regression discontinuity design. They are interested in the impact of a training programme D on annual earnings Y and thereby note that 'annual earnings in the previous year' is a very important predictor. They examine a randomised experiment which also contains an RDD and conclude that controlling for covariates is important for finite-sample performance. Their result highlights the importance of using pre-treatment covariates in the estimation of conditional mean counterfactuals. In their case for example, ignoring the pre-treatment covariate 'past earnings' causes a large bias in the conventional RDD estimates without covariates.

While efficiency gains and selection or sample biases are the main reasons for incorporating covariates, there may also be situations where the distribution of $F(X|Z)$ is truly discontinuous at z_0 for some variables X. In most cases, this may be an indication of a failure of the RDD assumptions. Sometimes, but not always, conditioning on these covariates restores the validity. In other words, like in the previous chapters, conditioning the necessary RDD-assumptions on X might render them more plausible (or at

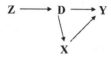

Figure 6.3 Direct and indirect impact of D on Y

least help to make them less implausible). Certainly, this argument is not that different from the 'balancing' argument above. Here we just say that even at z_0 (and not only when moving away from it) you may face what we called confounders in the previous chapters.

There are two major reasons why the distribution of (some) covariates may be discontinuous, due to confounding, or via a direct impact of Z on X. We first discuss the latter case. Here, covariates may help to distinguish direct from total treatment effects, recall Chapter 2. Note that many of the cases discussed imply different distributions of X for treated and non-treated, respectively. Such a situation is sketched in Figure 6.3; it shows a situation where the inclusion of covariates X helps to distinguish total from direct (or partial) effects. Note, though, that this approach only works if there are no unobservables that affect X and Y simultaneously.

Example 6.12 Recall Example 6.5. Black (1999) analysed the impact of school quality on housing prices by comparing houses adjacent to school–attendance district boundaries. School quality varies across the border, which should be reflected in the prices of apartments. Consider two plots of land of the same size which are adjacent to a school district boundary but on opposite sides of it. The school on the left happens by chance to be a good school. The school on the right by chance happens to be of poor quality supposing a completely random process. One is interested in the impact of school quality on the market price of a flat. Using the RDD approach, we compare the prices of houses left and right of the border. So this is an RDD with geographical borders. To use this approach, we must verify the assumptions. As with all geographical borders used in an RDD approach, one might be concerned that there could also be other changes in regulations when moving from the left-hand side to the right-hand side of the street. It seems though that school districts boundaries do in some states not coincide with other administrative boundaries such that these concerns can be dissipated. In this example there is a different concern, though: although, in contrast to individual location decisions, houses cannot move, the construction companies might have decided to build different types of houses on the left-hand side and the right-hand side of the road. If school quality was indeed valued by parents, developers would build different housing structures on the two sides of the boundary: on the side with the good school, they will construct larger flats with many bedrooms for families with children. On the side with the bad school, they will construct flats suitable for individuals or families with no or fewer children (of school age), i.e. smaller flats with fewer bedrooms. Hence, the houses on the two sides of the border may be different such that differences in prices not only reflect the valuation of school quality but also the differences in housing structures. Let i indicate a flat where Z_i indicates distance to the border. Y_i is the market price of the flat. D_i is the school quality associated with the region where the flat is located, and X_i are characteristics of the flat (number of bedrooms, size, garden, etc.). If school quality evolved completely randomly, D_i is not confounded. However, school quality D_i has two effects. Firstly, it has a direct effect on the value of the flat i. Secondly, it has an indirect effect via X_i. As discussed, because houses are built (or refurbished) differently on the two sides of the border, school quality has an effect on the characteristics X_i of the flat (number of bedrooms, size), which by itself has an effect on the market price. If we are interested in the valuation of school quality, we need to disentangle these effects. As Black (1999) wants to know the impact of school quality on market price for a flat of identical characteristics, he controls for the number of bedrooms, square footage and other characteristics of the apartments. This approach corresponds to Figure 6.3 and is only valid if there are no other unobservables related to X and Y.

Now let us consider an example where it is less clear whether to condition on X or not.

Example 6.13 Reconsider the impact of a summer school programme for poorly performing children, c.f. Matsudaira (2008). The fact that some pupils performed poorly but nevertheless were just above the cutoff z_0 for participation in the publicly subsidised summer school programme could lead their parents to provide some other kind of educational activities over the summer months. Let these be measured by X variables. Again, the X variables are intermediate outcomes and we might be interested in both: the total effect of the summer school programme and the direct effect after controlling for supplementary but privately paid activities X. In this example, conditioning on X is unlikely to work, though, because these activities are likely to be related to some unobservables that reflect parental interest in education, which itself is likely to be also related with the outcome variable Y. This makes the interpretation even harder.

Figure 6.4 indicates a situation where a change in Z also affects Y indirectly via X. In such a situation controlling for X is necessary since the 'instrumental variable' Z would otherwise have an effect on Y that is not channelled via D. Such a situation often occurs when geographical borders are used to delineate a discontinuity. Without loss of generality, in the following example we look at a discretised but not necessarily binary D.

Example 6.14 Brügger, Lalive and Zweimüller (2008) use the language border within Switzerland to estimate the effects of culture on unemployment. The language border (German and French) is a cultural divide within Switzerland, with villages to the left

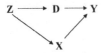

Figure 6.4 Two channels for the impact of Z on Y

and the right side of the border sharing different attitudes. The authors use highly dis-aggregated data (i.e. for each village) on various national referenda on working time regulations. The voting outcomes per community are used to define an indicator of the 'taste for leisure' as one particular indicator of the local culture. When plotting the 'taste for leisure' of a community/village against the distance to the language border, they find a discontinuous change at the language border. As 'taste for leisure' (treatment D) may also have an effect on the intensity of job search efforts and thus the duration of unemployment spells Y. They use commuting distance to the language border from each village as an instrument Z. A crucial aspect of their identification strategy is thus that changing the location of the village (e.g. from the German speaking to the French speaking side) only changes Y via the 'taste for leisure' D. Very importantly, the language border is different from administrative state borders, which implies that the same unemployment laws and regulations apply to the left and right side of the border. They also find that the distribution of many other community covariates X is continuous at the border: local taxes, labour demand (vacancies etc.), age and education structure etc. On the other hand, they also find discontinuities at the language border in the distribution of some other community characteristics X, mainly in the use of active labour market programmes and sanctions by the public employment services as well as in the number of firms. To avoid allowing these covariates to bias the estimate, they control for them.

This is an example of a convincing application of RDD: a language border that passes through an integrated labour market within the same legal environment where discontinuities in the distribution of community characteristics X are nevertheless observed at the border. Even though one can never exclude the possibility that not only X but also some unobserved characteristics U may have discontinuous distribution at the language border, if estimates remain stable after controlling for X, one is usually more confident that they would be also if one were able to control for U. Another example, where total and direct effects are often compounded occurs with the use of school entry cut-off dates.

Example 6.15 In most countries, the year when a child enters school depends on whether a child was born before or after a fixed cut-off date, e.g. 1 July. A child born before 1 July would enter school in this school year, whereas a child born after 1 July would enter school in the next school year. Comparing two children born close to the cut-off date, the child born before the cut-off enters school now, whereas the other child born a few days later enters school next year. The 'age of entry' in school thereby differs nearly a year. Usually, the assignment according to this regular school starting age is not strict and parents can advance or delay their child. Nevertheless, in most countries one observes a clear discontinuity in 'age of entry' around the cut-off, corresponding to a fuzzy design. This school-entry rule has been used in several research articles to estimate the returns to the years of education: in many countries, pupils have to stay in school compulsorily until a specific age, e.g. until their 16th birthday, after which they can drop out of education voluntarily. Children who entered school effectively one year later thus can drop out with less schooling than those who entered school at the younger age. This discontinuity is also visible in the data. One problem with this identification strategy, though, is that the birth cut-off date has several effects: not only is there an effect on the number of school years attended, but also on the age of school entry, which in itself not only affects the absolute age at the child at school entry but also the relative age within the class, i.e. the age compared to the schoolmates: children born before the cut-off date tend to be the youngest in the class, whereas those born after the cut-off are the oldest in the class. The relative age may be an important factor in their educational develop-ment. Hence, the birth date has several channels, and attribution of the observed effects to these channels is not possible without further assumptions. Fredriksson and Öckert (2006) aim to disentangle the effects of absolute and relative age at school entry. They are mainly interested in the effect of absolute age, without a change in relative age, because the policy question they are interested in is a nationwide reduction in school starting age, which obviously would reduce the school starting age for everyone without affecting the relative age distribution. They assume that the relative age effect is fully captured by the rank order in the age distribution within school and exploit the within school variation in the age composition across cohorts to estimate the relative age effect. Because of natural fluctuations in the age composition of the local school population and postponed or early entry of some school children, it is possible that children with the same age rank have quite different absolute ages (particularly for small schools in rural areas). They thus estimate the effect of changes in absolute age while keeping the age rank (X) constant. Fully non-parametric identification is not possible in this approach and their estimates therefore rely on extrapolations from their applied parametric model.

Now we consider the case of confounding. Figure 6.5 shows the classical case of confounding where there are variables X that determine Z and D or Y. An interesting example is when looking at dynamic treatment assignment. Past treatment receipt may affect the outcome as well as current treatment receipt, and the past value of the eligi-bility variable Z_{t-1} may be correlated with the current one. This scenario is depicted in Figure 6.6, which is a special case of Figure 6.5 for setting $X = Z_{t-1}$.

$$Z \longrightarrow D \longrightarrow Y$$

Figure 6.5 Confounded RDD (or IV) situation

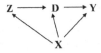

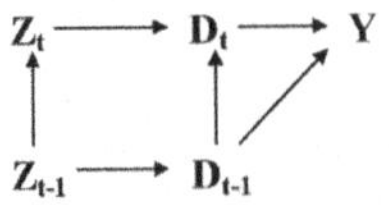

Figure 6.6 An example of dynamic treatment assignment

Example 6.16 Van der Klaauw (2008) analyses a policy where schools with a poverty rate above a certain threshold $z_{0,t}$ in year t receive additional subsidies, whereas schools below the threshold do not. The threshold $z_{0,t}$ changes from year to year. In addition to this simple assignment rule, there is one additional feature: schools which received a subsidy in the previous year continue to receive a subsidy for another year even if their poverty rate drops below $z_{0,t}$. This is called the 'hold-harmless' provision. Hence, treatment status D_t in time t depends on Z_t and the threshold $z_{0,t}$ as well as Z_{t-1} and the threshold of last year $z_{0,t-1}$. At the same time it is reasonable to expect that past poverty Z_{t-1} is related to current poverty Z_t.

In this situation of dynamic treatment assignment, one would like to control for D_{t-1}. If data on D_{t-1} is not available, one would like to control for Z_{t-1}. By this we ensure that individuals with the same values of the control variables have the same treatment history. Otherwise, we do not know whether we estimate the effect of subsidies for 'one-year' or the 'cumulative effect' of subsidies over several years. This, of course, is important for interpreting the results and to assess the cost benefit of the programme.

Example 6.17 Continuing with Example 6.16, consider a scenario where poverty rates Z_t are time-constant and also $z_{0,t}$ is time-constant. In this scenario, schools with $Z_t > z_{0,t}$ also had $Z_{t-1} > z_{0,t-1}$ and $Z_{t-2} > z_{0,t-2}$ etc. In other words, these schools qualified for the school subsidies in every year, whereas schools with $Z_t < z_{0,t}$ did not receive any subsidies in the past. In this situation, the simple RDD would measure the cumulative effects of subsidies over many years. Note that the distribution of past treatment receipt is discontinuous at $z_{0,t}$. On the other hand, if school poverty rates vary a lot over time (or $z_{0,t}$ varies over time), then it is more or less random whether schools with Z_t slightly above $z_{0,t}$ in t had been above or below $z_{0,t-1}$ in the past year. Hence, schools slightly above $z_{0,t}$ in t are likely to have had a similar treatment history in the past as those schools slightly below $z_{0,t}$ in t. In this case, the simple RDD measures the effect of one year of subsidy, and the treatment history is not discontinuous at $z_{0,t}$.

Hence, in one case we estimate the effect of current subsidies, whereas in the other case we estimate the effect of current and previous subsidies. To distinguish between these scenarios, we can control for D_{t-1}, D_{t-2}, etc. If data on past treatment status is not available we could control for Z_{t-1}, Z_{t-2}, etc. More complex treatment assignment rules are conceivable where controlling for past Z and/or D becomes important. e.g. a school may be entitled to a subsidy if $Z_t > z_{0,t}$ and if they have been above the poverty cutoff in at least five of the past ten years and have received subsidies for not more than three years in the past ten years. Such kind of rules can lead to discontinuities in treatment histories at $z_{0,t}$.

Confounding as in Figure 6.5 may also occur in other settings. Recall Example 6.9, the example of splitting school classes in Israel if class size exceeds 41 pupils. It can very well be that apart from class size there are also other differences, say in observable characteristics X, between the children in a grade with 40 versus 41 children. We might think of parents, typically with higher education, who care quite a bit about their children's education. Or think of wealthy parents who can organise longer journeys to school for their children. We should then be concerned about a confounding due to parents pulling their children out of school and sending them to other (maybe private) schools if they realise that their child would be in a class of (about) 40 pupils, whereas they might let them in if class size is only below 25 pupils. In those cases one must be worried that even when only using data 'at the threshold' (which already is often too restrictive in practice) is not sufficient to make Assumption RDD-3 or RDD-3* hold. As stated, conditioning on those confounders may offer a route to deal with this problem. If the RDD-3 or RDD-3* assumption holds conditional on observed confounders, we can eliminate biases present in the basic specification through these covariates. However, whether Assumption RDD-3 or RDD-3* holds conditional on covariates must be judged on substantive grounds, similarly as in Chapter 3 or 4. We cannot appeal to the 'local random experiment' any longer as we did in the previous subsections since we now have evidence for selective assignment. The thought experiment is to judge whether, conditional on X, we have a 'local random experiment' about z_0. If so, controlling for confounders will lead to consistent estimation.

Finally, accounting for covariates can be important when different data collection schemes have been used for individuals above the threshold z_0 versus those below z_0. In the summer remedial education example where one was interested in the effects on later outcomes Y, one can imagine that for participants in the summer camp data may be collected on site for all students, whereas data on students with $Z > z_0$ may be taken from a general purpose survey to reduce data collection costs. In those cases the distribution of X could easily differ between the $Z > z_0$ sample and the $Z < z_0$ sample.

Differences in the distributions of X could also arise as a result of differential *attrition*. This may be particularly relevant when estimating the medium to long-run effects of an intervention, where attrition is often a serious concern. Differential attrition obviously raises concerns about the validity of the identifying assumptions, yet controlling for covariates may still provide indicative information compared to abstaining from an evaluation at all. In many evaluations we may have access to short-term and to long-term follow-up data. Missing data is often minimal with the short-term follow-up data, such that the distributions of X are continuous at z_0 when analysing the short-term data. Yet, missing data can be a concern for the long-term follow-up, such that the distributions of X could be discontinuous at z_0 in the subpopulation with observed outcome data Y. In order to judge whether attrition is selective one could compare the short-term treatment effects with those short-term treatment effects obtained when using only those observations for whom also long-term follow up data exists. If both estimation approaches lead to similar results (i.e. for the full sample and for the complete-data sample), one would be less concerned about attrition based on unobservables. In the estimations, though, one would need to account for differences in observables X (e.g. age, gender etc.) in order to ensure that one is estimating the same parameter.

We have discussed various motivations why one sometimes wants to include covariates in the RDD approach. In many empirical applications covariates are indeed incorporated, yet in almost all applications they are added rather ad hoc in the linear regression (OLS or 2SLS) with a linear or (at most) second-order polynomial in Z, and just a linear term in X. Below we discuss an alternative approach that explains how covariates X can be included fully non-parametrically.

6.2.2 Identification of Treatment Effect with RDD and Covariates

Following the setup we have used so far, let $D_i \in \{0, 1\}$ be the binary treatment variable, Y_i^0, Y_i^1 the individual potential outcomes and $(Y_i^1 - Y_i^0)$ its treatment effect. The potential outcomes as well as the treatment effects are permitted to vary freely across individuals, so no constant treatment effect is assumed. As before, let Z_i be a variable that influences the treatment variable in a discontinuous way, and X_i comprise all further information on individual i that we would like to control for. No matter what the motivation for the inclusion of these covariates is, we account for them in always the same way. So for identification or estimation there is no need to differentiate along the different motivations; although they might be important for interpretation. We are again interested in a population with $supp(X) = \mathcal{X}$.

The definitions of sharp and fuzzy design are affected by the introduction of covariates in an obvious way: we simply require that $E[Y^d | X = x, Z = z]$ is continuous in z_0 for all $x \in \mathcal{X}$ while $E[D|X = x, Z = z]$ is not. In contrast, for the non-testable Assumptions RDD-3 and RDD-3*, the conditioning on X can have quite important implications. We discussed already examples that revealed that without conditioning on some X these assumptions might be too restrictive: either some confounders may degrade their credibility or they restrict the Z_i to be that close to z_0 that no reasonable sample size is available. Certainly, conditioning on X mitigates this problem only if the 'conditioned on X' versions of RDD-3 and RDD-3* are more credible.[14]

Then it is not surprising that we can identify a treatment effect conditional on (z_0, x) for any $x \in \mathcal{X}$ straightforwardly following (6.10), c.f. Exercise 2, namely by

$$\lim_{\varepsilon \to 0} E\left[Y^1 - Y^0 \,|X, D(z_0 + \varepsilon) > D(z_0 - \varepsilon), Z = z_0\right] = \frac{m_+(X) - m_-(X)}{p_+(X) - p_-(X)}, \quad (6.27)$$

where $m_+(x, z) = \lim_{\varepsilon \to 0} E[Y|X = x, Z = z + \varepsilon]$, $m_-(x, z) = \lim_{\varepsilon \to 0} E[Y|X = x, Z = z - \varepsilon]$ and $p_+(x, z)$, $p_-(x, z)$ being defined analogously with D replacing Y. Furthermore, at the boundary we simplify notation writing just $m_+(x), m_-(x), p_+(x), p_-(x)$ when $z = z_0$. The identification strategy is exactly the same as before, we just conditioned all expressions on X. As an exercise (Exercise 7), you can check that with (6.8) but conditioned on X. As the conditional local treatment effect for all compliers at (x, z_0) is

$$LATE(x, z_0) = E\left[Y^1 - Y^0 | X = x, Z = z_0\right] = \frac{m_+(x) - m_-(x)}{p_+(x) - p_-(x)}. \quad (6.28)$$

---

[14] It is difficult to say which version is more restrictive. For example, it might be very well that RDD-3 is fine, but conditioned on X_i, variables D_i and $(Y_i^1 - Y_i^0)$ become dependent; recall examples in Chapter 2.

It should not be hard to identify the unconditional effect for all compliers at z_0:

$$\lim_{\varepsilon \to 0} E\left[Y^1 - Y^0 \,|\, D(z_0 + \varepsilon) > D(z_0 - \varepsilon), Z = z_0\right]. \qquad (6.29)$$

We identify this effect by first controlling for X and thereafter averaging over it. Recall that for sharp designs, the population consists only of compliers by definition at least at z_0. For fuzzy designs however, you must ensure to integrate only over $f(x|compliers, z_0)$.

As discussed in Chapter 4, there are at least three reasons why also the unconditional effect (6.29) is interesting. First, for the purpose of evidence-based policymaking a small number of summary measures can be more easily conveyed to the policymakers and public than a large number of estimated effects for each possible X. Second, unconditional effects can be estimated more precisely than conditional effects. Third, the definition of the unconditional effects does not depend on the variables included in X (if it contains only pre-treatment variables). One can therefore consider different sets of control variables X and still estimate the same object, which is useful for examining robustness of the results.

It is typically assumed that the covariates X are continuously distributed, but this is an assumption made only for convenience to ease the exposition, particularly in the derivation of the asymptotic distributions later on. Discrete covariates can easily be included in X at the expense of a more cumbersome notation. Note that identification does not require any of the variables in X to be continuous. Only Z has to be continuous near z_0. We will see below that the derivation of the asymptotic distribution only depends on the number of continuous regressors in X as discrete covariates do not affect the asymptotic properties. As before, we must assume that only compliers, never- and always-takers exist. Assumptions RDD-1 and RDD-2 are assumed to hold conditional on X. We can summarise the additional assumptions for conditional RRD as follows:

Assumption RDD-4 Let $\mathcal{N}_\varepsilon$ be a symmetric ε neighbourhood about z_0 and let's partition $\mathcal{N}_\varepsilon$ into $\mathcal{N}_\varepsilon^+ = \{z : z \geq z_0, z \in \mathcal{N}_\varepsilon\}$ and $\mathcal{N}_\varepsilon^- = \{z : z < z_0, z \in \mathcal{N}_\varepsilon\}$. Then we need the following three conditions;

(i) *Common support*: $\lim_{\varepsilon \to 0} Supp(X|Z \in \mathcal{N}_\varepsilon^+) = \lim_{\varepsilon \to 0} Supp(X|Z \in \mathcal{N}_\varepsilon^-)$.

(ii) *Density at threshold*: $f_Z(z_0) > 0$.
$\lim_{\varepsilon \to 0} F_{X|Z \in \mathcal{N}_\varepsilon^+}(x)$ and $\lim_{\varepsilon \to 0} F_{X|Z \in \mathcal{N}_\varepsilon^-}(x)$ exist and are differentiable in $x \in \mathcal{X}$
with pdf $f_+(x|z_0)$ and $f_-(x|z_0)$, respectively.

(iii) *Bounded moments*: $E[Y^d|X, Z]$ is bounded away from $\pm$infinity *a.s.* over $\mathcal{N}_\varepsilon$, $d \in \{0, 1\}$.

Assumption RDD-4 (i) corresponds to the well-known common support assumption we discussed, e.g. for matching. It is necessary because we are going to integrate over the support of X in (6.27). If it is not satisfied, one has to restrict the LATE to be the local average treatment on the common support. Assumption RDD-4 (ii) requires that there is positive density at z_0 such that observations close to z_0 exist. We also assume the existence of the limit density functions $f_+(x|z_0)$ and $f_-(x|z_0)$ at the threshold z_0.

So far we have not assumed their continuity; in fact, the conditional density could be discontinuous, i.e. $f_+(x|z_0) \neq f_-(x|z_0)$, in which case controlling for X might even be important for identification and thus for consistent estimation. Assumption RDD-4 (iii) requires the conditional expectation functions to be bounded from above and below in a neighbourhood of z_0. It is invoked to permit interchanging the operations of integration and taking limits via the Dominated Convergence Theorem. This assumption could be replaced with some other kind of smoothness conditions on $E[Y^d|X, Z]$ in a neighbourhood of z_0.

Adding Assumption RDD-4 to Assumptions RDD-3* (or RDD-3) conditioned on X, the LATE for the subpopulation of local (at z_0) compliers is non-parametrically identified as

$$\lim_{\varepsilon \to 0} E\left[Y^1 - Y^0 \,|Z \in \mathcal{N}_\varepsilon, complier\right]$$

$$= \lim_{\varepsilon \to 0} \int E\left[Y^1 - Y^0 \,|X, Z \in \mathcal{N}_\varepsilon, complier\right] dF\left(X|Z \in \mathcal{N}_\varepsilon, complier\right) \quad (6.30)$$

by applying iterated expectations. Clearly, the distribution $F\left(X|Z \in \mathcal{N}_\varepsilon, compliers\right)$ among the local compliers is not identified since the type (complier, always-taker, etc.) is unobservable. However, by applying Bayes' theorem to $F\left(X|Z \in \mathcal{N}_\varepsilon, compliers\right)$ and replacing the first term in (6.30) with (6.27) before taking limits, several terms cancel and one obtains

$$\lim_{\varepsilon \to 0} E\left[Y^1 - Y^0 \,|Z \in \mathcal{N}_\varepsilon, complier\right] = \frac{\int \{m_+(x) - m_-(x)\} \{f_+(x|z_0) + f_-(x|z_0)\}dx}{\int \{p_+(x) - p_-(x)\} \{f_+(x|z_0) + f_-(x|z_0)\}dx},$$
$$(6.31)$$

which can be estimated from observables. Actually, the idea is exactly the same as discussed in the previous Chapters 3 and 4; we take the conditional LATE(z_0, X) from (6.27) and integrate it over X for given $Z = z_0$ (i.e. convoluted with the densities of X given z_0):

$$E\left[Y^1 - Y^0|Z = z_0\right] = \int \frac{m_+(x) - m_-(x)}{p_+(x) - p_-(x)} \cdot \frac{f_+(x|z_0) + f_-(x|z_0)}{2} dx. \quad (6.32)$$

Expression (6.32) differs from (6.31) in that it is an integral of a ratio and not a ratio of integrals. The results derived later do therefore not apply to (6.32). In practice, the expression (6.32) may be difficult to estimate in small samples as the denominator can be close to zero for some values of x. This bears the risk to integrate over some denominator values being close to zero and/or having a large variance. As in the former chapters, it can be shown that this is asymptotically equivalent to (6.31) where we integrate numerator and denominator separately.

So the treatment effect for the local compliers is identified as a ratio of two integrals. Similarly to the situation without covariates X, this represents the intention-to-treat (ITT) effect of Z on Y divided by the effect of Z on D. With covariates included, the numerator in (6.31) is the ITT effect of Z on Y, weighted by the conditional density of X at z_0. In the limit, the density of X conditional on Z being within a symmetric neighbourhood around z_0 is given by $\frac{f_+(x|z_0)+f_-(x|z_0)}{2}$. The denominator in (6.31) gives the fraction of compliers at z_0. So the ratio of integrals gives the ITT effect of Z on Y multiplied by the inverse of the proportion of compliers. This identifies the treatment effect for the compliers in the fuzzy design. Without any restrictions on treatment effect heterogeneity, it is impossible to identify the effects for always- and never-takers since they would never change treatment status in a neighbourhood of z_0.

For the estimation one proceeds as usual, starting with the non-parametric estimation of $m_+(\cdot)$, $m_-(\cdot)$, $p_+(\cdot)$ and $p_-(\cdot)$ at all points X_i. This can be done by local linear estimation; e.g. an estimate of $m_+(x)$ is the value of a that solves

$$\arg\min_{a,a_z,a_x} \sum_{i=1}^{n} \left(Y_i - a - a_z (Z_i - z_0) - a'_x (X_i - x) \right)^2 \cdot K_i 1_i^+ \tag{6.33}$$

where $1_i^+ = \mathbb{1}\{Z_i > z_0\}$ and a product kernel is used

$$K_i = K_i(x, z_0) = K\left(\frac{Z_i - z_0}{h_z}\right) \cdot \prod_{l=1}^{q} L\left(\frac{X_{il} - x_l}{h_x}\right), \tag{6.34}$$

where $q = dim(X)$ and K, L are univariate kernel functions with K a second-order kernel and L a kernel of order $r \geq 2$.

With all estimators $\hat{m}_+(\cdot)$, $\hat{m}_-(\cdot)$, $\hat{p}_+(\cdot)$ and $\hat{p}_-(\cdot)$ at hand we define

$$\hat{\alpha}_{CRDD} = \frac{\sum_{i=1}^{n} \left(\hat{m}_+(X_i) - \hat{m}_-(X_i) \right) \cdot K^*\left(\frac{Z_i - z_0}{h}\right)}{\sum_{i=1}^{n} \left(\hat{p}_+(X_i) - \hat{p}_-(X_i) \right) \cdot K^*\left(\frac{Z_i - z_0}{h}\right)}, \tag{6.35}$$

where $K_h^*(u)$ is a boundary kernel function, see below for details. For establishing the asymptotic properties of our non-parametric estimator we need some assumptions which we have seen in similar form in Chapter 2.

Assumption RDD-5

(i) The data $\{(Y_i, D_i, Z_i, X_i)\}$ are i.i.d. from $\mathbb{R} \times \mathbb{R} \times \mathbb{R} \times \mathbb{R}^q$.
(ii) Smoothness: The functions $m_+(x)$, $m_-(x)$, $p_+(x)$, $p_-(x)$ are r times continuously differentiable with respect to x with rth derivative Hölder continuous in an interval around z_0. Densities $f_+(x, z)$ and $f_-(x, z)$ are $r - 1$ times continuously differentiable with respect to x at z_0 with $(r - 1)$th derivative Hölder continuous in an interval around z_0. Furthermore, $m_+(x, z)$, $p_+(x, z)$ and $f_+(x, z)$ have two continuous right derivatives with respect to z at z_0 with second derivative Hölder continuous in an interval around z_0. Finally, $m_-(x, z)$, $p_-(x, z)$ and $f_-(x, z)$ have two continuous left derivatives with respect to z at z_0 with second derivative Hölder continuous in an interval around z_0.
(iii) The univariate Kernel functions κ and $\bar{\kappa}$ in (6.34) are bounded, Lipschitz and zero outside a bounded set; κ is a second-order kernel and $\bar{\kappa}$ is a kernel of order λ.
(iv) Bandwidths (a): The bandwidths satisfy h, h_z, $h_x \to 0$ and $nh \to \infty$ and $nh_z \to \infty$ and $nh_z h_x^L \to \infty$.

(v) Bandwidths (b): For getting optimal convergence rates for the conditional RDD estimator we need further $\lim_{n\to\infty} \sqrt{nh^5}c < \infty$, $\lim_{n\to\infty} \frac{h_z}{h} = c_z$ with $0 < c_z < \infty$, and
$$\lim_{n\to\infty} \frac{h_x^{r/2}}{h} = c_x < \infty.$$

(vi) Conditional variances: The left and right limits of the conditional variances $\lim_{\varepsilon\to 0} E\left[(Y - m^+(X, Z))^2 \,|\, X, Z = z + \varepsilon\right]$ and $\lim_{\varepsilon\to 0} E\left[(Y - m^-(X, Z))^2 \,|\, X, Z = z - \varepsilon\right]$ exist at z_0.

Define κ and $\bar{\kappa}$ as in Chapter 2, namely $\kappa_l = \int_{-\infty}^{\infty} u^l K(u)du$, $\bar{\kappa}_l = \int_{-\infty}^{\infty} u^l K^2(u)du$. Furthermore define $\dot{\kappa}_l(K) = \int_0^{\infty} u^l K(u)du$, $\ddot{\kappa}_l = \int_0^{\infty} u^l K^2(u)du$ and $\tilde{\kappa} = \frac{\kappa_2}{2} - \dot{\kappa}_1^2$. With symmetric kernel $\dot{\kappa}_0 = \frac{1}{2}$. And analogously we define $\eta_l = \int_{-\infty}^{\infty} u^l L(u)du$. Then the boundary kernel $K^*(u)$ could be set to $(\dot{\kappa}_2 - \dot{\kappa}_1 \cdot u)K(u)$. Now we can state the statistical (asymptotic) properties of the conditional RDD estimator $\hat{\alpha}_{CRDD}$.

THEOREM 6.2   *Under Assumptions RDD 1, 2, 3 (or 4) and 5 without (v), the bias and variance terms of $\hat{\alpha}_{CRDD}$ are of order*

$$Bias(\hat{\alpha}_{CRDD}) = O(h^2 + h_z^2 + h_x^\lambda)$$

$$Var(\hat{\alpha}_{CRDD}) = O\left(\frac{1}{nh} + \frac{1}{nh_z}\right).$$

Adding assumption RDD 5 (v), the estimator is asymptotically normally distributed and converges at the univariate non-parametric rate

$$\sqrt{nh}\left(\hat{\alpha}_{CRDD} - \alpha\right) \to N(\mathcal{B}, \mathcal{V})$$

with α being the true treatment effect, and where

$$\mathcal{B} = c\mathcal{B}_1 + cc_z^2\mathcal{B}_2 + cc_x^2\mathcal{B}_3$$

$$\mathcal{V} = \mathcal{V}_1 + \frac{1}{c_z}\mathcal{V}_2$$

where for $\Gamma = \int (p_+(x) - p_-(x)) \cdot \frac{f_-(x|z_0) + f_+(x|z_0)}{2}dx$

$$\mathcal{B}_1 = \frac{1}{\Gamma}\frac{\dot{\kappa}_2^2 - \dot{\kappa}_1\dot{\kappa}_3}{4\tilde{\kappa}\,f(z_0)} \int (m_+(x) - m_-(x) - \alpha\{p_+(x) - p_-(x)\})$$
$$\times \left(\frac{\partial^2 f_+}{\partial z^2}(x, z_0) + \frac{\partial^2 f_-}{\partial z^2}(x, z_0)\right)dx$$

$$\mathcal{B}_2 = \frac{1}{\Gamma}\frac{\dot{\kappa}_2^2 - \dot{\kappa}_1\dot{\kappa}_3}{2\tilde{\kappa}} \int \left(\frac{\partial^2 m_+(x)}{\partial z^2} - \frac{\partial^2 m_-(x)}{\partial z^2} - \alpha\left\{\frac{\partial^2 p_+(x)}{\partial z^2} - \frac{\partial^2 p_-(x)}{\partial z^2}\right\}\right)$$
$$\times \frac{f_-(x, z_0) + f_+(x, z_0)}{2f(z_0)}dx$$

$$\mathcal{B}_3 = \frac{\eta_r}{\Gamma} \int \sum_{i=1}^{q}\left[\left\{\frac{\partial^r m_+(x)}{r!\,\partial x_l^r} + \sum_{s=1}^{r-1}\frac{\partial^s m_+(x)}{\partial x_l^s}\omega_s^+ - \frac{\partial^r m_-(x)}{r!\,\partial x_l^r} - \sum_{s=1}^{r-1}\frac{\partial^s m_-(x)}{\partial x_l^s}\omega_s^-\right\}\right.$$

$$-\alpha \left\{ \frac{\partial^r p_+(x)}{r! \, \partial x_l^r} + \sum_{s=1}^{r-1} \frac{\partial^s p_+(x)}{\partial x_l^s} \omega_s^+ - \frac{\partial^r p_-(x)}{r! \, \partial x_l^r} - \sum_{s=1}^{r-1} \frac{\partial^s p_-(x)}{\partial x_l^s} \omega_s^- \right\} \right]$$

$$\times \frac{f_-(x, z_0) + f_+(x, z_0)}{2 f(z_0)} dx$$

$$\text{with } \omega_s^+ = \left\{ \frac{\partial^{r-s} f_+(X_i, z_0)}{s!(r-s)! \, \partial x_l^{r-s}} - \frac{\partial^{r-1} f_+(x_0, z_0)}{\partial x_l^{r-1}} \left(\frac{\partial^{r-2} f_+(x_0, z_0)}{\partial x_l^{r-2}} \right)^{-1} \frac{(r-2)!}{(r-1)! s!(r-1-s)!} \frac{\partial^{r-1-s} f^+(X_i, z_0)}{\partial x_l^{r-1-s}} \right\} \Big/$$

$f^+(X_i, z_0)$ and ω_s^- *defined analogously, and*

$$\mathcal{V}_1 = \frac{\dot{\kappa}_2^2 \ddot{\kappa}_0 - 2\dot{\kappa}_2 \dot{\kappa}_1 \ddot{\kappa}_1 + \dot{\kappa}_1^2 \ddot{\kappa}_2}{\Gamma^2 4\tilde{\kappa}^2 f^2(z_0)}$$

$$\times \int \{m_+(x) - \alpha p_+(x) - m_-(x) + \alpha p_-(x)\}^2 \cdot (f_+(x, z_0) + f_-(x, z_0)) \, dx$$

$$\mathcal{V}_2 = \frac{\dot{\kappa}_2^2 \ddot{\kappa}_0 - 2\dot{\kappa}_2 \dot{\kappa}_1 \ddot{\kappa}_1 + \dot{\kappa}_1^2 \ddot{\kappa}_2}{\Gamma^2 4\tilde{\kappa}^2 f^2(z_0)} \times \int \{f_+(x, z_0) + f_-(x, z_0)\}^2$$

$$\times \left\{ \frac{\sigma_Y^{2+}(x) - 2\alpha\sigma_{YD}^{2+}(X) + \alpha^2\sigma_D^{2+}(x)}{f_+(x, z_0)} + \frac{\sigma_Y^{2-}(x) - 2\alpha\sigma_{YD}^{2-}(X) + \alpha^2\sigma_D^{2-}(x)}{f_-(x, z_0)} \right\} dx,$$

where $\sigma_Y^{2+}(X) = \lim_{\varepsilon \to 0} E\left[(Y - m^+(X, Z))^2 \,|X, Z = z_0 + \varepsilon \right],$
$\sigma_{YD}^{2+}(X) = \lim_{\varepsilon \to 0} E\left[(Y - m^+(X, Z)) (D - p_+(X, Z)) \,|X, Z = z_0 + \varepsilon \right],$
$\sigma_D^{2+}(X) = \lim_{\varepsilon \to 0} E\left[(D - p_+(X, Z))^2 \,|X, Z = z_0 + \varepsilon \right]$ *and analogously for* $\sigma_Y^{2+}(X),$
$\sigma_{YD}^{2+}(X)$ *and* $\sigma_D^{2+}(X).$

In the sharp design everyone is a complier at z_0, i.e. $p_+(x, z_0) - p_-(x, z_0) = 1$, so the expression (6.31) simplifies to

$$\lim_{\varepsilon \to 0} E\left[Y^1 - Y^0 \,|Z \in \mathcal{N}_\varepsilon \right] = \int \{m_+(x) - m_-(x)\} \frac{f_+(x|z_0) + f_-(x|z_0)}{2} dx. \quad (6.36)$$

This is identical to the numerator of (6.31) (divided by 2 to normalise the density to one). As numerator and denominator of (6.31) will be estimated and analysed separately, one obtains automatically the asymptotic distribution of (6.36) for the sharp design: specifically: $\Gamma = 1$ and the terms $\sigma_D^{2+}, \sigma_D^{2-}, \sigma_{YD}^{2+}, \sigma_{YD}^{2-}$ and all derivatives of $p_+(x)$ and $p_-(x)$ are zero.

Instead of relying on assumption (6.9), we could alternatively base our identification on the assumption (6.8). Recall that both are now conditional on X. We do not analyse this further since most applied work either uses a sharp design (where Equations 6.8 and 6.9 are identical) or otherwise refers to (6.9).

Finally, instead of using (6.8) or (6.9) conditioned on X, one might be willing to strengthen these kinds of CIA assumptions to

$$Y_i^1, Y_i^0 \perp\!\!\!\perp D_i | X_i, Z_i \qquad \text{for } Z_i \text{ near } z_0. \quad (6.37)$$

This actually permits us to identify the treatment effect as

$$E\left[Y^1 - Y^0 | Z = z_0\right] = \int \left(E\left[Y|D = 1, X = x, Z = z_0\right]\right.$$

$$\left. - E\left[Y|D = 0, X = x, Z = z_0\right]\right) \frac{f_+(x|z_0) + f_-(x|z_0)}{2} dx.$$

Here the $E\left[Y|D, X, Z = z_0\right]$ can be estimated by a combination of the left- and right-hand side limit. This approach does no longer rely only on comparing observations across the threshold but also uses variation within either side of the threshold. This has a similar structure as (6.31) and (6.36)

Note that assuming (6.37), one can also estimate the entire potential outcome quantiles and distributions, cf. Chapter 7.

6.3   Plausibility Checks and Extensions

The main appeal of RDD approach rests on the idea of a local randomised experiment. This interpretation insinuates some checks and diagnostic tools in order to judge the plausibility of the identification assumptions. An obvious one is to obtain data from a time point before treatment was implemented (or even announced, to exclude anticipation effects) to see whether there was already a significant difference between groups (of type $E[Y|X, D = 1] - E[Y|X, D = 0]$) before the treatment started. This brings us back to the idea of DiD; see Section 6.3.3 for bias stability and plausibility checks. Recall also the discussion on checking for pseudo-treatment effects, e.g. in Chapter 4. In Section 6.1.1 we already gave some ideas about potential manipulation of Z; we start this section by explaining that issue more in detail. But before we begin, first notice that the concerns about self-selection, manipulation etc., in brief, most of the potential sources of identification problems due to sample selection biases have their origin in potentially heterogeneous treatment effects $(Y_i^1 - Y_i^0) \neq constant$. Consequently, the people might want to manipulate their Z_i or threshold z_0 along their expectations. If the treatment effect is expected to be positive for everybody, then one would expect a discontinuity in f_Z at z_0 in the form of an upward jump.

6.3.1   Manipulation of the Assignment Variable

Individuals and agents may be able to influence the value of Z and we might run into a risk for the validity of Assumption RDD-2. However, the main question is whether individuals have (perfect) control over shifting Z to the left or right of z_0 or whether there is still some randomness left such that even after manipulation they may end up left or right, and they cannot be sure where exactly. If agents know the threshold and can adjust their value of Z, then we observe a precise sorting around z_0 which should lead to a discontinuity in the distribution of the variable Z at the threshold. On the other hand, if individuals do not have precise control over Z or if they do not know the threshold z_0 in advance, the distribution of Z should be smooth. The intuition is that an enthusiastic individual i may attempt to modify or adjust his value of Z_i in his own interests, but even after such modifications we still have some randomness left so that $F_{Z|U}(z_0|u)$ is neither zero nor one (i.e. the individual may manipulate Z_i but does not have *full* control over it). In addition, $f_Z(z_0) > 0$ indeed implies that for some individuals it was a random event whether their Z happened to be larger or smaller than z_0. You can see that it is important to know whether individuals have information about z_0 in advance. If z_0 is unknown at the time of manipulation, then it is more likely that it will be random whether a Z ends up on the left or right of z_0. On the other hand, if z_0 is known, it is more likely that strategic manipulation around the threshold is not random.

Consider the situation where students have to attend a summer school if they fail on a certain math test. Some students may want to avoid summer school (and therefore aim to perform very well on the test), whereas others like to attend summer school (and therefore want to perform poorly on the test). The important point here is that the students are unlikely to sort exactly about the threshold. The reason is that even when they answer purposefully some of the test items correctly or incorrectly, they may not know with certainty how their final score would be and/or may not know the threshold value z_0. Hence, although the score Z_i may not truly reflect the ability of student i (and true ability may not even be monotonous in Z), among those with final score Z close to z_0 it is still random who is above and who is below.

On the other hand, the case is interesting for those who grade the exam. They have control over the outcome and they can manipulate the test scores. Nonetheless, there is still no need to worry as long as they do not know the value of z_0. For example, grading might be done independently by several people and z_0 is set such that, say, 20% of all pupils fail the test. In this case, exact manipulation around z_0 is nearly impossible. Certainly, if they know z_0 in advance, they can manipulate scores around the threshold. We distinguish two types of manipulations: (a) random manipulations and (b) selection on unobservables. As an example, suppose they attempt to reduce the class size of the summer school programme, so they may increase the scores of a few individuals who had scored slightly below z_0 so that now the students end up above z_0. If they select these students independently of their treatment effect, the RDD design would still be valid. But if the manipulation of the exam grading is based on the teacher's expectation (unobserved to the econometrician) of the individual treatment effects, then we expect this to lead to inconsistent estimates. An interesting observation is that such kind of manipulation often goes only in one direction which would imply a discontinuity of f_Z at z_0. Consequently, if we detect a discontinuity of f_Z at z_0 in the data, this might be a sign of possible manipulation.

Example 6.18 In Example 6.8, Anderson, Dobkin and Gross (2012) exploited the discontinuity around age 19 to estimate effects of insurance coverage. Clearly, individuals cannot manipulate their age but they can react in anticipation of their birthday, i.e. individuals could shift the timing of health care visits across the age of 19. Hence, individuals may shift the timing of healthcare visits from the uninsured period to the insured period. So they may 'stockpile' healthcare shortly before coverage expires. Such behaviour would confound the RDD estimates as they would capture mostly short-term inter-temporal substitution responses. The authors, however, found no evidence that individuals would shift the timing of healthcare visits in anticipation of gaining or losing insurance coverage.

Example 6.19 In earlier examples, the class size rule in Israel had been used to estimate the effects of small classes in school on later outcomes. A similar class size rule existed in Chile, which mandated a maximum class size of 45. This rule should lead to large drops in average class size at grade-specific enrolment levels of 45, 90, 135 etc. students. Histograms of school enrolment levels, however, show clear spikes, with higher numbers of schools at or just below these thresholds. This shows clear evidence for (at least some) precise sorting of schools around these thresholds: in order to avoid splitting classes as mandated by law (which would require more teachers and more class rooms) schools appear to be able to discourage some students from enrolling in their school. Such patterns raise doubts about the validity of the RDD assumptions since the schools being close to the left of the thresholds also contain those schools that deliberately intervened to avoid splitting classes. These might differ in observables and unobservables from those right to the threshold. One might nevertheless hope that controlling for covariates X might solve or at least ameliorate this problem. One could inspect if the conspicuous spikes in school enrolment remain after controlling for some covariates X or if they remain only in some subgroups.

So we have seen in several examples that when using RDD as the identification strategy, it is important to check if there is sorting or clumping around the threshold that separates the treated and untreated. This is particularly important when the thresholds that are used for selecting people are known to the public or to politicians, and people can easily shift their Z from below z_0 to above or vice versa. If individuals have control over the assignment variable Z or if administrators can strategically choose the assignment variable or the cut-off point, the observations may be strategically sorted around the threshold such that comparing outcomes left and right will not longer be a valid approach. Whether such behaviour might occur depends on the incentives and abilities to affect the values of Z or even z_0 (no matter whether it is the potentially treated of the agents responsible for conferring admissions). Generally, such sorting is unlikely if the assignment rule is unknown or if the threshold is unknown or uncertain, or if agents have insufficient time for manipulating Z. Generally, manipulation is only a concern if people have (perfect) control over the placing of their Z below or above z_0.

Example 6.20 Another example is a university entrance admission test (or GRE test) which can be taken repeatedly. If individuals know the threshold test score z_0, those scoring slightly below z_0 might retake the test, hoping for a better test result. Unless the outcomes of repeated tests are perfectly correlated, this will lead to much lower density f_Z at locations slightly below z_0 and much higher density above z_0. We might be then comparing people who took the test only once with those who repeatedly took the test, which might also be different on other characteristics. Hence, the RDD would most likely be invalid. Even if we used only people who took the test just once could be invalid as this would result in a very selective sample, where selection is likely to be related to the unknown treatment effect. The correct way to proceed is to use all observations and to define Z for each individual as the score obtained the first time the test was taken. Clearly, this will lead to a fuzzy design, where the first test score basically serves as an instrument for treatment, e.g. for obtaining the GRE. See Jepsen, Mueser and Troske (2009).

Let us finally come back to Example 6.3 and consider the problem of potential manipulation based on mutual agreement or on anticipation.

Example 6.21 Recall the example of the policy reform in Austria that provided a longer unemployment benefit duration in certain regions of Austria but only for individuals who became unemployed at age 50 or older. A clear concern is that employers and employees might collude to manipulate age at entry into unemployment. Firms could offer to wait with laying off their employees until they reach the age of 50, provided the employees are also willing to share some of their gains, e.g. through higher effort in their final years. In this case, the group becoming unemployed at the age of 49 might be rather different from those becoming unemployed at age 50. Therefore Lalive (2008) examines the histogram of age at entry into unemployment. If firms and workers agreed to delay a layoff until the age of 50, then the histogram should show substantially more entries into unemployment at age 50 than below. Non-continuity of the density at the threshold may indicate that employers and employees actively changed their behaviour because of this policy. This could induce a bias in the RDD if the additional layoffs were selective, i.e. if they had different counterfactual unemployment duration. Indeed, Lalive (2008) finds an abnormal reaction at the age threshold for women.

Another thing to check the above concerns on manipulation is to examine the exact process how the policy change was enacted. If the change in the legislation was passed rather unexpectedly, i.e. rapidly without much public discussion, it may have come as a surprise to the public. Similarly, if the new rules apply retrospectively, e.g. for all cases who had become unemployed six months ago, these early cases might not have been aware of the change in the law at the time they became unemployed; for more details on this see also Example 6.21.

6.3.2   Further Diagnostic Checks for RDD

Above we mainly talked about potential discontinuities of f_Z. But to justify the use of the RDD design, various plausibility checks can be helpful. As for the other methods, a first check is to verify that no other programmes are set in at or about the threshold z_0. For example, if we examine the effect of a certain law that applies only to firms with more than 10 employees ($z_0 = 11$), there might be other rules of law that also change at this threshold. More difficult is even the situation if other law changes happen not at but close to z_0, e.g. for firms with more than 8 employees: because for obtaining a sufficient sample size we would often like to include firms with 7, 8, 9 and 10 to our control group, but in order to do so we need that there is no such break at 8.

Next, simple graphical tools can be helpful for finding possible threats to the validity of the RDD. First, there should indeed be a discontinuity in the probability of treatment at z_0. Therefore, one can plot the functions $E[D|Z = z_0 + \varepsilon]$ and $E[D|Z = z_0 - \varepsilon]$ for $\varepsilon \in (0, \infty)$. One way of doing this, is to plot averages of D for equally sized non-overlapping bins along Z, on either side of the cut-off. It is important that these bins are either completely left or right of the cut-off z_0, such that there should be no bin that includes points from both sides of z_0. This is to avoid smoothing over the discontinuity at z_0, which, if the jump really existed, would be blurred by pooling observations from left and right. Similarly, we could plot the functions $E[Y|Z = z_0 + \varepsilon]$ and $E[Y|Z = z_0 - \varepsilon]$ for $\varepsilon \in (0, \infty)$. If the true treatment effect is different from zero, the plot should reveal a similar discontinuity at the same cut-off in the average outcomes. There should be only one discontinuity at z_0. If there happen to be other discontinuities for different values of Z, they should be much smaller than the jump at z_0, otherwise the RDD method will not work.

If one has access to data on additional covariates that are related to Y, say X, one can plot the functions $E[X|Z = z_0 + \varepsilon]$ and $E[X|Z = z_0 - \varepsilon]$ for $\varepsilon \in (0, \infty)$. An implication of the local randomised experiment interpretation is that the distribution of *all* pre-treatment variables should be continuous at z_0. Individuals on either side of the threshold should be observationally similar in terms of observed as well as unobserved characteristics. Hence, if we observe pre-treatment variables in our data, we can test whether they are indeed continuously distributed at z_0. If they are discontinuous at z_0, the plausibility of the RDD is reduced. One should note, though, that this last implication is a particular feature of Lee (2008, Condition 2b) and not of the RDD per se. But ideally, X should not have any discontinuity at z_0. If a discontinuity at z_0 is observed, one might be concerned about potential confounding and has to apply the RDD with covariates, i.e. one has to include (condition on) X.

Example 6.22 In the class size Example 6.19 in Chile, clear differences in student characteristics left and right of the thresholds were observed. Private school students to the left of the thresholds (who had larger classes) had lower average family incomes than the students right of the thresholds (in smaller classes). Hence, students were not only exposed to different class sizes; they were also different in background characteristics.

How to check for such a discontinuity at $E[X|Z = z_0]$? If the variance of X given Z is not too large and the sample of moderate size, a simple scatter plot of X versus Z often gives a very helpful visual impression. If the scatter plot is too blurred, non-parametric estimation of $E[X|Z = z_0 + \varepsilon]$ and $E[X|Z = z_0 - \varepsilon]$ can be helpful. Recall that if one uses kernel or local linear regression to estimate $E[X|Z = z_0 + \varepsilon]$ and $E[X|Z = z_0 - \varepsilon]$, one should be sure to use only data points with $Z_i > z_0$ for estimating $E[X|Z = z_0 + \varepsilon]$ and only data points with $Z_i < z_0$ for estimating

$E[X|Z = z_0 - \varepsilon]$, respectively. Otherwise, one would automatically smooth over z_0 and any discontinuity would be smoothed away (or get greatly diminished). In addition to visual inspection, we can also test formally for a discontinuity at z_0 by using the previous RDD regression estimators and plugging in the X covariate instead of the outcome variable.

Further diagnostic checks can be used if data on unaffected regions or periods are available. Such data can be used in several ways. First, referring to our discussion on manipulation of the assignment variable, one can analyse the density f_Z in those regions or time periods and examine if the pattern of the density around z_0 is different in these unaffected regions. Second, we could inspect if we find discontinuities in the conditional mean $E[X|Z]$ of pre-treatment covariates also in the unaffected regions. Finally, we could estimate pseudo treatment effects with these data. Finding a zero effect in such falsification tests would increase credibility in the RDD assumptions, even though they are not directly testing these assumptions.

In the next examples we see different examples of checking the conditional (mean) independence assumption: either looking for pseudo treatment effects in cross-section data, or using data from prior periods to see whether there were already differences between the two groups before treatment.

Example 6.23 Recall again Example 6.3. Lalive (2008) has the advantage of having control regions available that were not affected by the policy change. This permits to consider the histogram of age of those becoming unemployed in the treated regions compared to those in the non-treated regions. We could also look at an alternative Z, one that measures distance to the regional border (with $z_0 = 0$) to an adjacent region that is not subject to the policy. Now you could use either threshold (age 50 and/or border between regions) to estimate the treatment effect and compare the outcomes.

Recall further the concern mentioned in Example 6.21 that manipulation has taken place via anticipation. The implementation of the reform is strongly related to the history of the Austrian steel sector. After the Second World War, Austria nationalised its iron, steel and oil industries into a large holding company, the Oesterreichische Industrie AG (OeIAG). In 1986 a large restructuring plan was envisioned with huge lay-offs due to plant closures and downsizing, particularly in the steel industry. With such large public mass lay-offs planned, a social plan with extended unemployment benefit durations was enacted, but only in those regions that were severely hit by the restructuring and only for workers of age 50 and older with a continuous work history of at least 780 employment weeks during the last 25 years prior to the current unemployment spell. Only workers who lived since at least 6 months prior to the lay-off in the treatment regions were eligible for the extended benefits. In his analysis, only individuals who entered unemployment from a non-steel job were examined. The focus on non-steel jobs is that they should only be affected by the change in the unemployment benefit system, whereas individuals entering unemployment from a job in the steel industry were additionally affected by the restructuring of the sector. The identification strategy uses as threshold the border between treated and control regions. The 'region of residence' were harder to manipulate as the law provided access to extended benefits only if the person had lived in that region since, as stated, at least 6 months prior to the claim. Selective migration is still possible, but workers would have to move from control to treated regions well in advance.

Example 6.24 Lee (2008) examines the effect of incumbency on winning the next elections in the USA for the House of Representatives (1900 to 1990). He shows graphically that if in an electoral district the vote share margin of victory for the democratic party was positive at time t, it has a large effect of wining the elections in $t + 1$. On the other hand, if it was close to zero and thus more or less random whether the vote share happened to be positive or negative in t, conditional on being close to zero (our z_0), it should not be related to election outcomes before, e.g. in $t - 1$. In other words, for them the sign of the vote share margin in t should have no correlation with *earlier* periods. Again, this was examined graphically by plotting the Democratic Party probability victory in election $t - 1$ on the margin of victory in election t.

A different way to use observations from earlier periods is discussed in the next subsection. An alternative diagnostic test is suggested in Kane (2003) to inspect whether the RDD treatment effect estimates captured a spurious relationship. His idea is analysing the threshold z_0, i.e. where the threshold is actually placed and what to do if for some individuals it was not z_0. He suggests examining whether the actual threshold z_0 fits the data better than an alternative threshold nearby. If we express the estimator in a likelihood context, we obtain a log likelihood value of the model when exploiting the threshold z_0 and would similarly obtain a log likelihood value if we pretended that the threshold was $z_0 + c$ for some positive or negative value of c. Repeating this exercise for many different values of c, we can plot the log-likelihood value as a function of c. A conspicuous spike at $c = 0$ would indicate that the discontinuity is indeed where we thought it to be. Similarly, we could apply break-point tests from time series econometrics to estimate the exact location of the discontinuity point. Finding only a single break-point which in addition happened to be close to z_0 would be reassuring.

Finally, consider the case of mixed designs where nobody below z_0 is treated but some people above z_0 decide against treatment. Imagine you would like to estimate ATET for all people being treated and not only for the subpopulation at threshold z_0. In order to do so you need to assume in addition that

$$Y^0 \perp\!\!\!\perp D | X, Z \qquad \text{for } Z \geq z_0. \tag{6.38}$$

Then the selection-on-observables assumption would imply

$$\lim_{\varepsilon \to 0} E\left[Y | D = 0, X = x, Z = z_0 + \varepsilon\right] - \lim_{\varepsilon \to 0} E\left[Y^0 | D = 1, X = x, Z = z_0 + \varepsilon\right] = 0. \tag{6.39}$$

Since $\lim_{\varepsilon \to 0} E\left[Y^0 | D = 1, X = x, Z = z_0 + \varepsilon\right]$ is identified analogously to (6.11), provided that $E\left[Y^0 | X = x, Z\right]$ is continuous at z_0 and all x, (6.39) implies the testable equality

$$\lim_{\varepsilon \to 0} E\,[Y|D = 0, X = x, Z = z_0 + \varepsilon] = \lim_{\varepsilon \to 0} E\,[Y|X = x, Z = z_0 - \varepsilon]\,.$$

Hence, one can test (6.39) and thereby the joint validity of the RDD and the selection-on-observables assumption at z_0. Of course, non-rejection at z_0 does not ensure that selection-on-observables is valid at other values of z. We would nevertheless feel more confident in using assumption (6.38) to estimate ATET for the entire population. These derivations can immediately be extended to the case where Z is a proper instrumental variable, i.e. not only at a limit point. In other words, if $\Pr(D = 0|Z \leq \tilde{z}) = 1$ for some value $\tilde{z}$, the ATET can be identified.

6.3.3   DiD-RDD and Pseudo Treatment Tests

In many applications, we may also have access to pre-treatment outcome variables as in Example 6.23. So, similarly to the previous chapter, we have data on two time periods. We might have observed both $Y_{t=0}$ (from period 0 or *before* the treatment) and $Y_{t=1}$ (from period 1 *after* the treatment). As in the previous chapter, we could use the earlier time period as a falsification test by applying the RDD estimator to $Y_{t=0}$. This pseudo treatment effect should be zero since the treatment had not yet started in time period 0, unless the treatment already affected outcome earlier through anticipation. Alternatively, we could apply the RDD approach to changes over time $Y_{t=1} - Y_{t=0}$, whereby we would eliminate time-constant unobservables or small sample disbalances between the groups left and right of the threshold. This is the idea of RDD with difference-in-differences (DiD-RDD). This idea can help us to analyse the robustness of the estimated effects. Analogously to the previous chapter we replace Assumption RDD-2 with

Assumption DiD-RDD: $E[\Delta Y^d|Z = z]$ is continuous in z at z_0 for $d \in \{0, 1\}$ (6.40)

equivalently we can write,

$$\lim_{\varepsilon \to 0} E\left[Y_{t=1}^d - Y_{t=0}^d|Z = z_0 + \varepsilon\right] = \lim_{\varepsilon \to 0} E\left[Y_{t=1}^d - Y_{t=0}^d|Z = z_0 - \varepsilon\right].   (6.41)$$

We can also rewrite this common trend assumption as a bias stability assumption in the neighbourhood of z_0, i.e.

$$\lim_{\varepsilon \to 0} E\left[Y_{t=1}^d|Z = z_0 + \varepsilon\right] - \lim_{\varepsilon \to 0} E\left[Y_{t=1}^d|Z = z_0 - \varepsilon\right]$$
$$= \lim_{\varepsilon \to 0} E\left[Y_{t=0}^d|Z = z_0 + \varepsilon\right] - \lim_{\varepsilon \to 0} E\left[Y_{t=0}^d|Z = z_0 - \varepsilon\right].$$

In the sharp design, we showed in (6.16) that the (kernel weighted) regression of $Y_{t=1}$ on a constant, D, $(Z - z_0) D$ and $(Z - z_0) (1 - D)$ non-parametrically estimates the effect in the period $t = 1$. With two time periods $t = 0, 1$ and Assumption DiD-RDD, we would regress

$$Y \text{ on } constant, t, Dt, (Z - z_0) Dt, (Z - z_0) (1 - D)t,$$
$$(1 - t), D(1 - t), (Z - z_0) D(1 - t), (Z - z_0) (1 - D)(1 - t).$$

As before, the regression is done locally around z_0 using kernel weights $K_h(Z - z_0)$ with a bandwidth h, where we could also use the kernel weights (6.17) instead. Here we interacted all the regressors of (6.16) with t. Because all regressors are interacted with the two possible values of t, the result is numerically identical to estimating (6.16) separately in each time period. By rearranging the regressors we obtain the equivalent local linear regression

$$Y \quad \text{on} \quad constant, \quad t, \ D, \ Dt, \ (Z-z_0), \ (Z-z_0)D, \ (Z-z_0)t, \ (Z-z_0)Dt, \quad (6.42)$$

weighting each observation with kernel weights (6.17). Then, the coefficient on Dt is the DiD-RDD treatment effect estimate. Note that although we estimate a linear equation, no linearity assumption is required – as we have not needed it in the derivation. In most applied work, the uniform kernel is used for simplicity, and sample size is (re-)defined to be n_b, the number of observations with $|Z_i - z_0| \leq h$. Then, regression problem (6.42) is treated like a standard parametric one with sample size n_b. Yet, a boundary kernel is more appropriate.

Example 6.25 Recall Examples 6.3 and 6.23 of Lalive (2008). In his study he gives a nice application to study the effects of maximum duration of unemployment benefits in Austria combining RDD with difference-in-differences (DiD) estimation. We already discussed that he had actually two discontinuities he could explore for estimating the treatment effect of extended unemployment benefits: the one of age $z_0 = 50$, and the one at administrative borders as this law was employed only in certain regions. On top of it, Lalive (2008) has also access to the same administrative data for the time period before the introduction of the policy change. If the identification strategy is valid for that period, we should not observe a difference at the age nor at the region threshold before the policy change. So we can estimate pseudo-treatment effects like in the DiD case.

In this example also pre-programme data could be used for a *pseudo-treatment* analysis. The RDD compares either individuals on both sides of the age 50 threshold or geographically across the border between affected and unaffected regions. Using the same definitions of treatment and outcome with respect to a population that became unemployed well before the reform, one would expect a pseudo-treatment effect of zero, because the treatment was not yet enacted. If the estimate is different from zero, it may indicate that differences in unobserved characteristics are present even in a small neighbourhood across the border. On the one hand, this would reduce the appeal of the RDD assumptions. On the other hand, one would like to account for such differences in a DiD-RDD approach, i.e. by subtracting the pseudo-treatment effect from the treatment effect.

Analogous results can be obtained for DiD-RDD with a fuzzy design. A Wald-type estimator in the DiD-RDD setting is

$$\frac{\lim_{\varepsilon \to 0} E\left[Y_{t=1} - Y_{t=0} | Z = z_0 + \varepsilon\right] - \lim_{\varepsilon \to 0} E\left[Y_{t=1} - Y_{t=0} | Z = z_0 - \varepsilon\right]}{\lim_{\varepsilon \to 0} E\left[D | Z = z_0 + \varepsilon\right] - \lim_{\varepsilon \to 0} E\left[D | Z = z_0 - \varepsilon\right]}. \quad (6.43)$$

We could estimate this expression by estimating separately each conditional expectation nonparametrically e.g. by using local linear estimates as in (6.16). If we use the same bandwidths, we could also rewrite this as a 2SLS estimator. For simplicity, suppose a uniform kernel is used with the same bandwidth h everywhere. In other words, only observations with $|Z_j - z_0| \leq h$ are used, and all receive equal weights. With $1^+ = 1 - 1^- = \mathbb{1} \{Z \geq z_0\}$ we regress using 2SLS

$$Y \quad \text{on} \quad constant, \ t, \ D, \ Dt, \ (Z - z_0)1^+, \ (Z - z_0)1^-, \ (Z - z_0)1^+t, \ (Z - z_0)1^-t \tag{6.44}$$

with the following instruments for D: a constant, t, 1^+, 1^+t, $(Z - z_0)1^+$, $(Z - z_0)1^-$, $(Z - z_0)1^+t$ and $(Z - z_0)1^-t$. Here, 1^+ and 1^+t are the excluded instruments. Again, the coefficient of Dt gives the ATET at z_0 of the compliers. The reason why this is equivalent is that we could estimate (6.19) separately for both time periods. With only two time periods, the two separate regressions of (6.19) are identical to fully interacting the model (6.19) with t and fully interacting the list of instruments with t. Now, by rearranging the regressors we can estimate the treatment effect via (6.44). If we have multiple pre-treatment time periods, the regressor t may be replaced by a set of time dummies.

Example 6.26 Leuven, Lindahl, Oosterbeek and Webbink (2007) consider a programme in the Netherlands, where schools with at least 70% disadvantaged minority pupils received extra funding. The 70% threshold was maintained nearly perfectly, which would imply a sharp design. The existence of a few exceptions make the design nevertheless fuzzy, where the threshold indicator can be used as an instrument for treatment. Given the availability of pre-programme data on the same schools, difference-in-differences around the threshold can be used. The programme was announced in February 2000 and eligibility was based on the percentage of minority pupils in the school in October 1998, i.e. well before the programme started. This reduces the usual concern that schools might have manipulated their shares of disadvantaged pupils to become eligible. In that situation, schools would have to have anticipated the subsidy about one to one-and-a-half years prior to the official announcements. As a check of such potential manipulation, one can compare the density of the minority share across schools around the 70% cutoff. In case of manipulation, one would expect a drop in the number of schools which are slightly below 70% and a larger number above the cut-off. Data on individual test scores is available for pre-intervention years 1999 and 2000, and for post-intervention years 2002 and 2003, permitting a DiD-RDD. As a pseudo-treatment test the authors further examine the estimated effects when assuming that the relevant threshold was 10%, 30%, 50% or 90%. In all these cases the estimated effects should be zero since no additional subsidy was granted at those thresholds.

Finally, you might even have data that allow for a mixture of experimental, RDD and DiD approach. For example, in the pilot phase of PROGRESA, the participating households were selected in a two-stage design. First, communities were geographically selected in several states of Mexico. These communities were then randomly allocated either as treatment or control community. A baseline household survey was collected in all these communities. From these data a poverty score was calculated for each household and only households below this poverty score were eligible to conditional cash transfers. This provides a sharp RDD. Because of the collection of baseline data, i.e. data from the time before the conditional cash transfer programme started, it is possible to use DiD, experimental evaluation and RDD separately for the identification. The programme was later extended, and the calculation of the poverty score was also changed, such that various groups might have become beneficiaries later.

Example 6.27 Buddelmeyer and Skoufias (2003) exploit this possibility to judge the reliability of the RDD regression approach. The experimental data permits for a clean estimation approach with the baseline data also permitting to test for differences even before programme started. At the same time, one could also pretend that no data were available for untreated and randomly selected control communities, and to estimate effects by RDD using only the treatment communities (a pseudo non-treatment test). By comparing this to the experimental estimates, one can judge whether a simple non-experimental estimator can obtain similar results as a experimental design. One would usually consider the experimental results more credible. However, when comparing the results one has to bear in mind that they refer to different populations, which may limit the comparability of the estimates. Nevertheless, one could even conceive a situation where the RDD can help the experimental design. Suppose the households in the control communities expected that the pilot programme would also be extended to them in the near future such that they might have changed their behaviour in anticipation. Clearly, only the households below the poverty score should change the behaviour (unless there was belief that the poverty scores would be recalculated on the basis of future data collection) such that the RDD in the control communities would indicate such kind of anticipation effects.

6.4   Bibliographic and Computational Notes

6.4.1   Further Reading and Bibliographic Notes

The idea of RDD can be and has been extended to methods exploiting potential discontinuities in the derivatives of the propensity score. Another popular design is the so-called regression kink design. Identification is based here on a kinked assignment rule of treatment: Consider the simple model

$$Y = \alpha D + g(Z) + U,$$

where participation D depends on Z in a maybe continuous way, say $D = p(Z)$, but with a kink at z_0 while $g(Z)$ is continuous in z_0. Then

$$\alpha = \frac{\lim_{\varepsilon \to 0} \nabla E[Y|Z = z_0 + \varepsilon] - \lim_{\varepsilon \to 0} \nabla E[Y|Z = z_0 + \varepsilon]}{\lim_{\varepsilon \to 0} \nabla E[D|Z = z_0 + \varepsilon] - \lim_{\varepsilon \to 0} \nabla E[D|Z = z_0 - \varepsilon]}$$

with $\nabla E[\cdot|Z = z]$ denoting the first derivative with respect to z. This can certainly repeated for more complex models and introducing again fuzzy and mixed designs. An extensive discussion and overview is given in Card, Lee, Pei and Weber (2015).

In this chapter we have permitted for a situation where the density $f(X|Z)$ is discontinuous at z_0. However, as stated, if X contains only pre-treatment variables, such a discontinuity may indicate a failure of the RDD assumptions, see Lee (2008). We will briefly discuss below his approach assuming continuity of $f(X|Z)$ at z_0. Nevertheless, there could also be situations where $f(X|Z)$ is discontinuous and all conditions of RDD still apply. For example, such discontinuity can occur due to attrition, non-response or other missing data problems. Non-response and attrition are common problems in many datasets, particularly if one is interested in estimating long-term effects. Assuming 'missing at random' (MAR, or conditional on covariates X) is a common approach to deal with missing data; see e.g. Little and Rubin (1987). Although controlling for observed covariates X may not always fully solve these problems, it is nevertheless helpful to compare the estimated treatment effects with and without X. If the results turn out to be very different, one certainly would not want to classify the missing-data problem as fully innocuous.

While the MAR assumption requires that the missing data process depends only on observables, we could also permit that data might be missing on the basis of unobservable or unobserved variables, c.f. Frangakis and Rubin (1999) or Mealli, Imbens, Ferro and Biggeri (2004). The methods proposed in this chapter could be extended to allow for such missing data processes.

Further, differences in X could also be due to different data collection schemes, especially if different collection schemes may have been used for individuals above the threshold z_0 versus those below z_0. Why should this happen? In practice this is quite common as treated people are often monitored during the treatment and for a certain period afterwards, whereas control groups are often collected ad hoc in the moment when a treatment evaluation is requested.

Another reasons why one might want to control for X is to distinguish direct from indirect effects, recall our first sections, especially Chapter 2.

Example 6.28 For further discussion on separating direct from indirect effects see also Rose and Betts (2004). They examine the effects of the number and types of math courses during secondary school on earnings. They are particularly interested in separating the indirect effect of math on earnings, e.g. via increasing the likelihood of obtaining further education, from the direct effect that math might have on earnings. They also separate the direct effect of maths from the indirect effects via the choice of college major. See also Altonji (1995).

A different reason for controlling for X applies in a situation where a change in Z not only triggers changes in D but at the same time also changes in X. If we observe all the variables X that were affected, we can still apply the RDD after controlling for X. In such a situation controlling for X is necessary since the 'instrumental variable' Z would otherwise have a direct effect on Y. Such a situation often occurs when geographical borders are used to delineate a discontinuity. Recall Example 6.14 that was looking at the language border(s) within Switzerland to estimate the effects of culture on unemployment. In that example it turned out that the distribution of some community covariates X, others than language, are also discontinuous at the language borders. To avoid that these covariates bias the instrumental variable estimate, one needs to control for X.

Notice that Example 6.28 refers to treatments D that are no longer binary. We have discussed this problem already before and will come back to it later. The ideas outlined at the different chapters of this book typically carry over to the RDD case. This brings us to the question what happens if Z is discrete? Lee and Card (2008) examine this situation, when Z is measured only as a discrete variable. For example if we have $Z =$ *number of children*. In such a case, non-parametric identification is not plausible and a parametric specification is appropriate.

Let us now consider in a little more detail the approach of Lee (2008) assuming continuous $f(X|Z)$ in z_0. He gives an intuitive discussion of assumption (6.5) describing a selection mechanism under which it is true. Let U_i be unobservable characteristics of individual i and suppose that treatment allocation depends on some score Z_i such that $D_i = \mathbb{1}\{Z_i \geq z_0\}$. Let $F_{Z|U}$ be the conditional distribution function and f_Z the marginal density of Z. He proposes the conditions $f_Z(z_0) > 0, 0 < F_{Z|U}(z_0|u) < 1$ for every $u \in Supp(U)$, and that its derivative $f_{Z|U}(z_0|u)$ exists. The intuition is that every individual i may attempt to modify or adjust the value of Z_i in his own interest, but that even after such modification there is still some randomness left in that $F_{Z|U}(z_0|u)$ is neither zero nor one. In other words, (defiers excluded) each individual may manipulate his Z_i but does not have full control. Actually, $f_Z(z_0) > 0$ implies that for some individuals it was a random event whether Z happened to be larger or smaller than z_0.

Under this condition is follows that

$$E\left[Y^1 - Y^0|Z = z_0\right] = \int \left\{Y^1(u) - Y^0(u)\right\} \frac{f_{Z|U}(z_0|u)}{f_Z(z_0)} dF_U(u), \qquad (6.45)$$

which says that the treatment effect at z_0 is a weighted average of the treatment effect for all individuals (represented by their value of U), where the weights are the density at the threshold z_0. Those individuals who are more likely to have a value z_0 (large $f_{Z|U}(z_0|u)$) receive more weight, whereas individuals whose score is extremely unlikely to fall close to the threshold receive zero weight. Hence, this representation (6.45) gives us a nice interpretation of what the effect $E\left[Y^1 - Y^0|Z = z_0\right]$ represents.

Another implication of Lee's condition is that the distribution of all pre-treatment variables is continuous at z_0. If we observe pre-treatment variables in our data, we can test whether they are indeed continuously distributed at z_0 in order to check the plausibility of his assumption. One should note, though, that this last implication is a particular feature of his condition but not of the RDD per se.

The selection mechanism of Lee (2008) permits that individuals may partly self-select or even manipulate their desired value of Z, but that the final value of it still depends on some additional randomness. It permits some kind of endogenous sorting of individuals as long as they are not able to sort precisely around z_0. Recall the example in which individuals have to attend a summer school if they fail on a certain mathematics test. Some students may want to avoid summer school and therefore aim to perform well on the test, whereas others like to attend summer school and therefore perform poorly on the test. The important point is that students, however, are unlikely to sort exactly about the threshold.

6.4.2 Computational Notes

In the context of RDD to estimate the treatment effect at cut-off value(s) z_0,[15] one needs to use the local regression techniques around these cut-off point(s). In an empirical analysis one can consider three distinct steps: identification, bandwidth selection and estimation. These steps can be performed either in Stata or **R** software, with the latter providing more choices in terms of estimation of the local fits and bandwidth selection methods.

The package rdd in **R** has put together the tools one needs to undertake the estimation of RDD, both for sharp and fuzzy design. The counterpart command in Stata is rd, as a free contribution; see Nichols (2014) for more details. The main tool for identification of the RDD case is the graphical representation of the data. If there is a manipulation in Z, then the density of Z around the threshold is expected to be discontinuous. In this case it is not appropriate to use a general kernel density to check for discontinuity, the better option is to construct a histogram that has the cut-off points at the boundaries of its bins and then check the continuity of the distribution of Z. One can also use the DCdensity function from the rdd package that implements the McCrary (2008) sorting test, or plot.RD to plot the relationship of Z and the outcome Y. In the same manner, the distribution of X (covariates) can be tested be continuous in Z, and whether the distribution of D is discontinuous (as supposed). To plot X and D against Z you may use plot(z,x) and plot(z,D).

The estimation of the RDD treatment effect is quite sensitive to the bandwidth choice. There is no restrictive assumption on equality of the bandwidths at both sides of threshold z_0 to be equal. In empirical work this equality is used for the sake of simplicity. It simplifies the form of the objective function for bandwidth selection. Both packages rdd in **R** and rd in Stata use the same method of bandwidth selection proposed by Imbens and Kalyanaraman (2012).[16] **R** and Stata provide the estimation of the treatment effect with the their bandwidth, half and twice that bandwidth as a default. More options for bandwidth choices can be added manually by the user. A sensitivity test can be done in the end by trying different bandwidths. See also rddqte command.

---

[15] z_0 can be a scalar in case of a single cut-off point or a vector when we have multiple thresholds.

[16] In case of fuzzy design, $E[D|Z = z]$ is typically expected to be smoother (as a function of z) than $E[Y|Z = z]$, therefore the bandwidth choice for the former regression must be larger than the latter: $h_d > h_y$.

If one is interested to perform the estimation manually out of the aforesaid packages, recall first that the estimate of the treatment effect (in either sharp or fuzzy design) is the difference of two local regressions at the boundaries of the threshold. In **R** there are numerous functions that offer the local polynomial fit such as `locpoly` from the package `KernSmooth` or `npreg` from the package `np`. As in the RDD context we are mainly interested in the fit at the boundaries, it is advised to use the local linear or higher degree local polynomial for the fit. In `Stata` one can use the command `lpoly` or `locpoly` as a counterpart to fit a local polynomial regression. In any case, the standard errors or confidence intervals must then be obtained by bootstrap.

Moreover, one can construct weights around the cut-off point by using directly the function `kernelwts` from the `rdd` package in **R**. This is useful especially in cases where there is a mixed design. The choice of kernel can be set by the user in both software languages, but the estimation of the treatment is not very sensitive to this choice. In the `rdd` package and `rd` command, the default is to take the triangular kernel. For further practical guidance of the use and implementation see Imbens and Lemieux (2008), Lee and Lemieux (2010) or Jacob and Zhu (2012).

6.5   Exercises

1. For Figures 6.3 to 6.6 discuss the different conditional distributions and expectations. For which do you expect discontinuities at z_0?

2. Check the derivation (identification) of the LATE in Chapter 4. Then prove the equality (6.10); first under Assumption 2, then under Assumption 2'. You may also want to consult Section 2 of Imbens and Angrist (1994).

3. Recall the parametric model (6.23) for RDD with fuzzy designs. Imagine now one would model the propensity score as

$$E[D|Z] = \gamma + \bar{\Upsilon} + \lambda \cdot \mathbb{1}\{Z \geq z_0\}$$

with a parametrically specified function $\bar{\Upsilon}$. What would happen if we chose the same polynomial order for Υ and $\bar{\Upsilon}$, e.g. a third-order polynomial? Show that the solution to (6.23) is identical to instrumental variable regression of Y on a constant, D, Z, Z^2, Z^3. What are the excluded instruments?

4. Imagine we face several thresholds z_{0j}, $j = 1, 2, 3, \ldots$ at which treatment takes place (as discussed in Section 6.1.3). Imagine that for all these we can suppose to have sharp design. Consider now equation (6.22). How do you have to redefine D and/or the sample to be used such that we can still identify and estimate the ATE by a standard estimator for β?

5. Derive the asymptotics given in Theorem 6.1 for the case of sharp designs, i.e. when the denominator is not estimated (because it is known to be equal to 1).

6. Revisit Section 6.1.2. Ignoring further covariates X, give an estimator for the LATE(z_0) as in (6.10) in terms of a two-step least-squares estimator using always

the same bandwidth and uniform kernels throughout. Do this first for sharp designs, then for the case of fuzzy, and finally for mixed designs.

7. Take Assumption (6.8) but conditioned on X. Show that (6.28) holds.

8. Revisit Section 6.3: Make a list of the different plausibility checks, and discuss their pros and cons.

9. Revisit Section 6.2: Give and discuss at least two reasons (with examples) why the inclusion of additional covariates might be helpful in the RDD context.

7 Distributional Policy Analysis and Quantile Treatment Effects

In many research areas it is of first-order importance to assess the distributional effects of policy variables. For instance, policymakers will evaluate differently two training programmes having the same average effect on wages but whose effects are concentrated in the lower end of the distribution for the first one, and on the upper end for the second one. Therefore, instead of considering only average effects, it is often of considerable interest to compare the distributional effects of the treatment. An example which has received considerable public attention is 'educational equality' because many societies would prefer to provide every child with a fair chance into adult live. Let Y be a measure of cognitive ability (e.g. obtained from maths and language tests) and D may be the introduction of computers in classroom (teaching). The aim is rather to identify and estimate the entire distribution functions of Y^1 and Y^0 than just the mean difference. Even more evident, for many interventions in development economics we are interested in the distribution of income or in certain lower quantiles but not that much in the mean. Any analysis of inequality and/or poverty is plainly a question of quantiles and distributions – but not of averages. It is therefore obvious that the ability of quantile treatment effects (QTE) estimation to characterise the heterogeneous impact of variables on different points of an outcome distribution is appealing in many applications. Even if one is not primarily interested in the distributional impacts, one may still use the quantile method in order to reduce potential susceptibility to outliers. It is, for example, well known that median regression is robust to outliers while mean regression is not. All this together has motivated the recent surge of interest in identification and estimation of quantile treatment effects, using different sets of assumptions, particularly in the applied policy evaluation literature.

Example 7.1 For studying the *union wage premium*, Chamberlain (1994) regressed the log hourly wage on a union dummy for men with 20 to 29 years of work experience and other covariates. He estimated this premium first for the mean (by OLS), and then for different income quantiles ($\tau = 0.1, 0.25, 0.5, 0.75, 0.9$). The results were as follows:

OLS	$\tau = 0.1$	$\tau = 0.25$	$\tau = 0.5$	$\tau = 0.75$	$\tau = 0.9$
0.158	0.281	0.249	0.169	0.075	−0.003

For the moment we abstract from a causal interpretation. The results show that on average the wage premium is 16%, which in this example is similar to the premium for the

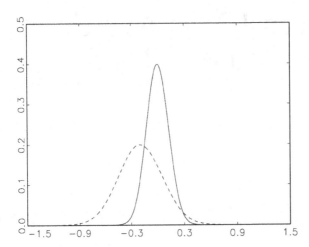

Figure 7.1 Hypothetical distributions of conditional log wages in the union (solid line) vs non-union sector (dashed line) along Example 7.1

median earner. For the lower quantiles it is very large and for the large quantiles it is close to zero. Figure 7.1 shows a (hypothetical) distribution of conditional log wages in the union and non-union sector, which shall illustrate the above estimates.

The main conclusion we can draw from this table and figure is: as expected, the biggest impact is found for the low-income group. But maybe more importantly, heterogeneity of the impact seems to dominate, i.e. the change of the distribution is more dramatic than the change of the simple mean.

Although there exists a literature on unconditional QTEs without including any confounders, we will often treat this as a special, simplified case. Indeed, we have seen in the previous sections that methods without covariates (X) require rather strong assumptions: either on the experimental design, i.e. assuming that treatment D (participation) is independent of the potential outcomes, or on the instrument Z, i.e. assuming that Z is independent of the potential outcomes but relevant for the outcome of D. And as before, even if one of these assumptions is indeed fulfilled, the inclusion of covariates can still be very helpful for increasing both the interpretability, and the efficiency of the estimators.

Before we come to the specific estimation of quantile treatment effects let us briefly recall what we have learnt so far about the estimation of distributional effects. In Chapter 2 we introduced the non-parametric estimators of conditional cumulative distribution functions (cdf) and densities in a quite unconventional way. We presented them as special cases of non-parametric regression, namely by writing $F(y|x) = E[\mathbb{1}\{Y \leq y\}|X = x]$, i.e. regressing $\mathbb{1}\{Y \leq y\}$ on X by smoothing around x with kernel weights $K_h(X-x)$ in order to estimate conditional cdfs, and by writing $f(y|x) = E[L_\delta(Y - y)|X = x]$ for estimating conditional densities (with a given kernel function L_δ, see Chapter 2 for details). The main advantage of this approach has been (in our context) that in all following chapters we could easily extend the identification and estimation of the potential mean outcomes $E[Y^d]$ (or $E[Y^d|X = x]$) to those of the potential outcome distributions $F(y^d)$ (or $F(y^d|x)$). This has been explicitly done only in some of the former chapters; therefore let us revisit this along the example of instrumental variable estimation of treatment effects.

We will re-discuss in detail the exact assumptions needed for IV estimation in Section 7.2.2. For the moment it is sufficient to remember that our population must be composed only of so-called *always takers* $T = a$ (always participate, $D_i \equiv 1$), *never takers* $T = n$ (never participate, $D_i \equiv 0$), and *compliers* $T = c$ (do exactly what the instrument indicates, $D_i = \mathbb{1}\{Z_i > 0\}$). IV methods never work if *defiers* exist (or *indifferent* subjects that by chance act contrary to the common sense). For the cases where they can be assumed to not exist, one can identify treatment effects at least for the compliers:

$$F_{Y^1|T=c} \quad \text{and} \quad F_{Y^0|T=c}.$$

For identifying distributions (and not 'just' the mean), we need the independent assumptions

$$(Y^d, T) \perp\!\!\!\perp Z \quad a.s. \quad \text{for } d = 0, 1. \tag{7.1}$$

This requires that Z is not confounded with D^0, D^1 nor with the potential outcomes Y^0, Y^1. Using basically the same derivations as in Chapter 4, it is easy to show that the potential outcome distributions for the compliers are identified then by the Wald-type estimator, i.e.

$$F_{Y^1|c}(u) = \frac{E\left[\mathbb{1}\{Y \leq u\} \cdot D|Z = 1\right] - E\left[\mathbb{1}\{Y \leq u\} \cdot D|Z = 0\right]}{E[D|Z = 1] - E[D|Z = 0]},$$

$$F_{Y^0|c}(u) = \frac{E\left[\mathbb{1}\{Y \leq u\} \cdot (D-1)|Z = 1\right] - E\left[\mathbb{1}\{Y \leq u\} \cdot (D-1)|Z = 0\right]}{E[D|Z = 1] - E[D|Z = 0]}.$$

Extensions to the case where we need to include some confounders X such that the assumptions above are fulfilled at least 'conditional on X' are straightforward. Then, by using similar derivations one can also show that the potential outcome distributions are identified by

$$F_{Y^1|c}(u) = \frac{\int E\left[\mathbb{1}\{Y \leq u\} \cdot D|X, Z = 1\right] - E\left[\mathbb{1}\{Y \leq u\} \cdot D|X, Z = 0\right] dF_X}{\int E[D|X, Z = 1] - E[D|X, Z = 0] dF_X},$$

$$F_{Y^0|c}(u) = \frac{\int E\left[\mathbb{1}\{Y \leq u\} \cdot (D-1)|X, Z = 1\right] - E\left[\mathbb{1}\{Y \leq u\} \cdot (D-1)|X, Z = 0\right] dF_X}{\int E[D|X, Z = 1] - E[D|X, Z = 0] dF_X}.$$

7.1 A Brief Introduction to (Conditional) Quantile Analysis

Today, there exists a considerable amount of literature on quantile regression. We aim neither to summarise nor to review this literature. But as quantile regression is not as well known as the mean regression, we give a brief introduction to some of the main ideas of estimation and interpretation, some of the typical problems, and the statistical properties of the estimators. Nonetheless, for a deeper insight to quantile analysis we also recommend consulting some introductory literature to quantile regression; see our bibliographical notes.

7.1.1   What Is Quantile Regression and Where Is It Good For?

As stated, so far we have mainly been interested in estimating the conditional mean function $E[Y|X]$, but now our focus lies in other parts of the distribution of $Y|X$. As stated, in order to estimate the entire distribution, we can use similar approaches as before, exploiting that

$$F_{Y|X}(a; x) = E\left[\mathbb{1}\{Y \leq a\} \,|X = x\right], \tag{7.2}$$

i.e. we obtain the entire distribution function by estimating (7.2) via mean regression of $\mathbb{1}\{Y \leq a\}$ for a grid over $supp(Y)$.

Recall then that a quantile of a variable Y is defined as

$$Q_Y^\tau = F_Y^{-1}(\tau) \equiv \inf\{a : F_Y(a) \geq \tau\}. \tag{7.3}$$

So, in principle one could invert the estimated cdf $\hat{F}$. However, in practice this can be quite cumbersome. Therefore, a substantial literature has been developed which aims to estimate the quantiles directly. We will later see that from a non-parametric viewpoint, though, these approaches are quite related. In contrast, for parametric models the estimation procedures are rather different.

If Y is continuous with monotonically increasing cdf, there will be one unique, say value a, that satisfies $F_Y(a) \geq \tau$ (or $F_Y(a) > \tau$ if strictly monotone). This is the case if F_Y has a first derivative f_Y (the density) with $f_Y(Q_Y^\tau) > 0$. Otherwise, the smallest value is chosen. Note that even if you allow for jumps in F, the cdf is typically still assumed to be right continuous, and thus the quantile function is left continuous. Consequently, given a random i.i.d. sample $\{Y_i\}_{i=1}^n$, one could estimate the quantile by

$$\hat{Q}_Y^\tau = \inf\left\{a : \hat{F}_Y(a) \geq \tau\right\},$$

and plug in the empirical distribution function of Y. Such an approach bears a close similarity with sorting the observed values Y_i in an ascending order. A main problem of this is that its extension to conditional quantiles, i.e. including covariates, is somewhat complex, especially if they are continuous. Fortunately there are easier ways to do so. Before we consider the most popular alternative quantile estimation strategy, let us discuss a few important properties of quantiles which will be used in the following.

First, according to the remark above about continuous Y, quantile functions Q_Y^τ are always non-decreasing in τ. They can nevertheless be constant over some intervals. Second, if Y has cdf F, then $F^{-1}(\tau)$ gives the quantile function, whereas the quantile function of $-Y$ is given by $Q_{-Y}^\tau = -F^{-1}(1 - \tau)$. Furthermore, if $h(\cdot)$ is a non-decreasing function on $\mathbb{R}$, then $Q^\tau h(Y) = h(Q^\tau Y)$. This is called *equivariance to monotone transformations*. Note that the mean does not share this property because generally $E[h(Y)] \neq h(E[Y])$ except for some special $h(\cdot)$ such as linear functions. On the other hand, for quantiles there exists no equivalent to the so-called *iterated expectation*

$E[Y] = E[E[Y|X]]$. Finally, recall that median regression is more robust to outliers than mean regression is.

Let us start now with the interpretation and estimation of parametric quantile regression. As stated, in most of the cases confounders are involved, so that we will examine conditional quantiles $Q^\tau_{Y|X}$ instead of unconditional ones. How can we relate this quantile function to the well-known (and well-understood) mean and variance (or scedasticity) function? The idea is as follows: imagine you consider a variable $U = Y - \mu(X)$ of the subjects' unobserved heterogeneity with distribution function $F(\cdot)$. If this conditional distribution function of Y depends on X only via the location $\mu(\cdot)$, then $F(y|x) = F(y - \mu(x))$ such that

$$\tau = F\left(Q^\tau_{y|x}|x\right) = F\left(Q^\tau_{y|x} - \mu(x)\right)$$

and we can write

$$Q^\tau_{y|x} = F^{-1}(\tau) + \mu(x).$$

If, however, it depends on X also via the scedasticity function $\sigma_u(\cdot)$, such that $F(y|x) = F(\frac{y - \mu(x)}{\sigma_u(x)})$, then we get

$$Q^\tau_{y|x} = \sigma_u(x) \cdot F^{-1}(\tau) + \mu(x). \tag{7.4}$$

The latter formula demonstrates that even if $\mu(x)$ was described by a simple linear model, $Q^\tau_{y|x}$ would not necessarily be linear in x; it depends also on $\sigma_u(x)$. If further higher moments of $F(y|x)$ like symmetry and kurtosis are also functions of X, then Equation 7.4 becomes even more complex. Consequently, even a most simple parametrisation of the mean function $\mu(\cdot)$ does not lead to a simple parametric model for the quantile. In order to get that, you would need rather strong functional form assumptions on all moments. This explains the increasing popularity of non-parametric estimation for conditional quantiles.

But for the sake of presentation we start with introducing the estimation of linear quantile regression. As already indicated above, unless X is discrete (with only few mass points), estimation by sorting and exact conditioning on X will be futile. Parametric assumptions can help; for example a linear model for the quantiles can be written as

$$Q^\tau_{Y|X} = \alpha^\tau + X'\beta^\tau \quad \Rightarrow$$
$$Y = \alpha^\tau + X'\beta^\tau + U \quad \text{with } Q^\tau_{U|X} = 0.$$

Before continuing with the discussion and estimation consider another example:

Example 7.2 When studying the demand for alcohol, Manning, Blumberg and Moulton (1995) estimated the model

$$\log consumption_i = \alpha + \beta_1 \log price_i + \beta_2 \log income_i + U$$

at different quantiles. Here, $income_i$ is the annual income of individual i, $consumption_i$ his annual alcohol consumption, and $price_i$ a price index for alcoholic beverages, computed for the place of residence of individual i. Hence, the latter varies only between individuals that live in different locations. For about 40% of the observations consumption was zero, such that price and income responses were zero for low quantiles. For larger quantiles the income elasticity was relatively constant at about 0.25. The price elasticity β_1 showed more variation. Its value became largest in absolute terms at $\tau \geq 0.7$, and very inelastic for low levels of consumption $\tau \leq 0.4$, but also for high levels of consumption $\tau \approx 1$. Hence, individuals with very low demand and also those with very high demand were insensitive to price changes, whereas those with average consumption showed a stronger price response. A conventional mean regression would not detect this kind of heterogeneity.

Consider the three examples of quantile curves given in Figure 7.2. For all three the line in the centre shall represent the median regression. Obviously, they are all symmetric around the median. To ease the following discussion, imagine that for all moments of order equal to or larger than three the distribution of Y is independent from X.

The first example (on the left) exhibits parallel quantile curves for different τ. This actually indicates homoscedasticity for U. The second example (in the centre) shows a situation with a linear scedasticity, i.e. of the form

$$Y = \alpha + X\beta + (\gamma + X\delta)\, U \text{ with } U \perp\!\!\!\perp X . \tag{7.5}$$

Clearly, for $\delta > 0$, the simple linear quantile models would cross if the X variable could take negative values. For example, if $\gamma = 0$ and $\delta > 0$, all conditional quantiles will path through the point $(0, \alpha)$. A more adequate version for such a quantile model is then

$$Q_{Y|x}^{\tau} = \begin{cases} \alpha + x\beta + (\gamma + x\delta)\, F^{-1}(\tau) & \text{if } \gamma + x\delta \geq 0 \\ \alpha + x\beta + (\gamma + x\delta)\, F^{-1}(1 - \tau) & \text{else} . \end{cases} \tag{7.6}$$

It is further clear that we can generate quantiles as indicated on the right side of Figure 7.2 by extending the scedasticity function in model (7.5) from a linear to a quadratic one. But nonetheless, generally a polynomial quantile function might give crossing quantiles as well.

Regarding estimation, if covariates are involved, then the estimation procedure is based on optimisation instead of using ordering. Nonetheless, for the sake of presentation let us first consider the situation without covariates. Define the *asymmetric loss (or check) function*

$$\rho_\tau(u) = u \cdot (\tau - 1\!1\{u < 0\}), \tag{7.7}$$

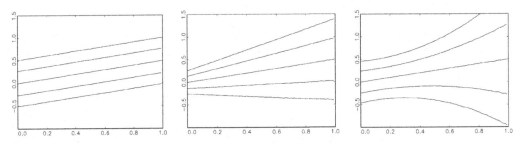

Figure 7.2 Three examples of quantile curves

and the optimisation problem

$$\arg\min_{\beta} E\left[\rho_\tau(Y - \beta)\right]. \tag{7.8}$$

In mean regression one usually examines the square loss function u^2, which leads to the least squares estimator. For the median $\tau = \frac{1}{2}$ the loss function (7.7) is the absolute loss function. For values $\tau \neq \frac{1}{2}$ it gives an asymmetric absolute loss function.[1]

Suppose that a density exists and is positive at the value Q_Y^τ, i.e. $f_Y(Q_Y^\tau) > 0$. Then it can be shown that the minimiser in (7.8) is in fact Q_Y^τ. To see this, suppose that the quantile Q_Y^τ is unique. The interior solution to $\arg\min_{\beta} E\left[\rho_\tau(Y - \beta)\right]$ is given by the first-order condition, i.e. setting the first-derivative to zero. Note that the first derivative is

$$\frac{\partial}{\partial\beta} \int_{-\infty}^{\infty} (Y - \beta) \cdot (\tau - 1\!\!1\,\{(Y - \beta) < 0\})\, dF_Y$$

$$= \frac{\partial}{\partial\beta} \left((\tau - 1) \int_{-\infty}^{\beta} (Y - \beta) dF_Y + \tau \int_{\beta}^{\infty} (Y - \beta) dF_Y \right).$$

Applying the Leibniz rule of differentiation gives

$$(\tau - 1) \int_{-\infty}^{\beta} (-1) dF_Y + \tau \int_{\beta}^{\infty} (-1) dF_Y + 0 - 0$$

$$= -(\tau - 1)\, F_Y(\beta) - \tau(1 - F_Y(\beta)) = F_Y(\beta) - \tau$$

which is zero for $F_Y(\beta) = \tau$. Hence, minimising $E\left[\rho_\tau(Y - \beta)\right]$ leads to an estimator of the quantile. An alternative interpretation is that β is chosen such that the τ-*quantile of* $(Y - \beta)$ is set to zero. Or in other words, it follows that

$$E\left[1\!\!1\,\{(Y - Q_Y^\tau) < 0\}\right] - \tau = 0.$$

An estimator of the quantile is thus

$$\hat{\beta}^\tau = \arg\min_{\beta} \sum_{i=1}^{n} \rho_\tau\, (Y_i - \beta). \tag{7.9}$$

In order to develop an intuition for this loss or objective function, let us illustrate the trivial cases of $\tau = \frac{1}{2}$ and sample sizes $n = 1, 2, 3$ and 4. An example of this situation is given in Figure 7.3. As the figure shows, the objective function is not differentiable everywhere. It is differentiable except at the points at which one or more residuals are zero.[2] The figures also show that the objective function is flat at its minimum when (τn) is an integer. The solution is typically at a vertex. To verify the optimality one needs only to verify that the objective function is non-decreasing along all edges.

---

[1] Hence, the following estimators are not only for quantile regression, but can also be used for other situations where an asymmetric loss function is appropriate. For example, a financial institution might value the risk of large losses higher (or lower) than the chances of large gains.

[2] At such points, it has only so-called *directional derivatives*.

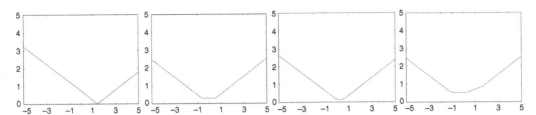

Figure 7.3 Objective function of (7.9) with ρ as in (7.7), with $\tau = \frac{1}{2}$ and sample sizes 1, 2, 3 and 4 (from left to right)

Similarly to the above derivation, if there is a unique interior solution one can show that when including covariates X, our estimator can be defined as

$$\arg\min_{\beta} E\left[\rho_\tau(Y - X'\beta)\right] = \arg zero_{\beta} E\left[\left(\tau - \mathbb{1}\left\{Y < X'\beta\right\}\right) \cdot X\right]. \qquad (7.10)$$

Now assume a linear quantile regression model with a constant 1 included in X,

$$Y = X'\beta_0^\tau + U \qquad \text{with } Q_{U|X}^\tau = 0.$$

In other words, at the true values β_0^τ the quantile of $(Y - X'\beta_0^\tau)$ should be zero. This suggests the linear quantile regression estimator

$$\hat{\beta}^\tau = \arg\min_{\beta} \frac{1}{n} \sum_{i=1}^{n} \rho_\tau\left(Y_i - X_i'\beta\right) \qquad \text{with } \rho_\tau \text{ as in (7.7).} \qquad (7.11)$$

Using the relationship (7.10) we could choose β to set the moment conditions

$$\left| \frac{1}{n} \sum_{i=1}^{n} \left(\tau - \mathbb{1}\left\{Y_i < X_i'\beta\right\}\right) \cdot X_i \right|$$

to zero. In finite samples, it will usually not be possible to set this exactly equal to zero, so we set it as close to zero as possible.

Example 7.3 Consider the situation for $\tau = 0.25$ without X. Suppose we have three data points. It will be impossible to find a β such that $\sum(\tau - \mathbb{1}\{Y_i < \beta\}) = 0$. To see this, rewrite this equation as $\frac{1}{3}\sum_{i=1}^{3} \mathbb{1}\{Y_i < \beta\} = 0.75$, which cannot be satisfied.

But certainly, for $n \to \infty$ the distance from zero will vanish. That is, for finite n the objective function (7.11) is not differentiable, whereas $E\left[\rho_\tau(Y - X'\beta)\right]$ usually is. The objective function (7.11) is piecewise linear and continuous. It is differentiable everywhere except at those values of β where $Y_i - X_i'\beta = 0$ for at least one sample observation. As stated, at those points the objective function has directional derivatives which depend on the direction of evaluation. If at a point $\hat{\beta}$ all directional derivatives are non-negative, then $\hat{\beta}$ minimises the objective function (7.11).[3]

---

[3] See Koenker (2005) for further discussion.

For analytical derivations one may prefer to consider

$$\frac{1}{n}\sum_{i=1}^{n}(\tau - \mathbb{1}\{Y < X'\beta\}) \cdot X$$

as an approximate derivative of the objective function (7.11) and apply similar approaches. For a differentiable objective function $Q_D(\beta)$ one often employs an expansion of the type

$$Q_D(\hat{\beta}) - Q_D(\beta_0) = \frac{\partial Q_D(\beta_0)}{\partial \beta'}(\hat{\beta} - \beta_0) + O\left((\hat{\beta} - \beta_0)^2\right),$$

where the last term vanishes in probability if the estimator is consistent. For a non-differentiable objective function one could use an approximate derivative Δ

$$Q_D(\hat{\beta}) - Q_D(\beta_0) = \Delta(\beta_0) \cdot (\hat{\beta} - \beta_0) + remainder$$

and impose sufficient regularity conditions such that

$$Q_D(\hat{\beta}) - Q_D(\beta_0) - \Delta(\beta_0) \cdot (\hat{\beta} - \beta_0)$$

converges to zero sufficiently fast.[4]

We already noticed the problem of quantile crossing when using linear quantile regression functions, recall Figure 7.2 and discussion. Certainly, by definition the quantile $Q^\tau_{Y|X}$ is non-decreasing in τ. However, this is not guaranteed for the estimates $\hat{Q}^\tau_{Y|X}$ if we estimate the quantiles by (7.11). Quantile crossing could happen either due to sampling variability or simply (and pretty often) due to misspecification of the model: if we assume a linear model, by definition, the quantile functions have to cross for some values of $X = x$ (though this may be outside the $supp(X)$), unless all quantile functions are parallel. Hence, quantile crossing could be used to test for misspecification. If crossing occurs at the boundary with a density f_X close to zero, there might be less concern. E.g. if years of education is positive throughout, we are not concerned if quantiles cross for some value $x \leq 4$. If, however, crossing occurs in regions where the density f_X is high, we must think about a respecification of the model, for example by including squares or higher-order terms.

To illustrate, let us turn to the example of the location-scale shift model, i.e. with $X_i \in \mathbb{R}^1$

$$Y_i = \alpha + X_i\beta + (\gamma + \delta X_i)U_i \text{ with } U_i \perp\!\!\!\perp X_i,$$

but only concentrating on the version where $\alpha = \beta = \gamma = 0$ and $\delta = 1$. The conditional quantiles of this model are linear in X for realisations unequal to zero; but at 0 the slope changes. At $X = 1$ the conditional quantile is $Q^\tau_{Y|X}(1) = F^{-1}_U(\tau)$, and at $X = -1$ it is $Q^\tau_{Y|X}(-1) = -F^{-1}_U(1 - \tau)$. Hence, the quantiles can be modelled as in (7.6) for which the slope changes at $X = 0$. Just assuming a linear model would be incorrect. The graphs in Figure 7.4 show the conditional $\tau = 0.75$ quantiles, on the left for standard normal U and on the right for uniform errors. Since the normal distribution is symmetric

---

[4] Rigorous proofs usually exploit the convexity of (7.11) and apply the convexity lemma of Pollard.

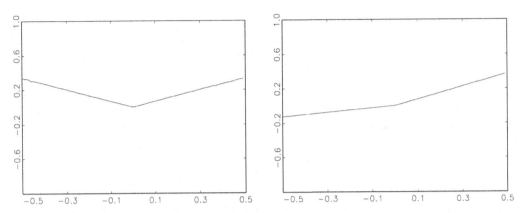

Figure 7.4 Example of 0.75 quantiles for model $Y_i = X_i U_i$ with U standard normal (see left) and uniform (see right)

about zero, the values of $F_U^{-1}(\tau)$ and $-F_U^{-1}(1 - \tau)$ are the same, and therefore the absolute value of the slope is the same to the left and right of zero in the left graph. In the right graph, the sign of the slope does not change, but its magnitude does though the conditional median would still be linear.

Once again, quantile crossing can occur for the estimated quantiles for many reasons. Interestingly, it is nevertheless ensured[5] that even if we estimate all quantile functions separately with a simple linear model (7.11), at least at the centre of the design points $\bar{X} = \frac{1}{n}\sum X_i$, the estimated quantile function $Q_{Y|X}^\tau(\bar{X}) = \bar{X}'\hat{\beta}^\tau$ is non-decreasing in $\tau \in [0, 1]$. On the other hand, if the assumed model was indeed correct, estimates that exhibit crossing quantiles would not be efficient since they do not incorporate the information that $Q_{Y|X}^\tau$ must be non-decreasing in τ. Algorithms exist that estimate parametric (linear) quantile regressions at the same time for all quantiles but modifying the objective function such that $Q_{Y|X}^\tau$ is non-decreasing in τ.

7.1.2 The Linear Regression Quantile Estimator

Well-developed algorithms based on a *linear programming* (LP) representation are available, which are particularly interesting if one wants to estimate β_0^τ for various τ. Rewrite the estimator (still using ρ_τ as defined in Equation 7.7) in the form

$$\hat{\beta}^\tau = \arg\min_\beta \sum_{i=1}^n \rho_\tau\left(Y_i - X_i'\beta\right)$$

$$= \arg\min_\beta \sum_{i=1}^n \tau\left(Y_i - X_i'\beta\right) \mathbb{1}\left\{Y_i > X_i'\beta\right\} - (1 - \tau)\left(Y_i - X_i'\beta\right) \mathbb{1}\left\{Y_i < X_i'\beta\right\}.$$

Hence, the estimator minimises a weighted sum of positive residuals. Consider residuals $r_{1i} = \left|Y_i - X_i'\beta\right| \mathbb{1}\left\{Y_i > X_i'\beta\right\}$ and $r_{2i} = \left|Y_i - X_i'\beta\right| \mathbb{1}\left\{Y_i < X_i'\beta\right\}$ such that

---

[5] See Theorem 2.5 of Koenker (2005).

$$\hat{\beta}^\tau = \arg\min_{\beta} \sum_{i=1}^{n} \tau r_{1i} + (1-\tau) r_{2i} \quad \text{with } r_{1i} - r_{2i} = Y_i - X_i'\beta \quad \text{where } r_{1i}, r_{2i} \geq 0$$

$$(7.12)$$

with only one of the two residuals r_{1i}, r_{2i} being non-zero given i. It can be shown that the solution is identical to the solution to an LP problem where minimisation is over β, r_1 and r_2. Now define the following LP problem:

$$\min_{z} c'z \quad \text{subject to} \quad Az = Y_n, \ z \in S, \qquad (7.13)$$

where $A = \left[X \vdots I \vdots -I \right]$ is a matrix of dimension $n \times (\dim(X) + 2n)$. The column vector c is $(\mathbf{0}'_{\dim(X)}, \tau \mathbf{1}'_n, (1-\tau)\mathbf{1}'_n)'$ with $\mathbf{1}_n$ being a vector of n ones. The column vector z is of length $\dim(X) + 2n$ and the set S is $I\!R^{\dim(X)} \times I\!R^{2n}_{+0}$. If z is set to $(\beta', r'_{1n}, r'_{2n})'$ this exactly reproduces the expression (7.12). In (7.13) the scalar $c'z$ is minimised over z where z satisfies the linear constraints $Az = Y_n$ and is non-negative, except for the first $\dim(X)$ components. The latter refer to the coefficients β whereas the former components represent the non-negative residuals r_{1i} and r_{2i}. Having expressed the minimisation problem in a canonical form as in (7.13), conventional linear programming (LP) algorithms can be used for estimating z and thereby β.[6]

As indicated, one is often interested in estimating β_0^τ for various values of τ, e.g. for all deciles or all percentiles. With a finite number of observations, only a finite number of estimates will be numerically distinct, see Exercise 1. In addition, the estimates $\hat{\beta}^\tau$ for different values of τ will be correlated, which is important if one wants to test for equality of the slopes. The fact that the estimates of all quantiles are numerically related also indicates that the algorithms to estimate many quantiles at the same time should be very fast if efficiently implemented. This is helpful if we want to estimate the conditional distribution by estimating 'all' percentiles.

For deriving confidence intervals and for testing hypotheses, the distribution of the estimated $\hat{\beta}^\tau$ needs to be known or estimated. Koenker (2005, chapter 3) derives the exact distribution for the linear quantile regression model, which are expensive to compute for large sample sizes. This gets even worse for the non-linear cases. So approximations based on asymptotic theory may be more helpful for large n.

For illustration purposes it is helpful to consider the case of i.i.d. errors, and to suppose a linear quantile regression model of type where X includes a constant 1,

$$Y = X'\beta_0^\tau + U, \qquad Q_{U|X}^\tau = 0.$$

Let $\hat{\beta}^\tau$ be an estimator obtained from the minimisation problem (see above) with $\tau \in (0, 1)$. Under the following assumptions one can establish its consistency and statistical properties:

Assumption Q1 Let F_i be the conditional cdf of Y_i (or simply the cdf of U_i), allowing for heteroskedasticity. Then we assume that for any $\varepsilon > 0$

---

[6] An introduction to these algorithms is given for example in Koenker (2005, chapter 6).

$$\sqrt{n}\left(\frac{1}{n}\sum_{i=1}^{n} F_i\left(X_i'\beta_0^\tau - \varepsilon\right) - \tau\right) \xrightarrow{n\to\infty} -\infty \quad \text{and}$$

$$\sqrt{n}\left(\frac{1}{n}\sum_{i=1}^{n} F_i\left(X_i'\beta_0^\tau + \varepsilon\right) - \tau\right) \xrightarrow{n\to\infty} \infty .$$

This condition requires that the density of the error term U at point 0 is bounded away from zero at an appropriate rate. If the density of U was zero in an ε neighbourhood, the two previous expressions would be exactly zero. The conditions require a positive density and are thus simple identification conditions. The next assumptions concern the data matrix X.

Assumption Q2 There exist real numbers $d > 0$ and $d' > 0$ such that

$$\liminf_{n\to\infty} \inf_{\|\beta\|=1} \frac{1}{n}\sum_{i=1}^{n} \mathbb{1}\left\{|X_i'\beta| < d\right\} = 0 , \qquad \limsup_{n\to\infty} \sup_{\|\beta\|=1} \frac{1}{n}\sum_{i=1}^{n} (X_i'\beta)^2 \le d' .$$

These conditions ensure that the X_i observations are not collinear, i.e. that there is no β such that $X_i'\beta = 0$ for every observed X_i. The second part of it controls the rate of growth of the X_i and is satisfied when $\frac{1}{n}\sum X_i X_i'$ tends to a positive definite matrix. Alternative sets of conditions can be used to prove consistency, e.g. by trading off some conditions on the density of U versus conditions on the X design.

Assumptions Q1 and Q2 are typically sufficient for obtaining consistency. For examining the asymptotic distribution of the estimator, stronger conditions are required. We still suppose the Y_i to be i.i.d. observations with conditional distribution function $F_i = F_{Y_i|X_i}$. For notational convenience we set $\xi_i^\tau = Q_{Y_i|X_i}^\tau$. Then we need to impose

Assumption Q3 The cdf F_i are absolutely continuous with continuous densities f_i uniformly bounded away from zero and infinity at the points $f_i(\xi_i^\tau)$ for all i.

Assumption Q4 There exist positive definite matrices $\mathcal{D}_0$ and $\mathcal{D}_1$ such that

$$\lim \frac{1}{n}\sum_{i=1}^{n} X_i X_i' = \mathcal{D}_0 , \quad \lim \frac{1}{n}\sum_{i=1}^{n} f_i(\xi_i^\tau) X_i X_i' = \mathcal{D}_1 \text{ and } \lim_{n\to\infty} \max_i \frac{1}{\sqrt{n}}\|X_i\| = 0 .$$

Then, with Assumptions Q3 and Q4, the estimated coefficients converge in distribution as

$$\sqrt{n}\left(\hat{\beta}^\tau - \beta_0^\tau\right) \xrightarrow{d} N\left(0, \tau(1-\tau)\mathcal{D}_1^{-1}\mathcal{D}_0\mathcal{D}_1^{-1}\right) .$$

The proof consists of three steps. First, it is shown that the function

$$Z_n(\delta) = \sum_{i=1}^{n} \rho_\tau\left(U_i - \frac{X_i'\delta}{\sqrt{n}}\right) - \rho_\tau(U_i) \text{ with } U_i = Y_i - X_i'\beta_0^\tau$$

is convex in δ and converges in distribution to a function $Z_0(\delta)$. Second, since $Z_0(\delta)$ is also convex, the minimiser is unique and $\arg\min Z_n(\delta)$ converges in distribution to $\arg\min Z_0(\delta)$. Third, it can be shown that $\sqrt{n}\left(\hat{\beta}^\tau - \beta_0^\tau\right)$ is equivalent to the minimiser of $Z_n(\delta)$. For the latter one has

$$Z_n(\delta) \xrightarrow{d} -\delta'W + \frac{1}{2}\delta'\mathcal{D}_1\delta \quad \text{with } W \sim N(0, \tau(1-\tau)D_0) .$$

Since the left- and right-hand sides are convex in δ with a unique minimiser, it follows

$$\arg\min Z_n(\delta) \xrightarrow{d} \arg\min\left(-\delta'W + \frac{1}{2}\delta'\mathcal{D}_1\delta\right) = \mathcal{D}_1^{-1}W \sim N(0, \tau(1-\tau)\mathcal{D}_1^{-1}D_0\mathcal{D}_1^{-1}).$$

(7.14)

Finally, the function $Z_n(\delta)$ is shown to be indeed minimised at the value $\sqrt{n}\left(\hat{\beta}^\tau - \beta_0^\tau\right)$. To see this, note that with a few calculations it can be checked that $Z_n(\sqrt{n}(\hat{\beta}^\tau - \beta_0^\tau)) = \sum_{i=1}^n \rho_\tau(Y_i - X_i'\hat{\beta}^\tau) - \rho_\tau(U_i)$. The first term achieves here its minimum as this is the definition of the linear quantile regression estimator. The second term does not depend on δ anyhow. Hence, $\arg\min Z_n(\delta) = \sqrt{n}\left(\hat{\beta}^\tau - \beta_0^\tau\right)$, which gives the asymptotic distribution of $\hat{\beta}^\tau$ thanks to (7.14).

Consider the simple case where X contains only a constant which represents the case of univariate quantile regression. Then

$$\sqrt{n}\left(\hat{\beta}^\tau - \beta_0^\tau\right) \xrightarrow{d} N\left(0, \frac{\tau(1-\tau)}{f_Y^2(Q_Y^\tau)}\right) .$$

(7.15)

The variance is large when $\tau(1-\tau)$ is large, which has its maximum at 0.5. Hence, this part of the variance component decreases in the tails, i.e. for τ small or large. On the other hand, the variance is large when the density $f_Y(Q_Y^\tau)$ is small, which usually increases the variance in the tails. If the density $f_Y(Q_Y^\tau)$ is pretty small, rates of convergence can effectively be slower than $\sqrt{n}$ because we expect to observe very few observations there.

Due to the normality in (7.15) one can easily extend the previous derivations to obtain the joint distribution of several quantiles, say $\hat{\beta}^\tau = (\hat{\beta}^{\tau_1}, \ldots, \hat{\beta}^{\tau_m})$:

$$\sqrt{n}\left(\hat{\beta}^\tau - \beta_0^\tau\right) \xrightarrow{d} N(0, \Omega) , \quad \Omega_{ij} = \frac{\min(\tau_i, \tau_j) - \tau_i\tau_j}{f\left(F^{-1}(\tau_i)\right) \cdot f\left(F^{-1}(\tau_j)\right)} , \Omega = \{\Omega_{ij}\}_{i,j}^{m,m} .$$

With similar derivations as those being asked for in Exercise 3 one can calculate the influence function representation of the linear quantile regression estimator which is (for $\tau \in (0, 1)$)

$$\sqrt{n}\left(\hat{\beta}^\tau - \beta_0^\tau\right) = \mathcal{D}_1^{-1}\frac{1}{\sqrt{n}}\sum_{i=1}^n X_i \cdot \left(\tau - \mathbb{1}\left\{Y_i - \xi_i^\tau < 0\right\}\right) + O\left(n^{-\frac{1}{4}}(\ln\ln n)^{\frac{3}{4}}\right);$$

see Bahadur (1966) and Kiefer (1967). It can further be shown that this representation holds uniformly over an interval $\tau \in [\varepsilon, 1 - \varepsilon]$ for some $0 < \varepsilon < 1$.

These $\hat{\beta}^\tau$ allow us to predict the unconditional quantiles of Y for a different distribution of X if the β^τ remain unchanged (or say returns to X and the distribution of U). In fact, as one has (Exercise 2)

$$Q_Y^\tau = F_Y^{-1}(\tau) \Leftrightarrow \int\left(\int \mathbb{1}\{Y \le Q_Y^\tau\}dF_{Y|X}\right)dF_X$$

$$= \int\left(\int_0^1 \mathbb{1}\{F_{Y|X}^{-1}(t|X) \le Q_Y^\tau\}dt\right)dF_X = \tau$$

(7.16)

you can predict Q_Y^τ from consistent estimates $\hat{\beta}^t$ for $F_{Y|X}^{-1}(t|X)$ with $t = 0 \leq t_1 < \cdots < t_J \leq 1$, t_1 being close to zero, and t_J close to one. You only need to apply the empirical counterpart of (7.16), i.e.

$$\hat{Q}_Y^\tau = \inf\left\{q : \frac{1}{n}\sum_{i=1}^{n}\sum_{j=1}^{J}(t_J - t_{j-1})\mathbb{1}\{x_i\hat{\beta}^{\tau_j} \leq q\} \geq \tau\right\}. \qquad (7.17)$$

Example 7.4 Melly (2005) used linear quantile regression methods to replicate the decomposition of Juhn, Murphy and Pierce (1993) for the entire distribution and not just for the mean. This allowed him to study the development of wage inequality by gender over the years 1973 to 1989 in the USA. More specifically, he simulated the (hypothetical) wage distribution in 1973 for a population with the characteristics' distribution observed in 1989 but quantile returns β_j^t $(j = 1, \ldots, J)$ as in 1973. As a result, he could quantify how much of the income inequality change was caused by the change in characteristics over these 16 years. Then he calculated the changes of the deviations of β^{τ_j} from the median returns, i.e. $\beta_{89}^{0.5} - \beta_{73}^{0.5} + \beta_{73}^{\tau_j}$, so that he could estimate the distribution that would have prevailed if the median return had been as in 1989 with the residuals distributed as in 1973. Taking all together, under these conditions he could calculate how much of the change from 1973 to 1989 in income inequality was due to the changes in returns and/or changes in X.

Alternatively, instead of using (7.16), (7.17) one could simply generate an artificial sample $\{y_j^*\}_{j=1}^m$ of a 'target population' with $\{x_j^*\}_{j=1}^m$ (say, in the above example you take the x from 1989) by first drawing randomly t_i from $U[0, 1]$, $j = 1, \ldots, n$, estimate from a real sample $\{(y_i, x_i)\}_{i=1}^n$ of the 'source population' (in the above example the population in 1973) the corresponding $\hat{\beta}^{t_j}$ and set afterwards $y_j^* := x_j\hat{\beta}^{\tau_j}$. Then the distribution of Y in the target population can be revealed via this artificial sample $\{y_j^*\}_{j=1}^m$; see Machado and Mata (2005).

Although the linear quantile regression presented above is doubtless the presently most widely used approach, we finally also introduce non-parametric quantile regression. Extensions to nonlinear parametric models have been developed, but it might be most illuminating to proceed directly to non-parametric approaches, namely to *local quantile regression*. Similar to the previous chapters, we will do this via local polynomial smoothing. Let us start with the situation where for a one-dimensional X_i we aim to estimate the conditional quantile function $Q_{Y|X}^\tau(x)$ at location $X = x$. A local linear quantile regression estimator is given by the solution a to

$$\min_{a,b} \sum \rho_\tau \{Y_i - a - b(X_i - x)\} \cdot K\left(\frac{X_i - x}{h}\right).$$

Extensions to higher polynomials are obvious but seem to be rarely used in practice. Note that local constant regression quantiles won't cross whereas (higher-order) local polynomials might do, depending on the bandwidth choice. Regarding the asymptotics,[7]

---

[7] They were introduced by Chaudhuri (1991) in a rather technical paper. Asymptotic bias and variance were not given there.

the convergence rate is known (see below), whereas the variance is typically estimated via simulation methods (namely jackknife, bootstrap or subsampling). Suppose that

$$Y = g(X) + U \quad \text{with} \quad Q_U^\tau = 0,$$

and g belonging to the class of Hölder continuous functions $C^{k,\alpha}$ (i.e. with k continuously differentiable derivatives with the kth derivative Hölder being continuous with exponent α). It has been shown that the estimate of the function $\hat{g}$ when choosing a bandwidth h proportional to $n^{-\frac{1}{2(k+\alpha)+\dim(X)}}$ converges to g almost surely as follows:

$$\|\hat{g} - g\| = O\left(n^{\frac{(k+\alpha)}{2(k+\alpha)+\dim(X)}} \cdot \sqrt{\ln n}\right).$$

This result is thus similar to non-parametric estimation of conditional expectation.

7.2 Quantile Treatment Effects

So far we have considered the estimation of $Q_{Y|X}^\tau$, i.e. the (quantile) relationship between observed variables. As argued throughout this book, the prime interest of empirical research does often not lie in estimating marginal but total effects, in our case the total causal effect of treatment D. Alternatively you may say that our interest is in estimating potential outcomes.

Let us again start with the simplest setup, where D is binary and $(Y^1, Y^0) \subset \mathbb{R}^2$ are the potential outcomes. We may be interested in the quantiles of these potential outcomes, i.e.

$$Q_{Y1}^\tau \text{ and } Q_{Y0}^\tau \quad \text{with } Q_{Yd}^\tau = \inf_q \Pr\left(Y^d \leq q\right) \geq \tau, \, d = 0, 1$$

(the τ quantiles of Y^d) or their difference – or even the distribution of the difference in outcomes Q_{Y1-Y0}^τ. But the latter is rarely of interest. Alternatively one might be interested in the direct effect of increasing the proportion of 'treated', say e.g. unionised workers in a country, $p = \Pr(D = 1)$ on the τ's quantile of the distribution of Y, say wages. Note that the coefficient from a single conditional quantile regression,[8] $\beta^\tau = F_Y^{-1}(\tau|D = 1) - F_Y^{-1}(\tau|D = 0)$, is generally different from

$$\partial Q^\tau(p)/\partial p = \left\{\Pr(Y > Q^\tau|D = 1) - \Pr(Y > Q^\tau|D = 0)\right\}/f_Y(Q^\tau). \quad (7.18)$$

The last equation can be obtained by implicit differentiation of

$$F_Y(Q^\tau) = p \cdot \left\{\Pr(Y \leq Q^\tau|D = 1) - \Pr(Y \leq Q^\tau|D = 0)\right\} + \Pr(Y \leq Q^\tau|D = 0)$$

and using

$$2 f_Y(Q^\tau) = p \cdot \left\{f_Y(Q^\tau|D = 1) - f_Y(Q^\tau|D = 0)\right\} + f_Y(Q^\tau|D = 0).$$

Most of the literature has focused on $Q_{Y1}^\tau - Q_{Y0}^\tau$ though it might equally well be interesting to look at Q_{Y1}^τ/Q_{Y0}^τ. Estimation of Q_{Y1}^τ and Q_{Y0}^τ only requires identifying

---

[8] See for example Firpo, Fortin and Lemieux (2009).

assumptions on the marginal distributions of Y^1 and Y^0, whereas estimation of $Q^\tau_{Y^1-Y^0}$ requires identifying assumptions on the joint distribution of Y^1 and Y^0. But as knowledge of the marginal distributions does not suffice for identifying the joint distribution, the latter is more challenging. Suppose that the distributions of Y^1 and Y^0 are exactly identical. Hence, the difference $Q^\tau_{Y^1} - Q^\tau_{Y^0}$ is zero for every quantile. This could be the case if the treatment effect is zero for every individual. However, this could also be the result of offsetting individual treatment effects, i.e. if some individuals had a negative treatment effect and others a positive one. Then, $Q^\tau_{Y^1-Y^0}$ could still be positive or negative because it looks at the distribution of the differences, whereas the difference in the quantiles $Q^\tau_{Y^1} - Q^\tau_{Y^0}$ simply measures the distance in the two outcome distributions.

For example, if the treatment does not change the ranks of the individuals, i.e. for any two individuals $Y^0_i > Y^0_j$ implies $Y^1_i > Y^1_j$, but $Y^0_i = Y^0_j$ implies $Y^1_i = Y^1_j$, then $Q^\tau_{Y^1} - Q^\tau_{Y^0}$ gives the treatment effect for an individual at rank τ in the outcome distribution. This is usually still different from $Q^\tau_{Y^1-Y^0}$ as the latter refers to quantiles of the effect, e.g. to the 90% person who gains the most from treatment. Another way to see this is to remember that the integral over all quantiles gives the expected value, i.e.

$$\int_0^1 Q^\tau_{Y^1} d\tau = E[Y^1] \quad \text{and} \quad \int_0^1 Q^\tau_{Y^1-Y^0} d\tau = E[Y^1 - Y^0].$$

We thus obtain the relationship

$$\int_0^1 \left(Q^\tau_{Y^1} - Q^\tau_{Y^0} \right) d\tau = E[Y^1 - Y^0] = \int_0^1 Q^\tau_{Y^1-Y^0} d\tau,$$

which does not provide us with information on $Q^\tau_{Y^1-Y^0}$ at a particular quantile τ.

However, for interpreting the QTE, it should be kept in mind that usually no rank invariance assumption on the outcome function $Y = \varphi(D, X, U)$ is imposed. Hence, we are not imposing that an individual who is at, say, the 90th percentile in the Y^1 distribution would also be at the 90th percentile in the Y^0 distribution. Therefore, even if the distribution of Y^1 first-order stochastically dominates Y^0 (if we have e.g. a rightward shift in wages), it is not certain that the wage of every individual would increase when treated. Someone at the 90th percentile in the Y^0 distribution might be at the 20th percentile in the Y^1 distribution. Hence, differences in the distributions do not provide a distribution of the individual treatment effects. They could help to bound the distribution of the individual treatment effects, but these bounds are often wide and uninformative. For being able to interpret quantile treatment effects as individual treatment effects, we would need some monotonicity assumption on $\varphi(\cdot, \cdot, U_i)$.

All in all, since quantile treatment effects (QTE) are an intuitive way to summarise the distributional impact of a treatment, we focus our attention on them:

$$\Delta^\tau = Q^\tau_{Y^1} - Q^\tau_{Y^0}. \tag{7.19}$$

This can be defined for the subpopulation of the treated, i.e. the QTE for the treated (QTET)

$$\Delta^\tau_{D=1} = Q^\tau_{Y^1|D=1} - Q^\tau_{Y^0|D=1}. \tag{7.20}$$

It is worthwhile noting that Q_{Y1}^τ and Q_{Y0}^τ (or $Q_{Y1|D=1}^\tau$ and $Q_{Y0|D=1}^\tau$ respectively) are often separately identified. Hence, instead of the difference Δ^τ one could also examine other parameters e.g. the treatment effect on inequality measures such as the interquantile spread. A typical inequality measure is the inter-decile ratio that can be defined as

$$\frac{Q_{Y1}^{0.9}}{Q_{Y1}^{0.1}} - \frac{Q_{Y0}^{0.9}}{Q_{Y0}^{0.1}} \qquad \text{or as} \qquad \frac{Q_{Y1}^{0.9}}{Q_{Y1}^{0.1}} \frac{Q_{Y0}^{0.1}}{Q_{Y0}^{0.9}}.$$

For the following discussion, is it important to distinguish between unconditional and conditional QTE. The unconditional QTE, see Equation 7.19, gives the effects of D in the population at large. The conditional QTE $\Delta_X^\tau = Q_{Y1|X}^\tau - Q_{Y0|X}^\tau$ gives the effect in the subpopulation of individuals with characteristics X, where X may contain a number of confounders as discussed in the previous chapters. Conditional and unconditional effects are interesting in their own rights. In some applications, the conditional effect Δ_X^τ may be of primary interest, e.g. when testing hypothesis on treatment effects heterogeneity. From a non-parametric perspective the conditional effect Δ_X^τ can only reach the non-parametric convergence rate and might therefore be subject to the curse of dimensionality unless additional structure like additivity is imposed. In sum, it typically is estimated with low precision if many variables are included in X, unless a functional form restriction is imposed.

The unconditional QTE, on the other hand, can be estimated – at least under certain regularity conditions – at $\sqrt{n}$ rate without any parametric restriction. One therefore expects more precise estimates for the unconditional QTE than for the conditional QTE. For purposes of public policy evaluation the unconditional QTE might also be of (more) interest because it can be more easily conveyed to policy makers (and the public) than conditional QTE with an X vector. Indeed, still today, conditional quantiles lead easily to confusion and misinterpretation. And as for the mean, a conditional quantile function is a multidimensional function. In contrast, the unconditional QTE summarises the effects of a treatment for the entire population and is a one-dimensional function.

We organise the rest of this chapter in a somewhat unconventional way. For randomised control trials the calculus of unconditional quantile treatment effects is trivial – you simply compare the quantiles of the observed Y^1 and Y^0 respectively. Therefore we directly consider quantile treatment effect estimation under CIA. When thinking of conditional QTE under CIA, then you are in the situation of standard quantile estimation, though it is performed for the treated and controls separately to afterwards compare the outcomes. It is therefore more interesting to see how we can estimate in an efficient way the unconditional QTE under CIA. This idea will be extended then to IV estimation of unconditional QTE. The section will conclude with comments on IV estimation of conditional QTE. We then dedicate an entire section to QTE estimation with RDD, for at least two reasons: 1. RDD-based QTE do not have an analogue in the standard quantile regression analysis; 2. they are particularly interesting, as typically, RDD estimators are quite sensitive to outliers whereas quantile estimation is not.

7.2.1   Quantile Treatment Effects under Selection on Observables

As stated, and following the structure of the book, we start with the selection-on-observables estimator of the unconditional QTE.[9] That is, we consider estimation of treatment effects when D is exogenous conditional on X (CIA for quantiles). Again, our identification strategy will be fully non-parametric, i.e. not depending on any functional form assumptions.

Clearly, if the selection problem can be solved by conditioning on a set of covariates X, say

$$Y^d \perp\!\!\!\perp D | X \tag{7.21}$$

and if common support $Supp(X|D) = Supp(X)$ is given, then the distribution of the expected potential outcome is identified as

$$F_{Yd}(a) = \int E\left[\mathbb{1}\left\{Y \le a\right\} | X, D = d\right] dF_X , \tag{7.22}$$

and the quantiles can be obtained by inverting the distribution function, i.e.

$$Q_{Yd}^\tau = F_{Yd}^{-1}(\tau) ,$$

provided that $F_{Yd}(\tau)$ is invertible. The latter is identical to saying that the quantile Q_{Yd}^τ is well defined, and therefore not a restriction but a basic assumption for QTE estimation. In order to estimate (7.22) you can now predict $E\left[\mathbb{1}\left\{Y \le a\right\} | X = x_i, D = d\right]$ for all observed individuals $i = 1, \ldots, n$ and their x_i by any consistent (e.g. non-parametric regression) method, and then take the average over the sample that represents your population of interest (namely all, or only the treated, or only the non-treated). Alternatively, weighting by the propensity score gives

$$F_{Yd}(a) = E\left[\frac{\mathbb{1}\left\{Y \le a\right\} \cdot \mathbb{1}\left\{D = d\right\}}{\Pr(D = d|X)}\right] , \text{ see (7.22)},$$

which can be estimated by

$$\frac{1}{n} \sum_{i=1}^{n} \mathbb{1}\left\{Y_i \le a\right\} \cdot \mathbb{1}\left\{D_i = d\right\} / \hat{\Pr}(D_i = d|X_i) .$$

These may be less precise in finite samples if the estimated probabilities $\Pr(D = d|X)$ are very small for some observed x_i. For the weighting by the propensity score, recall also Chapter 3 of this book.

Example 7.5 Frölich (2007b) used a propensity score matching estimator to analyse the gender wage gap in the UK. Along his data set he studied the impacts of using parametric vs nonparametric estimators, estimators that accounted for the sampling schemes at different stages of estimation, and how sensitive the results were to bandwidth and kernel choice (including pair matching). He controlled for various confounders like age,

---

[9] Compare also with Melly (2005), Firpo (2007) and Frölich (2007b).

full- or part-time employment, private or public sector, and the subject of degree of the individuals' professional education. He could show that the subject of degree explained the most important fraction of the wage gap. But even when controlling for all observable characteristics, 33% of the gap still remained unexplained.[10] Secondly, as expected, the gap increased with the income quantile, i.e. $Q^\tau_{Ym} - Q^\tau_{Yf}$ (with m = male, f = female) and Q^τ_{Ym}/Q^τ_{Yf} increased with τ.

These considerations were interesting for some applications and in general for identification. But as already discussed at the beginning of this chapter, if one is interested particularly in the difference between two quantiles and its asymptotic properties, then direct estimation of the quantiles might be more convenient than first estimating the entire distribution function. In order to do so, notice that the last equation implies that

$$\tau = F_{Yd}(Q^\tau_{Yd}) = E\left[\frac{\mathbb{1}\left\{Y \le Q^\tau_{Yd}\right\} \cdot \mathbb{1}\{D = d\}}{\Pr(D = d|X)}\right].$$

Hence, no matter whether (Y, X) comes from the treatment or control group we can identify Q^τ_{Yd} for any d by

$$Q^\tau_{Yd} = \arg\mathop{zero}_{\beta} E\left[\frac{\mathbb{1}\{Y < \beta\} \cdot \mathbb{1}\{D = d\}}{\Pr(D = d|X)} - \tau\right]. \tag{7.23}$$

This can be considered as the first order condition to

$$Q^\tau_{Yd} = \arg\min_{\beta} E\left[\frac{\mathbb{1}\{D = d\}}{\Pr(D = d|X)} \cdot \rho_\tau\,(Y - \beta)\right]. \tag{7.24}$$

Therefore, once we have estimated the propensity score $\Pr(D = d|X)$, we could use a conventional univariate quantile regression estimation routine with weights $\frac{\mathbb{1}\{D=d\}}{\Pr(D=d|X)}$. Note that all weights are positive so that our problem is convex and can be solved by Linear Programming.

All what we need in practice is to predict the propensity score function $\Pr(D = d|X = x_i)$ for all observed x_i, and to replace the expectation in (7.23) by the corresponding sample mean. Again, you could alternatively consider (7.22), substitute Q^τ_{Yd} for a, and estimate the unconditional quantile by

$$Q^\tau_{Yd} = \arg\mathop{zero}_{\beta} \int E\left[\mathbb{1}\{Y \le \beta\}|X, D = d\right] dF_X - \tau,$$

replacing $\int[\ldots]dF_X$ by averaging over consistent predictors of $E[\ldots|x_i, D = d]$.

---

[10] It should be mentioned that also the 'explained' part of the gap could be due to discrimination. It is known that branches or areas of knowledge that are dominated by men are systematically better paid than those dominated by women, independently from the years of education, demand, etc.

To see the relationship between (7.23) and (7.24), rewrite

$$E\left[\frac{\mathbb{1}\{D=d\}}{\Pr(D=d|X)}\rho_\tau\,(Y-\beta)\right]$$

$$= \tau E\left[\frac{\mathbb{1}\{D=d\}}{\Pr(D=d|X)}\,(Y-\beta)\right] - E\left[\frac{\mathbb{1}\{D=d\}}{\Pr(D=d|X)}\,(Y-\beta)\,\mathbb{1}\{Y<\beta\}\right]$$

$$= \tau E\left[\frac{\mathbb{1}\{D=d\}}{\Pr(D=d|X)}\,(Y-\beta)\right] - \int\int\int_{-\infty}^{\beta}\frac{\mathbb{1}\{D=d\}}{\Pr(D=d|X)}\,(Y-\beta)\,dF_{YXD}\,.$$

Differentiation with respect to β, using Leibniz rule, assuming that the order of integration and differentiation can be interchanged, and some simple algebra gives the first-order condition

$$0 = -\tau E\left[\frac{\mathbb{1}\{D=d\}}{\Pr(D=d|X)}\right]_. + \int\int\int_{-\infty}^{\beta}\frac{\mathbb{1}\{D=d\}}{\Pr(D=d|X)}dF_{YXD}$$

$$= -\tau + \int\int\int_{-\infty}^{\beta}\frac{\mathbb{1}\{D=d\}}{\Pr(D=d|X)}\,\mathbb{1}\{Y<\beta\}\,dF_{YXD}$$

$$= E\left[\frac{\mathbb{1}\{D=d\}}{\Pr(D=d|X)}\,\mathbb{1}\{Y<\beta\}\right] - \tau$$

which in turn gives (7.23).

When discussing the statistical properties of the estimators of the QTE Δ^τ for binary D, recall (7.19), based on the empirical counterparts of (7.23) or (7.24), we will directly consider the case in which the propensity scores $p(X_i)$ are predicted with the aid of a consistent non-parametric estimator. Let us use what we learnt about semi-parametric estimation in Section 2.2.3. The influence function ψ from (2.63) for estimating (7.23) with known $p(x)$ is

$$g_d^\tau(Y, X, D) = -\frac{(1-d)-D}{(1-d)-p(X)}\left(\mathbb{1}\{Y\le Q_d^\tau\}-\tau\right)/f_{Y^d}\,, \quad d=0,1.$$

Note that this is just the influence function of a common quantile regression times the (necessary) propensity weights. If we can non-parametrically estimate $p(x)$ sufficiently well (i.e. with a sufficiently fast convergence rate[11]), then (2.63) to (2.64) applies with $|\lambda|=0$, $m(x):=p(x)$ and $y:=d$ (in the last equation). We get that the adjustment factor for the non-parametric prior estimation is

$$\alpha_d^\tau(D, X) = -\frac{D-p(X)}{(1-d)-p(X)}E[g_d^\tau(Y)|X, D=d]\,.$$

Consequently our influence function is

$$\psi_d^\tau(Y, D, X) = g_d^\tau(Y, X, D) - \alpha_d^\tau(D, X)\,,$$

---

[11] As we discussed in previous chapters this requires either $dim(x) \le 3$ or bias reducing methods based on higher-order smoothness assumptions on $p(\cdot)$.

such that we can state

$$\sqrt{n}(\hat{\Delta}^\tau - \Delta^\tau) = \frac{1}{\sqrt{n}} \sum_{i=1}^{n} \psi^\tau(Y_i, D_i, X_i) + o_p(1) \xrightarrow[n \to \infty]{} N(0, V_\tau) \qquad (7.25)$$

$$\text{with} \quad V_\tau = E\left[\{\psi_d^\tau(Y, D, X)\}^2\right] = E\left[\{g_d^\tau(Y, X, D) - \alpha_d^\tau(D, X)\}^2\right]$$

$$= E\left[\sum_{d=0}^{1} \frac{Var\left[(\mathbb{1}\{Y \le Q_d^\tau\} - \tau)/f_{Yd}|X, D = d\right]}{(1-d) - p(X)}\right.$$

$$+ \left\{E[\frac{\mathbb{1}\{Y \le Q_0^\tau\} - \tau}{f_{Y0}}|X, D = 0]\right.$$

$$\left.\left. - E[\frac{\mathbb{1}\{Y \le Q_1^\tau\} - \tau}{f_{Y1}}|X, D = 1]\right\}^2\right].$$

A natural estimator for the variance is $\frac{1}{n}\hat{V}_\tau$ with $\hat{V}_\tau = \frac{1}{n}\sum_{i=1}^{n}\{\hat{g}_d^\tau(Y_i, X_i, D_i) - \hat{\alpha}_d^\tau(D_i, X_i)\}^2$, where $\hat{g}_d^\tau, \hat{\alpha}_d^\tau$ are simply g_d^τ, α_d^τ with all unknown parameter and functions being replaced by (non- or semi-parametric) estimates.

Let us finally remark that the same line of reasoning as above can be applied to the estimation of the QTET $\Delta_{D=1}^\tau$. The proposed estimator is defined as the difference between the solutions of two minimisations of sums of weighted loss functions:

$$\hat{Q}_{Y1|D=1}^\tau = \arg\min_q \sum_{i=1}^{n} \frac{D_i}{\sum_{l=1}^{n} D_l} \rho_\tau(Y_i - q), \text{ and}$$

$$\hat{Q}_{Y0|D=1}^\tau = \arg\min_q \sum_{i=1}^{n} \frac{1 - D_i}{\sum_{l=1}^{n} D_l} \frac{p(X_i)}{1 - p(X_i)} \rho_\tau(Y_i - q),$$

(for ρ_τ recall Equation 7.7) where again, in practice the propensity scores $p(x_i)$ have to be predicted.

7.2.2 Quantile Treatment Effects under Endogeneity: Instrumental Variables

If the number of control variables X observed is not sufficient to make the conditional independence assumption $Y^d \perp\!\!\!\perp D|X$ plausible, instrumental variable techniques may overcome the endogeneity problem. As in Chapter 4 we then consider a *triangular* non-separable model:

$$Y = \varphi(D, X, U), \qquad D = \zeta(Z, X, V), \qquad (7.26)$$

where φ and ζ are unknown functions, Z the instrumental variable(s), X additional control variables and the unobserved heterogeneity U and V possibly related. (Note that the control variables X are permitted to be correlated with U and/or V.) We assume Z to be excluded from the function φ, i.e. Z has no other relation with Y than via D. The corresponding potential outcomes are

$$Y^d = \varphi(d, X, U) \quad \text{and} \quad D^z = \zeta(z, X, V). \qquad (7.27)$$

As we already know from the previous chapters, the exclusion restriction in (7.26) is not sufficient to obtain identification. As we discussed in Chapter 4, one needs additionally the monotonicity assumption saying that the function ζ is *weakly monotonous* in z. Without loss of generality we normalise it to be increasing, i.e. assume that an exogenous increase in Z can never decrease the value of D (otherwise check with $-Z$).

Supposing that D is binary let us define

$$z_{min} = \min_{z \in Z} \Pr\left(D^z = 1\right) \quad \text{and} \quad z_{max} = \max_{z \in Z} \Pr\left(D^z = 1\right).$$

By virtue of the monotonicity assumption, $D_i^{z_{min}} < D_i^{z_{max}}$ for i being a complier, whereas $D_i^{z_{min}} = D_i^{z_{max}}$ for i being an always- or never-taker. (If Z is binary, clearly $z_{min} = 0$ and $z_{max} = 1$.) Identification of the effect on all compliers is obtained by those observations with $z_i = z_{min}$ and $z_i = z_{max}$, irrespective of the number of instrumental variables or whether they are discrete or continuous. The asymptotic theory requires that there are positive mass points i.e. that $\Pr(Z = z_{min}) > 0$ and that $\Pr(Z = z_{max}) > 0$. This rules out continuous instrumental variables, unless they are mixed discrete-continuous and have positive mass at z_{min} and z_{max}.

Again, the subgroup of 'compliers' is the *largest subpopulation* for which the effect is identified. If the instruments Z were sufficiently powerful to move everyone from $D = 0$ to $D = 1$, this would lead to the average treatment effect (ATE) in the entire population (but at the same time indicate that either $D|X$ is actually exogenous or $Z|X$ is endogenous, too). If Y is bounded, we can derive bounds on the overall treatment effects because the size of the subpopulation of compliers is identified as well. We focus on the QTE for the compliers:

$$\Delta_c^\tau = Q_{Y^1|c}^\tau - Q_{Y^0|c}^\tau \tag{7.28}$$

where $Q_{Y^1|c}^\tau = \inf_q \Pr\left(Y^1 \leq q \mid complier\right) \geq \tau$.

Summarising, identification and estimation is based only on those observations with $Z_i \in \{z_{min}, z_{max}\}$.[12] In the following we will assume throughout that z_{min} and z_{max} are known (and not estimated) and that $\Pr(Z = z_{min}) > 0$ and $\Pr(Z = z_{max}) > 0$. To simplify the notation we will use the values 0 and 1 subsequently instead of z_{min} and z_{max}, respectively. Furthermore, we will only refer to the effectively used sample $\{i : Z_i \in \{0, 1\}\}$ or in other words, we assume that $\Pr(Z = z_{min}) + \Pr(Z = z_{max}) = 1$. This is clearly appropriate for applications where the single instruments Z are binary. In other applications, where $\Pr(Z = z_{min}) + \Pr(Z = z_{max}) < 1$, the results apply with reference to the subsample $\{i : Z_i \in \{0, 1\}\}$.

By considering only the endpoints of the support of Z, recoding Z as 0 and 1, and with D being a binary treatment variable, we can define the same kind of partition of the population as in Chapter 4, namely into the four groups

---

[12] Differently from the Marginal Treatment Estimator in Chapter 4 we are not exploring variations in Y or of the complier population over the range of Z.

$T \in \{a, n, c, d\}$ (always treated, never treated, compliers, defiers) for which we need to assume

Assumption IV-1

(i) Existence of compliers:	$\Pr(T = c) > 0$
(ii) Monotonicity:	$\Pr(T = d) = 0$
(iii) Independent instrument:	$(Y^d, T) \perp\!\!\!\perp Z \mid X$
(iv) Common support:	$0 < \pi(X) < 1 \quad a.s.$

with $\pi(x) = \Pr(Z = 1 \mid X = x)$, which we will again refer to $\pi(x)$ as the 'propensity score', although it refers to the instrument Z and not to the treatment D.

Assumption IV-1 (i) requires that the instruments have some power in that there are at least some individuals who react to it. The strength of the instrument can be measured by the probability mass of the compliants. The second assumption reflects the monotonicity as it requires that D^z weakly increases with z for all individuals (or decreases for all individuals). The third part of the assumption implicitly requires an exclusion restriction ($\Rightarrow$ triangularity) and an unconfounded instrument restriction. In other words, Z_i must be independent from the potential outcomes of individual i; and those individuals for whom $Z_i = z$ is observed should not differ in their relevant unobserved characteristics from individuals j with $Z_j \neq z$. As discussed in Chapter 4, unless the instrument has been randomly assigned, these restrictions are very unlikely to hold. However, *conditional* on a large set of covariates X, these conditions can be made more plausible.

Note that we permit X to be *endogenous*. X can be related to U and V in (7.26) in any way. This may be important in many applications, especially where X contains lagged (dependent) variables that may well be related to unobserved ability U. The fourth assumption requires that the support of X is identical in the $Z = 0$ and the $Z = 1$ sub-population. This assumption is needed since we first condition on X to make the instrumental variables assumption valid but then integrate X out to obtain the unconditional treatment effects.[13] Let us also assume that the quantiles are unique and well defined; this is not needed for identification, but very convenient for the asymptotic theory.

Assumption IV-2 The random variables $Y^1 \mid c$ and $Y^0 \mid c$ are continuous with positive density in a neighbourhood of $Q^\tau_{Y^1 \mid c}$ and $Q^\tau_{Y^0 \mid c}$, respectively.

Under these two Assumptions IV-1 and IV-2, a natural starting point to identify the QTE is to look again at the distribution functions of the potential outcomes, which could then be inverted to obtain the QTEs for compliers, say $\Delta^\tau_c = Q^\tau_{Y^1 \mid c} - Q^\tau_{Y^0 \mid c}$. It can be shown that the potential outcome distributions are identified by

$$
\begin{aligned}
F_{Y^1 \mid c}(u) &= \frac{\int (E[\mathbb{1}\{Y \le u\}D \mid X, Z = 1] - E[\mathbb{1}\{Y \le u\}D \mid X, Z = 0]) \, dF(x)}{\int (E[D \mid X, Z = 1] - E[D \mid X, Z = 0]) \, dF(x)} \\
&= \frac{E[\mathbb{1}\{Y < u\}DW]}{E[DW]}
\end{aligned}
\tag{7.29}
$$

---

[13] An alternative set of assumptions, which leads to the same estimators later, replaces monotonicity with the assumption that the average treatment effect is identical for compliers and defiers, conditional on X.

$$F_{Y^0|c}(u) = \frac{\int (E[\mathbb{1}\{Y \le u\}(D-1)|X, Z=1] - E[\mathbb{1}\{Y \le u\}(D-1)|X, Z=0]) \, dF(x)}{\int (E[D|X, Z=1] - E[D|X, Z=0]) \, dF(x)}$$

$$= \frac{E[\mathbb{1}\{Y < u\}(1-D) W]}{E[DW]} \tag{7.30}$$

with weights

$$W = \frac{Z - \pi(X)}{\pi(X)(1 - \pi(X))} (2D - 1). \tag{7.31}$$

Here we have made use of the fact that for the proportion of compliers, say P_c, one has

$$P_c = \int (E[D|X, Z=1] - E[D|X, Z=0]) \, dF(x)$$

$$= E\left[\frac{E[DZ|X]}{\pi(X)} - \frac{E[D(1-Z)|X]}{1-\pi(X)} \right]$$

which with some algebra can be shown to equal $E[D\frac{Z-\pi(X)}{\pi(X)\{1-\pi(X)\}}]$. Hence, one could estimate the QTE by the difference $q_1 - q_0$ of the solutions of the two moment conditions

$$E\left[\mathbb{1}\{Y < q_1\} DW \right] = \tau E[(1-D) W] \quad \text{and} \quad E\left[\mathbb{1}\{Y < q_0\}(1-D) W \right] = \tau E[DW] \tag{7.32}$$

or equivalently (Exercise 4)

$$E\left[\{\mathbb{1}\{Y < q_1\} - \tau\} WD \right] = 0 \quad \text{and} \quad E\left[\{\mathbb{1}\{Y < q_0\} - \tau\} W(1-D) \right] = 0. \tag{7.33}$$

To see the equivalence to QTE estimation note that these moment conditions are equivalent to a weighted quantile regression representation, namely the solution of the following optimisation problem

$$(\alpha, \beta) = \arg\min_{a,b} E\left[\rho_\tau(Y - a - bD) \cdot W \right], \tag{7.34}$$

where $\rho_\tau(u) = u \cdot (\tau - \mathbb{1}\{u < 0\})$, as usual. In fact, a corresponds to $Q_{Y^0|c}^\tau$ and the solution for b corresponds to $\Delta_c^\tau = Q_{Y^1|c}^\tau - Q_{Y^0|c}^\tau$. Therefore, the weighted quantile estimator of $\hat{\Delta}_c^\tau$ is

$$(\hat{Q}_{Y^0|c}^\tau, \hat{\Delta}_c^\tau) = \arg\min_{a,b} \frac{1}{n} \sum_{i=1}^n \rho_\tau(Y_i - a - bD_i) \hat{W}_i \tag{7.35}$$

with $\hat{W}_i$ being as in (7.31) but with predicted $\pi(X_i)$ for individual i. A problem in practice is that the sample objective (7.35) is typically non-convex since W_i is negative for $Z_i \ne D_i$, and so will be $\hat{W}_i$. This complicates the optimisation problem because local optima could exist. The problem is not very serious here because we need to estimate only a scalar in the $D = 1$ population, and another one in the $D = 0$ population. In other words, we can write (7.35) equivalently as

$$\hat{Q}_{Y^1|c}^\tau = \arg\min_{q_1} \frac{1}{n} \sum_{i=1}^n \rho_\tau(Y_i - q_1) D_i \hat{W}_i \quad \text{and} \tag{7.36}$$

$$\hat{Q}_{Y^0|c}^\tau = \arg\min_{q_0} \frac{1}{n} \sum_{i=1}^n \rho_\tau(Y_i - q_0)(1 - D_i) \hat{W}_i.$$

These are two separate one-dimensional estimation problems in the $D = 1$ and $D = 0$ populations such that we can easily use grid-search methods supported by visual inspection of the objective function for local minima.

In order to state the asymptotic statistical properties of the QTE IV estimator, one needs some more assumptions, namely

Assumption IV-3 We assume the following conditions to hold:

(i) The data $\{(Yi; Di; Zi; Xi)\}_{i=1}^{n}$ are i.i.d. with $\mathcal{X} \subset \mathbb{R}^q$ being a compact set.
(ii) The propensity $\pi(x)$ is bounded away from 0 and 1 over the support $\mathcal{X}$ of X.
(iii) Smoothness of the unknown functions: in particular, $\pi(x)$ is two times continuously differentiable with a second derivative that is Hölder continuous; $f(x)$ is $(r-1)$ times continuously differentiable with its $(r-1)$th derivative being Hölder continuous; and $F_{Y|d,z,x}(y)$ is continuously differentiable with respect to y.
(iv) Uniform consistency of $\hat{\pi}(x)$, i.e. $\sup_{x \in \mathcal{X}} |\hat{\pi}(x) - \pi(x)| \longrightarrow 0$ in probability.

It is clear that there is a direct relation between dimension q and smoothness r due to the so-called curse of dimensionality in non- and semi-parametric estimation. The aim is – as in all our semi-parametric estimators – to keep the convergence rate of $\hat{\pi}$ sufficiently fast in order to get a $\sqrt{n}$ convergence rate for the QTE estimator. If we succeed, in the sense that the bias of $\hat{\pi}$ converges in a rate faster than $\sqrt{n}$ with a variance still going to zero, then we get

$$\sqrt{n}\left(\hat{\Delta}_c^\tau - \Delta_c^\tau\right) \longrightarrow N(0, V_\tau^{IV}) \quad \text{with} \tag{7.37}$$

$$V_\tau^{IV} = \frac{1}{P_c^2 f_{Y^1|c}^2(Q_{Y^1|c}^\tau)} E\left[\frac{p(X,1)}{\pi(X)} F_{Y|D=1,Z=1,X}(Q_{Y^1|c}^\tau)\left\{1 - F_{Y|D=1,Z=1,X}(Q_{Y^1|c}^\tau)\right\}\right]$$

$$+ \frac{1}{P_c^2 f_{Y^1|c}^2(Q_{Y^1|c}^\tau)} E\left[\frac{p(X,0)}{1-\pi(X)} F_{Y|D=1,Z=0,X}(Q_{Y^1|c}^\tau)\left\{1 - F_{Y|D=1,Z=0,X}(Q_{Y^1|c}^\tau)\right\}\right]$$

$$+ \frac{1}{P_c^2 f_{Y^0|c}^2(Q_{Y^0|c}^\tau)} E\left[\frac{1-p(X,1)}{\pi(X)} F_{Y|D=0,Z=1,X}(Q_{Y^1|c}^\tau)\left\{1 - F_{Y|D=0,Z=1,X}(Q_{Y^1|c}^\tau)\right\}\right]$$

$$+ \frac{1}{P_c^2 f_{Y^0|c}^2(Q_{Y^0|c}^\tau)} E\left[\frac{1-p(X,0)}{1-\pi(X)} F_{Y|D=0,Z=0,X}(Q_{Y^1|c}^\tau)\left\{1 - F_{Y|D=0,Z=0,X}(Q_{Y^1|c}^\tau)\right\}\right]$$

$$+ E\left[\frac{p(X,1)\vartheta_{11}^2(X) + (1-p(X,1))\vartheta_{01}^2(X)}{\pi(X)} + \frac{p(X,0)\vartheta_{10}^2(X) + (1-p(X,0))\vartheta_{00}^2(X)}{1-\pi(X)}\right]$$

$$- E\left[\pi(X)\{1-\pi(X)\}\left\{\frac{p(X,1)\vartheta_{11}(X) + (1-p(X,1))\vartheta_{01}(X)}{\pi(X)}\right.\right.$$

$$\left.\left. + \frac{p(X,0)\vartheta_{10}(X) + (1-p(X,0))\vartheta_{00}(X)}{1-\pi(X)}\right\}^2\right],$$

where $p(X,z) = \Pr(D = 1|X, Z = z)$ indicates a special conditional propensity, P_c the fraction of compliers, $\vartheta_{dz}(x) = \dfrac{\tau - F_{Y|D=d,Z=z,X}\left(Q_{yd|c}^\tau\right)}{P_c \cdot f_{yd|c}\left(Q_{yd|c}^\tau\right)}$, and

$$f_{Y^1|c}(u) = \frac{1}{P_c} \int f_{Y|X,D=1,Z=1}(u)p(X,1) - f_{Y|X,D=1,Z=0}(u)p(X,0)dF_X$$

$$f_{Y^0|c}(u) = \frac{-1}{P_c} \int f_{Y|X,D=0,Z=1}(u)\{1 - p(X,1)\} - f_{Y|X,D=0,Z=0}(u)\{1 - p(X,0)\}dF_X$$

the marginal densities of potential outcomes for the compliers. The variance contributions stem from two parts: first the weighting by W if the weights were known, and second from the fact that the weights were estimated. To attain $\sqrt{n}$ consistency, higher-order kernels are required if X contains more than three continuous regressors, else conventional kernels can be used. More precisely, the order of the kernel should be larger than $\dim(X)/2$. It can be shown that then the estimator reaches the semi-parametric efficiency bound, irrespectively of $\pi(x)$ being known or estimated with a bias of order $o(n^{-1/2})$.

Now remember that these weights W might sometimes be negative in practice, which leads to a non-convex optimisation problem. Alternatively one could work with modified, positive weights. These are obtained by applying an iterated expectations argument to (7.34) to obtain

$$(\alpha, \beta) = \arg\min_{a,b} E\left[\rho_\tau(Y - a - bD) \cdot W\right] = \arg\min_{a,b} E\left[\rho_\tau(Y - a - bD)E\left[W|Y,D\right]\right]$$

with the always positive (Exercise 5) weights

$$W^+ := E\left[W|Y,D\right] = E\left[\frac{Z - \pi(X)}{\pi(X)(1 - \pi(X))}|Y,D\right](2D - 1). \tag{7.38}$$

Hence, they can be used to develop an estimator with a linear programming representation. The sample objective function with W^+ instead of W is globally convex in (a,b) since it is the sum of convex functions, and the global optimum can be obtained in a finite number of iterations. However, we would need to estimate W^+ first. Although $W^+ = E\left[W|Y,D\right]$ is always non-negative, some predicted $\hat{W}_i^+$ can happen to be negative. In practice, the objective function would then be non-convex again. Since the probability that $\hat{W}_i^+$ is negative goes to zero as sample size goes to infinity, one can use the weights $\max(0, \hat{W}_i^+)$ instead. In other words, negative $\widehat{W_i^+}$ are discarded in the further estimation.

Similar to arguments discussed in the previous chapters, the covariates X are usually included to make the instrumental variable assumptions (exclusion restriction and unconfoundedness of the instrument) more plausible. In addition, including covariates X can also lead to more efficient estimates. Generally, with a causal model in mind, we could think of four different cases for the covariates. A covariate X can (1) causally influence Z and also D or Y, it can (2) influence Z but neither D nor Y, it can (3) influence D or Y but not Z, and finally (4) it may neither influence Z nor D nor Y.[14] In case (1), the covariate should be included in the set of regressors X because otherwise the estimates would generally be inconsistent. In cases (2) and (4), the covariate should

---

[14] There are also other possibilities where X might itself be on the causal path from Z or D or Y.

usually not be included in X as it would decrease efficiency and might also lead to common support problems. In case (3), however, inclusion of the covariate can reduce the asymptotic variance.[15]

Let us finally comment on the estimation of conditional QTE, i.e. the quantile treatment effect conditionally on X. When looking at non-parametric estimators, it should again be local estimators. Therefore, when X contains continuous regressors, fully non-parametric estimation will be slower than the $\sqrt{n}$ rate. The early contributions to the estimation of conditional QTE usually imposed functional form assumptions. They often imposed restrictions on treatment effect heterogeneity, e.g. that the QTE does not vary with X, which in fact often implies equality of conditional and unconditional QTE. With those kinds of strong assumptions one can again reach $\sqrt{n}$ consistency.

Let us briefly consider one popular version which can easily be extended to semi- and even non-parametric estimators.[16] We still apply the assumption of facing a monotone treatment choice decision function and can only identify the conditional QTE for compliers, i.e.

$$Q^{\tau}_{Y^1|X,c} - Q^{\tau}_{Y^0|X,c} \, .$$

Let us assume that conditional on X the τ quantile of Y in the subpopulation of compliers is linear, i.e.

$$Q^{\tau}(Y|X, T = c) = \alpha_0^{\tau} D + X'\beta_0^{\tau} \, , \tag{7.39}$$

where D and Z are binary. If the subpopulation of compliers were known, parameters α and β of such a simple linear quantile regression could be estimated via

$$\arg\min_{a,b} E\left[\rho_{\tau}\left(Y - aD - X'b\right)|T = c\right]. \tag{7.40}$$

Evidently, since we do not know in advance which observations belong to the compliers, this is not directly achievable. But as before, with an appropriate weighting function containing the propensity $\pi(X) = \Pr(Z = 1|X)$ it becomes a feasible task. First note that for any absolutely integrable function $\xi(\cdot)$ you have

$$E\left[\xi(Y, D, X)|T = c\right] P_c = E\left[W \cdot \xi(Y, D, X)\right], \tag{7.41}$$

with P_c being the proportion of compliers, and the weight

$$W = 1 - \frac{D(1 - Z)}{1 - \pi(X)} - \frac{(1 - D)Z}{\pi(X)}. \tag{7.42}$$

To see the equality of (7.41), realise that with D and Z binary and monotonicity in the participation decision (having excluded defiers and indifferent individuals), for P_a the proportion of *always-participants*, P_n the proportion of *never-participants*, and P_c that of *compliers*, we obtain

$$E\left[W \cdot \xi(Y, D, X)\right] = E\left[W \cdot \xi(Y, D, X)|T = c\right] P_c$$
$$E\left[W \cdot \xi(Y, D, X)|T = a\right] P_a + E\left[W \cdot \xi(Y, D, X)|T = n\right] P_n \, .$$

---

[15] Frölich and Melly (2013) show that the semi-parametric efficiency bound decreases in this situation.

[16] The version here presented is basically the estimator of Abadie, Angrist and Imbens (2002).

Inserting the definition of W and exploiting the exogeneity of IV Z gives

$$E\left[W \cdot \xi(Y, D, X)\right] = E\left[\xi(Y, D, X)|T = c\right] P_c .$$

This suggests the estimation of the coefficients α, β by a weighted quantile regression based on

$$\arg\min_{a,b} E\left[W \cdot \rho_\tau \left(Y - \alpha D - X'\beta\right)\right] , \qquad (7.43)$$

where P_c has been ignored as it does not affect the values where this function is minimised.

Since (7.40) is globally convex in (a, b), the function (7.43) is also convex as the objective function is identical apart from multiplication by P_c. But again, the weights W_i for individuals i with $D_i \neq Z_i$ are negative, and consequently the sample analogue

$$\arg\min_{a,b} \frac{1}{n} \sum W_i \cdot \rho_\tau \left(Y_i - a D_i - X_i' b\right) \qquad (7.44)$$

may not be globally convex in (a, b). Algorithms for such piecewise linear but non-convex objective functions may not find the global optimum and (7.44) does not have a linear programming (LP) representation. As in the case of IV estimation of the unconditional QTE, one may use the weights $W^+ := E\left[W|Y, D, X\right]$ instead of W, which can be shown to be always non-negative. This permits the use of conventional LP algorithms, but the estimation of the weights $E\left[W|Y, D, X\right]$ requires either additional parametric assumptions or high-dimensional non-parametric regression.[17] Unfortunately, as for W^+ the estimates $\widehat{E}\left[W|Y, D, X\right]$ could be negative, another modification is necessary before an LP algorithm can be used. One could also use the weights (7.31) instead of (7.42), both would lead to consistent estimation of α and β, but it is not clear which ones will be more efficient. For compliers, W varies with X whereas W^+ equals 1 for them. In any case, both types of weights would be generally inefficient since they do not incorporate the conditional density function of the error term at the τ quantile. Hence, if one was mainly interested in estimating a conditional QTE with a parametric specification, more efficient estimators could be developed.

7.3   Quantile Treatment Effects under Endogeneity: RDD

At the beginning of this chapter on quantile treatment effects we mentioned that even if one is not primarily interested in the distributional impacts, one may still use the quantile method to reduce susceptibility to outliers. This argument is particularly relevant for the regression discontinuity design (RDD) method since the number of observations close to the discontinuity threshold is often relatively small. This is why we dedicate here more space to QTE with RDD.

---

[17] Note that the weights $W^+ = E[W|Y, D]$ cannot be used, as conditioning on X is necessary here.

On the other hand, in Chapter 6 we came to know the so-called RDD approach as an alternative to the instrumental approach.[18] So one could keep this section short by simply defining the RDD as our instrument and referring to the last (sub)section. Instead, we decided to take this as an opportunity to outline a different estimation method, namely via numerically inverting the empirical cdf, while presenting some more details on the RDD-QTE estimation.

Let us first recall the definition of the two designs and definitions we are using in the RDD approach. One speaks of a *sharp* design if the treatment indicator D changes for everyone at the threshold z_0 of a given variable Z which typically represents the distance to a natural border (administrative, geographical, cultural, age limit, etc.). One could then write

$$D = \mathbb{1}\{Z \geq z_0\} . \tag{7.45}$$

In this sharp design, all individuals change programme participation status exactly at z_0. In many applications, however, the treatment decision contains some elements of discretion. Caseworkers may have some latitude about whom they offer a programme, or they may partially base their decision on criteria that are unobserved to the econometrician. In this case, known as the *fuzzy* design, D is permitted to depend also on other (partly observed or entirely unobserved) factors but the treatment probability changes nonetheless discontinuously at z_0, i.e.

$$\lim_{\varepsilon \to 0} E\left[D|Z = z_0 + \varepsilon\right] - \lim_{\varepsilon \to 0} E\left[D|Z = z_0 - \varepsilon\right] \neq 0 . \tag{7.46}$$

The fuzzy design includes the sharp design as a special case when the left-hand side of (7.46) is equal to one. Therefore the following discussion focusses on the more general fuzzy design.

Let $\mathcal{N}_\varepsilon$ be a symmetric ε neighbourhood about z_0 and partition $\mathcal{N}_\varepsilon$ into $\mathcal{N}_\varepsilon^+ = \{z : z \geq z_0, z \in \mathcal{N}_\varepsilon\}$ and $\mathcal{N}_\varepsilon^- = \{z : z < z_0, z \in \mathcal{N}_\varepsilon\}$. According to the reaction to the distance z over $\mathcal{N}_\varepsilon$ we can partition the population into five (to us already well-known) subpopulations:

$$
\begin{array}{llllll}
T_\varepsilon = a & \text{if} & D(z) = 1 & \forall z \in \mathcal{N}_\varepsilon^- & \text{and} & D(z) = 1 & \forall z \in \mathcal{N}_\varepsilon^+ \\
T_\varepsilon = n & \text{if} & D(z) = 0 & \forall z \in \mathcal{N}_\varepsilon^- & \text{and} & D(z) = 0 & \forall z \in \mathcal{N}_\varepsilon^+ \\
T_\varepsilon = c & \text{if} & D(z) = 0 & \forall z \in \mathcal{N}_\varepsilon^- & \text{and} & D(z) = 1 & \forall z \in \mathcal{N}_\varepsilon^+ \\
T_\varepsilon = d & \text{if} & D(z) = 1 & \forall z \in \mathcal{N}_\varepsilon^- & \text{and} & D(z) = 0 & \forall z \in \mathcal{N}_\varepsilon^+ \\
\text{and} \quad T_\varepsilon = ind & \text{if} & \multicolumn{4}{l}{D(z) \text{ is non-constant over } \mathcal{N}_\varepsilon^- \text{ or over } \mathcal{N}_\varepsilon^+ .}
\end{array}
$$

We have already discussed the groups at different places in this book. The fifth group (labelled indefinite) contains all units that react non-monotonously over the $\mathcal{N}_\varepsilon$ neighbourhood, e.g. they may first switch from $D = 0$ to 1 and switch then back for increasing values of z. Clearly, for binary IVs the definition of such a group would not have made

---

[18] Some may argue that this is not a different approach as one could interpret the RDD as a particular instrument. As we discussed in that chapter, the main promoters of this method, however, prefer to interpret it as a particular case of randomised experiments.

much sense. As in the RDD, Z itself is not the instrument but (if at all) $\mathbb{1}\{Z \geq z_0\}$, such a group might exist. For identification reasons, however, we must exclude them by assumption together with the defiers. Note that in the sharp design, everyone is a complier (by definition) for any $\varepsilon > 0$. We work with the following basic assumptions:

Assumption RDD-1 There exists some positive $\bar{\varepsilon}$ such that for every positive $\varepsilon \leq \bar{\varepsilon}$

(i) Compliers exist $\lim_{\varepsilon \to 0} \Pr(T_\varepsilon = c | Z = z_0) > 0$

(ii) Monotonicity $\lim_{\varepsilon \to 0} \Pr(T_\varepsilon = t | Z \in \mathcal{N}_\varepsilon) = 0$ for $t \in \{d, ind\}$

(iii) Independent IV $\lim_{\varepsilon \to 0} \Pr\left(T_\varepsilon = t | Z \in \mathcal{N}_\varepsilon^+\right) - \Pr\left(T_\varepsilon = t | Z \in \mathcal{N}_\varepsilon^-\right) = 0$

           for $t \in \{a, n, c\}$

(iv) IV Exclusion $\lim_{\varepsilon \to 0} F_{Y^1 | Z \in \mathcal{N}_\varepsilon^+, T_\varepsilon = t}(u) - F_{Y^1 | Z \in \mathcal{N}_\varepsilon^-, T_\varepsilon = t}(u) = 0$

           for $t \in \{a, c\}$

           $\lim_{\varepsilon \to 0} F_{Y^0 | Z \in \mathcal{N}_\varepsilon^+, T_\varepsilon = t}(u) - F_{Y^0 | Z \in \mathcal{N}_\varepsilon^-, T_\varepsilon = t}(u) = 0$

           for $t \in \{n, c\}$

(v) Density at threshold $F_Z(z)$ is differentiable at z_0 and $f_Z(z_0) > 0$.

These assumptions require that for every sufficiently small neighbourhood, the threshold acts like a local IV. Assumption RDD-1 (i) requires that $E[D|Z]$ is in fact discontinuous at z_0, i.e. we assume that some units change their treatment status exactly at z_0. Then, (ii) requires that in a very small neighbourhood of z_0, the instrument has a weakly monotonous impact on $D(z)$. Further, (iii) and (iv) impose the continuity of the types and the distribution of the potential outcomes as a function of Z at z_0. Finally, (v) requires that observations close to z_0 exist.

Under Assumption RDD-1 the distribution functions of the potential outcomes for local compliers are identified. Define $F_{Y^d|c}(u) = \lim_{\varepsilon \to 0} F_{Y^d | Z \in \mathcal{N}_\varepsilon, T_\varepsilon = c}(u)$ and as in Chapter 6, $1^+ = \mathbb{1}\{Z \geq z_0\} = 1 - 1^-$. Then we get that the distributions of the potential outcomes for the local compliers are identified as

$$F_{Y^1|c}(u) = \lim_{\varepsilon \to 0} \frac{E\left[\mathbb{1}\{Y \leq u\}\left(1^+ - p_\varepsilon\right) | Z \in \mathcal{N}_\varepsilon, D = 1\right]}{E\left[1^+ - p_\varepsilon | Z \in \mathcal{N}_\varepsilon, D = 1\right]}, \text{ and}$$

$$F_{Y^0|c}(u) = \lim_{\varepsilon \to 0} \frac{E\left[\mathbb{1}\{Y \leq u\}\left(1^+ - p_\varepsilon\right) | Z \in \mathcal{N}_\varepsilon, D = 0\right]}{E\left[1^+ - p_\varepsilon | Z \in \mathcal{N}_\varepsilon, D = 0\right]}, \tag{7.47}$$

where $p_\varepsilon = \Pr(Z \geq z_0 | Z \in \mathcal{N}_\varepsilon)$ for $\varepsilon > 0$. Taking together Assumption RDD-1 (v) and the symmetry of $\mathcal{N}_\varepsilon$, it follows by l'Hospital that $\lim_{\varepsilon \to 0} p_\varepsilon = \lim_{\varepsilon \to 0} \Pr(Z \geq z_0 | Z \in \mathcal{N}_\varepsilon) = \frac{1}{2}$. This would simplify the above formulae to

$$F_{Y^1|c}(u) = \lim_{\varepsilon \to 0} \frac{E\left[\mathbb{1}\{Y \leq u\}\left(2 \cdot 1^+ - 1\right) | Z \in \mathcal{N}_\varepsilon, D = 1\right]}{E\left[2 \cdot 1^+ - 1 | Z \in \mathcal{N}_\varepsilon, D = 1\right]}, \text{ and}$$

$$F_{Y^0|c}(u) = \lim_{\varepsilon \to 0} \frac{E\left[\mathbb{1}\{Y \leq u\}\left(2 \cdot 1^- - 1\right) | Z \in \mathcal{N}_\varepsilon, D = 0\right]}{E\left[2 \cdot 1^- - 1 | Z \in \mathcal{N}_\varepsilon, D = 0\right]}. \tag{7.48}$$

In Monte-Carlos simulations, however, it turned out that the estimators for the potential distributions performed better when a non-parametric estimator for p_ε was used. The reasons for this could be many, and can therefore not be discussed here.[19]

As in the *sharp* design everyone with 1^+ has $D = 1$ and vice versa, i.e. everyone is a complier at z_0, the potential outcomes in the population is identified as

$$F_{Y^1}(u) = \lim_{\varepsilon \to 0} E\left[\mathbb{1}\{Y \le u\} | Z \in \mathcal{N}_\varepsilon, D = 1\right] \text{ and}$$
$$F_{Y^0}(u) = \lim_{\varepsilon \to 0} E\left[\mathbb{1}\{Y \le u\} | Z \in \mathcal{N}_\varepsilon, D = 0\right].$$

Analogously to the above, for the potential cdf one obtains from Assumption RDD-1 also the identification formulae for the quantiles of the potential outcomes for the local compliers, namely

$$Q^\tau_{Y^1|c} = \lim_{\varepsilon \to 0} \arg\min_q E\left[\rho_\tau (Y - q)(1^+ - p_\varepsilon) | Z \in \mathcal{N}_\varepsilon, D = 1\right], \text{ and}$$
$$Q^\tau_{Y^0|c} = \lim_{\varepsilon \to 0} \arg\min_q E\left[\rho_\tau (Y - q)(p_\varepsilon - 1^+) | Z \in \mathcal{N}_\varepsilon, D = 0\right],$$

where $\rho_\tau(u) = u \cdot (\tau - \mathbb{1}\{u < 0\})$ is the check function. Again one could try with $p_\varepsilon = 0.5$.

Regarding the quantile treatment effects (QTE) $\Delta^\tau_{QTE} = Q^\tau_{Y^1|c} - Q^\tau_{Y^0|c}$, we could identify it directly as

$$\left(Q^\tau_{Y^0|c}, \Delta^\tau_{QTE}\right) = \lim_{\varepsilon \to 0} \arg\min_{a,b} E\left[\rho_\tau (Y - a - bD)(1^+ - p_\varepsilon)(2D - 1) | Z \in \mathcal{N}_\varepsilon\right],$$

$$(7.49)$$

which corresponds to a local linear quantile regression. Hence, the quantiles can be obtained by univariate weighted quantile regressions. Despite its simplicity one should note that the objective function of the weighted quantile regression is not convex if some of the weights are negative. Conventional linear programming algorithms will typically not work. Instead of repeating the discussion and procedures from the last sections for this modified context, we will briefly study the non-parametric estimators for the distribution functions, and give the corresponding quantile estimators resulting from inverting these distribution functions afterwards.

The distribution functions can be estimated by local regression in a neighbourhood of z_0. More specifically, let K_i be some kernel weights depending on the distance between Z_i and z_0, and on a bandwidth h that converges to zero. Then, with a consistent estimator for p_ε, e.g. $\sum_i 1^+_i K_i / \sum K_i$, a natural estimator for the distribution function $F_{Y^1|c}$ is (Exercise 7)

---

[19] Note that having in (7.47) 1^+ in the numerator and denominator, but in (7.48) the 1^- is not an erratum; see Exercise 6.

$$\hat{F}_{Y^1|c}(u) = \frac{\sum_{i=1}^{n} \mathbb{1}\{Y_i \leq u\} D_i \left(1_i^+ - \hat{p}_\varepsilon\right) K_i}{\sum_{i=1}^{n} D_i \left(1_i^+ - \hat{p}_\varepsilon\right) K_i}$$

$$= \frac{\dfrac{\sum_{i:1_i^+=1} \mathbb{1}\{Y_i \leq u\} D_i K_i}{\sum_{i:1_i^+=1} K_i} - \dfrac{\sum_{i:1_i^+=0} \mathbb{1}\{Y_i \leq u\} D_i K_i}{\sum_{i:1_i^+=0} K_i}}{\dfrac{\sum_{i:1_i^+=1} D_i K_i}{\sum_{i:1_i^+=1} K_i} - \dfrac{\sum_{i:1_i^+=0} D_i K_i}{\sum_{i:1_i^+=0} K_i}}. \tag{7.50}$$

This is certainly just a modified version of the Wald estimator. Let us define for a random variable V the right limit $m_V^+ = \lim_{\varepsilon \to 0} E[V|Z = z_0 + \varepsilon]$ and the left limit $m_V^- = \lim_{\varepsilon \to 0} E[V|Z = z_0 - \varepsilon]$. Imagine now that in (7.50) variable V represents either $\mathbb{1}\{Y \leq u\} \cdot D$, or $\mathbb{1}\{Y \leq u\} \cdot (1 - D)$, or $(1 - D)$, or D. In all cases V has bounded support such that the previously defined limit functions are bounded, too. The suggested estimator is

$$\hat{F}_{Y^1|c}(u) = \frac{\hat{m}^+_{\mathbb{1}\{Y \leq u\}D} - \hat{m}^-_{\mathbb{1}\{Y \leq u\}D}}{\hat{m}^+_D - \hat{m}^-_D}.$$

Similarly, for the non-treatment outcome we can use

$$\hat{F}_{Y^0|c}(u) = \frac{\hat{m}^+_{\mathbb{1}\{Y \leq u\}(1-D)} - \hat{m}^-_{\mathbb{1}\{Y \leq u\}(1-D)}}{\hat{m}^+_{1-D} - \hat{m}^-_{1-D}}.$$

If we want to apply local linear weights, which appears appropriate here since we are effectively estimating conditional means at boundary points (from the left and right side of z_0), each of our m_V^+ is estimated as the value of a that solves

$$\arg\min_{a,b} \sum_{i=1}^{n} \{V_i - a - b(Z_i - z_0)\}^2 \, 1_i^+ K\left(\frac{Z_i - z_0}{h}\right).$$

Analogously m_V^- can be estimated by using only observations to the left of z_0. This can be applied to all the four above-discussed versions of V.

As usual, in order to use the estimator, draw conclusions, construct confidence intervals, etc. it is quite helpful to know the statistical properties of the estimator(s). In order to state them, we first have to specify some more regularity conditions.

Assumption RDD-2 The following conditions are assumed to hold.

(i) The data $\{(Y_i, D_i, Z_i)\}$ are i.i.d. with $\mathcal{X}$ being a compact set.

(ii) Smoothness and existence of limits: the left and right limits of the functions $E[\mathbb{1}\{Y \leq u\}|Z, D = 0]$, $E[\mathbb{1}\{Y \leq u\}|Z, D = 1]$ and $E[D|Z]$ exist at z_0, and these functions are twice continuously differentiable with respect to Z at z_0 with second derivatives being Hölder continuous in a left and a right ε-neighbourhood of z_0, and uniformly on a compact subset of $\mathbb{R}$, say $\mathcal{Y}$.

(iii) The density f_Z is bounded away from zero, and is twice continuously differentiable at z_0 with a second derivative being Hölder continuous in an ε-neighbourhood of z_0.

(iv) The fraction of compliers $P_c = m_D^+ - m_D^-$ is bounded away from zero.

(v) For bandwidth h it holds that $nh \to \infty$ and $\sqrt{nh} \cdot h^2 \to \Xi < \infty$.

(vi) Kernel K is symmetric, bounded, zero outside a compact set and integrates to one.

These conditions were already discussed in Chapter 6. Recall that condition (iv) is equivalent to assuming that we have a strong instrument in an IV context, and condition (v) balances bias and variance of the estimator. This way, for $\Xi > 0$, squared bias and variance are of the same order. One may want to modify this to obtain faster rates for the bias.

To simplify the notation, the same bandwidth is used for all functions on both sides of the threshold. The method does certainly also allow for different bandwidths as long as the convergence rates of the bandwidths are the same. Recall the definitions of the kernel constants: $\kappa_l = \int u^l K(u)du$, $\dot{\kappa}_l = \int_0^\infty u^l K(u)du$, $\tilde{\kappa} = \dot{\kappa}_2 \dot{\kappa}_0 - \dot{\kappa}_1^2$, and $\ddot{\mu}_l = \int_0^\infty u^l K^2(u)du$. Then we can state:

THEOREM 7.1   *If Assumptions RDD-1 and 2 are satisfied, the estimators $\hat{F}_{Y^0|c}(u)$ and $\hat{F}_{Y^1|c}(u)$ of the distribution functions for the compliers, i.e. $F_{Y^0|c}(u)$ and $F_{Y^1|c}(u)$, jointly converge in law such that*

$$\sqrt{nh_n}\left(\hat{F}_{Y^j|c}(u) - F_{Y^j|c}(u)\right) \longrightarrow G^j(u), \qquad j \in \{0,1\},$$

in the set of all uniformly bounded real functions on $\mathcal{Y}$, sometimes denoted by $\ell^\infty(\mathcal{Y})$, where the $G^j(u)$ are Gaussian processes with mean functions $b_j(u) =$

$$\frac{\bar{\mu}_2^2 - \bar{\mu}_1\bar{\mu}_3}{2\bar{\mu}} \frac{\Xi}{P_c}\left\{\frac{\partial^2 m^+_{\mathbb{1}\{Y \leq u\}(D+j-1)}}{\partial z^2} - F_{Y^j|c}(u)\frac{\partial^2 m^+_D}{\partial z^2}\right.$$

$$\left. -\frac{\partial^2 m^-_{\mathbb{1}\{Y \leq u\}(D+j-1)}}{\partial z^2} + F_{Y^j|c}(u)\frac{\partial^2 m^-_D}{\partial z^2}\right\},$$

where $\frac{\partial^2 m^+_V}{\partial z^2} = \lim_{\varepsilon \to 0}\frac{\partial^2 E[V|Z=z_0+\varepsilon]}{\partial z^2}$ for a random variable V, and $\frac{\partial^2 m^-_V}{\partial z^2}$ the analogous left limit,[20] and covariance functions ($j, k \in \{0,1\}$),

$$v_{j,k}(u, \tilde{u}) = \frac{\bar{\mu}_2^2\ddot{\mu}_0 - 2\bar{\mu}_2\bar{\mu}_1\ddot{\mu}_1 + \bar{\mu}_1^2\ddot{\mu}_2}{\bar{\mu}^2}\frac{1}{P_c^2 f_Z(z_0)}\left(\omega^+_{j,k}(u,\tilde{u}) + \omega^-_{j,k}(u,\tilde{u})\right),$$

with $\omega^+_{j,k}(u,\tilde{u}) = \lim_{\varepsilon \to 0}Cov\{(D+j-1)\left(\mathbb{1}\{Y \leq u\} - F_{Y^j|c}(u)\right),$

$$(D+k-1)\left(\mathbb{1}\{Y \leq \tilde{u}\} - F_{Y^k|c}(\tilde{u})\right)|Z \in \mathcal{N}_\varepsilon^+\}$$

and $\omega^-_{j,k}(y, \tilde{y})$ the analogous left limit.[21]

So the estimators of the distribution functions evaluated at a particular value $u \in \mathcal{Y}$ are asymptotically jointly normally distributed, i.e.

$$\sqrt{nh_n}\left(\hat{F}_{Y^j|c}(u) - F_{Y^j|c}(u)\right) \sim N\left(b_j(u), v_{j,j}(u,u)\right), \qquad j \in \{0,1\}.$$

---

[20] Note that the first fraction is a constant that depends only on the kernel, e.g. $-\frac{11}{190}$ for the Epanechnikov.

[21] Note that the first fraction is a constant that depends only on the kernel, e.g. $\frac{56832}{12635}$ for the Epanechnikov.

The bias functions $b_j(u)$ disappear if we choose $\Xi = 0$, and thereby choose an under-smoothing bandwidth for the functions to be estimated. This has the advantage of simplifying the asymptotics. The asymptotic covariances are the sum of the covariances of the estimated functions rescaled by $P_c^2 f_Z(z_0)$.

A possible way to characterise the treatment effect on the outcome Y consists in estimating the distribution treatment effect (DTE) for compliers, say Δ_{DTE}^u, by $F_{Y^1|c}(u) - F_{Y^0|c}(u)$. A natural estimator is $\hat{\Delta}_{DTE}^u = \hat{F}_{Y^1|c}(u) - \hat{F}_{Y^0|c}(u)$ for which it can be shown that under Assumptions RDD-1 and 2, it converges in $\ell^\infty(\mathcal{Y})$ to the Gaussian process

$$\sqrt{nh_n}\left(\hat{\Delta}_{DTE}^u - \Delta_{DTE}^u\right) \longrightarrow G^1(u) - G^0(u)$$

with mean function $b_1(u) - b_0(u)$ and covariance function $v_{1,1}(u, \tilde{u}) + v_{0,0}(u, \tilde{u}) - 2v_{0,1}(u, \tilde{u})$.

Let us turn to the quantile treatment effects. They have a well-defined asymptotic distribution only if the outcome is continuous with continuous densities. One therefore needs the additional

Assumption RDD-3 $F_{Y^0|c}(u)$ and $F_{Y^1|c}(u)$ are both continuously differentiable with continuous density functions $f_{Y^0|c}(u)$ and $f_{Y^1|c}(u)$ that are bounded from above and away from zero on $\mathcal{Y}$.

One could estimate the quantile treatment effects by the sample analog of (7.49). But also this minimisation problem is a non-convex optimisation problem because some weights are positive while others are negative. This requires grid searches or algorithms for non-convex problems. But they do not guarantee to find a global optimum. Instead, one can follow a more direct strategy by inverting the estimated distribution function. There one might find a similar problem, in particular that the estimated distribution function is non-monotone, i.e. $\hat{F}_{Y^j|c}(u)$ may decrease when we increase u. But this is only a small sample problem because the assumed monotonicity ensures that the estimated distribution function is asymptotically strictly increasing. A quick and simple method to monotonise the estimated distribution functions is to perform some re-arrangements. This does not affect the asymptotic properties of the estimator but allows us to invert it. These procedures typically consist of a sequence of closed-form steps and are very quick.

THEOREM 7.2   *If Assumptions RDD-1 to 3 are satisfied, the estimators $\hat{Q}_{Y^0|c}(\tau)$ and $\hat{Q}_{Y^1|c}(\tau)$ jointly converge in $\ell^\infty((0,1))$ to the Gaussian processes*

$$\sqrt{nh_n}\left(\hat{Q}_{Y^j|c}(\tau) - Q_{Y^j|c}(\tau)\right) \longrightarrow -f_{Y^j|c}\left(Q_{Y^j|c}(\tau)\right)^{-1} G^j\left(Q_{Y^j|c}(\tau)\right)$$

$$:= \tilde{G}^j(\tau), j \in \{0, 1\}$$

with mean function $\tilde{b}_j(\tau) = -f_{Y^j|c}\left(Q_{Y^j|c}(\tau)\right)^{-1} b_j\left(Q_{Y^j|c}(\tau)\right)$, and covariance function $\tilde{v}_{j,k}(\tau, \tilde{\tau}) = f_{Y^j|c}\left(Q_{Y^j|c}(\tau)\right)^{-1} f_{Y^k|c}\left(Q_{Y^k|c}(\tilde{\tau})\right)^{-1} v_{j,k}\left(Q_{Y^j|c}(\tau), Q_{Y^k|c}(\tilde{\tau})\right)$ with b_j and $v_{j,k}$ as in Theorem 7.1. Furthermore, for the estimator $\hat{\Delta}_{QTE}^\tau$ of the QTE for the compliers one has

$$\sqrt{nh_n}\left(\hat{\Delta}_{QTE}^\tau - \Delta_{QTE}^\tau\right) \longrightarrow \tilde{G}^1(\tau) - \tilde{G}^0(\tau)$$

with mean function $\tilde{b}_1(\tau) - \tilde{b}_0(\tau)$ and covariance function $\tilde{v}_{1,1}(\tau, \tilde{\tau}) + \tilde{v}_{0,0}(\tau, \tilde{\tau}) - 2\tilde{v}_{0,1}(\tau, \tilde{\tau})$.

It can also be shown that smooth functionals of both distribution functions satisfy a functional central limit theorem. This is very helpful in practice as we will see in Example 7.6. First let us state the theory:

THEOREM 7.3 *Let $\xi\left(u, F_{Y^0|c}, F_{Y^1|c}\right)$ be a functional taking values in $\ell^\infty(\mathcal{Y})$ that is differentiable in $\left(F_{Y^0|c}, F_{Y^1|c}\right)$ tangentially to the set of continuous functions with derivative (ξ'_0, ξ'_1).[22] If Assumptions RDD-1 and 2 are satisfied, then the plug-in estimator $\hat{\xi}(u) \equiv \xi\left(u, \hat{F}_{Y^0|c}, \hat{F}_{Y^1|c}\right)$ converges in $\ell^\infty((0,1))$ as follows:*

$$\sqrt{nh_n}\left(\hat{\xi}(u) - \xi(u)\right) \longrightarrow \xi'_0(u) G^0(u) + \xi'_1(u) G^1(u).$$

This is very useful in many situations where the interest is directed to a derivative or a parameter of the distribution. Let us look at cases where the Lorenz curve or the Gini coefficient of the income distribution are the objects of interest.

Example 7.6 We apply Theorem 7.3 in order to derive the limiting distribution of the estimators of the Lorenz curves and the Gini coefficients of the potential outcomes. Their estimates are defined as

$$L^j(\tau) = \frac{\int_0^\tau Q_{Y^j|c}(t)\,dt}{\int_0^1 Q_{Y^j|c}(t)\,dt}, \qquad \hat{L}^j(\tau) = \frac{\int_0^\tau \hat{Q}_{Y^j|c}(t)\,dt}{\int_0^1 \hat{Q}_{Y^j|c}(t)\,dt}.$$

The Hadamard derivative of the map from the distribution function to the Lorenz curve can be found e.g. in Barrett and Donald (2009). Using their result one obtains the limiting distribution for a simple plug-in estimator, i.e.

$$\sqrt{nh_n}\left(\hat{L}^j(\tau) - L^j(\tau)\right) \longrightarrow \frac{\int_0^\tau \tilde{G}^1(t)\,dt - L^1(\tau)\int_0^1 \tilde{G}^1(t)\,dt}{\int_0^1 Q_{Y^1|c}(t)\,dt} =: \mathcal{L}(\tau) \quad (7.51)$$

with $\tilde{G}^j$ defined as in Theorem 7.2, mean function

$$b^l_j(\tau) = \frac{\int_0^\tau \tilde{b}_j(t)\,dt - L^j(\tau)\int_0^1 \tilde{b}_j(t)\,dt}{\int_0^1 Q_{Y^j|c}(t)\,dt}$$

and covariance function

$$v^l_{j,k}(\tau, \tilde{\tau}) = \frac{1}{\int_0^1 Q_{Y^j|c}(t)\,dt \int_0^1 Q_{Y^k|c}(t)\,dt}$$

$$\cdot \left(\int_0^\tau \int_0^{\tilde{\tau}} \tilde{v}_{j,k}(t,\tilde{t})\,d\tilde{t}dt + L^j(\tau) L^k(\tilde{\tau}) \int_0^1 \int_0^1 \tilde{v}_{j,k}(t,\tilde{t})\,d\tilde{t}dt \right.$$

$$\left. -L^j(\tau) \int_0^1 \int_0^{\tilde{\tau}} \tilde{v}_{j,k}(t,\tilde{t})\,d\tilde{t}dt - L^k(\tilde{\tau}) \int_0^\tau \int_0^1 \tilde{v}_{j,k}(t,\tilde{t})\,d\tilde{t}dt \right).$$

---

[22] What is exactly demanded is the so-called Hadamard or compact differentiability; see, for example, Gill (1989), page 100.

The Gini coefficient is defined and estimated by

$$g^j = 1 - 2 \int_0^1 L^j(t)\, dt, \qquad \hat{g}^j = 1 - 2 \int_0^1 \hat{L}^j(t)\, dt \ .$$

Our plug-in estimator is asymptotically normally distributed with bias $-2 \int_0^1 b_j^l(t)\, dt$ and variance $4 \int_0^1 \int_0^1 v_{j,k}^l(t, \tilde{t})\, d\tilde{t} dt$, and

$$\sqrt{nh_n} \left\{ \hat{g}^j(\tau) - g^j(\tau) \right\} \to 2 \int_0^1 \mathcal{L}(t)\, dt \ , \quad \text{see (7.51) for definitions.}$$

For the same reasons discussed in the previous chapters and sections it can be useful to incorporate additional covariates X. We recommend to do this in a fully non-parametric way and then suppose that Assumption RDD-1 holds conditionally on X. Even if one believes that the RDD is valid without conditioning, one might want to check the robustness of the results when covariates are included. As before, including covariates might increase the precision of the estimates. Another reason for incorporating covariates applies when the threshold crossing at z_0 itself affects them. Under certain conditions we can separate then the direct from the indirect effects by controlling for X but first obtain the conditional treatment effect. The common support restriction will then identify the unconditional effects which are obtained as usual by integrating the conditional treatment effect over X. So we need then

Assumption RDD-4 Suppose Assumption RDD-1 (i), (ii) and (v). Suppose further that Assumption RDD-1 (iii) and (iv) are true conditionally on X. Further assume:

(vi) Common support $\quad \lim_{\varepsilon \to 0} Supp(X|Z \in \mathcal{N}_\varepsilon^+) = \lim_{\varepsilon \to 0} Supp(X|Z \in \mathcal{N}_\varepsilon^-)$

Under these assumptions, similar expressions as in the Theorems above are obtained, but the weights are now functions of $p_\varepsilon(x) = \Pr(Z \geq z_0 | X = x, Z \in \mathcal{N}_\varepsilon)$, and one has

$$\left(Q_{Y^0|c}^\tau, \ \Delta_{QTE}^\tau \right)$$
$$= \lim_{\varepsilon \to 0} \arg\min_{a,b} E \left[\rho_\tau \left(Y - a - bD \right) \frac{1^+ - p_\varepsilon(X)}{p_\varepsilon(X)(1 - p_\varepsilon(X))} (2D - 1) | Z \in \mathcal{N}_\varepsilon \right].$$

This shows that the unconditional QTE can be estimated via a simple weighted quantile regression where the covariates X only enter in the weights via $p_\varepsilon(x)$. Again, the weights in the previous expression are sometimes positive and sometimes negative such that conventional linear programming algorithms fail because of the potential non-convexity.

7.4   Bibliographic and Computational Notes

7.4.1   Further Reading and Bibliographic Notes

Koenker and Bassett (1978) proposed and derived the statistical properties of a parametric (linear) estimator for conditional quantile models. Due to its ability to capture heterogeneous effects, its theoretical properties have been studied extensively, and it has been used in many empirical studies. Chaudhuri (1991) analysed non-parametric estimation of conditional QTE. A more recent contribution is Hoderlein and Mammen (2007), who consider marginal effects in non-separable models.

Linear instrumental variable quantile regression estimates have been proposed for example by Abadie, Angrist and Imbens (2002), Chernozhukov and Hansen (2005), and Chernozhukov and Hansen (2006). Chernozhukov, Imbens and Newey (2007) and Horowitz and Lee (2007) have considered non-parametric IV estimation of conditional quantile functions. Furthermore, instead of exploiting monotonicity in the relationship predicting D, alternative approaches assume a monotonicity in the relationship determining the Y variable. Finally, in a series of papers, Chesher examines non-parametric identification of conditional distributional effects with structural equations, see Chesher (2010) and references therein.

Regarding the bandwidth choice, note that for semi-parametric estimators the first-order asymptotics do often not depend on the bandwidth value, at least as long as sufficient smoothness conditions are fulfilled and all necessary bias reduction methods were applied in the non-parametric step. This has the obvious implication that the first-order asymptotics is not helpful for selecting bandwidth values. Therefore, on the one hand, those methods would have to be based on second-order approximations. On the other hand, it is well known that in practice these approximations are of little help for finite samples. Taking all together it must be said that the bandwidth choice problem is so far an open field.

Frölich and Melly (2013) discuss the relationship between existing estimators. For example, Abadie, Angrist and Imbens (2002) are interested in parametrically estimating conditional QTE (with a simple linear model). One could be attempted to adapt that approach to estimating unconditional QTE by using the weights (7.42) but no X in that parametric specification. However, this approach would not lead to consistent estimation as it would converge to the difference between the τ quantiles of the treated compliers and non-treated compliers, respectively:

$$F_{Y^1|c,D=1}^{-1}(\tau) - F_{Y^0|c,D=0}^{-1}(\tau).$$

This difference is not very meaningful as one compares the Y^1 outcomes among the treated with the Y^0 outcomes among the non-treated. Therefore, in the general case the weights (7.42) are only useful to estimate conditional quantile effects. If one is interested in non-parametric estimation of the unconditional QTE, one should use the weights in (7.31) but not those in (7.42). When X is the empty set, e.g. in the case where Z is randomly assigned, then the weights (7.31) and those in (7.42) are proportional such that both approaches converge to the same limit.

Often, when people speak about distributional effects, they are thinking of changes in the distribution of $Y = \varphi(X, U)$ caused by a new distribution of X but keeping the distribution of U unchanged. That is, we are in the situation where the impact of D on Y happens exclusively through X. Note that in such a situation you are not necessarily interested in studying a causal effect of X on Y; you are rather interested in the change of F_Y to F_Y^* caused by a change from F_X to F_X^*. This implicates that you take the latter change (i.e. F_X^*) as known or at least as predictable. Often one speaks also of F_X and F_Y

as being the distributions of the source population, whereas F_X^*, F_Y^* denote those of the target population. Of interest are certainly only those target distributions whose changes (from F_Y to F_Y^*) are exclusively caused by the change from F_X to F_X^*.

In Section 7.1.2 we already saw the two approaches proposed by Machado and Mata (2005) and Melly (2005), recall equations (7.16), (7.17) for the latter one. For a related approach compare also with Gosling, Machin and Meghir (2000). Firpo, Fortin and Lemieux (2009) aim to estimate the partial effects on F_Y caused by marginal changes of F_X. For the case of quantiles these could be approximated via the regression of (under certain conditions analytically) equivalent expressions containing the re-centred influence function of the Y-quantiles on X. They study this approach for parametric and non-parametric estimation methods. Chernozhukov, Fernández-Val and Melly (2013) review the problem, summarise the different approaches in a joint formal framework, and discuss inference theory under general conditions.

Having in mind that $F_Y(y) = \int F(y, x)dx = \int F(y|x)dF_X$ can be well approximated by $\frac{1}{n} \sum_{i=1}^{n} F(y|x_i)$, all you need for predicting $F_Y^*(y) = \int F^*(y|x)dF_X^* \approx \frac{1}{n^*} \sum_{i=1}^{n^*} F^*(y|x_i)$ is a reasonable predictor for $F^*(y|x)$ together with either a given distribution F_X^* or a sample $\{x_i\}_{i=1}^{n^*}$ from the target population. In the existing methods it is assumed that $F^*(y|x)$ can be estimated from the available data, or simply that $F_Y^*(y) = E[F(y|X^*)]$, which is, for example, the case if for $Y = \varphi(X, U)$, you have also $Y^* = \varphi(X^*, U)$ with U independent from X and X^*. Note that this does not exclude the dependence of the conditional moments of Y on X, but the moment functions must be the same for the pair (Y^*, X^*). Some might argue that this would be a strong restriction; others might say that this is exactly what counterfactual distributions are. For a simple though quite flexible and effective way to implement this idea, see Dai, Sperlich and Zucchini (2016). The asymptotic properties for a purely non-parametric predictor of $F_Y^*(y)$ based on this idea are studied in Rothe (2010).

7.4.2   Computational Notes

As explained in this chapter, the quantile treatment effect is mainly referred to the difference in the quantile of the potential outcomes, either in form of a ratio or as an absolute difference.

The function (quantile) in **R**, and the command _pctile in Stata can be used as starting points to calculate the sample quantiles of the (potential) outcomes. This is useful in the absence of covariates and under randomised design.

In the presence of covariates, and under the assumption of selection on observables, one needs to fit quantile regressions. In **R**, the package quantreg provides a rich library of useful functions. The rq function from this package allows to estimate the linear quantile regression function, whereas nlrq offers non-linear quantile regression estimates. Furthermore, lprq calculates local polynomial quantile regression estimates. The package also contains a function kuantile, which mimics the generic function quantile but is faster in calculating the sample quantiles when handling a large sample. For further references, see the manual on CRAN.

For some of the routines one first needs to obtain predictions for the propensity scores (as also explained in earlier chapters). These propensity score predictions are used to calculate the weights $W = \frac{\mathbb{1}\{D=d\}}{Pr(D=d|x)}$. To obtain a quantile Q^{τ}_{Yd} you run a univariate quantile regression using rq and setting the option weights=W. To construct the standard errors and confidence interval you can use the bootstrap function boot.rq from that package.

The corresponding commands for these function in Stata, are qreg, iqreg, sqreg, bqreg that provide quantile regression, interquartile range regression, simultaneous quantile regression and bootstrapped quantile regression, respectively. Among these commands only qreg accepts the use of weights, and sqreg and bsqreg calculate a variance-covariance estimator (via bootstrapping).

Since quantile treatment effect under endogeneity and the presence of a plausible instrumental variable, say Z, is equivalent to the solution of $(\hat{Q}^{\tau}_{Y0}, \Delta^{\tau}) = $ arg min$_{a,b} \frac{1}{n} \sum_{i=1}^{n} \rho_{\tau}(Y_i - a - bD_i)\hat{W}_i$ one can first calculate some weights, say $\hat{W} = \frac{z - \pi(x)}{\pi(x)(1-\pi(x))}(2D - 1)$ and then proceed with the univariate estimation of the weighted quantiles with the techniques mentioned above. Moreover, the function qregspiv from the package library("McSpatial") in **R** allows to run the quantile IV estimation for any model with one endogenous explanatory variable; the function was originally created to deal with special AR models. In Stata the command ivreg can handle up to two endogenous treatment variables.

For quantile Diff-in-Diff estimation see this section in Chapter 5. For the case of estimating the quantile treatment effect in the regression discontinuity design, the corresponding Stata codes exist under the command rddqte, see Frölich and Melly (2008), Frölich and Melly (2010), and Frandsen, Frölich and Melly (2012) for more details. To install the ado and helpfiles go to http://froelich.vwl.uni-mannheim.de/1357.0.html. To use similar techniques in **R** one can make use of the function lprq mentioned above.

7.5   Exercises

1. Consider the estimation of β^{τ} in the linear quantile regression problem; recall Equation 7.11. One may often be interested in estimating β^{τ}_0 for various different values of τ, e.g. for all deciles or all percentiles. Show that with a finite number of observations, only a finite number of estimates will be numerically distinct. You may start with a sample of just two observations. Then try to estimate the median and the quartiles.

2. Prove Equation 7.16 using substitution.

3. *Asymptotics using the GMM framework:* Under certain regularity conditions, the GMM framework can be used to show

$$\sqrt{n}\left(\hat{\beta}^{\tau} - \beta^{\tau}_0\right) \xrightarrow{d} N(0, \Sigma_{\tau}),$$

with $\Sigma_{\tau} = \tau(1 - \tau) \cdot E\left[f_{U|X}(0|X) \cdot XX'\right]^{-1} \cdot E\left[XX'\right] \cdot E\left[f_{U|X}(0|X) \cdot XX'\right]^{-1}$.

If one is willing to strengthen the assumption $Q^\tau_{U|X} = 0$ to be satisfied for every quantile $\tau \in (0, 1)$, which implies full independence between U and X, the variance matrix simplifies to

$$\Sigma_\tau = \frac{\tau\,(1-\tau)}{f_U\,(0)^2} \cdot E\left[XX'\right]^{-1}.$$

Derive the asymptotic variance using the results for exactly identified GMM estimators:

$$E\left[(\tau - \mathbb{1}\left\{Y < X'\beta_0\right\}) \cdot X\right] = 0.$$

4. Show that estimators resulting from conditions (7.33) are equivalent to those resulting from conditions (7.32).

5. Show that the weights W^+ defined in (7.38) are indeed positive.

6. Note that in (7.47) you have 1^+ in the numerator and denominator. Therefore, in (7.48) you would also expect 1^+, and this would be correct. Proof that (7.48) with 1^- substituting 1^+ is equivalent to the present formula.

7. Derive the estimator and formulae given in (7.50).

8. Discuss standard problems that occur in parametric quantile regression that disappear when using local constant estimators. Which of these problems can also occur (locally) when using local linear estimation?

8   Dynamic Treatment Evaluation

In the preceding chapters, we examined the impact of a treatment D on an outcome variable Y. The treatment started at some point in time t_0 and the outcome variable was measured some time later, say $t_0 + t$, for both the treated and a control group. We usually would control for variables X_{i,t_0} measured at or until time t_0, e.g. employment and earnings histories. Only with the Difference-in-Difference method have we tried so far to explore the dynamics; for all the other methods time was largely ignored.

In the evaluation of labour market programmes, we could think of $Y_{t_0+t}^d$ as the employment status at some point in time. Alternatively, we could pursue a duration or hazard model perspective e.g. to examine the outflow of unemployment. The expected value of $Y_{t_0+t}^d$ would then be the survival probability. In the latter case, we would measure only the impact on outflows, but would not consider the impact on repeated unemployment.

Until now we have not considered sequential treatment processes of decisions or outcomes. One could even go a step further, combining the time someone is unemployed before he participates in a training programme, and its effect on the time he afterwards waits for a job – or simply the effect on the hazard rate.

Although the literature on dynamic treatment effect estimation is rapidly increasing, too, we can only give here some basic ideas of its modelling and estimation approaches. The existing literature looks to a good part extremely technical. Our aim is to give here some intuitive insights; this certainly implicates several simplifications and limitations. A much more general but also technical review on dynamic treatment effects can be found in Abbring and Heckman (2007).

8.1   Motivation and Introduction

While in several settings the framework of the previous chapters may well apply, in others a more careful treatment of time and dynamic treatment allocation is needed. As an example, consider a few issues that come up with the evaluation of active labour market policy:

Example 8.1 The time t_0 when a programme starts might itself be related to unobserved characteristics of the unemployed person. Therefore, t_0 might often itself be an important control variable. Here t_0 might reflect calendar time (e.g. seasonal effects) as well as process time (e.g. current unemployment duration).

The time t_1 when participation in a programme ends might often be already an outcome of the programme itself. A person who finds employment while being in a training programme would naturally have a shorter programme duration $t_1 - t_0$ than a person who did not find a job during that period. In other words, if someone finds a job during training he would stop training earlier than planned. The fact of having found a job is then the reason for the short treatment duration, and not its outcome. That means we cannot say that because of the short treatment duration he found a job.

It can be seen from this example that, for this reason, it is often advisable to measure the impact of the beginning of a treatment t_0 and not of the end t_1. Nevertheless, one might also be interested in the effects of the duration $t_1 - t_0$ of the programme. A possible shortcut is to use the length of *intended programme duration* as a measure that may be more likely to be exogenous, conditional on X_{t_0}. The confounding variables often include time-varying variables as well. Then, a more explicit modelling may be necessary.

Example 8.2 Ashenfelter (1978) noted that the decision to participate in active labour market programmes is highly dependent on the individual's previous earnings and employment histories. Recent negative employment shocks often induce individuals to participate in training programmes. Hence the employment situation in the months before the programme starts is an important determinant of the programme participation decision but is also likely to be correlated with the potential employment outcomes.

As mentioned above it may often be important to include the time t_0 as a variable to control for. Certainly, for the non-participation (the control group) there is no natural starting date. As an imperfect solution, one may simulate potential start times for these non-participants.

Example 8.3 Recall Example 8.2. Since usually no explicit start time can be observed for the 'non-participation' treatment, the employment situation in the months before the programme started is undefined for them. To solve this problem, Lechner (1999) suggested drawing hypothetical start times for the 'non-participants' from the distribution of start times among the participants, and to delete the 'non-participant' observations for whom the assigned start time implies an inconsistency. Thus, if unemployment is a basic eligibility condition for participation in an active labour market programme, individuals with an assigned start time after the termination of their unemployment spell are discarded, because participation could not have been possible at that date. Lechner (2002b) analysed the assignment of hypothetical start times further. Instead of drawing dates from the unconditional distribution of start times, he also considered drawing from the distribution conditional on the confounding variables. This conditional distribution can be simulated by regressing the start times on the covariates and fitting the mean of the conditional distribution at the covariate values of the respective non-participant. In his application both methods led to similar results.

An alternative to simulation approaches is to shorten the length of the treatment definition window to make participants and non-participants more alike. The *treatment definition window* is the time period that is used to define the treatment status in a static model. At the beginning of this window, eligibility to the treatment is defined, and thus the risk set of observations who could start treatment with probability between zero and one is determined. At the end of the window it is clear who started treatment during this period. Such a window is usually defined with respect to process time.

Example 8.4 Recall Examples 8.2 and 8.3, and think of an unemployed person registered at a certain day. A treatment definition window of length '1 day' would define an individual as treated if a programme started on the first day of unemployment. Everyone else would be defined as non-treated. Similarly, a treatment definition window of length '1 day' applied to day 29 of their unemployment would define as treated everyone who starts treatment on day 29 and as untreated who does not (certainly only using the individuals who are still registered unemployed at day 29). Treatment is undefined for those not in the risk set, i.e. those individuals that are no longer unemployed or already started training. The risk set contains only those individuals who are eligible and could potentially be assigned to a programme.

For an extremely short treatment definition window, e.g. of one day like in this example, there would be only very few treated observations such that estimation might be very imprecise. In addition, the treatment effects are likely to be very small and may not be of main interest: they would measure the effect of starting a programme today versus 'not today but perhaps tomorrow'. Many of the non-treated might actually receive treatment a few days later so that this situation would be similar to a substitution bias in an experimental setting where people in the control group get a compensation or a different treatment. In certain situations, however, the effect of treatment today versus 'not today but perhaps tomorrow', may indeed be the effect of interest.

Example 8.5 In Frölich (2008) this is the case. There the choice problem of a caseworker in the employment office is considered. At every meeting with the unemployed person, the caseworker aims to choose the optimal action plan including e.g. the choice among active labour market programmes. In the next meeting, the situation is reconsidered and different actions might be taken. The caseworker might choose 'no programme' today, but if the unemployed person is still unemployed four weeks later, a different action (i.e. different treatment) might be appropriate then.

A very large treatment definition window of e.g. *one year* (that would define as treated everyone who started a programme in the first year and as untreated who did not enter a programme during the entire first year) might be the treatment effect of most interest.

The problem for identification, however, is that the definition is 'conditioning on the future', using the language of Fredriksson and Johansson (2008). From the onset of the treatment definition window, one could imagine two competing processes: the one of being sent to a programme, and the one of finding a job. Even for two persons exactly identical in all their characteristics, it may happen by chance that the first person finds a job after eight weeks whereas the other person would have found a job after ten weeks but was sent to a programme already after nine weeks. In this case, the first person would be defined as non-treated, whereas the second would be defined as treated. This clearly introduces a problem because for otherwise identical individuals – and supposing for the moment a zero (or say, no) treatment effect – the untreated are those who were lucky in finding a job early, whereas the treated are the unlucky who did not find a job so soon. In the extreme case of a very long treatment definition window, you may even imagine a case where all the non-treated could be those who found a job before the programme started, whereas all the treated would be those who could have found a job at some time but the programme happened to start before. Clearly, such a situation leads to biased estimates, in favour of the so-defined non-treated. Hence, if there would be no differences in unobservables between treated and non-treated, apart from differences in luck in the dynamic assignment process, the estimated treatment effects are downward biased. This bias is likely to be most severe if every unemployed person eventually has to participate in some programme, unless he finds a job before then. On the other hand, the bias would be expected to be smaller if the probability of eventually ending up in treatment (if no other event happened) is clearly below one.

In most applications, the sign of the bias is unclear since there might also be other systematic differences between treated and non-treated in addition to differences in luck in the dynamic assignment process. That is, there might be other unobserved reasons for why individuals did not get treated even though the haven't found a job.

To overcome this problem of *conditioning on the future*, one has to shorten the length of the treatment definition window. But this is likely to introduce again the problem that many of those defined as non-treated may have actually been treated shortly thereafter, as discussed above. One solution is to analyse the sensitivity of the final estimates to alternative definitions of this window. If the length of the window is shortened, bias due to *conditioning on the future* decreases but variance increases. At the same time, however, many non-treated may shortly thereafter have become treated what blurs the treatment effect definition as discussed above. If the data available permits, one can measure how many people have been affected. For the interpretation of the estimated effects, one should therefore always examine which share of the non-treated actually received treatment in the period thereafter (i.e. how many people that were classified as non-treated actually received treatment thereafter). If this fraction is small, we are more confident that we measure the effect of treatment versus no-treatment and not of treatment today versus 'not today but perhaps tomorrow'.[1]

We will discuss two possible approaches to deal with this conditioning-on-the-future problem. First we discuss *discrete-time dynamic models*, which mitigate the problem. However, when we return to treatment definition windows of a very short length like

---

[1] For a nice example, see Lechner, Miquel and Wunsch (2011).

one day, a week or maybe a month, then this could be handled by a *continuous-time model* approach that attempts to aggregate the effects over time. This latter approach seems particularly natural if the outcome variable Y is the survival probability, e.g. in single-spell unemployment data.

Example 8.6 Fredriksson and Johansson (2008) suggest a non-parametric hazard model to estimate the effects of treatment start for each day, from which the survival functions of the potential outcomes can be derived. The intuition is as follows. Consider again a training programme for unemployed people. At every day t (in process time) the risk set consists of those people who are still unemployed and have not yet entered training. These people are at risk of entering training on day t and of finding a job (or say, exiting unemployment) on day t. It is assumed that these are random events with equal probability for all individuals still in the risk set, perhaps conditional on some observed covariates X_t. I.e. after controlling for X_t and conditional on still being in the risk set, selection into treatment is only based on white noise. In other words, it is assumed that there are no unobserved confounders after controlling for X_t and the risk set. Hence, the hazard rates into treatment and into employment can be estimated non-parametrically, from which the potential survival functions can be deduced.

Continuous time models often avoid the *conditioning on the future* problem. However, they require certain restrictions on treatment effect heterogeneity, which are not needed in discrete time models. This will become obvious from the following discussion of problems in which the number of possible treatment sequences would be infinite in continuous time.

Before starting, let us add one more reason why in various situations static models could be insufficient for treatment effect evaluation. As already indicated at the beginning of this chapter, in many applications we might be interested in the effects of sequences of programmes; a first programme, say A, is followed by another programme, say B. You also might want to compare that sequence with its inverse, i.e. starting with programme B followed by programme A. Since purely the fact that a second treatment was applied may already be an outcome of the (successful or unsuccessful) first programme, disentangling such effects is very difficult or simply impossible in a static model. To avoid these kind of problems, one could focus on estimating the effects of the first programme (measured from the beginning of the first programme) while considering the second programme as an endogenously evolving outcome of this first one. One would thereby estimate the total effect of the first programme together with any possibly following subsequent programme. From this example we already notice that intermediate outcome variables, i.e. Y_t for some values of t, might be important variables that affect the sequence of treatment choice. But as discussed in previous chapters, a general rule from the static model is that one should usually never control for variables already affected by the treatment. We will see below that some type of controlling for these variables is nonetheless important or even unavoidable here. If we further want to disentangle the effects of each programme (e.g. A and B), then we certainly need a more complex model setup.

8.2   Dynamic Potential Outcomes Model

Introducing a time dimension into the evaluation framework can be done in two ways: either by considering sequences of treatments over a number of discrete time periods (of finite lengths), or by considering time as continuous. We start by examining a modelling framework for discrete time periods, which permits a wide range of possible treatment sequences, different start times, different treatment durations etc. This model may often be directly applicable if treatments can start only at certain fixed points in time, e.g. quarterly,[2] or when data is observed only for discrete time periods.[3] When treatments can start in (almost) continuous time, this model may nevertheless have several advantages over an explicit incorporation of continuous time in that it does not impose strong restrictions on treatment effect heterogeneity. Time is partitioned into discrete periods where different sequences of treatments can be chosen.

Example 8.7 Lechner and Miquel (2010) study the impact of government sponsored training in Western Germany on finding a job during the nineties. They define the first month of unemployment between January 1992 and December 1993 being the reference period (i.e. their period zero). Since in the data there is not enough variation over time to analyse monthly movements they aggregate the monthly information to quarterly information. They consider the following three possible states until finding a job: participating in a vocational training programme paid by the employment office (T), participating in a retraining programme paid by the employment office to obtain a vocational degree in a different occupation (R), or simply remaining unemployed receiving benefits and services (U). Observing a single unemployment spell over one year, there are many sequences possible like for example UUUU, RRRR, TTTT but also UTTT, UURR, etc., but also shorter sequences if the individual has found a job after less than four quarters. Lechner and Miquel (2010) study only the differences between the effects of RRRR, TTTT and UUUU on being employed one (respectively four) year(s) later.

Because the treatment effects are not restricted across treatment sequences, the model cannot be directly extended to continuous time as there would be an infinite number of different sequences. Hence, for most of these sequences the number of observations would be zero. Clearly, for continuous time more restrictions will be required, as will be discussed later. In applications, time could almost always be considered as discrete because information is typically aggregated over periods (hours, days, weeks, moths, etc.). The important points are how many observations are observed entering in treatment in a particular time period, and how many different treatment sequences can be examined.

---

[2] In the evaluation of school education policies, each school year would be a discrete time period.
[3] Similarly, primary education, lower secondary and upper secondary education can be considered as a sequence.

Flexible multiperiod extensions of the potential outcomes model has been developed since a while in biometrics.[4] In this chapter we focus on the exposition and extensions of Lechner and Miquel (2001), Lechner and Miquel (2010), and Lechner (2008), which are much closer in spirit and notation to the rest of this book as directed towards applications in social sciences. Identification is based on sequential conditional independence assumptions, which could also be called sequential 'selection on observables' assumptions. As we will see, for identification it is often important to be able to observe *intermediate outcomes* variables. Such information may be available in administrative data of unemployment registers. In many other applications this information does usually not exist, and it would therefore be important to collect such data as part of the evaluation strategy.

To introduce the basic ideas, suppose that there are time periods τ and that in each time period either a treatment 0 or 1 can be chosen. From this setup, the extensions to many time periods and multiple treatments will be straightforward. The outcome variable is measured at some time t later. In addition, there is an initial period for which information on covariates is available before any treatment has started. I.e. a time period zero exists where none of the treatments of interest has already started, and where we can measure potentially confounding variables (before treatment). More precisely, we define a period 0. Treatments could have happened before, but we will not be able to identify their effects.

Recall Example 8.7 studying labour market programmes: at the beginning of the spell, every observed person is unemployed, and we have some information measured at that time about the person and previous employment histories. Let $D_\tau \in \{0, 1\}$ be the treatment chosen in period τ, and let $\underline{D}_\tau$ be the sequence of treatments until time τ with $\underline{d}_\tau$ being a particular realisation of this random variable. The set of possible realisations of $\underline{D}_1$ is $\{0, 1\}$. The set of possible realisations of $\underline{D}_2$ is $\{00, 10, 01, 11\}$. The possible realisations of $\underline{D}_3$ are 000, 001, 010, 011, 100, 101, 110, 111, etc. We define potential outcomes as $Y_T^{\underline{d}_\tau}$ which is the outcome that would be observed at some time T if the particular sequence $\underline{d}_\tau$ had been chosen. In the following we use the symbols t and τ to refer to treatment sequences, and the symbol T for the time when the outcome is measured.

Hence, with two treatment periods we distinguish between $Y_T^{\underline{d}_1}$ and $Y_T^{\underline{d}_2}$. The observed outcome Y_T is the one that corresponds to the sequence actually chosen. To be specific about the timing when we measure these variables, we will assume that treatment starts at the beginning of a period, whereas the outcome Y (and also other covariates X introduced later) are measured at the end of a period. We thus obtain the observation rule, i.e. the rule linking potential outcomes to observed outcomes:

$$Y_1 = D_1 Y_1^1 + (1 - D_1) Y_1^0$$
$$Y_2 = D_1 Y_2^1 + (1 - D_1) Y_2^0$$
$$= D_1 D_2 Y_2^{11} + (1 - D_1) D_2 Y_2^{01} + D_1 (1 - D_2) Y_2^{10} + (1 - D_1)(1 - D_2) Y_2^{00}.$$

---

[4] See, for example, Robins (1986), Robins (1989), Robins (1997), Robins (1999), Robins, Greenland and Hu (1999) for discrete treatments, and Robins (1998), Gill and Robins (2001) for continuous treatments.

To be clear about the difference between Y_2^{11} and Y_2^1: the potential outcome Y_2^{11} is the outcome that a particular individual i would have realised at the end of the second period if by external intervention this person was sent to the sequence 11. The potential outcome Y_2^1 is the outcome that this individual i would have realised at the end of the second period if by external intervention this person was sent first to the programme 1 and thereafter chose for the second period whatever this person was about to choose. I.e. the first period is set by external intervention whereas the treatment in the second period is determined according to the selection process of the individual or the case-worker, given the assignment of the first programme. Note that the choice of the second programme may be influenced by the first programme. This means

$$Y_T^1 = D_2^1 Y_T^{11} + (1 - D_2^1) Y_T^{10}, \tag{8.1}$$

where D_2^1 is the potential treatment choice in the second period if the programme in the first period D_1 was set to 1. Analogously, D_3^1 is the programme in period three if the first programme was set to one, and D_3^{11} the programme in period three if the treatment in the first two periods was set to one. By analogy we obtain,

$$Y_T^1 = D_2^1 D_3^1 Y_T^{111} + (1 - D_2^1) D_3^1 Y_T^{101} + D_2^1 (1 - D_3^1) Y_T^{110} + (1 - D_2^1)(1 - D_3^1) Y_T^{100},$$

or as another example

$$Y_T^{11} = D_3^{11} Y_T^{111} + (1 - D_3^{11}) Y_T^{110}.$$

The observed outcome Y_T corresponds to the outcome if the person herself selected the entire sequence of programmes.

Example 8.8 We might be interested in the effects of school inputs on cognitive development. One could consider education as a sequence of school years. However, there is usually rather limited variation from one year to the next, such that many of the sequences may be hard to identify. A more interesting approach would be to consider education as a sequence of kindergarten, primary education, lower secondary education, upper secondary education, tertiary education. Along this sequence quite a number of different input sequences could be considered. E.g. private versus public school, small versus large classes, traditional schooling versus strong emphasis on education in foreign languages, low versus high teacher salary, etc. Several interesting research questions arise then. Are investments into schooling complementary or substitutive? Do early investments into pre-school increase the returns to further schooling or reduce the returns (i.e. diminishing marginal returns)? If a fixed budget is available, at which stage should it be invested most? One could compare a sequence with many expenditures at the beginning (e.g. small classes) and lower expenditures later on versus the opposite sequencing.

The observed schooling sequence clearly evolves endogenously and the decisions about the next step almost certainly depend on the success in the previous steps. The strategy outlined below is based on sequential conditional independence assumptions, which requires data on the test scores or grades in the previous periods, which we denote as covariates X. For example, the type of secondary school a child attends clearly depends on the schooling outcomes (grades, test scores) at the end of primary school, and without observing these grades or scores, identification would be very difficult.[5]

Before turning to endogeneity problems, identifying and estimating issues, we first discuss various average treatment effects that could be interesting to consider. To make discussion easier, we do this reflexion along the example of labour market programme sequences considering some typical sequences:

You may focus on the *starting times* (or *timing*) of treatments: for some individuals, a programme starts later, for others earlier in an unemployment spell. For those who never participate in a training programme, their 'starting date' would be undefined. Suppose we define time in quarters. We could then compare sequences such as 001 to 0001, i.e. to compare a programme start in the third quarter of unemployment versus in the fourth quarter of unemployment. Comparing the sequence 1 versus 001 helps to examine the effect of starting the programme in the first days of unemployment or only after half a year. We could also compare the sequences 1 to 000, where the latter group refers to not receiving any treatment during the first nine months. Another option is comparing a sequence 00 to 01, which is the effect of receiving treatment in the second quarter versus not receiving it in the second quarter but perhaps immediately after.[6] When examining the 'effects of waiting', we might also require some minimum programme duration, e.g. to compare 11 to 0011 or 111 to 00111. Note that for several of these comparisons the warning of Fredriksson and Johansson (2008) that 'conditioning on the future' may introduce a bias will still apply in principle. To mitigate the extent of such biases (though its direction can often be conjectured in empirical applications) the length of the time periods should be kept short. If the amount of data available permits, one may want to use months rather than quarters when defining the sequences. If the amount of data is limited, one could examine various alternative definitions of the length of the time window (months, quarters) and compare the estimation results. For the shorter time periods, the results should be less biased, but may be more variable.

The interest could also target on *treatment durations*: To examine the effects of different durations of treatment, we could compare the sequences 010 to 011, for example. We already referred to the potential endogeneity of the treatment duration in evaluation studies if subjects can drop out during the treatment. If the treatment is unpleasant or sends a signal, individuals will seek to leave the programme while it is underway. This attrition is, however, already an effect of the programme.[7] In some situations this may be the effect of most interest. In other situations the effect of realised durations may be more interesting, though. We might thus be interested in comparing 1 versus 11, or alternatively also 10 versus 110. Whereas the former comparison refers to treatments

---

[5] Another example in Lechner (2004) considers the labour supply effects of different fertility sequences, e.g. two children in the first period and zero in the second period versus one child in each period.

[6] This last example is used in Sianesi (2004) and Fredriksson and Johansson (2008) and is applied in Frölich (2008).

[7] One way to circumvent this problem in the static model is to consider the effects of planned durations only, e.g. in Lechner, Miquel and Wunsch (2011).

with a minimum duration of at least one or two periods, the latter comparison refers to treatments with a duration of exactly one or two periods.

Finally, one might want to study the effect of *sequences of treatments*: We could be interested in various sequences of treatments, e.g. 010001 versus 0101. Particularly when we extend the previous setup to allow for several treatment options, e.g. {0, 1, 2, 3} in each period, for example, no assistance, job search assistance, training and employment programmes, it is interesting to compare a sequence 123 to 132 or 101 to 1001. Should one start with training or with an employment programme? If one programme has been completed, should one start with the next one, or leave some time in between in order to permit individuals to focus on their own job search activities? The application of the static model as covered in the previous section, breaks down when selection into the second and any subsequent programmes is influenced by the outcome of the previous programmes. Then these intermediate outcomes have to be included to control for selection.

Hence, a large number of sequences could be interesting. However, when specifying such sequences, one should keep in mind that the longer the treatment sequences specified, the fewer observations will be in the data that have exactly followed this sequence. Hence, one could run into small sample problems even with a data set of several thousand observations. An additional complication will arise when comparing two rather different sequences, e.g. 1110 to 00001110. It is quite likely that those individuals who followed a very specific sequence such as 00001110 may be relatively homogenous in their X characteristics. If also the participants in 1110 are relatively homogenous, the common support between these two participant groups will be relatively small. After deleting observations out of common support, the treatment effect between 00001110 and 1110 might thus depend on only a very specific subpopulation, which reduces external validity.

Another concern with very long sequences is that in case we get identification via some (sequential) conditional independence assumptions, we have to include the vector of covariates $X_0, X_1, \ldots$, up to $X_{\tau-1}$ for identifying the effect of a sequence $\underline{d}_\tau$, which may contain an increasing number of variables when τ is increasing. So the number of covariates becomes too large, one may perhaps only include, say, four lags $X_{t-1}, X_{t-2}, X_{t-3}, X_{t-4}$ as they may be picking up most of the information contained in the past X.

As a further component to the model, one often wants to include covariates X_t which are time-varying; we denote by $\underline{X}_t$ the collection of X_t variables up to time period t. The $\underline{X}_t$ may also include the outcome variables up to Y_t. Hence, we permit that the variables X_t are already causally influenced by the treatments, and we could even define potential values $X_t^{\underline{d}_\tau}$ for these. Remember that we observe X_t at the end of a period. Hence, at the beginning of a period τ, the values of X_t up to $\tau - 1$ are observed. In the examples on active labour market policies given above, X_t could be (among other variables) the employability of the unemployed person. The caseworker assesses the employability of his unemployed client, and this assessment can change over time. If training programmes are effective, one would expect that the employability should increase after having participated in training. Certainly, also other issues such as motivation, psychological status or family composition can also change over time, see for example Lechner and Wiehler (2011) on the interactions between labour market programmes and fertility.

We now can define a large number of different average treatment effects. Let $\underline{d}'_{\tau'}$, $\underline{d}''_{\tau''}$ and $\underline{d}'''_{\tau'''}$ be three sequences of possibly different lengths τ', τ'', τ'''. Define the treatment effect by

$$\alpha_T^{\underline{d}'_{\tau'}, \underline{d}''_{\tau''}}(\underline{d}'''_{\tau'''}) = E[Y_T^{\underline{d}'_{\tau'}} - Y_T^{\underline{d}''_{\tau''}} \mid \underline{d}'''_{\tau'''}] \qquad \text{for} \qquad \tau''' \leq \tau', \tau'',$$

which is the treatment effect between sequence $\underline{d}'_{\tau'}$ and $\underline{d}''_{\tau''}$ for the subpopulation that is observed to have taken sequence $\underline{d}'''_{\tau'''}$. Note that the three sequences $\underline{d}'_{\tau'}$, $\underline{d}''_{\tau''}$ and $\underline{d}'''_{\tau'''}$ can differ in the length and in the types of the treatments. Hence, we could be comparing two sequences of the same length, e.g. 01 versus 10, as well as sequences of different lengths, e.g. 01 versus 1. The latter example corresponds to the effect of a delayed treatment start, i.e. the treatment starting in period 2 versus period 1. The sequence $\underline{d}'''_{\tau'''}$ defines the subgroup for which the effect is defined. We supposed $\tau''' \leq \tau', \tau''$ since there is little interest in the effect for a (sub-)population which is more finely defined than the two sequences for which the causal effect is to be determined. The identification conditions would also be stronger.

If $\tau''' = 0$, this gives the dynamic average treatment effect (DATE)

$$\alpha_T^{\underline{d}'_{\tau'}, \underline{d}''_{\tau''}} = E[Y_T^{\underline{d}'_{\tau'}} - Y_T^{\underline{d}''_{\tau''}}],$$

whereas the dynamic average treatment effect on the treated (DATET) would be obtained when $\underline{d}'''_{\tau'''} = \underline{d}'_{\tau'}$

$$\alpha_T^{\underline{d}'_{\tau'}, \underline{d}''_{\tau''}}(\underline{d}'_{\tau'}) = E[Y_T^{\underline{d}'_{\tau'}} - Y_T^{\underline{d}''_{\tau''}} \mid \underline{d}'_{\tau'}],$$

and the dynamic average treatment effect on the non-treated (DATEN) would be obtained when $\underline{d}'''_{\tau'''} = \underline{d}''_{\tau''}$

$$\alpha_T^{\underline{d}'_{\tau'}, \underline{d}''_{\tau''}}(\underline{d}''_{\tau''}) = E[Y_T^{\underline{d}'_{\tau'}} - Y_T^{\underline{d}''_{\tau''}} \mid \underline{d}''_{\tau''}].$$

Without any restrictions on effect heterogeneity, these effects could be very different.

Further, we only consider the case where $T \geq \max(\tau', \tau'')$, which means that we only consider as final outcome variables the periods after the completion of the sequence. It would not make sense to consider explicitly the case for $T < \max(\tau', \tau'')$ because we assume that treatments can have an effect only on future periods but not on earlier ones. We will refer to this as the assumption of *no anticipation effects*. If we were expecting anticipation effects, we would have to re-define the treatment start to the point were the anticipation started. For example, if we observed in the data that an unemployed person started a training programme in June, but we also know that this person was already informed by early May about this programme, then we could consider May as the date where treatment started. If the date of referral and the date of programme start are very close together, and the date of referral is not observed, the possible anticipation effects can hopefully be ignored.

If we cannot assume that participation is exogenous, i.e. we do not face randomised experiments, then we need to control for the confounders. Under certain conditions discussed below the treatment effects can be identified by sequential controlling for them. Note that these treatment effects can also be identified within strata defined by any strictly exogenous covariates X. Strata defined by covariates that are causally affected by the treatment will require a more careful consideration and usually stronger identification conditions.

From the above definitions we obtain a useful result that helps to relate various treatment effects to each other, for example when we examine the relation between the expected outcomes for different lengths of the conditioning set $\underline{d}'''_{\tau'''}$. Define $(\underline{d}'''_{\tau'''}, v_1, v_2, \ldots, v_\delta)$ as a sequence of length $\tau''' + \delta$ which starts with the subsequence $\underline{d}'''_{\tau'''}$ followed by the $(0-1)$ treatments $v_1, v_2, \ldots, v_\delta$. By iterated expectations we obtain, with a slight abuse of notation, that

$$E\left[Y_T^{\underline{d}'_{\tau'}} \mid \underline{d}'''_{\tau'''}\right] = \sum_{v_1=0}^{1} \cdots \sum_{v_\delta=0}^{1} E\left[Y_T^{\underline{d}'_{\tau'}} \mid (\underline{d}'''_{\tau'''}, v_1, v_2, \ldots, v_\delta)\right] \qquad (8.2)$$
$$\cdot \Pr\left(D_{\tau'''+1} = v_1, \ldots, D_{\tau'''+\delta} = v_\delta \mid \underline{d}'''_{\tau'''}\right).$$

This implies that if a treatment effect is identified for a finer population, i.e. defined by a longer sequence τ''', then it will also be identified for the coarser population by a simple weighted average. In other words, if we can estimate the probabilities and expectations on the right-hand side, then we automatically get an estimate for the courser potential mean outcome on the left-hand side. It is also clear then that identification for finer sub-populations will in general be more difficult.

8.2.1 Equivalence to Static Model

To gain some intuition we consider first very strong assumptions that permit us employing the tools of a simple static model. In the next subsection we will then relax these assumptions. Let Θ_τ be the set of all possible treatment sequences up to period τ. First note that if only a binary treatment is available in each period, the cardinality of Θ_τ is 2^τ.

We start with a pretty strong version of CIA for our treatment models, namely we assume that all potential outcomes for all possible treatment sequences $\underline{d}_\tau$ are independent of the actual sequence $\underline{D}_\tau$ conditional on X_0.

Assumption SCIA   Strong conditional independence assumption

$$Y_T^{\underline{d}_\tau} \perp\!\!\!\perp \underline{D}_\tau \mid X_0 \qquad \forall \, \underline{d}_\tau \in \Theta_\tau \qquad (8.3)$$

together with a common support condition:[8]

$$0 < \Pr\left(\underline{D}_\tau = \underline{d}_\tau \mid X_0\right) < 1 \qquad a.s. \qquad \forall \, \underline{d}_\tau \in \Theta_\tau. \qquad (8.4)$$

---

[8] Recall that *a.s.* means *almost surely*, i.e. the statement is true for all values of x_0 except for a set that has measure (or say, probability to be observed) zero. More formally, this expression means that $\Pr\left(\Pr\left(\underline{D}_\tau = \underline{d}_\tau \mid X_0\right) \in (0,1)\right) = 1 \qquad \forall \, \underline{d}_\tau \in \Theta_\tau.$

With this assumption we suppose that accounting for the information X_0 observed at time zero, the entire treatment sequence taken later is independent from their potential outcomes. This includes that all important information the agent has about his future potential outcomes (and does therefore influence his decisions on treatment participation) is already contained in X_0. In other words, we assume that the researcher has enough information in the beginning of the initial period so that treatment assignment in every period can be treated as random conditional on X_0. Such an assumptions is reasonable for example for a scheme where the assignment of all treatments is made in the initial period and is not changed subsequently. Or, more precisely, any revision of the original treatment plan has not been triggered by the arrival of new information that is related to the potential outcomes. Hence, the choices do not depend on time varying X and also not on the outcomes of the treatments in the previous periods, because the complete treatment sequence is chosen[9] initially based on the information contained in X_0.

For many situations this assumption can be rather strong and will therefore be relaxed in the next subsection(s). But it is helpful to understand the implications of this assumption. As shown in Lechner and Miquel (2001), with the above assumptions all treatment effects up to period τ are identified, including DATET and DATEN as well as for coarser subpopulations. It also includes identification of effects of the type

$$E[Y_T^{111} - Y_T^{000} \,|\underline{D}_\tau = (101)],$$

where the population for which the effect is identified has no common *initial subsequence* with the potential outcomes that are compared. I.e. we need to identify the outcome Y_T^{000} for those who have sequence 101. The two sequences 101 and 000 already differ in the first element. As we will see later, such effects are much harder to identify when the conditional independence assumption is relaxed.

The above setup essentially boils down to the multiple programme approach of the static model. There are $\underline{d}_\tau \in \Theta_\tau$ different types of treatments (in this case sequences), and controlling for X_0 eliminates the selection bias problem. Hence, the conventional matching or re-weighting approach of the multiple treatment evaluation approach can be applied here.

For comparison with the later subsections, we also note that the assumption (8.3) can equivalently be written sequentially as

$$Y_T^{\underline{d}_\tau} \perp\!\!\!\perp D_t | X_0, \underline{D}_{t-1} \qquad \forall\, t \leq \tau \quad \text{and} \quad \underline{d}_\tau \in \Theta_\tau. \tag{8.5}$$

Hence, conditional on the treatment sequence until $t - 1$, the choice of treatment D_t only depends on X_0 and some random noise or information that is not related to the potential outcomes. Again, this assumption implies an essentially static treatment regime because any new information related to the potential outcomes that might be revealed after period 0 does not play a role in the selection process.

---

[9] What it actually meant is that if the complete treatment sequence had been chosen initially, we would not get systematically different treatment sequences than those observed.

8.2.2   Sequential Conditional Independence Assumptions

The previous discussion examined some identifying conditions which are likely to be too restrictive in many applications. Specifically, they did not permit sequential treatment selection to depend on intermediate outcome variables. In the following we will relax this point of the assumption. We first consider a sequential conditional independence assumption which permits to control for endogenous variables, including intermediate outcome variables.

Assumption WDCIA   Weak dynamic conditional independence assumption

$$Y_T^{\underline{d}_\tau} \perp\!\!\!\perp D_t | \underline{X}_{t-1}, \underline{D}_{t-1} \qquad \forall\, t \le \tau \quad \text{and} \quad \underline{d}_\tau \in \Theta_\tau, \tag{8.6}$$

$$0 < \Pr\left(D_t = d_t | \underline{X}_{t-1}, \underline{D}_{t-1}\right) < 1 \qquad a.s. \qquad \forall\, t \le \tau \quad \text{and} \quad d_t \in \{0, 1\}, \tag{8.7}$$

where X_t may include Y_t.

This assumption is weaker than the previous one as it does permit selection to depend on observable variables that are functions of the outcomes of previous treatments. To see whether such an assumption is plausible, we have to know which variables influence changes in treatment status as well as outcomes and whether they are observable. When considering only two periods, the WDCIA means

(a) $Y_T^{\underline{d}_2} \perp\!\!\!\perp D_1 | X_0 \qquad\qquad \forall\, \underline{d}_2 \in \Theta_2$

(b) $Y_T^{\underline{d}_2} \perp\!\!\!\perp D_2 | \underline{X}_1, D_1 \qquad \forall\, \underline{d}_2 \in \Theta_2$

(c) $0 < \Pr\left(D_1 = 1 | X_0\right) < 1 \qquad \text{and} \qquad 0 < \Pr\left(D_2 = 1 | \underline{X}_1, D_1\right) < 1 \qquad a.s.,$

where $\underline{X}_1$ may include Y_1. Under this assumption, the first selection is not related to the potential outcomes conditional on X_0. Similarly, it is assumed that the second treatment selection is not related to the potential outcomes conditional on all the variables observed up to that point. These control variables include X_0, X_1, the treatment choices (D_1) made so far, and usually also the *intermediate outcome* variable Y_1. In a certain sense this is similar to the static model but with the additional aspect that we include intermediate outcome variables in certain steps of the estimation. This of course requires that information on these intermediate outcome variables is available.

The common support assumption (8.7) requires that each treatment path is observed in the data. E.g. the second part states that for all values of $(\underline{X}_1 = x, D_1 = d)$ with non-zero density, both choices, $D_2 = 0$ and $D_2 = 1$, should have positive probability. Note that this common support condition needs to hold only sequentially and is thus weaker than

$$\Pr\left(D_1 = d_1, D_2 = d_2 | \underline{X}_1\right) > 0 \qquad a.s. \qquad \text{for all } d_1, d_2 \in \{0, 1\}. \tag{8.8}$$

As an example, certain values of $\underline{X}_1$ may have zero density when $D_1 = 1$, but may have positive density when $D_1 = 0$. Suppose that for these values of $\underline{X}_1$ we have that $\Pr\left(D_2 = 1 | \underline{X}_1, D_1 = 1\right) = 0$. For the values of $\underline{X}_1$ together with $D_1 = 1$, the common support condition (8.7) would still be satisfied because the conditioning set has zero probability mass. On the other hand, (8.8) would not be satisfied.

Example 8.9 Recall our examples on active labour market policy but now thinking of a training programme that prohibits repeated participation. Then the eligibility status (included in the vector of confounders X_1) will never be one if $D_1 = 1$, whereas it has positive probability to be one if $D_1 = 0$. Hence, $\Pr\left(D_2 = 1|X_1 = eligible, D_1 = 1\right)$ is zero, and the event $(X_1 = eligible, D_1 = 1)$ has probability zero. On the other hand, (8.8) would not be satisfied because $\Pr(D_1 = D_2 = 1|X_1 = eligible) = 0$ but $X_1 = eligible$ happens with positive probability.

Still, the common support assumption may be rather restrictive in many applications. Suppose participation in treatment is permitted only for unemployed persons. Then

$$\Pr(D_2 = 1|D_1, Y_1 = \text{no longer unemployed}) = 0,$$

which implies that it is impossible to observe individuals with $D_2 = 1$ for those who found a job after the first training.

To better understand what is identified by WDCIA (8.6) consider $E[Y_T^{11}|D_1 = 0]$ in the simple two-period model example above. Using iterated expectations and WDCIA with respect to the first period, we can write

$$\begin{aligned}
E\left[Y_T^{11}|D_1 = 0\right] &= E\left[E\left[Y_T^{11}|X_0, D_1 = 0\right] |D_1 = 0\right] \\
&= E\left[E\left[Y_T^{11}|X_0, D_1 = 1\right] |D_1 = 0\right] \\
&= E\left[E\left[E\left[Y_T^{11}|X_0, X_1, D_1 = 1\right] |X_0, D_1 = 1\right] |D_1 = 0\right] \\
&= E\left[E\left[E\left[Y_T^{11}|X_0, X_1, D_2 = 11\right] |X_0, D_1 = 1\right] |D_1 = 0\right] \\
&= E\left[E\left[E\left[Y_T|X_0, X_1, D_2 = 11\right] |X_0, D_1 = 1\right] |D_1 = 0\right] \\
&= \int E\left[Y_T|X_1, D_2 = 11\right] dF_{X_1|X_0, D_1=1} dF_{X_0|D_1=0}.
\end{aligned}$$

This result shows on the one hand that this potential outcome is identified and also suggests a way for estimating it. We first need to estimate $E\left[Y_T|X_1, D_2 = 11\right]$ nonparametrically and then to adjust it *sequentially* for the distributions $dF_{X_1|X_0,D_1=1}$ and $dF_{X_0|D_1=0}$. As discussed later this adjustment can be done via matching or weighting. The estimator is more complex than in the static model as we have to adjust for differences in the X distribution twice. Generally, when we were to consider treatment sequences of length τ we would have to adjust τ times.

More generally, under the WDCIA assumption the population average potential outcomes

$$E[Y_T^{\underline{d}_\tau}]$$

are identified for any sequence $\underline{d}_\tau$ of length $\tau \leq T$ if the necessary conditioning variables are observed. Also all average outcomes for any sequence $\underline{d}_\tau$ in the subpopulation of individuals who participated in treatment 0 or 1 in the first period

$$E[Y_T^{\underline{d}_\tau} |D_1 = d_1]$$

are identified then. The situation becomes more difficult, however, if we are interested in the average effect for a subpopulation that is defined by a longer sequence (especially with $D_1 = D_2 = 0$). The relevant distinction between the populations defined by treatment states in the first and, respectively, subsequent periods is that in the first period, treatment choice is random conditional on exogenous variables, which is the result of the initial condition stating that $D_0 = 0$ holds for everybody. In the second and later periods, randomisation into these treatments is conditional on endogenous variables, i.e. variables already influenced by the first part of the treatment. WDCIA has an appeal for applied work as a natural extension of the static framework. However, W-CIA does not identify the classical treatment effects on the treated if the sequences of interest differ in the first period.

In contrast to the stronger assumption (8.3) of the previous subsection, the SCIA, not all treatment effects are identified anymore. Observing the information set that influences the allocation to the next treatment in a sequence together with the outcome of interest is sufficient to identify average treatment effects (DATE) even if this information is based on endogenous variables. However, this assumption is not sufficient to identify the treatment effect on the treated (DATET). To understand why it is not identified, it is a useful exercise to attempt to identify $E[Y_T^{00}|D_2 = 11]$ by iterated expectations, see Exercise 4. The reason is that the subpopulation of interest (i.e. the participants who complete the sequence) has evolved (i.e. been selected) based on the realised intermediate outcomes of the sequence. This result is quite different from the static model, where identification of ATET is often considered to be even easier than identification of ATE.

Nevertheless some effects can also be identified for finer subpopulations. The first result refers to comparisons of sequences that differ only with respect to the treatment in the last period, i.e. that they have the same *initial subsequence* until $\tau - 1$ and differ only in period τ. This is basically the same result as before, but with time period $\tau - 1$ playing the role of time period 0 before, the period up to which the treatment sequence still coincides. In this case the endogeneity problem is not really harmful, because the potentially endogenous variables $\underline{X}_{\tau-1}, \underline{Y}_{\tau-1}$, which are the crucial ones to condition on for identification, have been influenced by the same past treatment sequence at time $\tau - 1$ when comparing the two sequences. It can be shown[10] that, given WDCIA, the potential outcome is identified if the sequences $(\underline{d}_{\tau-1}, d'_\tau)$ and $(\underline{d}_{\tau-1}, d''_\tau)$ are identical except for the last period, i.e.

$$E[Y_T^{(\underline{d}_{\tau-1}, d'_\tau)} \mid \underline{D}_\tau = (\underline{d}_{\tau-1}, d''_\tau)] \tag{8.9}$$

is identified. By the result (8.2) for coarser subpopulations, this also implies that

$$E[Y_T^{(\underline{d}_{\tau-1}, d'_\tau)} \mid \underline{D}_{\tau-1} = \underline{d}_{\tau-1}] \tag{8.10}$$

is identified. To give some examples, $E[Y_T^{11}]$, $E[Y_T^{11}|D_1 = 0]$, $E[Y_T^{11}|D_1 = 1]$ and $E[Y_T^{11}|\underline{D}_2 = 10]$ and $E[Y_T^{11}|\underline{D}_2 = 11]$ are identified, but neither $E[Y_T^{11}|\underline{D}_2 = 00]$

---

[10] See, for example, Lechner and Miquel (2001, theorem 3b).

nor $E[Y_T^{11}|\underline{D}_2 = 01]$. Hence, the ATET between the sequences 10 and 01 is thus not identified.

The result given in (8.10) extends actually to the cases where we consider longer sequences for outcome Y. Once the WDCIA is given, all what is needed is that the initial (sub-)sequence of Y is identical to the sequence of D we condition on. Formally spoken, for a sequence $\underline{d}_{\tau-w}$ where $1 \leq w < \tau$, and a longer sequence that starts with the same subsequence $(\underline{d}_{\tau-w}, d_{\tau-w+1}, \ldots, d_{\tau})$, given WDCIA, the average potential outcome

$$E[Y_T^{(\underline{d}_{\tau-w}, d_{\tau-w+1}, \ldots, d_{\tau})} | \underline{D}_{\tau-w} = \underline{d}_{\tau-w}] \tag{8.11}$$

is identified. Of course, the relevant subpopulations for which identification is obtained could be coarser, but not finer. Compared to (8.9) the conditioning set for the expected value is 'one period shorter'. The identification of sequences that differ for more than one period is more difficult: The conditioning variables $\underline{X}_{\tau-1}, \underline{Y}_{\tau-1}$ needed to make participants comparable to non-participants in the specific sequence might be influenced by all events during the sequence. However, since the sequences differ, also these events can differ, leading to some additional loss of identification.

Example 8.10 Recall the two periods examples from above. It is clear that the WDCIA implies that $Y_T^{11} \perp\!\!\!\perp D_2 | X_1, X_0, D_1$. Together with

$$Y_T^{11} \perp\!\!\!\perp D_1 | X_1, X_0 \tag{8.12}$$

one could conclude $Y_T^{11} \perp\!\!\!\perp (D_1, D_2) | X_1, X_0$. However, the WDCIA (8.6) does (and shall) not imply (8.12). The implication of (8.12) is clearly visible from the graph in Figure 8.1 (where for ease of exposition we ignored D_0 and X_0). Generally, we would like to permit X_1 to be potentially affected by D_1 since X is measured at the end of the period, whereas treatment D starts at the beginning of the period, but conditioning on X_1 as in (8.12) 'blocks' a part of the total effect of D_1 on Y_T. In other words, X_1 is an outcome variable of D_1 and thereby conditioning on it is an unreasonable condition. and (8.12) can only be true if there is no causal effect running through X_1. In other words, D_1 is not permitted to have any effect on X_1.

For the identification of $E[Y_T^{11}|D_1]$ this was no problem, but for example for $E[Y_T^{11}|\underline{D}_2]$, cf. also Exercise 8.6, this becomes important because X_1 determines the population of interest in the second period. Hence, on the one hand, we would have to condition on X_1 to control for the selection in the second period. On the other hand, we are not permitted to condition on this variable as this could invalidate independence for the selection in the first period.

Figure 8.1 Causality graph for condition (8.12)

In order to identify more than 'just' (8.11) but also DATET, DATEN, or other treatment effects, one has to restrict the potential endogeneity of X_τ, resulting in a stronger sequential independence assumption. In fact, recall (8.11), for $w = 1$ we are aiming for a condition that allows us to identify all effects up to period τ.

Assumption SDCIA Strong dynamic conditional independence assumption

(a) $(Y_T^{d_\tau}, X_t) \perp\!\!\!\perp D_t | \underline{X}_{t-1}, \underline{D}_{t-1}$ 	$\forall\, t \leq \tau - 1$ and $\underline{d}_\tau \in \Theta_\tau$,

(b) $Y_T^{d_\tau} \perp\!\!\!\perp D_t | \underline{X}_{t-1}, \underline{D}_{t-1}$ 	$t = \tau$ and $\underline{d}_\tau \in \Theta_\tau$,

(c) $0 < \Pr\left(\underline{D}_t = \underline{d}_t | \underline{X}_{t-1}\right) < 1$ 	$a.s.$	$\forall\, t \leq \tau$ and $\underline{d}_\tau \in \Theta_\tau$.

Compare now SDCIA with the two-period presentation of WDCIA (given directly below the original assumption). Note that assumption (a) implies that $Y_T^{d_2} \perp\!\!\!\perp D_1 | X_0, X_1$ as can be shown by simple calculations. Together with the assumption (b) we thus have that $Y_T^{d_2} \perp\!\!\!\perp (D_1, D_2) | \underline{X}_1$. This follows because $A \perp\!\!\!\perp (B, C)$ is equivalent to $A \perp\!\!\!\perp B|C$ together with $A \perp\!\!\!\perp C$. With this assumption we can derive for $E[Y_T^{11} | \underline{D}_2 = 00]$ that

$$E\left[Y_T^{11} | \underline{D}_2 = 00\right] = E\left[E[Y_T^{11} | X_1, X_0, \underline{D}_2 = 00] \,| \underline{D}_2 = 00\right]$$

$$= E\left[E[Y_T^{11} | X_1, X_0, D_1 = 0] \,| \underline{D}_2 = 00\right] = E\left[E[Y_T^{11} | X_1, X_0, D_1 = 1] \,| \underline{D}_2 = 00\right]$$

$$= E\left[E[Y_T^{11} | X_1, X_0, \underline{D}_2 = 11] \,| \underline{D}_2 = 00\right] = E\left[E[Y_T | X_1, X_0, \underline{D}_2 = 11] \,| \underline{D}_2 = 00\right].$$

Clearly, the same can be done for $E\left[Y_T^{00} | \underline{D}_2 = 11\right]$. This result has two implications: First, the DATET is identified. Second, we simply have to adjust for the distribution of X_1 and X_0 simultaneously, and can therefore use the methods we learnt for the static model with multiple treatments. In other words, we do not have to resort to more complex sequential matching or weighting methods (that are discussed in detail later when only using WDCIA).

Part (a) of the SDCIA further implies that $X_1 \perp\!\!\!\perp D_1 | X_0$, i.e. the variable X_1 which is observed at the end of the first period is not influenced by D_1 which in turn starts at the beginning of the first period. Hence, the X_t still have to be exogenous in the sense that D_t has no effect on X_t. This (eventually) prohibits to include intermediate outcomes in X_t. In other words, treatment assignment is typically decided each period based on initial information, treatment history and new information that is revealed up to that period. But it is not permitted that the information revealed has been caused by past treatments. The participation decision may be based on the values of time varying confounders observable at the beginning of the period, as long as they are not influenced by the treatments of this period. Hence, X_t is still exogenous, which thus does not allow Y_t to be included in X_t.

Note that this is a statement in terms of observed variables and its implication can be related to causality concepts in time series econometrics. It says that X_1 is not Granger-caused by previous treatments. This condition is a testable implication of SDCIA, which on the one hand is an advantage, but on the other hand suggests that SDCIA may be stronger than strictly necessary.

We will discuss alternative representations in terms of potential values of $X_1^{d_1}$, i.e. of the values of X_1 that would be observed if a particular treatment had been applied. Some might think that SDCIA (a) says that $X_1^{d_1} = X_1^{d_1'}$ but these two statements are definitely not equal. To examine alternative representations of the CIA assumptions in terms of potential values, we first turn back to the WDCIA. When using WDCIA, no explicit exogeneity condition is required for the control variables. This may be surprising, because it is a well-known fact that if we include, for example, the outcome in the list of control variables, we will always estimate a zero effect.[11] Obviously, a CIA based on observable control variables which are potentially influenced by the treatment is not the 'best' representation (in terms of a representation whose plausibility is most intuitively and easily be judged in a given application) of the identifying conditions, because it confounds selection effects with other endogeneity issues. Sometimes it helps to get its own mind clear when expressing the conditions really needed in terms of potential confounders. For example, the WDCIA implies for the second period

$$E[Y_T^{\underline{d}_\tau}|\underline{X}_1, D_1 = 1] = E[Y_T^{\underline{d}_\tau}|\underline{X}_1, \underline{D}_2 = 11].$$

Equivalently one could work with an expression in terms of potential confounders, i.e.

$$E[Y_T^{\underline{d}_\tau}|\underline{X}_1^{d_1=1}, D_1 = 1] = E[Y_T^{\underline{d}_\tau}|\underline{X}_1^{\underline{d}_2=11}, \underline{D}_2 = 11].$$

This shows that the WDCIA is in fact a set of joint assumptions about selection and endogeneity bias.

We close this subsection discussing alternative sets of assumptions for WDCIA and SDCIA expressed in terms of potential confounders (and called WDCIA-P, and SDCIA-P respectively). We concentrate only on versions for the simple two periods model to focus on the key issues. It can be shown that these assumptions are strongly related to the original versions given above. Nevertheless, neither does WDCIA directly imply this new WDCIA-P nor vice versa. The same applies to SDCIA and SDCIA-P. One can show that the same treatment effects are identified under WDCIA and WDCIA-P. All in all, the following assumptions are not exactly equivalent to our previous discussion, but almost. They provide an intuition into how we might interpret WDCIA and SDCIA, but are not testable.

Assumption WDCIA-P Weak dynamic conditional independence based on potential confounders

(a) $Y_T^{\underline{d}_2} \perp\!\!\!\perp D_t | \underline{X}_{t-1}^{\underline{d}_2}, \underline{D}_{t-1}$ $\qquad \forall t \le 2$ and $\underline{d}_2 \in \Theta_2$

(b) $F(X_0^{\underline{d}_2}|D_1 = d_1) = F(X_0^{d_1}|D_1 = d_1)$ $\qquad \forall \underline{d}_2 \in \Theta_2$ $\qquad\qquad$ (8.13)

(c) $F(X_1^{d_1,d_2'}|X_0^{d_1,d_2'}, D_1 = d_1) = F(X_1^{d_1}|X_0^{d_1}, D_1 = d_1)$ $\qquad \forall \underline{d}_2 \in \Theta_2,$

where X_t may include Y_t. The common support requirement remains the same as before.

---

[11] See, for example, Rosenbaum (1984), Rubin (2004) and Rubin (2005) on this so-called endogeneity bias.

The conditional independence condition (a) looks like before but now formulated in terms of potential confounders. What is new are the exogeneity conditions given afterwards. Intuitively, (8.13) states that given D_1, D_2 should have no effect on (the distribution of) the confounders in period 0, and if also given $X_0^{d_1}$, then D_2 should have no effect on confounders in period 1, cf. (c). A somewhat stronger assumption which implies this, is if the treatment has no effect on the confounders before it starts, i.e. $X_0^{\underline{d}_2} = X_0^{\underline{d}_2'}$ for any $\underline{d}_2$ and $\underline{d}_2'$ and also $X_1^{d_1,d_2} = X_1^{d_1,d_2'}$ for any d_2 and d_2'. This rules out anticipation effects on the confounders. In the jargon of panel data econometrics, the values of X_t are 'pre-determined'. They may depend on past values of the treatment sequence, but not on the current value or future values of D_t. Overall, this implies that we do not only rule out anticipation effects on the outcome variable, as this would not permit identification anyhow, but also anticipation effects on the confounders X.

The requirements for the strong dynamic CIA are nearly equivalent representation in terms of confounders:

Assumption SDCIA-P Strong conditional independence based on potential confounders

$$(a)\ (Y_T^{\underline{d}_2}, X_1^{\underline{d}_2}) \perp\!\!\!\perp D_1 | X_0^{\underline{d}_2} \qquad \forall\, \underline{d}_2 \in \Theta_2$$

$$(b)\ Y_T^{\underline{d}_2} \perp\!\!\!\perp D_2 | X_1^{\underline{d}_2}, D_1 \qquad \forall\, \underline{d}_2 \in \Theta_2$$

$$(c)\ F(X_0^{\underline{d}_2'} | D_2 = \underline{d}_2) = F(X_0^{\underline{d}_2} | D_2 = \underline{d}_2) \qquad \forall\, \underline{d}_2, \underline{d}_2' \in \Theta_2 \qquad (8.14)$$

$$(d)\ F(X_1^{\underline{d}_2'} | X_0^{\underline{d}_2'}, D_2 = \underline{d}_2) = F(X_1^{\underline{d}_2} | X_0^{\underline{d}_2}, D_2 = \underline{d}_2) \qquad \forall\, \underline{d}_2, \underline{d}_2' \in \Theta_2.$$

In contrast to WDCIA-P, the above exogeneity conditions require that $X_1^{d_1,d_2} = X_1^{d_1',d_2'}$ for any values of d_1, d_1', d_2, d_2'. This means not only that the causal effect of D_2 on X_1 is zero as before (no anticipation) but also that the causal effect of D_1 on X_1 is zero. Hence, X_t is assumed to not be affected by current nor future values of D_t. This assumption goes much beyond the no-anticipation condition required for WDCIA-P by ruling out the use of intermediate outcomes as conditioning variables. Hence, as already remarked when discussing SDCIA before, the identification essentially boils down to the static model with multiple treatments, which, if deemed reasonable, makes estimation much simpler. In many applications SDCIA is likely to be too strong. However, in cases where the new information X_t does influence outcomes as well as the choice of treatment in the next period, and this new information is so far not influenced by the evolving of the treatment history, then SDCIA can be plausible.

8.2.3   Sequential Matching or Propensity Score Weighting

So far we have only spoken about identification. As one might have noticed, all average potential outcomes (which in turn give the various average effects of treatment sequences by comparing them) were expressed in conditional means and (sometimes also) conditional probabilities. Assuming that you have already read the previous chapters on matching and propensity score weighting, the estimation is straightforward once you can express the mean of all needed potential outputs in terms of expectations of observed outputs. We can then proceed accordingly to the main estimation ideas of matching and propensity score weighting, only extended now by the hyperindices, indicating to which treatment sequence the (observed) variables refer to. In fact, all above identified effects can be considered as weighted averages of the observed outcomes in the subgroup experiencing the treatment sequence of interest. As an example we have already shown that

$$E\left[Y_T^{11}|D_1 = 0\right] = \int\int E\left[Y_T|\underline{X}_1, \underline{D}_2 = 11\right] dF_{X_1|X_0,D_1=1} dF_{X_0|D_1=0}$$

$$\text{or,} \quad E\left[Y_T^{11}\right] = \int\int E\left[Y_T|\underline{X}_1, \underline{D}_2 = 11\right] dF_{X_1|X_0,D_1=1} dF_{X_0}. \quad (8.15)$$

From here on we can obviously apply the same non-parametric (matching) estimators as in the static case.

In practice, though, there might be some complications which can pose problems (given that we are only provided with finite samples). We already mentioned that if we consider very long sequences, e.g. 10 versus 0000010, then the number of observations who actually experienced these sequences can be very small. We have further discussed that the observations in very long sequences are likely to be more homogenous such that the common support for the comparison of two sequences may be rather small. Another potential problem is that often we will have to control for continuous variables in our sequential matching estimation: While we can estimate dF_{X_0} in (8.15) simply by the empirical distribution function of X_0, this would not be possible for $dF_{X_1|X_0,D_1=1}$ if X_0 contains a continuous variable. If one were to impose parametric forms for $dF_{X_1|X_0,D_1=1}$ and dF_{X_0}, this would trivially become much simpler. This problem is actually not present if one were to assume SDCIA. In that case, one could identify

$$E\left[Y_T^{11}|\underline{D}_2 = 00\right] = \int E\left[Y_T|\underline{X}_1, \underline{D}_2 = 11\right] dF_{X_1,X_0|\underline{D}_2=00},$$

$$E\left[Y_T^{11}|D_1 = 0\right] = \int E\left[Y_T|\underline{X}_1, \underline{D}_2 = 11\right] dF_{X_1,X_0|D_1=0} \text{ and}$$

$$E\left[Y_T^{11}\right] = \int E\left[Y_T|\underline{X}_1, \underline{D}_2 = 11\right] dF_{X_1,X_0},$$

where $D_1 = 0$ and $\underline{D}_2 = 00$ have positive probability mass. Hence, with SDCIA we obtain a simpler estimator. Of course, since the SDCIA implies the WDCIA, the methods (outlined below) for WDCIA are also applicable here. This could in fact be used as a specification check for those parameters that are identified under SDCIA but also under WDCIA.

In the sections on propensity score matching and/or weighting we discussed that these approaches are often taken as a semi-parametric device to improve the estimators' performance.[12] For the problem considered here this is even more attractive, if not necessary, due to the above-mentioned problem that arises when continuous confounders

---

[12] It is semi-parametric if, as often done in practice, the propensity score is estimated parametrically.

are present. Similarly to matching, the propensity score weighting estimator is straightforward; only the notation complicates a bit. Defining $p^{d_1}(x_0) = \Pr(D_1 = d_1 | X_0 = x_0)$ and $p^{d_2|d_1}(\underline{x}_1) = \Pr(D_2 = d_2 | \underline{X}_1 = \underline{x}_1, D_1 = d_1)$ we have

$$E\left[\frac{Y_T}{p^{1|1}(\underline{X}_1)p^1(X_0)} \Big| \underline{D}_2 = 11\right] \cdot \Pr(\underline{D}_2 = 11)$$

$$= \int \frac{\Pr(\underline{D}_2 = 11)}{p^{1|1}(\underline{X}_1)p^1(X_0)} E\left[Y_T | \underline{X}_1, \underline{D}_2 = 11\right] dF_{X_1, X_0 | \underline{D}_2 = 11}$$

$$= \int \frac{\Pr(\underline{D}_2 = 11)}{p^{1|1}(\underline{X}_1)p^1(X_0)} E\left[Y_T | \underline{X}_1, \underline{D}_2 = 11\right] \frac{\Pr(D_2 = 1 | X_1, X_0, D_1 = 1)}{\Pr(D_2 = 1 | D_1 = 1)} dF_{X_1, X_0 | D_1 = 1}$$

$$= \int \frac{\Pr(D_1 = 1)}{p^1(X_0)} E\left[Y_T | \underline{X}_1, \underline{D}_2 = 11\right] dF_{X_1 | X_0, D_1 = 1} dF_{X_0 | D_1 = 1}$$

$$= \int \frac{\Pr(D_1 = 1)}{p^1(X_0)} E\left[Y_T | \underline{X}_1, \underline{D}_2 = 11\right] dF_{X_1 | X_0, D_1 = 1} \frac{\Pr(D_1 = 1 | X_0) dF_{X_0}}{\Pr(D_1 = 1)}$$

$$= \int E\left[Y_T | \underline{X}_1, \underline{D}_2 = 11\right] dF_{X_1 | X_0, D_1 = 1} dF_{X_0} = E\left[Y_2^{11}\right],$$

which is identical to (8.15). Hence, a natural estimator is

$$\left\{\sum_{i:\underline{D}_{2,i}=11} \hat{w}_i Y_T\right\} \Bigg/ \left\{\sum_{i:\underline{D}_{2,i}=11} \hat{w}_i\right\} \quad \text{where } \hat{w}_i = \frac{1}{\hat{p}^{1|1}(\underline{X}_1)\hat{p}^1(X_{0,i})}.$$

The conditional probabilities can be estimated non-parametrically. But when the sequences become very long, parametric estimation might be more advisable because the number of observations who have followed exactly this sequence decreases, but the list of control variables $\underline{X}_\tau$ gets longer. Similarly,

$$E\left[Y_T^{11} | D_1 = 0\right] = E\left[\frac{Y_T}{p^{1|1}(\underline{X}_1)p^1(X_0)} \cdot p^0(X_0) \Big| \underline{D}_2 = 11\right] \cdot \frac{\Pr(\underline{D}_2 = 11)}{\Pr(D_1 = 0)}.$$

Though we have derived here expressions for the means of the potential outcome for 'two times treated', i.e. sequence 11, the procedure works the same for sequences 00, 01 and 10. Various matching estimators based on nearest-neighbour regression are examined in Lechner (2008).

Turning to propensity score matching, it can be shown that the propensity scores also satisfy a balancing property which can make sequential matching estimation somewhat simpler. (Else you might match directly with the conditioning variables.) The idea is as follows: note that for the two-period case under the WDCIA one has

$$Y_T^{d_2} \perp\!\!\!\perp D_1 | p^1(X_0) \quad \text{and} \quad Y_T^{d_2} \perp\!\!\!\perp D_2 | p^{1|D_1}(\underline{X}_1) \tag{8.16}$$

(cf. Exercise 5) but also[13]

$$Y_T^{d_2} \perp\!\!\!\perp D_2 | p^{1|D_1}(\underline{X}_1), D_1 \quad \text{and} \quad Y_T^{d_2} \perp\!\!\!\perp D_2 | p^{1|D_1}(\underline{X}_1), p^1(X_0), D_1. \tag{8.17}$$

---

[13] In fact, instead of $p^{d_i}(x_i)$ one can also use any balancing scores $b(x_i)$ with the property that $E\left[p^{d_i}(X_i) | b_i(X_i)\right] = p^{d_i}(X_i)$.

Hence, we can augment the propensity score with additional control variables that we deem to be particularly important for the outcome variable, with the aim to improve small sample properties. In addition to that, it means that we can use the same propensity score when estimating the effects separately by gender or age groups, for example. We obtain

$$E\left[Y_T^{11}\right] = \int \int E\left[Y_T | p^{1|1}, p^1, D_2 = 11\right] dF_{p^{1|1}|p^1, D_1=1} dF_{p^1},$$

so that a potential estimator would be

$$\frac{1}{n}\sum_{i=1}^{n}\left(\frac{\sum_{j:D_{1,j}=1} m^{11}(p_j^{1|1}, p_j^1) \cdot K\left(\frac{p_j^1 - p_i^1}{h}\right)}{\sum_{j:D_{1,j}=1} K\left(\frac{p_j^1 - p_i^1}{h}\right)}\right),$$

where $m^{11}(p^{1|1}, p^1) = \widehat{E}\left[Y_T | p^{1|1}, p^1, D_2 = 11\right]$.

If more than two time periods are examined, more propensity scores are needed. This means that the dimension of the (non-parametric) matching estimator is increasing with the length of the treatment sequence even if we use a parametrically estimated propensity score. The reason is that when we are interested in Y^{11}, then we have to control for $p^{1|1}$ and p^1 (in the matching). When Y^{111} is of interest, we will need $p^{1|11}$ and $p^{1|1}$ and p^1. In fact, the minimum number of propensity scores needed corresponds to the length of the treatment sequence; actually, the number of propensity scores needed for a treatment sequence $\underline{d}_\tau$ equals τ.

A crucial assumption in the above model was the common support, i.e. that $0 < \Pr\left(D_2 = 1 | \underline{X}_1, \underline{D}_1\right) < 1$ almost surely. In other words, for every value of X_0 and X_1 there should be a positive probability that either $D_2 = 1$ or $D_2 = 0$ is chosen. In some applications, the set of possible treatments might, however, depend on the value of X_1. For example, if we examine a particular training programme for unemployed, the treatment option $D_2 = 1$ might not exist for someone for whom X_1 indicates that this person is not unemployed anymore. Here, the set of available treatment options in a given time period t varies with X_{t-1}, and the model discussed so far would have to be adjusted to this setting.

8.3 Duration Models and the Timing of Treatments

What happens if the outcome of interest is *time* or say, the *duration* to change from a given state (e.g. unemployment) to another (e.g. getting employed)? One might study for example what are the patterns of unemployment duration or even what are the factors which influence the length of an unemployment spell. Other examples are the duration from a political decision to its implementation, or the impact of tuition fees on the duration of university studies. These are the sorts of questions that duration (or survival) analysis is designed to address. Statistical methods have been developed over a long time in other disciplines (biometrics, technometrics, statistics in medicine, etc.). In econometrics, however, it is still much less used.

For this reason, before we start to study the impact of (dynamic) treatment on duration, we first give a brief introduction (in Section 8.3.1) to some basic definitions and concepts in duration analysis. Afterwards, in Section 8.3.2 we introduce the concept of *competing risks* which is fundamental for our analysis of treatment effect estimation on durations.

8.3.1   A Brief Introduction to Duration Analysis in Econometrics

Let Y be now the *duration of a process*, or the *time to exit from a state*. The aim is to study the distribution of Y, and later on the impact of a certain covariate (indicating the treatment) on it. We denote the duration density function by $f(t)$ and the duration distribution function by $F(t) = \Pr(Y < t) = \int_{s=0}^{t} f(s)ds$. The latter actually represents the probability of exit from the state by time t with density $f(t) = \frac{dF(t)}{dt}$. Then, the *probability of survival* in a state to at least time t is simply $S(t) = \Pr(Y > t) = 1 - F(t)$. For continuous time this is equal to $S(t) = \Pr(Y \geq t)$. The *median duration, $t = M$*, is then defined by $S(M) = 0.5$.

However, in duration analysis the basic building block in duration modelling is the *exit rate* or *hazard function*, denoted by $\lambda(t)$. It represents the *instantaneous exit rate* from the state at time t, and is the ratio of the duration density to the complement of the duration distribution function at time t, as will be shown below. In discrete terms one has $\Pr(t \leq Y \leq t + dt | Y \geq t)$, giving an average probability of $\frac{\Pr(t \leq Y \leq t + dt | Y \geq t)}{dt}$.

More specifically, for discrete time we can write

$$F(t) = \Pr(Y \leq t) = \sum_{l=1}^{t} \Pr(Y = l) = \Pr(Y < t + 1),$$

$$S(t) = \Pr(Y > t) = 1 - \sum_{l=1}^{t} \Pr(Y = l) = \Pr(Y \geq t + 1),$$

(the so-called *survival function*) and the hazard rate (cf. Exercise 6) as

$$\lambda(t) = \Pr(Y = t)/\Pr(Y \geq t) = \Pr(Y = t)/\{1 - \Pr(Y \leq t - 1)\}. \tag{8.18}$$

For continuous time we converge to the hazard rate $\lambda(t)$, specifically

$$\lambda(t) = \lim_{dt \to 0} \left\{ \frac{P(t \leq Y \leq t + dt | Y \geq t)}{dt} \right\} = \lim_{dt \to 0} \frac{1}{dt} \left\{ \frac{P(t \leq Y \leq t + dt, Y \geq t)}{P(Y \geq t)} \right\}$$

$$= \lim_{dt \to 0} \frac{1}{dt} \left\{ \frac{P(t \leq Y \leq t + dt)}{P(Y \geq t)} \right\} = \lim_{dt \to 0} \frac{1}{dt} \left\{ \frac{P(Y \leq t + dt) - P(Y \leq t)}{P(Y \geq t)} \right\}$$

$$= \frac{1}{S(t)} \lim_{dt \to 0} \left\{ \frac{P(Y \leq t + dt) - P(Y \leq t)}{dt} \right\} = \frac{1}{S(t)} \lim_{dt \to 0} \left\{ \frac{dP(Y \leq t)}{dt} \right\}$$

$$= \frac{1}{S(t)} \lim_{dt \to 0} \left\{ \frac{dF(t)}{dt} \right\} = \frac{f(t)}{S(t)}.$$

A first simple concept of duration dependence is to talk of *negative duration dependence* when $\frac{d\lambda(t)}{dt} < 0$. Conversely, positive duration dependence is present where $\frac{d\lambda(t)}{dt} > 0$. Typical examples are strike duration for negative, and unemployment duration for positive duration dependence. Clearly, the potential patterns of duration dependence depend on the form of $\lambda(t)$ which is therefore often considered as the main building block of duration analysis. The simplest hazard rate has constant exit rate (zero duration dependence), but generally $\lambda(t)$ may neither be constant nor monotonic.

As part of the audience might not be familiar with duration analysis, some basic relationships between functions could be interesting to be mentioned. From above, we have that

$$\lambda(t) = \frac{f(t)}{S(t)} = \frac{1}{S(t)}\frac{dF(t)}{dt} = \frac{1}{S(t)}\left[-\frac{dS(t)}{dt}\right] = -\frac{d\,log\,S(t)}{dt} = -\frac{d\,log[1-F(t)]}{dt}.$$

So, integrating $\lambda(\cdot)$ to t gives

$$\Lambda(t) = \int_{s=0}^{t}\lambda(s)ds = \int_{s=0}^{t}-\frac{d\,log[1-F(s)]}{ds}ds = [-log[1-F(s)]]_0^t$$
$$= -log[1-F(t)] + log[1-F(0)] = -log[1-F(t)]$$
$$= -log\,S(t)\quad\text{since}\quad F(0) = 0.$$

You may think of $\Lambda(t)$ as the sum of the risks you face going from duration 0 to t. We can thus express the survival function and the density in terms of the hazard rate by rearranging

$$S(t) = \exp\left[-\int_{s=0}^{t}\lambda(s)ds\right],\text{ and}\tag{8.19}$$

$$f(t) = \exp\left[-\int_{s=0}^{t}\lambda(s)ds\right]\lambda(t).\tag{8.20}$$

It is obvious then that for continuous time $F(t) = \exp[-\Lambda(t)]$, indicating that $\Lambda(t)$ has an exponential distribution with parameter 1, and $log\,\Lambda(t)$ an extreme value Type 1 (or *Gumbel*) distribution with density $f(\epsilon) = \exp[\epsilon - \exp(\epsilon)]$. Similarly to the above calculations it can be shown that for discrete time the probability $\Pr(Y = t)$ can be expressed in terms of the hazard. Let us consider some typical examples of distributions used in duration analysis.

Example 8.11 The classical example in basic statistics courses is the exponential distribution. It has a constant hazard rate specification where $\lambda(t) = \lambda_0$ for $\lambda_0 > 0$. To derive $S(t)$, note first that $\frac{d\,log\,S(t)}{dt} = -\lambda_0$. This implies $log\,S(t) = k - \lambda_0 t$ for some k. Hence, for a given $K > 0$

$$S(t) = \exp(k - \lambda_0 t) = K\,\exp(-\lambda_0 t) = \exp(-\lambda_0 t)$$

because $S(0) = 1$. It follows that

$$\Lambda(t) = \lambda_0 t,\qquad f(t) = \lambda_0\exp(-\lambda_0 t),$$
$$F(t) = \frac{\lambda(t) - f(t)}{\lambda(t)} = \frac{\lambda_0 - \lambda_0\exp(-\lambda_0 t)}{\lambda_0} = 1 - exp(-\lambda_0 t).$$

This exponential distribution is clearly a quite restrictive specification whose major drawback is the zero duration dependence. We also say that this process has *no memory* because the time already elapsed has no impact on the future hazard or remaining survival time.

Example 8.12 Another classical example is the Weibull distribution. The Weibull hazard rate is defined as

$$\lambda(t) = \lambda_0 \gamma (\lambda_0 t)^{\gamma - 1} \quad \text{or} \quad a \gamma t^{\gamma - 1} \quad \text{for} \quad a = \lambda_0^\gamma$$

with $\lambda_0, \gamma > 0$ (as negative exit rates do not exist), giving survival function and derivative of the hazard

$$S(t) = \exp[-(\lambda_0 t)^\gamma], \qquad \frac{d\lambda(t)}{dt} = \lambda_0^2 \gamma * (\gamma - 1) * (\lambda_0 t)^{\gamma - 2}.$$

The median duration can be calculated by

$$S(M) = \exp[-(\lambda_0 M)^\gamma] = 0.5 \implies M = \frac{\log(2)^{1/\gamma}}{\lambda_0}.$$

The hazard is positive for $\gamma > 1$ and negative for $\gamma < 1$. So the parameter γ defines the sign and degree of duration dependence. Note, however, that the Weibull is monotonic in t, for $\gamma > 1$ monotonically increasing, and for $\gamma < 1$ monotonically decreasing.

The Weibull distribution is quite popular as it allows to model a positive or a negative duration dependence. However, it is just a one-parameter generalisation of the exponential distribution and does not allow for a change of the sign of the hazard. This is different for the next example.

Example 8.13 The log logistic distribution is another, though still one-parameter, generalisation of the exponential distribution with hazard rate

$$\lambda(t) = \frac{\lambda_0 \gamma (\lambda_0 t)^{\gamma - 1}}{1 + (\lambda_0 t)^\gamma} \quad \text{for} \quad \lambda_0, \gamma > 0$$

$$\text{or} = a \gamma t^{\gamma - 1} \left(1 + a t^\gamma\right)^{-1} \quad \text{for} \quad a = \lambda_0^\gamma.$$

We can now distinguish three cases: for $\gamma = 1$ it is monotonically decreasing from a at $t = 0$ to zero when $t \to \infty$; for $\gamma < 1$ it is monotonically decreasing but unbounded for $t \to 0$; and for $\gamma > 1$ it is increasing until $t = \{(\gamma - 1)/\gamma\}^{1-\gamma}$ but then decreasing to 0. With the alternative a-notation we have

$$\int_0^t \lambda(s)ds = \log(1 + at^\gamma) = -\log[(1 + at^\gamma)^{-1}],$$

$$F(t) = 1 - (1 + at^\gamma)^{-1},$$

$$S(t) = \frac{1}{(1 + (\lambda_0 t)^\gamma)}$$

$$f(t) = a\gamma t^{\gamma-1}(1 + at^\gamma)^{-2}.$$

One conclusion is that $log(t)$ has logistic distribution (Exercise 7) with density

$$g(y) = \gamma \exp\{\gamma(y - \mu)\} / [1 + \exp\{\gamma(y - \mu)\}]^2,$$

expectation $\mu = -\gamma^{-1}log(a)$, and variance $\pi^2/(3\gamma^2)$. This is why it is called *log-logistic*.

In Figure 8.2 you see graphical examples of the exponential, Weibull and log-logistic distribution. It can now also be seen why it is much easier to look at a hazard rate than looking at the survival (or cumulative distribution) function to see and understand the differences.

For estimating the unknown parameter of the particular distribution we can obviously resort to maximum likelihood methods. Even if we start out from the specification of the hazard, thanks to (8.20) we always get immediately the density (for the continuous case) or the probability (for the discrete case), see (8.18) we need. More specifically, take t as continuous and consider a sample of n observed (completed) durations $t_1, t_2, \ldots, t_n$ within a sample period. Given a parametric form for $\lambda(\cdot)$ that is fixed up to an unknown finite-dimensional parameter θ, the density for t_i is $f(t_i; \theta) = \lambda(t_i; \theta) \cdot S(t_i; \theta)$ which yields a likelihood and corresponding log-likelihood of

$$L(\theta) = \prod_{i=1}^{n} f(t_i; \theta) = \prod_{i=1}^{n} \lambda(t_i; \theta) \cdot S(t_i; \theta),$$

$$l(\theta) = \sum_{i=1}^{n} \ln f(t_i; \theta) = \sum_{i=1}^{n} \ln \lambda(t_i; \theta) + \sum_{i=1}^{n} \ln S(t_i; \theta). \tag{8.21}$$

Now, maximum likelihood estimation to obtain an estimator θ is straightforward.

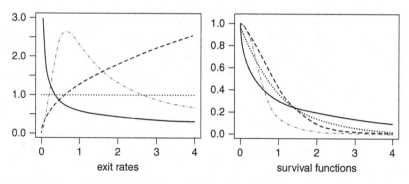

exit rates   survival functions

Figure 8.2 Hazard rates (left figure) and survival functions (right figure) for exponential with $\lambda_0 = 1$ (dotted), Weibull with $\lambda_0 = 1.4$, $\gamma = 0.5$ (solid), respectively with $\lambda_0 = 0.9$, $\gamma = 1.5$ (dashed), and log-logistic with $\lambda_0 = 1.9$, $\gamma = 2.7$

So far we supposed that all t_i represented completed durations. Problems arise in practice when data are censored or truncated, as is often the case in duration analysis. Sometimes one may not observe completed durations but *right-censoring*, and sometimes one may not observe the start of the event but *left-censoring*. Furthermore, for some individuals one may observe *multiple durations* over the period of the sample. This causes dependency in the data but can also help with some identification issues. One speaks of *multi-spell data*, else of *single-spell data* then.

Typical sampling schemes are *flow sampling* and *stock sampling*. In the former we randomly sample from individuals that enter(ed) the initial state at a given point in time during time interval $[0, b]$. As at some point we have to stop observing them, it is subject to right censoring. In case of *stock sampling* we observe individuals that are in initial state at time point b. Then we do not necessarily know when they started but we follow them up to their exit. Clearly, these data are subject to left censoring or even truncation.

Let us first discuss the problem of right-censoring, i.e. considering the situation in which some in the sample $t_1, t_2, \ldots, t_n$ are right-censored. Each individual my have his own censoring time, say c_i; and let $\delta_i \in \{0, 1\}$ indicate whether the observed duration is completed $\delta_i = 1$ or not $\delta_i = 0$. Then we can proceed similarly to the estimation of a Tobit model in mean regression: we know that for the censored observations one has $Y > t_i$ with probability $S(t_i; \theta)$, i.e. individual i has survived in the initial state until to the end of the study. For the non-censored individuals we are provided with the full information and can use $f(t_i; \theta)$. The new likelihood and corresponding log-likelihood are therefore

$$L_r(\theta) = \prod_{\delta_i=1} f(t_i; \theta) \prod_{\delta_i=0} S(t_i; \theta) = \prod_{\delta_i=1} \lambda(t_i; \theta) S(t_i; \theta) \prod_{\delta_i=0} S(t_i; \theta),$$

$$l_r(\theta) = \sum_{\delta_i=1} \ln f(t_i; \theta) + \sum_{\delta_i=0} \ln S(t_i; \theta) = \sum_{\delta_i=1} \ln \lambda(t_i; \theta) + \sum_{i=1}^{n} \ln S(t_i; \theta). \quad (8.22)$$

For the consistency of this maximum likelihood estimator it is needed that the latent duration is distributed independently from c_i and the starting point, say a_i, from the initial state.

Left-censoring can be treated equivalently, but for left-truncation we would need some more information. Imagine now, durations t_i were only observed for people being (still) in the initial status at time b, i.e. observed conditional on $t_i > l_i$ (for $l_i > 0$), where $l_i = b - a_i$ with a_i being, as above, the starting point. Where l_i is known you can work with the conditional density

$$f(t_i | t_i > l_i; \theta) = \frac{\lambda(t_i; \theta) S(t_i; \theta)}{S(l_i; \theta)}$$

to calculate the log-likelihood (in the absence of right-censoring). In sum this gives the log likelihood

$$l_l(\theta) = \sum_{i=1}^{n} \ln \lambda(t_i; \theta) + \sum_{i=1}^{n} [\ln S(t_i; \theta) - \ln S(l_i; \theta)]. \quad (8.23)$$

Of course, the problem is the need to know l_i (respectively b and a_i).

Finally, combining the left-truncation with right-censoring gives the log-likelihood

$$l_{lr}(\theta) = \sum_{\delta_i=1} \ln f(t_i; \theta) + \sum_{\delta_i=0} \ln S(t_i; \theta) - \sum_{i=1}^{n} \ln S(l_i; \theta). \qquad (8.24)$$

When having grouped data, typically some methods are used that are different from the discrete time or parametric continuous time models above. One could say that people often tend to directly apply non-parametric methods. The idea is actually pretty simple. Having grouped data means that the time bar is divided into $M + 1$ intervals: $[0, b_1), [b_1, b_2), \ldots, [b_M, \infty)$, where the b_m are given (in practice: chosen by the empirical researcher) for all m. We record the observations now in terms of exits E_m in m's interval, $[b_{m-1}, b_m)$. Let N_m be the people still at risk in that period, i.e. still alive in the initial state. Then a trivial estimator for the exit rate is obviously for all m, $\hat{\lambda}_m = E_m/N_m$. Similarly,

$$\widehat{\Pr}(Y > b_m | Y > b_{m-1}) = (N_m - E_m)/N_m \text{ and } \widehat{S}(b_m) = \prod_{r=1}^{m} (N_r - E_r)/N_r. \qquad (8.25)$$

This is the so called *Kaplan–Meier* estimator. It is consistent when assuming that for increasing sample size the number of observations in each interval increases, too. In practice it means that in each interval we have a 'reasonable' large number N_r.

As already discussed in other chapters, for our purpose it is quite helpful – if not necessary – to include covariates in the model. We will see that basically all we have learnt above does still apply though the notation changes. The most crucial points are the definition of a conditional hazard, and the assumptions on the covariates that are to be included.

An important first distinction is to separate covariates x_i into those that are time-invariant covariates, i.e. that do not depend on the period of duration, and time-varying covariates (x_{it}). Typical examples for the former are evidently gender of the individual, or the level of school qualification (for adults). The time-varying covariates, however, have to be handled with care. As we did in the previous chapters, one typically prefers to assume that the included covariates are not influenced by the considered process; they have to be exogenous.

Example 8.14 Consider unemployment duration. If Y is the length of time unemployed, measured in weeks, then $\lambda(20)$ is (approx.) the probability of finding a job between weeks 20 and 21. Here, 'finding a job' reflects the fact that the person was unemployed until week 20 but has changed his status in week 21. The probability (= percentage) refers to the population being still unemployed in week 20. Typical covariates contain *education, labour market experience, marital status, gender, race and number of children*, but also macro variables like *rules governing unemployment benefits and unemployment rate*. If measured at the beginning of the unemployment spell and unchanged during the stay in this state, they might be considered as time-invariant. When we observe these covariates over time (i.e. as real time-varying covariates), then problems start when there is a feedback from duration on them (as e.g. for marital status). If, however, there is only a feedback from a change in X on Y, then it is manageable.

For the ease of presentation we start with the inclusion of time-invariant covariates. Furthermore, we assume that the conditional distribution of the latent duration $t_i^*|x_i$ is independent of c_i, a_i (potential censoring and the starting point). Then the most popular modelling approach, at least in continuous time, is the *proportional hazard* (PH) specification: for some parametric *baseline hazard* $\lambda_0(t)$ consider

$$\lambda(t; x) = g(x) \cdot \lambda_0(t), \qquad g(x), \lambda_0 > 0 \tag{8.26}$$

with an unknown (maybe pre-specified up to a vector β of unknown parameters) function $g(\cdot)$ which is called *systematic* part. A typical choice is $g(x) = \exp(x'\beta)$. Then, $log\{\lambda(t; x)\} = x'\beta + \ln \lambda_0(t)$, and the elements of β measure the semi-elasticity of the hazard with respect to their corresponding element in vector x. The definition of the survival function becomes

$$S(t) = \exp\left[-\int_{s=0}^{t} \exp(x'\beta)\lambda_0(s)ds\right] = \exp\left[-\exp(x'\beta)\int_{s=0}^{t} \lambda_0(s)ds\right]$$

$$= \exp\left[-\exp(x'\beta)\Lambda_0(t)\right].$$

This way we get again standard formulations for (log-) likelihoods which can be used for maximum likelihood estimation of the PH. One reason for its popularity is that for proportional hazards, Cox (1972) derived the *partial maximum likelihood estimation* method for β. Its advantage is that it does not require the knowledge of $\lambda_0(t)$, i.e. no further specification of the exact distribution of duration: It is defined (for completed observations) as being the maximum of

$$L(\beta) = \prod_{t_i} \exp(x_i'\beta)/ \sum_{j \in R_i} \exp(x_j'\beta) \tag{8.27}$$

where R_i is the set of individuals under risk at time t_i, and 'i' is the individual with the event at t_i.

Example 8.15 Recall Example 8.12, and the Weibull hazard specification $\lambda(t) = f(t)/S(t) = a\gamma t^{\gamma-1}$. If we substitute $g(x) = \exp\{\beta_0 + x'\beta\}$ for a in order to model the dependency on x, then we obtain a proportional hazard with $\lambda_0(t) = \gamma t^{\gamma-1}$.
Even more generally, with $g(x) = \exp\{\beta_0 + x'\beta\}$ we obtain for the baseline hazard

$$log\left\{\int_0^t \lambda_0(s)ds\right\} = -\beta_0 - x'\beta + \epsilon \tag{8.28}$$

with ϵ having the extreme value Type 1 distribution; recall the discussion after Equations 8.19 and 8.20.

This shows also a link to regression analysis of duration. However, in Equation 8.28 the ϵ only represents the purely random variation in the duration outcome; it does not capture any other individual heterogeneity. Therefore we will later on introduce the so-called *mixed proportional hazard*.

An alternative to the popular proportional hazard is the idea of *accelerated hazard* functions (AHF), also called accelerated failure time models. For a given parametric hazard model (like the exponential or Weibull) one simply replaces λ_0 by

$$\lambda_0 = \exp(x'\beta).$$

Modifications and extensions can be various.

Example 8.16 For the Weibull distribution, cf. Example 8.12, this gives

$$\lambda(t; x) = \lambda_0 \gamma (\lambda_0 t)^{\gamma-1} = \exp(x'\beta)\gamma(\exp(x'\beta)t)^{\gamma-1}.$$

For the exponential hazard with no duration dependence, cf. Example 8.11, we have simply $\lambda(t) = \lambda_0 = \exp(x'\beta)$. This gives expected duration time

$$E[Y|X] = \frac{1}{\exp(x'\beta)}$$

which for 'completed' durations is often estimated by a linear regression model as

$$-\log(t) = x'\beta + v, \qquad \text{with error term } v \text{ fulfilling certain assumptions.}$$

Other distributions suitable for AHF models include the log-normal, generalised gamma, inverse Gaussian distributions, etc. Among them, the generalised gamma distribution is quite flexible as it is a three-parameter distribution that includes the Weibull, log-normal and the gamma. Their popularity, however, is less oriented along their flexibility but along the availability of software packages, or the question whether its survival function has an analytic closed form.

In Example 8.15 we saw that it would be desirable to include also unobserved heterogeneity between individuals in the PH model. This can be done straightforwardly and leads to the so-called *mixed proportional hazard* (MPH) models:

$$\lambda(t; x, v) = g(x)\lambda_0(t)v, \qquad g(x), v, \lambda_0 > 0 \tag{8.29}$$

with a time-invariant (i.e. only individual specific) random effect v with distribution $F_v(v)$ and $E[v] < \infty.$[14] For identification (and estimation) it is typically assumed that the observed covariates x are independent from the unobserved heterogeneity v. For a complete set of technical assumptions in order to non-parametrically identify the MPH, see for example van den Berg (2001). Compared to the regression equation in Example 8.15 we have now

$$\log \int_0^t \lambda_0(s)ds = -\beta_0 - x\beta - \log v + \epsilon$$

---

[14] Sometimes it is also set $E[v] = 1$ if one wants to identify a scale for $g(x)$ and/or $\lambda_0(t)$. Else one has to normalise these functions.

which is much more flexible than that resulting from the PH, but still more restrictive than a regression with an arbitrary (finite variance) error term.

For calculating the maximum likelihood, note that when $t_i(x_i, v_i) \sim F(t|x_i, v_i; \theta)$, and $v \sim F_v(v; \delta)$ with a finite dimensional unknown parameter δ, then

$$t_i|x_i \sim H(t|x_i; \theta, \delta) = \int_0^\infty F(t|x_i, v; \theta)\, dF_v(v; \delta).$$

This means, one would work with H or $h = dH/dt$ (instead of F, f) for the construction of the likelihood. As a byproduct we have (suppressing δ)

$$f(t|x) = \lambda(t; x)S(t|x) = \int_0^\infty \lambda(t; x, v)S(t|x, v)dF_v(v)$$

which gives for the (M)PH the hazard function

$$\lambda(t; x) = g(x)\lambda_0(t)E[v|Y > t, x].$$

It can be shown that its duration dependence is more negative than the one of $\lambda(t; x, v)$.

But how to choose the distribution of the unobserved heterogeneity F_v among survivors? Heckman and Singer (1984) study the impact of the choice on the parameter estimates and propose a semi-parametric estimator. Abbring and van den Berg (2007) show that for a large class of MPH models this distribution converges to a gamma distribution.

Example 8.17 If we use gamma-distributed heterogeneity, then we can find the distribution of completed $t_i|x_i$ for a broad class of hazard functions with multiplicative heterogeneity. Set $\lambda(t; x, v) = v \cdot g(t|x)$ without further specification, and $v \sim \Gamma(\delta, \delta)$, such that $E[v] = 1$ and $Var[v] = \delta^{-1}$. Recall the density of the Gamma distribution: $\delta^\delta v^{\delta-1} \exp\{-\delta v\}/\Gamma(\delta)$ and that for $t|x, v$ we have

$$F(t|x_i, v_i) = 1 - \exp\left\{-v_i \int_0^t g(s|x_i)ds\right\} = 1 - \exp\left\{-v_i\varrho(t; x_i)\right\},$$

where $\varrho(t; x_i) = \int_0^t g(s|x_i)ds$. Set $\varrho_i = \varrho(t; x_i)$, then plugging-in gives

$$H(t_i|x_i; \theta, \delta) = \int_0^\infty \left[1 - \exp\{-v\varrho_i\}\right]\delta^\delta v^{\delta-1} \exp\{-\delta v\}/\Gamma(\delta)dv$$

$$= 1 - [\delta/(\delta + \varrho_i)]^\delta \int_0^\infty (\delta + \varrho_i)\delta v^{\delta-1} \exp\{-v(\delta + \varrho_i)\}/\Gamma(\delta)dv$$

$$= 1 - [\delta/(\delta + \varrho_i)]^\delta = 1 - [1 + \varrho_i/\delta]^{-\delta}$$

since $E[v] = 1$. This gives for any $g(t|x)$

$$H(t|x_i; \delta) = 1 - [1 + \varrho_i/\delta]^{-\delta} \quad \text{and} \quad h(t|x_i; \delta) = g(t|x_i)[1 + \varrho_i/\delta]^{-\delta}$$

as duration distributions to work with.

For grouped duration data, cf. the Kaplan–Meier estimator introduced above, the inclusion of time-invariant covariates is quite straightforward for parametrically specified hazards $\lambda(t; x)$ that are specified up to a finite-dimensional parameter θ. For a moment let us assume not to suffer from any censoring. Again, we have the timeline divided into $M + 1$ intervals $[0, b_1), [b_1, b_2), \ldots, [b_M, \infty)$, where the b_m are given. Then we can estimate θ by maximising the likelihood

$$\prod_{i=1}^{n}\{1 - \tilde{b}_{m_i}(x_i; \theta)\} \prod_{l=1}^{m_i-1} \tilde{b}_l(x_i; \theta) \quad \text{where} \quad \tilde{b}_l(x_i; \theta) := \exp\left\{-\int_{b_{l-1}}^{b_l} \lambda(s; x)\, ds\right\}.$$

That is, we sum up the exits in each time interval. For right censored observations i, we can simply drop $\{1 - \tilde{b}_{m_i}(x_i; \theta)\}$ from the likelihood.

In the Kaplan-Meier estimator without covariates we considered constant exit rates in each interval. Here we have allowed for a continuous function $\lambda(\cdot)$; but nonetheless use only its integral $\tilde{b}_m$. Quite popular are the *piece-wise-constant proportional hazards* with $\lambda(t; x) = g(x)\lambda_m$ for $m = 1, \ldots, M$ and $g(\cdot) > 0$ to be specified. Such a specification causes discontinuities in the time dimension but only in theory, because even if λ_0 is continuous, for proportional hazards we will only work with $\int_{b_m}^{b_{m-1}} \lambda_0(s)ds$. For the common specification $g(x) = \exp(x'\beta)$ one obtains $\tilde{b}_m(x; \beta) = \exp[-\exp(x'\beta)\lambda_m(b_m - b_{m-1})]$.

We finally turn to hazard models conditional on time-varying covariates. For notational convenience we denote therefore the covariates by $x(t), t \geq 0$. There exist various definitions of the hazard function with slight modifications of the conditioning set. For our purposes it is opportune to work with the following: We (re)define the hazard by

$$\lambda\{t; X(t)\} = \lim_{dt \searrow 0} \Pr\left(t \leq Y < t + dt | Y \geq t, X\{u\}_0^t\right) / dt, \qquad (8.30)$$

where $X\{u\}_0^t$ denotes the path of X over the time period $[0, t]$. This requires that the entire path of X is well defined whether or not the individual is in the initial state.

A further necessary condition for a reasonable interpretation (at least in our context) of the model and its parameters is to rule out feedback from the duration to (future) values of X. One would therefore assume that for all t and $s > t$

$$\Pr\left(X\{u\}_t^s | Y \geq s, X(t)\right) = \Pr\left(X\{u\}_t^s | X(t)\right). \qquad (8.31)$$

One speaks then also of *strictly exogenous* covariates.[15] One speaks of *external* covariates if the path of the X is independent of whether or not the agent is in or has left the initial state. Note that these have always a well-defined paths and fulfil Assumption (8.31).

In the context of (mixed) proportional hazard models, however, it is more common to say that $X(t)$ *is a predictable process*. This does not mean that we can predict the whole future realisation of X; it basically means that all values of the covariates for the hazard at t must be known and observables just before t. In other words, the covariates

---

[15] The covariates are then also *sequentially exogenous*, because by specification of $\lambda\{t, X(t)\}$ we are conditioning on current and past covariates.

at time t are influenced only by events that have occurred up to time t, and these events are observable.[16]

Example 8.18 Time invariant covariates like gender and race are obviously predictable. All covariates with fully known path are predictable. A trivial example is age, but there one might argue that this is equivalent with knowing the birth date and thus being equivalent to a time-invariant covariate. Another example are unemployment benefits as a function of the elapsed unemployment duration. If these are institutionally fixed, then the path is perfectly known and thus predictable. It is less obvious for processes that can be considered as random. A stochastic X is predictable in the above defined sense if its present value depends only on past and outside random variation. As a counterexample serves any situation where the individual has inside information (that the researcher does not have) on future realisations of X, that affect the present hazard. In other words, predictability of X does not necessarily mean that the empirical researcher or the individual can predict its future values; but it means that both are on the same level of information as far as it is relevant for the hazard.

Regarding the use of time-varying covariates in proportional hazard models, one should say that, strictly speaking, proportional hazards with time-varying covariates do not exist: the impact of time and covariates is no longer separable. Nevertheless, models of the form

$$\lambda(t; X(t), v) = g\{X(t)\}\lambda_0(t)v$$

are called *mixed proportional hazard with time-varying covariates*. Again, the unobserved heterogeneity v is typically assumed to be time invariant. Estimation, especially if the distribution of v is assumed to be known (up to a finite-dimensional parameter), is possible via maximum likelihood methods because all above presented relations between hazards, survival functions and densities do still hold such that, having specified the hazard, you also have specified the distribution.

8.3.2   From Competing Risks Models to Treatment Effects in Duration Analysis

So far we only considered the competition between two states, for example to be unemployed or not. Especially in medicine, however, when studying the success of a therapy, then there is obviously always the risk of dying due to a different reason, because no patient lives for ever. The same holds certainly also true for many problems in technometrics as most machines will break after a while even if we only focus on one particular bolt. This leads us to the concept of looking at *cause-specific* hazards or cause-specific density functions. In the literature one often calls the integral of a cause-specific density the *cumulative incidence function*, or *subdistribution*, or *marginal probability* or *crude incidence*. While the overall hazard rate is still defined (with continuous time) as

---

[16] For people being familiar with time series and panel data analysis it might be quite helpful to know that *predictability* of process X is basically the same as *weak exogeneity* of X.

$$\lambda(t; x) = \lim_{dt \to 0} \Pr(t \le Y < t + dt | Y \ge t, x) / dt$$

for the cause-specific case we simply add an indicator for the cause, say $k \in \{1, 2, \ldots, M\}$:

$$\lambda_k(t; x) = \lim_{dt \to 0} \Pr(t \le Y < t + dt, K = k | Y \ge t, x) / dt. \qquad (8.32)$$

From the law of total probability one has immediately $\lambda(t; x) = \sum_{k=1}^{M} \lambda_k(t; x)$. Accordingly you get

$$S_k(t|x) = \exp\{-\Lambda_k(t; x)\}, \quad \Lambda_k(t; x) = \int_0^t \lambda_k(s; x) ds \qquad (8.33)$$

from which we can conclude $S(t|x) = \prod_{k=1}^{M} S_k(t|x)$. Analogously, the cause-specific density is

$$f_k(t|x) = \lim_{dt \to 0} \Pr(t \le Y < t + dt, K = k|x) / dt = \lambda_k(t; x) S(t|x) \qquad (8.34)$$

with $f(t|x) = \sum_{k=1}^{M} f_k(t|x)$. Similarly we can proceed for the case when time is discrete. Consequently, with the density at hand, all parameter specified in this model can be estimated by maximum (log-)likelihood, no matter whether you directly start with the specification of the density or with modelling the hazard or the cumulative incidence function. And again, in case of right censoring you include for completed observations the density, and for censored observations only the survival function. For left-truncation you can again derive the density conditional on being not truncated like we did before.

Typically used names for this model are *multiple exit* or *multivariate* duration models. But often one speaks of *competing risks models* because the different causes of failure are competing for being the first in occurring. In case we are only interested in one of them, a natural approach would be to classify all the others as censored observations. This decision certainly depends very much on the context, i.e. whether one is interested in the over-all or just one or two cause-specific exit rates. The way of modelling the overall and/or the cause-specific hazards can be crucial. For example, understanding the duration effects of a therapy on different subgroups, interventions can be targeted for those who most likely benefit at a reasonable expense. A most obvious approach is to apply (M)PH models to the cause-specific hazards.[17] If using the Cox (1972) PH specification for each cause-specific hazard function, then the overall partial likelihood is just the product of the M partial likelihoods one would obtain by treating all other causes of failure alike censored cases. The extension to mixed proportional hazards, i.e. including unobserved individual (time invariant) heterogeneity V that may vary over individuals and/or cases, works as before. But it can easily render the estimation problem infeasible when the assumed dependence structure among the V_{ik} gets complex. The extensions to more complex dependence structures or to more flexible functional forms is generating a still-growing literature on competing risks models, their modelling, estimation and implementation.

---

[17] An also quite popular approach is to model explicitly the cumulative incidence function; see Fine and Gray (1999).

In what follows we only concentrate on the problem of identifying the treatment effect in a bivariate ($M = 2$) competing risks model. We consider the population being in the initial status, e.g. unemployment, and are interested in measuring the effect of a treatment on the exit rate, e.g. the duration to find a job. The complication is that those people leaving the initial status are no longer eligible for treatment. In other words, there are four observed situations thinkable: you never get treated and you never find a job; you get treated but you do not find a job; you find a job after treatment; you find a job before a treatment has taken place. For each you observe the duration Y of 'staying in the initial state', and D 'waiting in the initial state for treatment'.

So we denote by D the *treatment time* which typically refers to the point in time the treatment is initiated. Like in the previous chapters we are interested in Y^d, i.e. the potential duration to change the state (e.g. find a job) given a certain $d \geq 0$. As usual, for the observed duration we have $Y = Y^D$. What we can identify from a reasonable large data set without further specifying a model are the probabilities

$$\Pr(Y > y, D > d, Y > D) = \Pr(Y > y, D > d | Y > D) \cdot \Pr(Y > D) \text{ and}$$
$$\Pr(Y > y, Y < D) = \Pr(Y > y | Y < D) \cdot \Pr(Y < D).$$

In our example $\Pr(Y < D) = 1 - \Pr(Y > D)$ just indicates the proportion of people who found a job before starting with a training programme, and $\Pr(Y > y | Y < D)$ the cumulative distribution function within this group. Now, if the treatment effect can be revealed from these probabilities, then one says it is identifiable. Similarly to the previous chapters, the causal model is given by the pair ($\{Y^d; d \geq 0\}, D$). The hazard for the potential outcomes is defined the same way as we defined hazard functions before, namely by

$$\lambda_{Y^d}(t) = \lim_{dt \to 0} \Pr\left(t \leq Y^d < t + dt | Y^d \geq t\right) / dt, \qquad (8.35)$$

with its integral $\Lambda_{Y^d}(t) = \int_0^t \lambda_{Y^d}(y)dy$.

Abbring and van den Berg (2003b) showed that, unfortunately, to each causal model specification exists an observationally equivalent specification, say ($\{\tilde{Y}^d; d \geq 0\}, \tilde{D}$), that satisfies randomised assignment, i.e. $\{\tilde{Y}^d; d \geq 0\} \perp\!\!\!\perp \tilde{D}$, and *no anticipation*. In other words, the two probabilities $\Pr(Y > y, D > d, Y > D), \Pr(Y > y, Y < D)$ could be produced equally well from models with and without a treatment effect. Consequently, without a structural model and a clear rule of *no anticipation*, one cannot detect a treatment effect from observational data. In fact, in order to be able to identify a treatment effect under plausible assumptions, we need to have some observable variation over individuals or strata. This can either be multiple spells or observable characteristics X.

Clearly, after all we have seen above, the possibly most appealing structure seems to be the mixed proportional hazard with unobserved heterogeneity V and either multiple spells or observable covariates X. We proceed as we did in the former chapters, i.e. start without observable characteristics X. We assume to have observed for each individual or strata at least two spells, say $(Y_1, D_1), (Y_2, D_2)$, and for the ease of notation only use these two. While the unobserved heterogeneity is allowed to change over time but must be unique for an individual or strata (therefore indexed below by Y), the treatment effect can be different for the different spells. A useful model is then given by

$$\lambda_{Y_k}(t; D_k, V) = \begin{cases} \lambda_{0,Y_k}(t)V_Y(t) & \text{if } t \le D_k \\ \lambda_{0,Y_k}(t)\alpha_k(t, D_k)V_Y(t) & \text{if } t > D_k \end{cases} \quad k = 1, 2, \quad (8.36)$$

where the $\lambda_{0,Y_k}(\cdot)$, $V_Y(\cdot)$ are integrable on bounded intervals. For identification one has to either normalise the baseline hazards or V_Y; for convenience (but without loss of generalisation) let us set $\lambda_{0,Y_1} = 1$. Note that the model is restrictive for the treatment effects α_k in the sense that it must not depend on individual characteristics except those captured by D_k.

Then, the identification strategy is very similar to all what we have seen in former chapters; in particular, we need a kind of conditional independence assumption:

Assumption CIA-PH1 (*conditional independence assumption for competing risks models with multiple spells*): $Y_1 \perp\!\!\!\perp (Y_2, D_2)|(D_1, V_Y)$ and $Y_2 \perp\!\!\!\perp (Y_1, D_1)|(D_2, V_Y)$.

This looks weaker than what we had so far as we no longer ask for something like $Y_k \perp\!\!\!\perp D_k$ or $Y_k \perp\!\!\!\perp D_k|V_Y$. The latter, however, is already quite a weak requirement as it does not specify what we can put in V_Y and what not. Assumption CIA-PH1 seems to be even weaker, but again we will only be able to identify treatment effects if each individual or strata was exposed twice to the same experiment. This is a situation we never considered in earlier chapters.

Now define N_d as being our treatment indicator, i.e. $N_d(y) = 0$ if $y < d$ and $= 1$ else, and $\{N_d(t) : 0 \le t \le Y\}$ being our treatment history until Y. Then it can be shown that for $Y_{(1)} := \min\{Y_1, Y_2\}$ in model (8.36) it holds

$$\Pr\left(Y_1 = Y_{(1)} \Big| Y_{(1)}, V_Y, \{N_{d_1}(t) : 0 \le t \le Y_{(1)}\}, \{N_{d_2}(t) : 0 \le t \le Y_{(0)}\}\right)$$

$$= \begin{cases} \left[1 + \lambda_{0,Y_2}(Y_{(1)})\right]^{-1} & \text{if } D_1, D_2 > Y_{(1)} \\ \left[1 + \lambda_{0,Y_2}(Y_{(1)})/\alpha_1(Y_{(1)}, D_1)\right]^{-1} & \text{if } D_1 < Y_{(1)} < D_2 \\ \left[1 + \lambda_{0,Y_2}(Y_{(1)})\alpha_2(Y_{(1)}, D_2)\right]^{-1} & \text{if } D_1 > Y_{(1)} > D_2 \\ \left[1 + \lambda_{0,Y_2}(Y_{(1)})\alpha_2(Y_{(1)}, D_2)/\alpha_1(Y_{(1)}, D_1)\right]^{-1} & \text{if } D_1, D_2 < Y_{(1)} \end{cases}$$

$$= \Pr\left(Y_1 = Y_{(1)} \Big| Y_{(1)}, \{N_{d_1}(t) : 0 \le t \le Y_{(1)}\}, \{N_{d_2}(t) : 0 \le t \le Y_{(0)}\}\right)$$

recalling that we set $\lambda_{0,Y_1} = 1$. The last equation is obvious as none of the expressions depends on V_Y. This is extremely helpful because the last expression can be directly estimated from the data by the observed proportions with $Y_1 = Y_{(1)}$ in the sub-samples defined by the conditioning set. Then, $\lambda_{0,Y_2}(\cdot)$ can be obtained for all observed $y_{(1)}$ in the first group, afterwards $\alpha_1(\cdot)$ for all $(y_{(1)}, d_1)$ observed in the second group, etc. Actually, having four equations for only three functions, they might even be overidentified.[18] This gives the estimator; for further inference one may use for example wild bootstrap in order to get variance estimates and confidence intervals.

In practice one is often interested in studying the hazard function of treatment(s) D. At the same time, when thinking of models with common factors in the unobservable

---

[18] We say 'might be' because this also depends on the availability of observations in each group and further specification of the unknown functions.

parts (V_Y, V_D) one typically drops the time dependence of V. This leads us to the next model:

Take the hazard from (8.36) but replace $V_Y(t)$ by V_Y, and add

$$\lambda_{D_k}(t; V_D) = \lambda_{0,D_k}(t)V_D, \quad k = 1, 2. \tag{8.37}$$

One assumes that $(V_D, V_Y) \in \mathbb{R}_+^2$ have finite expectations but are not $\equiv 0$, come from a joint (often specified up to some parameter) distribution G, further $\Lambda_{0,D_k} = \int_0^t \lambda_{0,D_k}(s)ds < \infty$ and $\Lambda_{0,Y_k} = \int_0^t \lambda_{0,Y_k}(s)ds < \infty$ for all $t \in \mathbb{R}_+$. Suppressing index k, treatment effect $\alpha : \mathbb{R}_+^2 \to (0, \infty)$ is such that $\mathcal{A}(t, d) = \int_d^t \alpha(s, d)ds < \infty$ and $\tilde{\mathcal{A}}(t, d) = \int_d^t \lambda_{0,Y}(s)\alpha(s, d)ds < \infty$ exist and are continuous on $\{(t, d) \in \mathbb{R}_+^2 : t > d\}$. Again, to have full identification and not just up to a multiplicative scale, you also need to normalise some of the functions; e.g. you may say set $\Lambda_{0,D}(t_0) = \Lambda_{0,Y}(t_0) = 1$ for a given t_0, instead of setting $\lambda_{0,Y_1} = 1$.[19] It is clear that adding (8.37) to (8.36) will simplify rather than complicate the identification of the treatment effect. The estimation strategy for (8.36) does not change. Depending on the estimation procedure one might or not modify the conditional independence assumption as follows:

Assumption CIA-PH2 (*conditional independence assumption for competing risks models with multiple spells*): $(Y_1, D_1) \perp\!\!\!\perp (Y_2, D_2)|V$.

In the so far considered model we allowed the treatment effect to be a function of time that may vary with (D_k). Alternatively, one could allow the treatment to depend on some unobserved heterogeneity but not on D_k (apart from the fact that treatment only occurs if the time spent in the initial status has exceeded D_k) for example of the form

$$\lambda_{Y_k}(t; D_k, V) = \begin{cases} \lambda_{0,Y_k}(t)V_Y & \text{if } t \le D_k \\ \lambda_{0,\Delta_k}(t)V_\Delta & \text{if } t > D_k \end{cases} \quad k = 1, 2 \tag{8.38}$$

with normalisation $\Lambda_{0,\Delta_k}(t_0) = 1$ for an a priori fixed $t_0 \in (0, \infty)$, and $V = (V_Y, V_D, V_\Delta)$ has joint distribution $\tilde{G}$. Then the treatment effects α_k are obtained from the fraction $\{\lambda_{0,Y_k}(t)V_\Delta\}/\{\lambda_{0,Y_k}(t)V_Y\}$.

It can be shown that under Assumption CIA-PH2 all functions in either model, (8.37) or (8.38), can be identified in the sense that they can be expressed in terms of the following four probabilities:

$$\Pr(Y_1 > y_1, Y_2 > y_2, D_1 > d_1, D_2 > d_2, Y_1 > D_1, Y_2 > D_2)$$
$$\Pr(Y_1 > y_1, Y_2 > y_2, D_2 > d_2, Y_1 < D_1, Y_2 > D_2)$$
$$\Pr(Y_1 > y_1, Y_2 > y_2, D_1 > d_1, Y_1 > D_1, Y_2 < D_2)$$
$$\Pr(Y_1 > y_1, Y_2 > y_2, Y_1 < D_1, Y_2 < D_2).$$

Note that these are equivalent to the following four expressions (in the same order)

$$\Pr(Y_1 > y_1, Y_2 > y_2, D_1 > d_1, D_2 > d_2|Y_1 > D_1, Y_2 > D_2) \cdot \Pr(Y_1 > D_1, Y_2 > D_2)$$
$$\Pr(Y_1 > y_1, Y_2 > y_2, D_2 > d_2|Y_1 < D_1, Y_2 > D_2) \cdot \Pr(Y_1 < D_1, Y_2 > D_2)$$

---

[19] So far we had to restrict the hazard over the entire timescale because heterogeneity V was allowed to vary over time.

$$\Pr(Y_1 > y_1, Y_2 > y_2, D_1 > d_1 | Y_1 > D_1, Y_2 < D_2) \cdot \Pr(Y_1 > D_1, Y_2 < D_2)$$
$$\Pr(Y_1 > y_1, Y_2 > y_2 | Y_1 < D_1, Y_2 < D_2) \cdot \Pr(Y_1 < D_1, Y_2 < D_2)$$

which can all be estimated from a sufficiently rich data set. In fact, we have simply separated the sample into the four groups $(Y_1 > D_1, Y_2 > D_2)$, $(Y_1 < D_1, Y_2 > D_2)$, $(Y_1 > D_1, Y_2 < D_2)$, $(Y_1 < D_1, Y_2 < D_2)$ whose proportions are the probabilities in the second column. In the first column we have probabilities that also correspond to directly observable proportions inside each corresponding group. We said 'from a sufficiently rich data set' because it requires that for all values of possible combinations of (y_1, y_2, d_1, d_2) we are provided with sufficiently many observations (or you merge them in appropriate intervals) to obtain reliable estimates of these probabilities (i.e. proportions). To avoid this problem one would typically specify parametric functions for the baseline hazards and distribution G, and $\tilde{G}$ respectively, in order to apply maximum likelihood estimation.

In Abbring and van den Berg (2003c) are given some indications on how this could be estimated non-parametrically. Else you simply take parametrically specified hazard models and apply maximum likelihood estimation. The same can basically be said about the next approaches.

Quite often we do not have multiple spells for most of the individuals or strata but mostly single spells. In order to simplify presentation, imagine we use only one spell per individual (or strata) from now on. Then we need to observe and explore some of the heterogeneity; say we observe characteristics X. Obviously, to include them in the above models gives the original mixed proportional hazard model with observable (X) and non-observable (V) covariates. The potential outcomes would be durations $Y^{x,v,d}$ and $D^{x,v}$ with $Y = Y^{X,V,D}$, $Y^d = Y^{X,V,d}$, and $D = D^{X,V}$. When using those characteristics as control variables one arrives to a kind of conditional independence assumption that is much closer to what we originally called the CIA. Specifically,

Assumption CIA-PH3 (*conditional independence assumption for competing risks with single spells*): $Y^{x,v,d} \perp\!\!\!\perp D^{x,v}$, *and the distribution of* $(Y^{x,v,D^{x,v}} \perp\!\!\!\perp D^{x,v})$ *is absolutely continuous on* $\mathbb{R}_+^2$ *for all* (x, v) *in* $supp(X, V)$.

On the one hand, this seems to be more general than all CIA versions we have seen so far, as it allows to condition on unobservables V. On the other hand, recall that for the MPH one typically needs to assume independence between X and V; something that was not required for matching, propensity score weighting, etc. What also looks new is the second part of the assumption. It is needed to allow for remaining variation, or say, randomness for treatment and outcome: while (X, V) include all joint determinants of outcomes and assignment, like information that triggers relevant behaviour responses, they fully determine neither Y nor D.

An easy way to technically specify the *no anticipation* property we need in this context, is to do it via the integral of the hazard:

Assumption NA (*no anticipation*): *For all* $d_1, d_2 \in [0, \infty]$ *we have* $\Lambda_{Y^{x,v,d_1}}(t) = \Lambda_{Y^{x,v,d_2}}(t)$ *for all* $t \leq \min\{d_1, d_2\}$ *and all* (x, v) *in* $supp(X, V)$.

Again we give two examples of MPH competing risks models that allow for the identification of the treatment effect; one allowing the treatment effect to be a function of time that may depend on (X, D), and one allowing it to depend on (X, V) but not on D. The first model has a standard mixed proportional hazard rate for D, but a two-case one for Y:

$$\lambda_D(t; X, V) = \lambda_{0,D}(t)g_D(X)V_D \tag{8.39}$$

$$\lambda_Y(t; X, V, D) = \begin{cases} \lambda_{0,Y}(t)g_Y(X)V_Y & \text{if } t \le D \\ \lambda_{0,Y}(t)g_Y(X)\alpha(t, D, X)V_Y & \text{if } t > D \end{cases} \tag{8.40}$$

with $V = (V_D, V_Y) \in \mathbb{R}_+^2$, joint distribution G independent of X, finite expectation but not $V \equiv 0$. Functions $g_D, g_Y, \lambda_{0,D}, \lambda_{0,Y} : \mathcal{X} \to (0, \infty)$ are normalised at an a priori fixed x_0, e.g. $g_Y(x_0) = g_D(x_0) = 1$, and $\lambda_{0,Y}, \lambda_{0,D}$, and α fulfil the same regularity conditions as before (given after equation (8.37)). Then it is not hard to see that, given Assumptions CIA-PH3 and NA, conditional on (X, V), the outcome Y and treatment D are only dependent through function $\alpha(\cdot)$. This function can therefore be interpreted as the treatment effect of D on Y. The only additional assumption you need for identifying it is

Assumption SP1 *The systematic parts, namely g_Y, g_D exhibit different variations in x.*[20]

All together, with these assumptions we can identify $\Lambda_{0,D}, \Lambda_{0,Y}, g_D, g_Y, G$ and $\mathcal{A}$ from the probabilities $\Pr(Y > y, D > d, Y > D), \Pr(Y > y, Y < D)$ and therefore from the data. The derivative of $\mathcal{A}$ reveals the treatment effect $\alpha(t, d, x)$.

As before, one might criticise that the treatment effect does not allow for heterogeneity based on unobservables V. One can get this still, but at the price of no heterogeneity over treatment D. This alternative model has a standard mixed proportional hazard rate for D like model (8.39)–(8.40), but like (8.38) a more flexible one for Y, i.e.

$$\lambda_D(t; X, V) = \lambda_{0,D}(t)g_D(X)V_D \tag{8.41}$$

$$\lambda_Y(t; X, V, D) = \begin{cases} \lambda_{0,Y}(t)g_Y(X)V_Y & \text{if } t \le D \\ \lambda_{0,\Delta}(t)g_\Delta(X)V_\Delta & \text{if } t > D \end{cases} \tag{8.42}$$

with $V = (V_D, V_\Delta, V_Y) \in \mathbb{R}_+^3$, $E[V_D V_\Delta] < \infty$ but not $V \equiv 0$, with a joint (typically specified up to some parameter) distribution $\tilde{G}$ independent of X, and else the same regularity conditions and normalisations as for model (8.39)–(8.40), here also applied to $g_\Delta, \lambda_{0,\Delta}$.

Clearly, the treatment effect is now

$$\alpha(t, x, V_Y, V_\Delta) := \frac{\lambda_{0,\Delta}(t)g_\Delta(x)V_\Delta}{\lambda_{0,Y}(t)g_Y(x)V_Y}$$

$$\alpha(t, x) = \int_0^\infty \frac{\lambda_{0,\Delta}(t)g_\Delta(x)u}{\lambda_{0,Y}(t)g_Y(x)v} d\tilde{G}(u, v) \tag{8.43}$$

---

[20] Technically one would say: $\{(g_Y(x), g_D(x)); x \in \mathcal{X}\}$ contains a non-empty open two-dimensional set in $\mathbb{R}^2$.

Assumption SP2 *The image of the systematic part* g_Δ, $\{g_\Delta(x); x \in \mathcal{X}\}$ *contains a non-empty open interval in* $\mathbb{R}$.

It can be shown that Assumptions CIA-PH3, NA, SP1 and SP2 together guarantee the identification of $\Lambda_{0,D}, \Lambda_{0,Y}, \Lambda_{0,\Delta}, g_D, g_Y, g_\Delta, \tilde{G}$ from the probabilities $\Pr(Y > y, D > d, Y > D), \Pr(Y > y, Y < D)$, and therefore the treatment effect (8.43).

While it is true that these are non-parametric identification results – some would speak of semi-parametric ones because we imposed clear separability structures – most of the estimators available in practice are based on parametric specifications of these MPH models. Consequently, once you have specified the hazard functions and G, respectively $\tilde{G}$, you can also write down the explicit likelihood function. Then a (fully) parametric maximum likelihood estimator can be applied with all the standard tools for further inference. The main problems here are typical duration data problems like censoring, truncation, etc. These, however, are not specific to the treatment effect estimation literature but to any duration analysis, and therefore not further treated in this book. For the simpler problems we already indicated how to treat censoring and truncation, recall Section 8.3.1.

Example 8.19 Abbring, van den Berg and van Ours (2005) study the impact of unemployment insurance sanctions on the duration to find a job. In the theoretical part of the article they construct the Bellman equations for the expected present values of income before and after the imposition of a sanction as a result of the corresponding optimal job search intensities s_1 (before), s_2 (when sanction is imposed). Under a set of assumptions on functional forms and agent's rational behaviour they arrive at hazard rates

$$\lambda_{Y_k} = \lambda_{0,Y} s_k \{1 - F(w_k)\}, \qquad k = 1, 2$$

for given reservation wages w_1, w_2. In the empirical study they specify them for a large set of observable covariates x by

$$\lambda_Y = \lambda_{0,Y}(t) \exp\{x'\beta_Y + \alpha \mathbb{1}\{d < t\}\} V_Y$$

i.e. with an exponential systematic part. The difference between the hazards before and after treatment is reduced to just a constant treatment effect for all individuals, treatments and durations. The model is completed by the hazard function for treatment, specified as

$$\lambda_D = \lambda_{0,D}(t) \exp\{x'\beta_D\} V_D.$$

For the baseline hazards $\lambda_{0,Y}(t), \lambda_{0,D}(t)$, are taken piecewise constant specifications with prefixed time intervals, and for G, the distribution of V_Y and V_D, a bivariate discrete distribution with four unrestricted point mass locations. When they estimated their model (no matter whether for the entire sample or separated by sectors), they found a significant positive α throughout, i.e. in all cases the imposition of sanctions increased significantly the re-employment rate.

The research on non- and semi-parametric estimation is still in progress. But even the parametric models are so far not much used in empirical economics; as indicated at the beginning. Actually, most of the empirical studies with competing risks structure can be found in the biometrics and technometrics literature.

8.4   Bibliographic and Computational Notes

8.4.1   Further Reading and Bibliographic Notes

As we could see in Section 8.2.3, estimation of the discrete dynamic potential outcome model is possible by sequential matching or by sequential inverse probability weighting (IPW). Lechner (2008) examines the finite sample properties of sequential matching, whereas IPW weighting estimators are considered in Lechner (2009). These two papers also discuss in detail the finite sample issues that arise in the implementation of the common support restriction. The definition of the common support region has to be adjusted period by period with respect to the conditioning variables. Recall also the comments on the implementation of common support conditions in Chapter 3 in the context of propensity score weighting. Which of these approaches tends to be more reliable in finite samples is still an unresolved question, but the study of Lechner (2004) concludes in favour of matching-based ones.

How does the understanding and identification of causality in the sequential treatment literature relate to causality in time series econometrics? Lechner (2006), for example, relates the above concept (Section 8.2) of causality based on potential outcomes to concepts of causality frequently found in time series econometrics. In the concept of causality advocated by Granger and Sims, a variable D_t is causing Y_{t+1} if the information D_t helps to obtain better predictions of Y_{t+1} given all other information available. Consider the *Granger–Sims non-causality*

$$D_t \text{ does not GS-cause } Y_{t+1} \qquad \text{iff} \qquad Y_{t+1} \perp\!\!\!\perp D_t | Y_t, D_0, Y_0$$

and the *potential outcome non-causality*

$$D_t \text{ does not GS-cause } Y_{t+1} \qquad \text{iff} \qquad F_{Y_{t+1}^{d_t'}}(u) = F_{Y_{t+1}^{d_t'}}(u).$$

Lechner (2006) shows that neither of these two definitions of non-causality implies the other. However, if the W-CIA holds (including the common support assumption) than each of these two definitions of non-causality implies the other. Hence, if we can assume W-CIA, both definitions can be used to test for non-causality, and they can be interpreted in the perspective that seems to be more intuitive.

Turning to Section 8.3, nowadays, the literature on duration analysis is quite abundant. A general, excellent introduction to the analysis of failure time data is given in Kalbfleisch and Prentice (2002) and Crowder (1978), of which the latter puts the main emphasise on multivariate survival analysis and competing risks, i.e. what has been considered here. A detailed overview on duration analysis in economics was given in Lancaster (1990). A more recent review of duration analysis in econometrics can be found in van den Berg (2001).

Competing risks models have been in the focus of biometrical research since many decades, see for example David and Moeschberger (1978). You can find a recent, smooth introduction in Beyersmann and Scheike (2013). Mixture models and Cox regression was applied already very early to competing risks models, see e.g. Larson and Dinse (1985) or Lunn and McNeil (1995). However, as stated, there is still a lot of research going on. A recent contribution to the inclusion of time-varying covariates is e.g. Cortese and Andersen (2010), a recent contribution to semi-parametric estimation is e.g. Hernandez-Quintero, Dupuy and Escarela (2011). Abbring and van den Berg (2003a) study the extension of the hazard function-based duration analysis to the use of instrumental variables. Although they argue that they generally doubt the existence of instruments fulfilling the necessary exogeneity conditions, they provide methods in case an intention to treat is randomised but compliance is incomplete. The identification presented in Abbring and van den Berg (2003b) was essentially based on the results for competing risks models introduced in Abbring and van den Berg (2003c) and Heckman and Honoré (1989).

In this chapter we almost strictly divided the dynamic treatment effect estimation into two sections: one section considered discrete time in which several treatments, different treatment durations, and its timing was analysed regarding its impact on any kind of outcome. Another section considered only durations, namely the impact of the duration until treatment takes place on the duration of leaving an initial state. In the first section (Section 8.2) we have presented matching and propensity score estimators extended for the dynamic case and multiple treatments; in the second section (Section 8.3) we only have worked with tools known from duration analysis. The estimator proposed by Fredriksson and Johansson (2008) uses elements of both approaches. They consider a discrete time framework but are interested in the impact of the timing of treatment on duration, i.e. the estimation problem considered in Section 8.3. However, for this they use (generalised) matching estimators.

8.4.2   Computational Notes

As the methods for analysing dynamic treatment in Section 8.2 are from an estimation perspective basically the same we studied in the former chapters (depending on the available data and assumptions used), we can also refer to the corresponding sections regarding implementation and available software packages. However, explicit implementations of sequential methods (matching or weighting) are so far not available but done by sequential application of the respective estimators.

When searching appropriate packages for Section 8.3, one may concentrate on software available for dynamic treatment with time dimension, i.e. the duration or survival methods. For example, in Stata the main command is stteffects; it allows for parametric model specifications with an outcome model that is Weibull or a weighted mean, potentially with Weibull censoring, and a logit treatment model. The treatment effects can be estimated using regression adjustment (referring to correction by confounders), inverse-probability weights (i.e. the propensity weighting), inverse-probability-weighted regression adjustment (related to the ideas of double robust estimation), and weighted regression adjustment. However, the estimators implemented in stteffects do not adjust for left-truncation, so it cannot be used for delayed-entry data; it can neither be used with time-varying covariates or multiple-record data. For further assumptions see also its help file and description. Similarly, a rapidly increasing number of packages and commands is available in **R**; see e.g. the survival package, the OIsurv and the KMsurv package.

As we have seen, also in duration analysis the causal inference basically resorts to existing methods, in this case developed for competing risks and multi-state models. We therefore refer mainly to the paper of de Wreede, Fiocco and Putter (2011) and the book of Beyersmann, Allignol and Schumacher (2012), and the tutorial of the **R** package mstate by Putter, Fiocco and Geskus (2006) and Putter (2014); all publications explicitly dedicated to the estimation of those type of models with the statistics software **R**.

It should be mentioned, however, that this is presently a very dynamic research area on which every year appear several new estimation methods, programme codes and packages, so that it is hardly possible to give a comprehensive review at this stage.

8.5   Exercises

1. Give examples in practice where we cannot estimate the treatment effects by any method of the previous chapters.

2. Give the explicit formula of (8.2) for $\tau''' = 2, \delta = 3$ in the binary treatment case and discuss examples.

3. Give examples of identification problems with the SCIA in Subsection 8.2.1 (i.e. potential violations or when and why it could hold).

4. Show that the WDCIA is not sufficient to predict $E[Y_T^{00}|D_2 = 11]$.[21] What can be followed for DATET? Give additional assumptions that would allow it to be identified.

5. Show that from WDCIA it follows that (8.16) and (8.17).

6. Show for the discrete case that the probability $\Pr(T = t)$ and the cumulative distribution function $F(t)$ can be expressed in terms of the hazard rate $\lambda(t)$.

7. Recall Example 8.13 and show that for the given hazard rate, $log(t)$ has a logistic distribution. Calculate also the mean.

8. Discuss how you could estimate non-parametrically the probabilities given below model (8.38).

9. Several of the estimation procedures proposed or indicated here were based on sequential (or multi-step) estimation. Discuss how to apply resampling methods in order to estimate the final (over all steps) variance of the treatment effect estimator.

---

[21] Hint: Show that it cannot be written in terms of $E[Y_T^{11}|\cdot,D_2 = 11]$, which would correspond to the observable outcome $E[Y_T|\cdot,D_2 = 11]$.

Bibliography

Abadie, A. (2005): 'Semiparametric Difference-in-Differences Estimators', *The Review of Economic Studies*, 72, 1–19.

Abadie, A., J. Angrist and G. Imbens (2002): 'Instrumental Variables Estimates of the Effect of Subsidized Training on the Quantiles of Trainee Earnings', *Econometrica*, 70, 91–117.

Abadie, A. and G. Imbens (2006): 'Large Sample Properties of Matching Estimators for Average Treatment Effects', *Econometrica*, 74, 235–267.

  (2008): 'On the Failure of the Bootstrap for Matching Estimators', *Econometrica*, 76, 1537–1557.

  (2011): 'Bias-Corrected Matching Estimators for Average Treatment Effects', *Journal of Business and Economic Statistics*, 29, 1–11.

  (2016): 'Matching on the Estimated Propensity Score', *Econometrica*, 84, 781–807.

Abbring, J. and J. Heckman (2007): 'Econometric Evaluation of Social Programs Part III: Distributional Treatment Effects, Dynamic Treatment Effects, Dynamic Discrete Choice, and General Equilibrium Policy Evaluation', in *Handbook of Econometrics*, ed. by J. Heckman and E. Leamer, pp. 5145–5303. Amsterdam and Oxford: North-Holland.

Abbring, J. and G. van den Berg (2003a): 'The Identifiability of the Mixed Proportional Hazards Competing Risks Model', *Journal of the Royal Statistical Society (B)*, 65, 701–710.

  (2003b): 'The Nonparametric Identification of Treatment Effects in Duration Models', *Econometrica*, 71, 1491–1517.

  (2003c): 'Social Experiments and Instrumental Variables with Duration Outcomes', *Journal of the Royal Statistical Society (B)*, 65, 701–710.

  (2007): 'The Unobserved Heterogeneity Distribution in Duration Analysis', *Biometrika*, 94, 87–99.

Abbring, J., G. van den Berg and J. van Ours (2005): 'The Effect of Unemployment Insurance Sanctions on the Transition Rate from Unemployment to Employment', *The Economic Journal*, 115, 602–630.

Aitchison, J. and C. Aitken (1976): 'Multivariate Binary Discrimination by the Kernel Method', *Biometrika*, 63, 413–420.

Alatas, V., A. Banerjee, R. Hanna, B. Olken, R. Purnamasari and M. Wai-poi (2013): 'Self Targeting: Evidence from a Field Experiment in Indonesia', *MIT Working Paper*.

Albert, J. (2012): 'Distribution-Free Mediation Analysis for Nonlinear Models with Confounding', *Epidemiology*, 23, 879–888.

Altonji, J. (1995): 'The Effects of High School Curriculum on Education and Labor Market Outcomes', *Journal of Human Resources*, 30, 409–438.

Anderson, M., C. Dobkin and T. Gross (2012): 'The Effect of Health Insurance Coverage on the Use of Medical Services', *American Economic Journal: Economic Policy*, 4(1), 1–27.

Angrist, J. (1998): 'Estimating Labour Market Impact of Voluntary Military Service using Social Security Data', *Econometrica*, 66, 249–288.

Angrist, J., G. Imbens and D. Rubin (1996): 'Identification of Causal Effects using Instrumental Variables', *Journal of American Statistical Association*, 91, 444–472 (with discussion).

Angrist, J. and A. Krueger (1991): 'Does Compulsory School Attendance Affect Schooling and Earnings?', *Quarterly Journal of Economics*, 106, 979–1014.

    (1999): 'Empirical Strategies in Labor Economics', in *Handbook of Labor Economics*, ed. by O. Ashenfelter and D. Card, pp. 1277–1366. Amsterdam: North-Holland.

Angrist, J. and V. Lavy (1999): 'Using Maimonides Rule to Estimate the Effect of Class Size on Scholastic Achievement', *Quarterly Journal of Economics*, 114, 533–575.

Angrist, J. & Pischke (2008): Mostly Harmless Econometrics. An empiricist's companion. Princeton University Press.

Arias, O. and M. Khamis (2008): 'Comparative Advantage, Segmentation and Informal Earnings: A Marginal Treatment Effects Approach', IZA discussion paper, 3916.

Arpino, B. and A. Aassve (2013): 'Estimation of Causal Effects of Fertility on Economic Wellbeing: Evidence from Rural Vietnam', *Empirical Economics*, 44, 355–385.

Ashenfelter, O. (1978): 'Estimating the Effect of Training Programmes on Earnings', *Review of Economics and Statistics*, 6, 47–57.

Athey, S. and G. Imbens (2006): 'Identification and Inference in Nonlinear Difference-in-Differences Models', *Econometrica*, 74, 431–497.

Bahadur, R. (1966): 'A Note on Quantiles in Large Samples', *Annals of Mathematical Statistics*, 37, 577–580.

Bailey, R. (2008): *Design of Comparative Experiments*. Cambridge: Cambridge University Press.

Baron, R. and D. Kenny (1986): 'The Moderator-Mediator Variable Distinction in Social Psychological Research: Conceptual, Strategic, and Statistical Considerations', *Journal of Personality and Social Psychology*, 6, 1173–1182.

Barrett, G. and S. Donald (2009): 'Statistical Inference with Generalized Gini Indices of Inequality and Poverty', *Journal of Business & Economic Statistics*, 27, 1–17.

Barrios, T. (2013): 'Optimal Stratification in Randomized Experiments', discussion paper, Harvard University OpenScholar.

Becker, S. and A. Ichino (2002): 'Estimation of Average Treatment Effects Based on Propensity Scores', *The Stata Journal*, 2, 358–377.

Beegle, K., R. Dehejia and R. Gatti (2006): 'Child Labor and Agricultural Shocks', *Journal of Development Economics*, 81, 80–96.

Begun, J., W. Hall, W. Huang and J. Wellner (1983): 'Information and Asymptotic Efficiency in Parametric-Nonparametric Models', *Annals of Statistics*, 11, 432–452.

Belloni, A., V. Chernozhukov, I. Fernández-Val and C. Hansen (2017): 'Program Evaluation and Causal Inference with High-Dimensional Data', *Econometrica*, 85, 233–298.

Belloni, A., V. Chernozhukov and C. Hansen (2014): 'Inference on Treatment Effects after Selection among High-Dimensional Controls', *Review of Economic Studies*, 81, 608–650.

Benini, B., S. Sperlich and R. Theler (2016): 'Varying Coefficient Models Revisited: An Econometric View', in *Proceedings of the Second Conference of the International Society for Nonparametric Statistics*. New York, NY: Springer.

Benini, G. and S. Sperlich (2017): 'Modeling Heterogeneity by Structural Varying Coefficients Models', Working paper.

Bertrand, M., E. Duflo and S. Mullainathan (2004): 'How Much Should We Trust Differences-in-Differences Estimates?', *Quarterly Journal of Economics*, 119, 249–275.

Beyersmann, J., A. Allignol and M. Schumacher (2012): *Competing Risks and Multistate Models with R*. New York, NY: Springer.

Beyersmann, J. and T. Scheike (2013): 'Classical Regression Models for Competing Risks', in *Handbook of Survival Analysis*, pp. 157–177. CRC Press Taylor & Francis Group.

Bhatt, R. and C. Koedel (2010): 'A Non-Experimental Evaluation of Curricular Effectiveness in Math', mimeo.

Bickel, P., C. Klaassen, Y. Ritov and J. Wellner (1993): *Efficient and Adaptive Estimation for Semiparametric Models*. Baltimore, MD: John Hopkins University Press.

Black, D., J. Galdo and J. Smith (2005): 'Evaluating the Regression Discontinuity Design using Experimental Data', *mimeo*, Ann Arbor, MI: University of Michigan.

Black, D. and J. Smith (2004): 'How Robust is the Evidence on the Effects of College Quality? Evidence from Matching', *Journal of Econometrics*, 121, 99–124.

Black, S. (1999): 'Do "Better" Schools Matter? Parental Valuation of Elementary Education', *Quarterly Journal of Economics*, 114, 577–599.

Blundell, R. and M. C. Dias (2009): 'Alternative Approaches to Evaluation in Empirical Microeconomics', *Journal of Human Resources*, 44, 565–640.

Blundell, R. and J. Powell (2003): 'Endogeneity in Nonparametric and Semiparametric Regression Models', in *Advances in Economics and Econometrics*, ed. by L. H. M. Dewatripont and S. Turnovsky, pp. 312–357. Cambridge: Cambridge University Press.

Bonhomme, S. and U. Sauder (2011): 'Recovering Distributions in Difference-in-Differences Models: A Comparison of Selective and Comprehensive Schooling', *The Review of Economics and Statistics*, 93, 479–494.

Brookhart, M., S. Schneeweiss, K. Rothman, R. Glynn, J. Avorn and T. Stürmer (2006): 'Variable Selection for Propensity Score Models', *American Journal of Epidemiology*, 163, 1149–1156.

Brügger, B., R. Lalive and J. Zweimüller (2008): 'Does Culture Affect Unemployment? Evidence from the Barriere des Roestis', mimeo, Zürich: University of Zürich.

Bruhn, M. and D. McKenzie (2009): 'In Pursuit of Balance: Randomization in Practice in Development Field Experiments', Policy Research Paper 4752, World Bank.

Buddelmeyer, H. and E. Skoufias (2003): 'An evaluation of the Performance of Regression Discontinuity Design on PROGRESA', IZA discussion paper, 827.

Busso, M., J. DiNardo and J. McCrary (2009): 'Finite Sample Properties of Semiparametric Estimators of Average Treatment Effects', Unpublished manuscript, University of Michigan and University of Californa-Berkeley.

(2014): 'New Evidence on the Finite Sample Properties of Propensity Score Matching and Reweighting Estimators', *Review of Economics and Statistics*, 58, 347–368.

Cox, D. (1972): 'Regression Models and Life-Tables', *Journal of the Royal Statistical Society (B)*, 34, 187–220.

Cameron, C. and P. Trivedi (2005): *Microeconometrics: Methods and Applications*. Cambridge: Cambridge University Press.

Card, D., J. Kluve and A. Weber (2010): 'Active Labour Market Policy Evaluations: A Meta-Analysis', *Economic Journal*, 120(548), F452–F477.

Card, D. and A. Krueger (1994): 'Minimum Wages and Employment: A Case Study of the Fast-Food Industry in New Jersey and Pennsylvania', *American Economic Review*, 84, 772–793.

Card, D., D. Lee, Z. Pei and A. Weber (2015): 'Inference on Causal Effects in a Generalized Regression Kink Design', IZA discussion paper No 8757.

Carpenter, J., H. Goldstein and J. Rasbash (2003): 'A novel boostrap procedure for assessing the relationship between class size and achievement', *Applied Statistics*, 52, 431–443.

Carroll, R., D. Ruppert and A. Welsh (1998): 'Local Estimating Equations', *Journal of American Statistical Association*, 93, 214–227.

Cattaneo, M. (2010): 'Efficient Semiparametric Estimation of Multi-Valued Treatment Effects under Ignorability', *Journal of Econometrics*, 155, 138–154.

Cattaneo, M., D. Drucker and A. Holland (2013): 'Estimation of Multivalued Treatment Effects under Conditional Independence', *The Stata Journal*, 13, 407–450.

Cerulli, G. (2012): 'treatrew: A User-Written STATA Routine for Estimating Average Treatment Effects by Reweighting on Propensity Score', discussion paper, National Research Council of Italy, Institute for Economic Research on Firms and Growth.

——— (2014): 'ivtreatreg: A Command for Fitting Binary Treatment Models with Heterogeneous Response to Treatment and Unobservable Selection', *The Stata Journal*, 14, 453–480.

Chamberlain, G. (1994): 'Quantile Regression, Censoring and the Structure of Wages', in *Advances in Econometrics*, ed. by C. Sims. Amsterdam: Elsevier.

Chan, K., S. Yam and Z. Zhang (2016): 'Globally Efficient Nonparametric Inference of Average Treatment Effects by Empirical Balancing Calibration Weighting', *Journal of the Royal Statistical Society (B)*, 78, 673–700.

Chaudhuri, P. (1991): 'Global Nonparametric Estimation of Conditional Quantile Functions and their Derivatives', *Journal of Multivariate Analysis*, 39, 246–269.

Chay, K., P. McEwan and M. Urquiola (2005): 'The Central Role of Noise in Evaluating Interventions that Use Test Scores to Rank Schools', *American Economic Review*, pp. 1237–1258.

Chen, X., O. Linton and I. van Keilegom (2003): 'Estimation of Semiparametric Models when the Criterion Function is Not Smooth', *Econometrica*, 71, 1591–1608.

Chernozhukov, V., I. Fernandez-Val and A. Galichon (2007): 'Quantile and Probability Curves Without Crossing', MIT working paper.

Chernozhukov, V., I. Fernández-Val and B. Melly (2013): 'Inference on Counterfactual Distributions', *Econometrica*, 81, 2205–2268.

Chernozhukov, V. and C. Hansen (2005): 'An IV Model of Quantile Treatment Effects', *Econometrica*, 73, 245–261.

——— (2006): 'Instrumental Quantile Regression Inference for Structural and Treatment Effect models', *Journal of Econometrics*, 132, 491–525.

Chernozhukov, V., G. Imbens and W. Newey (2007): 'Instrumental Variable Estimation of Nonseparable Models', *Journal of Econometrics*, 139, 4–14.

Chesher, A. (2003): 'Identification in Nonseparable Models', *Econometrica*, 71, 1405–1441.

——— (2005): 'Nonparametric Identification under Discrete Variation', *Econometrica*, 73, 1525–1550.

——— (2007): 'Identification of Nonadditive Structural Functions', in *Advances in Economics and Econometrics*, ed. by R. Blundell, W. Newey and T. Persson, pp. 1–16. Cambridge: Cambridge University Press.

——— (2010): 'Instrumental Variable Models for Discrete Outcomes', *Econometrica*, 78, 575–601.

Claeskens, G., T. Krivobokova and J. Opsomer (1998): 'Asymptotic Properties of Penalized Spline Estimators', *Biometrika*, 96, 529–544.

——— (2009): 'Asymptotic Properties of Penalized Spline Estimators', *Biometrika*, 96, 529–544.

Cleveland, W., E. Grosse and W. Shyu (1991): 'Local Regression Models', in *Statistical Models in S*, ed. by J. Chambers and T. Hastie, pp. 309–376. Pacific Grove: Wadsworth & Brooks.

Collier, P. and A. Höffler (2002): 'On the Incidence of Civil War in Africa', *Journal of Conflict Resolution*, 46, 13–28.

Cortese, G. and P. Andersen (2010): 'Competing Risks and Time-Dependent Covariates', *Biometrical Journal*, 52, 138–158.

Cox, D. (1958): *Planning of Experiments*. New York: Wiley.

Croissant, Y. and G. Millo (2008): 'Panel Data Econometrics in R: The plm Package', *Journal of Statistical Software*, 27(2).

Crowder, M. (1978): *Multivariate Survival Analysis and Competing Risks*. CRC Press Taylor & Francis Group.

Crump, R., J. Hotz, G. Imbens and O. Mitnik (2009): 'Dealing with Limited Overlap in Estimation of Average Treatment Effects', *Biometrika*, 96, 187–199.

Curie, I. and M. Durban (2002): 'Flexible Smoothing with P-Splines: A Unified Approach', *Statistical Science*, 2, 333–349.

Dai, J., S. Sperlich and W. Zucchini (2016): 'A Simple Method for Predicting Distributions by Means of Covariates with Examples from Welfare and Health Economics', *Swiss Journal of Economics and Statistics*, 152, 49–80.

Darolles, S., Y. Fan, J. Florens and E. Renault (2011): 'Nonparametric Instrumental Regression', *Econometrica*, 79:5, 1541–1565.

Daubechies, I. (1992): *Ten Lectures on Wavelets*. Philadelphia, PA: SIAM.

David, H. and M. Moeschberger (1978): *The Theory of Competing Risks, Griffins Statistical Monograph No. 39*. New York, NY: Macmillan.

de Wreede, L., M. Fiocco and H. Putter (2011): 'mstate: An R Package for the Analysis of Competing Risks and Multi-State Models', *Journal of Statistical Software*, 38, 1–30.

Dette, H., A. Munk and T. Wagner (1998): 'Estimating the Variance in Nonparametric Regression – What is a Reasonable Choice?', *Journal of the Royal Statistical Society, B*, 60, 751–764.

Dette, H., N. Neumeyer and K. Pilz (2006): 'A Simple Nonparametric Estimator of a Strictly Monotone Regression Function', *Bernoulli*, 12, 469–490.

Dette, H. and K. Pilz (2006): 'A Comparative Study of Monotone Nonparametric Kernel Estimates', *Journal of Statistical Computation and Simulation*, 76, 41–56.

Donald, S. and K. Lang (2007): 'Inference with Difference-in-Differences and Other Panel Data', *Review of Economics and Statistics*, 89, 221–233.

Duflo, E. (2001): 'Schooling and Labor Market Consequences of School Construction in Indonesia: Evidence from an Unusual Policy Experiment', *American Economic Review*, 91, 795–813.

Duflo, E., P. Dupas and M. Kremer (2015): 'Education, HIV, and Early Fertility: Experimental Evidence from Kenya', *The American Economic Review*, 105, 2757–2797.

Duflo, E., R. Glennerster and M. Kremer (2008): 'Using Randomization in Development Economics Research: A Toolkit', in *Handbook of Development Economics*, ed. by T. Schultz and J. Strauss, pp. 3895–3962. Amsterdam: North-Holland.

Edin, P.-A., P. Fredriksson and O. Aslund (2003): 'Ethnic Enclaves and the Economic Success of Immigrants – Evidence from a Natural Experiment', *The Quarterly Journal of Economics*, 118, 329–357.

Eilers, P. and B. Marx (1996): 'Flexible Smoothing with B-Splines and Penalties', *Statistical Science*, 11, 89–121.

Engel, E. (1857): 'Die Produktions- und Konsumtionsverhältnisse des Königsreichs Sachsen', *Zeitschrift des statistischen Büros des Königlich Sächsischen Ministeriums des Inneren*, 8, 1–54.

Fan, J. (1993): 'Local Linear Regression Smoothers and their Minimax Efficiency', *Annals of Statistics*, 21, 196–216.

Fan, J. and I. Gijbels (1996): *Local Polynomial Modeling and its Applications*. London: Chapman and Hall.

Field, C. and A. Welsh (2007): 'Bootstrapping Clustered Data', *Journal of the Royal Statistical Society (B)*, 69, 366–390.

Fine, J. and R. Gray (1999): 'A Proportional Hazards Model for the Subdistribution of a Competing Risk', *Journal of the American Statistical Association*, 94:446, 496–509.

Firpo, S. (2007): 'Efficient Semiparametric Estimation of Quantile Treatment Effects', *Econometrica*, 75, 259–276.

Firpo, S., N. Fortin and T. Lemieux (2009): 'Unconditional Quantile Regressions', *Econometrica*, 77, 935–973.

Florens, J. (2003): 'Inverse Problems and Structural Econometrics: The Example of Instrumental Variables', in *Advances in Economics and Econometrics*, ed. by L. H. M. Dewatripont and S. Turnovsky, pp. 284–311. Cambridge: Cambridge University Press.

Florens, J., J. Heckman, C. Meghir and E. Vytlacil (2008): 'Identification of Treatment Effects Using Control Functions in Models With Continuous, Endogenous Treatment and Heterogeneous Effects', *Econometrica*, 76:5, 1191–1206.

Frandsen, B., M. Frölich and B. Melly (2012): 'Quantile Treatment Effects in the Regression Discontinuity Design', *Journal of Econometrics*, 168, 382–395.

Frangakis, C. and D. Rubin (1999): 'Addressing Complications of Intention-to-Treat Analysis in the Combined Presence of All-or-None Treatment-Noncompliance and Subsequent Missing Outcomes', *Biometrika*, 86, 365–379.

(2002): 'Principal Stratification in Causal Inference', *Biometrics*, 58, 21–29.

Fredriksson, P. and P. Johansson (2008): 'Dynamic Treatment Assignment: The Consequences for Evaluations using Observational Data', *Journal of Business and Economics Statistics*, 26, 435–445.

Fredriksson, P. and B. Öckert (2006): 'Is Early Learning Really More Productive? The Effect of School Starting Age on School and Labor Market Performance', *IFAU Discussion Paper 2006:12*.

Frölich, M. (2004): 'Finite Sample Properties of Propensity-Score Matching and Weighting Estimators', *Review of Economics and Statistics*, 86, 77–90.

(2005): 'Matching Estimators and Optimal Bandwidth Choice', *Statistics and Computing*, 15/3, 197–215.

(2007a): 'Nonparametric IV Estimation of Local Average Treatment Effects with Covariates', *Journal of Econometrics*, 139, 35–75.

(2007b): 'Propensity Score Matching without Conditional Independence Assumption – with an Application to the Gender Wage Gap in the UK', *Econometrics Journal*, 10, 359–407.

(2008): 'Statistical Treatment Choice: An Application to Active Labour Market Programmes', *Journal of the American Statistical Association*, 103, 547–558.

Frölich, M. and M. Lechner (2010): 'Exploiting Regional Treatment Intensity for the Evaluation of Labour Market Policies', *Journal of the American Statistical Association*, 105, 1014–1029.

Frölich, M. and B. Melly (2008): 'Quantile Treatment Effects in the Regression Discontinuity Design', *IZA Discussion Paper*, 3638.

(2010): 'Estimation of Quantile Treatment Effects with STATA', *Stata Journal*, 10, 423–457.

(2013): 'Unconditional Quantile Treatment Effects under Endogeneity', *Journal of Business & Economic Statistics*, 31, 346–357.

Gautier, E. and S. Hoderlein (2014): 'A Triangular Treatment Effect Model with Random Coefficients in the Selection Equation', Working Paper at Boston College, Department of Economics.

Gerfin, M. and M. Lechner (2002): 'Microeconometric Evaluation of the Active Labour Market Policy in Switzerland', *Economic Journal*, 112, 854–893.

Gerfin, M., M. Lechner and H. Steiger (2005): 'Does Subsidised Temporary Employment Get the Unemployed Back to Work? An Econometric Analysis of Two Different Schemes', *Labour Economics*, 12, 807–835.

Gill, R. (1989): 'Non- and Semi-Parametric Maximum Likelihood Estimators and the von Mises Method (Part 1)', *Scandinavian Journal of Statistics*, 16, 97–128.

Gill, R. and J. Robins (2001): 'Marginal Structural Models', *Annals of Statistics*, 29, 1785–1811.

Glennerster, R. & Takavarasha, K. (2013): Running Randomized Evaluations: A Practical Guide. Princeton University Press.

Glewwe, P., M. Kremer, S. Moulin and E. Zitzewitz (2004): 'Retrospective vs. Prospective Analyses of School Inputs: The Case of Flip Charts in Kenya', *Journal of Development Economics*, 74, 251–268.

Glynn, A. and K. Quinn (2010): 'An Introduction to the Augmented Inverse Propensity Weighted Estimator', *Political Analysis*, 18, 36–56.

Gonzalez-Manteiga, W. and R. Crujeiras (2013): 'An Updated Review of Goodness-of-Fit Tests for Regression Models', *Test*, 22, 361–411.

Gosling, A., S. Machin and C. Meghir (2000): 'The Changing Distribution of Male Wages in the U.K.', *Review of Economics Studies*, 67, 635–666.

Gozalo, P. and O. Linton (2000): 'Local Nonlinear Least Squares: Using Parametric Information in Nonparametric Regression', *Journal of Econometrics*, 99, 63–106.

Graham, B., C. Pinto and D. Egel (2011): 'Efficient Estimation of Data Combination Models by the Method of Auxiliary-to-Study Tilting (AST)', NBER Working Papers No. 16928.

(2012): 'Inverse Probability Tilting for Moment Condition Models with Missing Data', *Review of Economic Studies*, 79, 1053–1079.

Greene, W. (1997): *Econometric Analysis*, 3rd edn. New Jersey: Prentice Hall.

Greevy, R., B. Lu, J. Silver and P. Rosenbaum (2004): 'Optimal Multivariate Matching Before Randomization', *Biostatistics*, 5, 263–275.

Gruber, S. and M. van der Laan (2012): 'tmle: An R Package for Targeted Maximum Likelihood Estimation', *Journal of Statistical Software*, 51(13).

Hahn, J. (1998): 'On the Role of the Propensity Score in Efficient Semiparametric Estimation of Average Treatment Effects', *Econometrica*, 66(2), 315–331.

Hahn, J. and G. Ridder (2013): 'Asymptotic Variance of Semiparametric Estimators with Generated Regressors', *Econometrica*, 81(1), 315–340.

Hahn, J., P. Todd and W. van der Klaauw (1999): 'Evaluating the Effect of an Antidiscrimination Law Using a Regression-Discontinuity Design', NBER working paper, 7131.

Hall, P., R. Wolff and Q. Yao (1999): 'Methods for Estimating a Conditional Distribution function', *Journal of American Statistical Association*, 94(445), 154–163.

Ham, J. and R. LaLonde (1996): 'The Effect of Sample Selection and Initial Conditions in Duration Models: Evidence from Experimental Data on Training', *Econometrica*, 64, 175–205.

Ham, J., X. Li and P. Reagan (2011): 'Matching and Nonparametric IV Estimation, A Distance-Based Measure of Migration, and the Wages of Young Men', *Journal of Econometrics*, 161, 208–227.

Hansen, C. (2007a): 'Asymptotic Properties of a Robust Variance Matrix Estimator for Panel Data when T is Large', *Journal of Econometrics*, 141, 597–620.

(2007b): 'Generalized Least Squares Inference in Panel and Multilevel Models with Serial Correlation and Fixed Effects', *Journal of Econometrics*, 140, 670–694.

Härdle, W., P. Hall and H. Ichimura (1993): 'Optimal Smoothing in Single-Index Models', *Annals of Statistics*, 21, 157–193.

Härdle, W. and S. Marron (1987): 'Optimal Bandwidth Selection in Nonparametric Regression Function Estimation', *Annals of Statistics*, 13, 1465–1481.

Härdle, W., M. Müller, S. Sperlich and A. Werwatz (2004): *Nonparametric and Semiparametric Models*. Heidelberg: Springer Verlag.

Härdle, W. and T. Stoker (1989): 'Investigating Smooth Multiple Regression by the Method of Average Derivatives', *Journal of American Statistical Association*, 84, 986–995.

Hastie, T. and R. Tibshirani (1990): *Generalized Additive Models*. London: Chapman and Hall.

Have, D. S. T. T. and P. Rosenbaum (2008): 'Randomization Inference in a GroupRandomized Trial of Treatments for Depression: Covariate Adjustment, Noncompliance, and Quantile Effects', *Journal of the American Statistical Association*, 103, 271–279.

Haviland, A. and D. Nagin (2005): 'Causal Inferences with Group Based Trajectory Models', *Psychometrika*, 70, 557–578.

Hayes, A. (2009): 'Beyond Baron and Kenny: Statistical Mediation Analysis in the New Millennium', *Communication Monographs*, 76, 408–420.

Heckman, J. (2001): 'Micro Data, Heterogeneity, and the Evaluation of Public Policy: Nobel Lecture', *Journal of Political Economy*, 109, 673–748.

(2008): 'Econometric Causality', *International Statistical Review*, 76, 1–27.

Heckman, J. and B. Honoré (1989): 'The Identifiability of the Competing Risks Model', *Biometrika*, 76, 325–330.

Heckman, J., H. Ichimura and P. Todd (1998): 'Matching as an Econometric Evaluation Estimator', *Review of Economic Studies*, 65, 261–294.

Heckman, J., R. LaLonde and J. Smith (1999): 'The Economics and Econometrics of Active Labour Market Programs', in *Handbook of Labor Economics*, ed. by O. Ashenfelter and D. Card, pp. 1865–2097. Amsterdam: North-Holland.

Heckman, J. and B. Singer (1984): 'A Method for Minimizing the Impact of Distributional Assumptions in Econometric Models for Duration Data', *Econometrica*, 52, 277–320.

Heckman, J. and J. Smith (1995): 'Assessing the Case for Social Experiments', *Journal of Economic Perspectives*, 9, 85–110.

Heckman, J. and E. Vytlacil (1999): 'Local Instrumental Variables and Latent Variable Models for Identifying and Bounding Treatment Effects', *Proceedings National Academic Sciences USA, Economic Sciences*, 96, 4730–4734.

(2007a): 'Econometric Evaluation of Social Programs Part I: Causal Models, Structural Models and Econometric Policy Evaluation', in *Handbook of Econometrics*, ed. by J. Heckman and E. Leamer, pp. 4779–4874. Amsterdam and Oxford: North-Holland.

(2007b): 'Econometric Evaluation of Social Programs Part II: Using the Marginal Treatment Effect to Organize Alternative Econometric Estimators to Evaluate Social Programs, and to Forecast their Effects in New Environments', in *Handbook of Econometrics*, ed. by J. Heckman and E. Leamer, pp. 4875–5143. Amsterdam and Oxford: North-Holland.

Heckman, N. (1986): 'Spline Smoothing in a Partly Linear Model', *Journal of the Royal Statistical Society, B*, 48, 244–248.

Henderson, D., D. Millimet, C. Parmeter and L. Wang (2008): 'Fertility and the Health of Children: A Nonparametric Investigation', *Advances in Econometrics*, 21, 167–195.

Henderson, D. and C. Parmeter (2015): *Applied Nonparametric Econometrics*. Cambridge: Cambridge University Press.

Hernan, M., B. Brumback and J. Robins (2001): 'Marginal Structural Models to Estimate the Joint Causal Effect of Nonrandomized Trials', *Journal of American Statistical Association*, 96, 440–448.

Hernandez-Quintero, A., J. Dupuy and G. Escarela (2011): 'Analysis of a Semiparametric Mixture mowl for competing risks', *Annals of the Institute of Statistical Mathematics*, 63, 305–329.

Hirano, K., G. Imbens and G. Ridder (2003): 'Efficient Estimation of Average Treatment Effects Using the Estimated Propensity Score', *Econometrica*, 71, 1161–1189.

Hoderlein, S. and E. Mammen (2007): 'Identification of Marginal Effects in Nonseparable Models without Monotonicity', *Econometrica*, 75, 1513–1518.

   (2010): 'Analyzing the Random Coefficient Model Nonparametrically', *Econometric Theory*, 26, 804–837.

Hoderlein, S. and Y. Sasaki (2014): 'Outcome Conditioned Treatment Effects', working paper at John Hopkins University.

Holland, P. (1986): 'Statistics and Causal Inference', *Journal of American Statistical Association*, 81, 945–970.

Hong, H. and D. Nekipelov (2012): 'Efficient Local IV Estimation of an Empirical Auction Model', *Journal of Econometrics*, 168, 60–69.

Horowitz, J. and S. Lee (2007): 'Nonparametric Instrumental Variables Estimation of a Quantile Regression Model', *Econometrica*, 75, 1191–1208.

Huber, M., M. Lechner and A. Steinmayr (2013): 'Radius Matching on the Propensity Score with Bias Adjustment: Tuning Parameters and Finite Sample Behaviour', Discussion paper at the University of St Gallen.

Huber, M., M. Lechner and C. Wunsch (2013): 'The Performance of Estimators Based on the Propensity Score', *Journal of Econometrics*, 175, 1–21.

Ichimura, H. (1993): 'Semiparametric Least Squares (SLS) and Weighted SLS Estimation of Single-Index Models', *Journal of Econometrics*, pp. 71–120.

Imai, K. (2005): 'Do Get-Out-of-the-Vote Calls Reduce Turnout?', *American Political Science Review*, 99, 283–300.

Imai, K., L. Keele and T. Yamamoto (2010): 'Identification, Inference and Sensitivity Analysis for Causal Mediation Effects', *Statistical Science*, 25, 51–71.

Imai, K. and I. Kim (2015): 'On the Use of Linear Fixed Effects Regression Estimators for Causal Inference', working Paper at Princeton.

Imai, K., G. King and C. Nall (2009): 'The Essential Role of Pair Matching in Cluster-Randomized Experiments, with Application to the Mexican Universal Health Insurance Evaluation', *Statistical Science*, 24, 29–53.

Imai, K., G. King and E. Stuart (2008): 'Misunderstandings between Experimentalists and Observationalists about Causal Inference', *Journal of the Royal Statistical Society (A)*, 171, 481–502.

Imbens, G. (2000): 'The Role of the Propensity Score in Estimating Dose-Response Functions', *Biometrika*, 87, 706–710.

   (2001): 'Some Remarks on Instrumental Variables', in *Econometric Evaluation of Labour Market Policies*, ed. by M. Lechner and F. Pfeiffer, pp. 17–42. Heidelberg: Physica/Springer.

(2004): 'Nonparametric Estimation of Average Treatment Effects under Exogeneity: A Review', *Review of Economics and Statistics*, 86, 4–29.

Imbens, G. and J. Angrist (1994): 'Identification and Estimation of Local Average Treatment Effects', *Econometrica*, 62, 467–475.

Imbens, G. and K. Kalyanaraman (2012): 'Optimal Bandwidth Choice for the Regression Discontinuity Estimator', *Review of Economic Studies*, 79 (3), 933–959.

Imbens, G. and T. Lemieux (2008): 'Regression Discontinuity Designs: Guide to Practice', *Journal of Econometrics*, 142, 615–635.

Imbens, G. and W. Newey (2009): 'Identification and Estimation of Triangular Simultaneous Equations Models Without Additivity', *Econometrica*, 77, 1481–1512.

Imbens, G., W. Newey and G. Ridder (2005): 'Mean-Squared-Error Calculations for Average Treatment Effects', unpublished.

Imbens, G. and D. Rubin (2015): *Causal inference in Statistics and in the Social and Biomedical Sciences*. Cambridge: Cambridge University Press.

Imbens, G. and J. Wooldridge (2009): 'Recent Developments in the Econometrics of Policy Evaluation', *Journal of Econometric Literature*, 47, 5–86.

Jacob, R. and P. Zhu (2012): 'A Practical Guide to Regression Discontinuity', discussion paper, www.mdrc.org.

Jepsen, C., P. Mueser and K. Troske (2009): 'Labor-Market Returns to the GED Using Regression Discontinuity Analysis', mimeo, x(x).

Juhn, C., K. Murphy and B. Pierce (1993): 'Wage Inequality and the Rise in Returns to Skill', *Journal of Political Economy*, 101, 410–442.

Kalbfleisch, J. and R. Prentice (2002): *The Statistical Analysis of Failure Time Data*. Wiley Series in Probability and Statistics, Hoboken, NJ: Wiley.

Kane, T. (2003): 'A Quasi-Experimental Estimate of the Impact of Financial Aid on College-Going', *NBER Working Paper Series* 9703, 1–67.

Kasy, M. (2013): 'Why Experimenters Should Not Randomize, and What They Should Do Instead', discussion paper, Harvard University OpenScholar.

Kernan, W., C. Viscoli, R. Makuch, L. Brass and R. Horwitz (1999): 'Stratified Randomization for Clinical Trials', *Journal of Clinical Epidemiology*, 52, 19–26.

Kiefer, J. (1967): 'On Bahadur's Representation of Sample quantiles', *Annals of Mathematical Statistics*, 38, 1323–1342.

King, G., E. Gakidou, N. Ravishankar et al. (2007): 'A Politically Robust Experimental Design for Public Policy Evaluation, with Application to the Mexican Universal Health Insurance Progam', *Journal of Policy Analysis and Management*, 26, 479–506.

King, G. and I. Zeng (2006): 'The Dangers of Extreme Counterfactuals', *Political Analysis*, 14, 131–159.

Klein, R. and R. Spady (1993): 'An Efficient Semiparametric Estimator for Binary Response Models', *Econometrica*, 61, 387–421.

Kluve, J. (2010): 'The Effectiveness of European Active Labor Market Programs', *Labour Economics*, 17, 904–918.

Koenker, R. (2005): *Quantile Regression*. Cambridge: Cambridge University Press.

Koenker, R. and G. Bassett (1978): 'Regression Quantiles', *Econometrica*, 46, 33–50.

Köhler, M., A. Schindler and S. Sperlich (2014): 'A Review and Comparison of Bandwidth Selection Methods for Kernel Regression', *International Statistical Review*, 82, 243–274.

Koshevnik, Y. and B. Levit (1976): 'On a Non-Parametric Analogue of the Information Matrix', *Theory of Probability and Applications*, 21, 738–753.

Lalive, R. (2008): 'How Do Extended Benefits Affect Unemployment Duration? A Regression Discontinuity Approach', *Journal of Econometrics*, 142, 785–806.

Lalive, R., J. Wüllrich and J. Zweimüller (2008): 'Do Financial Incentives for Firms Promote Employment of Disabled Workers: A Regression Discontinuity Approach', mimeo, *University of Zürich*.

LaLonde, R. (1986): 'Evaluating the Econometric Evaluations of Training Programs with Experimental Data', *American Economic Review*, 76, 604–620.

Lancaster, T. (1990): *The Econometric Analysis of Transition Data*. Cambridge: Cambridge University Press.

Langrock, R., N. Heidenreich and S. Sperlich (2014): 'Kernel-Based Semiparametric Multinomial Logit Modelling of Political Party Preferences', *Statistical Methods and Applications*, 23, 435–449.

Larson, M. and G. Dinse (1985): 'A Mixture Model for the Regression Analysis of Competing Risks Data', *Applied statistics*, 34, 201–211.

Lechner, M. (1999): 'Earnings and Employment Effects of Continuous Off-the-Job Training in East Germany after Unification', *Journal of Business and Economic Statistics*, 17, 74–90.

(2001): 'Identification and Estimation of Causal Effects of Multiple Treatments under the Conditional Independence Assumption', in *Econometric Evaluation of Labour Market Policies*, ed. by M. Lechner and F. Pfeiffer, pp. 43–58. Heidelberg: Physica/Springer.

(2002a): 'Program Heterogeneity and Propensity Score Matching: An Application to the Evaluation of Active Labor Market Policies', *Review of Economics and Statistics*, 84, 205–220.

(2002b): 'Some Practical Issues in the Evaluation of Heterogeneous Labour Market Programmes by Matching Methods', *Journal of the Royal Statistical Society (A)*, 165, 59–82.

(2004): 'Sequential Matching Estimation of Dynamic Causal Models', Universität St Gallen Discussion Paper, 2004–06.

(2006): 'The Relation of Different Concepts of Causality in Econometrics', Universität St Gallen Discussion Paper, 2006–15.

(2008): 'Matching Estimation of Dynamic Treatment Models: Some Practical Issues', in *Advances in Econometrics, Volume 21, Modelling and Evaluating Treatment Effects in Econometrics*, ed. by T. Fomby, R. Carter Hill, D. Millimet, J. Smith and E. Vytlacil, Emerald Group Publishing Ltd, pp. 289–333.

(2009): 'Sequential Causal Models for the Evaluation of Labor Market Programs', *Journal of Business and Economic Statistics*, 27, 71–83.

(2011): 'The Estimation of Causal Effects by Difference-in-Difference Methods', *Foundations and Trends in Econometrics*, 4, 165–224.

Lechner, M. and R. Miquel (2001): 'A Potential Outcome Approach to Dynamic Programme Evaluation: Nonparametric Identification', Universität St Gallen Discussion Paper, 2001–07.

(2010): 'Identification of the Effects of Dynamic Treatments by Sequential Conditional Independence Assumptions', *Empirical Economics*, 39, 111–137.

Lechner, M., R. Miquel and C. Wunsch (2011): 'Long-Run Effects of Public Sector Sponsored Training in West Germany', *Journal of the European Economic Association*, 9, 742–784.

Lechner, M. and S. Wiehler (2011): 'Kids or Courses? Gender Differences in the Effects of Active Labor Market Policies', *Journal of Population Economics*, 24(3), 783–812.

Lee, D. (2008): 'Randomized Experiments from Non-Random Selection in U.S. House Elections', *Journal of Econometrics*, 142, 675–697.

Lee, D. and D. Card (2008): 'Regression Discontinuity Inference with Specification Error', *Journal of Econometrics*, 142, 655–674.

Lee, D. and T. Lemieux (2010): 'Regression Discontinuity Designs in Economics', *Journal of Econometrics*, 142, 615–674.

Leuven, E., M. Lindahl, H. Oosterbeek and D. Webbink (2007): 'The Effect of Extra Funding for Disadvantaged Pupils on Achievement', *Review of Economics and Statistics*, 89, 721–736.

Leuven, E. and B. Sianesi (2014): 'PSMATCH2: Stata Module to Perform Full Mahalanobis and Propensity Score Matching, Common Support Graphing, and Covariate Imbalance Testing', *Statistical Software Components*.

Li, Q. and J. Racine (2007): *Nonparametric Econometrics – Theory and Practice*. Princeton, NJ: Princeton University Press.

Little, R. and D. Rubin (1987): *Statistical Analysis with Missing Data*. New York, NY: Wiley.

Loader, C. (1999a): 'Bandwidth Selection: Classical or Plug-In?', *Annals of Statistics*, 27, 415–438.

(1999b): *Local Regression and Likelihood*. New York, NY: Springer.

Lu, B., E. Zanuto, R. Hornik and P. Rosenbaum (2001): 'Matching with Doses in an Observational Study of a Media Campaign against Drug Abuse', *Journal of the American Statistical Association*, 96, 1245–1253.

Lunceford, J. and M. Davidian (2004): 'Stratification and Weighting via the Propensity Score in Estimation of Causal Treatment Effects: A Comparative Study', *Statistics in Medicine*, 23, 2937–2960.

Lunn, M. and D. McNeil (1995): 'Applying Cox Regression to Competing Risks', *Biometrics*, 51, 524–532.

Machado, J. and J. Mata (2005): 'Counterfactual Decomposition of Changes in Wage Distributions Using Quantile Regression', *Journal of Applied Econometrics*, 20, 445–465.

Mammen, E. (1991): 'Estimating a Smooth Monotone Regression Function', *Annals of Statistics*, 19, 724–740.

(1992): *When Does Bootstrap Work: Asymptotic Results and Simulations. Lecture Notes in Statistics 77*. New York, NY and Heidelberg: Springer Verlag.

Manning, W., L. Blumberg and L. Moulton (1995): 'The Demand for Alcohol: The Differential Response to Price', *Journal of Health Economics*, 14, 123–148.

Markus Frölich & Martin Huber (2017): Direct and indirect treatment effects-causal chains and mediation analysis with instrumental variables, J. R. Statist. Soc. B (2017), 79, Part 5, pp. 1645–1666.

(2018): Including Covariates in the Regression Discontinuity Design, Journal of Business & Economic Statistics, forthcoming DOI: 10.1080/07350015.2017.142154

Markus Frölich, Martin Huber, Manuel Wiesenfarth (2017): The finite sample performance of semi- and non-parametric estimators for treatment effects and policy evaluation, Computational Statistics and Data Analysis 115 (2017) 91–102

Markus Frölich and Blaise Melly (2010): Estimation of quantile treatment effects with STATA, Stata Journal, 10 (3), 423–457.

Matsudaira, J. (2008): 'Mandatory Summer School and Student Achievement', *Journal of Econometrics*, 142, 829–850.

McCrary, J. (2008): 'Manipulation of the Running Variable in the Regression Discontinuity Design: A Density Test', *Journal of Econometrics*, 142, 698–714.

Mealli, F., G. Imbens, S. Ferro and A. Biggeri (2004): 'Analyzing a Randomized Trial on Breast Self-Examination with Noncompliance and Missing Outcomes', *Biostatistics*, 5, 207–222.

Melly, B. (2005): 'Decomposition of Differences in Distribution Using Quantile Regression', *Labour Economics*, 12, 577–590.

Meyer, B. (1995): 'Natural and Quasi-Experiments in Economics', *Journal of Business and Economic Statistics*, 13, 151–161.

Miguel, E. and M. Kremer (2004): 'Worms: Identifying Impacts on Education and Health in the Presence of Treatment Externalities', *Econometrica*, 72, 159–217.

Miguel, E., S. Satyanath and E. Sergenti (2004): 'Economic Shocks and Civil Conflict: An Instrumental Variables Approach', *Journal of Political Economy*, 112, 725–753.

Moffitt, R. (2004): 'The Role of Randomized Field Trials in Social Science Research: A Perspective from Evaluations of Reforms of Social Welfare Programs', *American Behavioral Scientist*, 47, 506–540.

(2008): 'Estimating Marginal Treatment Effects in Heterogeneous Populations', *Annales d'Economie et de Statistique*, 91/92, 239–261.

Mora, R. and I. Reggio (2012): 'Treatment Effect Identification Using Alternative Parallel Assumptions', WP Carlos III de Madrid, Spain.

Moral-Arce, I., S. Sperlich and A. Fernandez-Sainz (2013): 'The Semiparametric Juhn-Murphy-Pierce Decomposition of the Gender Pay Gap with an application to Spain', in *Wages and Employment: Economics, Structure and Gender Differences*, ed. by A. Mukherjee, pp. 3–20. Hauppauge, New York, NY: Nova Science Publishers.

Moral-Arce, I., S. Sperlich, A. Fernandez-Sainz and M. Roca (2012): 'Trends in the Gender Pay Gap in Spain: A Semiparametric Analysis', *Journal of Labor Research*, 33, 173–195.

Nadaraya, E. (1965): 'On Nonparametric Estimates of Density Functions and Regression Curves', *Theory of Applied Probability*, 10, 186–190.

Neumeyer, N. (2007): 'A Note on Uniform Consistency of Monotone Function Estimators', *Statistics and Probability Letters*, 77, 693–703.

Newey, W. (1990): 'Semiparametric Efficiency Bounds', *Journal of Applied Econometrics*, 5, 99–135.

(1994): 'The Asymptotic Variance of Semiparametric Estimators', *Econometrica*, 62, 1349–1382.

Newey, W. and J. Powell (2003): 'Instrumental Variable Estimation of Nonparametric Models', *Econometrica*, 71, 1565–1578.

Nichols, A. (2007): 'Causal Inference with Observational Data', *The Stata Journal*, 7, 507–541.

(2014): 'rd: Stata Module for Regression Discontinuity Estimation. Statistical Software Components', discussion paper, Boston College Department of Economics.

Pagan, A. and A. Ullah (1999): *Nonparametric Econometrics*. Cambridge: Cambridge University Press.

Pearl, J. (2000): *Causality: Models, Reasoning, and Inference*. Cambridge: Cambridge University Press.

Pfanzagl, J. and W. Wefelmeyer (1982): *Contributions to a General Asymptotic Statistical Theory*. Heidelberg: Springer Verlag.

Pocock, S. and R. Simon (1975): 'Sequential Treatment Assignment with Balancing for Prognostic Factors in the Controlled Clinical Trial', *Biometrics*, 31, 103–115.

Politis, D., J. Romano and M. Wolf (1999): *Subsampling*. New York, NY: Springer.

Powell, J., J. Stock and T. Stoker (1989): 'Semiparametric Estimation of Index Coefficients', *Econometrica*, 57, 1403–1430.

Putter, H. (2014): 'Tutorial in Biostatistics: Competing Risks and Multi-State Models Analyses Using the mstate Package', discussion paper, Leiden University Medical Center.

Putter, H., M. Fiocco and R. Geskus (2006): 'Tutorial in Biostatistics: Competing Risks and Multi-State Models', *Statistics in Medicine*, 26, 2389–2430.

Racine, J. and Q. Li (2004): 'Nonparametric Estimation of Regression Functions with Both Categorical and Continuous Data', *Journal of Econometrics*, 119, 99–130.

Ravallion, M. (2008): 'Evaluating Anti-Poverty Programs', in *Handbook of Development Economics*, ed. by T. Schultz and J. Strauss, pp. 3787–3846. Amsterdam: North-Holland.

Reinsch, C. (1967): 'Smoothing by Spline Functions', *Numerische Mathematik*, 16, 177–183.

Rice, J. (1986): 'Convergence Rates for Partially Splined Estimates', *Statistics and Probability Letters*, 4, 203–208.

Robins, J. (1986): 'A New Approach to Causal Inference in Mortality Studies with Sustained Exposure Periods – Application to Control of the Healthy Worker Survivor Effect', *Mathematical Modelling*, 7, 1393–1512.

(1989): 'The Analysis of Randomized and Nonrandomized AIDS Treatment Trials Using a New Approach to Causal Inference in Longitudinal Studies', in *Health Service Research Methodology: A Focus on Aids*, ed. by L. Sechrest, H. Freeman and A. Mulley, pp. 113–159. Washington, DC: Public Health Service, National Center for Health Services Research.

(1997): 'Causal Inference from Complex Longitudinal Data. Latent Variable Modelling and Applications to Causality', in *Lecture Notes in Statistics 120*, ed. by M. Berkane, pp. 69–117. New York, NY: Springer.

(1998): 'Marginal Structural Models', *Proceedings of the American Statistical Association*, 1997, 1–10.

(1999): 'Association, Causation, and Marginal Structural Models', *Synthese*, 121, 151–179.

Robins, J., S. Greenland and F. Hu (1999): 'Estimation of the Causal Effect of a Time-varying Exposure on the Marginal Mean of a Repeated Binary Outcome', *Journal of the American Statistical Association*, 94, 687–700.

Robins, J. and A. Rotnitzky (1995): 'Semiparametric Efficiency in Multivariate Regression Models with Missing Data', *Journal of American Statistical Association*, 90, 122–129.

Robins, J., A. Rotnitzky and L. Zhao (1995): 'Analysis of Semiparametric Regression Models for Repeated Outcomes in the Presence of Missing Data', *Journal of American Statistical Association*, 90, 106–121.

Robins, J. M., A. Rotnitzky and L. Zhao (1994): 'Estimation of Regression Coefficients When Some Regressors Are Not Always Observed', *Journal of the American Statistical Association*, 90, 846–866.

Roodman, D. (2009a): 'How to Do xtabond2: An Introduction to Difference and System GMM in Stata', *The Stata Journal*, 9, 86–136.

(2009b): 'A Note on the Theme of Too Many Instruments', *Oxford Bulletin of Economics and Statistics*, 71, 135–158.

Rose, H. and J. Betts (2004): 'The Effect of High School Courses on Earnings', *Review of Economics and Statistics*, 86, 497–513.

Rosenbaum, P. (1984): 'The Consequences of Adjustment for a Concomitant Variable That Has Been Affected by the Treatment', *Journal of Royal Statistical Society (A)*, 147, 656–666.

(2002): *Observational Studies*. Heidelberg: Springer Verlag.

Rothe, C. (2010): 'Nonparametric Estimation of Distributional Policy Effects', *Journal of Econometrics*, 155, 56–70.

Rothe, Christoph & Firpo, Sergio, 2013. "Semiparametric Estimation and Inference Using Doubly Robust Moment Conditions," IZA Discussion Papers 7564, Institute for the Study of Labor (IZA).

Rotnitzky, A. and J. Robins (1995): 'Semiparametric Regression Estimation in the Presence of Dependent Censoring', *Biometrika*, 82, 805–820.

(1997): 'Analysis of Semiparametric Regression Models with Non-Ignorable Non-Response', *Statistics in Medicine*, 16, 81–102.

Rotnitzky, A., J. Robins and D. Scharfstein (1998): 'Semiparametric Regression for Repeated Outcomes With Nonignorable Nonresponse', *Journal of the American Statistical Association*, 93, 1321–1339.

Roy, A. (1951): 'Some Thoughts on the Distribution of Earnings', *Oxford Economic Papers*, 3, 135–146.

Rubin, D. (1974): 'Estimating Causal Effects of Treatments in Randomized and Nonrandomized Studies', *Journal of Educational Psychology*, 66, 688–701.

(1980): 'Comment on "Randomization Analysis of Experimental Data: The Fisher Randomization Test" by D. Basu', *Journal of American Statistical Association*, 75, 591–593.

(2001): 'Using Propensity Scores to Help Design Observational Studies: Application to the Tobacco Litigation', *Health Services and Outcomes Research Methodology*, 2, 169–188.

(2004): 'Direct and Indirect Causal Effects via Potential Outcomes', *Scandinavian Journal of Statistics*, 31, 161–170.

(2005): 'Causal Inference Using Potential Outcomes: Design, Modeling, Decisions', *Journal of American Statistical Association*, 100, 322–331.

(2006): *Matched Sampling for Causal Effects*. Cambridge: Cambridge University Press.

Ruppert, D. and M. Wand (1994): 'Multivariate Locally Weighted Least Squares Regression', *Annals of Statistics*, 22, 1346–1370.

Särndal, C.-E., B. Swensson and J. Wretman (1992): *Model Assisted Survey Sampling*. New York, NY, Berlin, Heidelberg: Springer.

Schwarz, K. and T. Krivobokova (2016): 'A Unified Framework for Spline Estimators', *Biometrika*, 103, 121–131.

Seifert, B. and T. Gasser (1996): 'Finite-Sample Variance of Local Polynomials: Analysis and Solutions', *Journal of American Statistical Association*, 91, 267–275.

(2000): 'Data Adaptive Ridging in Local Polynomial Regression', *Journal of Computational and Graphical Statistics*, 9, 338–360.

Shadish, W., M. Clark and P. Steiner (2008): 'Can Nonrandomized Experiments Yield Accurate Answers? A Randomized Experiment Comparing Random and Nonrandom Assignments', *Journal of the American Statistical Association*, 103, 1334–1344.

Sianesi, B. (2004): 'An Evaluation of the Swedish System of Active Labor Market Programs in the 1990s', *Review of Economics and Statistics*, 86, 133–155.

Speckman, P. (1988): 'Kernel Smoothing in Partial Linear Models', *Journal of the Royal Statistical Society (B)*, 50, 413–436.

Sperlich, S. (2009): 'A Note on Nonparametric Estimation with Predicted Variables', *The Econometrics Journal*, 12, 382–395.

(2014): 'On the Choice of Regularization Parameters in Specification Testing: A Critical Discussion', *Empirical Economics*, 47, 275–450.

Sperlich, S. and R. Theler (2015): 'Modeling Heterogeneity: A Praise for Varying-coefficient Models in Causal Analysis', *Computational Statistics*, 30, 693–718.

Staniswalis, J. (1989): 'The Kernel Estimate of a Regression Function in Likelihood-Based Models', *Journal of American Statistical Association*, 84, 276–283.

Stein, C. (1956): 'Efficient Nonparametric Testing and Estimation', in *Proceedings of the Third Berkeley Symposium on Mathematical Statistics and Probability*, vol. 1. Berkeley, CA: University of California Press.

Stone, C. (1974): 'Cross-Validatory Choice and Assessment of Statistical Predictions', *Journal of Royal Statistical Society (B)*, 36, 111–147 (with discussion).

    (1980): 'Optimal Rates of Convergence of Nonparametric Estimators', *Annals of Statistics*, 8, 1348–1360.

    (1982): 'Optimal Global Rates of Convergence for Nonparametric Regression', *Annals of Statistics*, 10, 1040–1053.

Tan, Z. (2006): 'A Distributional Approach for Causal Inference Using Propensity Scores', *Journal of the American Statistical Association*, 101, 1619–1637.

    (2010): 'Bounded, Efficient and Doubly Robust Estimation with Inverse Weighting', *Biometrika*, 97, 661–682.

    (2013): 'Variance Estimation under Misspecified Models', working paper at the Department of Statistics, Rutgers University.

Telser, L. (1964): 'Iterative Estimation of a Set of Linear Equations', *Journal of the American Statistical Association*, 59, 845–862.

Tibshirani, R. and T. Hastie (1987): 'Local Likelihood Estimation', *Journal of American Statistical Association*, 82, 559–567.

Utreras, F. (1985): 'Smoothing Noisy Data under Monotonicity Constraints Existence, Characterization and Convergence Rates', *Numerische Mathematik*, 47, 611–625.

van den Berg, G. (2001): 'Duration Models: Specification, Identification, and Multiple Durations', in *Handbook of Econometrics*, pp. 3381–3460. Amsterdam: North Holland.

van der Klaauw, W. (2002): 'Estimating the Effect of Financial Aid Offers on College Enrollment: A Regression-Discontinuity Approach', *International Economic Review*, 43, 1249–1287.

    (2008): 'Breaking the Link between Poverty and Low Student Achievement: An Evaluation of Title I', *Journal of Econometrics*, 142, 731–756.

Wahba, H. (1990): *Spline Models for Observational Data*. Philadelphia, PA: SIAM.

Wald, A. (1940): 'The Fitting of Straight Lines if Both Variables are Subject to Error', *Annals of Mathematical Statistics*, 11, 284–300.

Wand, M. (2003): 'Smoothing and Mixed Models', *Computational Statistics*, 18, 223–249.

Watson, G. (1964): 'Smooth Regression Analysis', *Sankhya*, 26:15, 175–184.

Wooldridge, J. (2002): *Econometric Analysis of Cross Section and Panel Data*. Cambridge, MA: MIT Press.

Yatchew, A. (2003): *Semiparametric Regression for the Applied Econometrician*. Cambridge: Cambridge University Press.

Zhao, Z. (2004): 'Using Matching to Estimate Treatment Effects: Data Requirements, Matching Metrics, and Monte Carlo Evidence', *Review of Economics and Statistics*, 86, 91–107.

Zhou, S., X. Shen and D. Wolfe (1998): 'Local Asymptotics for Regression Splines and Confidence Regions', *Annals of Statistics*, 26, 1760–1782.

Index

Printed in the United States
By Bookmasters